LITERACY DISORDERS
Holistic Diagnosis and Remediation

Anthony V. Manzo
University of Missouri-Kansas City

Ula C. Manzo
School District of Kansas City, Missouri

Harcourt Brace Jovanovich College Publishers
Fort Worth   Philadelphia   San Diego   New York   Orlando   Austin   San Antonio
Toronto   Montreal   London   Sydney   Tokyo

Editor in Chief	Ted Buchholz
Acquisitions Editor	Jo-Anne Weaver
Developmental Editor	Laurie Runion
Senior Project Editor	Steve Welch
Production Manager	Cynthia Young
Senior Book Designer	Serena B. Manning
Cover Art "Paper Dolls"	Joan Truckenbrod
Cover Designer	Linda Harper
Text Designer	Paula Goldstein

Dedication

*To our teachers and mentors
in diagnosis and remediation:*

➤ ➤   ◄ ◄

Frank P. Greene

Gerald G. Glass

Harvey Alpert

Harold Tanyzer

Address for Editorial Correspondence: Harcourt Brace Jovanovich College Publishers, 301 Commerce Street, Suite 3700, Fort Worth, TX 76102.

Address for Orders: Harcourt Brace Jovanovich, Inc. 6277 Sea Harbor Drive, Orlando, FL 32887. 1-800-782-4479, or 1-800-433-0001 (in Florida).

Printed in the United States of America

Library of Congress Catalog Card Number: 92-81852

ISBN: 0-15-500287-2

6 7 8 9 0 1 2 039 9 8 7 6 5 4 3

SECTION I

PRIMER ON LITERACY NEEDS

Literacy Needs and Literacy Providers

1

> "*We always pass failure on the way to success.*"
> MICKEY ROONEY

> ➤ **LOOK FOR IT**
>
> This chapter tells the story of the relationship of the rising demands and roles in contemporary life, to the rising demands on and roles available to literacy providers.

Remedial Reading

The term "remedial reading," according to Nila Banton Smith (1965), was first used in an article by Uhl in 1916. The title of that article still defines one of the most basic functions of diagnostic and remedial reading: "The Use of Results of Reading Tests as Bases for Planning Remedial Work" (in Johnston & Allington, 1991). The term "remedial" first described the nature of the instruction given to disabled readers. A semantic shift has resulted in the current shortening of the term to where it now appears to be an attribute of a person. While broadly accepted now as another way of saying that one is a disabled reader who has been or is receiving remedial instruction, the shift also suggests that the disability is a trait that interacts with everything else that a child is and could be. There seems to be an element of truth in this perception,

3

since such disabilities do influence every act of reading, and hence every effort to become a literate and independent person. In a manner of speaking, reading does seem to sum one up.

Reading Sums Us Up

When a child looks down at a page of print, there are several invisible factors and forces that sit down with him or her. There is previous ancestry, as embodied in genetic makeup. There are the influences of immediate family, friends, acquaintances, and even the general mood of the country. There are the voices of the child's prior successes and failures: not merely with reading, but with school and life in general. There also are the child's own priorities and personal "felt needs." Together, these influences determine how much the student is willing and able to bring to the printed page—and, therefore, how much is likely to be derived from it.

With so many factors and forces influencing the "simple" act of reading, it is little wonder that difficulties arise. Most students have occasional reading difficulties that are overcome with a little extra effort and classroom-based instruction. For a percentage of students, however, the difficulties are *serious* and

Reading Sums Us Up

We look for ourselves in what we read.
(Much recent research indicates that sex differences, as depicted here, are neither stereotypic nor culturally imparted, but are real and possibly innate.)

persistent, and can correctly be called *disorders*. The numbers and types of problems and disorders that can be labelled and deemed to warrant remedial attention are arguable: definitions and classifications of "reading disorders" are based on how "reading" is defined. The complexity of the reading act is evident in the introductory definition offered next. We will return to the issue of defining "reading disorders" shortly.

Reading Defined

Reading can be defined as the act of *simultaneously* reading the lines, reading between the lines, and reading beyond the lines.* "Reading the lines" is the process of decoding the words in order to reconstruct the author's *basic* message. "Reading between the lines" is the process of making inferences in order to reconstruct the author's *implied* messages. This requires an understanding of the internal logic of the facts presented, as well as an understanding of connotative and figurative language. "Reading beyond the lines" is the process of judging the *significance* of the author's message, and constructively applying it to other areas of knowledge and experience. This process often extends beyond the author's original intent. Box 1.1 offers an example of reading the lines, reading between the lines, and reading beyond the lines.

The study of reading problems has tended to focus in great measure on "reading the lines," to a lesser degree on "reading between the lines," and to a far lesser degree on "reading beyond the lines." As a result, the field has developed very precise ways to assess and treat word analysis problems, and reasonably effective ways to measure literal and inferential comprehension. There are, however, *no* agreed upon means of assessing students' ability to read "beyond the lines." Our ability to measure only one or two dimensions of a robust, three-dimensional process has tended to produce a distorted "picture" of the reading process, reading needs, and reading diagnosis. Since we tend to teach what we are able to measure, there is little attention to the higher-order needs of remedial readers. Remedial reading instruction tends to focus *only* on decoding and basic comprehension, but seldom offers opportunities for students to see reading as a springboard for thinking and creating. Further, there is a *great* lack of commitment to identifying youngsters who do not have conventional remedial reading problems, but who may have serious higher-order reading deficiencies. A notable exception to this was a study by Iver Moe and Frank Nania (1959) that showed many proficient readers to lack flexibility in reading rate.

In an effort to improve this picture, this text presents that which is known about the diagnosis and treatment of reading disorders on *each* of these three

*It is uncertain who first used these terms to define the basic functions of reading. We are inclined to accept the suggestion of Michael McKenna (personal communication) that it was Edgar Dale in the early 1940s.

BOX 1.1

Three Levels of Reading

Excerpt:
An Old Crab said to her son, "Why do you walk sideways like that, my son? You ought to walk straight." The Young Crab replied, "Show me how, dear mother, and I'll follow your example." The Old Crab tried, but tried in vain, and then saw how foolish she had been to find fault with her child.

Reading the lines:
This is a story about a mother crab trying to get her young son to walk in a straight line. The youngster asks his mother to show him how. When she can not, she realizes that it is foolish to think that he could do something she could not do.

Reading between the lines:
This is a story that demonstrates that example is better than criticism.

Reading beyond the lines (Some of many possibilities):
We tend to project our insecurities onto our children. Surely happiness begins with accepting what we are. The best preparation for teaching is to begin by knowing oneself.

---

levels. It probably will take considerable additional research and thinking before this all comes together smoothly. Nevertheless, you should find the reporting of even as much as is now known to be interesting and clarifying of your current understandings of reading disorders. For example, a look at the larger picture reveals that there is a great similarity in the profiles of some conventional remedial readers and of children who read too much or with excellent literal comprehension (Casale, 1982; Huttenlocher & Huttenlocher, 1973). You will read more about this ahead, along with evidence for how some attempts to build higher-order comprehension in remedial readers actually has been shown to improve more basic and resistant problems in learning how to read. So, while this chapter remains focused on more introductory concepts, such as the current and expanding scope and history of diagnosis and remediation, the remainder of the text is set in the fuller context of literacy education, aptly reflected by the popular quote from Francis Bacon:

> To spend too much time in studies is sloth; to use them too much for ornament is affection; to make judgment wholly by rules is the humor of a scholar. . . . Read not to contradict or confute; nor to believe and take for granted; nor to find talk and discourse; but to weigh and consider. Some books are to be tasted, others to

be swallowed, and some few to be chewed and digested. . . . Reading maketh a full person; conference a ready person; and writing an exact person.

In contemporary language, one could say that "reading education" is coming to mean attention to reading, language, thinking, and social-emotional maturity. Consider now how this already is being reflected in the scope of current research and practice in remedial reading.

The Scope of Remedial Reading

One way to get a quick overview of the field of remedial reading is to answer the question, "Who needs remedial help?" Not many years ago, the answer to this question was thought to be clear: *students whose reading test scores were below a certain criterion level, based on their IQ and grade level.* Today, remedial readers are defined more in terms of their reading *process*, and their personal and literacy orientation. Peter Johnston and Richard Allington's recent review of the literature on remediation offers these examples:

- Remedial readers are unreflective, and do not self-monitor or self-correct (Brown, 1980; Torgesen, 1982)
- Remedial readers are less positive about reading and writing—less inclined to write independently (Anderson, Wilson, & Fielding, 1988; Juel, 1988)
- Remedial readers are less likely to actively construct meaning and see patterns in reading and writing (Johnston & Winograd, 1985; Vellutino, 1987)
- Remedial readers are less persistent when faced with frustrating text (Andrews & Debus, 1978; Chapin & Dyck, 1976)
- Remedial readers are far less strategic or flexible in the way they read (Diener & Dweck, 1978; Torgesen, 1982)
- Remedial readers have low self-esteem, reflected in a tendency to make negative statements about themselves while performing tasks (Diener & Dweck, 1978).

(Johnston & Allington, 1991, p. 999)

Johnston and Allington further point out that children *labelled* "remedial readers" have tended to *remain* remedial readers. This puzzling but widely documented fact was a motivating force behind recent efforts to define the reading process better. Clearer understandings of what reading "is" have suggested the need to revise our definitions of "remedial." When a comprehensive view of the reading process is taken, it becomes clear that *all* of us reach points at which we could benefit from some remedial assistance, *many* of us have fairly frequent remedial needs, and a few of us have extensive remedial needs (see "Functional Literacy" ahead). This realization alone illustrates that where literacy needs are concerned, we're all in this together! The distant "they" of illiterates vs. literates is more illusion than fact. There really is no such thing as a remedial reader; there are only people with remedial needs. This expanded scope of remedial reading will be further clarified as we now take a closer look at three current trends in the field of reading: conceptualizing reading as an interactive process that readers go through to understand the printed page; a preference for the term "literacy needs" over "reading needs"; and an increased awareness of the increasing levels of literacy required to deal with the spiralling complexity of daily life.

Reading as an Interactive Process

As previously suggested, reading is no longer viewed as a mere objective reconstruction of the author's message. Rather, it is viewed as a highly subjective interaction of the reader's prior knowledge, perceptions, and purposes with those of the author. This process of "reading beyond the lines," as it was referred to earlier, can result in understandings that are even greater than the author intended. At other times, the reader and writer may fail to connect for one of several reasons. The reader may have inadequate vocabulary or prior knowledge about the subject. The writer's own ideas may be inadequately formed, or presented in a way that assumes more knowledge than the reader reasonably could have. This view of reading as an *interactive process* is reflected in the fact that there now is a popular technical term for failures on the part of the writer as well as the reader: when writing is unnecessarily difficult, or requires too much of the reader, it is called "inconsiderate text."

Literacy Needs vs. Reading Needs

Another current trend in the way reading is viewed is evident in the growing preference for the term *literacy* over *reading*. The implication of this semantic shift is that the purpose of education is not merely to produce individuals who are not illiterate, but to produce more individuals who *are literate*, in the traditional sense of being able to *read, write, speak, listen,* and most of all, *think* in ways that are critical and imaginative. Needless to say, when reading is defined to include these four additional aspects of human development, this effectively increases the number and types of problems and disorders that need to be diagnosed and remediated. A good example of this can be seen in recent developments in the area known as functional literacy. A brief account of these developments provides the basis for understanding the expanding nature of current literacy efforts.

Functional Literacy

Functional literacy refers to the level of learning at which one is able to read well enough to negotiate life's everyday activities and demands. In recent years, however, the criteria for functional literacy has become a moving target. Each time we collect our will and resources to take aim at it, it spirals upward. The fact that it keeps moving predictably upward is causing educators to believe that we need to get out ahead of it, thereby preventing the next "literacy crisis." A

SECTION III

Principles and Practices of Remediation   201

SECTION II

Detecting Literacy Disorders   37

Contents

that will help you to understand the basic physiology of reading and learning processes.

In any undertaking of this type, there are many people to thank. We are especially grateful to Jo-Anne Weaver, Acquisitions Editor at Harcourt Brace Jovanovich, for helping to set us on this course; to Siriwan Ratanakarn and Fengfang Lu for research assistance; to all who agreed to have us cite and reproduce portions of their work; to Laurie Runion for good counsel; to the HBJ editorial and art staff; and to the following reviewers, who so generously shared their professional expertise: Jeanne Chall, Harvard University; J. Richard Chambers, Boston University; Cathy Collins, Texas Christian University; Lane Gauthier, University of Houston; Gerald Glass, Adelphi University; Roselmina Indrisano, Boston University; Michael McKenna, Georgia Southern University; Jane Meeks, Old Dominion University; and Leo Schell, Kansas State University.

One expert reviewer of the pre-publication manuscript for this book observed that it probably would define diagnosis and remediation in the '90s. Whether this actually will be the case will be decided by you who use it.

AVM/UCM

Preface

Literacy Disorders presents diagnostic and remedial reading as a challenging and dynamic discipline and points out how your involvement and participation can shape its future. The text covers the traditional material as well as some topics that are enjoying a resurgence of popularity and some that are unique among books of this type. The major topics included are as follows:

- *understanding the reading process as the basis for remediation*
- *conducting comprehensive assessment*
- *strategic reading—the flexible use of reading strategies*
- *providing for broad-based literacy needs, including spelling and handwriting*
- *providing for higher-order literacy needs, including study, writing, and aspects of effective thinking*

If there is a fundamental assumption in this field, it is that effective diagnosis and remediation requires *reflective teaching*—the *flexible* use of testing and teaching strategies. Three features of this book promote this key objective teaching. One is an emphasis on laying out the *concepts* that underlie most testing and teaching procedures. This concept-based approach is intended to equip the professional educator to meet unanticipated situations and job roles. The second feature is the use of *heuristics* for teaching and testing. Heuristics are methods that induce reflective thinking and ongoing self-education; they cause one to learn by doing. The third feature is a repeated emphasis on three types of teacher/student conversation that are inherently self-educating or heuristic: the instructional conversation, the diagnostic dialogue, and the therapeutic dialogue.

The theme of reflective teaching supports a major movement in education to empower teachers with sound knowledge and choices. Reflective teaching is based on the premise that while teaching has a scientific basis, it remains the responsibility of each teacher to exercise fair judgment in its interpretation. The pages ahead report the scientific findings and many of the experiences and interpretations of the authors and of many other clinicians and teachers. Your initial interpretations will no doubt evolve as you teach and experience.

We expect that you will find *Literacy Disorders* to be quite "reader friendly." Each chapter is introduced with a relevant quotation, an outline of the chapter, and a focusing introduction called *Look For It*. Within the chapter, you will find *Figures* that illustrate the complex points and *Boxes* that provide additional supportive information or exercises designed to deepen and personalize your connection to the material. Finally, each chapter closes with a brief summary called *Looking Back,* and a section called *Looking Ahead* to connect you to the next chapter. There also are interesting and useful appendices. One provides explicit help with assessment and contains information you will need to assess many aspects of affect. Other appendices provide a graded word list for teaching vocabulary, proverbs that can be used to improve comprehension and abstract thinking, an annotated bibliography of materials for improving higher-order thinking in remedial level readers, and a handy primer and critique on the brain brief history of the definition of functional literacy illustrates what has happened, how it is altering our professional priorities, and how we are attempting to address the situation. Until about three generations ago, most people were able to go through their entire lives as self-sufficient individuals with little more than the ability to read some labels and sign their names. At about the time of the first World War, it became necessary to be able to read a newspaper and listen to the radio in order to monitor and understand life-affecting world and local events, and to cope with changing job demands. Reading also became an increasingly popular way to enjoy the little leisure time that was available. The compounding effects of the Great Depression and the birth of modern technology, along with a continuing shift away from purely menial to mechanically assisted work further increased reading demands. In grade level equivalents, you could say that the children of the pre-World War I era could have gotten by with a second to third grade reading level, whereas their children needed an astonishing sixth to eighth grade reading level. That translates into about a four-grade increase in education needed to be functionally "literate" in less than one generation. This could be called the first great literacy crisis.

The onset of World War II and the continuing increase in the sophistication of the equipment of war and industry further accelerated the demand for a literate citizenry. Even higher levels of reading proficiency and knowledge were needed to work with others on tasks that also required cooperation and effective communication. It was about this time that the number of attorneys needed began to grow astronomically, not to handle any real increase in crime, but to deal essentially with contract law and various forms of disputes related to failed efforts to communicate effectively with one another and work cooperatively. By 1955, although people were essentially the same, educators projected that everyone would need a high school education and equivalent reading ability in order to function in the years ahead. When the Russians launched Sputnik just two years later, it raised questions about this literacy target again. Nonetheless, as late as 1965, estimations of projected earnings made by the Labor Department still were given in terms of projected income with vs. without a *high school* diploma; now, projected income is based on high school vs. *college* education, and the differences between these levels has become staggering. Only 15 years ago, according to the U.S. Department of Labor Statistics, a person graduating from college could expect to earn twice as much as a person with a high school education. Today, a college education is worth up to 4 times as much, and, incredibly, it is projected that by the time the children we are now teaching reach the work force it will be worth *17* times as much. This is not the difference between lower, middle, and upper middle class, but the difference between the "haves" and the "have-nots."

Soaring literacy requirements have underscored the need to reconceptualize "remedial reading." In particular, it is clear that almost everyone now suffers from some form of *specific functional illiteracy*. Box 1.2 gives an idea of how well you, with a college education, are handling today's "basic" functional literacy requirements.

BOX 1.2

Functional Literacy Questionnaire

Directions: Place a check beneath the best estimation of how well you can do each of the items listed below.

	VERY WELL	WELL	NOT WELL
1. programming your clock radio and VCR			
2. filling out and filing your own federal and state income tax returns			
3. understanding and voting on local referenda issues			
4. understanding and voting on issues related to foreign affairs			
5. understanding and acting on the growing barrage of information on nutrition, health, and exercise			
6. understanding and dealing effectively with the many facets of owning a car (purchase and payment options, driver's license, license plates, city stickers, local and state taxes, safety inspections, maintenance, and the many questions related to insurance)			
7. understanding, to the level of thinking critically and creatively about the literature and current options being expressed in your own field			
8. remembering and analyzing what you have read or studied			
9. writing business letters, notes, memoranda, academic papers, and professional reports, each with proper style and formatting			

Let us now take a brief look at the recent history of remedial reading. This should help you get a better perspective on the role you might wish to play in it.

Recent and Continuing History of Remedial Reading

Remedial reading, for much of its early life, was a "pull-out" program. Students were taken from their regular classrooms for individual or small group tutoring. Since the need for these programs often was an afterthought, schools were not designed to accommodate them. Not surprisingly, reading specialists often operated in inadequately ventilated rooms, in basements, if not in oversized broom closets. This "add-on" picture is changing as we come to grips with the sheer size of the need. Today's reading teacher needs to be a major player in the school, and in at least three other theaters of social activity: 1) helping students feel more whole and functionally literate; 2) securing democratic life by helping students continue to be well-informed for the rest of their lives; and 3) addressing higher-order as well as basic literacy needs that every citizen needs to conduct personal life and vote intelligently.

The reasons that remedial reading specialists can continue to be major players in the educational process is largely attributable to the quality of the basic principles underlying the field and its practices. The basic principles that underlie remedial reading, now nearly 100 years old, are being applied in a wider variety of contexts than ever before. These principles are an integral part of the philosophy and practices of fields and programs such as Learning Disabilities, Chapter I, mainstreaming, class within a class, Reading Recovery (described ahead), and other forms of preventative, corrective, and compensatory education from preschool to college levels. Ironically, interest in these new fields and programs has temporarily dimmed the realization that the basic principles of remedial reading are still viable and have served as a dependable beacon by which to find our way in meeting these newer regions of demand. No matter how current and past movements and programs are viewed, and some do view "remedial reading" as archaic, it still will fall on tomorrow's literacy specialists to come up with the means of providing for school and lifetime literacy needs of all who attend school, including those with limited English proficiency, those who are slow to learn, and those who are, at least on the surface, resentful of learning. This will require considerable imagination and involvement outside of the traditional classroom. Three recent occurrences illustrate how a movement toward this broadened state of involvement already is under way.

- There is a nationwide movement to make all government materials more readable. (For more information, write to: "Simply Stated," Document Design Center, 1055 Jefferson St., Washington, DC 20007.)
- Educational psychologists and reading specialists have created a new field, called "text technology," which is dedicated to finding the most effective

---

BOX 1.3

Facts About University-Based Reading Clinics

1. Male clients outnumber females by a 3-to-1 ratio.
2. Most clients are in the 7-12 age range.
3. Over 90% are individually treated.
4. Clinics tend to operate during summers only.
5. Parents make over 80% of referrals to clinics.
6. More than half have insufficient space.
7. Clinics tend to have very good relationships with public schools.
8. Clinics tend to provide excellent training in diagnosis.
9. Regarding instruction in the 6-9 age range:
   a. writing is heavily emphasized.
   b. decoding instruction was strong, with analytic phonics being emphasized three times as much as synthetic phonics.
   c. readiness, sight words, and oral language received more emphasis than explicit comprehension instruction.
10. Regarding instruction in the 10-13 age range:
    a. comprehension and content area reading and study skills are most heavily emphasized.
    b. writing also is heavily emphasized.
    c. sight vocabulary, decoding, and oral language dropped a bit in emphasis, but still are held to be important.
11. Regarding instruction in the 14-17 age range:
    a. the major emphasis is comprehension, content area reading, and reference skills.
    b. oral language, writing, and reading rate receive "some" emphasis.
    c. word analysis receives only token attention.
12. There is heavy emphasis at all levels on building positive attitudes.
13. Computers are used in only 19% of clinics (at that time).
14. The most frequently used methods and approaches (again at that time) are: Language Experience Approach (87%); "linguistic patterns" (no other elaboration available) (52%); Fernald VAK(T) (37%); Directed Reading-Thinking Activity (31%); basal reading series (6%).

Boder & Wiesendanger (1986)

---

means of writing, organizing, structuring, and displaying instructional text for remedial, average, and even above average readers.

- There is a growing concentration of effort on how to diagnose and correct not mere literal level reading problems, but anything and everything that may impede progress toward reading, language, thinking, content knowledge, and social-emotional maturity.

The latter point is evident in the research of Lois A. Boder and Katherine D. Wiesendanger (1986) on university-based reading clinics, as summarized in Box 1.3. Of course, many of the traditional statistics and roles that have characterized remedial reading operations also clearly remain true in their findings.

As a final preparation for study in the remainder of this text, it is advisable to pause and collect your thoughts on your still forming perspective of the field, and the roles you might come to play in it.

Personal Professional Perspectives and Roles

Much of what is gleaned from any situation is decided by one's initial perspective. The simplest way to get a sense of your current perspective is to try to determine what you see yourself doing professionally. An outline and critique of some basic job descriptions in the field of reading diagnosis and remediation is provided below to help you get a realistic look at your options. There are essentially eight career roles for individuals with a profound working knowledge of reading process and related literacy skills. Rate each of these on a scale of 1 (lowest) to 7 (highest) according to your *current interest level*. Discuss and compare your ratings with those of others as a way to clarify and "reality test" your present views and initial decisions.

YOUR RATING	ROLES
_____	1. An elementary, middle, or secondary school classroom teacher who wishes to be knowledgeable about how to screen and refer youngsters for special help, and to provide in-class assistance to special needs students
_____	2. An elementary, middle, or secondary school teacher who teaches one or two reading classes per day in addition to other duties
_____	3. An elementary, middle, secondary, or college teacher who is a full-time reading/study skills specialist and may also have duties in a reading and writing laboratory or center
_____	4. A site-based reading or literacy resource specialist whose primary responsibility is to confer on a regular basis with other teachers, assisting them in addressing the reading, writing, and related literacy needs of their students. The resource specialist may also teach several "pull-out" students whose needs can not be fully met in the regular classroom.
_____	5. A learning disabilities teacher or specialist who works with a reading specialist or who is personally responsible for the identification and treatment of learning disabled students
_____	6. A school or central office based administrator who has experience and expertise in detecting and meeting the full literacy needs of children

YOUR RATING	ROLES

_____ 7. A central office reading resource teacher who primarily serves as an assistant to a director or coordinator and serves several schools from a district office. This person may assist school-based reading specialists with individual student testing and treatment recommendations; provide inservice training and demonstration lessons; assist with the selection, purchase, and distribution of materials; and generally act as the chief liaison between the school-based specialist and the school district's reading and/or language arts coordinators.

_____ 8. A coordinator or director of reading and/or language arts, for elementary, middle, and/or secondary schools, depending upon the size of the district and the needs and expectations of the community. This person primarily is responsible for overall program quality. S/he may recommend methods and materials, arrange for and/or provide inservice training, articulate the roles and responsibilities of other reading and/or language arts personnel, and help the superintendent and school board understand and meet the needs of all of the district's children.

Whichever of the above roles happens to define your present or future professional life, the one thing that will serve you above all else on the long term is a profound, conceptual knowledge of the "business."

> ⟩   **_LOOKING BACK_**   ⟨

The chapter explained and illustrated how spiralling literacy demands continue to keep remedial reading programs necessary and vital. The chapter also illustrated how this vitality is reflected in the shift in terminology from "reading" to "literacy;" the implication being that the latter term is more indicative of the broader scope of concerns, such as for language, thinking, writing, and social-emotional adjustment that now are attended to as part of the reading curriculum. Finally, the chapter offered some critical guidance in helping you determine which of a variety of roles you might choose in identifying your place in this traditional—though still emerging—field.

➤ *LOOKING AHEAD*

The next chapter lays out the conceptual bases of the field and will bring you "up to speed" on what is known about the reading process, particularly as it relates to diagnosis and remediation. It also tells about how various groups and movements, or schools of thought, are earnestly attempting to address the nation's literacy needs.

2

Models of Reading and Approaches to Literacy Disorders

> ➤ *LOOK FOR IT*

This chapter provides the organizational framework for the remainder of the text by addressing the two most fundamental questions underlying reading diagnosis and remediation: *Why do literacy disorders occur?* and *How should literacy disorders be treated?*

The first question is answered in largely theoretical terms. The second question is answered much more practically here and throughout the remainder of the text in terms of how theories and models are translated into practices or treatments. The chapter begins with an explanation of how current theories, or "models," of reading explain reading process and reading disorders.

Current and Emerging Models of Reading: Implications to Diagnosis and Remediation

Reading occurs inside the head. It becomes partially observable when one reads aloud, but oral reading is only the end effect of a complex and highly integrated process. A "model" of the reading process is a theoretical statement, often accompanied by graphic illustrations, of what happens inside the head when one reads.

Understanding the reading process helps us more accurately identify causes of reading problems. Better diagnosis of reading problems, in turn, helps us select and implement more effective remedial strategies. Models of reading generally fall into three general categories: bottom-up models, top-down models, and interactive models. Each is a way of seeing what "happens" when one reads. Each also has implications for how to teach reading and what one should do to correct reading problems.

Every practitioner as well as theoretician is routinely involved in model building. More importantly, whether we realize it or not, our attitudes and behaviors as teachers are strongly influenced by our implicit model. One well-known model builder, Harry Singer (researcher on the substrata factor theory of reading), once noted that his son's fourth grade teacher revealed her implicit model of reading when she said that the boy was bright and capable but not yet quite ready to engage in the close-knit act of reading. According to Singer, the boy's teacher was saying that she believed in a "developmental model of reading;" that is, one that places great stock in physical and emotional maturation more so than exposure and instruction (Singer, 1985).

As you read about each of the three categories of models, try to determine which model seems to be most compatible with your views and current context.

Bottom-Up Models

Bottom-up models picture reading as a step-by-step process that begins with letter perception, moves on to recognition of phonetic elements, then words, groups of words, and finally sentence, paragraph, and passage meaning. The reader's job is to process these units accurately and promptly. Mastery of each successive reading subskill is the means and the basic formula for achieving reading competency (Gough & Cosky, 1977). These models have been called text-driven, meaning that the page is the meaning giver, and the reader is the meaning receiver. Theoretical support for bottom-up models is derived from two sources: the "automaticity (or rapid word recognition) theory" of reading set forth by LaBerge & Samuels (1974), and the analysis of huge bodies of research by Jeanne Chall (1967), Connie Juel (1991), Marilyn Adams (1991), and others who have routinely concluded that approaches to beginning reading that stress phonics tend to produce greater initial gains, and fewer remedial readers (Chall, 1967). Additional support for bottom-up models can be inferred from Holmes and Singer's (1961) "substrata factor" theory of reading. This theory, based on data collected from students at different grade and ability levels, proposed that early reading success was a product of several strata of factors, such as mental age, chronological age, and conceptual ability at one level, and then by mastery of word recognition and spelling skill, etc. at the next level, and so on to several possible interacting levels. The substrata factor theory also contains a developmental feature that says that some skills may recede in importance at a certain grade level, and that then a different cluster of factors may assume more or less importance as one progresses to the next age/grade level. This developmental feature is cited by the supporters of "mastery learning" to mean that one can not master the next set of substrata factors if one hasn't mastered an earlier set. It also is cited by those opposed to mastery learning as evidence that mastery of lower order skills may not be evident or necessary when a student has progressed to the next higher level of operation.

In any case, the basic objection to bottom-up models is that they are unable to explain the effects of context on speed of reading, an effect that has been observed under experimental conditions to be natural, and therefore should be apparent in a good model (Stanovich, 1980; Wesson, Vierthaler, & Haubrich, 1989). Also, when interpreted into practice, bottom-up approaches don't seem to reconcile well with human motivation. They tend to stress putting the reader's own interests and agenda on hold while he or she concentrates a great deal of energy and attention just on learning how to decode, or reach "automaticity." It has been further noted that bottom-up models seem to continue to stress accuracy in word analysis and literal comprehension long after word recognition has been mastered, and often to the detriment of language and thinking development. Samuels (1983), as well as others who have constructed bottom-up models, have routinely denied these characterizations as exaggerations or distortions of this position. Nevertheless, there are some bottom-up approaches to instruction that do deserve criticism since they can lapse into mind-numbing routines. The "linguistic approach" (Bloomfield & Barnhardt, 1962; Fries, 1963) to teaching reading, for example, uses "stories" carefully composed to control the introduction of new phonic elements. The result is "stories" like the following:

The cat sat on the mat.
The rat sat on the mat.
The cat and the rat
    sat on the mat.
The cat had a hat.
The rat had a hat.
The cat had a hat on the mat.

It was largely in reaction to instructional practices of this type that top-down models began to emerge. You may not be surprised to learn that some of these may have gone too far in the opposite direction; however, it also may be short-sighted to say that there can never be a place for such controlled texts in special circumstances.

Top-Down Models

Top-down models view reading as a search for meaning. 100% accuracy in word recognition is not as important as getting the general sense of what one is reading. For example, if the printed words are, "He was delighted," it is not so important if a child reads "He was very happy." Top-down models suggest that such renditions are better thought of as "miscues" rather than as "errors." The reader is making use of several cue systems to produce an oral version of the printed message: in addition to letter cues, the reader appears to be applying context and prior personal experiences to produce a meaningful translation. Supporters of top-down models consider this type of "miscue" to indicate a reading *strength*, rather than a word recognition weakness.

Proponents of top-down models have evolved some general guidelines for reading instruction. These guidelines have come to be known as the Whole Language approach. The term "approach" refers to the expressions or operations that come to be associated with a given philosophy. This approach stresses the importance of creating an "authentic" literate environment, rather than a highly didactic or "teachy" one. The idea is that a literate environment will be conducive to reading, writing, and language development, and will provide many timely opportunities for children to learn to read as they are drawn into reading through their natural inclinations to use language and to grapple with meaning in whatever form it presents itself. The key distinguishing feature of this approach, from a classroom point of view, is that it provides instruction on an incidental basis rather than in a planned, sequential way. Jerome Harste, et.al. (1982) represents the prevailing attitude of whole language enthusiasts when he says that children first internalize what reading is, then they take steps toward decoding (as cited in Swaby, 1989).

It has been suggested by some that bottom-up models of reading tend to describe what *beginning* readers do, whereas top-down models tend to describe what *proficient* readers do. Empirical findings, however, suggest that this distinction is not entirely accurate. In a study that compared several of the reading behaviors of poor and fluent readers, Just & Carpenter (1980) discovered that fluent readers concentrated more on words and word parts to build meaning, whereas poorer readers relied more on the context to guess at how to read the words. This finding seems especially laden with meaning where remedial instruction is concerned, a point that will come up again in considering the next type of model.

Interactive models of reading clearly are the most widely supported. Even those who are proponents of essentially top-down or bottom-up models are quick to say that they too basically hold to an interactive view. This is not surprising, since interactive models include both reconstructive and constructive operations. Interactive models also have shortcomings, but these are being corrected with each refinement.

Interactive Models

Interactive models say that a reader decides on a word's meaning by a combination of top-down and bottom-up processing approaches. The term interactive refers to the interaction of different information sources available to readers, not as is often suggested as an interaction between reader and text (see the non-interactive model ahead for a clarification). The four primary sources of information are:

- the phonetic features of letters, known as *orthography*
- the sentence structure features of language, known as *syntax*
- the meanings of language, known as *semantics*
- the meanings each of us carries with us from *human experience*

One of the better known interactive models of reading was proposed by Rumelhart (1977). In this model, Rumelhart articulated what has been the prominent position of most educators for some time.

Here is how a reading scenario would be described from the perspective of an interactive model. A student is reading the following: "Mary had a little lamb, whose fleece was white as snow." When the student gets to "fleece" this word may look unfamiliar, so s/he slows down to consider it. The student wonders, "Is it pronounced *flees* or *fleecy*?" Then, remembering the rhyme s/he has heard and recited before, realizes, "Oh, that's what that word is that I've been saying, and that's how it's spelled." In this process, sometimes called analytic phonics, the student deduces how to say a word by a combination of initial consonant sounds and context cues until the word is recognized as one already in the child's listening or reading vocabulary. Typically, the reader then continues with some related, human-experience-searching thoughts, such as, "Just what is a *fleece* anyway?" Using the context again, the student seeks meaning: the context here suggests that it is another word for fur, because lambs usually have a white coat, and the student has seen storybook pictures of Mary and her little lamb.

In this apparently simple example, the child has conducted a complex interactive analysis. A top-down approach initiated the reading, as the child used what was known to enter the text. Then, on encountering an unfamiliar printed word, the child switched to a bottom-up approach, using some knowledge of phonics and sentence structure to predict and confirm the pronunciation of a word that had been, until that point, part of an incompletely comprehended string of language. Continuing this bottom-up analysis, the child noted and visualized the printed form of the new word, and finally, switching again to a top-down approach, reflected again on the context to confirm and clarify its meaning. This view of the reading process strongly resembles Thorndike's early description of reading as a problem-solving process (1917).

It is this problem-solving aspect of the interactive model that has fueled a growing interest in promoting higher-order literacy. The importance of *reasoning*, at even the most literal levels of reading, underscores the importance of promoting higher-order thinking even among remedial level readers. Additionally, it is evident that any attempt to "read the lines" is greatly aided by the ability to "read between the lines" and even further aided by efforts of "reading beyond the lines," where initial levels of reading can be enriched by world knowledge, personal interests, and curiosity.

Interactive models have several other implications for detecting and treating literacy problems and disorders. One is that one's ability to learn from reading can be improved simply by increasing the one's general fund of information, or domain knowledge (Pearson & Fielding, 1991). This principle was demonstrated rather dramatically in a recent unpublished study by Manzo, Manzo, and Smith (in preparation), in which at-risk fourth graders in an inner-city school were shown to have made much greater gains on a wide variety of measures of reading and academic achievement when they were taught *concepts* and related interdisciplinary *content* as well as reading skills. Another implication of the interactive model is that reading should be taught with an emphasis on independent strategies for monitoring and "fixing up" comprehension when it appears to be faltering. This emphasis is a central feature of the "Interactive-Compensatory Model," an interactive model that has special significance to the diagnosis and treatment of literacy disorders, and is therefore described in more detail.

Interactive-Compensatory Model

The Interactive-Compensatory model proposes that a student with a deficiency at any level of reading generally will compensate for it by drawing on a perceived strength at another level of reading (Stanovich, 1980, 1986a). In practical terms, this simply means that when a reader has a word recognition deficiency, s/he probably will resort to available higher-order knowledge structures in an attempt to compensate for those weaknesses. In other words, weak readers tend to use context, pictures, prior knowledge, and prediction to compensate for poor letter-sound relationship skills. This model explains the findings of Just and Carpenter (1980), referenced above, and further suggests the apparent need to give remedial students training in how to use each of these cuing systems (Juel, 1991).

On a slightly more speculative note, we take the Stanovich model and the Just and Carpenter findings to suggest further that where readers have difficulty with higher-order reading—that is, poor levels of inferential, evaluative, and applied reading—they too will resort to compensation by overanalyzing every word and phrase. In serious cases, we have observed such students engaged in such an obsessive degree of analysis that they tended to turn up seeming ambiguities in even the simplest of statements, and especially so where even the slightest inference was called for. Two extreme examples of this odd condition, called hyperlexia and Williams syndrome, are discussed in the chapter on severe reading disabilities.

In general, the interactive-compensatory model of reading seems to suggest that instruction for readers with either basic or higher-literacy deficiencies should not dissuade them from relying on their perceived strengths when they are in a difficult reading situation, but that they also need to be helped to face up to their weaknesses and tackle them with a well-thought-out plan. This critical understanding is more fully discussed in the chapter on principles of remediation. Consider now one other, less popular, view that is also something of a model.

Hayes's Non-Interactive Model

David A. Hayes (1990) argues that reading is not complex at all. "Put simply," he says, "reading is thinking about the referents of symbols marked on a surface" (p. 2). He adds that it proceeds by a sequential synthesis of symbol interpretations and culminates in thoughts formed from these interpretations.

Hayes does not believe that youngsters need to be taught to "introspect the reading act" (p. 4) since, in his view, it can not be done while you are reading anyway. He also does not believe that we "interact with a text" as if there was a give and take between reader and author. No such interaction is possible. The text, he says, is fixed in print—it is inert. The reader must do everything to get meaning from the page. It should be noted that the interactive model of reading originally referred only to the reader interactively, or selectively, using top-down and bottom-up processes.

Hayes maintains that if we think critically about reading, we would conclude that it simply is a process of "thoughtfully interpreting symbols displayed in a text" (p. 5).

We find sense and a little comfort in Hayes's view, but believe, too, that his differences with others stem largely from words and metaphors that have been taken too literally, rather than from real conceptual differences. Nonetheless, he probably is correct when he suggests that words invite confusion and have led to such "wrong-headed" propositions as the belief that reading is too complex to ever understand; that introspection on the act of reading while engaged in reading, empowers reading; and that proficient reading is, in any literal sense, an interaction between a reader and an author. Hence, while Hayes's point is well taken, it is necessary to remain focused on acquiring a broad understanding of the field by reviewing the major ideas, precepts, and movements that have come to influence how diagnosis and remediation are understood and conducted. To achieve this, we shall now review the major schools of thought in the field, beginning with a brief account of "traditional diagnosis and remediation," a time-honored school of thought that was built on several of the propositions espoused by Hayes.

Schools of Thought

A school of thought is a contextualized theory; it includes relevant information about the people behind the idea, and about the evolution of the idea from its inception to current applications. This kind of contextualization of a theory often reveals the practical shortcomings of approaches that may otherwise seem theoretically sound. In fact, impractical and unsound theories and approaches have been known to win widespread popularity through the sheer personal magnetism of their creators. Revelations of this type should arm you to:

- establish realistic expectations of yourself, your colleagues, and your students;
- develop more astute powers of critical analysis;
- develop a more constructive problem-solving outlook in dealing with literacy needs;
- get a preliminary grasp of some of the umbrella concepts that comprise the major approaches to detecting and treating literacy disorders.

Traditional Diagnosis and Remedial Reading

Turn of the century physicians were among the first to describe severe cases of reading disability. At about the same time, psychologists were undertaking the initial investigations into the nature of reading disability (Dearborn, 1906; Huey, 1908; Quartz, 1897). These investigations were furthered by significant advances in the measurement of reading and "intellectual capacity." The first professional books on reading diagnosis and remediation were written by Clarence T. Gray (1922) and William S. Gray (1925). The influence of medicine, however, was not lost. In fact, it was Arthur Gates, a medical school dropout, who firmly implanted the "medical model" into the reading business by writing more than 100 articles and studies on reading, including several widely used basic textbooks (Schell, 1988).

The medical model is sometimes maligned for the fact that it ostensibly assumes that there is a defect in the reader (Lipson & Wixon, 1991), which it flatly does not. It also deals more with the loss or damage to a mature ability than with the problem of poor acquisition of that ability. Gates and others were aware of these imperfections of "fit," but suggested that this analog still was the most appropriate approach to diagnosing and treating reading disorders. The medical model of diagnosis and remediation simply says that before a reading problem can be effectively treated, it is necessary to classify it in terms of its major symptoms and *probable causes*. In order to identify causes, it is necessary to understand and be able to identify many of the possible factors that might contribute to reading failure, and to consider the comparative weightings and interactions of these factors in a given case. From the early 1920s until the late 1960s, most of the work in diagnosis and remediation was clinic-based, and *psychoeducational* in nature—reading specialists were psychologists who specialized in education, or educators with a broad knowledge of psychology. This connection had all but atrophied by the early 1970s, and is only now being renewed (as you will read ahead).

Implementation of the medical model of diagnosis and remediation calls for initial screening of all students to categorize their developmental progress and identify those who might be in need of specialized assistance, including preventive assistance (Putnam, 1991). Students who are reading far ahead of age-grade expectations are classified as "advanced" readers (a designation seldom used, but potentially useful). Students reading at a level that is consistent with their age, grade level, and IQ are categorized as "developmental" readers. Students needing extra instructional assistance are categorized as "corrective" readers (those who are six months to approximately one and a half years below their expectancy level), or as "remedial" readers (those who are approximately two years or more below their expectancy level). Students with the greatest need are then referred to a reading specialist for a more intensive diagnosis of their apparent reading problems. Typically, these youngsters become the reading specialist's primary obligation and usually are "pulled out" of class on a regular basis for special instruction until their reading problems are corrected, and they can function in a regular classroom. In order to assist the remedial students in this catch-up effort, the classroom teacher is expected to coordinate methodology and grouping practices with the recommendations of the reading specialist. The classroom teacher also collaborates with the reading specialist to design instructional procedures that will best meet the needs of corrective and developmental students. Only recently has attention been paid to "advanced" or gifted readers.

While basically sound in theory, certain practical problems have been said to arise sometimes with this approach. They include the following:

- The classroom teacher's plans for the class may conflict with the reading specialist's interpretation of the special needs of the few.
- The child may miss important class time when attending the pull-out remedial sessions.
- The negative effects of labelling the child may overshadow the positive effects of the remedial sessions.
- Diagnosis and remediation may be isolated from classroom operations, the very place where adjustments and application most need to occur.
- The controlled reading level and reduced content load of typical remedial materials may have little motivational value, and actually deprive the child of needed opportunities to engage in educationally challenging tasks.
- The accent placed on detecting remedial problems often tends to reduce the emphasis that could be placed on early identification and prevention of reading problems.

- The classroom teacher, in deferring to the reading specialist, may actually begin to do *less* with reading, rather than more, and reading may become increasingly isolated from the other language arts.
- Diagnosis, under this approach, may be of variable quality, sometimes being limited simply to characterizing the child's already obvious reading deficiencies.

Years of experience with traditional diagnosis and remediation have increased the field's wisdom in how to ease some of these potential ill effects. Two innovations are especially worth noting here. One is the evolution of a powerful idea called diagnostic-teaching (Gable, et.al., 1990; Valencia, 1991; Zabroske & Klever, 1991) that stresses having the teacher conduct lessons that are designed to disclose and treat reading and related literacy needs simultaneously in the conventional classroom. The other is the continued evolution of the reading specialist into a reading consultant and/or reading resource teacher. In this approach, sometimes called "push-in" (Reynolds, Wang, & Walbert, 1987), the resource teacher helps identify students with reading needs and then helps teachers provide for those students' special needs within the classroom. A third development, which draws heavily on the wisdom of the first two, is called Content Area Reading, an approach that is often unrealized for its contribution to prevention, diagnosis, and remediation.

The Content Area Reading Movement

Initially, the content area reading movement has focused largely on the secondary schools. Content area reading (CAR) developed largely in answer to a question frequently posed by frustrated teachers: "How can I help my students study and learn from books that they can hardly read?" The idea that youngsters who have *learned to read* still need to be taught to *read to learn* was first launched almost 70 years ago (Gray, 1922). Over the last 30 years, pursuit of this concept has stimulated the development of an impressive body of ideas and practices, many of which are applicable for any teacher at any level.

Early Efforts: The Compensation Principle

Some early efforts in this field, as in most new fields of study, led to incomplete or impractical answers and blind alleys. One incomplete answer was the concept of simply helping poor readers to *compensate* for their weak reading. Rather than building independence, things were adjusted to their needs. By the mid-1960s, typical compensations included:

- purchasing multiple textbooks at varying difficulty levels for a single course
- rewriting textbooks to lower their difficulty levels
- developing lessons in ways that required poorer readers to read less
- audiotaping texts and tests for poorer readers
- simply advising poorer readers to take a watered-down version of a particular course.

Seeing the folly in this type of compensation as a *primary* approach to remediation, the content area reading movement shifted its perspective. Rather than merely helping students compensate for their inability to read and learn from textbooks, it refocused its efforts on helping them build their reading power. While the compensation model was never entirely abandoned, the CAR movement remains firmly based on two principles of empowerment that form part of the basis for many contemporary literacy efforts.

Two Principles of Empowerment

Much is being written about empowerment in recent years (c.f. Pierce, 1991; Carr & Williams, 1991; Burnett, 1991; Levesque & Prosser, 1991). The first principle of empowerment could be called "The Making of Strategic Readers." A "strategy," in this context, refers to what a reader might say to himself or herself before, during, and/or after reading. According to this principle, reading power is built by engaging students in a process of understanding, observing, and then internalizing and practicing effective reading strategies. This process involves a certain degree of self-monitoring while reading, and practice in selecting and using appropriate "fix-up" strategies when comprehension seems to be faltering.

The second principle of empowerment could be called "The Rule of Contiguity." "Contiguity" means being close together. Since students' reading difficulties arise in the content classroom, it is the content teacher who is close at hand to provide assistance at the most receptive and "teachable moment." Hence, the content area reading movement has provided most of the basic methodology for seizing the moment and making the most of it.

Notice that both of these principles cast the teacher as a model and coach in how to read and think effectively more so than as a didactic giver of information. In this approach, the student is seen essentially as an apprentice who has come to the workbench of a teacher craftsman, who is a dedicated, lifelong student of a subject. The challenge has been to come up with heuristics that bring about an instructional conversation between teacher and students that advances understanding and mediation of text.

The recent advancement of the learning disabilities movement, with required mainstreaming of special needs students, has given considerable impetus to content area reading methods, though the LD movement remains more philosophically wedded to a compensatory model. The reasons for this philosophical difference are interesting and instructive.

The Learning Disabilities Movement

From its onset, the learning disabilities movement has been more of a political and social movement than an educational one. Its early supporters were primarily middle- and upper-class parents eager to attribute the underachievement of their children to something other than low intelligence or emotionality. For example, Nelson Rockefeller, former governor of New York and member of one of the wealthiest families in the world, was said to have been dyslexic. Neal

Bush, the son of President and Mrs. George Bush, also had "a touch of dyslexia," according to Mrs. Bush. Even the fictitious son of the highly educated Cliff and Claire Huckstable of "The Cosby Show" developed dyslexia when he went on to college.

Mothers across the country, some with seriously handicapped children, joined together with those who had children with traditional reading and learning problems, and through their well-leveraged positions, pressured state legislatures and the federal government into passing laws requiring that special accommodations be provided for all of these "handicapped" children, from the elementary grades through the college level. Public Law 94–142 covered elementary and high school, and Public Law 504 was written to cover their needs through the college level.

Surprisingly enough, this legislation was written, debated, and passed without the development of a clear conceptual or operational definition of learning disabilities. The closest thing to a definition was a statement that a child was "learning disabled" if:

- there was a discrepancy between his or her intellectual ability and academic achievement;
- this discrepancy was *not* due primarily to lack of cultural opportunity or to psychological disorders; and,
- the discrepancy could, therefore, be assumed to be the result of some form of neurological deficit.

Since a neurological deficit is a physical condition, this definition permitted "learning disabilities" to be brought in under the rules and accommodations that were being set up for the physically handicapped. The most important of these rules called for all handicapped children to be accommodated in a "least restrictive environment." This meant that they were to be "mainstreamed" into regular classrooms. Moreover, mainstreaming was to be accompanied by highly specialized testing, professional consultation, and complete "individual educational plans," known as I.E.P.'s, for each mainstreamed handicapped student. Thus, the mainstreaming of the physically handicapped also came to provide these identical services for all L.D. students, and in a socially acceptable way. Unfortunately, while this model tends to lighten the burden on the L.D. student and his or her parents, it increases it to unrealistic levels on schools and teachers—particularly given the fact that over 80% of children diagnosed as L.D. have mild to serious reading disabilities (Kirk & Elkins, 1975; Lyon, 1985).

There are glaring problems with the existing definition of learning disability. The most fundamental problem is that it is difficult if not impossible to *distinguish* a neurological problem from a psychoeducational one with existing tests and technology. Nonetheless, the 94–142 law calls for the clear separation of those with primarily emotional needs from those with more constitutional problems. As a result, the thousands of school children who are diagnosed as learning disabled each year often are treated as if they are free of psychological disorders. This does not reconcile with the long established fact that about 13% of the general population has serious psychological problems, and another 40%

or more has mild psychological disorders. The definitions and regulations of the current system, in all likelihood, are masking the psychological problems of many children who are categorized as learning disabled.

On a more positive note, the L.D. movement has raised everyone's sensibilities to the fact that many children and grown-ups alike do have legitimate literacy and learning needs, and that some of these need to be accommodated, since they probably can not all be remediated. There also is the fact that L.D. specialists have been quite willing to adopt and adapt whatever works. They have and continue to access the literature in the field of reading, and they are leading the way in some related areas that have hampered remedial reading efforts in the past. They are, for example, leading the way in the design and implementation of "push-in" procedures for helping children in the regular classroom. They are doing this with interdisciplinary teams who draw up I.E.P.'s for each child found to be in need. They also have revived interest in seeking the etiology of a learning problem as a fundamental part of planning an instructional program (Sawyer & Wilson, 1979). As a coincidence of this, the L.D. movement also has built further support for the cognitive processing approach to the treatment of reading disorders.

The Cognitive Processing Approach

The cognitive processing approach examines reading from the point of view of information acquisition and concept formation. The idea is that reading and learning disabilities essentially are cognitive processing problems. From this perspective, most reading and learning problems may appear to be some form of language problem, but in actuality are thinking problems, or "cognitive dysfunctions." In order to fix the reading problem, you must fix the underlying thinking problem. Reading skills, in other words, are viewed as a broader class of cognitive skills (Crowder, 1982).

Diane Sawyer (1975) offered a means of inferring a child's ability to read effectively while also aptly stating the underlying thesis of the cognitive processing approach when she said:

> Comprehension is grounded in thinking skills. We can not expect any child to exhibit a greater depth of comprehension in listening or reading than the child is able to demonstrate in manipulative and verbal interactions (1975, p. 1089).

This school of remediation, which is known in Canada and New Zealand as the "cognitive-adaptationist" approach to remediation, also draws heavily on concepts such as metacognition and explicit feedback to students on the reading strategies they seem to be using and what alternatives there are to consider. (See Clare Brett & Carl Bereiter [1989] for an example of this approach in an extended clinical report of a single third-grade boy.)

This explanation of reading problems is compatible with that of the learning disabilities movement, but for the fact that in L.D. the root cause is presumed to be neurological. This arguable point aside, the L.D. movement draws heavily on the concept structure and the language of this approach. Problems in word recognition and analysis, for example, are said to stem from "successive process-ing deficiencies"—that is, the reader can not take in a sequence of sound units and synthesize them into recognizable words. Comprehension problems are said to stem from "simultaneous processing" deficiencies—that is, the reader can not deal, more or less at the same time, with letter sounds, word meanings, sentence structure, new information, and personal reflections (Leong & Haines, 1978; Leong, 1980).

Many of the methodologies offered in this book are compatible with this approach. However, the approaches recommended in this text tend to differ in the degree to which cognitive processing deficiencies are viewed as a cause or merely a correlate of reading and literacy disorders. In other words, strictly speaking, cognitive processing deficits may be neither a cause nor an effect, but a simultaneous problem that interacts with and complicates most reading and related language functions.

In order to help the teacher and diagnostician determine the extent to which a reading-learning problem may be interacting with a cognitive deficiency, it is useful to look next at the psychoeducational approach to reading and related literacy disorders. This school of thought is of potentially great significance since it provides a common ground for understanding higher-order as well as basic literacy needs.

Psychoeducational Approach to Reading Disorders

There are several variations on this approach to reading disorders. The basic belief is that psychological processes best explain how well one reads, what one reads, and what one understands from what is read. Psychological processes, therefore, are held to be accountable for at least some reading disorders.

Early reading specialists were strong supporters of this view. Many, such as Roma Gans (1941), Arthur Gates (1941), Helen Robinson (1946), and William S. Gray (1948) were trained as psychologists as well as educators. While there is a rising interest once again in this perspective (Gentile & McMillian, 1987; Johnston, 1985; Oka & Paris, 1986; Manzo 1977a, 1987), it is a view that has largely been ignored, though never discredited. Ironically, the use of newer branches of psychology, first behavioral psychology and, more recently, cognitive psychol-ogy, have dimmed the perceived value of exploring the psychodynamics sur-rounding a child's inner life as an area of concern and possible adjustment. The dwindling of interest in this realm is at least in part due to the way in which the subject is treated in most current diagnostic and remedial reading textbooks. Typically, the question is posed as to how we can know whether an emotional problem is the cause of reading failure or a symptomatic by-product of it. We suspect, and will elaborate in other chapters ahead, that this intimidating ques-tion has a relatively simple answer: It can not be known for sure, but it is possible to make a reasonable determination and, in either case, we the reading educators should feel obliged to do all that we reasonably can to promote greater personal-social adjustment while providing reading instruction—our clear primary responsibility. There are three simple reasons why we should do this. First, more than half the elements involved in comprehension and higher-order literacy, or reading maturity, are affective and attitudinal (Holmes & Singer, 1961). Second, the emotional health and well-being of children is one of the principle obligations of education. Third, our research paradigms and models of remedial assistance are inadequate without reasonable account of these factors. Karen Wixson and Margorie Lipson (1991) further reflect the coming of change in this regard with this statement from their recent review of the research literature on reading disabilities: "In the future, studies will need to address not only the relationships between metacognition, motivation and cognition, but also whether changes in *affect* and strategy use have enduring benefits for reading achievement" (1991, p. 556). In line with this belief, you will find assessment instruments and teaching methods described ahead that were designed to sharpen the teacher's and reading specialist's psychological sense without converting them into psychologists, or pseudo-therapists.

There are respectable arguments against a psychoeducational approach to the diagnosis and treatment of reading disabilities as summarized below:

1. On a theoretical basis, opponents point out that it remains questionable as to which behaviors, drives, and forces are the result of nurture, or life experience and psychology, and which are constitutional, or the result of chemical and anatomical dispositions that are inherited. In other words, if someone is born with a certain temperamental suit, it is a given, and there is no sense in wasting time characterizing an affect that is essentially unchangeable.
2. On a practical level, psychology introduces too much subjectivity into reading evaluation. It also can skew the treatment of reading disabilities to psychologists rather than to educators.
3. In a related vein, psychologists, counselors, and psychiatrists, as with all other professionals, are largely drawn to their fields for deeply personal reasons, such as to address their own psychological needs and interests. This has resulted in theories and practices which have tended to be biased to people who, generally, are highly verbal, middle class, and white. It also has resulted in the frequently cited study from the 1950s (original source unknown) that psychologists and psychiatrists tend to diagnose and treat their own personality and trait conditions no matter what their clients may need and, therefore, assumes that educators would fall into the same trap.
4. Teachers and school-based personnel simply do not have a charter from the community to collect personal information and to "intervene" in the lives of children and adults.
5. It is unrealistic to think that the huge numbers of children who are in school can be provided for under such a comprehensive educational and psychological model.

Of course, the "pro" side of all this tends to argue that a little of anything *is* better than nothing, and that imperfect systems that are vital should not be abandoned, but improved. There also is a growing realization that the most respected professions are those that do not shy away from murky and difficult issues.

The next approach takes a strong language-based view, while avoiding psychological language and assessment. Nonetheless, it does reflect a good deal of concern for basic psychological and developmental processes. It was known as the "psycholinguistic" approach to reading instruction from the late 1960s to the mid-1970s, but now is better known as the whole language approach.

The Whole Language Approach

The whole language approach to reading has not been fully defined yet in terms of its relationship to diagnosis and remediation. Its origins lie largely in a reaction to what is perceived as the senseless aspects of traditional instruction (McKenna, Robinson, & Miller, 1990). Nonetheless, there are several meaningful themes in this approach that have strong implications for how one might conduct diagnosis and remediation.

The basic idea for this approach was supported initially in a study in which Kenneth Goodman (1967) showed that youngsters made *fewer* miscues and other word calling errors when encountering words in a sentence context than when reading those same words off a list. The chief criticism of this study is that these results seem obvious. More clues, such as are provided by context, will *almost* always yield greater accuracy than fewer clues, as when a word must be faced as a separate entity (Blanchard, 1983). Further, it does not follow from this that the best way to teach children to read words accurately is to present them *only* in context. In fact, Gerald Glass (1973), among others, argues that emphasis on context can lead young readers to become inattentive to letter and sound cues. This, in turn, increases the number of words that are misread, and further distorts the very context the student is being taught to rely on to decode words. This point aside, Goodman, Bird, and Goodman (1991), as well as Smith (1979), and other proponents of this essentially top-down approach have evolved a set of guidelines for reading diagnosis and instruction that have strongly influenced theory and practice.

The major contribution of this approach to diagnosis has been to urge a more careful analysis of oral reading errors to determine whether in fact these might not be better classified as *miscues*—or misspoken words with intact semantic meanings. This practice alone has greatly strengthened respect for the child's inclination to interact with the page in a more top-down—or concept and personal meaning—driven way, rather than in a purely sound-to-word driven—or bottom-up—way.

The contribution of whole language to remediation may be summarized in this way: 1) teach to children's strengths, not to their weaknesses; and, 2) children should be engaged in meaningful interactions of the type from which language springs naturally. When engaged in this way, the assumption is that children will be more responsive to language in all its forms, and they will be inclined to speak more precisely, listen more attentively, and learn to read more accurately, since reading is little more than recorded language and thought. For this reason, among others, whole language enthusiasts stress writing alongside, or even before, formal reading instruction, a practice many remedial specialists are once again coming to support. Sondra Holt and Frances O'Tull (1989) were able to show significant differences in vocabulary, comprehension, and writing when low SES background students engaging in "Sustained Silent Reading" (described ahead in the text) and writing were compared with those in a traditional basal.

There are several accounts ahead of how this message is influencing contemporary diagnostic and remedial procedures. (For further information on the roots, theory, and practices associated with whole language, the reader may wish to see: Yetta Goodman [1989], and Angela Jagger & Kathy Harwood [1989].) In general, whole language is best thought of as a philosophical position or value system that stresses principles of language learning as a chief guide to professional conduct. The same can be said of the next approach, which embraces many of its tenets, though it is more firmly rooted in the tradition of diagnostic and remedial reading.

The Holistic Approach

The holistic, or whole-child, approach is not the least bit new; it is merely a theme, or beacon, to guide choices from all other perspectives. The term holistic, or whole-child, is chosen here in an attempt to find an acceptable term that synthesizes psychoeducational, psycholinguistic, cognitive processing, and behavioral approaches to traditional diagnosis and remediation. It is pragmatic, but not completely eclectic, since it is driven by a very specific set of values that are defined below as "precepts." This approach, in many ways, merely is a more recent evolutionary stage of traditional diagnosis and remediation. The only reason it may seem unfamiliar is that it was all but lost for many years in conventional reading and language arts circles, though it never completely disappeared from remedial reading circles; the diagnosis and treatment of real disabilities seems to have a way of keeping professionals child-centered despite other rising and falling fads and themes. The theme of the holistic approach very simply is to *put kids first!* This means we teach children to read, rather than teaching reading or language to children. The significance of this seemingly slight semantic shift is demonstrated best in the jobs that this approach is willing to take on. These include concerns and objectives that tend to go unattended to by most other approaches to literacy education. The child-first orientation is best grasped by a review of its basic operations and concerns, most of which should seem very familiar.

Precepts of the Holistic Approach

There are essentially seven precepts that underlie the holistic approach:

1. A reading disability rarely takes place in a vacuum. Where a reading disability exists, there probably are at least a few other aspects of the child's life and development that are either being affected or that are contributing factors causing the reading problem to reach serious proportions.

Diagnosis and remediation need not be limited to treating simple reading deficiencies, but should be driven by concern for a child's physical, language, thinking, and social-emotional well-being as well (Gann, 1945; Gray & Rogers, 1956; Manzo & Casale, 1980; Searfoss & Readence, 1989; Rabin, 1991).

It is necessary to engage in a very broad and systematic assessment of a child with a reading disability. This assessment should include appraisal of potentially relevant—though slight and often overlooked—"trace elements" of reading, language, thinking, and social-emotional progress (Manzo & Casale, 1981; Manzo & Manzo, 1990a), such as the ability to take and offer critical feedback. Rude and Oehlkers have pointed out that the very term "diagnosis" suggests that "it consists not only of a knowledge of students' assets and liabilities in reading but also an assessment of the student as a person" (1984, p. 68).

Remediation, as a general rule, should attempt to address the total needs of the child, not merely the most surface or symptomatic expressions of it.

Diagnosis and remediation should be extended, wherever circumstances permit, to include higher-literacy needs of remedial-level youngsters, and to the needs of seemingly proficient readers such as those with poor critical thinking abilities and even those who may read too much (Casale, 1982; Manzo & Manzo, 1990).

Every effort should be made to involve the cognitive, affective, and the often overlooked sensorimotor domains in diagnosis and in remediation. Affective, in this context, refers as much to social situational as to deep emotional factors (Camperell, 1982; Vygotsky, 1962). Sensorimotor here should be taken in its broadest sense to mean the physical-behavioral aspects of learning as referred to by developmental psychologists such as Piaget.

Whenever possible, the student should participate in planning, monitoring, and seeing to his or her own progress.

A New Eclecticism

The whole-child approach is philosophically akin to what is coming to be called the "new paradigm" in geo-political circles where Eastern and Western cultures and forms of government are now melding into new forms. It is this "new eclecticism" that holds to a policy of inclusion rather than exclusion of alternate views. It respects and attempts to learn from past traditions. It is, in effect, less intent on criticizing and wiping out other views as in seeing them fully tested, supported, and assimilated into a growing collective wisdom. It seems to be dawning on everyone that "new" movements in education, as well as in other fields, have tended to belittle veterans, casting them in the role of dinosaurs who must be changed or let go.

The new eclecticism, of which the holistic approach is a part, seems to begin more willingly with a sense of respect for conventions, or the experience and know-how of veterans, and welcomes their voice in the process of charting change or invention. In short, it has a high regard for innovation, but especially so when the *invention* rests firmly on time-tested *conventions*. The "graying" of

America could add more strength to this movement than any additional rhetoric might hope to achieve.

The next approach focuses on *preventing* reading problems among children who are judged to be at-risk. Early prevention sometimes is proposed as an alternative to diagnosis and remediation, but in fact it is meant to be the first order of business in the diagnostic-remedial model. It can even be argued that it is the natural complement to it.

Early Prevention Approach

There is a longstanding belief among educators that early intervention, before a child even begins formal reading instruction, can prevent failure in reading. Over the years, this has taken many forms.

It began with the "reading readiness" question: At what age should children be taught to read to minimize the number who will fail to achieve? For a long time, the most popularly held answer was given not in chronological terms, but as a mental age of 6.5 years.

Subsequent thinking was to designate a clear "prereading" stage and to develop certain prereading skills as a best means of ensuring success once formal reading instruction commenced. This plan had several holes; chief among the problems was the fact that children increasingly were coming to school with a good deal of knowledge about what reading was and even how to do it. Teale (1986), for example, found that some, mostly middle-class children, were coming with as much as ten times the exposure to reading as the children of low-income families.

Ironically, the current and most poplar impression of how to conceptualize early reading and best prevent initial reading failure was written and named over twenty-five years ago. It was called "emergent literacy" by Marie Clay (1966). Clay's work, which was originally done in New Zealand, has evolved into a complete program of early detection and intense tutoring. The program, called Reading Recovery (Clay, 1985) is now being enthusiastically received in the USA.

It is important to realize that the huge investments that have been made in American programs such as Head Start and Chapter I were developed in this same preventative mode. The popularization of the term "children at-risk" is an indication of the level of interest and commitment on the part of American educators in providing early compensatory assistance to youngsters who faced the greatest probability of failure.

These programs are unheralded "successes." This has not been apparent, however, due to the mushrooming numbers of children who are at-risk as a result of dramatic increases in social and political problems such as teenage pregnancy, children born with drug addiction, single parent homes, and budget crunches that are reducing the availability of funds for such programs. In other words, even the most successful programs of early detection and prevention will not be able to reach all children at that time, nor attend to needs that arise

---

BOX 2.1

Self-Profile: Personal Orientation Toward Diagnosis and Remediation

Directions: Make a bar graph by drawing a horizontal line out to the level of your current belief in each of the approaches listed below. Compare and contrast your responses with others', then mark with an "x" any changes in perception you may have come to as a result of discussion and further reflection.

LEVEL OF PERSONAL
ORIENTATION: 0   1   2   3   4   5   6   7   8   9

          (NONE)   (HIGH)

APPROACH:

Traditional

Content Area Reading

Learning Disabilities

Cognitive Processing

Psychoeducational

Whole Language

Holistic (New Eclectic)

---

subsequently. In a manner of speaking, all subsequent diagnostic and remedial efforts are in the spirit of "reading recovery"—or attention to immediate needs in an effort to prevent subsequent failure.

While the focus of the remainder of this text will be on diagnosing and treating those who have "failed," realize that by this we mean that the system too may have failed; a point that Johnson and Allington (1991) make repeatedly in their recent review of the literature on diagnosis and remediation. Pause now to take stock of how you feel about each of the basic approaches presented, and see how your personal orientation toward diagnosis and remediation is forming by completing the self-profile in Box 2.1. To do this effectively probably will require going back and highlighting some of the chief points of these approaches or philosophies.

➤ **LOOKING BACK** ◄

The chapter laid the foundations for understanding currently agreed upon and disputed areas of practice in diagnosis and remediation. This was done by first describing the three basic models of reading upon which practices typically are based, and then by reviewing the nine "schools of thought" through which they tend to find expression. The holistic, or "new eclecticism" was acknowledged as the "school" of choice. It is a philosophy that emphasizes the education of the whole child, and the selection of materials and methods from all other schools on the purely pragmatic basis of whether they meet an apparent need.

➤ **LOOKING AHEAD**

Having surveyed some of the more traditional, current, and emerging themes in contemporary *diagnosis and remediation* of literacy disorders, the next chapter hones in on the specifics of diagnosis. Staying with the theme of providing a conceptual basis for reflective teaching, the chapter attempts to impart a sense of the "diagnostic process" in general terms, followed by a compatible set of specific guiding principles, models, and foundational procedures that underlie most diagnostic practices.

SECTION II

DETECTING LITERACY DISORDERS

Diagnostic Process, Principles, Models, and Procedures

39

> **➤ LOOK FOR IT**

Expect a thorough grounding in diagnosis. The challenging nature of the process becomes apparent in a review of recommended principles and models that are offered to guide it, and in detailed accounts of the underpinning concepts and procedures that are followed in reaching diagnostically sound determinations. Look, too, for an account of the emerging potential in various forms of computerized diagnosis.

Diagnostic Process

The diagnostic process, according to Angela Jaggar (1985), is high-level problem solving that requires the teacher to engage in profound and resourceful thinking. The word "diagnosis" itself reveals this; it is from the Greek, meaning "to know thoroughly." In its original form, it implies taking something apart, or "looking through" an object to see its inner workings (Liddell & Scott, 1940). Today, diagnosis means examining a flawed operational system to uncover the nature of a problem so as to be better able to correct it and add to the knowledge base necessary for solving similar problems. There is an important connotation in diagnostic process that all conclusions should be considered provisional, or subject to modification. Diagnosis of reading and learning problems are especially provisional, since:

- the reading process itself is filled with unknowns;
- we can never completely know someone else;
- each person is in a state of change even while we are studying him/her (this is especially true of children for whom each day is an experiment with different ways to feel, to think, and to be); and
- any slight new piece of information can cause all other information to be realigned to form an entirely different picture than the one suggested by the first cache.

In short, the diagnostic process amounts to doing investigative research on a single individual. As such, it requires a great deal of knowledge, experience, sensitivity, adroitness, wisdom, objectivity, and even some prognosticating—or looking into the future to predict long-term effects of a current situation.

To paraphrase Thorndike's (1917) definition of the problem-solving act in comprehension, diagnosis "is a very elaborate procedure involving a weighing of each of many elements in a case, their organization in proper relations one to another, the selection of certain of their connotations, and the rejection of others, and the cooperation of many forces to determine a likely cause and course of action."

Diagnosis is not easily mastered, although there are masters from whom much can be learned. Several of them have left us with a legacy of their learnings and insights in the form of their teachings, articles, books, and assessment instruments and protocols. The citations in this text were selected to provide a vicarious apprenticeship with these masters-of-the-craft. To maximize the value of these vicarious learnings, we suggest that you also should:

- be attentive to the experiences that are shared with and channeled to you by your course instructor;
- seek a variety of classroom teaching experiences at different levels and in different settings;
- develop a special attentiveness to students with special needs;
- stay abreast of the literature of the field throughout your career;
- take advantage of opportunities to conduct and be part of diagnostic case studies;
- reflect on and compare notes on cases with peers and veteran diagnosticians; and
- make a commitment to being a lifelong student of the craft, even if you do not expect to practice it regularly.

There are several situations, or circumstances in which diagnostic process may be undertaken. These are organized into levels of diagnosis.

Levels of Diagnosis

There are five circumstances in which diagnostic assessment may be undertaken. These are presented here as nonexclusive categories that tend to increase hierarchically in level of sophistication after the first one which, it can be argued, may be the most difficult since it occurs in the most active and potentially distracting setting.

1. **Diagnostic Teaching**. The teacher, at this level of assessment, conducts lessons that are carefully designed to reveal and improve specific reading and related literacy needs *simultaneously*. Several examples of this approach are described in the chapters ahead. Examples include: "Reading Recovery," an early detection and intervention program; "portfolio analysis" of children's classwork; the "Informal *Textbook* Inventory," for upper grade students; and the ReQuest procedure, a comprehension improvement method that has developed a rich and instructive clinical history.

2. **Diagnostic Screening**. This level of diagnosis typically is an extension of a schoolwide assessment. It is a means of quality control that relies most heavily on standardized tests to establish how groups of youngsters compare with national norms and with other comparable groups. Standardized evaluation also allows instructional innovations to be evaluated against a national yardstick. Diagnostic screening also can provide teachers with some benchmark information on students that is useful in initial grouping, in determining what more needs to be ascertained, and other aspects of instructional decision making.

3. **Survey Diagnosis**. This level of diagnosis is undertaken when a student has been identified by a screening device, or where no other information is available due to the absence of school records. Typically, survey diagnosis is

done with quick and short forms of well established tests. Several examples are discussed in the chapter ahead including the Wide Range Achievement Test, the San Diego Quick Test, and the Slosson IQ test.

4. **Intensive Diagnosis**. An intensive diagnosis is warranted when prior levels of assessment have revealed a problem that appears to be more serious and/or long-standing. Intensive diagnosis is characterized by an in-depth evaluation. It tends to involve a variety of individually administered tests, and a more holistic examination of the child from a variety of perspectives and, ideally, by more than one person. It often involves use of informal inventories, such as those developed by Silvaroli (1976), DeSanti, Casbergue, & Sullivan (1986), Burns & Roe (1985), and others that are detailed in the next chapter.

5. **Dynamic Diagnosis**. Dynamic diagnosis typically is a part of an extended clinical, or intensive evaluation that is undertaken when a routine intensive diagnosis has not proven to be useful. It can take a good deal of time, and can involve the "free-form" use of standardized tests and/or the use of specialized teaching episodes to create a diagnostic dialogue that can uncover very specific areas of need. Better standardized tests now incorporate suggestions for how to undertake such dialogues in their test manuals. For an example, see the manual for the Gates-MacGinitie Reading Tests, which illustrates how users can discover when a student may be overrelying on "prior knowledge" to answer comprehension questions (MacGinitie & MacGinitie, 1989, pp. 38–39). The manual also provides helpful hints for addressing related problems. Carney and Cioffi's (1990) dynamic assessment approach, described in a later chapter, serves a good procedural example of this level of diagnosis in action.

Diagnosis: Yes or No?

It may seem obvious that diagnosis is undertaken in order to prescribe and apply the most effective remedy. But this is not an unchallenged principle. In fact, you can almost guarantee that you will be asked why you do, or should do, diagnoses. Several respected reading specialists have answered this question by saying things like, "I don't. Why should I test a kid to death when it is already apparent that he can not read? I'd rather get on with teaching him/her and seeing what works." Others have said, "Abysmally little can be learned about a student's real needs just by administering a battery—more like a battering—of tests in a sterile and static environment." Still others have argued that, "An ounce of prevention is worth a pound of cure, so choose the best methods to teach initial reading, and avoid all that testing and remediation afterwards."

This sampling of statements probably represents some very real frustrations with some occasionally abusive practices, rather than with the basic principles of diagnosis and remediation. Nonetheless, there are entire school systems operating without diagnostic and remedial services, largely because educators are not well versed in just what diagnosis is, and what the arguments are for and against it. The next few passages are offered to help you fill and meet this informational need wherever you might encounter it.

Diagnosis: No!

While some of the reasons that have caused some professionals to turn away from diagnosis are implicit in the discussion above, there are these elaborations and additional reasons for saying "No!" to diagnosis:

- Reading disorders are apparent from simple observation; therefore, extensive testing is not necessary.
- Conventional clinical diagnostic processes are artificial, tedious for the child, usually conducted by a person other than the teacher, and therefore are likely to yield findings that are inaccurate and unreliable.
- Diagnostic findings and recommendations are only rarely even communicated to the classroom teacher.
- Testing takes time away from teaching; let's substitute a "diagnostic teaching" approach that permits reading assessment to be conducted simultaneously with instruction.
- We can eliminate the need for all but an occasional survey assessment of a child's reading progress by relying upon good preventative approaches to early reading that build on a child's natural language and promote enjoyment of reading and writing.

The latter position was given a recent boost in Volume 2 of the *Handbook of Reading Research* (Barr, et.al., 1991). In it, Johnson and Allington say that:

> ...the unavoidable conclusion, then, is that the most sensible way to improve remedial reading [that is, diagnosis and remediation] is to eliminate the need for it in the first place. (1991, p. 1001)

To this list of "professional" reasons for saying "no" to diagnosis, a few others can be added that can be called self-centered and perhaps naive. These typically are expressed as follows:

- I learned to read without all of this testing and retesting; therefore, so can others.
- I find great joy in reading, and so will every child if given a fair exposure.
- I don't know much about psychology, psycholinguistics, or special methods; nonetheless, I've succeeded in teaching many children to read.

The controversy over the relative importance of diagnosis is not entirely new. Almost three decades ago, Ruth Strang (1964) concluded that there seemed to be two extreme positions with regard to diagnosis and remediation. Those against diagnosis described the process as follows:

> The teacher or clinician starts with the problem as the student presents it and begins immediately to help him solve it. As he observes and works with the student, he learns more about his manner of reading, the skills he has mastered, and those in which he is still deficient. If he feels the need for some special source of information, such as an intelligence test, a reading test, or a home visit, he secures it. Thus, diagnosis is interwoven with instruction and practice in reading. (p. 8)

Those who took a strong position for diagnosis recommended:

...obtaining as much information as possible before beginning to work with the individual. Data are gathered from existing records; parents and students are interviewed; intelligence and achievement tests are administered, scored, and interpreted. This information is then reviewed and summarized before one attempts any remedial work. (pp. 7-8)

With these two approaches in mind, let's look more closely now at the case *for* diagnosis.

Diagnosis: Yes!

The case for clinical reading diagnosis, as suggested earlier, is simple and inherent in the process; it is to collect and scrutinize information related to the nature and likely origins of a reading problem, and then to continue the labor to find the best possible means of remedying it. The intent of diagnosis is not to compete with instructional time but to ensure that such time is not wasted in ineffective, or occasionally even counter-effective ways. Determining the exact nature of a student's reading problems is a step toward correcting previously ill-spent time. Bloom, Hastings, and Madaus (1971) have pointed to five frequently cited goals of diagnostic assessment, to which we have added a sixth:

1. To acquire and interpret evidence needed to improve learning and teaching.
2. To obtain process information to be added to the usual final (or product-oriented) examination.
3. To clarify the significant goals and objectives of education as reflected in student progress.
4. To obtain a quality control measure to determine whether each step of the instructional process has been working or needs to be changed.
5. To acquire a way to compare and contrast teaching procedures.
6. To get objective information to offset the overly subjective, and occasionally misleading, information gained from classroom teachers.

Curiously, critics of clinical diagnosis see the last point on objectivity as being at odds with being responsive to student needs, when in fact it is a sincere way to ascertain what those needs might be, rather than presuming to know.

Furthermore, while it is true that the examiner is careful not to step outside standardized assessment procedures during test administration, the skilled diagnostician is equally careful about establishing a relationship with a student by attempting to develop that very real but rather indescribable commodity known as "rapport." Throughout the diagnostic process, the effective diagnostician is able to lead an individual into and out of the examiner/examinee setting as necessary, maintaining a strong teacher/student relationship as a base. The skilled diagnostician also tries to remain aware of the differences between testing and teaching, when analyzing test scores obtained under standardized conditions and when recommending remedial actions. Most importantly, the diagnostician confers with the student regarding diagnostic findings and recommendations, imparting a sense of confidence that the reading difficulties are understandable, manageable, and correctable.

The final reason for conducting a diagnostic workup is the fact that it anchors efforts to grasp and provide for educational needs to the classic scientific method for problem-solving:

1. State the problem — look at available information about the student, interview key individuals, including the student him/herself, draw some initial conclusions about the seriousness of the reading problem, and make hypotheses regarding possible correlates and causes of the problem.
2. Gather the facts — conduct tests of relevant factors, taking on the role of objective examiner as necessary to obtain reliable measures.
3. Form a testable hypothesis — taking all information into account, determine the nature and probable causes of the reading problem, and design recommendations for remedial intervention.
4. Test the hypothesis — observe the effects of the remedial program.
5. Draw conclusions — determine whether the intervention has been effective, or whether a new hypothesis is needed.

Let us now consider some of specific principles to guide effective diagnostic problem solving.

Diagnostic Principles

Unlike inflexible rules, principles are flexible concepts derived from considerable human experiences and knowledge. Presented here are thirteen principles of diagnosis that have been deduced from a host of clinical cases, research reports, and plain human experience. Notice that some of these guidelines may seem paradoxical, or apparently contradictory of one another. The reason they do is because they parallel reality, which is a delicate balance of paradoxes that often need to be disentangled and reconciled with one another before essential truths can be revealed. Willingness to puzzle through these seeming paradoxes also builds the understandings, competence, and intuition necessary for becoming a high-level problem solver, and respected professional.

The thirteen principles, stated here in brief form, can be said to guide diagnosis. An elaboration of each follows.

1. Diagnosis should have instructional change as its major purpose.
2. Diagnosis should draw on subjective experience, but be conducted objectively.
3. Diagnosis should relate test patterns to observation.
4. Diagnosis should be selective.
5. Diagnosis should be heuristic.
6. Diagnosis should be cross-referenced.
7. Diagnosis should be continuous.
8. Diagnosis should determine the seriousness of the problem.
9. Diagnosis should be holistic.
10. Diagnosis should be parsimonious.
11. Diagnosis should include prognosis.

12. Diagnostic process needs to involve the student.
13. Diagnosis should search for strengths as well as weaknesses.

Thirteen Principles of Diagnosis

1. *Diagnosis should have instructional change as its major purpose.* Diagnosis is undertaken when a formal screening process or referral indicates that a student is not making optimal progress. The purpose of diagnosis is to alter the student's environment in ways that will enable him or her to make better progress. Diagnosis should not be undertaken unless there is a willingness to alter the instructional environment. There are two ways to ensure this: a) be sure that formal diagnosis is preceded by instruction that includes diagnostic teaching; and b) remind yourself that the word "therefore" should implicitly follow each reported test finding.

2. *Diagnosis should draw on subjective experience, but be conducted objectively.* There is no contradiction in this statement, it is only another paradox for the reflective professional. It simply means that every little bit of human experience can become a voice from the past to help you find your way through a diagnostic workup, but you must make every effort not to have the voice inside you drown out the voice of the student before you.

In other words, it can be quite all right to say to yourself at some point, "Why, this child is just like my brother—he just doesn't do his homework, and he is reckless and irresponsible!" With this visceral response, you have found a point of reference for the child before you. Now, however, the professional diagnostician must dig deeper and raise questions like: "How is he different from my brother?"; and "Was my brother really irresponsible, or did he only appear that way to me—perhaps because I was too serious, and constantly being his big brother/sister?" When this more introspective set of questions is completed, some stronger hypothesis should have been formed. This should then be checked wherever possible, against a second opinion from someone who is different in nature from the first diagnostician or teacher. When the process is completed, the diagnostician should know the child better, his/her brother better, and him/herself better. In this way, the diagnostician's "subjective" inner voice has been made more objective, and every similar case encountered will benefit from the diagnosticians enriched understanding and intuition—or "secondary sense learnings," as the learning theorist D.O. Hebb once referred to this rather remarkable human capacity to gather, abstract, generalize, store, and apply experiences and insights to new problems and situations (1949).

3. *Diagnosis should relate test patterns to observations.* This simply means that patterns observed in testing and those derived from classroom behavior and out-of-school life should reconcile with one another in some logical manner. This is a twofold job involving some data collection, conversations with students, and a lot of thinking. The thinking aspect is enhanced by several of the the next guiding principles.

4. *Diagnosis should be selective.* It should include assessment of all factors pertinent to a student's problem, but avoiding tests of irrelevant factors. With regard to "all factors pertinent," the diagnosis should consider more than the

reading problem alone. It should consider possible contributing factors as well. With regard to "avoiding tests of irrelevant factors," the diagnosis should attempt to rule out all measures of factors that clearly do not contribute to the individual student's problem.

The strong implication of this principle is that there is no single series of measures that can be routinely applied to every student. As you will see in the next principle, however, there is ample justification for using a core of familiar instruments with some regularity.

5. *Diagnosis should be heuristic.* A heuristic is a structural, or procedural, change in the way things are typically done that tends to stimulate and evoke discovery and insights. One way to ensure that this can occur during diagnosis is to develop familiarity with a collection of tests and methods of observation. The Informal Reading Inventory (IRI) (detailed in the next chapter) is a good example of a well-established assessment heuristic, although a departure from conventional classroom teaching. Familiarity in this case provides an examiner with a great storehouse of interpretive power built on past experiences and connections with the IRI. To amplify the heuristic effect from established instruments, select a second instrument or method of assessment that does *not* seem to be called for, just to see what new relevant questions or thoughts this structural change might suggest that you could not have foreseen. This might be anything from a five-item spelling test to a quick appraisal of affect. This guiding principle is based on the realization that if a child has a persistent and mysterious learning problem, a calculated "shot in the dark" could provide the unexpected insight needed to unlock the mystery. Remember, too, that diagnosis need not rely solely on a collection of tests and inventories. It also can and should include opportunities for "planned" incidental observation and discussion. Veteran diagnosticians say that their greatest insights often are gleaned from the structural changes that arise in informal conversations that occur in the space between the words "Let's take a break" and "Are you ready to resume testing?" The question of just what constitutes a useful heuristic can be very personal; however, some initial hints on how to select appropriates ones for testing or teaching are offered in Figure 3.1.

6. *Diagnosis should be cross-referenced.* Important diagnostic conclusions should never be drawn from single measures. Indications from any one test or observation should be cross-referenced with the student's performance on other tests and with reported observations of the student's behavior in the classroom, in peer settings, and at home. A good way to guide your conclusions is to imagine that the things you will say will be checked by an editor and a research staff before they will be permitted to go public. This precept should not inhibit you from expressing suppositions and conjectures; simply be certain to express them as suppositions in need of further verification.

7. *Diagnosis should be continuous.* Continuous diagnosis means two things: each teacher needs a system for continuously monitoring student progress, and that once a formal diagnosis has been conducted by an in-house specialist, the specialist has an obligation to follow up on the diagnosis, both to verify the findings and to monitor student progress. The teacher's chief means of conducting continuous diagnosis is through diagnostic-teaching. The chief means by which the diagnostician meets the spirit of "continuous diagnosis" is by sup-

FIGURE 3.1

Hints for Selecting Procedures that have Heuristic Value

Select testing and teaching procedures that. . .

- are structurally different from conventional interactions
- offer opportunity for students to reciprocate—or to respond freely as well as in a measured and controlled way
- provide feedback on a variety of behaviors
- are relatively easy to do and, therefore, to learn from
- can be adapted to other contexts, or can be replicated in other subject and skill areas
- urge reflective inquiry and more effective problem solving by virtue of the breadth or depth of information they provide
- lead students and teachers to interact with one another in authentic and respectful ways

Several testing and teaching procedures and clinical anecdotes are cited ahead, and give a more concrete sense of heuristic properties in action. For more general information on heuristics in reading and the language arts, see: Manzo and Manzo, 1990a; Marzano, 1991.

---

porting the formal diagnosis with some clinical teaching, or dynamic interaction of the type described by Carney and Cioffi (1990), discussed in the next chapter.

8. *Diagnosis should determine the seriousness of the problem.* The diagnostician is expected to make two important determinations: how acute, or severe, the problem is, and how chronic, or long-standing—and therefore resistant—to change it is. This is decided in a number of ways. The primary means is by comparing actual achievement levels over time with capacity levels. The analysis of differences between these two types of measures is called "discrepancy analysis." Mathematical formulas for discrepancy analysis are presented ahead in the text.

9. *Diagnosis should be holistic.* This principle is widely accepted as a concept, but not widely followed in practice. It advises us to look at the whole person, and try to determine if he or she is making relatively even progress toward reading, language, thinking, and social-emotional maturity. The message here is that overall human development is the primary goal of schooling, and that reading is merely our focus area or touch-point of responsibility.

10. *Diagnosis should be parsimonious.* Parsimony, in this context, means the cautious expenditure of explanation. A parsimonious conclusion is one that starts with the simplest and most economical hypothesis, rather than one that is overly expansive or farfetched. A useful way to remember this principle is provided by the maxim: When you hear hoofbeats, think horses, not zebras!

11. *Diagnosis should include prognosis.* Looking ahead, especially at life after school, can be a valuable means of understanding what more, if anything, needs to be done for a child. School puts everyone under pressure. Grading systems are inherently harsh. They tend to call up defensive postures and even biochemical responses that are narrowing and self-destructive. Some individuals respond

by compulsively completing every assignment and striving to ace every test. Others respond by missing assignments, and eventually succumbing, in stages that resemble near-death experiences, to the "fact" that they are failures. Our sense is that during the prolonged school experience, more than 60% of the school-age population eventually comes to feel terribly inadequate; 50% simply because they are attending schools obsessed with having everyone on grade level when they happened to have been born with an IQ of 100 or less, and therefore can be said to be doing "just fine" if their best efforts are yielding below average grades.

The wise diagnostician will permit his or her mind to run ahead and to try to see the future. This can have a frightening effect sometimes, as when you see a child whose anger and frustration is monumental and building. For the most part, however, it should permit you to say things that are comforting to both parents and children, since most of us do go on to lead successful and productive lives despite what happens to us in school.

12. *Diagnostic process needs to involve the student.* This principle of diagnosis is on the "cutting edge" of the still evolving field of diagnosis. The idea is that diagnosis should not be "done to" students, it should be "done with" them. To make this shift, it is necessary to learn to engage in "diagnostic dialogues," that is, to converse with students by encouraging them to reflect on their learning behaviors, as well as participating in the selection and development of appropriate remedial strategies. It is not farfetched to have students participate to a degree in selecting the diagnostic tests that could be taken. Chapter 6 features how students can be conferred with, and reported to, rather than conferred about and reported on.

13. *Diagnosis should be the search for strengths as well as weaknesses.* This principle is of greatest importance to whole-language advocates, since they hold that remediation is best achieved through strengths rather than by teaching to weaknesses (Goodman, Bird, & Goodman, 1991). It also is a cornerstone function of the whole-child approach of this book. This emphasis is most clearly evident in the worth placed on discovering needs and hidden areas of strength in thinking between and beyond the lines. This topic is discussed more fully in Chapter 10 on comprehension and in Chapter 13 on higher-order literacy skills (see especially the Informal Reading-Thinking Inventory, an experimental instrument designed for this purpose).

Metadiagnostics

In addition to the basic principles of diagnosis stated above, it is helpful to have a diagnostic *model* as a heuristic to guide one's efforts in collecting, processing, and discovering meaning in the paradoxical and overlapping information brought together in a diagnosis. This mental guiding and monitoring helps one better grasp what is known, decipher what is not known, and decipher what more may need to be known. An effective diagnostic model raises the examiner's awareness of his or her own mental processes, thereby refining what might be called the examiner's metadiagnostic skills.

The next section opens with such a plan. It describes 4-D Diagnostic Model, a heuristic system for diagnostic discovery. The remainder of the text is organized around this model.

Diagnostic Models

The creation of appropriate categories is always a landmark development in any area of knowledge, particularly in one requiring the collection, organization, and interpretation of large amounts of data. Categories are the building blocks of specialized schemata, or the "slots" used to receive and process information.

Weiner and Cromer (1967) have provided educators with such a set of categories. These categories offer a simple and useful way to guide individual diagnosis or group assessment. Their chief value is in seeing whether an evaluation has become overloaded in one area and underrepresented in another, thus creating an unbalanced picture. The 4-D Diagnostic Model helps achieve better balance by providing a reminder to gather information related to the four major areas of possible human dysfunctions:

- Defects
- Deficiencies
- Disruptions
- Differences

Defects

The *Defect* category refers to innate or constitutional factors. These typically include various aspects of mental aptitude and functioning, such as hearing, vision, neurological organization, chemistry, or any other physical factors that might impede reading progress. This category reminds us to collect general medical information on such things as blood pressure, anemia, headaches, and allergies. The negative weight of these on reading and learning is often overlooked. Allergies such as hay fever, for example, probably account for more erratic brain activity and disorientation during fall and spring than all other neurological problems combined. Nonetheless, it is treated as unimportant because it is common. Specific instruments and methods for assessing or otherwise inferring the nature of several of these factors are discussed in the chapters ahead.

Deficiencies

Deficiencies typically are the most closely monitored and assessed category. This category includes reading, language, academic skills, and all subject knowledge areas. Most of the standardized and informal testing done in schools, and, in truth, in clinics, amounts to little more than repeated measures of these same factors. There is, however, another dimension of this area that could be especially important in diagnosing a variety of literacy disorders. It is the inclusion of those academic "trace elements" factors alluded to in a previous chapter. These subtle, though highly influential elements of progress toward reading, language, and thinking maturity include factors such as:

- inclination and skill in thinking abstractly
- ability to critique and be critiqued (or give and take constructive criticism)
- inclination and ability to read between and beyond the lines
- inclination and ability to deal with ambiguities
- tendency toward self-examination (metacognitive operations)
- inclination to think about and refine understandings of the world about oneself (schema-building)

Many trace elements factors are measurable with conventional test formats, some of which are detailed in the chapter on higher-order literacy disorders, though most are revealed from observations and self-reports of the type described in the next three chapters.

Disruptions

Disruptions are interruptions to learning that occur in the affective, or feeling, domain. This category is used by Weiner and Cromer to refer to *internal-emotional* factors that cause intrusive thoughts or disruptions to attention and, therefore, thinking, reading, and learning. Educators also can use this category as a schema slot for collecting information related to external-emotional disruptions such as a distressing family condition, unruly school situations, or extended exposure to some emotionally unstable individuals (siblings, teachers, ministers, parents, peers, neighbors). This aspect of the Disruption category reminds us that young people are extremely impressionable, and that occasionally someone will pull up close to a child and slowly convolute the youngster's behavior and mental health in much the same way as a pebble in the shoe affects even the will to walk (see the Reflective Box ahead for an

---

REFLECTIVE BOX 1

Intruders

Imagine that you are a relatively shy sixth grader and a new student joins your class. This child is assigned to share your locker and sits in front of you for most of the day. The child is unkempt, rarely bathes, and is not well-mannered.

How might such a situation impact your schoolwork, your comprehension and responses to textual material, and general emotional health and well-being? How would you, as a child, handle or cope with the situation?

Now think about how a similar situation might arise in adult life with a new neighbor of the same sort. How would you feel? How might it affect your daily life? How would you handle or cope with the situation?

Compare perspectives and responses with others.

---

exercise in understanding the force of such emotional intrusions). The chapters ahead offer specific suggestions on how to assess and otherwise improve your ability to recognize and comment on factors in the affective domain. Some of these systems have a rich tradition in education and are no more demanding than it is to be a keen observer.

The next category addresses a collection of more subtly influencing factors.

Differences

Differences are mismatches between the student and the general assumptions of schools and teachers. These typically include language, social, cultural, attitudinal, and learning-style differences. Such factors rarely are the sole cause of a reading or learning disability, but they can be serious contributing or aggravating conditions. This category of factors usually conjures concerns related to the effects of social-cultural differences between minority groups and core-culture based schools. It also, however, should conjure concerns about:

1. shifts in lifestyles that render the typical assumptions about the lives and experiences of any group of children to be significantly different from the actual facts of their lives; and,
2. learning-style variables that may negatively influence literacy functions (e.g., higher than normal levels of impulsivity or hyperactivity that make careful reading and spelling difficult; lower than normal levels of impulse or hypoactivity accompanied by incomplete assignments and poor school grades).

In general, it can be said that while Differences, or life, language, and learning-style factors, may not account for a great proportion of the difficulties seen in the general population of students, this category is likely to have considerably greater impact on an already susceptible population of remedial and learning impaired youngsters. Ekwall and Shanker (1988) refer to this as a "heroic" area of investigation, since it can be so demanding and uncertain an area to assess and accommodate. Some survey techniques and instruments are detailed in the chapters ahead to help you to decide if further investigation of this category might be warranted for a given individual or group of youngsters.

While the 4-D Model primarily serves as a reminder of how to get a balanced diagnostic picture of a student, it also can be used to enhance flexible thinking and interpretation of data that has already been collected.

Four D's Help with Interpretation

The 4-D Model helps with interpretation when each category is used as a perspective for re-*viewing* the same information. If it was learned, for example, from a conventional spelling test that a child's spelling was very poor, with little correspondence between sounds and symbols, this would, at first sight, appear to be a deficiency, that is, a simple phonics skill deficit.

By moving this same information around, like a gameboard piece, into each of the other categories, other hypotheses suggest themselves. Considered from the Defect category, it could suggest a condition tied to a specific neurophysiological deficit (the particulars of this are discussed further under the title "Dyslexia and Related Learning Disabilities"). When considered from the point of view of the Disruption category, very poor spelling could be suggestive of extremely high levels of impulsivity and/or a lack of willingness to operate within expected boundaries—in other words, another possible example of an ever present emotionally disruptive force in reading, learning, and thinking. Curiously, excellent spelling also has been said to be indicative of higher levels of neurosis. Finally, when poor spelling is considered from the vantage point of the Difference category, it could be taken to mean that concern for spelling simply has taken a rear seat to a highly imaginative mind and artistic temperament; just as excellent spelling could mean an unusual brain organization (see Williams syndrome in the chapter on dyslexia for an extreme example).

It might appear on first blush that the ability to find a possible meaning for most every test score in most every category is a weakness rather than a strength of the 4-D Model. This does not turn out to be the case, however. Once two or three pieces of information have been considered from each of these four perspectives, you will find that a pattern begins to form that confirms some hypotheses and refutes others. If no pattern takes shape, you will know that more testing and observing needs to be done and, more importantly, what type of testing and observing, and toward what ends. If, after all of this, you still are in a quandary, then you are entitled, even obliged, to say what every teacher and diagnostician must learn to say: "We don't know yet what the causes are of this child's reading/learning problems; however, we think we have narrowed it down to this or this, and we believe that it is best treated in the following manner at this time." This last gesture tends to make diagnosis humbling, but it also reinvites the potentially significant participation of the child, the classroom teacher, and the parents or guardians.

Now, let us consider four of the most fundamental procedural concepts underlying diagnostic operations. These help us to get an operational picture of the reader's M.O.—or Mode of Operation.

Diagnostic Procedures

There are essentially four procedural concepts that permit us to get a reader's M.O. These are:

- discrepancy analysis
- study of corollary conditions or co-symptoms
- expectancy or capacity determination
- reader subtyping

Discrepancy

The traditional basis for detecting any literacy disorder is to establish a certifiable discrepancy between what should be and what is. Each time assessment is made, a null hypothesis is implicitly tested. The null hypothesis is that there will be no educationally significant difference between those factors in the individual or the group being tested and the typical way those factors are commonly known to relate. Thus, if IQ and reading performance are measured, the two are expected to be highly and positively correlated in all groups and in any given individual. If they are not, the discrepancy is noted and an explanation is sought.

Thus, the procedural concept underlying discrepancy analysis is that an individual's score should parallel or correlate with the pattern found in group testing. This is a fair operational assumption, but since it is based on probability, it can only be a guideline, not a rule, and it will vary in individual cases. Nonetheless, diagnosticians need to be well schooled in the nature of relationships, or correlations in order to interpret what certain discrepancies might be saying.

Correlations

Correlations are statistically established probabilities that two things are likely to be related to one another, either positively (in the same direction) or negatively (in an opposite direction). Correlations typically are expressed on a scale from zero (no correlation) to plus or minus one (a perfect correlation).

For example, it is well known that those who smoke have a high rate of lung cancer. Therefore, if days of life were correlated with heavy, moderate, and nonsmoking, we would expect to see a fairly strong negative correlation between the amount one smokes and the number of days of life enjoyed (probably in the range of −.60). Causation, however, is not easy to establish, although it is fair to infer it. The purpose of correlations is to permit inferences to be drawn.

Reasonably then, the skillful diagnostician must know what relationships exist, and understand what inferences can reasonably be drawn from those relationships. Here, in summary form, are some thumbnail relationships dealing with reading and related skills, and some guidelines for interpreting correlations that we have tended to find useful.

Estimated Correlations of Reading and Related Literacy Functions

These estimates are gleaned from hundreds of studies, though they can vary markedly from one study to another, based largely on the test instruments used. These relationships also vary somewhat at different stages of development. Many other correlates of reading are discussed and developed in the chapters ahead.

- Attitudes toward reading are significantly, though not overwhelmingly, related to reading performance and progress (about a .40 level of correlation).
- Listening and silent reading comprehension are so highly related that they can be called essentially the same process (about .90 level of correlation).
- Oral reading comprehension (where the student reads) and silent reading comprehension also are highly correlated, though less so than with listening (about .70).

- Rate of reading tends to be rather highly correlated to reading comprehension and vocabulary (about .50).
- Vocabulary and reading comprehension are highly related (about .75).
- Spelling is not predictably related to anything important beyond fourth grade level.
- Writing tends to be somewhat related to comprehension and vocabulary (.35).
- Critical thinking tends to be solidly correlated to comprehension but to a degree that varies with the nature of the comprehension test (.30 to .60).
- IQ is most highly correlated to vocabulary (about .80), next most to reading comprehension (about .70), critical thinking (about .50), speed of reading (.35), and in no predictable way to spelling. The correlation of reading and writing is not clearly enough established to offer a report at this time.

Thumbnail Guidelines for Interpreting Correlations

Correlations of reading disability are often filled with paradoxes. Relationships between any two things should always be taken as a data-based suggestion that these two factors are interacting in one of several possible ways. This perspective is essential to proper interpretation and writing of a diagnostic report. Four ways are illustrated here that have significance for diagnoses and remediation.

Related as Travellers
A and B simply are travelling side-by-side, but they are not influencing one another as much as are they both influenced by a third factor that may be more causative. For example, if A was spelling, and B was phonic knowledge, then C could be "high impulsivity"—a factor that often reduces attention to details.

Artifactually Related
A and B clearly are correlated, but their interaction—or effect on one another— is not profound. Their relationship depends more on how the factors are measured or taught. For example, spelling and writing ability typically are correlated if spelling is included in the means by which good writing is assessed. It also may show up as being a significant factor if spelling is overemphasized in the teaching of writing so as to reduce emphasis on the writing process as a means of searching for meaning, as opposed to merely an act of wordcrafting.

Obvious But Overlooked Relationship
Sometimes, there is an intrinsic cause and effect relationship between two things that simply is unappreciated. For example, the relationship between "prior knowledge" and "ability to acquire new knowledge" is profound. However, since both of these also are related to things such as IQ and cultural opportunity, their influence on one another often is overlooked. If knowing something directly causes one to be able to know more, and not knowing tends to keep us from learning new things, then it should be apparent that a greater emphasis should be placed on fact and knowledge acquisition in remedial situations. Nonetheless, remedial education is alarmingly light on stressing information and

concept acquisition, a point that is developed more fully elsewhere in the text. It is notable, however that educators are not alone in overlooking the obvious. For example, it took several studies to "discover" that the three greatest essentials of good health could not be gotten in the average hospital — good nutrients, light exercise, and uninterrupted sleep.

Mathematically Weak But Significant

In this situation, A and B are statistically significantly correlated, but at some weak level that does not appear to have any educational significance, until that relationship is more carefully examined. The area of trace elements affecting reading maturity, mentioned previously, is a good example. Trace elements factors, such as the willingness to accept criticism and level of curiosity, may not have a great correlation with initial success in learning to read, but it is apparent that they are root factors in being able to read and think to higher levels, and therefore of critical importance in the life-long process of making progress toward reading, language, thinking, and social-emotional maturity.

The simple point is that weak correlations can be educationally significant correlations nonetheless. If you would like to sharpen your understanding of how things can be related, read or take courses covering these technically related topics in statistics, particularly in parametric and nonparametric correlations, partial and curvilinear correlations, multiple regression, discriminant function analysis, and factor analysis.

The concepts of Discrepancy and Correlation are brought together next in the third basic idea that underlies all diagnosis, the deceptively simple idea of expectancy.

Expectancy

Underlying all diagnosis is the implicit question: How well could this child be *expected* to read if there were no other impediments?

Determining what someone *might* be able to do as a reader is not easy, but it can be estimated due to a strong and fortuitous relationship between reading and listening, and reading and IQ. The very high correlations between reading and listening, and reading and IQ, make it possible to construct tests and formulas that estimate potential to read from ability to listen as an indicator of potential to learn.

Consider first how the relationship of reading to listening can be used to this practical advantage.

Listening-Based Capacity Estimates

Comparable passages with established readability levels are presented to students. The student is questioned on his/her comprehension of these graded passages under two conditions. In one condition, the student orally reads the passage and answers questions posed by the examiner on his/her oral comprehension. In the second condition, the examiner reads the passage while the

FIGURE 3.2

Capacity Estimate: Listening

Oral reading comprehension	4.5
Aural (listening) comprehension	5.5
Growth expectancy	1.0

student listens and then tries to recall what was read without prompt, and/or with short-answer comprehension questions.

Scores from the two conditions are expected to be comparable. Where the listening score is higher, this is taken to be an indication of the student's greater capacity to learn from instruction (see Figure 3.2). Where the reading score is higher, no inferences are drawn about capacity. It is either taken to be an anomaly, or an indication that the student was seriously distracted by his/her own oral reading, an uncommon but not completely unusual occurrence.

Listening capacity assessment is routinely done as part of an Informal Reading Inventory, a testing strategy covered fully in the next chapter. Listening capacity has some limitations. It tends to overclassify beginning readers as "remedial," since they obviously can listen better than they can read, and it occasionally causes very advanced, fluent readers to be categorized as "overachievers," since they tend to read better than they listen (personal communication from Michael McKenna, 1991).

IQ-Based Capacity Estimates

IQ-based estimates of reading capacity typically are constructed of formulas that take into account factors such as chronological age, years in school, and current reading status. The predictive value of any of these is necessarily influenced by the validity and reliability of the measurement instruments that are entered into the formulas.

There are three widely used expectancy formulas presented here. The intertwined notions of IQ and mental age are briefly developed first since this forms the conceptual foundation for determining expected grade level performance.

Intelligence, or general ability, tests are based upon a ratio of mental and chronological age (IQ=MA/CA x 100). That is, the more mental age exceeds chronological age, the higher the IQ. A mental age score is obtained by comparing a student's score on a mental abilities test with the average scores of students at different age levels. Thus, mental age can also be easily calculated from knowledge of IQ and chronological age by the following formula:

$$MA = \frac{IQ \times CA}{100}$$

For reasons discussed in a moment, several IQ test makers have abandoned "mental age" scores in recent times. Nonetheless, the underlying concept remains intact, and mental age still is the conceptual basis for estimating intelligence.

To illustrate, when an 8-year-old child has a measured IQ of 120, he or she has performed cognitive tasks at the level of an *average* child of 9.6 years. Similarly, if an 8-year-old has a measured IQ of 80, the child's performance is roughly comparable to that of the *average* 6.4-year-old.

The major objection to the use of mental age is that it may give the misimpression that mental age somehow equals maturity level, when in fact it merely is a rough index of the rate at which learning typically occurs at each age level. Keeping this precaution in mind, here are the three formulas that are the most widely used in educational assessment.

Harris's Reading Expectancy Formula

Albert Harris (1961) seems to have been the first to apply the idea of an expected grade score. It is obtained simply by subtracting 5 from the mental age, which you will recall, is determined by an IQ test. Thus, Harris' simple formula is

$$\text{Reading Expectancy} = \text{MA} - 5$$

The 5 in the formula represents the number of years which passed before the child entered school. Accordingly, an 8-year-old third grader with an IQ of 120, which according to IQ to MA charts translates into an MA of 9.6, would have a Reading Expectancy grade equivalent of 4.6, or 1.6 years above typical age-grade placement.

This simple formula has been revised by Harris and Sipay (1985) to be slightly more accurate and now is as follows:

$$\text{REA (Reading Expectancy Age)} = \frac{2\text{MA} + \text{CA}}{3}$$

To aid in the interpretation of scores, Harris has suggested that the differences between Reading Achievement grade scores (RA) and Reading Expectancy Age (REA) should be considered of greater or lesser significance at different grade levels. Accordingly, a lesser difference at the lower grade levels is considered more significant than at a higher grade as shown below:

Grade 1-3:   REA exceeds RA by 6 mo. (.5 yr)
Grade 4-5:   REA exceeds RA by 9 mo. (.75 yr)
Grade 6+:   REA exceeds RA by 1 year or more

The next formula, developed by Bond and Tinker, uses IQ instead of MA, and puts a greater emphasis on years in school.

Bond and Tinker's Formula

Since IQ scores are in more common use than MA scores, Bond and Tinker (1973) offered a formula for calculating reading expectancy (RE) directly from an IQ score without reference to mental age. They also constructed their formula to circumvent the problem of subtracting 5, the estimated number of preschool years. This is accomplished by adding a new factor to the formula called "years in school." This eliminates the variability related to when the child actually may have begun school. The formula looks like this:

$$RE = \text{Years in School} \times \frac{IQ + 1}{100}$$

The significant discrepancies suggested by Bond and Tinker are:

Grade 1 - RE exceeds RA by .50
Grade 2 - RE exceeds RA by .66
Grade 3 - RE exceeds RA by .75
Grade 4 - RE exceeds RA by 1.00
Grade 5 - RE exceeds RA by 1.50
Grade 6+ - RE exceeds RA by 2.00

The Reading Age Expectancy approach used by Harris and Sipay has been shown to be a better predictor of actual reading achievement for the fourth and fifth graders they studied than was the years-in-school method used by Bond and Tinker (Dore-Boyce, Misner, & McGuire, 1975). At higher grade levels, it would seem that the Bond and Tinker approach might prove more accurate since years-in-school becomes increasingly predictive of IQ, vocabulary, and all other aspects of scholastic achievement beyond the tenth grade level where lower IQ students would have begun to drop out.

The next formula is slightly more complex, though somewhat more reliable than either Harris and Sipay or Bond and Tinker. It also is more widely used in LD circles where it is known as an estimate of general learning capacity.

Myklebust's "Learning Quotient"

The comparison of current achievement with expected achievement is of central importance to learning disabilities' specialists. This led Myklebust (1968a), one of the early workers in that field, to develop a somewhat more complex technique for making this comparison. To use this technique, an individual's "Expectancy Age" (EA) first is calculated from Mental Age (MA), Chronological Age (CA), and Grade Age (GA):

$$EA = \frac{MA + CA + GA}{3}$$

[where Mental Age is expressed in years to the nearest tenth, as derived from an intelligence test as shown below, Chronological Age is the child's actual age in years, and Grade Age is the average age of a child at that grade level].

The Mental Age used, when scores from the Wechsler IQ test are available, should be derived from *either* the Verbal IQ score *or* the Performance IQ score; *whichever is higher.* The assumption is that the higher score is the most representative of the individual's true capacity level. The higher IQ score is translated into an MA by the simple calculation of:

$$MA = \frac{\text{Verbal or Performance IQ} \times CA}{100}$$

The final step in obtaining a "Learning Quotient" is to divide Achievement Age (score on a reading achievement test + 5.2) by the Expectancy Age obtained above:

$$LQ = \frac{AA}{EA}$$

A student with an LQ of below 89 would be considered learning disabled, according to Myklebust's criteria.

Flaw in Discrepancy/Expectancy

There is an obvious flaw in rigidly applying the rule of discrepancy. It is the implicit assumption that the measures taken of "capacity" and of "performance" are accurate. Of these, the capacity measure is the most challengeable. It has been noted that IQ scores can not be trusted to measure real capacity, and even listening capacity measures tend to suffer from "Matthew effect" (Stanovich, 1986b)—that is, the notion of reciprocal causation, or where poor reading interacts with weak cognitive development so that the bright get sharper and the unbright get duller. This has led some to argue that diagnosis of reading disability should be based solely on whether there is a decoding deficit, irrespective of "intellectual capacity" (Siegel, 1988, 1989). This position generally makes sense. However, practical considerations may warrant the development of priorities as to who can be served fully, and who may not be. In such situations, it may be useful to use IQ or listening capacity to help determine where resources are best directed. This is not as harsh as it appears, since the youngsters falling outside the range of the reading and LD specialist are not forgotten, but generally fall within the province of programs for the mentally retarded or developmentally disabled. Nonetheless, inadequacies in the current means of determining discrepancy or expectancy suggest that there should be one other class of "formulas" for making these determinations—called "Clinical Estimation."

Clinical Estimation

As a teacher and future reading and/or LD specialist, you eventually will store and call upon a good deal more subtle and sophisticated information in the appraisal of human capacity than any formula could ever take into account. Your judgement creates a unique and dynamic formula that matures with each experience.

We suggest, therefore, that you use the formulas presented, and other guidelines suggested in this book as heuristics, or means of stimulating the development of your own intuitive powers to make informed judgements and design appropriate "trial teaching" episodes (see especially the Informal Reading-Thinking Inventory in a later chapter). This experimental instrument is being designed to inform and evoke the intuitive power for such judgments.

Were it not for intuition, no one would ever have tried to teach Helen Keller much of anything, let alone how to read. The results of that effort, called the VAKT method, are told in a chapter ahead on treating severe reading disabilities. By the same token, formulas can build intuitive process by calling our attention to what easily could be overlooked. It was through the use of a discrepancy formula in a graduate class simulation that one of the authors came to discover greater potential in a 30-year-old nonverbal teacher (who, as it turned out, was raised by mute parents) than had been realized, even by him, in his many years of previous schooling. In this way, the formula was the heuristic that caused the writer to become wiser in looking for human potential, even where it might be masked by adult appearances.

Subtyping, the next topic, is another heuristic that can help in determining the reader's M.O.

Subtyping: Another Means of Getting the Reader's M.O.

The classification, or subtyping, of readers is another way to describe and understand a reader's *modus operandi* — or means of thinking and operating when faced with typical reading demands. The idea is to permit the teacher or diagnostician to access the most appropriate categories of materials and treatments. The process of subtyping can go on as long as the teacher or diagnostician has slots, or schemata, for filing meaningful information.

Subtyping is a process of characterizing and sorting behaviors according to some large grid, or set of generalizations. The idea is to continue to do so until the grids get smaller and more particular to the person before you. It is a system of specifying from some initially larger generalization. The process of subtyping is analogous to learning someone's gender, then ethnic makeup, then the region of the country that they have come from, and then down to increasingly smaller categories of slight but potentially telling information — such as whether they like dogs or cats better. With each categorization, some expectations are suggested, others refuted, and still others refined, until a clear and unique picture comes into focus. Needless to say, this process always must be undertaken with caution since it involves a good deal of subjectivity, and most of us harbor a perverse though natural inclination to overgeneralize from limited information.

Here now are some basic methods of subtyping. As we look at these, remember to keep one additional category open in each system proposed, one called "UNIQUELY" — this is where you should note the nuances of difference between the actual person being observed and the assumptions of the category. The first system of categorizing is the most widely used — the reader level subtyping.

Reader Level Subtyping

All readers can be subtyped into one of these four categories, each of which can contain some further subclassifications.

Developmental Reader. This is the student whose word recognition, comprehension, vocabulary, and rate of reading are appropriately aligned with capacity indicators such as IQ, listening comprehension, age, and grade placement. A reader can also be said to be "exceeding developmental expectations."

This type of apparently precocious behavior typically goes unnoted, but it can be expected to occur as a statistical artifact about 2-3% of the time. Some writers, such as Rude and Oehlkers (1984) have suggested a fifth category called "advanced" to cover this possibility.

Corrective Reader. This is the student whose reading behaviors show some or all aspects of reading to be *mildly* below expectations (six months to a year). Such readers typically are assisted in the regular classroom setting.

Remedial Reader. There are two or three subtypes of remedial readers, depending on what is considered: those who are mildly remedial, or approximately one and a half to two years below grade level expectancy in some aspect of reading; those who are severely remedial, or more than two years below reasonable expectations; and those who are so severely remedial that the next category described seems appropriate.

Severely Disabled, or Dyslexic, Readers. This classification is used where there is evidence that solid efforts have been made to teach the child to read, and that two of the three diagnostic indicators below have been confirmed:

1. The student has little or no phonic sense (dysphonetic).
2. The student has little or no ability to recognize words at sight despite training (dyseidetic).
3. The student tends to learn only what is taught, but fails to couple this with previous learnings and to reach a synergy, or growth beyond the simple sum of the lessons (non-generative learner).

The chapter on severe reading disabilities/dyslexia further fleshes out these ideas and terms. Methods of subtyping have been unchanged for many years. Recently, however, a new and more sophisticated system has begun to evolve. This newer approach attempts to classify remedial readers by the processes they use to read. Malicky and Norman (1988) are leading this line of research, which is reported here for its heuristic value to professional thinking and research.

Reading Processes Subgroups

Using a clinical reading population as their base, Malicky and Norman (1988) factor analyzed miscues, re-tellings, and reading level variables to reveal six potentially significant "processing factors" that might come to be used to classify remedial readers. Their findings, while still a bit tentative, correspond well with the interactive theory of reading, and therefore pick up some further validation from this source.

Their results suggest that remedial (and perhaps other) readers can be categorized into seven possible styles of reading based on how they decoded words and recalled what they read.

1. Those who use "integrative processing *during* reading" as their chief mode of reading. That is, they use context clues along with background information to decode words and get meaning. The miscues of this group tend to be consistent with author meaning. This process group did not correlate with reading level (poorer readers were as likely to use this process as were better readers).
2. Those who use "integrative processing *after* reading" as their chief mode of

reading. That is, they use the text and background knowledge to infer text-implied meanings. This process group did correlate with reading level (poorer readers were less likely to do this than good readers).

3. Those who use "print-based processing" as their chief mode of reading. That is, they tended to over-rely on graphic cues, without moving beyond print to meaning. Like those in category 2, this process group also correlated with reading level (poorer readers were also more likely to over-rely on graphic cues than were better readers).

4. Those who use "text-based processing" as their chief mode of reading. That is, they tended to rely on the text for meaning, without associating new information with appropriate prior knowledge (most poor readers would do this, but also some good readers; see the discussion of "literalness" in Chapter 13 for an elaboration on how this processing style, or mode of operation, may have important implications in detecting a major type of high-literacy disorder).

5. Those who use "monitoring" as their chief mode of reading. That is, they tended to rely on self-correction of errors. Malicky and Norman found this category difficult to interpret due to the way the data was collected, and therefore concluded that further study was required before anything more could be said about it.

6. Those who use "knowledge-based processing" as their chief mode of reading. That is, they would use background knowledge and experience to elaborate on recalls from the text, even to the extent of displacing exact recalls from the text.

Further research seems needed before these modes of operating as readers are fully understood. There is little doubt, however, that this is a much more sophisticated system of classification, with more implications for instruction than anything now available.

Computerized Diagnosis: An Emerging Potential

Though largely an unrealized potential at this time, computerized assessment has made considerable progress in recent years. Much of this progress stems from the evolution of so-called "expert systems" that employ "artificial intelligence" (AI) programs. AI is another way of saying smart machines that, in a manner of speaking, are able to "learn." They do this by adding prior cases to their database and altering their diagnostics accordingly. There is nothing quite this sophisticated available yet in reading; however, there are two developments that are immediately useful and available:

• Computer assisted diagnosis. Michael C. McKenna (1986, 1987) has designed an Apple II compatible program that is both educationally and technologically sophisticated. McKenna's system requests information on a broad range of factors bearing on literacy acquisition, such as: parental support, student attitude, and even type of materials in use. It then makes a diagnosis and provides recommendations. Though "live" experts may disagree with the machine's diagnosis and suggestions, the exercise has powerful and proven

---

REFLECTIVE BOX 2

Writing-to-Learn-What-You-Think

It has been said that "all writing is like a plunge into the unknown." We take this to mean that writing can be a means by which to deepen and enrich learning, to connect random impressions into some dependable markers to pilot your professional work. Work through some of your thoughts on diagnosis by writing a brief essay (about 500 words) on one of the statements below.

1. Diagnosis begins with a teacher's first lesson.
2. The diagnosis can't be completely right if it was completely predictable.
3. The scientific method offers a proper grounding for diagnosis and remediation.
4. Subtyping is moving closer to our more refined knowledge of the reading process.
5. The principle of diagnosis which says the most to me is . . .

---

heuristic value in fine-tuning diagnostic skills (McKenna, 1991; Vinsonhaler, Weinshank, Wagner, & Polin, 1987).

- Interactive computer programs. Interactive computer systems are the other major area of development. Unlike systems where the teacher collects and enters the information, interactive systems are used by students. These systems are essentially automated workbooks that score, store, and interpret information while the student does exercises (McLoughlin & Lewis, 1990). This type of system is on the verge of making a quantum leap. Computers now are capable, within certain parameters, of being diagnostic teachers. This is done through the availability of branching programs that, based on initial student responses, call up simplifications, elaborations, and limitless associative chains (Blanchard & Rottenberg, 1990). This option, which was well along in development in mathematics by the late 1960s, is even further enhanced now by the availability of the technology to branch to nonprint forms. Such "hypermedia" options permit words in print to be converted into spoken words, pictures, and illustrations, and even videotaped segments of standard lectures and films. When these options are put in the control of the student, such systems are ready to enhance self-monitoring and teach whenever students are ready to learn. They are "on demand teaching" systems comparable to the "on demand feeding" systems that governed the feeding of infants until modern times when it was felt that this was detrimental to child discipline. Ironically, books offer the same option, but tend to be more linear and less responsive. It will be interesting to see if these options enhance or detract from the willingness of youngsters to read.

McKenna (1991) reports another recent development with implications for both diagnosis and remediation. It involves linking computers to eye-tracking cameras. With such devices recording and assessing eye movements as an indicator of pauses, regressions, and such, it becomes possible to determine problems that readers may be having with types of print, classes of words or ideas, sentence structures, etc. (McConkie & Zola, 1987). Robert Cutler and Carroll Truss (1989) have designed a sophisticated program that helps youngsters with word pronunciation and meanings as they read text at the computer, while keeping track of the words called up and the child's reading rate.

There are two other possibilities with computers that are elaborated elsewhere in the text. One is a clinic electronic bulletin board that would allow teachers and clinicians to share problems and solutions. The other is an annotation exchange system that would allow students and others to exchange letters or comments with one another about what they have read, and to survey these annotations before reading a selection or book in order to get some literal help or a proper perspective.

As we prepare to go to press, there is a report of a new computer diagnostic system that looks very promising. See John E. McEneaney, "Computer-assisted diagnonis in reading: An expert systems approach" in the *Journal of Reading* 1992, Volume 36, No.1, pp. 36–47.

➤ *LOOKING BACK* ◄

After presenting arguments, pro and con, to the question of whether diagnosis was worth the bother, the chapter answered in the affirmative. It then covered aspects of process, principles, and models that inform diagnostic procedures. This section described the Weiner-Cromer Diagnostic Model as the organizational framework for the rest of the text. The chapter went on to detail several of the most traditional procedural underpinnings of diagnosis, namely: discrepancy, correlational relationships, expectancy, and subtyping. The chapter concluded with a discussion of computerized diagnosis, and a promising procedural option.

➤ *LOOKING AHEAD*

The next two chapters are designed to provide you with knowledge of the specific assessment devices and procedures that are available for use in the diagnosis of reading and related literacy disorders. The next chapter covers the heart of remedial reading, the diagnosis of reading and language related deficits. The one following details the assessment of defects, disruptions, and differences.

4

Detecting and Assessing Literacy Deficits

> ➤ *LOOK FOR IT*

This chapter opens with a general discussion of testing—types of "lures" that are available. It then focuses on specific assessment of possible deficiencies in word analysis, reading comprehension, vocabulary, rate of reading, and study skills. It also gives fair attention to speaking, writing, listening, and to certain aspects of metacognition and schema. The heart of the chapter is a focus on means and methods for measuring specific reading and literacy factors.

Primer on Testing

Testing is a lot like fishing. Often you have to try several different kinds of lures to discover what might be under those sometimes murky waters. There are three conventional methods of discovering what is under the murky waters: standardized, criterion-referenced, and informal testing. In practice, the differences among these forms and formats can become blurred by who is using them and what they choose to call them. Nonetheless, the differences are worth noting since they do provide a matrix for organizing thoughts and available options.

Standardized Tests

This type of test is norm-referenced, which means that some large and presumably representative sampling of students was given the test to establish reference points for the percentage of correct answers students could be expected to make at different age or grade levels. These percentages then become benchmarks for interpreting the raw scores of others who may be given the test.

Norm-referenced, or standardized test scores, typically are expressed as grade equivalents, percentiles, or stanines. A grade equivalent score indicates that a student's raw score is the same as the average score of the sample students in a certain grade level. It is reported in a whole number and a tenth to represent some portion of the year. Thus, 5.5 is equivalent to fifth grade, fifth month of school. There has been strong objection by some to the use of grade equivalent scores since these might imply that there is a fixed level of performance that should be expected at each age and grade level; exercise appropriate cautions and qualifications in referring to these. A percentile score is another way of indicating how a student's raw score relates to the sample population. A raw score, for example, may be checked against a table that might show that score to be in the 57th percentile. This is another way of saying that the score is better than 57% of those in the sample group and not as good as 43%. Sometimes, special norms are calculated to determine how that same raw score compares with the average score of students from similar regional, socioeconomic, or ethnic backgrounds. Finally, there is the stanine (or, standard nine) score. This system was devised to get a sense of the band in which a student is operating. This is done by taking a raw score and checking it against a statistical table. Should the score be equivalent to the fourth stanine, then that student's performance on the test is in the fourth of nine possible segments, or one stanine below the fifth stanine, which is the standardized average score for stanine rankings.

There are limitations to standardized testing, despite their generally higher levels of validity (assurance that they measure what they say they measure), and reliability (dependability that the score made will not vary greatly from one test situation to the next). Ironically, the limitations of standardized testing most frequently cited are not necessarily corrected by either criterion-referenced or informal testing. Therefore, think of the limitations stated below as precautions in interpreting all forms of testing:

1. Tests tend to measure the easy things, things that usually can be inferred from classwork and simple observation (e.g., level of comprehension, IQ, achievement).
2. The validity and reliability of an individual student's score can not always be trusted since tests usually are based on group norms that can misrepresent an individual's performance, and also can vary widely, if not wildly, when individuals are retested with alternate forms of the same instrument.
3. Most standardized tests tend to provide a measure of a student's highest level of performance, or frustrational level, rather than of instructional or independent levels (to determine a student's instructional reading level from a standardized test score, subtract one year from the score; to establish independent level, subtract one and a half to two years).
4. High and low scores on tests can be especially misleading since scores rarely are on an equal interval basis, and only relatively few items tend to distinguish performances at upper and lower ranges (the difference between the 75th and the 95th percentiles may be just two or three items, and similarly so between the 10th and the 30th percentiles).
5. Most tests are not of much help in offering insights into how and why someone responded the way they did. While they offer huge amounts of quantitative information, there is little that is qualitative, and therefore useful in instructional planning.

Limitations such as these only further serve to explain why it is necessary for teachers and reading specialists to be well versed in testing and to be able to use a variety of testing methods and devices to cross-verify initial findings. It is largely as a result of this ongoing need that the next two types of tests, the criterion referenced and informal, evolved.

Criterion-Referenced Tests

In contrast to standardized tests, this type of test presumably does not compare students to one another, but to some clearly defined objective. Mastery tests, for example, are a form of criterion-referenced testing. Such tests now are being widely used by various states to ascertain whether a student has achieved "minimum competencies" in certain basic skills and operations. They also are used by state departments to convey a clear message as to what government, business, and society expect schools to accomplish. Unlike standardized tests, whose items are carefully guarded, most criterion-referenced tests are constructed by converting curriculum guides and objectives into test items.

The credibility of virtually "teaching to the test" is maintained by the fact that most criterion-referenced tests represent essential minimum competencies and that they are implicitly normed. Criteria are established from samples of students whose scores provide the state test makers with some benchmarks of the age and grade levels at which mastery should reasonably be expected. Even where this type of "norming" is not followed, the mastery criteria approximate it by drawing from general knowledge of what children should know and be able to do at certain age and grade levels.

In short, unlike standardized tests that attempt to measure generalized states of knowledge, criterion-referenced tests tend to assess basic and often pragmatic skills, such as reading driver's manuals and following directions. Informal tests, the next consideration, also could be considered criterion-based but tend to have a different purpose and orientation.

Informal Tests

There are many types of "informals." Some are criterion-referenced, and some are even standardized. Informals, however, have one characteristic that distinguishes them from the first two types. They are intentionally heuristic. That is, they are constructed for the specific purpose of causing diagnostic insights to occur from sharpened observations of, and interactions with, needy students.

While teachers may construct their own "informal" tests from established guidelines, it usually makes more sense to select one from those that are commercially available. Most commercially prepared informals have a rich history and background of use in clinical and school settings. The use of some such informals also permits teachers and clinicians to better communicate with one another about a student's needs in very specific terms, and with some common points of reference.

Several examples are given ahead in the chapter on the use of commercial informals as a means of stimulating and communicating clinical insights. Before looking at these, let us first consider some very informal means of assessing general reading level using Quick Tests.

Quick Tests of Overall Reading

There are three popular "quick means" to assess overall reading ability: the rule of thumb, word list estimation, and cloze passage appraisal.

Rule of Thumb

A student is given a one-hundred word passage to read orally from a selection with a known difficulty level. The instructor makes a fist that can not be seen. Then, each time the student makes an obvious error, the fingers of the hand, ending with the thumb, are opened until all words are read. If one or two fingers are raised, then the material probably is at the student's independent reading level. If 3 or 4 are used, it is at the student's instructional level. If the thumb and more become necessary, the material is becoming too difficult to learn from. Be liberal in what you count as errors. Do not, for example, count repetitions and word substitutions that do not distort meaning. Susan Glazer (1984), a master clinician at Rider College (NJ), suggests that *students* be taught the rule of thumb as a means of helping them increase their metacognitive sensitivity and in selecting their own reading materials. Robert Gunning (1979) recommends this same procedure to attain a readability index, or estimate of the difficulty of reading material, a practice that has been verified by Victor Nell (1988).

Word List Estimations

There is a reliable and high correlation between recognizing words in isolation and in identifying them in context. This fact makes it possible to infer general reading level quite accurately from sets of graded word lists. Such word lists are typically compiled from basal readers and empirically established lists such as Thorndike and Lorge's *The Teacher's Word Book of 30,000 Words* (1944), and a more recent list researched by Dale and O'Rourke (1976; 1981). The Dale and O'Rourke Living Word Vocabulary list includes more than 44,000 items and was used as a guide for controlling the difficulty level of *The World Book Encyclopedia*. It provides a grade level for every word listed and the percentage of students who can be expected to know the word at that grade level. It also provides different grade level estimates for the same word when it has different meanings (see Figure 4.1). The chapter on vocabulary acquisition provides further information on uses of this word list in teaching and assessing vocabulary and concept knowledge.

There is a seeming irony to keep in mind when using word list estimations: Students typically are less accurate in recognizing words in isolation than in context; nonetheless, most word list estimations of reading levels tend to be a bit

FIGURE 4.1

Dale & O'Rourke Word List Excerpt

Grade	Score	Word	Meaning
04	87%	bar	piece of soap/candy
06	67%	bar	block or barrier
12	75%	bar	separate measure

on the high side. This well-known fact was further demonstrated in a study that compared grade placement on the word list of the *Wide Range Achievement Test* with levels derived from more conventional reading tests (Bristow, Pikulski, & Pelosi, 1983).

Although teachers and reading specialists usually prefer and recommend a word list, these choices tend to be based most on what is familiar and available. There is no definitive evidence that one word list is better than another. The most familiar word lists include the following:

Harris-Jacobson Core lists (Harris Jacobson, 1982)
Peabody Individual Achievement Test (Dunn & Markwardt, 1970)
Queens College Tests (Harris, 1970)
San Diego Quick Assessment (LaPray & Ross, 1969)
Slosson Oral Reading Test (Slosson, 1963)
Word list from the Wide Range Achievement Test (Jastak & Jastak, 1978)

The San Diego Quick Assessment has become one of the most popular of these lists since it was made available at no cost by LaPray and Ross (1969). It is presented in detail in Figure 4.2.

There is one other quick test of decoding ability that is especially worth the note of teachers of remedial reading since it does a better job of eliciting responses from children who have stopped trying due to excessive failure.

The Name Test

Recently, Patricia Cunningham (1990) has proposed a new "quick test" based on children's ability to decode names (see Figure 4.3). The use of names has certain advantages over conventional word lists and nonsense word lists. Names tend to invite better effort from the children. Most names are familiar, and therefore, in the child's listening vocabulary. This is important in decoding since it is by checking one's attempts at decoding a word against our recognition of having heard it that tells us that we probably have pronounced the word correctly.

There are no set norms yet for the Name Test. The test, however, has been found to be very reliable (.98). Procedures for administering and scoring the Name Test are described below.

Preparing the Instrument.

1. Type or print legibly the 25 names on a sheet of paper or card stock. Make sure the print size is appropriate for the age or grade level of the students being tested.
2. For students who might perceive reading an entire list of names as being too formidable, type or print the names on index cards, so they can be read individually.
3. Prepare a protocol (scoring) sheet. Do this by typing the list of names in a column and following each name with a blank line to be used for recording a student's responses.

FIGURE 4.2

San Diego Quick Assessment

PREPARATION

1. Prepare word list cards by typing each of the following lists of words on a large index card. Leave ample space between words so that you can easily point to each word as you administer the test. Type the grade-level designations on the *back* of each card for your reference only. The word card lists can be laminated for durability.
2. Prepare typed word list sheets, with space to write the student's responses beside each word.

WORD LISTS

Preprimer		**Primer**		**Grade 1**	
see	_____	you	_____	road	_____
play	_____	come	_____	live	_____
me	_____	not	_____	thank	_____
at	_____	with	_____	when	_____
run	_____	jump	_____	bigger	_____
go	_____	help	_____	how	_____
and	_____	is	_____	always	_____
look	_____	work	_____	night	_____
can	_____	are	_____	spring	_____
here	_____	this	_____	today	_____

Grade 2		**Grade 3**		**Grade 4**	
our	_____	city	_____	decided	_____
please	_____	middle	_____	served	_____
myself	_____	moment	_____	amazed	_____
town	_____	frightened	_____	silent	_____
early	_____	exclaimed	_____	wrecked	_____
send	_____	several	_____	improved	_____
wide	_____	lonely	_____	certainly	_____
believe	_____	drew	_____	entered	_____
quietly	_____	since	_____	realized	_____
carefully	_____	straight	_____	interrupted	_____

Grade 5		**Grade 6**		**Grade 7**	
scanty	_____	bridge	_____	amber	_____
certainly	_____	commercial	_____	dominion	_____
develop	_____	abolish	_____	sundry	_____
considered	_____	trucker	_____	capillary	_____
discussed	_____	apparatus	_____	impetuous	_____
behaved	_____	elementary	_____	blight	_____
splendid	_____	comment	_____	wrest	_____
acquainted	_____	necessity	_____	enumerate	_____
escaped	_____	gallery	_____	daunted	_____
grim	_____	relativity	_____	condescend	_____

Grade 8

capacious _____
limitation _____
pretext _____
intrigue _____
delusion _____
immaculate _____
ascent _____
acrid _____
binocular _____
embankment _____

Grade 9

conscientious _____
isolation _____
molecule _____
ritual _____
momentous _____
vulnerable _____
kinship _____
conservatism _____
jaunty _____
inventive _____

Grade 10

zany _____
jerkin _____
nausea _____
gratuitous _____
linear _____
inept _____
legality _____
aspen _____
amnesty _____
barometer _____

Grade 11

galore _____
rotunda _____
capitalism _____
prevaricate _____
risible _____
exonerate _____
superannuate _____
luxuriate _____
piebald _____
crunch _____

ADMINISTRATION

1. Begin with a card that is at least two years below the student's grade placement.
2. Ask the student to read the words aloud. If he or she misreads *any* words on the list, drop to easier lists until the student makes *no* errors. This indicates the base reading level.
3. Write down all incorrect responses, or use diacritical marks on your copy of the test. For example, *lonely* might be read and recorded as *lovely* or *apparatus* as *a-per´-a-tus*.
4. Encourage the student to read words he or she does not know so that you can identify the techniques used for word identification.
5. Have the student read from increasingly difficult lists until he or she misses at least three words on one of the lists.
6. Identify the student's independent, instructional, and frustration levels using the following interpretation criteria:

> **Independent level** = no more than one error on a list
> **Instructional level** = two errors on a list
> **Frustration level** = three or more errors on a list

LaPray and Ross (1969)

Administering the Name Test.

1. Administer the Name Test individually. Select a quiet, distraction-free location.
2. Explain to the student that s/he is to pretend to be a teacher who must read a list of names of students in the class. Direct the student to read the names as if taking attendance.

3. Have the student read the entire list. Inform the student that you will not be able to help with difficult names, and encourage s/he to, "make a guess if you are not sure." This way you will have sufficient responses for analysis.
4. Write a check on the protocol sheet for each name read correctly. Write phonetic spellings for names that are mispronounced.

Scoring and interpreting the Name Test.

1. Count a word correct if all syllables are pronounced correctly regardless of where the student places the accent. For example, either Yo'/lan/da or Yo/lan'/da would be acceptable.
2. For words where the vowel pronunciation depends on which syllable the consonant is placed with, count them correct for either pronunciation. For example, either Ho/mer or Hom/er would be acceptable.
3. Count the number of names read correctly, and analyze those mispronounced, looking for patterns indicative of decoding strengths and weaknesses.
4. As a benchmark of performance, you can expect the average second grader to score 23 out of 50.

Cloze Passage Testing

The term "cloze" has come to refer to any activities in which students are asked to fill in missing words in passages. The term was coined by Wilson Taylor (1953) who was using this fill-in-the-blanks activity to try to measure the psychological trait of "closure" (the tendency to complete missing elements of an incomplete stimulus and recognize it as a meaningful whole). Taylor's cloze test was not a good measure of closure, but he did find that it had a strong correlation with

---

FIGURE 4.3

The Name Test

Jay Conway	_____	Wendy Swain	_____
Tim Cornell	_____	Glen Spencer	_____
Chuck Hoke	_____	Fred Sherwood	_____
Yolanda Clark	_____	Flo Thornton	_____
Kimberly Blake	_____	Dee Skidmore	_____
Roberta Slade	_____	Grace Brewster	_____
Homer Preston	_____	Ned Westmoreland	_____
Gus Quincy	_____	Ron Smitherman	_____
Cindy Sampson	_____	Troy Whitlock	_____
Chester Wright	_____	Vance Middleton	_____
Ginger Yale	_____	Zane Anderson	_____
Patrick Tweed	_____	Bernard Pendergraph	_____
Stanley Shaw	_____		

P. Cunningham (1990)

FIGURE 4.4

Standard Cloze Passage Test

PREPARATION OF THE TEST
Select a passage of about 300 words from a selection of known difficulty level. Copy the first sentence with no deletions. Then select a word at random in the second sentence. Delete this word and every fifth word thereafter until 50 words have been deleted. Finish the sentence containing the 50th blank, and copy the next sentence with no deletions. The blanks should be typed lines five spaces long, and numbered from 1 to 50. Students record their responses on numbered answer sheets.

ADMINISTRATION OF THE TEST
When ready to give the test, inform students that the task will be difficult, but that 60% accuracy is a good score. Demonstrate the task of filling in the blanks for the child.

SCORING THE TEST
Count the number of actual words filled in correctly. Do not count synonyms. Multiply this number by 2 (since there are 50 items) to get the percent correct.

INTERPRETING THE RESULTS
A score above 60% indicates that the material is within the child's independent reading level. Scores between 40% and 60% indicate that the material is within the child's instructional reading level. Scores below 40% tend to indicate that the material is in the child's frustration level. It is best to allow a plus or minus 5 percentage point spread for error of measurement on each of these bands of scores.

---

reading comprehension. As a result, the Standard Cloze Passage Test, developed later by Bormuth (1965), can be used to obtain a quick estimate of a student's ability to comprehend material at a given difficulty level. It yields a score indicating that the material used for the test is at the student's independent, instructional, or frustration level. The cloze format effectively taps into the student's familiarity with the subtle language redundancy patterns within a passage (Weaver & Kingston, 1963). A more recent study by Michael McKenna and Kent Layton (1990) seems to confirm that it also can be a trustworthy measure of comprehension from one sentence to another, a notion that had been challenged by earlier research by Victor Culver, and associates (1972). There are many variations on the cloze format, and many effective instructional uses. For purposes of diagnostic screening, however, the most reliable and valid results will be obtained when using the Standard Cloze Passage Test in the manner described in Figure 4.4. Adaptations of the format, such as varying the length, using alternative procedures for deleting words, or accepting synonyms, tend to invalidate the scoring criteria.

The issue of accepting or not accepting synonyms has been the subject of a good deal of controversy and research. For informal evaluation of a student's cloze test responses, there is value in analyzing the extent to which "reasonable guesses," including synonyms, were used, as compared with word choices that failed to indicate comprehension of the test passage. Several early studies did, in fact, show somewhat greater validity and internal consistency when synonyms were accepted in scoring (McKenna, 1976; Porter, 1978; Schoelles, 1971). For formal uses of the cloze test, where the object is to obtain standardized measures, it should be kept in mind that the results of synonym scoring have proven to be unreliable across raters. William Henk and Mary L. Selders (1984), who did a definitive study of this issue, concluded that "there does not seem to be any overt reason to credit synonyms on a cloze test" (1984, p. 286).

The next level of assessment of overall reading is rather ironically referred to as Informal Reading Inventories. While having humble beginnings as teacher-constructed instruments, "informals" now are published, quasi-standardized, and tend to be very precise in terms of how each should be administered, scored, and interpreted.

Informal Reading Inventories (IRI's)

Emmett Betts, one of the founders of contemporary reading instruction, is most often credited with the development of IRI's. In point of fact, Betts did not design these informals alone — they evolved through the work of many others. It is his criteria, however, that still provide the chief guidelines for their interpretation. The word "informal" remains appropriate, since the purposes of IRI's still are very pragmatic and classroom oriented. These purposes include the following:

1. Establish students' independent, instructional, and frustration levels in reading and listening.
2. Estimate student capacity to learn to read (from listening level).
3. Group students for reading and related activities.
4. Appraise progress in word analysis, oral reading fluency, and comprehension, although the latter has been challenged.
5. Permit some up-close observations of children operating under a variety of reading tasks and levels of demand.

The initial four objectives are often referred to as the *quantitative analysis* portion of IRI's, whereas the latter one is thought of in terms of *qualitative analysis*, or focused "kid watching." There is another aspect to qualitative analysis, referred to as "miscues," which is discussed further ahead in this chapter.

Formalizing Informals

Originally constructed by teachers, primarily from available basal materials, IRI's were found to have shortcomings that were more correctable when commercially prepared. Chief among the problems of teacher prepared IRI's were the following shortcomings:

1. Readability levels of the excerpts were found to be inaccurate (Bradley & Ames, 1977).

2. Questions often were shown not to be passage dependent (Schell, 1991).
3. When a school changed basals, the predictive or matching value of the IRI's fell off too sharply (Baumann, 1988a,b).
4. Constructing the IRI's took an inordinate amount of teacher time and energy.

For these reasons, it generally is more cost effective to buy one of the several excellent and commercially available IRI's. Several popular IRI's are listed further ahead in this chapter. Should you wish to construct an IRI, you will wish to consult some suggestions assembled in Box 4.1, from Michael C. McKenna (1983) and William J. Valmont (1972).

IRI: Structure

An IRI usually is divided into two main parts. Part I consists of graded word lists, and Part II contains graded paragraphs for silent and/or oral reading. Word lists and paragraphs usually start at the preprimer level, and extend at least through grade 8 (Harman, 1982). Most commercial IRI's, in addition, provide the following materials:

1. A manual of directions for administering the test, scoring, and interpreting students' performances.
2. Student test materials for Part I—graded word lists; and Part II—graded reading and listening passages.
3. Record forms of the graded word lists and graded reading passages for the test administrator.
4. A summary sheet form for recording test results.

IRI: General Administration Protocols

The graded word lists are administered first. The child's performance on the graded word lists provides an estimate of his/her word recognition abilities, with indications of specific areas of weakness in word recognition. This opening section of the test helps the test administrator determine the level of difficulty at which to begin the graded paragraphs portion of the test.

Administering Part I: Graded Word Lists

1. Establish a comfortable atmosphere and congenial rapport with the student before proceeding with the inventory.
2. Give the student an idea of why s/he is taking the test. For example, "This test will help me know what book you can read best." Also tell the child that you will write things down so you can remember how well s/he did. Some people have the student write his/her name on the test booklet. Your name and the date should also be placed on the booklet.
3. Present the student's copy of the graded word lists, starting at the preprimer level, and say, "Pronounce each word for me. If you are not sure or do not know the word, at least tell me what you *think* it is."

BOX 4.1

Suggestions for Constructing and Using IRI's

1. Do not assume that the stories in basal readers all represent the assigned readability level. Check readability with one or more of the better formulas.
2. Make sure the passages in each sequence are from the same general interest area, preferably one of moderate to high interest for both boys and girls of the ages at which the IRI will be given. It is a good idea to ask students individually about their interest in the subjects in the inventory. Make your inquiries prior to a student's exposure to the passages.
3. In writing questions, (1) state each clearly and simply; (2) limit the number of types; (3) avoid yes/no questions and questions stated in the negative; (4) avoid questions that overlap, or are dependent on one another; (5) begin questions with who, what, when, how, and why; (6) avoid multiple choice questions.
4. Ensure the passage dependency of questions by "field testing" them on some of your brighter students or by using an adult standard; i.e., would an adult be able to answer this question without reading the question.
5. Use the Betts criteria, but do not adhere to them too rigidly. Keep these points in mind: (1) in the lower grades, be lenient with the oral accuracy criteria when comprehension is good; (2) always look for signs of actual frustration in the student's behavior; and (3) when comprehension scores are between 65% and 75%, interpret the performance as instructional unless there is evidence of frustration.
6. Do not consider the quality (semantic acceptability) of miscues in obtaining initial scoring levels. However, do consider quality in subjectively evaluating overall patterns once the levels have been determined, concentrating on miscues made at and below the instructional level.
7. If there is a difference between oral and silent comprehension scores, use the higher of the two.
8. For miscue analysis, do not allow students to read passages silently before oral reading. When oral accuracy is at frustration level and silent comprehension is at the instructional level, consider the level as instructional.
9. At the secondary level, beware of commercial inventories that include passages at each of grades 7-12. If constructing your own IRI, combine the upper levels in pairs, 5-6, 7-8, 9-10, 11-12. When evaluating the performance of secondary students, give far more credence to silent comprehension than to oral accuracy scores.

4. The teacher should record all responses on the inventory record as indicated. When a list has been completed, ask the student to pronounce each word missed (e.g., "Tell me number 4 again.") Do not follow this procedure if the list is obviously too difficult.
5. Discontinue the testing when the student is unable to correct 5 of the 20 words in any list. Remember, the reading levels are not determined by this test, so additional testing does not improve the student's score.
6. Total the number of correct and corrected responses, and multiply by 5. Record the total percentage at the bottom of each column tested. Later, these percentages will be recoded on the front summary sheet.
7. Since the word list takes very little time to administer, it can be used as a quick screening device. Pupils can be roughly classified as having word recognition ability above, at, or below grade level.

Marking System for Graded Word Lists   *Meaning*

1. and ___*an*✓___   (error, same error on second trial)

2. big ___*t*___   (correct)

3. can ___*dk*___   (don't know–no correction)

4. when ___*then*ᵗ___   (error, corrected on next trial)

5. now ___*0*ᵗ___   (word skipped, corrected on 2nd trial)

Administering Part II: Graded Paragraphs

This portion of the IRI is intended to provide an estimate of the child's independent, instructional, and frustration levels in reading and listening. The reading passages further help in identifying specific instructional needs related to contextual reading and passage comprehension.

1. For primary levels, begin at the highest level at which the child scored 100% on the word list. Students reading at higher levels can be started at the level where the student made the first uncorrected error on the word recognition test.
2. Ask the student to read out loud for you and tell the student that you will ask several questions about what was read after the story is finished.
3. Introduce the oral reading passage by reading the motivation statement preceding the actual passage. Then have the child read the title and the passage from the student booklet. Record any incorrect responses in the space above the sentence or words on the teacher's record sheet of the passage.

4. Four types of word errors generally are recorded and counted to determine the reading level of the student:

   a. words pronounced by the teacher   a cr*P*owded room

   b. words omitted   a(crowded)room

   c. words added   a, *big* crowded room

   d. words substituted   a *crowned* crowded room

5. Count as an error any word to which the pupil adds or omits an ending unless the student's oral language reflects the same omission type.
6. Count the same error only *once* no matter how many times the error is repeated. If a repeated word is unknown to the student and the word is essential to the story comprehension, the word should be pronounced for the student.
7. Observations about fluency, word-by-word reading, finger pointing, signs of tension, etc., should be recorded in the margin or at the bottom of the page.
8. Hesitations between words and phrases are recorded with slashes—He/saw/the//pirate—one slash per second. Words or phrases which are repeated should be underlined. Neither hesitations nor repetitions are counted as errors.
9. Multiple or consecutive errors are counted as a single error when the second or later errors are brought about in order to maintain grammatical agreement:

   He is
   (They are going . . .)

10. Errors that are corrected by the child are recorded but *not counted as errors*:

    was
    (He saw a pig.   =   "He was a pig . . . He saw a pig.")

11. In order to identify specific types of comprehension difficulties, comprehension questions on each passage are labeled to indicate the type of thinking required. For example:
    I   Inference
    F   Factual
    PR   Picture Recognition
    V   Vocabulary

12. Following the oral reading, the student booklet should be closed and the comprehension check of the story started. The comprehension check may be undertaken in one or more formats (discussed further ahead). For ease of presentation, we assume here that the comprehension check is conducted with conventional short answer questions read to the student. Questions may be rephrased as long as the new wording does not provide additional clues.

13. All responses should be recorded. If a student's response is the same as the suggested answer (provided in brackets), the printed answer may be underlined to indicate this equivalence. Any different wording should be written just above or just below the suggested answer. Responses may be studied later to check the accuracy of the original scoring, or to analyze the reasoning used by the student.

14. A question should be repeated if the student does not give an answer related to the question. (e.g., "Listen to the question again..."). Record a "Q" to indicate that the question has been repeated and write down the new response.

15. When scoring questions, use [+] for correct, and [0] for incorrect responses. If a question indicates that a multiple response is required, such as "name two ways.[. .]," full credit can be given only if the specified number of correct responses are provided. On such questions, partial credit may be awarded for partial responses (half credit for only one correct response). The question may be repeated if the student names just one. IRI manuals often provide several suggested answers for comprehension questions.

16. Testing is discontinued when the accuracy reaches frustration level or the student attains 50% or less in comprehension. Scoring guides are generally provided on the recording booklet. In the event that the student reaches frustration level through inaccurate reading, the comprehension questions are usually administered. Inaccurate reading does not always mean that the student will be equally poor in comprehension.

17. The basic directions should not be changed. However, the teacher may reasonably test a level above estimated frustration when the score drops rapidly or when the first score is very low.

18. Examples to indicate that further testing is warranted:

Billy J.				The first score is at frustration
	Word List	WR	Comp.	level, but the Word Recognition scores suggest he is a better reader
PP	100%	89%	60%	than Preprimer. Further testing
P	90%	97%	100%	confirms that the score was not
1(2)	80%	94%	90%	a true indication of his reading ability.

Joe M.				Joe reached frustration level at 4th; however, the drop between 3 and 4 seems unusual. Testing was continued and the results indicate that the 50% was not a true score.
	Word List	WR	Comp.	
3	90%	98%	90%	
4	85%	94%	50%	
5	80%	96%	80%	

Mary				In this case, the continued testing still indicates a comprehension problem.
	Word List	WR	Comp.	
3	90%	98%	90%	
4	85%	96%	50%	
5	80%	94%	40%	

IRI: Establishing Levels and Interpreting Results

Emmett Betts (1946) is said to have first suggested the most popularly used criteria for using student scores on comprehension of grade level reading passages to determine the level at which the student is likely to read at independent, instructional, and frustration levels. His student, Patsy Aloysius Killgallon (1942), conducted a study that focused on the most critical criterion—that for "instructional level." The criteria found in her study for accuracy of words in context was 93.9, very close to the 95% level suggested by Betts. The complete Betts-Killgallon criteria are shown in Figure 4.5.

FIGURE 4.5

Criteria for Determining Reading Levels

I. *Independent reading level*—easy reading
   A. Word recognition in isolation—90%–100% in the "flash" condition
   B. Word recognition in context—99%
   C. Comprehension—90% or better on 10 question inventories, 80% where there are five questions
   D. Freedom from tensions such as frowning, body movements, etc.
   E. Freedom from finger-pointing, subvocalization, and/or lip movement
   F. Acceptable reading posture
   G. Oral reading should be rhythmical, in a conversational tone, and with correct interpretation of punctuation
   H. Silent reading comprehension should surpass oral reading comprehension

II. *Instructional reading level* — guided reading
   A. Word recognition in isolation — 75%–89% in the "flash" condition
   B. Word recognition in context — 95%
   C. Comprehension — a minimum score of 75% (interpreted as 70% on 10-question tests and 60% on 5-question tests)
   D. Freedom from body movements, finger-pointing and/or lip movement
   E. Acceptable reading posture
   F. Oral rereading is mostly rhythmical, conversational, and with correct interpretation of punctuation, and a reasonable eye-voice span
   G. Silent reading can be sustained since word difficulty and concept load are challenging but manageable
III. *Frustration level* — nonproductive reading
   A. Word recognition in isolation — 50% or less in the "flash" condition
   B. Word recognition in context — 90% or less
   C. Comprehension — 50% or less
   D. Evidence of compensations: finger-pointing, guessing, gross inferencing from graphic clues
   E. Defense mechanisms apparent: withdrawal, crying, attempts at distraction, and/or refusal to read
   F. Oral reading is too poor to permit comprehension and should be discontinued
   G. Lack of enthusiasm, comprehension below oral reading, and disengagement
IV. *Listening Capacity Level* — potential to read with understanding
   A. Comprehension — 75% or better
   B. Discussion of material parallels the complexity of the selections
   C. Ability to supply information pertinent to the topic from experience
   D. Precise and meaningful use of words — from context of selection
   E. Able to sustain attention to duration of selection

Modified from Robert E. Leibert
UMKC Division of Reading Education

Four examples of student IRI test results are given on pgs. 84–87 to provide practice in using these criteria to establish reading levels. Each example is followed by a brief explanation of how the levels were established and the instructional implications of each type of reading performance.

In the first example, the levels have been provided for you. In the three following examples, you are encouraged to complete the interpretation before comparing your reasoning against the explanation provided. Each example illustrates a different type of problem you are likely to encounter.

For Example 2, cover the interpretation, and see if you can identify the three levels. After you have worked out what you think the levels are, compare your conclusions with those in the interpretation provided.

Challenges to Reading Levels

Several investigations and reviews have challenged, but mostly verified, the Betts-Killgallon criteria (Beldin, 1970); Jongsma and Jongsma, 1981; McKenna,

---

Example 1: Billy, Grade 2

Grade Level	Part I Graded Word List % of Words Correct	Part II Percent		Label	
		WR	Comp	WR	Comp
PP	100				
P	100				
1	100	99	100	IND	IND
2	85	96	60	INST	INST
3	80	85	50	FRUST	FRUST

IND __1__   INST __2__   FRUST __3__

[Notes: Only the information from Part II, Word Recognition and Comprehension is used to determine levels; the Comprehension score is usually based on 5 questions per passage.]

INTERPRETATION:
Billy's scores decline evenly. Each level exactly meets the stated criteria. Billy should receive instruction at the second reader level. A balanced reading lession (DRA or DR-TA) should provide Billy with the needed instruction to improve contextual reading and comprehension.

1983; Pikulski, 1974; Pikulski and Shanahan, 1982; Powell and Dunkeld, 1971; and Walter, 1974). Of these challenges, Powell (1978) did find differences for words in context at instructional level that are notable.

Essentially, what Powell found was that youngsters at lower grade levels could tolerate higher levels of error in word recognition and still have good comprehension. This oddity probably is explainable in two ways. One is that young children's knowledge base often surpasses their word analysis skills. This enables them to answer some comprehension questions correctly with little or no information from the passage, and despite many word recognition errors. The second explanation is that word analysis skill tends to be underestimated on some widely used IRI's (such as Ekwall's, 1974, and Gilmore's & Gilmore's, 1968) that count more things as errors, including noncontext distorting *miscues*, discussed ahead.

Miscue Analysis

Kenneth Goodman (1973) developed a system he called miscue analysis as a way to better understand and interpret the types of problems children encounter in reading. Miscue analysis is based on the psycholinguistic model of reading, which proposes that reading is a complex process of making predictions based on minimal clues and continuously checking the "sense" of these predictions. Traditional procedures for recording and scoring IRI's called for recording *every* deviation the reader made from an exact and fluent reading, including repetitions of

Example 2: Shara, Grade 5

GRADE LEVEL	PART I GRADED WORD LIST % OF WORDS CORRECT	PART II PERCENT		LABEL	
		WR	COMP	WR	COMP
3	100				
4	100	99	100	IND	IND
5	90	97	100	I/I	IND
6	80	94	100	INST	IND
7	80	91	90	I/F	IND
8	40	88	80	FRUST	IND

IND ___   INST ___   FRUST ___

INTERPRETATION:

The highest level that meets the criteria for independent level is 4th. The 5th level is between instructional and the independent levels and is not reported. Even though the comprehension performance is higher than needed, the sixth level is the highest level where the accuracy criterion is met. Sixth level is the instructional level. Seventh level is betwen instructional and frustration levels and like the 5th is not reported. To reach frustration level, only one of the two areas (WR or Comp) needs to meet the criterion for frustration level. Shara's accuracy reaches the frustration level at the 8th level and even though her comprehension is still acceptable, the 8th level is considered the frustration level.

Shara should either be placed at the sixth reader level for instruction, or if above grade level readers are not available, she should receive an enriched library reading program.

words or phrases, self-corrections, and lengthy pauses. Goodman proposed that these types of "errors" were not of equal importance. Errors such as repetitions, self-corrections, and pauses, in fact, often are indications that the reader is trying to create meaning, rather than simply decoding. Goodman proposed that, at the very least, all errors should be thought of not as "errors," but as "miscues"— erroneous attempts to make use of available clues to meaning—and that those miscues that do not tend to distort meaning, such as repetitions, self-corrections, and pauses, should not be counted in the total word recognition score. Further, miscues could be analyzed to learn more about the degree to which the reader is functioning as a meaning-maker, rather than simply as a word decoder.

This second level of analysis is based on the premise that readers use different, and increasingly sophisticated, types of cues as they progress from beginning reading to mature reading. In order of sophistication, these include:

1. *Orthographic cues.* At this level, the reader is using individual letters and letter clusters to predict words. Beginning readers have to rely almost exclusively on these cues, making their reading slow and painstaking.

Example 3: Albert, Grade 5

Grade Level	Part I Graded Word List % of Words Correct	Part II Percent		Label	
		WR	Comp	WR	Comp
PP	100	100	60	IND	INST
P	100	100	60	IND	INST
1	95	100	60	IND	INST
2	90	100	60	IND	INST
3	90	97	40	IND	FRUST

IND __   INST __   FRUST __

Interpretation:

Independent level requires that both word recognition and comprehension meet the criteria. Albert never responded well enough to the comprehension questions to meet the comprehension criterion for independent level at any level tested. Independent level is then labeled as N.E. (Not Established) or N.D. (Not Determined). This testing simply did not establish a level. Second reader level is designated as instructional level even though the accuracy is excellent. Third reader level becomes frustration level because of comprehension inadequacies.

Albert needs to be instructed at the second reader level with emphasis on developing comprehension. His instructional materials should be drawn from appropriate high interest, controlled vocabulary materials. An alternative approach would be the Language Experience Approach based on extended experiences (*e.g., picture interpretation, etc.)

2. *Syntactic cues.* As readers acquire a vocabulary of words that can be recognized on sight, they are able to use elements of syntax, or sentence structure, to make predictions while reading.
3. *Semantic cues.* At the highest level readers use semantics, or *meaning,* as their primary guide while reading.

To emphasize the importance of interpreting oral reading "errors" as indications of the reader's ability to use these increasingly sophisticated sets of cues, Goodman somewhat jokingly has called reading a "psycholinguistic guessing game." Figure 4.6 illustrates the process of evaluating miscues in terms of these cue systems, as opposed to interpretation based on simple error count.

Yetta Goodman and Carolyn Burke attempted to simplify miscue analysis in an instrument called the Reading Miscue Inventory (1972) . The Reading Miscue Inventory is based on having a student orally read an extended passage while the examiner carefully records miscues. In interpreting the miscues recorded, the examiner asks nine qualitative questions of each miscue, such as:

Example 4: Michelle, Grade 2

GRADE LEVEL	PART I GRADED WORD LIST % OF WORDS CORRECT	PART II PERCENT		LABEL	
		WR	COMP	WR	COMP
PP	90	88	60	FRUST	INST
P	85	99	100	IND	IND
1	60	90	60	FRUST	INST
2		88	40	FRUST	FRUST

IND __   INST __   FRUST __

INTERPRETATION:

This testing illustrates two situations. Notice that Michelle read at frustration level (accuracy) at the preprimer level. Notice, however, that her word identification scores (word list) are reasonably strong through the primer level. The word list performance suggests that Michelle should not have been frustrated so soon. In this case, the teacher continued testing and confirmed that the first reading was not valid. A reason for this is that Michelle may have been asked to read the first passage before she was ready for the testing situation.

The second situation encountered is that Michelle's performance shows no instructional level. Primer level is rated as the independent level and the very next level, first level is frustration level. The examiner tested another level to be certain that her performance wouldn't change as in the beginning.

These results may be related to the testing situation, that is, there were too many distractions in the room, the pupil may have been missing out on a special event or the pupil may have been very anxious about the testing situation. Two actions are recommended. First, estimate the instructional as being between the IND and FRUST levels (e.g., Ind = P; INST = P(1); FRUST = 1) and on another day try the student in both reading groups (levels) to determine which is the better placement.

Is there a dialect variation in the miscue?
How much alike are the word and the miscue in appearance?
Does the miscue change the meaning?

The readers' comprehension is then compared with their ability to maintain meaning in their miscues.

There have been several challenges to the practicability of miscue analysis. Hood (1975-76) questioned the reliability of the scoring procedure. Groff (1980) has argued that the scoring is too subjective. Leslie and Osol (1978), Williamson and Young (1974), and Wixson (1979) have shown that the types of miscues

FIGURE 4.6

Using Miscue Analysis vs. Simple Error Count to Interpret Oral Reading Performance

Student A

waispe
The wasps buzzed around my head, as mad as could be, but they

Here *string*
couldn't get through to sting me.

Student B

fell *hand* *cell*
The wasps buzzed around my head, as mad as could be, but they

wouldn't *in* *stal*
couldn't get through to sting me.

Student C

flew
The wasps buzzed around my head, as mad as could be, but they

could not *in* *hurt*
couldn't get through to sting me.

Student A made 4 miscues, not counting repetitions and pauses (including these would make a count of 6 "errors"). The student seems to be using *orthographic* cues alone to predict unknown words. For each of the 4 miscalled words, the student substituted a word that begins with the same letter, and 2 of the 4 substitutions had the same ending letter. None of the substitutions preserved meaning, and only one was a syntactically appropriate substitution.

Student B made 5 miscues, not counting repetitions, pauses, and self-corrections (including these would make a count of 8 "errors"). The student seems to be using primarily *semantic* cues. Only 2 of the 5 miscalled words began with the same letter as the word in the text, and only one had the same ending letter. Only one of the substitutions preserved meaning, and all were syntactically appropriate substitutions (verbs for verbs, nouns for nouns, etc.)

Student C made 6 miscues, not counting pauses (including this would make a count of 7 errors). The two omissions did not alter the meaning, nor did any of the 4 substitutions. The substitutions were syntactically and semantically appropriate substitutions.

Counting "errors" alone, Student C would be judged the poorest reader, and Student A the best. Using miscue analysis, the evaluation is reversed.

students make change dramatically at the instructional as compared to the frustration levels of reading. The most practical objection, however, has been voiced by Hittleman (1978) and Weaver (1988): the unwieldy two hours needed to administer, score, and interpret the inventory.

Despite these objections, the concept of the miscue analysis has had a dramatic impact on IRI testing. Most commercially published IRI's are designed to evaluate children's word recognition skills through a qualitative analysis of their oral reading, rather than a simple sum of "errors." Even without extensive miscue analysis, the concept of interpreting oral reading "errors" in the context of the degree to which the student is attempting to make meaning from print can guide and inform the diagnostician's judgement. Several simplified forms of miscue analysis also have been developed. Among the more notable are inventories by Bean (1979), Cunningham (1984), Siegel (1979), Tortelli (1976), Christie (1979), and Pflaum (1979).

Cautions in the Use of IRI's

Several researchers have been tireless workers in analyzing many of the assumptions of informal reading inventories. Here, in brief form, are some of the findings and recommendations of Frederick Duffelmeyer and associates, and Robert E. Leibert.

- Nearly 50% of graded passages on IRI's they studied did not have explicitly stated main ideas (Duffelmeyer & Duffelmeyer, 1989).
- The vast majority of vocabulary questions on IRI's do not function properly: "they had an unacceptable level of passage independence, i.e, the meaning of the target words used in the selections tended to be familiar to students" (Duffelmeyer, Robinson, & Squier, 1989, p 147).
- An inordinate number of comprehension questions on IRI's are unintentionally passage independent, i.e., they are better answered from prior knowledge than from the textual clues provided (Duffelmeyer, 1980b; Duffelmeyer, Long, & Kruse, 1987). To combat such weaknesses in IRI testing, Robert Leibert (1982) recommends that trial lessons be conducted that link findings to instruction. For example, if word power initially is identified as the instructional need, the introduction of new words should produce better accuracy during oral reading. Conversely, "a pupil whose needs stem from contextual reading rather than word power should not profit from the previous lesson" (Leibert 1985, p. 114).

Widely Used Commercial Informal Reading Inventories

There are several excellent commercial IRI's. These are frequently revised and improved. Some of the more popular ones include:

Analytical Reading Inventory (Woods & Moe, 1981)
Burns and Roe Informal Reading Inventory (Burns & Roe, 1985)
Diagnostic Reading Scales (Spache, 1972)

Durrell Analysis of Reading Difficulty (Durrell, 1980)
Standard Reading Inventory (McCracken, 1966)
Diagnostic Reading Inventory (Jacobs & Searfoss, 1979)
The Contemporary Classroom Reading Inventory (Rinsky & deFossard, 1980)
Classroom Reading Inventory (Silvaroli, 1976)

For an alternative to standard IRI's, see the DeSanti Cloze Reading Inventory (DeSanti, Casbergue, & Sullivan, 1986), which uses cloze passages for testing rather than conventional questions; Goodman and Burk's Miscue Analysis (previously discussed); the Qualitative Inventory (Scott, Foresman, 1990); and the Informal Reading-Thinking Inventory (discussed in the last chapter of the text).

Reflective Box 1

To get a better grasp of some of the subtle and unusual possibilities that exist in interpreting diagnostic data, it is useful to ask three or four people, preferably representing different backgrounds and gender, some questions about their own reading habits and behaviors. Here are two questions that often elicit information that is particularly helpful in interpreting IRI results: Do you find that your oral and silent reading fluency are about the same, or is one considerably better than the other? How about comprehension when reading orally or silently? (Answer these questions first as you think others will answer them. Then get ready to revise your thinking.)

IRI Extensions and Refinements

There have been several extensions and refinements of the IRI protocol. Three are presented here. The first two are variations on Content Reading Inventories (Carvell, 1980; Readence, Baldwin, & Bean, 1981), or Informal Textbook Inventories (Manzo & Manzo, 1990a).

Informal Inventory for Adolescents

Martha A. Kinney and Ann L. Harry (1991) have attempted to design an IRI that better assesses the reader, the text, and the task as faced by adolescents. To these ends, they suggest the following modifications to create the Adolescent's IRI:

1. *Text characteristics.* Sample three areas of text characteristics: content, structure, and language. To accomplish this, it is necessary to use a 500-700 word sample that uses obvious structures, and for the teacher to make a hierarchical outline that reflects passage organization, main ideas, and supporting details.
2. *Reader characteristics.* The adolescent reader essentially is in what Chall (1983c) labels "Stage 3, Reading to Learn the New." Since this is characterized by the

ability to bring prior knowledge and experience to the reading task, it is necessary to assess this pertinent factor. Kinny and Harry suggest two ways to do this: a) have students tell or write out all they think they know about two or three central concepts of the selection; and b) have students give oral or written definitions of key words and terms.

3. *Task demands.* Identify and evaluate specific tasks and processes (or skills) that are necessary for content reading. Kinney and Harry (1991) identify and suggest these: a) main ideas, as determined by comparing students' oral and written recalls with the hierarchical outline previously made by the teacher; and b) establishing cohesion, as determined by either of two tasks—referent identification (e.g., identifying the words in the text that pronouns refer back to, as originally suggested by Irwin [1986] and Baumann [1986]), and inference questions requiring integration of two or more pieces of text.

Informal Textbook Inventory (ITI)

The Informal Textbook Inventory is an open book test. It is group administered and involves assessment and implicit teaching of basic study skills. Essentially, it asks students to answer an array of questions that help in determining whether they know how to use their textbooks and related resources effectively. Any question not answered correctly is indicative of a specific need.

1. **Constructing the ITI.**
   (a) Organization and Structure of the Text:
       -Develop three to five questions that students can answer by referring to *organizational elements* of the text: the index, table of contents, glossary, appendixes, or other text sections.
       -Develop three to five questions about *how the text is structured.*
   (b) Basic Comprehension: Select a short portion of the text that contains an *important concept* with supporting details and at least one graph, chart, or picture. (The same selection can be used for the following section on applied comprehension.)
       -Develop one or two fill-in or multiple choice questions that direct students to state or select the *main idea* of the material read.
       -Develop three or more fill-in, multiple choice, or matching questions about *specific factual details* that support the main ideas in the selection.
       -Develop three or more fill-in, multiple choice, or matching questions that direct students to state or select a definition for key *vocabulary* terms used in the selection.
       -Develop one or more questions requiring students to state or select an *interpretation of a graph, chart, or picture* that adds information not explicitly stated in the selection.
   (c) Applied Comprehension: Questions in these sections can be based on the same text selection used above.
       -Develop one or more questions requiring students to *draw valid conclusions* based on the information presented.

-Develop one or more questions that require students to *evaluate and apply information* from the text in terms of their own experiences, values, and existing knowledge base.

2. **Administering the ITI.** Before asking students to tackle the ITI, explain some of its features and purposes. It is not a "test" in the usual sense of the word; every text differs slightly from every other, and this is a way to find out how well students will be able to use this particular text. Also, point out that answers will be discussed as a group, for each student should attempt to complete the worksheets as thoroughly and accurately as possible in order to yield a quality assessment of the appropriateness and value of the text. Provide adequate time for all students to complete the inventory. It may take two or more class periods, and students who finish early should be provided with an alternate activity.

3. **Evaluating the Results of the ITI.** After all students have finished the ITI's, collect and score the tests. A total score need not be recorded on the students' papers, since the purpose of the test is to identify strengths and weaknesses in the various subsections. For diagnostic purposes, any error is taken as a sign of need in that category. Much of the diagnostic value of the inventory comes from the discussion of the items when the tests are returned to students. This discussion can take from one-half to three full class periods, depending on student abilities and the difficulty of the text.

Informal Reading-Thinking Inventory (IR-TI)

Miscue analysis changed the way reading specialists looked at word recognition behaviors, but comprehension assessment has remained virtually the same since the IRI was first described by Betts in 1936. The Informal Reading-Thinking Inventory (IR-TI) described in Chapter 13 on Higher Order Literacy represents one attempt to enhance the comprehension assessment capacity of the conventional IRI.

One aspect of the IR-TI is particularly appropriate for consideration here since it can be used with any IRI. It is the addition of a means of recording and reporting level of "engagement" in the diagnostic conversation. This ratio score is determined by adding a check or a minus to each question a student answers based on whether the response is congruent or incongruent with the question. All correct responses are congruent, or relevant to the conversation. Incorrect responses, however, may be congruent (related but incorrect) or incongruent (unrelated as well as incorrect). An increase in congruent responses is a sound sign that the student is engaged and that a two-way conversation is taking place. Accordingly, as the ratio of congruent responses grows, even where responses may still be incorrect, the diagnostic conversation can be said to be growing in strength and efficacy.

This measure is particularly important when note is taken of the fact that remedial students, even those in a one-to-one tutoring situation, have been found to answer about 80% of their teacher's questions with totally incongruent responses (Manzo, 1969a). In other words, they are hardly engaged, and therefore cannot possibly begin to learn.

Additional to the Quick Tests and IRI's, several specialized methods and instruments have been developed to further assess and verify aspects of word decoding, vocabulary, comprehension, and rate. Representative means of handling each of these in a variety of test formats are presented next.

Test Formats for Assessing Reading-Specific Factors

Knowledge of test formats is another way to develop clinical skill. The format of a test, or the way a question is posed, can be a matter of little or great importance. Generally speaking, the rank ordering of test scores of a given group of students will not vary greatly if a question is asked in one way or another if the format is made easier, everyone's grades will go up about the same, and vice versa. Nonetheless, test format can be an important factor where remedial readers are concerned. Remedial readers, by definition, have learning impairments that may cause them to respond differently, if not divergently, to the same basic item posed even in a slightly different manner.

There are three basic ways to prepare yourself to informally ascertain the impact of a particular format:

1. Note the format used by a given test to assess a particular factor.
2. Check the known relationship of a test format to other possible formats by checking the test manual under "concurrent validity"—it should contain reports of correlations of the test with others that measure the same factor in similar and different ways.
3. Become familiar with alternate formats so that you can select alternative tests, or reframe questions in an alternate format when engaged in a diagnostic or instructional conversation.

Look now at the variety of popular test formats used to assess the major areas of reading. You may also find it useful to note the general criteria used in selecting a good test item (see Figure 4.7).

FIGURE 4.7

General Criteria for a Good Test Item

1. About 50% of all students would get the item correct (although some easier and some more difficult items are needed to make an overall test discriminating at the lower and upper ends of the scale).
2. Each of the foils should attract "fair play" (none should be so apparently incorrect that almost no one chooses it).
3. Response to an item should have a .50 or higher correlation with total test score performance.

Assessing Word Decoding

There are five common ways of assessing word recognition and analysis skills.

1. Present words in isolation under two conditions: "Flash" (usually under two seconds) and "untimed" or delayed (usually up to 10 seconds) and record the student's response.

   Flash
   car (student response: *cat*)

   Delayed
   car (student response: *car*)

2. Present a string of simple words and have the student indicate which word is either similar or opposite; e.g., which means the same as the first word:

   car   kitten   train   automobile   watch   over

3. Have the student read the object word in a familiar context:

   "Dad and Mom got into the *car*."

4. Have the student try to blend and/or substitute a letter or letters in a cluster to form a new word:

   a. *squ* + *irrel* = _____;
   b. Read this word: *batter*. Now remove the "**b**" in your mind and replace it with an "**h**". What word do you have now?

5. Have students read nonsense words to see how well they handle certain phonic elements (e.g., *lome*; *glight*; *knipe*). Record their attempts: *lo-may; glitch; knip*.)

Assessing Vocabulary

Depending upon what you are willing to count, there are four or five levels of vocabulary: speaking, reading, writing, listening, and "visual." During childhood, listening and speaking vocabularies appear to be dominant. With further schooling, all aspects of vocabulary grow, but reading vocabulary tends to grow the most, since written language contains the greatest reservoir of factual, technical, and literary information. "Visual vocabulary," as it has been called by Debes (1962), is composed of mental representations of reality that are usually photovisual surrogates for words. These surrogates, or stand-ins for conventional words, are mental pictures of things we know about but for which we do not yet have easily available words. In a sense, these vague mental pictures may be necessary prerequisites or early stages in learning new words.

The predominant method for assessing word knowledge is to ask for a definition. This is the method of choice, for example, on the Weschler IQ tests discussed in the next chapter. However, there are five acceptable ways, according to Rapaport (1950), to define words:

1. by giving a synonym (e.g., childish, for puerile).
2. by classifying (e.g., man is a "rational animal").

3. by enumerating words to which it relates (e.g., *spices* are cinnamon, cloves, paprika, etc.).
4. by providing an example (e.g., pointing to the object and saying—"goat").
5. by operationally defining it—telling what to do to experience or recognize it (e.g., your *heart* is that thing you feel thumping in your chest).

Other formats, or methods for identifying words, include the following:

1. Selecting a similar or opposite word from a string of choices.
2. Selecting a definition from available multiple choices.
3. Matching columns of words with synonyms or brief definitions.
4. Identifying a picture that represents a word (as in the Peabody Picture Vocabulary Test described in the next chapter).

In general, unaided recalls are considerably more difficult than aided recalls or recognition type questions. There are nagging problems in vocabulary assessment that we have not yet found adequate means of handling. Chief among these is distinguishing the conceptual quality of someone's vocabulary. This is a problem since knowing how rich a student's concepts are helps the teacher know whether to proceed largely with drill and label work, or to stress the concepts underlying key vocabulary before teaching "labelling." Similarly, there is no differential test of vocabulary. That is, one telling the possible categories of the words that a student might be deficient in (e.g. sensory related terms, historical terms, arithmetic terms).

In general, vocabulary is about the most important assessment that can be made in school and in intensive diagnosis. There is even evidence that vocabulary is the one factor that tends to remain the most stable following most emotional and even brain traumas. This makes it a good "capacity to learn" measure following head injury or emotional upheaval (source unknown).

Detecting Reading Comprehension Deficits

Assessment of deficits in reading comprehension can become unwieldy since comprehension, as previously indicated, means reading the lines, reading between the lines, and, to an extent, reading beyond the lines. Collectively, these functions involve:

1. prior knowledge
2. innate curiosity
3. interests
4. ability to deal with elements of language, punctuation, and style
5. inclination and ability to think abstractly
6. inclination and ability to recognize and use elements of rhetorical, or organizational, format
7. inclination and ability to draw inferences
8. inclination and ability to think critically and inventively
9. inclination and ability to monitor and attempt to fix one's own comprehension when it appears to be faltering.

Formulating Questions

The traditional means of assessing comprehension is to frame questions that reflect taxonomies of the cognitive domain. Several such taxonomies have been synthesized into the eight cognitive domain type questions illustrated below:

1. *Recognition questions.* Recognition questions require identifying the answers from available choices (Mary had a little: a. goat; b. ham; c. dog; d. lamb)
2. *Recall questions.* Recall questions require remembering answers with very little prompting (Where was the battle of Bull Run fought? — Answer: at Bull Run Creek in Virginia)
3. *Translation questions.* Translation questions entail transferring something from one symbolic form to another (Can you describe this picture?; Can you tell in your own words what the author said in this paragraph?; Can you say what you just heard in your own words?).
4. *Inference questions.* Inference questions have the reader combine available textual information to reach an answer that is logical and implicit but not explicitly stated in the passage (What is the relationship between Jack and Joseph in this story?)
5. *Conjecture questions.* Often seen as a subset of inference, conjecture questions require that the reader read between the lines to make an inferential "leap" beyond what can be inferred from stated facts alone. (As we read ahead, do you suppose that Brent and Nancy will be friends again?)
6. *Explanation questions.* Explanation questions require verification of a previous point. These may involve reference to the text and/or to other sources (Why do you think Brent and Nancy will be friends again?).
7. *Application questions.* Application questions require critical and constructive thinking and problem solving (In similar circumstance, how might a person like Brent avoid hurting a friend's feelings?).
8. *Evaluation questions.* Evaluation questions are a specialized type of application question that requires critical thinking, aesthetic sense, and personal judgement (How do you feel about the story? The characters? The style of writing? The moral?).

These question types need not be asked in a linear order from lowest to highest levels. In fact, it is advisable to sometimes ask evaluative questions first. This format more closely resembles natural conversation and tends to be more inviting. Traditional tests, such as IRI's and most standardized tests tend to ask questions that presumably tap main ideas, supporting details, and relatively low level inferences. Responses to such questions are so highly correlated with one another that little tends to be learned of any differential diagnostic value. In general, then, these questions are best treated as belonging to the same class, namely questions that establish a student's reconstructive level of comprehension.

The question formats that can be used to measure comprehension may vary in order of difficulty, as follows:

1. true/false and multiple choice, or other recognition-type questions

2. questions that require recall of information
3. questions that require oral or written retelling of major points

While true/false and multiple choice testing dominate most conventional testing situations, retelling formats are widely used in clinical remedial situations. They are held to be better representations of what readers are doing most typically when reading silently (Schell, 1988; Gauthier, 1990).

There are certain other formats that are not easily classified by question type but that provide essentially the same information. One of the most popular has students fill in words missing in a piece of extended text by choosing the replacement words from two or three available choices. This format, used by the Gates-MacGinitie test and the Degrees of Reading Power Test, may look like a cloze passage test, but it tends to yield results that more closely approximate conventional multiple choice questioning. The explanation for this appears to be that the reader draws more from context and passage meaning than occurs on cloze passage tests where the reader depends more on syntactical and other language clues in making replacements.

The real diagnostic value of this type of test is reached when the examiner asks students to try to explain why they might have selected one replacement word over another. It is wise to ask this question of some items that the student has answered correctly as well as incorrectly. This tends to reduce the student's impression that s/he simply chose the wrong answer and now should choose a different one. When a student has great difficulty explaining his/her choices, it can be useful to model this "think-aloud" process with an example or two.

Retellings

An alternative to questioning, for comprehension assessment, is retelling—simply asking the reader to recall all they can about the passage. Ringler and Weber (1984) suggest the following retelling prompts:

- Tell me what you have read, using your own words.
- What is the text about?
- Tell me as much information as you can about what you have just read.

Retellings can be evaluated in a number of ways. Clark (1982) suggested this simple system:

- Break the passage into pausal units, placing a slash wherever a good reader would normally pause during oral reading. These boundaries typically fall at punctuation marks and at connectives such as *and*, *but*, and *because*. During the student's retelling, check each pausal unit recalled. Give the student credit for responses that capture the gist of the unit. A percent score can then be obtained from number of total units compared to number of units recalled.
- Rate the level of importance for each pausal unit by assigning a 1 to the most important units, a 2 to the next most important units, and a 3 to the least important units. This can be simplified by reading through the passage first to identify the most important units (1's), and then again to identify the least

important units. The remaining units are assigned as 2's. To score this aspect of retelling, add the value of each of the pausal units recalled by the student, and divide by the number of units recalled, to obtain the average importance level of units recalled.

- Record the order in which the pausal units are recalled by numbering them in the order in which they are retold. Sequence of retelling is evaluated subjectively, on a scale of 1-5, with 1 being low and 5 high.

Studies have indicated that the initial recall in acceptable retellings averages from 33–50% — much lower than the 75–90% criterion required by the IRI questioning protocol (Clark, 1982). After initial retelling has been recorded, general prompts can be given to determine whether the student has offered all that he or she remembers. These prompts should not be directed to specific information in the passage, but simply encourage the student to tell more, if they can. Lipson and Wixson (1991) suggest these questions for prompting recall:

- Tell me more about what you have read.
- Tell me more about what happened.
- Tell me more about the people you just read about.
- Tell me more about where this happened.

Box 4.2 provides a sample retelling recording/scoring form following Clark's format.

Retellings can be evaluated for other dimensions of comprehension and application of active reading strategies. See Box 4.3 and 4.4 for two formats developed by Pia Irwin and Judy N. Mitchell (1983, 1989) for scoring and evaluating retellings.

As useful as retellings can be, the task does introduce some problems of its own. It can be influenced, for example, by the reader's learning style: "Sequential" learners have an obvious advantage over "simultaneous" processors. It can be influenced, too, by common shyness. And, it is very much influenced by prior training: Students who have only been exposed to conventional question-answer strategies will have less expectation for what is meant by "retelling" than those exposed to methods, such as the Guided Reading Procedure (see Chapter 10 on comprehension), that inculcate an expectation for unprompted recall.

The Durrell Analysis of Reading Difficulty is an instrument with a rich tradition of using retellings in assessment. The Durell test is most meaningful when students are forewarned that a complete retelling will be asked for. This usually is done with a simple prompt, such as "Try to tell me everything you can recall from what you are about to read." Some examiners add "and in the order it was presented." For scoring purposes, the selection simply is reproduced in segments down a page for marking purposes (See Box 4.2). This permits the examiner to note a number of possible aspects of the retelling: its accuracy under unprompted and prompted conditions, its sequence, the relative importance of various points recalled, and other more elaborate post-retelling analyses, such as whether the retelling contained the features of a story grammar (c.f., Nancy

BOX 4.2

Sample Retelling Evaluation Format

To Record Unaided Retelling: Record a "1" in the Recall Sequence column for the first unit the student recalls, followed by numbers, in sequence, in that column to indicate the order in which units are recalled. This provides a record of which units were recalled as well as the sequence in which they were recalled.

  To Record Prompted Retelling: Place a check (✔) in the Prompted Retelling column beside each unit the student recalls upon being prompted for further recollections. This will provide a record of units that were repeated, and units that were added upon prompting.

Importance Level	The Fox and the Lion	Recall Sequence	Prompted Retelling
2	1. One day, a fox met a lion.	_____	_____
1	2. The fox had never seen a lion before.	_____	_____
1	3. The fox was terrified by the lion's large size and big mouth.	_____	_____
3	4. He was ready to die with fear.	_____	_____
2	5. After a time he met the lion again,	_____	_____
1	6. and was still frightened,	_____	_____
2	7. but not so much as he had been when he first met the lion.	_____	_____
2	8. When he saw the lion for the third time,	_____	_____
1	9. he was far from being afraid.	_____	_____
1	10. He went up and began to talk to the lion as if he had known the lion all his life.	_____	_____

Unaided Retelling Scores
Total number of units: (10)

Number of units recalled initially: ___

Percent of units recalled initially: ___

Sequence evaluation: (Subjective ___ rating, 1-5, with 1 being the lowest, 3 average, and 5 highest)

Average Level of Importance of ___ units: recalled initially (1-5 with 1 being lowest, 3 average, and 5 highest)

Prompted Recall Scores
Number of units recalled initially: ___

Percent of units recalled with ___ prompts: (should be at least 20% higher than percent of units recalled initially)

from the Informal Reading-Thinking Inventory (experimental edition), Anthony Manzo, Ula Manzo, Michael McKenna

BOX 4.3

A Schema for Scoring Retellings: The Retelling Profile

Directions: Indicate with a checkmark the extent to which the reader's retelling includes evidence of the following information:	low none	moderate degree	high degree	degree
1. Retelling includes information directly stated in text.				
2. Retelling includes information inferred directly or indirectly from text.				
3. Retelling includes what is important to remember from text.				
4. Retelling provides relevant content and concepts.				
5. Retelling indicates reader's attempt to connect background knowledge to text information.				
6. Retelling indicates reader's attempt to make summary statements or generalizations based on text that can be applied to the real world.				
7. Retelling indicates highly individualistic and creative impressions of, or reactions to, the text.				
8. Retelling indicates the reader's affective involvement with the text.				
9. Retelling demonstrates appropriate use of language (vocabulary, sentence structure, language conventions).				
10. Retelling indicates reader's ability to organize or compose the retelling.				
11. Retelling demonstrates the reader's sense of audience or purpose.				
12. Retelling indicates the reader's control of the mechanics of speaking or writing.				

Interpretation: Items 1-4 indicate the reader's comprehension of textual information; items 5-8 indicate metacognitive awareness, strategy use, and involvement with text; items 9-12 indicate facility with language and language development.

Mitchell & Irwin (1989)

BOX 4.4

Judging the Richness of Retellings

The Level Descriptors below can be used to evaluate, and assign a rating to, student retellings. The Summary of Level Descriptors provides a charted version of the criteria for each of the levels.

LEVEL DESCRIPTORS
Level   Criteria for establishing level in checklist below

Level	Criteria
5	Student generalizes beyond text; includes thesis (summarizing statement), all major points, and appropriate supporting details; includes relevant supplementations; shows high degree of coherence, completeness, comprehensibility.
4	Student includes thesis (summarizing statement), all major points, and appropriate supporting details; includes relevant supplementations; shows high degree of coherence, completeness, comprehensibility.
3	Student relates major ideas; includes appropriate supporting details and relevant supplementations; shows adequate coherence, completeness, comprehensibility.
2	Student relates a few major ideas and some supporting details; includes irrelevant supplementations; shows some degree of coherence; some completeness; the whole is somewhat comprehensible.
1	Student relates details only; irrelevant supplementations or none; low degree of coherence; incomprehensible.

5 = highest level   1 = lowest level

SUMMARY OF LEVEL DESCRIPTORS

	Level 5	4	3	2	1
Generalizes beyond text	X				
Thesis (summarizing) statement	X	X			
Major points	X	X	X	?	?
Supporting ideas	X	X	X	X	?
Supplementations	relevant	relevant	relevant	irrelevant	irrelevant
Coherence	high	good	adequate	some	poor
Completeness	high	good	adequate	some	poor
Comprehensibility	high	good	adequate	some	poor

Irwin and Mitchell (1983)

FIGURE 4.8

Oral and Silent Reading Rates

ORAL READING RATE		SILENT READING RATE	
Grade Level	*words per minute*	*Grade*	*words per minute*
1.8	30-54	2	86
2.8	66-104	3	116
3.8	86-124	4	155
4.8	95-130	5	177
5.8	108-140	6	206
6.8	112-145	7	215
7.8	122-155	8	237
8.8	136-157	9	252
		12	251

Gilmore & Gilmore (1968)

Marshall, 1983) and other such aspects of effective communication and involvement.

Beth Davey and associates (1989) have provided these additional points of information from their considerable research on formats and factors involved in comprehension assessment:

- Timed testing tends to bias outcomes against less skilled readers (Davey, 1988a).
- Poor readers and deaf readers tend to perform comparably to good readers on multiple choice tests but far worse on free response items (Davey & LaSasso, 1984).
- Being able to look back during question answering tends to enhance scores on the free response items but not on multiple choice tests (Davey, 1989).
- Good readers tend to profit more from look-backs than poor readers (Davey, 1987, 1988b; Davey & LaSasso, 1984).

Davey (1989) speculates that the latter two findings suggest that poor readers do not have good test-taking strategies—often preferring to leave an item blank rather than going to their own heads when the answer is not explicitly stated.

Most of the formats discussed above are fine for assessing reconstructive reading. The assessment of constructive reading is slightly more difficult because answers tend to be less clearly black or white, and scoring systems more open to challenge. More will be said about this in a later chapter that looks a little more carefully at recent efforts to assess and treat these higher-order literacy needs.

Reading Rate: An Overlooked Measure of Reading Progress

Rate of reading is generally undervalued as a diagnostic indicator since attention is detracted from it by the many other oral reading and comprehension problems that remedial-level students seem to possess. Rate of reading, however, can be a good indicator of progress, and a surprisingly good bet as an ingredient in a program to stimulate gains in overall reading fluency and comprehension (Erickson & Krajenta, 1991). Reading rate tends to grow in rather predictable increments through the grades. Figure 4.8 shows average oral reading rate gains from grade level 1.8 to 8.8, and silent reading rate from grades 2 to 12.

Reading rate typically should be calculated with a passage that is between a student's instructional and independent reading levels. When done orally, it is best to sample rate twice on two different passages of about 50-75 words each. These rates then should be combined and averaged. Rate is determined by noting lapsed time with an accurate stopwatch. Rate is calculated by converting minutes into seconds and dividing words read into time. This yields words per second, which then must be recalculated into words per minute (WPM) by multiplying by 60 seconds.

Example:

	# words	time
Oral Passage #1	55	1 min., 20 sec.
Oral Passage #2	59	1 min., 30 sec.

2 min., 50 sec. = 170 seconds
114 words / 170 seconds = .67 words per second
.67 words per second × 60 seconds = 40 words per minute

The process is easier but more obscured when passages are read silently. Under the latter process, students are given a passage to read silently and simply told to circle the word they are up to when you say "MARK" after precisely one minute of reading. The teacher, or student, then counts the number of words read in one minute of lapsed time to determine rate in words per minute. Again, an average of two samples will yield a more reliable estimate of rate.

Silent reading rate, as can be seen in Figure 4.8, tends to level off at about 250 words per minute by the end of middle school, not increasing throughout the high school years even though most students are quite capable of reading with equally high comprehension at rates between 300 and 400 words per minute (Carver, 1982). Thus, most students can benefit from instruction in reading rate. The broad goal of any focused instruction in reading rate, however, should be to improve reading *flexibility*, as much as reading *speed*. Flexibility refers to altering rate according to the *purpose* for reading and the *difficulty* level of the material. It is measured as the difference between words per minute in simple and difficult materials (Moe & Nania, 1959).

Instruction in reading rate and flexibility is particularly justified when other aspects of reading, such as vocabulary or comprehension, have shown improvement, but rate remains unchanged. Under these conditions, reading rate usually can be quickly improved through simple focused practice, since the lagging reading rate probably represents a lingering habit more so than a deficiency. A simple chart of progress, showing reading rate in words per minute on a sequence of reading passages of comparable type and difficulty, can provide incentive for focused practice in reading rate.

We turn now to the measurement of the related literacy areas of listening, speaking, writing, and study skills.

Test Formats for Assessing Reading-Related Literacy Functions

Listening

As stated earlier, following word identification, the processes of comprehending speech and print do not differ (Sticht et.al., 1974). This "unitary process" view suggests that words *heard* and words *seen* share more or less the same basic storehouse of known words. Therefore, having a student listen to a passage and then respond to questions about it is a straightforward and reliable way of establishing listening comprehension. It also provides a rather solid indication of capacity to read and comprehend (Durrell, 1969; Carroll, 1977; Sinatra, 1990).

There are two clear implications of this unitary view of listening and reading: one is that students who have comparable reading and listening comprehension probably are reading about as well as can be expected, and therefore would profit most from a program that emphasizes vocabulary and knowledge building; the second is that students with superior listening ability probably need a program to correct their basic word identification skills as well as opportunities to listen as someone else reads so that their vocabularies and fund of knowledge do not decline further during their period of reading deficiency.

There are some notable cautions in this seemingly tight relationship between visual and listening comprehension—the two processes may diverge at some point. "For example," notes Richard Sinatra (1990), "the processing of lengthy, connected text may require processing strategies that are qualitatively different from the strategies used in the processing of aural discourse" (p. 126). In other words, it is easy to pause, rest, and reflect while reading longer passages, while it is difficult to impossible to do this while listening. Samuel Miller and Donald E. Smith (1990) found the relationships of oral reading, silent reading, and listening to vary among low, average, and superior readers. Oddly, listening comprehension was equal to oral reading in lower readers, though both were superior to silent reading. In average readers, listening was equal to silent reading, and both superior to oral reading. For high achieving readers, oral comprehension was equal to silent and both were superior to listening. These findings were based on the Analytical Reading Inventory, and may vary with other instruments. See the section on improving listening in the chapter on study reading for some useful pointers for students in how to listen better and how to get the teacher to pause, restate, and otherwise be a more considerate speaker. Other aspects of listening, as related to hearing and auditory perception, are addressed in the next chapter under the defect category.

Speaking

It has long been recognized that there is a potentially important relationship between speech defects and severe reading disabilities. Several studies point to the fact that over 20% of severely disabled readers also have speech impediments. Oddly, few are stutterers, though, as might be expected, most are male (Klasen, 1972). Quite possibly, both reading and speech impediments go back to a common origin, and are different aspects of one basic disorder.

There are two classes of speech impediments, one related to delayed speech and another to the production of odd sounding speech. In general, when speech sounds are odd, it is wise to follow up with a careful hearing test (see the next chapter). The child may well be reproducing the sounds he or she hears.

More commonly, however, unusual speaking is a form of delayed speech. In such cases, a student's speech production will tend to include sounds such as labial "r's" as in "wabbit" for "rabbit," and add-on's such as "th's", as in "li*th*ening" for "listening." In such cases, it is more parsimonious to think that the problem is extended "baby-talk," and probably more emotionally driven, than related to serious speech, hearing, or neurological deficits. "Baby-talk" usually is related to delayed physical maturation, or ambivalence about growing up, and therefore a sign of emotional dependency—a frequent correlate of deficient reading (H. Robinson, 1946). The literature of the field is very sparse on diagnosing, interpreting, and treating the co-symptoms of speech impediment and reading disability. Better working relationships obviously need to be developed between speech and reading people at all levels.

There also is no means we are aware of for routinely assessing the compositional side of speech, such as its relevance and coherence. This is done, however, in writing, the next topic.

Writing

The recent literature on reading and language arts dwells on the fact that reading and writing are profoundly connected. Nonetheless, the two are not so predictably related that performance in one can be reliably inferred from knowing the other. In other words, knowing a child reads well does not guarantee that s/he will write well. Nor does knowing that a child writes well predict that s/he will read with solid and inferentially accurate comprehension. Obviously, children who read well tend to write better, though not necessarily more imaginatively, than children of average reading ability. In general, children who read poorly do tend to compose and write poorly, though again, not necessarily. When writing is clearly superior to reading, it is appropriate to suspect that there is minimal brain dysfunction, or some complex emotional source of the disparity. However, on rare occasions, it can be a function of a specific aptitude to encode and articulate well despite poor decoding and even listening comprehension. For further explanation, see the section on brain functions in the chapter on dyslexia and related learning disabilities.

Difficulty in establishing a clear quantitative relationship between reading and writing stems from several factors. These include the following:

1. There is no commonly agreed upon way to assess writing.
2. Most methods of writing assessment are not properly weighted to take into account factors that are not of equal importance (such as content and grammar).
3. Most methods of assessment contain a great deal of subjectivity.
4. Assessment is not based upon a concensually agreed upon set of norms or criteria.
5. Assessment does not tend to include separate appraisal of what are called the five stages of the writing process (planning, drafting, revising, editing, and publishing).
6. There is no assessment system that provides for the various stages or levels of development of students at different age and grade levels.

There have been many attempts to assess writing by some easy quantification scheme. These are not totally ineffective, but they do tend to leave too much unaccounted for. For example, Hunt (1965) determined that the length of each clause, or T-unit, as he called them, was a good indication of syntactical maturity and overall writing. Lundsteen (1979) countered with the point that would be clear to any observer: "It is not how long you make them, but how you make them long."

Thus, at this time, writing is best assessed informally, holistically, and subjectively. Basically, this is done by looking at a piece of writing and estimating, from your knowledge and experience, whether it is primitive, below average, average, above average, or advanced for the student's age and grade level.

To sharpen your ability to make these judgements, we recommend that you compare and discuss your appraisals with the judgements of others, and use some of the other means suggested below. These are detailed under the title Informal Writing Inventory, though we do not mean to suggest by this terminology that this system has the history and tradition of an IRI. It does, however, offer a fair means of estimating current level of writing and specific areas of possible instruction.

The IWI's described in Figures 4.9 and 4.10 assess some of the key features of the writing process (planning, drafting, revising, editing, and publishing) as well as certain expectations at different age/grade levels. Collect samples of writing about every 30 days to chart progress. Offer students the opportunity to keep their best work in a portfolio (see Portfolio Analysis in Chapter 6).

For your further information, there are these other sources of information and instruments for assessing writing:

General:

1. *Evaluating and Improving Written Expression*, Janice K. Hall (1988)
2. *Evaluating Writing: Describing, Measuring, and Judging*, Charles Cooper and Lee Odell (1977)

Text Analysis Systems (word and clause counts):

3. Hunt's (1965) T-Units
4. Mellon's (1969) sentence length and complexity

Rating Scales:

5. Diederich (1974) — ideas, organization, wording, flavor
6. *Carlson Analytical Survey*, and *Sparkling Words*, Carlson (1965) — story structure, novelty, emotion, individuality, and style

Peer and Self-Evaluation:

7. *Reading, Writing, and Rating Stories*, Beaven (1977) — a technique reported to result in gains in writing equal to those from teacher evaluations

Standardized Diagnostic Tests

8. *Picture Story Language Test*, Myklebust (1965) — intermediate to high school levels
9. *Test of Written Language*, Hammill and Larsen, (1983) — intermediate level
10. *Diagnostic Evaluation of Writing Skills*, Weiner (1980) — intermediate level

An additional system for evaluating writing, based on the quality of thinking exhibited, is presented in the chapter on diagnosing and treating higher-order literacy needs and functions.

FIGURE 4.9

Informal Writing Inventory: Primer to Fourth Grade (also for upper grade students with more limited skills)

1. Have the student write out his or her own name and address (if able). Rank for:

	primitive	below average	average	above average	advanced
A. accuracy	1	2	3	4	5
B. legibility	1	2	3	4	5
C. spelling	1	2	3	4	5
D. placement on page (top left or center of page is best)	1	2	3	4	5
E. comments _____					

2. Have the student speak or write a description of something that is pictured (see illustration). Record and rank for:

	primitive	below average	average	above average	advanced
A. accuracy (details)	1	2	3	4	5
B. reasonable sequence	1	2	3	4	5
C. cogency (lack of irrelevancies)	1	2	3	4	5
D. English usage	1	2	3	4	5
E. comments _____					

EXAMPLE
Name: Lana
Grade: 5

Directions: Describe the drawing below in about 25 words. Make up a title for this descriptive essay.

DESCRIPTION:

One day it was a gril name Jan
She was latte for school She got up
and took a qick bath Slipt her cothes on
and took her book to her friend doght [gave]
her a cookie Jan Said Tankeyou. She was
at scool and her theacher claect the home
work: The End   (collected)

TITLE: Home work for school

IWI PROFILE

A. accuracy (details) $\frac{2}{}$
B. reasonable sequence $\frac{3}{}$
C. cogency (lack of irrelevancies) $\frac{3}{}$
D. English usage $\frac{2}{}$
E. comments: Lana reacted to the picture, rather than *describing* it. Her story was coherent and sequential otherwise, though, strictly speaking, not cogent, since the entire piece is irrelevant. Attention to directions, spelling, and punctuation need some attention.

3. Invite the student to complete several sentences (see examples). Record and rank for:

	primitive	below average	average	above average	advanced
A. relevancy	1	2	3	4	5
B. English usage	1	2	3	4	5
C. comments					

EXAMPLES

1. Cats make me. . .

student response:	relevancy	English usage
(a) sneeze and choke	5	4
(b) run	4	4

2. I wish that I could. . .

student response:	relevancy	English usage
(a) go with my sister	4	3
(b) eat al thats I wanted	4	2

---

4. Have the student try to fill in a missing word from five sentences read to him. Record and rank for:

	primitive	below average	average	above average	advanced
A. accuracy (allow the student to change his mind)	1	2	3	4	5
B. syntax compatibility					
C. semantics					
D. prior knowledge					
E. comments					

EXAMPLES

The cat and the _____ were chased off by the store owner.

Incorrect student answers and evaluations:

	"mouse"	"street"
accuracy	2	1
syntax compatibility	5	1
semantics	4	2
prior knowledge	4	2

---

5. Dictate two to five sentences, repeating each three times. Rate the student's transcription of the sentences for:

	primitive	below average	average	above average	advanced
A. accuracy	1	2	3	4	5
B. spelling and punctuation	1	2	3	4	5
C. penmanship	1	2	3	4	5
D. comments					

6. Have a student tell you a story for two minutes. Offer the student three topic choices, and provide a minimum of ten minutes for the student to prepare for what they wish to say. Record the story told, and rate for:

	primitive	below average	average	above average	advanced
A. imagination	1	2	3	4	5
B. sequence	1	2	3	4	5
C. story form (beginning, middle, end)	1	2	3	4	5
D. internal logic (coherence)	1	2	3	4	5
E. overall quality	1	2	3	4	5
F. comments _____					

7. Read or play back the story to the child, and ask what, if anything, they might like to revise. Limit the revision period to ten minutes. Make suggested revisions without unnecessary comments, and rate the revised story for:

	primitive	below average	average	above average	advanced
A. inclination to correct	1	2	3	4	5
B. quality of corrections	1	2	3	4	5
C. comments _____					

Study Skills

Study skills is a generic name given to a host of means and methods for operating more efficiently and to greater depths of learning and recall. Study skills can be initiated at the prereading stage, but they are mostly intended to guide silent reading and improve retention after reading. Study skills are most observable, and therefore most measurable, in situations that require notetaking, long-term recall, and evidence of efficient use of time.

There are four popular means for assessing study skills: standardized tests, informal inventories, observational systems, and self-report inventories. Many schools have at least one standardized measure of study skills available on students in the form of the "Work-Study Skills" subtest of the Iowa Test of Basic Skills (Hieronymus, Hoover, and Lindquist, 1986). This test, and the similar ones of other major standardized test-makers, generally offer measures of a student's ability to:

- read and interpret maps, charts, graphs, and tables;
- use various parts of a book; and
- use standard reference materials such as dictionaries, encyclopedias, and almanacs.

This potentially vital information can usually be found in a student's cumulative record file.

There are published informal instruments, such as McWilliams and Rakes' "Content Inventories: English, Social Studies, and Science" (1979). There also is the Informal Textbook Inventory format, described above, for teachers to make

FIGURE 4.10

Informal Writing Inventory: Fifth Grade to High School Level

1. Have students write a simple description (word translation) of a picture. Rate for:

	primitive	below average	average	above average	advanced
A. accuracy (details)	1	2	3	4	5
B. organization	1	2	3	4	5
C. usage/spelling/punctuation	1	2	3	4	5
D. overall	1	2	3	4	5
E. comments _____					

2. Have students make up a four- to-eight-sentence discussion between a youngster and a mother as the youngster is about to leave the house. Rate for:

	primitive	below average	average	above average	advanced
A. imagination	1	2	3	4	5
B. sequence	1	2	3	4	5
C. usage/spelling/punctuation	1	2	3	4	5
D. overall	1	2	3	4	5
E. comments _____					

3. Have students write a summary of a passage (250-500 words) at the student's independent to instructional reading level. Rate for:

	primitive	below average	average	above average	advanced
A. accuracy	1	2	3	4	5
B. sequence	1	2	3	4	5
C. absence of irrelevancies	1	2	3	4	5
D. usage/spelling/punctuation	1	2	3	4	5
E. overall	1	2	3	4	5
E. comments _____					

4. Have the student write a critical-evaluative piece on a topic, such as "What I think of vegetarians" or a reaction piece to a statement such as "There surely is life on neighboring planets." Rate for:

	primitive	below average	average	above average	advanced
A. maturity of judgement	1	2	3	4	5
B. accuracy of facts	1	2	3	4	5
C. usage/spell/punctuation	1	2	3	4	5
D. overall	1	2	3	4	5
E. comments _____					

EXAMPLE
Name: Cindy
Grade: 7

Directions: Indicate whether you "totally disagree," "disagree," "partially agree," "agree," or "totally agree" with the statement that follows. Then explain why you feel as you do.
"There surely is life on neighboring planets."

> I totally disagree with this because if there were I think we would know about it by now. also there cant possibly be any because the planet in front of ours is too hot & the one behind ours is too cold.

Ratings
A. maturity of judgement   4
B. accuracy of facts   2
C. usage/spelling/punctuation   2
D. overall   3
E. comments: Cindy shows some immature but basically sound scientific thinking. Punctuation needs some work.

5. Have student offer a constructive resolution to a problem, such as: "What can be done about the enormous amount of waste the society generates?", or "What can you do if someone decides to give you the silent treatment for no good reason?" Rate for:

	primitive	below average	average	above average	advanced
A. maturity	1	2	3	4	5
B. inventiveness	1	2	3	4	5
C. accuracy and relevance of facts	1	2	3	4	5
D. usage/spelling/punctuation	1	2	3	4	5
E. overall	1	2	3	4	5
F. comments _____					

their own study skills inventory using a class text. The procedure by which this is constructed and administered provides an excellent example of diagnostic-teaching, since it is administered as an open book test that then becomes a series of lessons on how to use a text and related references efficiently and effectively.

Observational systems, the third assessment approach, typically are built upon a checklist that also is intended to guide teachers in the observing and appraising of student abilities to do things such as: use a book effectively, employ appropriate retention strategies (underlining, notetaking, memorizing), and make effective use of maps, charts, and graphs to aid comprehension. Douglas B. Rogers' (1984) Study-Reading Skills Checklist is one of the better known criterion-referenced, observational systems (see Figure 4.11).

Finally, there are several self-report scales, such as the Study Habits Checklist of Preston and Botel (1981). One of the oldest of these, the SSHA, or Survey of Study Habits and Attitudes (Brown & Holtzman, 1967) has been standardized on 7th to 12th graders, and, after 35 years of use, still is available from the publisher, Psychological Corporation.

Measures of certain other factors related to study skills already have been covered in the chapter (rate of reading and writing), and two others are covered immediately ahead, metacognition and schema.

Metacognition

The act of monitoring one's own thinking practices, or metacognition, is almost a prerequisite to the effective use of study skills. Study skills, after all, implies the intentional selection by a student of the most effective and efficient strategies for reading, noting, and recalling information. Metacognition, as previously noted, is based upon self-knowledge, task knowledge, and self-monitoring, or, knowing *when* you know, knowing *what* you know, knowing what you *need to know*, and (this is where the study skills aspect really clicks in) *knowing what must be done* to improve comprehension, rate, recall, or some other aspect of faltering learning (Brown, Campione, & Day, 1981; Manzo & Manzo, 1990a; Sanacore, 1984; Wagoner, 1983).

Since metacognition is a strand of self-examination that can and should run through all aspects of living and learning, it is potentially visible, and therefore measurable, in a variety of ways. However, student metacognitive functioning, like miscues in oral reading, appear to vary with the difficulty level of the material, and therefore require some thoughtful interpretation.

The assessment of metacognition took two significant steps forward with a seminal study by Scott G. Paris and Meyer Myers II (1981) and the development, by Maribeth Cassidy Schmitt (1990), of the Metacognition Strategy Index (see Figure 4.12). Schmitt's inventory was found to correlate well with other indices and measures of metacognitive awareness and comprehension: .48 with the Index of Reading Awareness (Paris, Cross, & Lipson, 1984); .50 with an error detection task (finding irrelevant or contradictory elements in a passage); and .49 with a cloze task (Schmitt, 1988). Lonburger (1988) reported a very respectable internal reliability of .87 for the MSI.

Prior to taking the test, students are told: "Think about what kinds of things you can do to help yourself understand a story better before, during, and after you read it. Read each of the lists of four statements and decide which one of them would help you the most. There are no right answers. It is just what you think would help the most." There is only one choice in each item that indicates appropriate metacomprehension strategy awareness, and it yields a score of 1 point.

FIGURE 4.11

Rogers' Study-Reading Skills Checklist

	DEGREES OF SKILL		
	Absent	*Low*	*High*

I. Special study-reading comprehension skills
  A. Ability to interpret graphic aids
    Can the student interpret these graphic aids?

	Absent	Low	High
1. maps			
2. globes			
3. graphs			
4. charts			
5. tables			
6. cartoons			
7. pictures			
8. diagrams			
9. other organizing or iconic aids			

  B. Ability to follow directions
    Can the student follow. . .

	Absent	Low	High
1. simple directions?			
2. a more complex set of directions?			

II. Information location skills
  A. Ability to vary rate of reading
    Can the student do the following?

	Absent	Low	High
1. scan			
2. skim			
3. read at slow rate for difficult materials			
4. read at average rate for reading level			

  B. Ability to locate information by use of book parts
    Can the student use book parts to identify the
    following information?

	Absent	Low	High
1. title			
2. author or editor			
3. publisher			
4. city of publication			
5. name of series			
6. edition			
7. copyright date			
8. date of publication			

    Can the student quickly locate and understand
    the function of the following parts of a book?

	Absent	Low	High
1. preface			
2. forward			
3. introduction			
4. table of contents			
5. list of figures			
6. chapter headings			
7. subtitles			

8. footnotes
9. bibliography
10. glossary
11. index
12. appendix

C. Ability to locate information in reference works
   Can the student do the following?
   1. locate information in a dictionary
      a. using the guide words
      b. using a thumb index
      c. locating root word
      d. locating derivations of root word
      e. using the pronunciation key
      f. selecting word meaning appropriate to passage under study
      g. noting word origin

   2. locate information in an encyclopedia
      a. using information on spine to locate appropriate volume
      b. using guide words to locate section
      c. using index volume

   3. use other reference works such as:
      a. telephone directory
      b. newspapers
      c. magazines
      d. atlases
      e. television listings
      f. schedules
      g. various periodical literature indices
      h. others (_____)

D. Ability to locate information in the library
   Can the student do the following?
   1. locate material by using the card catalog
      a. by subject
      b. by author
      c. by title

   2. find the materials organized in the library
      a. fiction section
      b. reference section
      c. periodical section
      d. vertical file
      e. others (_____)

III. Study and retention strategies
   A. Ability to study information and remember it
      Can the student do the following?
      1. highlight important information
      2. underline important information
      3. use oral repetion to increase retention
      4. ask and answer questions to increase retention

5. employ a systematic study procedure (such as SQ3R)
6. demonstrate effective study habits
   a. set a regular study time
   b. leave adequate time for test or project preparation
   c. recognize importance of self-motivation in learning

B. Ability to organize information

Can the student do the following?
   1. take notes
   2. note source of information
   3. write a summary for a paragraph
   4. write a summary for a short selection
   5. write a summary integrating information from more than one source
   6. write a summary for a longer selection
   7. make graphic aids to summarize information
   8. write an outline of a paragraph
   9. write an outline for a short selection
   10. write an outline for longer selections
   11. write an outline integrating information from more than one source
   12. use the outline to write a report or to make an oral report

Rogers (1984)

The MSI can be administered orally or silently. It is designed to measure strategies specific to narrative, more so than expository, comprehension. However, items can be adapted to use with content textbooks. The inventory assesses behaviors that fit within six broad categories:

a) predicting and verifying (item nos. 1, 13, 14, 15, 16, 18, 23)
b) previewing (item nos. 2, 3)
c) purpose setting (item nos. 5, 7, 21)
d) self questioning (item nos. 6, 14, 17)
e) drawing from background knowledge (item nos. 8, 9, 10, 19, 24, 25)
f) summarizing and applying fix-up strategies (item nos. 11, 12, 20, 22)

See Figure 4.13 for Schmitt's suggestions for how to use and interpret the MSI.

Another significant development in metacognitive strategy selection that is commercially available is the *Strategy Assessments* tests by Donna Alvermann, Connie A. Bridge, Barbara A. Schmidt, Lyndon W. Searfoss, and Peter Winograd (1988). The *Strategy Assessments* tests are designed to assess a student's knowledge and choice of reading strategies essential to comprehension and higher-

FIGURE 4.12

Metacognition Strategy Index (MSI)

I. In each set of four, choose the one statement that tells a good thing to do to help you understand a story better *before* you read it.

1. Before I begin reading, it's a good idea to:
   A. See how many pages are in the story.
   B. Look up all of the big words in the dictionary.
   C. <u>Make some guesses about what I think will happen in the story.</u>
   D. Think about what has happened so far in the story.

2. Before I begin reading, it's a good idea to:
   A. <u>Look at the pictures to see what the story is about.</u>
   B. Decide how long it will take me to read the story.
   C. Sound out the words I don't know.
   D. Check to see if the story is making sense.

3. Before I begin reading, it's a good idea to:
   A. Ask someone to read the story to me.
   B. <u>Read the title to see what the story is about.</u>
   C. Check to see if most of the words have long or short vowels in them.
   D. Check to see if the pictures are in order and make sense.

4. Before I begin reading, it's a good idea to:
   A. Check to see that no pages are missing.
   B. Make a list of the words I'm not sure about.
   C. <u>Use the title and pictures to help me make guesses about what will happen in the story.</u>
   D. Read the last sentence so I will know how the story ends.

5. Before I begin reading, it's a good idea to:
   A. <u>Decide on why I am going to read the story.</u>
   B. Use the difficult words to help me make guesses about what will happen in the story.
   C. Reread some parts to see if I can figure out what is happening if things aren't making sense.
   D. Ask for help with the difficult words.

6. Before I begin reading, it's a good idea to:
   A. Retell all of the main points that have happened so far.
   B. <u>Ask myself questions that I would like to have answered in the story.</u>
   C. Think about the meanings of the words that have more than one meaning.
   D. Look through the story to find all of the words with three or more syllables.

7. Before I begin reading, it's a good idea to:
   A. Check to see if I have read this story before.
   B. <u>Use my questions and guesses as a reason for reading the story.</u>
   C. Make sure I can pronounce all of the words before I start.
   D. Think of a better title for the story.

*Underlined responses indicate metacognition strategy awareness

8. Before I begin reading, it's a good idea to:
   A. Think of what I already know about the pictures.
   B. See how many pages are in the story.
   C. Choose the best part of the story to read again.
   D. Read the story aloud to someone.

9. Before I begin reading, it's a good idea to:
   A. Practice reading the story aloud.
   B. Retell all of the main points to make sure I can remember the story.
   C. Think of what the people in the story might be like.
   D. Decide if I have enough time to read the story.

10. Before I begin reading, it's a good idea to:
    A. Check to see if I am understanding the story so far.
    B. Check to see if the words have more than one meaning.
    C. Think about where the story might be taking place.
    D. List all of the important details.

II. In each set of four, choose the one statement that tells a good thing to do to help you understand a story better *while* you are reading it.

11. While I'm reading, it's a good idea to:
    A. Read the story very slowly so that I will not miss any important parts.
    B. Read the title to see what the story is about.
    C. Check to see if the pictures have anything missing.
    D. Check to see if the story is making sense by seeing if I can tell what's happened so far.

12. While I'm reading, it's a good idea to:
    A. Stop to retell the main points to see if I am understanding what has happened so far.
    B. Read the story quickly so that I can find out what happened.
    C. Read only the beginning and the end of the story to find out what it is about.
    D. Skip the parts that are too difficult for me.

13. While I'm reading, it's a good idea to:
    A. Look all of the bit words up in the dictionary.
    B. Put the book away and find another one if things aren't making sense.
    C. Keep thinking about the title and the pictures to help me decide what is going to happen next.
    D. Keep track of how many pages I have left to read.

14. While I'm reading, it's a good idea to:
    A. Keep track of how long it is taking me to read the story.
    B. Check to see if I can answer any of the questions I asked before I started reading.
    C. Read the title to see what the story is going to be about.
    D. Add the missing details to the pictures.

*Underlined responses indicate metacomprehension strategy awareness

15. While I'm reading, it's a good idea to:
    A. Have someone read the story aloud to me.
    B. Keep track of how many pages I have read.
    C. List the story's main character.
    D. <u>Check to see if my guesses are right or wrong.</u>
16. While I'm reading, it's a good idea to:
    A. Check to see that the characters are real.
    B. <u>Make a lot of guesses about what is going to happen next.</u>
    C. Not look at the pictures because they might confuse me.
    D. Read the story aloud to someone.
17. While I'm reading, it's a good idea to:
    A. <u>Try to answer the questions I asked myself.</u>
    B. Try not to confuse what I already know with what I'm reading about.
    C. Read the story silently.
    D. Check to see if I am saying the new vocabulary words correctly.
18. While I'm reading, it's a good idea to:
    A. <u>Try to see if my guesses are going to be right or wrong.</u>
    B. Reread to be sure I haven't missed any of the words.
    C. Decide on why I am reading the story.
    D. List what happened first, second, third, and so on.
19. While I'm reading, it's a good idea to:
    A. See if I can reconize the new vocabulary words.
    B. Be careful not to skip any parts of the story.
    C. Check to see how many of the words I already know.
    D. <u>Keep thinking of what I already know about the things and ideas in the story to help me decide what is going to happen.</u>
20. While I'm reading, it's a good idea to:
    A. <u>Reread some parts or read ahead to see if I can figure out what is happening if things aren't making sense.</u>
    B. Take my time reading so that I can be sure I understand what is happening.
    C. Change the ending so that it makes sense.
    D. Check to see if there are enough pictures to help make the story ideas clear.

III. In each set of four, choose the one statement that tells a good thing to do to help you understand a story better *after* you have read it.

21. After I've read a story it's a good idea to:
    A. Count how many pages I read with no mistakes.
    B. Check to see if there were enough pictures to go with the story to make it interesting.
    C. <u>Check to see if I met my purpose for reading the story.</u>
    D. <u>Underline the causes and effects.</u>

*Underlined responses indicate metacomprehension strategy awareness

22. After I've read a story it's a good idea to:
    A. Underline the main idea.
    B. <u>Retell the main points of the whole story so I can check
       to see if I understand it.</u>
    C. Read the story again to be sure I said all of the words right.
    D. Practice reading the story aloud.
23. After I've read a story it's a good idea to:
    A. Read the title and look over the story to see what it is about.
    B. Check to see if I skipped any of the vocabulary words.
    C. <u>Think about what made me make good or bad predictions.</u>
    D. Make a guess about what will happen next in the story.
24. After I've read a story it's a good idea to:
    A. Look up all of the big words in the dictionary.
    B. Read the best parts aloud.
    C. Have someone read the story aloud to me.
    D. <u>Think about how the story was like things I already knew about
       before I started reading.</u>
25. After I've read a story it's a good idea to:
    A. <u>Think about how I would have acted if I were the main character
       in the story.</u>
    B. Practice reading the story silently for practice of good reading.
    C. Look over the story title and pictures to see what will happen.
    D. Make a list of the things I understood the most.

*Underlined responses indicate metacomprehension strategy awareness

Schmitt (1990)

---

order thinking. Assessment is based on: Think Ahead, Think While Reading, Think Back, and Strategy Summary. Each assessment requires students to read one or more selections and answer a series of questions based on text(s) with open-ended response possibilities. Following are a few suggestions for how to make such homemade measures. Much of this comes from work in progress at the University of Missouri-Kansas City's Center for Studies in Higher Order Literacy.

The means we are proposing for assessing metacognition is to take items from routine tests of vocabulary, comprehension, and content knowledge and ask students to go back over them immediately following testing and mark each item with their best estimations of whether they thought they knew the correct answer. One way to do this is to have students use the following marking key:

(+) I'm fairly certain that this is correct
(0) I'm uncertain of this response
(−) I'm probably wrong on this item

FIGURE 4.13

Use and Interpretation of the MSI

INTERPRETING THE MSI

The results of the MSI can be used to help teachers design programs of reading comprehension instruction for individual students. Following is a MSI class record for a hypothetical fourth-grade class. Included are the students' scores for each of the six clusters of items, total MSI score, and percentile rank for the comprehension subtest of a standardized achievement test. MSI results can be interpreted both quantitatively and qualitatively. Following are descriptions of the decision making processes for Linda and Emily in the fourth-grade class.

Class Record for Fourth Graders

MSI DATA

	P/V (7)	Pre (2)	Pur (3)	Que (3)	B/K (6)	S/FU (4)	Total (25)	COMPREHENSION PERCENTILE	TEACHER OBSERVATIONS
Linda A.	6	2	2	3	5	4	22	89	A strong, competent reader performing at a higher level on all reading comprehension tasks.
Emily B.	2	0	1	1	1	1	6	12	Struggles with most reading tasks; tends to over-rely on the graphophonic cue system.
Dwayne B.	6	2	2	2	4	3	19	17	A capable student and a good decoder, but he has difficulty in many comprehension tasks; does not always seem to apply skills well.
Constance C.	3	0	1	2	1	2	9	67	A good reader with no apparent problems in reading comprehension.

Key:
P/V = Predicting and Verifying   Que = Self Questioning
Pre = Previewing   B/K = Drawing from Background Knowledge
Pur = Purpose Setting   S/FU = Summarizing and Applying Fix-Up Strategies
The number of items within each metacomprehension category is indicated by parentheses.

Linda A.   Linda performed at a high level on the MSI, selecting 22 out of 25 responses that are indicative of metacomprehension awareness. Further, her standardized test score suggests that she is a skilled comprehender, and her teacher's opinion of Linda's abilities was consistent with both of these findings. Thus, the MSI served to affirm the teacher's belief that Linda was a competent, strategic reader.

Emily B.   Emily's performance on the MSI suggests low strategic awareness, and her performance on the standardized test suggests a low general performance in reading comprehension. Emily's teacher sees her struggling with reading comprehension and also notes that Emily tends to focus on accurate word pronunciation during reading rather than reading for meaning. As a result, Emily's miscues tend to be semantically unacceptable though they are good phonic representations of the words she attempts to pronounce. Consistent with this finding is Emily's tendency to select responses on the MSI that were related to word identification (e.g., she chose "Sound out words I don't know," "Check to see if the words have long or short vowels in them").

In addition, Emily tended to select responses that were inappropriate with the phase of reading. For example, for item 6, which probed for a before reading behavior, Emily selected "Retell all of the main points that have happened so far," a during or after reading behavior. This suggests that she is unaware of when to select specific strategies for use. Emily's teacher concludes that she would benefit from a program of instruction that involves explicit teaching of metacomprehension strategies and when to apply those strategies; the program of instruction should also enable Emily to achieve a balance in drawing from graphophonic and meaning cues.

Schmitt (1990)

This approach has the advantage of assessing the metacognitive process separate from comprehension products measurement. The value of such an advantage, should it hold up in future research,* was stated well by Scott G. Paris and Peter Winograd (1990) when they noted that: "It is gratuitous to attribute performance variation to levels of metacognition when it can only be inferred from performance itself. Attributions to good or poor metacognition when it is not measured independently are simply attributes to the 'ghost in the machine' and add no psychological explanation" (p. 20).

Based on use of the "response self-appraisal" method, we estimate that metacognition above the fifth grade level should correspond to the actual number of correct responses in the following proportions:

(+) 70% or more estimated as correct should be correct.
(0) 40% of those items judged uncertain should be correct.
(−) 60% or more estimated as incorrect should be incorrect.

An overall congruency rating (between appraisals and rating on each item) can be recorded and used as a pretest score against which to measure possible progress following instruction. "Think-alouds," where a student attempts to externalize their thought processes, offer another way to listen-in, diagnostically,

*Preliminary results from one study by our colleague, Siriwan Ratanakarn of Bangkok University, suggest that self-appraisals are excellent predictors of students' overall performance on an informal reading inventory.

on a student's metacognitive processing. Cloze passage exercises are an espe-cially effective medium for eliciting think-alouds. Here is a recommended pro-cedure for using cloze in this way:

1. Identify 3–5 passages of varying difficulty.
2. Make 2 cloze passage type tests from *each* of these: one with every 5th word deleted and one with every 9th word deleted, up to 25 deletions. Be sure that the first sentence is left intact.
3. Read the passage that has the 9th-word deletions and is closest to that student's independent level. Ask the student to orally suggest replacement words. Record responses and periodically, about 5 times throughout the oral examination, ask the student questions such as:
   > Do you think that you are understanding these so far?
   > Do you think that you came up with the correct word here?
   > What made you guess that word?
   > How are you trying to figure out which word to say? What is helping you?
4. Administer the *same passage*, but with 5th-word deletions in a silent reading mode. Ask the students to give their estimations of their correctness by marking above each word they replace whether that word is probably correct (+), or incorrect (-). Do not use "uncertain" with cloze. It is too easy to say "uncertain" for items on this test.
5. Score by: a. accepting reasonable synonyms; b. comparing a student's estima-tion of correctness on each item with actual correctness.

There is another, even more informal, approach to think-alouds. Students are asked to read short text segments (a few sentences will do) and then to verbalize their mental processes, including unrelated thoughts occurring while they try to puzzle out the text (Afflerbach & Johnston, 1986; Davey, 1983; Ericsson & Simon, 1980). To gain further insights into student self-monitoring and thought processes, students can be asked to perform certain conventional reading operations and comment aloud on their thinking about these. Opera-tions such as summarizing, predicting, verifying, relating information to prior knowledge, and evaluating the material to determine if they like it, are all good means of eliciting clues to internal processing.

This same process can be done in a silent reading and writing mode. Simply mark off and number certain sections of text—words, phrases, sentences, or paragraphs, and have students stop at these points and write out "anything and everything you are thinking at this point" (Baumann, 1988).

Schema Assessment

Schema theory is based on the assumption that print itself conveys no meaning (Adam & Collins, 1977), but rather provides the readers with the stimuli for both reconstructing the author's meaning, extending meaning and thought, and building new schemata. Schema also is a reference to "subtext," or the under-standings that authors assume that readers have available when they read.

It has been suggested that words in text are like the buttons on a push-button telephone: they connect us with the information, concepts, and functions that we need to follow and build upon an author's message (Rude & Oehlkers, 1984).

To be able do this for the wide variety of things we read and need to think about, the reader must "call up" a variety of different schemata to give meaning to, and build meaning on, even the simplest of messages. A message, for example, such as: "A stitch in time saves nine" requires:

- prior knowledge (when and where in history or in personal experience that failure to act in a timely way resulted in serious problems and many times more effort and work)
- cultural orientation (this adage is very "western," and assertive)
- ability to form abstractions and follow metaphors (how a "stitch" represents decisiveness and action)
- appropriate vocabulary (the precise definition of "stitch")
- a healthy emotional outlook (avoiding undue anxieties or distortions of the intended meaning),
- an understanding of the world (as a place where timeliness often is important).

If the six words in the above proverb were thought of as just one phone number, it can be readily seen that assessing schema means dialing up all of the factors and working systems mentioned above. Fortunately, from the standpoint of assessment, several of these factors tend to be highly correlated, and therefore they can be inferred from one another.

The easiest way to assess general schema is to take a measure of the reader's fund of general or topical knowledge. Most standardized tests, and criterion-referenced tests, offer such measures in each content or subject domain. A student's grades in school are another easy indication of prior knowledge, although this is less trustworthy, since good learners are not always good students, nor vice versa.

Several other indices may be brought together to get a solid index of general schema. These include the following measures discussed in the chapters ahead:

- the Information, Comprehension, and Vocabulary subtests of the Weschler IQ Test
- the Peabody Picture Vocabulary Test
- the Proverbs Comprehension and Abstract Thinking Tests
- the Manzo Bestiary Inventory of personal schema (or social-emotional perception)
- the Cultural Compatibility Inventory
- recognition (usually multiple choice) measures of topical knowledge
- interviews of personal topical knowledge

Curiously, Sheila W. Valencia, et.al. (1990) did not find the latter two to be highly correlated, but concluded that the recognition test measures are adequate for assessing a specific body of information, whereas the interview opens a broader window on a student's knowledge.

FIGURE 4.14

Rating Scale for Language Functioning

Rating	Function Areas of Language and Thought
_____	1. Instrumental language—used to get things and for satisfying needs
_____	2. Regulatory language—used to control and direct others
_____	3. Interactional language—used for establishing and maintaining relationships with others
_____	4. Personal language—used to express aspects of temperament, personality, or individuality
_____	5. Imaginative language—used to create and describe one's own perspective or world view
_____	6. Informative language—used to convey information, including how one is experiencing the world
_____	7. Heuristic language—used to find things out, wonder, question, and hypothesize
_____	8. Overall language—the skillful and appropriate use of the others

In general, there is no aspect of living and learning that does not interact with our various schemata and world view, and therefore, cannot be tapped to gain insight into the breadth, depth, and content of this basic function. On the other hand, equal educational opportunity clearly is rooted in acquiring some of the common branches of learning, referred to as the "core curriculum" (Camperell, 1984).

Language-Thinking Functions

It is not widely appreciated, but it is possible to unobtrusively assess several specific aspects of language-thinking functions. If you are inclined to do so, you will be interested in this brief critique of noteable efforts.

Katherine Maria (1990) reminds us that the chief purpose of all speaking and writing is communication. Within this main purpose, M.A. Halliday (1975) has delineated several categories of language functioning. We find that by using a seven-point scale (1 low, 4 medium, 7 high) it is possible to derive a fairly sophisticated profile of a student's oral and written language proficiency and overall thinking (see Figure 4.14). It is best to use this scaling system over several samples. The samples are especially useful in keeping anecdotal records, and in reporting. Awareness of these functions also serves as a reminder to the teacher to elicit each type of language, thereby providing students with appropriate practice in thinking and articulating effectively in each function area noted.

To provide an additional index of proficiency with language, administer either an oral or written cloze passage test at the student's instructional level (McKenna & Robinson, 1980). A score higher or lower than that established on an IRI measure of word recognition and silent reading comprehension would indicate average, above, or below level of familiarity with language patterns and syntax.

> **LOOKING BACK**   <

A traditional centerpiece in a textbook on diagnosis and remediation, this chapter opened with a primer on tests and measurements. It then provided quick ways to estimate reading levels, followed by more exacting methods that included the individually administered Informal Reading Inventory (IRI), and the group Informal Textbook Inventory. The chapter concluded with an extensive section on test formats for assessing decoding, vocabulary, comprehension, listening, writing, study skills, metacognition, schema, and language-thinking functions. Knowledge of such options is expected to provide you with the savvy needed to assess reading related literacy functions and to compare and cross-verify findings as suggested by need.

> **LOOKING AHEAD**

The next chapter is an emersion in some of the issues as well as the means for assessing defects, disruptions, and differences. It most thoroughly treats the assessment of "intellectual capacity" as popularly determined by verbal and nonverbal measures. However, it also offers some very concrete ways to assess vision, hearing, possible neurological insult, and differences in learning and lifestyles that affect literacy acquisition.

Detecting Literacy Defects, Disruptions, and Differences

5

> **"We must make an effort to overcome the tendency in education to encourage the learner to understand everything but himself."**
> ARTHUR JERSILD

> ➤ *LOOK FOR IT*

This chapter addresses the assessment of nonreading specific factors that can impede wholesome literacy development. These factors are grouped into three categories:

Defects — or physical impediments
Disruptions — or emotional interferences
Differences — or life, language, and learning style variations

Information on these three D's can be gathered through observations, interviews, and assessment instruments. This chapter focuses on assessment instruments that are available for determining the severity level of problems in theses areas. Observation and interview systems are considered separately and in some detail in the next chapter.

Defects

There are many physical factors that can impede literacy development. These are evaluated under the Defect category and can include any or all of the following constitutional factors:

1. vision
2. hearing
3. neurological considerations
4. intellectual capacities and aptitudes

As you consider factors within the Defect category, keep these guiding questions in mind:

- In what way does this factor influence reading progress?
- How serious does a problem have to be before reading is influenced?
- Since the problem is a physical one, how might it be physically corrected or accommodated?
- Even though the factor is largely physical, to what extent can it be, or has it been, influenced by environmental factors?

Vision

Vision is the physical ability of the eyes to see clearly and accurately. The term "acuity" is used to refer to the clarity of the physical reception of stimuli, without regard for any mental interpretive processes. The ability to see things at a distance is called "far-point acuity." Far-point acuity typically is tested with the Snellen Eye Chart — the familiar poster showing rows of letters that get smaller and smaller as you read downward. The measurement of far-point acuity is expressed in terms of one's relative ability to read the letters on the Snellen chart from twenty feet away. Thus, the expression "20/20" vision means that one can read all of the letters from 20 feet away. A person with 20/80 vision sees the letters on the chart as if it were 80 feet away, or 4 times as far. Many children have far-point acuity in the 20/200 range, and some as great as 20/400 or more. These children see the chalkboard as if it were at the other end of a very long and dimly lit hallway.

The greatest period of deterioration of far point vision takes place during the school years, between the ages of 6 and 18. Near-point vision, or the ability to see close up, typically is not a serious problem until adulthood. Children with poor far-point vision need to be checked at least once a year if they are to remain in visual contact with the chalkboard and maintain attention in class. We have spoken to adults who claim to have "lost" up to 3 years of schooling because their uncorrected acuity problems had them develop rich fantasy lives to cope with endless hours of being out of touch with classroom activities. The road back from such visual isolation can be difficult. It often requires some form of behavioral reconditioning to reverse such old habits of "daydreaming" and put away these enticing "personal soap-operas." It also may require an extraordinary effort to catch up on the knowledge and skills that have been missed or underdeveloped.

The Effect of Vision Problems on Reading

Intensive reading workups have traditionally included a complete visual screening. Oddly, over 50 years of research has failed to show that there is *any* visual problem that is causatively linked to reading disorders in any predictable way. Only one, weak binocular fusion, comes close. Weak binocular fusion is the inability of both eyes to comfortably bring and hold together an image on a printed page. Children with this problem often experience visual fatigue (asthaenopia). It is suspected that this side-effect of reading may cause these children to avoid sustained reading. However, it has recently been realized that a severe fusion problem usually results in such sharp discomfort that the brain automatically corrects the problem by suppressing vision in one eye and subconsciously turning visual tasks such as reading over to the other (see the related problem of Amblyopia in Box 5.1 on Visual Impediments).

Optometrists have experimented with several forms of visual training for children with weak binocular fusion, including means of either strengthening the weak eye, forcing its suppression, or improving binocular fusion. There is no scientific evidence that these methods influence reading in any positive way, although they do result in improvements in certain visual tracking and fusion tasks, and there are many clinical and anecdotal reports of the uplifting effects of such training on morale, self-esteem, and grades. A new development in the area of visual training for reading is capturing national interest. This development, called Scotopic Sensitivity Training, is discussed in the chapter on dyslexia. Certain other aspects of visual training are addressed in the chapter on Remedies for Defects, Differences, and Disruptions.

Vision Testing

Instruments most frequently used for visual screening in reading diagnoses are the Bausch and Lomb School Vision Tester and the Keystone Telebinocular Test. The manuals of these and other visual testing systems give precise details about screening for a variety of visual impairments (see Box 5.1). Where screening test results indicate the possibility of a significant vision problem, the child should be referred for professional testing. In diagnostic reporting and conferencing, keep in mind that these *screening* instruments, by definition, are not as reliable as specialized tests. They can detect the possibility of a problem, but results tend to vary from one testing situation to another. This is partly because children with poor vision have difficulty interpreting and expressing what they are seeing as they go through the items on a vision test. Children with vision problems also will tend to have lower test results if the test immediately follows a visually taxing activity. For this reason, where vision problems are suspected, it can be worthwhile to test before and following a visually taxing task. When a visual anomaly is found, referred, and professionally corroborated, it still is wise to check again at intermittent periods (about every three months) for signs of improvement or further deterioration.

BOX 5.1

Visual Impediments

Refractive, or light focusing, problems

1. Hyperopia or farsightedness. The ability to see at far point but poor near point vision (the 14 inch typical reading distance from the eye).
2. Myopia or nearsightedness. The ability to see things at near point but not at far point.
3. Astigmatism or blurred vision. Usually found with hyperopia or myopia, astigmatism is a defect in the eye's ability to focus on both a vertical and horizontal axis. It can aggravate fusion problems.

Fusion, or binocular, focusing problems

4. Aniseikonia. The images seen in each eye appear unequal in size.
5. Strabismus. The eyes do not fuse well due to a tendency of the eyes to turn inward (estropia, or cross-eyedness), or outward (exotropia), or where one turns higher than the other (hypertropia), or lower (hypo-tropia).
6. Suppression. One eye's message is not transmitted, or not accepted, by the brain.
7. Amblyopia or lazy eye. This is a form of mild to severe atrophy and loss of acuity that tends to occur in a suppressed eye.

The dilemma regarding just how much time and energy to put into vision testing in reading diagnosis is not easy to resolve. Some researchers have concluded that vision appears to have a significant influence on reading. Ekwall and Shanker (1988), for example, report that four years of records at a University Reading Clinic revealed that about 50% of their disabled readers had visual problems that had not been previously detected. On the other hand, Miles Tinker, one of the leading researchers on the relationship between vision and reading, came to a different conclusion. At 80 years of age, while addressing a plenary session of the National Reading Conference in 1968, Dr. Tinker said, "After 50 years of interest and personal research in the connection between reading and vision, I find *none*." Similarly, the first author can vividly remember giving an oral reading test to a brain-injured child who was blind in one eye, and whose other eye "roamed" as she read. Nonetheless, she moved her head, and moved the book, and literally chased the words in order to say them.

While she was determined to read, and *did*, we realize that for most other children this extreme visual handicap could have been crushing. Other clinicians have reported that some children, who otherwise have good vision when they had been checked by optometrists or ophthalmologists (M.D.'s), show signs of a "visual hysteria" condition in which emotional upset leads to tunnel vision and reduced visual acuity. Clinical insights such as these, ironically, seem to provide one of the best justifications for continuing to do visual screening as part of a reading diagnosis. It can induce a diagnostic dialogue that creates incidental opportunities to speak to and hear from the student.

While vision is a physical factor, visual *perception* is a mental one: it is the brain's interpretation of visual stimuli. For this reason, visual perception is addressed ahead under neurological factors.

Hearing

With over 95% of human learning occurring through or in cooperation with listening, it should come as no surprise to learn that a severe hearing loss can have a devastating effect on reading and intellectual development. Fortunately, only about one in every thousand youngsters is deaf; however, approximately five in every thousand have severe hearing loss, and about 45 in every thousand have mild hearing loss (Davis & Silverman, 1970). Thus, an average-sized elementary school, with 500 students, is likely to have about 26 youngsters with hearing problems, and most high schools, with two or three times the total number of students, will have two or three times that number of students with hearing problems.

On an anecdotal level, an experience with a youngster in our own neighborhood provided more dramatic evidence of the need for regular screening tests for hearing acuity than any research we have read. A neighbor's son had been labelled as "weird" by the other children. As he grew older and bigger he began to "put off," if not intimidate, people in the neighborhood by standing too close and staring at them while they spoke. His own speech was oddly loud and booming. He developed a fascination with magic tricks and complicated

Houdini-like escapes. After a poor showing in school, he dropped out and tried to join the navy. It was at that time, when the boy was 17 years old, that it was discovered that he had severe hearing deficiencies in certain frequency ranges. Most extraordinary, however, was the fact that his mother was a school nurse. The simple conclusion to be drawn from this case is that hearing problems can be masked, and present misleading symptoms; therefore, hearing needs to be checked on a routine basis.

There are two aspects of hearing that are traditionally evaluated: *auditory acuity* — the ability to hear clearly and accurately, and *auditory discrimination* — the ability to distinguish similarities and differences in sounds of letters and words. It is arguable whether auditory discrimination should be evaluated as a hearing problem since it is an auditory perceptual task that is influenced by learning more than hearing. The two do become intertwined, however, since hearing losses in certain frequency ranges will result in poor auditory discrimination and even production of certain distinct speech sounds. It also is notable that most hearing losses can be traced back to birth difficulties or early illness, and therefore may be taken, in combination with other supporting evidence, as a possible "soft sign" of neurological impairment.

The Effect of Hearing Problems on Reading

Hearing loss can be expected to have some clear causative impacts on reading behaviors. These typically include the following:

- Poor phonics skill acquisition
- Weak fund of general information
- Strained participation in class discussions
- Poor listening vocabulary and weakened overall speaking, reading, and writing vocabularies

Hearing Testing

There are several means of detecting auditory acuity problems, and even certain auditory perceptual deficits. The first means is by simple observation. There is a comprehensive list of symptoms of hearing loss that have been known and recommended to teachers for many years (Ekwall & Shanker, 1988). These include observing a child:

1. Cupping a hand behind an ear to amplify sound.
2. Complaints of ringing or buzzing in the ear.
3. Staring and inattention.
4. Drainage or discharge from ears and sinus cavities.
5. Head tilting while listening.
6. Listening with mouth open.
7. Frequent head colds and earaches.
8. Failing to respond to oral directions.
9. Speaking in unnatural voice tones.
10. Unusual enunciation of familiar words.

Another informal means of assessing hearing loss is with the so-called "Whisper test."

Whisper Test

1. Construct five sentences of easy directions, find a quiet corner, and have the student listen and do what you then say.
2. Sit immediately behind the student and read these to him or her in the following order and with decreasing volume.
   A. To the right ear in a normal speaking voice: "Raise the left hand on the other side of your body."
   B. To both ears in lower voice: "Raise the same hand you just raised."
   C. To the left ear in a lower voice: "Raise the hand on this side of your body."
   D. In a whisper to the right ear: "Raise the hand on this side of your body."
   E. In a lower whisper to both ears: "Raise both hands above your head."

The whisper test can be made somewhat more precise by using a tape recorder with numbered units on the volume control. After each directional sentence, lower the volume to a predesignated setting. It also can be done in quicker fashion. Simply state a phrase in a medium-low voice from a distance of about 15 feet and continue to repeat it at the same volume while moving closer about 2 feet at a time until the student can repeat it. The more legitimate alternative to informal assessment is to use specially calibrated instruments for evaluation of hearing.

Instrument Testing

There are devices called *audiometers* with earphones that are scientifically constructed and calibrated to make sounds at different pitches or frequencies, and at different decibel levels. These devices have specific instructions and scoring forms to guide auditory evaluation (see the record form shown in Figure 5.1). Notice that the critical speech area is from about 500 to 3,000 cycles per second, though most people can hear sounds between 125 and 8,000 cycles per second. It is notable that youngsters with hearing losses in the 500 and higher frequency ranges are more likely to have problems in the early days of schooling since this higher range is more typical of the female voice, which usually is the one heard most from birth through the first six years of schooling. In general, a hearing loss under 15 decibels is not considered serious, and can be accommodated merely with better seating.

Hearing testing devices that are available for school and clinical use are very sensitive to fluctuations in temperature and humidity, and generally need to be recalibrated about every six months. Children suspected of having hearing loss should be retested by a physician or at a speech and hearing clinic.

FIGURE 5.1

Maico Audiogram Record Sheet

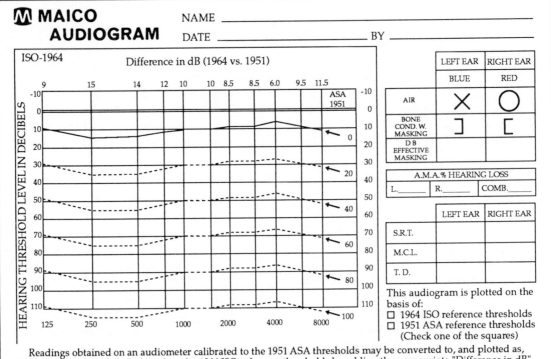

Auditory Discrimination Testing

Auditory discrimination testing is based on the ability to distinguish differences and *likeness* (which usually is more difficult to do) between sets of sounds or words:

/gr/	&	/br/
/say/	&	/hay/
/lie/	&	/lie/

The most widely used tests of auditory discrimination include:

Wepman's Auditory Discrimination test;
Goldman-Fristoe-Woodcock test of Auditory Discrimination;
Kimmell-Wahl Screening test of Auditory Perception.

While these tests have been used for many years in reading evaluations, several studies have shown that:

- they do not correlate well with early reading success (Dykstra, 1966);
- they do not correlate well with one another (Koenke, 1978);
- testing can be complicated by a variety of factors, such as dialect, prior knowledge and experience, vocabulary, and examiner bias (Geissal & Knafle, 1977).

We continue to recommend the use of a quick test of auditory discrimination nonetheless for these counterbalancing reasons:

- The test can be used as an indirect evaluation of possible hearing losses in the various sounds in the speech range.
- Auditory discrimination can be a vital skill in a reading program that relies heavily on phonics.
- The testing protocol gives the examiner another look at the child engaged in a different task.
- Where need suggests, the information gained can be combined with the results of the Digit Span subtest of the WISC IQ test (discussed ahead in the chapter), and patterns of errors on IRI's and word lists to yield indices of auditory discrimination, auditory memory, auditory segmentation, auditory blending, and overall auditory perception.

Auditory perception, like visual perception, is a brain function. We now shall consider how perceptual processes are used as a basis for inferring neurological organization and possible neurological damage.

Neurological Considerations

Neurological defects can be caused by hereditary factors, physiological (anatomy and chemistry) factors, or trauma from physical injury or disease. None of these causal factors is easily determined, although medical science has made a good deal of progress in recording and studying images of brain functions. Such developments and functions are discussed in greater detail in a later chapter on severe reading disabilities, or dyslexia.

Determinations about brain functioning have traditionally been *inferred* by educators and psychologists essentially from visual-perceptual and fine motor tasks. More recently, the evaluation of verbal fluency has been shown to provide highly reliable evidence of brain dysfunction (see the discussion of the Naming Test in the chapter on severe reading disabilities). Again, visual-perceptual functioning, a brain task, should not be confused with sight, a visual-anatomical task.

In visual-perceptual screening, children generally are shown a form or figure and asked to reproduce it. The assumption is that the reproduction will be fairly accurate and properly oriented on the page if the child is neurologically, developmentally, and emotionally sound, and that the reproduction will be distorted, misplaced, or rotated if there are constitutional problems in any of these realms.

Figure 5.2 shows a typical set of patterns that a child might be asked to duplicate and illustrates some distortions that would signal potential difficulty.

FIGURE 5.2

Visual-Perceptual Copy Tasks Used to Infer Neurological Organization

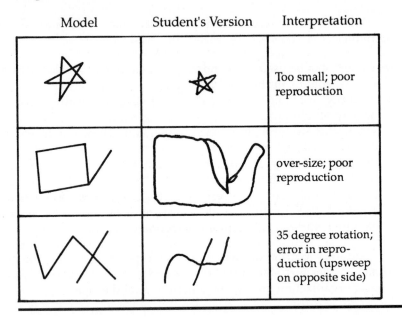

Model	Student's Version	Interpretation
		Too small; poor reproduction
		over-size; poor reproduction
		35 degree rotation; error in reproduction (upsweep on opposite side)

The problem with these inferential systems is that they do not distinguish easily among neurological, developmental, and emotional dysfunctions. In practice, these tests are sometimes treated as if they are sure "soft signs" of neurological disorganization. Examination of test manuals indicates that they routinely state that precautions should be exercised in forming conclusions about neurological or reading disorders from the test protocols. The fact that the relationship between visual-perceptual deficits and reading disability is inconclusive is drawn from research showing that programs designed to improve visual-perceptual "tracking," eye-hand-motor coordination, and visual-perceptual discrimination generally have no short- or long-term effects on reading (Leibert & Sherk, 1970).

In general, visual-perceptual screening still appears to be worthwhile since it does reveal dysfunction, even if it is uncertain as to whether the problem revealed is neurological, emotional, or both. Since neither of these problems, nor the reading problem, is improved by a program of visual-perceptual *training*, it seems wise to exercise great caution in recommending or conducting such training without some other compelling reason to do so.

Several tests of visual-perceptual functioning are marketed as part of visual-perceptual training programs. The two most widely known and used tests in reading and learning diagnosis that are not part of a training program are:

1. the Bender Visual Motor Gestalt Test (Bender, 1946), using the Koppitz scoring system, and
2. the Minnesota Percepto-Diagnostic Test (Fuller, 1969).

The latter is based on the student's ability to reproduce a drawn figure fairly accurately and without rotation on the page. We have found that some apparent rotations can be explained by the way the student turns the paper when he/she is drawing. When administering visual-perceptual tests, be sure that the student, the paper, and the test protocol are all properly oriented before and during the task. In a related vein, it has been experimentally shown that another common indicator of neurological dysfunction, namely reversals in children's writing, largely disappear if a line is drawn down the center of the page and the child is asked to reproduce the words, letters, or figures being reversed on the side of the page that causes the child to cross his or her body mid-line (Zaslow, 1966). Zaslow showed this to be true even with children who were known to be seriously brain damaged.

Suspicion of neurological dysfunction may be further inferred or refuted from a variety of other tests, subtests, and observational schedules. The House-Tree-Person test (Buck & Jolles, 1966), for example, asks the child to draw a picture of a house, a tree, and a person and then uses these protocols to infer a great many things about the child's intelligence, developmental history, emotional well-being, and neurological organization. There are several books and manuals offering years of clinical trials and observations on the H-T-P. Figure 5.3 offers an example of what has been learned about organicity, or brain dysfunction, and the drawing of a person. The Wechsler IQ test described in this chapter also permits inferences of neurological dysfunction, usually from significant discrepancies between the child's overall verbal and performance (or nonverbal) aptitudes, and/or from erratic performance on selected subtests.

Hints of possible neurological dysfunction or odd neurological organization may even be reasonably inferred from IRI protocols, such as when a child shows a great disparity between comprehension and word recognition, or between whole word recognition and phonic word attack skills, or a vast difference between reading and spelling. Three ways of further verifying a supposition of neurological dysfunction are:

1. Ask the child to tell about his reading problem from his perspective — what he/she can and can't seem to do.
2. Engage the child in a "think-aloud" (see ahead in the chapter for details).
3. Carefully recheck the child's cumulative school records and information from interviews for signs of illness, trauma, or abnormal developmental patterns or unusual abilities as well as disabilities (see Williams' Syndrome in the chapter on dyslexia for an example).

Let's look now at the assessment of intelligence, an aspect of brain functioning that can further help in distinguishing between attitude deficiencies and possible neurological and/or psychological disorders.

FIGURE 5.3

Indices of Neurological Disorders

1. much erasing
2. little improvement in quality of picture
3. usually a side-view; simple and concrete figure
4. frequently broken, sketchy, and irregular lines
5. unclosed or incomplete parts

Buck and Hammer, 1969, p. 175

IQ Assessment

An important consideration in a reading-learning diagnosis is the *rate* at which a student is likely to be able to reach mastery of the the varied tasks involved in decoding, comprehending, remembering, and transferring. Rate of learning is essentially what is determined by an IQ test.

Interpretation of IQ Scores

Intelligence Quotient scores, or *estimates* of intellectual capacity, are derived by translating raw scores into standard scores with an average of 100. By definition, then, almost half of the population is expected to be above 100, and almost half below. Scores between 80 and 119 are considered to be within the statistically "normal" range, since two-thirds of the population have scores within this range. Approximately 17% of scores fall above that range and 17% below. Because a certain degree of error in testing is unavoidable, and because IQ scores tend to be viewed with a certain degree of awe, a student's IQ score should be reported as falling within a certain "band," rather as a numerical score. The descriptive "bands" recommended by the widely used Wechsler IQ tests are:

69 & below	Mentally Deficient
70 - 79	Borderline Deficient
80 - 89	Low Average
90 - 109	Average
110 - 119	High Average
120 - 129	Superior
130 - 145	Very Superior

As previously suggested, the factor that IQ tests measure is general *rate of learning*. In attempting to understand why some of us learn faster than others, researchers have defined many subfactors of cognitive learning. J.P. Guilford (1967), for example, defined 120 separate cognitive factors in his "Structure of Intellect" model. Recent neurolinguistic research on what has come to be called the "discrete zones" hypothesis is verifying the high level of specificity of most brain functions (the chapter on Severe Reading Disabilities/Dyslexia treats this topic in considerable depth). Commonly used IQ tests, however, are still quite limited in scope. Noticeably absent from these tests are assessments of intellectual factors such as: originality, creativity, artistic ability, social intelligence, and even common sense. Emerald Dechant made this additional point about such testing: "IQ tests do not discriminate between ignorance and stupidity" (1968, p.10). In other words, there is an important difference between not having been taught and having been taught but having failed to learn.

While many of the factors that are not measured by IQ tests have a clear relationship to success in the real world, it is *rate of learning* that looms largest in schooling, where the struggle is to get everyone going in about the same direction at about the same pace. This also explains why most IQ tests are timed. When time constraints are removed from an IQ test, scores tend to become much less discriminating, and much more homogeneous.

In general, there are these things that can be said about most IQ tests: about 70% of what they measure seems to be genetically determined; measures of intellectual prowess vary in fairly predictable ways across ethnic and socio-economic groups; about 30% of IQ test performance can be profoundly influenced by nurture, environment, and training; and measures of IQ do not assess many valued intellectual functions, such as the ability to think fairly, objectively, creatively, and with good common sense.

Uses of IQ Scores

A review of the IQ-based methods used for detecting possible impediments to reading and learning, and the tests that popularly are used for marking these determinations follow.

The first, and most obvious use of the IQ test is to determine "mental age" and from this to infer the rate of a student's learning by the age-grade equivalent that student might be *expected* to achieve. This, as shown previously in the section on expectancy formulas, is a simple matter of multiplying IQ by chronological age and dividing by 100.

$$MA = \frac{IQ \times CA}{100}$$

Example:

$$MA = \frac{110 \times 10}{100} = 11 \text{ years}$$

As the example above illustrates, a 10-year-old child (and in the fifth grade), with an IQ of 110 would have the mental age of an 11-year-old, and therefore would be expected to read closer to the performance level of sixth graders who are eleven. There are obvious limitations to the concept of mental age: a 10-year-old with a MA of 18 can not reasonably be said to be as intellectually mature as an 18-year-old. In general, as mental age increases, the difference between successive years decreases, making the concept of little value for older children and adults.

There are 3 popular ways of estimating IQ. One is based on verbal aptitude, another on performance tasks, and a third on visual-perceptual tasks. The latter two are sometimes taken together as a nonverbal group. In general, the verbal scores tend to be the better predictors of reading and school learning.

IQ tests can be used in complex ways, such as to examine for evidence of scatter, or variability among various subtests. Such analyses are done in an effort to pinpoint areas of specific cognitive weakness and strength.

Finally, subtest scores can be grouped in certain ways to look more closely at cognitive aptitudes that are represented by a certain logical or factor analytically created cluster. Each of the five possibilities is described next along with the type of IQ tests that are most often used in making such analyses.

Verbal Aptitude Approach to IQ Assessment

This approach to IQ assessment is based largely on richness of vocabulary. The most popular and easily administered of these is the Peabody Picture Vocabulary Test (PPVT) (Dunn, 1970 and revisions).

The PPVT is one of the only untimed IQ tests; nonetheless, it only takes about 15 minutes to administer. It is applicable from 3 years of age to adulthood.

Subjects are asked to identify one of four pictures on a plate in response to an examiner's directions. The IQ scores yielded tend to be a bit higher than on other full range IQ tests. The items with human content have also been found to be more difficult than those with nonhuman content, especially for children with known personal-social adjustment problems (Shipe, Cromwell, & Dunn, 1964, as cited in Dunn, 1965). This suggests that a certain amount of emotionality can be disruptive to thinking, even with fairly innocuous stimuli.

Some clinicians have reported that the test has some cultural biases, but these are not so serious as to negate its predictive value. Contrary to most expectations, minority group children, in our experience, tend to do better on the PPVT than on other types of IQ measures.

There is another form of IQ testing that is also largely based on verbal aptitude but whose questions probe areas of arithmetic and, at lower levels, even eye-hand motor coordination. The most notable of these is the Slosson IQ test (1974; 1982) which contains items for subjects aged 2½ years to adulthood. The Slosson is a quick test that was constructed to parallel the verbal portion of the more comprehensive Stanford-Binet IQ test described ahead. It takes only 30 minutes to administer and is highly correlated with the Stanford-Binet, but has never won the same level of respectability. It contains items such as the following:

- Which of these three circles is smallest?
- How are a pig and a dog different?
- Say: "Jump down!" Good. Now listen carefully and say exactly what I say: "Mary shouted to Tim, 'Quick, father is coming, jump down!' "
- What is meant by infectious disease?

Listening Capacity

As indicated in a previous chapter, the simple act of orally reading graded passages to students and then checking their comprehension of those passages is widely accepted as a measure of *reading capacity*, or the level to which one can be expected to read. However, such measures are not necessarily the best predictors of whether a student will actually make such gains from instruction (Gauthier, 1988). (See the previous chapter for details on how to use the IRI to measure listening capacity and, by inference, how to derive an estimate of IQ as well.)

Visual-Perceptual Approach to IQ Assessment

This approach to IQ assessment is supposed to be the most culturally fair since there is no apparent need for language. Subjects must study patterns and make determinations such as which of several possible figures best completes a pattern or which figure in a pattern is different from the others shown (Figure 5.4).

This format is used as a part of a variety of IQ tests. However, the Standard Progressive Matrices (Raven, 1938) and the Columbia Mental Maturity test (Baurgimeister, Blum, & Lorge, 1972) are based entirely on perceptual tasks. The Raven's is a group administered test that is best used with subjects in the upper intermediate grades to the college level, whereas the Columbia is individually administered and is ideal for young children.

Perceptually based IQ tests do have certain drawbacks. They have a generally lower correlation with full scale IQ tests than do verbal tests. They tend to underestimate students who are impulsive and those who are overly perfectionistic. Young African-American children have been known to struggle even to understand the task (Jensen, 1980, p.652). East Asians, on the other hand, tend to do quite well with this task (Weiss, 1980). Those who work with patterns, such as seamstresses and engineers, do especially well with this approach to IQ testing. The task also is quite susceptible to "training effects." Subjects' scores tend to rise significantly with any level of exposure to the task.

FIGURE 5.4

Perceptual Quotient Test

Directions: Look at the first row and decide which picture is different from the others. Mark the letter on the answer sheet.

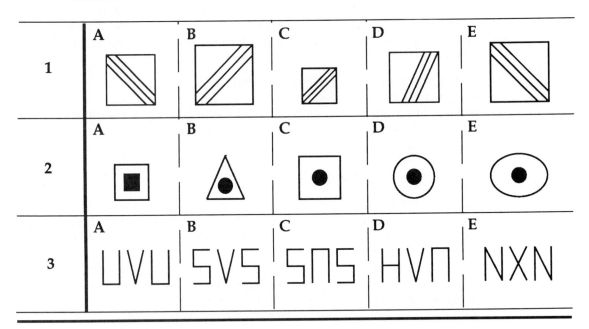

In general, it is misleading to think of these tests as culturally fair. The testing task assumes a certain type of cultural orientation and familiarity with a certain set of language patterns to guide thinking and problem-solving. Efforts to improve visual-perceptual functioning generally are successful but do not seem to transfer to reading. Jensen (1980) argued that these tests are the best available measure of "pure" intelligence. On the other hand, an analysis of over 20 studies led one researcher to conclude that these tests are better referred to as measures of "Perceptual Quotient" (PQ) (Burke, 1958). J. C. Raven, the British psychologist, seemed to agree with this conclusion in an early manual accompanying his Standard Progressive Matrices test (Raven, 1960).

Comprehensive, or Verbal AND Performance Based, IQ Assessment

IQ tests of this type are designed for individual administration. They often require a good deal of training and regular practice in administration; there are too many judgements to be made and things to be manipulated to administer these tests validly without training, practice, and routine usage.

The Stanford-Binet Intelligence Scale (1973) is the historical predecessor of most of these tests. It was first developed in the early 1900s by Simon Binet to help the French government determine which children would profit most by additional schooling. It is standardized on subjects from 2½ years old to adulthood. However, it yields only one overall IQ score. The Weschler Intelligence Scales for Children - Revised (WISC-R, 1974), on the other hand, contains the same type of items but groups them into 12 subtests (two categories of 6 subtests each). Scores yielded include a Verbal IQ, Performance IQ, and a combined Full Scale IQ, in addition to the 12 subtest scores. These subscores make discrepancy and pattern analysis possible, and are largely responsible for the overwhelming popularity of the test. There are separate WISC tests available for very young children and adults; respectively they are called the Weschler Preschool and Primary Scale of Intelligence (WPPSI) and the Weschler Adult Intelligence Scale (WAIS). A brief description of the Subtests of the WISC-R follows.

Six Verbal Subtests of the WISC-R

1. *Information* (30 items). This subtest is composed of a wide spectrum of general information type questions. It effectively measures "prior knowledge" and aspects of schema, and therefore has a high correlation with reading and academic achievement. It has been found to be significantly influenced by experiential background, memory, auditory deficits, and certain emotional and cultural orientational factors such as intellectual ambition.

2. *Similarities* (17 items). This subtest is made up of pairs of words. The student is asked to tell how the two things are the same. ("How are a pear and a pig alike?") This task is very nearly a "pure" measure of abstract verbal reasoning, and is recognized as the best measure of verbal aptitude. Oddly, analogical thinking is a factor that is highly influenced by training, yet few reading programs provide this type of instruction. (See the Proverbs Mastery Paradigm for a related means of assessing and teaching abstract thinking.)

3. *Arithmetic* (18 items). This subtest consists of word problems that are presented orally and must be solved without the use of pencil and paper. Each item is timed and may be repeated only once. Performance on this subtest is affected by attention deficits, intrusive thoughts, computational weaknesses, as well as math and general anxiety. Related training in arithmetic computation often will strengthen test performance and, in fact, provide a more accurate indicator of potential rather than achievement. The Arithmetic subtest is a solid, though often overlooked, predictor of reading and academic success.

4. *Vocabulary* (32 words). This subtest calls for definitions. Words are arranged in an ascending order of difficulty, beginning with concrete and familiar terms and rising to words of greater abstractness and lower frequency of occurrence. Variable credit is given based upon the accuracy and extensiveness of the definitions given. Of all subtests on the WISC-R, Vocabulary has the highest correlation with the Full Scale IQ score, and is the best predictor of reading and academic success.

5. *Comprehension* (17 items). This subtest measures social intelligence, and "world view" — the highest stage of literacy, by some accounts (Chall, 1983c). It measures common sense reasoning and problem-solving skills ("What would you

do if you saw a child alone in a car with the engine running?"). In a manner of speaking, this subtest assesses the primary purpose of going to school: to learn how to learn from experience as well as instruction, and to be able to transfer and apply all learnings in a wide variety of circumstances. Scores are affected by cultural opportunity, socialization, inclination to think practically, self-reliance, and overall personal-social maturity. Impulsive students sometimes will do poorly because they are inattentive to the question. Highly compulsive students also tend to do poorly as a result of inability to tolerate ambiguous tasks. This subtest *seems* similar to reading tasks that require critical and evaluative thinking; however, the authors have looked for this relationship in data from several studies, and have not found strong correlation between the two factors (Manzo & Casale-Manzo, 1981).

6. *Digit Span* (14 number series). This subtest is optional, but is almost always included in reading and learning evaluations. It simply requires the subject to repeat, in order, a series of numbers given at 1 per second intervals. It also requires repeating number series backwards. Forward repetition seems to be a measure of "associative" intelligence and results in even performance among youngsters of all social and ethnic groups; whereas, numbers backwards requires a higher level of attention, cognitive operation, and task orientation and shows up in larger differences among various socioeconomic and ethnic/racial groups (Jensen, 1980). It has also been called a measure of stress tolerance and control over intrusive thoughts. This subtest does not have a high correlation with the Full Scale IQ score, but as suggested above, appears to participate as a sequencing task in early reading development.

Six Performance Subtests of the WISC-R

1. *Picture Completion* (26 incomplete pictures). The child must study a picture and find some subtle missing element, such as eyelashes on a human face or a hand on a clock. It presumably measures visual discrimination, visual memory, and attention to details. It does not, however, have a high correlation with the Full Scale IQ score. It seems to be a distinct mental ability that is said to tap into "spatial awareness" (Goldberg, Schiffman, & Bender, 1983). Impulsive children generally tend to do poorly, though some seem to be especially alert and do quite well. Moderately perfectionistic students tend to do especially well on this task, as do children with high artistic aptitudes.

2. *Picture Arrangement* (12 series comic strip-like pictures). The child, in this subtest, is asked to uncover the story behind a group of pictures and then to arrange the pictures in sequence. There are time limits and credit given for rapid completion. The task requires attention to visual details to reconstruct the plot structure of the story. Generally, this task is easily mastered with age, so scoring has been tied to speed of response for children over 8 years old. This subtest is not correlated in any significant way with Full Scale IQ, or school success. Clinicians use the subtest as an opportunity to observe a child doing a comprehension and sequencing task.

3. *Block Design* (11 two-color designs are constructed from 4, 6, or 9 blocks). The child is shown a design or a picture and asked to construct a three dimensional block design just like it. This subtest provides the purest measure of abstract, nonverbal intelligence and correlates most highly with the total Performance IQ score. Youngsters with known neurological and severe emotional disorders tend to have their lowest scores on this subtest. Block Design scores are strongly influenced by time limitations, since, given enough time, most youngsters can make most designs. Clinicians tend to use this task to observe whether a child works essentially on a trial-and-error (or bottom-up) basis, or takes a more conceptual (or top-down) approach. (Another excellent test using block design, the Goldstein-Scheerer [1964] is constructed to offer further opportunity to learn how much support, or cuing, a youngster may need to complete such tasks.)

4. *Object Assembly* (4 puzzles of familiar objects). The subject is asked to assemble puzzles of familiar objects. Each puzzle assembly is timed, with bonus points for rapid assembly, or partial credit given for incomplete assembly at the end of the time limit. The emphasis on timed performance makes this subtest a measure of rate of learning, more so than power or depth of learning. The task also is said to be a measure of visual-spatial closure skills and attention to details. As with Block Design, the task is considered most useful for the opportunity it provides to observe trial-and-error versus reflective problem solving. The subtest also is considered diagnostically useful in identifying organic damage, particularly to the right hemisphere, as well as in detecting serious psychiatric disorders. It does not correlate well with general intelligence, nor with reading, except to a slight degree in young children.

5. *Coding* (2 different forms, one of 45 symbols for children below 8 years old, another of 95 items for youngsters above 8 years old). Children are asked to copy a certain symbol into small box each time they see a matching number (1-* 2-+ 3-0). The task requires rapid copying in a limited time and is another measure of rate of learning, but also of willingness to do a relatively meaningless task. It presumably measures speed of movement, accuracy, visual-sequential memory, visual-motor integration, discrimination, and shifting. Depressed scores, relative to other subtests, can be taken as a diagnostic indicator of poor motor coordination, tendency to perseverate (uncontrolled motor persistence), high impulsivity, or inadequate orientation and preparation for doing paper and pencil tasks. Coding does not correlate well with Full Scale IQ, or associative intelligence, but has been called a good predictor of clerical skills.

6. *Mazes* (an optional test of 9 mazes of increasing difficulty that must be completed without raising the pencil off the paper). This subtest, first developed by Porteus (1956), was intended to be a culturally fair test of IQ. It presumably measures problem-solving ability, and ability to plan ahead before moving. It has relatively weak correlations with Full Scale IQ and with other subtests. It is useful, however, in getting a more accurate fix on the mental abilities of youngsters with IQ's below 95. Observations of children taking the Mazes subtest reveal their ability to understand and follow direc-

tions and to learn from one trial to the next. Mazes scores typically will improve purely as a function of having done the task before.

Reshuffling WISC Subtests

A. Bannatyne (1974) has suggested that the Wechsler Scales make more sense in educational diagnosis when they are grouped into four categories rather than two. The categories suggested are as follows:

Acquired Knowledge	Information, Vocabulary, Arithmetic
Verbal Conceptualization	Similarities, Vocabulary, Comprehension
Spatial	Picture Completion, Block Design, Object Assembly
Sequential	Arithmetic (again), Digit Span, Coding

Despite the wide use of the WISC, there is no agreed upon pattern of weakness that has been clearly tied to reading deficiencies. However, there is a pattern frequently cited for learning disabilities, and reading deficiencies associated with learning disabilities. Not surprisingly, it also is tied to organicity, or neurological factors. This pattern is referred to as the ACID test. It refers to lower scores in *Arithmetic, Coding, Information,* and *Digit Span* (Kaufman, 1976).

Value of the WISC

It might seem odd that a test continues to be used in reading diagnosis when it does not yield a predictable subtest pattern. There are three reasons for this, two are historical, and the other logical.

The historical reasons stem from the fact that the WISC was one of the first IQ tests of its type. Secondly, it was developed by a psychologist, not an educator. Weschler developed it for use in a psychiatric ward at Bellview Hospital in New York City. It originally was called the Weschler-Bellview IQ test. This may explain why the test contains so many tasks related to social adjustment and emotional maturity (such as Comprehension, Picture Arrangement, and Object Assembly). It also may explain why it does not measure more of the things that are more specifically germane to reading and learning. Several test makers have tried to challenge the WISC's supremacy with more educationally oriented tests. Despite the special relevance of most of these, none has yet won wide acceptance. The chief challengers are:

Woodcock-Johnson Psychoeducational Battery - Cognitive Abilities (WJPEB-CA)
Kaufman Assessment Battery for Children (K-ABC)
McCarthy Scales of Children's Abilities (MSCA)

The third reason for the continued popularity of the WISC despite its uncertain predictiveness of reading disability also may explain why the other tests continue to have difficulty in challenging it. It is the fact that there is a rich literature and clinical lore of experience associated with the WISC. That lore, passed down in classes, clinics, and apprenticeship has become invaluable in trying not so much to find a pattern of reading disability, but in understanding a given reading disabled student. The WISC provides a familiar and common frame of reference for comparing clinical notes on how reading disabled children differ from one another, rather than in how they are the same. Most clinicians agree that it is wise to encourage the development and use of other instruments that might better reflect the needs and concerns of educators, but it also is agreed that it would be unwise to sever a 50-year-old connection and common frame of reference.

Let's turn now to the matter of affect, or the assessment of a child's personal-emotional schema. It is here, deep within the child, that the chief factors often can be found that are responsible for disrupting and convoluting comprehension, classroom learning, and understanding of one's own experiences.

Disruptive Thinking

To the keen eye, a person's every choice and expression can be interpreted into a sharper understanding of the person's psychological organization. Such "kid watching," as it is being called at the school level, assumes that teachers have the schemata necessary to see and read significance into what they are observing. In point of fact, some people can do this rather easily and others can not. Everyone, however, can get better at "seeing" and dealing with the complex nature of children and their ranging ways of being, feeling, and acting. The tests, inventories, and methods presented next are intended as "eye-openers," or heuristics, to help one develop better insights into the psychoeducational aspects of reading, learning, and living. Before reviewing these tools, it is appropriate to consider what one might be looking for.

Emotional Characteristics Associated with Reading Disorders

Several emotionally charged behaviors have been linked to reading and learning disorders. The checklist described in Figure 5.5 is compiled from Albert Harris and Edward Sipay (1980), Edward Poostay and Ira Aaron (1982), Anthony Manzo (1987), and Helen M. Robinson's classic study, "Why Children Fail in Reading" (1946).

Gaining Psychological Insight

There are several psychological instruments that can be used to understand a child. Each of these is based in some way on the theory of projection, a concept that research has shown to be operative in comprehension in a variety of ways (Lipson, 1982, 1983; Pichert & Anderson, 1977; Waern, 1977a, b).

Projection means that someone will reflect and project his/her inner feelings when asked to respond to any open-ended question or stimuli. In the Rorschach test, for example, inkblots are shown and the subject is encouraged to say what they "see." Whatever he/she says is taken as an expression of what occupies, if not preoccupies, his/her mind. Interpretation of inkblots is very difficult, since it generally takes a great deal of knowledge and experience as a psychologist to

FIGURE 5.5

Checklist of Emotional Characteristics Associated with Reading Disorders

_____   1. open hostility and refusal to learn

_____   2. disinclination to accept popular societal values, often accompanied by identification with "maverick" adults or peers

_____   3. hyper-sensitivity to anything that may be interpreted as criticism

_____   4. displaced hostility transferred from sibling, parental, or peer relationships

_____   5. resistance to the ambitions of parents

_____   6. subconscious desire to remain dependent (reading is a natural road to knowledge and independence)

_____   7. lack of self-confidence and self-respect resulting in easy discouragement

_____   8. subconscious fear that success will breed resentment from underachieving parents and friends

_____   9. extreme distractability or restlessness

_____   10. preoccupation with a private inner world

_____   11. gender confusion when accompanied by fear, denial, and need to counter-indicate

_____   12. sexual abuse, accompanied by hopelessness from need for help but fear of consequences of disclosure

_____   13. over-controlling nature

_____   14. obsessive-compulsive tendencies and behaviors

_____   15. social isolation (also associated with excessive reading)

make sense out of such free-form responding. In contrast, other tests narrow the range and reduce the difficulty of interpretation. They do this in a variety of ways, such as by telling the child what to draw as in the House-Tree-Person test (Buck & Jolles, 1966), or showing him/her pictures of people where the mood is ambiguous and the subject decides if the person is happy or sad, or whatever. The most widely known of this type is the Thematic Apperception Test, originally developed by Morgan and Murray (1935), and updated by John McClelland, et al. (1976). To get a mental image of the task, picture the enigmatic look of the Mona Lisa, then ask "What is she thinking?" or "What happened just prior to this picture?" Whatever comes to mind as one begins to answer these questions will reflect more of what is on one's mind than is in the picture. Of course, it still is no simple matter to determine the meanings of these projective associations.

Instruments that are the more accessible and useful to educators tend to take a more direct and less ambiguous tack. The California Psychological Inventory (CPI) (Gough, 1975), for example, is based on the widely used adult Minnesota Multiphasic Personality Inventory (Hathaway and McKinley, 1967) and uses a very direct approach. The CPI consists of 480 statements to which true-or-false responses are made. Items then are analyzed and yield scores on 18 different psychological factors. These include factors such as Dominance, Sociability, Sense of Well-Being, and even the very factor being discussed here, Psychological-mindedness—or the degree to which one is given to understanding human psychology, inner needs, and motivation.

Most of these instruments were developed or normed primarily with adults in mind, or they tend to contain scales on factors that are difficult for nonpsychologists to understand or interpret. There are some forms of emotional testing, however, that are more accessible and that are easily interpretable by any professional who works with people and wishes to develop greater psychological insight. These include the Incomplete Sentences, the Adjective Check List, and the Manzo Bestiary (Best'-ee'-ary) Inventory. Each of these is described in a form that should permit you to explore it for yourself.

Incomplete Sentences

Sentence completion procedures were used as early as the 1800s, but it is Julian Rotter who has provided us with a simple, although relatively subjective, means of assessing general emotional adjustment.

Simply create a series of incomplete sentences, ask students to complete them (either in written or oral form), and then judge on a zero to six scale the extent to which each response strikes you as healthy (0-2), neutral (3-4), or unhealthy (5-6) (Graham & Lilly, 1984); Figure 5.6, below, highlights some examples. Higher scores are suggestive of high emotionality and, therefore, a greater tendency to distort information in reading and listening.

Figure 5.7 gives an additional example of an incomplete sentence inventory developed by John E. George (1990).

Adjective Checklists

Direct and uncomplicated, adjective checklists are not so much scored as perused to get a sense of how a person may see him/herself. The Inventory shown

FIGURE 5.6

Incomplete Sentences

Test Item	Sample Student Response	Score
I believe that family life	stinks	6
I believe that art is for	sissies	5
I believe that reading is	OK	2
The thing I really enjoy is	I don't know	5
My best friend is	sometimes not to be trusted	3
When I get older	I'll do better	1
	TOTAL	22 (High emotionality)

(a healthy score for 6 items would be about 12; a mildly disruptive would be as high as 18)

FIGURE 5.7

George Incomplete Sentence Inventory

1. Today I feel _____

2. When I have to read, I _____

3. I get angry when _____

4. To be grown up _____

5. My idea of a good time _____

6. I wish my parents _____

7. School is _____

8. I can't understand why _____

9. I feel bad when _____

10. I wish teachers _____

11. I wish my mother _____

12. To me, books _____

13. My friends think I _____

14. I like to read about _____

15. On weekends I _____

16. I'd rather read than _____

17. I hope I'll never _____

18. I wish people wouldn't _____

19. When I grow up _____

20. I'm afraid _____

21. Comic books _____

22. When I take my report card home _____

23. I do my best when _____

24. Most brothers and sisters _____

FIGURE 5.7

George Incomplete Sentence Inventory (*continued*)

25. I won't know how _____

26. When I read math _____

27. I feel proud when _____

28. I wish my father _____

29. I like to read when _____

30. I would like to be more like _____

31. I often worry about _____

32. I wish I could _____

33. Reading about science _____

34. I look forward to _____

35. I wish _____

36. I'd read more if _____

37. When I read out loud _____

38. I'm sorry that _____

39. If I could be any animal it would be _____

40. Reading is _____

Reproduced with permission of John E. George, University of Missouri—Kansas City

in Figure 5.8 has students respond to the same words in terms of the way they "think they are" and the way they "would like to be." The greater the difference between these two ratings, the poorer the individual's self-concept and self-worth.

Students often will give some powerful clues as to what their real agenda is in the way they respond to the second condition—"would like to be." The teacher who understands these responses is likely to grasp the student's most basic emotional needs and drives, and hence be better equipped to respond empathetically to these in instructional and informal settings.

FIGURE 5.8

Adjective Checklist

Name _____   Date _____

Directions: To achieve a greater level of self-knowledge, start at the left first and check the column under "This is the way I am." Then, go back and check under "This is the way I'd like to be" in the same way.

THIS IS THE WAY I AM			THIS IS THE WAY I'D LIKE TO BE		
nearly always	about half the time	just now and then	nearly always	about half the time	just now and then
_____	_____	_____ Friendly	_____	_____	_____
_____	_____	_____ Brave	_____	_____	_____
_____	_____	_____ Honest	_____	_____	_____
_____	_____	_____ Thoughtful	_____	_____	_____
_____	_____	_____ Obedient	_____	_____	_____
_____	_____	_____ Careful	_____	_____	_____
_____	_____	_____ Fair	_____	_____	_____
_____	_____	_____ Mean	_____	_____	_____
_____	_____	_____ Lazy	_____	_____	_____
_____	_____	_____ Truthful	_____	_____	_____
_____	_____	_____ Smart	_____	_____	_____
_____	_____	_____ Polite	_____	_____	_____
_____	_____	_____ Clean	_____	_____	_____
_____	_____	_____ Kind	_____	_____	_____
_____	_____	_____ Selfish	_____	_____	_____
_____	_____	_____ Helpful	_____	_____	_____
_____	_____	_____ Good	_____	_____	_____
_____	_____	_____ Cooperative	_____	_____	_____
_____	_____	_____ Cheerful	_____	_____	_____
_____	_____	_____ Jealous	_____	_____	_____
_____	_____	_____ Sincere	_____	_____	_____
_____	_____	_____ Studious	_____	_____	_____
_____	_____	_____ Loyal	_____	_____	_____
_____	_____	_____ Likeable	_____	_____	_____
_____	_____	_____ A good sport	_____	_____	_____
_____	_____	_____ Useful	_____	_____	_____
_____	_____	_____ Dependable	_____	_____	_____
_____	_____	_____ Bashful	_____	_____	_____
_____	_____	_____ Happy	_____	_____	_____
_____	_____	_____ Popular	_____	_____	_____
_____	_____	_____ Simple	_____	_____	_____
_____	_____	_____ Flexible	_____	_____	_____

(Original authors unknown)

Manzo Bestiary Inventory

The MBI is a social-psychological traits inventory (Manzo, 1975b) on which school-age students express varying degrees of identification with selected animals. The inventory can be administered orally or silently, individually or in a group (see Figure 5.9).

FIGURE 5.9

Manzo Bestiary Inventory*

Name _____   Date _____

A. Which of the animals listed below would you least or most like to be? Use this 5-point scale to show your likes and dislikes:

> 1 – least
> 2 – rarely
> 3 – sometimes
> 4 – often
> 5 – most

(You may use a zero [0] if you do not know what an animal is.)

___ 1. horse	___ 13. tiger	___ 25. duck
___ 2. dog	___ 14. pheasant	___ 26. peacock
___ 3. squirrel	___ 15. horse	___ 27. squirrel
___ 4. pheasant	___ 16. goat	___ 28. swan
___ 5. cow	___ 17. turtle	___ 29. falcon
___ 6. rooster	___ 18. alligator	___ 30. dove
___ 7. lion	___ 19. porpoise	___ 31. snake
___ 8. chicken	___ 20. leopard	___ 32. elephant
___ 9. moose	___ 21. hog	___ 33. eagle
___ 10. penguin	___ 22. wolf	___ 34. hippopotamus
___ 11. owl	___ 23. giraffe	___ 35. fox
___ 12. badger	___ 24. mink	___ 36. coyote

B. Look back over your strongest choices (4's and 5's). Put *six* of them into the order that you *most* prefer:

1st _____   4th _____

2nd _____   5th _____

3rd _____   6th _____

C. Write the names of the *two* animals you like *least*:

low _____

lowest _____

*Pheasant, horse, and squirrel are repeated to provide a quick check of internal reliability. See Appendix A for details.

Animal choices have been empirically linked to common associations, as well as to a variety of other factors such as reading, writing, and two aspects of motivation: *appetitive* motivation—the desire to achieve something and or attain some personal goal; and *aversive* motivation—the desire to avoid failure or other negative consequences. This list of adjective associations and related factors for each animal is provided in Appendix A.

Review of a person's animal choices tends to reveal the descriptive words and, therefore, the thoughts and feelings through which that person filters his/her experiences, including reading, listening, and school life. A look into the nature of someone's "filtration system" generally reveals something about how that person is experiencing reality and, thus, why a gentle stroke to one child can appear as a sharp poke to another. Stick figure representations of the person under four basic human conditions can be used to illustrate the impact of this "filtration system" on reading, learning, and social situations (see Figure 5.10).

If you are in doubt, as you sometimes will be, about just which traits should be associated with a given animal chosen by a particular student, ask the student questions such as "What do you picture when you think about [the animal's name]?"

The MBI is a useful way to build psychological-mindedness, or orientation and insight into human needs and motivation. Full instructions for administering, scoring, and interpreting findings can be found in Appendix A. Chapter 6 also offers an example of how findings may be expressed in a diagnostic report, should you wish to do so.

The MBI was originated for use with children, and to provide a basis for more keenly observing and noting personal-social and school adjustment. The best way to build the knowledge base and confidence necessary to interpret any psychological instrument is to administer it to persons you already know quite well. In this way, you use existing schemata to further enhance schemata. If you wish to become more insightful in detecting deeper psychological factors, see the *Luscher Color Test* (translated by Ian Scott, 1969). This adult-oriented test asks subjects to select eight colors in the order of their choice. Color choices then are matched with interpretive statements that are quite useful and self-instructional in explaining motivation and behavior. We believe that you will find the instrument useful with upper elementary students as well.

Personal Traits Records

If the use of any psychological instruments seems foreign or foreboding, consider trying the personal traits record reports such as were widely used on cumulative record files in years past (see Figure 5.11 as an example).

Simple subjective record systems such as these make it possible to estimate whether a student is making reasonable progress toward maturity in independence, self-control, responsibility, and social adjustment. Factors such as these often become much more predictive of long-term progress in learning, lifetime reading, and productive living than do IQ or grade point averages.

FIGURE 5.10

MBI Stick Figures (with notes from research findings on choices shown)

IDEAL SELF

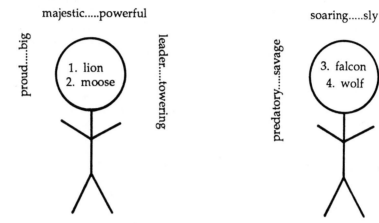

majestic.....powerful

proud.....big

leader.....towering

1. lion
2. moose

TYPICAL SELF

soaring.....sly

predatory.....savage

fierce.....wild

3. falcon
4. wolf

Notes: weak writing, high self-directed motivation, low fear of consequences

Notes: high self-directed motivation, weak language skills, some fearfulness

RESTRAINED SELF

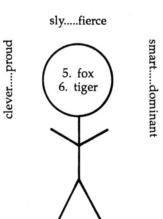

sly.....fierce

clever.....proud

smart.....dominant

5. fox
6. tiger

FEARED SELF

peaceful.....graceful

gentle.....lovely

graceful.....beautiful

1. dove
2. swan

Notes: strong vocabulary, strong comprehension, high fearfulness, high self-directedness

Notes: fears being female, fearful

Case report: a 10-year-old boy with brash, nongraceful behavior, poor school grades, poor oral reading (teacher recommended remedial reading), and erratic scores on the Iowa Test of Basic Skills: 95th percentile on Vocabulary; 85th percentile on Comprehension; 18th percentile on Language Skills (grammatical usage).

FIGURE 5.11

Personal Traits Record (High School Form)

TEACHER/EVALUATORS:
Name: Johnston, Sara   Year: 1961-62
Name: Clark, Mark   Year: 1962-63
Name: Coleson, Andrew   Year: 1963-64
Name: Walker, James   Year: 1964-65

Personal Traits	Year	(high) 5	4	3	2	(low) 1
Work Habits	1961-62			✔		
	1962-63				✔	
	1963-64					✔
	1964-65				✔	
Responsibility	1961-62			✔		
	1962-63			✔		
	1963-64				✔	
	1964-65					✔
Self-Control	1961-62		✔			
	1962-63			✔		
	1963-64				✔	
	1964-65				✔	
Getting Along with Others	1961-62					✔
	1962-63				✔	
	1963-64				✔	
	1964-65			✔		

It is always a hard sell, due to our regard for privacy, but we would add a slot to Figure 5.11 for "normal/abnormal behaviors." This may not bear on reading progress, but it definitely would help bring attention, and possibly timely help, to youngsters who are signaling inclination toward self-destructive or violent behaviors in the future. Suicide, murder, and other violent acts seldom explode without early signals. A holistic philosophy of education suggests that at least this modest effort to observe and possibly counter such problems should be a reasonable priority.

Chapter 11 treats this and the next topic, Differences, in the context of rather traditional reading practices. Differences are not always distinguishable in practical terms from disruptions since the surface expressions can be much the same.

Differences

All schooling, whether we realize it or not, is based on a set of assumptions. Predominant among these is the assumption of certain common learnings, or shared experiences, concepts, and values. Additional to these common learnings, or "Reading Facilitating Experience," as John George (1975) called them, is the unspoken expectation that we all will learn in about the same way. A sensitive school program realizes that such assumptions may not hold true for a given individual and seeks means by which to identify and address differences that put such students at risk (Beane, 1990).

Although the concept of "differences" receives a good deal of attention in the literature on learning styles and multicultural education, it still is in its infancy in terms of assessment and practice. The treatment here begins with the controversial issue of learning styles, and then takes up the more traditional realm of common-learnings, now also known as "cultural literacy" or "cultural compatibility."

Learning Styles

Learning styles issues in reading, also technically known as "aptitude-treatment interactions" (Cronbach & Snow, 1977; Curry, 1990), have come to focus mainly on modality preference. Robert Mills (1965) pioneered the assessment of modality preference with the development of the Learning Methods Test (Mills, 1970, revised).

The Mills Test

The Mills test helps the teacher identify 40 words that a student between the primary and third grade levels does not know, and then teaches and tests the student on these words in sets of 10 in 4 different ways over 5 days. Each teaching session is 15 minutes long. The methods are characterized as: phonic, visual, kinesthetic, and combined visual-auditory-kinesthetic.

Robert Mills and others who have attempted to refine these tests, such as Maria Carbo (1984 a, b, c), offer some interesting findings in support of the principle of matching students to style of teaching. Several key aspects of their findings have been hotly disputed (c.f. Ceprano, 1981; Kampwirth & Bates, 1980; Tarver & Dawson, 1978).

Currently there is insufficient proof of a significant interaction between modality preference and method of teaching to justify whole scale testing and matching. Three factors, however, continue to command the attention of remedial specialists to these developments. For one thing, Public Law 94-142 requires that "a specific statement describing the child's *learning style* be included in the Individual Educational Plan (IEP) for a handicapped student." This could be written off as a mere by-product of the social-political forces that created this legislation were it not for two other considerations. An overwhelming majority of LD specialists believe in modality testing and preference (as reported in Ekwall & Shanker, 1988), and there is, as stated previously, a certain compelling logic to the significance of issues in learning styles, especially where disabled readers and learners are concerned. The argument for it is based on the proposition that optimal results in learning anything are most likely to be achieved when an individual's learning style is carefully matched with the instructional methods used (Witkin, et al., 1977). Others are unconvinced that such matching needs to be done; they argue that children may actually grow to greater independence by mismatching. This paradox has led Snow and Lohman (1984) to suggest matching for the initial stages of learning, and systematic mismatching thereafter. The most current theoretical position has shifted even further. It now is being argued that the best learning style is the absence of any identified style or consistency of approach, with the emphasis on teaching children and being flexible in using the style or approach that best matches the content or objective rather than the individual learner (Kirby, 1988; Pask, 1988; & Curry, 1990).

The Learning Preference Inventory

The emphasis that appears best to us at this time is to build some alternative ways of teaching that simply permit us to meet a broader variety of human style variations, needs, and capacity levels. To this end, we began some time ago to develop and use an informally administered Learning Preference Inventory (Manzo, Lorton, & Condon, 1975; Manzo & Casale, 1983). This inventory, to which we have recently added four additional approaches and a checklist of eleven elements, seems to help both teacher and students to grow in their sense of the options that are available for conducting lessons in a variety of interesting—though not necessarily exotic or quirky—ways (see Box 5.2 for a copy of the Inventory).

The Learning Preference Inventory (LPI) is not limited to early age-grade ranges or to modality issues as are most other learning styles inventories; however, it is apparent that some methods are more suitable for some age-grade levels than others. The LPI should be scored with the expectation that a student should feel relatively comfortable (3's or higher on a 5-point scale) with each of the teaching-learning styles represented, and should be especially comfortable with the mode most used by his or her teachers or the mode that is especially necessary due to the nature of what is being taught at a given age and grade level. The chief thing to know about learning style preference is whether a student has a strong dislike for a commonly used mode of presentation, or that a student's most preferred mode of learning is one that is seldom if ever used, and therefore ought to be included at least some of the time. Learning style preference generally is a problem only for a small percentage of students with very specific needs. As noted previously, however, students who are at risk for other reasons, or those who are already failing, are likely to be the ones who need the most compatible environment. The greatest concern from the point of view of instructional planning is to be careful not to develop a remedial program

BOX 5.2

Learning Preferences Inventory

Directions: Choose the statement that best matches how you feel about each way of learning described. Circle the number that best matches your feeling about each.

1. strongly dislike
2. dislike
3. no strong feelings for or against
4. like
5. like very much

TEACHING/LEARNING METHODS

1. **Lecture Learning**: The teacher does most of the talking. Questions are permitted, but there generally is little discussion.
   How do you feel about the Lecture Learning method?
   Circle one:
   1   2   3   4   5

2. **Lecture/Discussion**: The teacher talks briefly, then answers and raises questions in class discussion.
   How do you feel about the Lecture/Discussion method?
   Circle one:
   1   2   3   4   5

3. **Inquiry Lesson:** The teacher names a topic, then the class questions the teacher to discover the important information on that topic. The teacher finally tells the class what important questions they may have failed to ask.

How do you feel about the Inquiry Lesson method?

Circle one:

1   2   3   4   5

4. **Incidental Teaching:** Most skills are taught as they appear to be needed. For example, a spelling, reading, or writing lesson may be taught on the spot in a social studies class because the students seem to need it at that time.

How do you feel about the Incidental Teaching method?

Circle one:

1   2   3   4   5

5. **Casual Learning:** Games are played or activities done to improve certain skills and attitudes.

How do you feel about the Casual Learning method?

Circle one:

1   2   3   4   5

6. **Individual Learning**: Each student is given different work to do based on need. The work must be completed before going to a higher level. This type of learning can involve workbooks.
   How do you feel about the Individual Learning method?
   Circle one:
   1   2   3   4   5

7. **Student Reporting**: Individual students are responsible for finding and presenting information to the class on assigned topics.
   How do you feel about the Student Reporting method?
   Circle one:
   1   2   3   4   5

8. **Group Work**: Small groups are assigned topics to look up and discuss. Their findings are then shared with the entire class.
   How do you feel about the Group Work method?
   Circle one:
   1   2   3   4   5

9. **Individual Tutoring:** The teacher works with one student (or a small group) while the remainder of the class does some other activity.
How do you feel about the Individual Tutoring method?
Circle one:
1   2   3   4   5

10. **Team Teaching:** Two or more teachers work together to teach a class. They discuss different points of view in front of the group. The class participates in the discussion.
How do you feel about the Team Teaching method?
Circle one:
1   2   3   4   5

11. **Role-playing (simulation)**: Students are guided in actually experiencing something and then discussing what they have learned.
How do you feel about the Role-playing method?
Circle one:
1   2   3   4   5

12. **Mental Picturing (imaging):** Students attempt to learn by trying to see a word or an idea in their minds, or by making an actual picture of it.
How do you feel about the Mental Picturing method?
Circle one:

1   2   3   4   5

13. **Movement (kinesthetic):** Students try to learn something by moving their hands in a tracing movement or by acting out a certain word or idea in order to remember it.
How do you feel about the Movement method?
Circle one:

1   2   3   4   5

14. **Hearing and Saying (Recitation training):** Students learn by having something said while they look at it, then say it, and then repeat the whole thing until they have got it down.
How do you feel about the Hearing and Saying method?
Circle one:

1   2   3   4   5

15. **Hands-on:** Students are asked to do or make something that aids in learning.
How do you feel about the Hands-on method?
Circle one:

1   2   3   4   5

Check each thing that you *would* like to see happen more or less often in the classroom. Circle one number for each item

Circle one:

	much less	less	slightly more	more	much more
16. repeating	1	2	3	4	5
17. faster pacing	1	2	3	4	5
18. moving around	1	2	3	4	5
19. writing	1	2	3	4	5
20. drawing	1	2	3	4	5
21. reading	1	2	3	4	5
22. being read to	1	2	3	4	5
23. student talking	1	2	3	4	5
24. use of TV & recordings	1	2	3	4	5
25. field trips	1	2	3	4	5

around "learning style" needs that are difficult to determine and match, at the expense of more tried and true methods of instruction.

To maximize the value of the LPI, in instructional planning, administer it to students, then take it yourself in two ways: first as you would prefer to learn, and then as you tend to teach. A simple comparison of these three perspectives will result in a valuable diagnostic conversation with yourself about how best to serve student needs.

Other Differences

While attention to learning style preference has properly been called a "heroic effort" (Ekwall & Shanker, 1988, p. 108) for teachers, there can be little argument about the need to reach a greater level of compatibility between youngsters and the hidden requirements and assumptions of school, the next "difference" topic.

Let's begin by noting some of the basic assumptions that schools tend to make about children. These often need to be reviewed in relation to a given student or group of students who are not reaching their learning potentials.

Common Assumptions About Students

- A child of 5–6 years is expected to have a secure understanding of what a mother and a father are, that books contain word recordings of speech, and that school is the place where one comes to learn how to read and write.
- A child of 7–10 years is expected to have a secure self-image; to have mastered certain basic Piagetian concepts such as "conservation"—that is, the realization that things may change in form though not in substance (physically, a piece of clay is the same weight whether in the shape of a ball or a platter); to understand that words are read from left to right; and to derive meaning from most syntactical and grammatical forms encountered in reading and listening.
- Beyond 11 years old, schools begin to make quantum leaps in terms of what youngsters are expected to know and understand. It is assumed, for example, that youngsters have a tangible grasp of what a business, a college, or a work place is; of abstract concepts such as democracy; of appropriate and inappropriate behavior; and of certain common feelings and sentiments, such as that reading is pleasant and informative, and that sitting for long periods of time in school and being attentive can be a bit troublesome but that it will be rewarding.

Checking Assumptions: The Difference Inventory

The primary purpose of the Differences category is to remind us to check out the relationship between our assumptions and the facts in order to determine if the difference category might be a source of literacy and learning problems. Once sensitized to the issue, most elements of difference can be identified by simple observation, interview, and reflection, others may require some instruments to guide investigation.

An instrument that we find useful in this regard is the Difference Inventory (Meeks, Eanet, & Manzo, 1976). This instrument is relatively easy to use, and can be given in oral or silent reading form (see Boxes 5.3 and 5.4). One should also feel free to reword items to meet situational needs. For purposes of interpretation, it generally should be assumed that a student will respond to each item with a 4 or a 5 on a five-point scale. Any deviations, therefore, are notable as potential areas of difference from the assumptions of most schools. Some additional criteria have been established for cases where differences are most likely to have an impact on literacy and related academic development (Meeks, Eanet, & Manzo, 1976). These are discussed ahead.

BOX 5.3

Difference Inventory of School Compatibility
Student Form

Anthony V. Manzo
Jane W. Meeks
Marilyn G. Eanet

Directions: Study each statement below. On a scale of one (1) to five (5), rank the extent to which you think each statement describes you or expresses the way you feel:

1 = **Not like you**
2 = **Slightly like you**
3 = **Somewhat or occasionally like you**
4 = **A good deal, but not completely, like you**
5 = **Very much like you**

* *

_____   1. I like being the way I am.
_____   2. I am pleased with the way I look.
_____   3. I feel sure of myself most of the time.
_____   4. Generally, I think I am pleasant to be with.
_____   5. I feel content most of the time.
_____   6. I take pride in my work.
_____   7. I do not mind speaking before a group of students or adults.
_____   8. I believe that I will become better at almost everything I do as I grow older.
_____   9. I seldom do things that I am really sorry for.
_____   10. I try to avoid students who are constantly getting into trouble.
_____   11. When I become frustrated in school, I double my effort.
_____   12. I would rather do something of medium difficulty than something that is too easy or too difficult.
_____   13. When I have failed to learn the first time, I try again and again.
_____   14. I rarely blame others for my failures.
_____   15. I try to improve myself by watching to see what other successful people are doing.
_____   16. I do not believe in gaining popularity just by getting attention.
_____   17. I believe that accuracy and care are important in most things I do.

BOX 5.3

Difference Inventory of School Compatibility (*continued*)

_____ 18. When I read school-like materials, I try to remember all that I can.

_____ 19. I tend to do what the teacher thinks is best.

_____ 20. I have a few close friends and several acquaintances.

_____ 21. School is a good place for making friends.

_____ 22. When things go wrong, I feel that I can get them straightened out.

_____ 23. If I don't understand something, I ask questions until I do.

_____ 24. The whole idea of learning new things appeals to me.

_____ 25. I enjoy hearing people tell about themselves.

_____ 26. Poetry can be interesting.

_____ 27. I enjoy reading and hearing stories.

_____ 28. I feel that it is important to write well.

_____ 29. I like arithmetic.

_____ 30. I try to speak clearly and distinctly.

_____ 31. I like work that requires care and precision.

_____ 32. I could enjoy being a librarian.

_____ 33. I like to work with others.

_____ 34. I would rather listen than talk.

_____ 35. I like conservative and reserved clothing.

_____ 36. I like the color blue.

_____ 37. I like plants and animals.

_____ 38. The members of my family usually eat one meal a day together.

_____ 39. Reading is an important leisure time activity in our home.

_____ 40. I live with two parents or guardians.

_____ 41. I have travelled for fun and vacation.

_____ 42. I like educational TV shows.

_____ 43. I eat breakfast.

_____ 44. I get plenty of sleep (at least 7 hours).

_____ 45. We receive several magazines at home.

_____ 46. I personally know some professional people (teachers, doctors, lawyers).

_____ 47. I have relatives who have graduated from college.

_____ 48. I have relatives who own their own homes.

_____ 49. I know people who own a business.

_____ 50. The English that we speak at home is about the same as you would hear on television.

_____ 51. I probably will go to college or a trade school after high school.

BOX 5.3

Difference Inventory of School Compatibility (*continued*)

_____ 52. Most of the people I know belong to a church.

_____ 53. I probably could become a congressman(woman) if I really tried.

_____ 54. I believe that it is possible for me to become mayor of this city.

_____ 55. I feel that I will become something like: an insurance agent, a hairdresser, or a health-care worker.

_____ 56. I feel that I am working toward a better life.

_____ 57. I feel I probably will have my own business someday.

_____ 58. I might become a newspaper reporter.

_____ 59. I might become a teacher or professor.

_____ 60. I believe in saving for a rainy day.

_____ 61. I would do extra credit projects in school.

_____ 62. I see my future in athletics.

_____ 63. I might become a performing artist—an actor, musician, showman, etc.

_____ 64. I generally feel proud of my race and culture.

_____ 65. Other people also tend to think highly of my race and culture.

_____ 66. I feel as if I know many of the characters we read about in books.

_____ 67. I can often identify with the main character in a story.

_____ 68. I don't mind sitting still and listening in class.

_____ 69. The type of food served in school is pretty much like the type we eat at home.

_____ 70. I get a lot of encouragement to do well in school.

_____ 71. I can usually get help with my school work when I need it.

_____ 72. I don't really mind doing homework.

Interestingly, the greatest value in administering an instrument such as the Difference Inventory is not in the scores that it yields, but in the diagnostic conversation that it brings about with students on a variety of issues and aspects of life and learning. The discussion often induces a kind of mature exchange that builds appreciation in the student for someone caring enough to ask about him or her, and empathy and even friendship in the teacher/examiner. This is almost always reflected in the diagnostic write-up, and in subsequent instructional decisions.

BOX 5.4

Interpretation of the Difference Inventory

The Difference Inventory originally was devised for use in a survey of the reading needs of middle school students attending city schools with a multi-ethnic population. It has since been used and quasi-normed with youngsters in a wide variety of situations and circumstances (Meeks, Eanet, & Manzo, 1976). The instrument tends to reveal the extent to which student self-confidence, background, experiences, values, and attitudes are the same or different from the preconceptions and standard expectations upon which school programs tend to be based. The instrument not only gives an indication of the degree to which students differ, but how they differ as well.

The first 25 statements are a self- and social-concept scale based on the paradigmatic, or basic, questions: "Do you like yourself?" "How much?" "In what ways?" The low end of the normal range for achieving students is 75% compatibility on these items, for an average of 3.75 per item and 94 out of a possible 125 as a raw score on the 25 items. Students scoring at 70% compatibility or below on the first 25 items tend to be in a high-risk to fail category. There are exceptions to this generalization. Some students compensate for feelings of insecurity and inadequacy by making exaggerated statements of self-worth. This is not uncommon among Afro-American youngsters. Similarly, it is not uncommon for foreign-born East Asians to *under*state how they really feel about themselves.

Items 26–72 measure feelings, lifestyle, and related socio-educational factors that tend to influence academic achievement. These are important, since a look at the assumptions of most schools reveals that school tends to be Anglo, sedentary, family/church/order-oriented, and based on the belief that students have had fair opportunities to sample life's alternatives. Past data suggest that percentage scores also should be in the 75% range, or about 3.75 per item. Working class urban youngsters tend to score about 70%, while working class suburban students score about 73%. Students who go on to post-secondary education tend to score above 77%, and those that go on to graduate school above 79%. As a rule of thumb, students scoring at 68% or below on items 26–72 appear to be at a high-risk to fail (Meeks, Eanet, & Manzo, 1976).

Items 26–72 may be further grouped in the following ways:

1. Temperament and hope. This category gives evidence that an individual is at ease and ready for the next step in development, which in Abraham Maslow's Hierarchy of Needs Scale would be cognitive and aesthetic pursuits. Analysis of individual responses often produces insights into a student's areas of interest and motivation. Examples: I like poetry; I feel it is important to write well.
2. Familiarity with life options. Are students aware of possible choices and options for professional, business, or trade vocations? This is becoming

> ## BOX 5.4
>
> ### Interpretation of the Difference Inventory (*continued*)
>
> increasingly important as fewer youngsters get to see adults engaged in their occupations. Examples: I know people who own a business; I feel that I could become something like an insurance agent, hairdresser, or health-care worker; I could be a mayor.
>
> 3. Exposure to cognitive and aesthetic pursuits. This category reveals if the student has had broadening experiences, and comfort with textual material. Examples: I have travelled for fun and vacation; We receive several different kinds of magazines at home; I enjoy poetry; I can often identify with the main character in a story.
> 4. Family unit. Does the student's family function as a traditional unit? Examples: The members of my family usually eat one meal a day together; I live with two parents or guardians.
> 5. Biological needs. Are the basic physical and nutritional needs of the student as expected? Examples: I eat a good breakfast; I get plenty of sleep (at least 7 hours).
> 6. Family expectations identified with cultural strata. How closely does the student identify with the culture and values typical of middle America? Examples: I like conservative and reserved clothing; I like plants and animals; I like the color blue (symbol of serenity and security).

> ➤   **LOOKING BACK**   ◄
>
> The chapter covered issues and methods for assessing vision, hearing, neurological considerations, IQ, emotionality, and learning and lifestyle differences. Most instruments were presented as survey forms that could be used to make referrals, or as heuristics to build your own insights and wisdom about the relevance of a factor to literacy in general or to a specific student.

> ### ➤ LOOKING AHEAD
>
> The next chapter continues in the same vein. However, it focuses more on observations, interviews, and conferences with children, parents, and other teachers. It covers the gamut from "intake" interviewing to final conferencing. Look especially for recommendations of actual phrasing that some master diagnosticians and clinicians tend to use in such complex interactions.

Observing, Interviewing, Conferring, Reporting

> "Many have eyes, but few can see."
> SHAKESPEARE

➤ **LOOK FOR IT**

The ability to "see" comes from making a mental commitment to do so. Observing, or "professional seeing," requires even further commitment, since it implies objective recording and reflecting. Much of what it takes to be a skilled professional is based on the proposition that you must intentionally seek out certain heuristics—or evokers—that will key you to see and understand better the literacy and related needs of children. Several instruments were suggested in the previous chapter as specific means of helping you see and reflect better upon a variety of students' literacy, learning, and personal-social adjustment needs. This chapter further explores methodological heuristics for enhancing the professional skill of "seeing" with a keen eye. These tend to be compatible with the role of the diagnostician, but are not incompatible with that of the classroom teacher.

Methods for enhancing professional "seeing" can be divided into front-end, in-process, and reflective systems. Front-end systems tend to rely on early observing and interviewing. In-process systems tend to rely on more systematic observations using checklists, rating scales, observational schedules, anecdotal accounts, and portfolio analysis. Reflective systems tend to rely on conferencing (with parents, teachers, and children) and report writing. Of course, these systems are intertwined. For this reason, the topic of observing is taken up first, since it often provides the point of departure for more intensive observation, interviewing, and subsequent testing and reporting.

Observing

Physical scientists essentially are professional observers. They watch and study nature as a means of learning how it gets things done, and as a way of understanding the physical world. Sociologists and anthropologists play this same role where people are concerned. Sociologists, anthropologists, and some psychologists who observe people in their natural state, for essentially the same reasons as do physical scientists, are called ethnographers. Much of the methodology of observation being used in contemporary education is derived from ethnography. Since educators are involved with their subjects in a more interactive way, they also must engage in a more sophisticated form of observing that may be called improvisational observing. This type of observing tends to be more naturalistic and unobtrusive (Moore, 1983), and it permits the observation of contextualized "peak performances" (Wood, 1988, p. 440) as balancing points for the pressurized, de-contextualized type of assessment that is sometimes served up by conventional testing. Descriptions and examples of ethnographic and improvisational systems are described ahead.

Ethnographic Observing (Kid Watching)

A recent study by Eula Monroe, Arden Watson, and Debra Tweddell (1989) made it clear that teachers can be very accurate in predicting children's IQ's, oral comprehension, and reading test scores. Hence, ethnographic research, observing, or "kid watching," as Yetta Goodman (1985) has referred to it, can be a powerful tool in diagnosis, because it tends to:

- occur in conditions that are more representative of typical functioning.
- have the benefit of a context and a human mind to see children for who they are.
- be open-ended, and continue until the observer is satisfied that what is being observed is truly characteristic of the learner.

However, there can be problems with free-form observations. They can become biased by the observer's subconscious psychological occupations, and they require a strong background of knowledge. Angela Jaggar (1985) suggests that teachers make clear decisions before observing, as to what they will attend to, as well as how, when, and where they will do the observing. Checklists and observational schedules help to overcome both of these problems by calling attention to behaviors that have been found to be important in prior research and clinical experience. This helps the observer to record more objectively and focus on relevant behaviors. Checklists also make it possible for the same person and others to review the observations from more reflective and different perspectives.

In slight counterpoint, the teacher can and should be open to understanding the teaching-learning process better with each interaction and from each pupil we experience. See Box 6.1 for an example from Carol Kirk (1990) of what she learned from teaching "Mitch."

Checklists and Rating Scales

Checklists are a means of guiding "seeing." They can be simple or very complex. They usually require a mere check to indicate that a certain behavior has been observed. Box 6.2 offers a fairly comprehensive list of Reading Behaviors. This larger list can be abbreviated, and more than one student's name listed so that you may observe three to five youngsters at a time.

Rating scales provide an even more structured and specific level of observation and evaluation. These are better used by someone who is not involved in an interaction. Box 6.3 offers an example of a rating scale that is useful in monitoring classroom participation, which often is a bellwether, or leading indicator, of academic and social-emotional health.

There are other indicators of personal-social *maladjustment* that are offered by some writers. Eldon Ekwall and James Shanker (1988), for example, list eighteen such indicators. These range from "Fails to sustain interest and effort" to "Exhibits nail-biting" (p. 267). Lists of inappropriate behaviors generally are of little value since it is impossible to make a list of all possible deviant behaviors. Furthermore, any behavior may be "deviant" to a greater or lesser degree depending upon situational elements: whether the behavior was contextually inappropriate, whether it was excessive, and whether it is part of a larger pattern of irregular development. One means of collecting a fair sampling and context for making these determinations is keeping anecdotal records.

Anecdotal Records

Anecdotal records once were the preferred means of gaining insight into students. Within the last 30 years, these subjective records came to be replaced by objective test records. Now, as we have begun to see the error in relying on test data alone, anecdotal records are being rediscovered as a valuable means of helping us not lose sight of the larger picture (namely, the pupil) more so than just his or her reading progress.

At best, anecdotal records are unbiased notes, written by the teacher, that represent the child's typical mode of behavior. They can be made any time the teacher observes behaviors that are notably characteristic of the student, or

> ## BOX 6.1
>
> ### Lessons from Mitch
>
> Mitch. "Remedial." Behind in reading, behind in writing ever since I first taught him in seventh grade. Mitch came to me again his junior year.
>
> "I hear you're teaching Advanced Comp next semester," he begins.
>
> "Yes."
>
> "I want to be in your class. Can I?"
>
> Mitch? In Advanced Comp? Could he have come so far?
>
> Mitch is a mind reader. "I know I can do it! I want to try and work for at least a *D*."
>
> "Oh boy!" I think. I take the safe road. "Let me think about it," I say, buying time. "I'd like to talk to your language arts teacher and your counselor. If you do this, let's make sure you'll succeed."
>
> "OK. I'll come back tomorrow."
>
> And he does. "I'm ready," he beams.
>
> How can I tell him that his basic-level sophomore composition teacher emphatically proclaimed, "No way!"? That his guidance counselor laughed?
>
> Mitch makes matters worse. "You have to let me try," he begs. "I want to prove to my dad and to myself that I can do this."
>
> He's right. His expectations are high. Mine must match them. I say yes. What have I done?
>
> Mitch's first rough piece is a bust. Short, choppy, rife with incomplete sentences. Yet, it has potential. I am experimenting, adapting a writer's workshop to the high school. Mitch is in a collaborative writing group with Erin, an excellent writer, and three other students. Mitch shares his piece. Response to content is very positive. Mitch's piece is interesting, real and humorous, but disjointed. Erin offers to help. She shows Mitch how to combine sentences so that his piece flows. When I see his final draft, it is wonderful. I share Mitch's piece with the class, using his pen name, Jack Daniels, but everyone knows who wrote it because Mitch's glow lights up the whole room.
>
> Mitch taught me the importance of giving students at risk of failure a chance to stretch themselves toward new goals. Mitch, like many students at risk, wanted to take control of his life. I had to give him that opportunity. It is ironic that students who are considered to be at risk have long stopped taking risks in school. It is the teacher who must make it "safe" to take risks again.
>
> Three critical factors in successful writing classrooms are time, ownership, and response, according to Mary Ellen Giacobbe (Atwell, 1987). Mitch taught me just how important each of these factors is.
>
> *Kirk (1990)*

BOX 6.2

Reading Behaviors Checklist

EMERGENT LITERACY	YES	NO
Listens to stories read	—	—
Knows what a book is	—	—
Hears likenesses in words	—	—
Hears differences in words	—	—
Understands reading is done from left to right	—	—
Hears sounds at beginnings of words	—	—
Hears sounds at ends of words	—	—
Knows basic concepts (such as small, medium, & large)	—	—
Sees likenesses in letters	—	—
Sees differences in letters	—	—
Sees likenesses in words	—	—
Sees differences in words	—	—
Identifies letters of the alphabet	—	—
Can write name	—	—
Can tell a story in sequence	—	—
Provides endings for incomplete sentences	—	—
Has a basic sight vocabulary	—	—
Visually examines words	—	—
Notes details of words	—	—

WORD RECOGNITION & MEANING	YES	NO
Has meaning vocabulary equal to age-grade expectations	—	—
Identifies words by their configuration	—	—
Identifies words by recognition of initial sounds	—	—
Pronounces phonic elements	—	—
Uses phonic elements to identify words	—	—
Notes endings of words (s, ed, ing, ly, est, 's)	—	—
Identifies root words	—	—
Identifies parts of compound words	—	—
Uses parts of compound words to identify new word	—	—
Identifies prefixes	—	—
Uses prefixes to identify new words	—	—
Identifies suffixes	—	—
Uses suffixes to aid word pronunciation	—	—
Identifies significant letter clusters	—	—
Uses syllables to aid word pronunciation	—	—
Uses context clues to aid word recognition	—	—
Uses context clues to aid vocabulary growth	—	—

> ## BOX 6.2
>
> ### Reading Behaviors Checklist (*continued*)
>
> | Comprehension | Yes | No |
> |---|---|---|
> | Can follow oral directions | — | — |
> | Can follow written directions | — | — |
> | Uses wide vocabulary in oral expression | — | — |
> | Identifies main idea in a selection | — | — |
> | Recalls details of a story | — | — |
> | Recalls sequence of events in story | — | — |
> | Identifies main characters in story | — | — |
> | Summarizes main points in a selection | — | — |
> | States inferences drawn from a selection | — | — |
> | Applies what is read | — | — |
> | Thinks critically | — | — |
> | Thinks constructively | — | — |
>
> | Writing | Yes | No |
> |---|---|---|
> | Can write a meaningful sentence | — | — |
> | Can write a meaningful paragraph | — | — |
> | Can write a meaningful story | — | — |
> | Can write a meaningful summary | — | — |
> | Can write a meaningful reaction | — | — |
>
> | Attitudes Toward Literacy | Yes | No |
> |---|---|---|
> | Selects books voluntarily | — | — |
> | Requests favorite stories | — | — |
> | Asks questions related to his reading | — | — |
> | Discusses ideas gained from reading | — | — |
> | Expresses ideas gained from reading through creative art | — | — |
> | Listens during oral reading | — | — |
>
> *Flood and Lapp (1989)*

behaviors that seem to be out of character, or behaviors that illustrate a student's response to a certain kind of task or stimulus. In this sense, anecdotal observations are like voice activated tape recorders that are also smart: they not only go on when there is sound, but when the sounds being emitted are potentially meaningful and significant.

Anecdotal records should be brief, factual accounts that more or less speak for themselves. The simplest way to remind yourself to make these is to prepare

---

BOX 6.3

Class Participation

	VERY LOW	LOW	AVERAGE	HIGH	VERY HIGH
1. Is ready for discussion	1	2	3	4	5
2. Listens when others speak	1	2	3	4	5
3. Answers correctly when called	1	2	3	4	5
4. Volunteers to answer	1	2	3	4	5
5. Volunteers questions	1	2	3	4	5
6. Volunteers relevant comments	1	2	3	4	5
7. Speaks without noticeable nervousness or domination	1	2	3	4	5
8. Particpates without thoughtless domination	1	2	3	4	5
9. Shows insightful thinking	1	2	3	4	5
10. Accepts critical feedback	1	2	3	4	5

Flood and Lapp (1989)

---

some index cards, as shown in Figure 6.1 below, and to fill one out on every student at least twice a semester. If you are a reading specialist, you might ask a student's teacher(s) to fill out a few in a shorter period of time: one or two per month for several months.

Earl Cheek, Rona Flippo, and Jimmy Linsey (1989) suggest using the same cards to make brief, unscheduled anecdotal accounts: simply flip over one of the cards, then record and date pertinent comments. For example:

9/15   Joe handed in his first completed assignment this term.
10/10   I hadn't noticed before, but Mark moves his lips and moves his finger to keep his place when he reads silently.

For a more compact method of recording anecdotal observations, try the single folder system. Use a plain 8½ x 11 inch folder and 5 x 8 inch file cards: one card for each student in a class. Tape the first card lengthwise on the bottom left side of the folder. Then tape the next card lengthwise about 1/2 inch higher. Continue taping cards at half inch intervals up to the top of the left-hand side of the folder, then repeat the process to prepare the right-hand side. When the folder is complete, write each child's name on the visible half-inch border of a card, making an easily visible flip-up card for each child, as shown in Figure 6.2.

FIGURE 6.1

Sample Cards: Anecdotal Observation

	Date: 10/12
Name: James Bean	**Observer**: Sawyer
Place & Situation: Library/Book selection	
Observation: Looks around at everyone else, but not at books. Finally picked up a book when he realized that I might be watching him.	
Interpretation: More people than task oriented	

Name: Nancy New	**Observer**: Sawyer
Place & Situation: Class discussion of science selection	
Observation: Quick to speak up in science, but says things that are largely irrelevant. Nancy doesn't speak up as quickly in literature discussions, but her responses are more relevant.	
Interpretation: When Nancy is uncertain of herself, she appears to compensate by being more aggressive. I wonder if I should bring this to her attention(?)	

Informal observations can be noted on self-adhesive stickers, and affixed to the cards when time permits.

There is another form of anecdotal record that the student participates in collecting, and is designed to mark progress more than to note deviancy. It is based on the classic concept of portfolio collection.

Portfolio Assessment

Artists rely on portfolios to show what they can do and how they have progressed through various stages and periods. A resume prepared for a job or in consideration of a promotion is based on the same principle—showing where you've been, where you are, and where you could be going. Faced with years of continuous schooling, and with so much of their lives in front of them, students deserve no less.

Portfolios for Students

Portfolio assessment is a simple means by which a student begins to collect his or her best works, as well as some works that simply are representative of earlier stages of learning. These can be essays, homework assignments, class tests,

FIGURE 6.2

Anecdotal Record Folder

ELAINE, A.	MEGAN, M.
DERRICK, B.	RANDY, M.
JANELLE, B.	CHRISTOPHER, N.
PATRICIA, C.	NANCY, N.
CALVIN, D.	SAM, N.
HAKEEM, D.	BELINDA, N.
STEPHEN, E.	WILL, O.
WALTER, F.	SCOTT, P.
COURTNEY, F.	FRANKLIN, R.
VALERIE, H.	WHITNEY, R.
MARVIN, H.	THOMAS, T.
JOHN, K.	RICHARD, V.
CAREY, L.	EDWARD, V.
LAURIE, L.	DARLENE, W.

artistic representations, or even extra-curricular productions: anything the student feels to be representative of developing skills and abilities, or just meaningful experiences.

The single most important value of a portfolio is that it provides a tangible place to store signs of progress more so than just the errors and false-starts made while acquiring a skill. It is also something that the students have control over—something that they do for themselves rather than merely for others.

Teacher and student critiques or comments and evaluations may be added to the portfolio for a further dimension of meaning. Here is a sample teacher comment:

Jackie and I agree that this account of her problems with keeping her bike "unbro-ken" is one of the most amusing and best things she has written to date.

Mrs. Serronne, 10/10/91

Portfolio collection obviously is something that is best done in the classroom. Generally, they are kept in an easily accessible part of the room, unlike grade books and permanent records that are secretive and stored elsewhere. However, a special reading teacher can set up folders for her students as a depository for their good works and, in the process, begin to collect some alternative and balancing impressions of each student. Portfolios can be especially revealing when students are asked to add a few sentences indicating either what they thought about while they were doing a certain project, or why they selected a particular item for inclusion in their portfolio. Here are examples of student notations of this type:

All I could think of while I was doing this report on our dirty rivers was how can I convince my father to stop fishing and forcing us to eat his big catch.

I included this tape recording of myself in the class play because I thought I was pretty good. I also was hoping to keep it as a reminder of how I have changed when I get older.

The value of portfolios in building a more holistic view of children and in understanding the effective and counter-effective aspects of schooling is just beginning to be appreciated. One thing, however, already is clear: portfolios build self-esteem and internal motivation by offering authentic reasons to do good work. Students learn the virtues of improvement as they initiate, revise, and embellish drafts of their own work, as opposed to the conventional cycle of writing or cramming, and then being criticized and having to accept a grade gamely. Portfolios are especially suitable for at-risk students for whom a self-guidance system is a necessity more than a nicety. Portfolios tend to create every desirable kind of interaction between teacher and student: diagnostic dialogue, instructional conversation, and a natural therapeutic dialogue. Some examples of items for inclusion in student portfolios are listed in Figure 6.3. For additional information on this emergent area of literacy assessment see: Au, Scheu, Kawakami, and Hermann (1988); Lucas (1988); Valencia (1990); Wolf (1980).

Portfolios for Parents

James Flood and Diane Lapp (1989) recommend portfolios for parents. This recommendation reflects sensitivity and insight into the larger issue of how at-risk children are perceived by their parents. Schools typically offer parents a picture of their children's progress that is based on summative evaluations: class grades and standardized test scores. Flood and Lapp point out that children operating close to their potentials, but who still have low percentile scores on standardized tests, will appear to parents to be hopelessly "behind" and not making progress. A portfolio assembled for such parents permits the teacher and the child to show that it is largely the child's *pace* that is slower, but that progress may still be occurring. This is a point that the student can benefit from as well. It can be done very simply, by presenting "before and after" examples of writing, types of spelling and vocabulary words being tackled, and representative passages of reading material. These can be charted to dramatize effort and progress further, even while the student's percentile ranking may not have changed markedly (see Figure 6.4).

FIGURE 6.3

Anatomy of a Student Portfolio*

- Periodic anecdotal accounts from teachers
- Quarterly writing samples from a variety of perspectives and across genre: journal writing, personal narrative, fiction, nonfiction, poetry
- Evidence of progress in spelling
- Evidence of progress in comprehension checks and on content tests
- Protocols from IRI or IR-TI (see Chapter 13)
- Taped oral readings
- Drawings
- Photographs of self or photographs taken by student

*Concept from Lois Bridges Bird (1991)

FIGURE 6.4

Charting Children's Growth in Reading: Alternatives to Standardized Tests
A. Charting a Child's Growth in Reading a Single Text

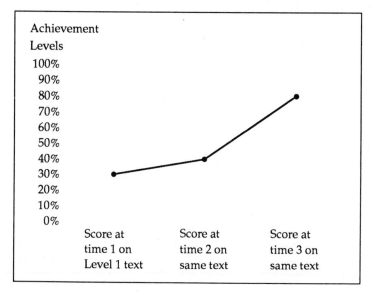

FIGURE 6.4

Charting Children's Growth in Reading: Alternatives to Standardized Tests (*continued*)

B. Charting a Child's Progress on Texts of Increasing Difficulty

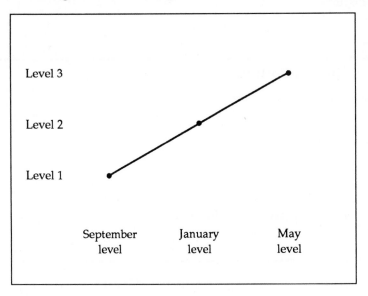

C. Charting a Child's Growth in Voluntary Reading

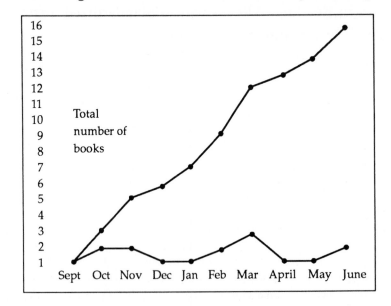

Flood & Lapp (1989)

Improvisational Observing

Improvisational observing refers to the use of nonstandard *procedures* with standardized test formats or protocols. The examiner exercises a clinical option to probe beyond conventional test protocols to induce a student's peak performance, or to uncover how the student operates under different levels of challenge. Through improvisational observing, the examiner can fill in missing pieces of information that could not be collected in a standardized test format nor by routine observation. This often can provide a more realistic assessment of a student's actual level of instructional need. It is, in effect, a way to reach a more qualitative type of "instructional reading level."

The improvisational approach has a long history in testing and teaching (Barr, Sadow, & Blackowizc, 1990; Cioffi & Carney, 1983, 1990; Clay, 1985; Durrell, 1955; Hamilton, 1983; Johnston, 1987; Paratore & Indrisano, 1987). The notion is based on a supposition that was best stated by Feuerstein (1979) in work on intellectual assessment:

> The potential for being modified by learning should be the object of focus in psychometric assessment. This potential can be measured only by an active, involved, and involving process, and can never be revealed by a static enumeration of existing abilities. Indeed, one wonders why it has taken us so long to realize that the only way to assess potential for change is to attempt to modify the examinee in some way, while measuring the extent of the change and the means by which this was attained. (as cited in Carney & Cioffi, 1990, p. 49)

John Carney and Grant Cioffi (1990), who call this type of improvisation "dynamic assessment," have developed some guidelines for its use (see Figure 6.5). An example of these guidelines in operation in assessing level of need in word analysis and recognition is shown in Box 6.4.

Observing Teachers and Children

Rounding out the topic of observations is the pioneering work of Rita Bean, William Cooley, R. Tony Eichelberger, Meryl Lazar, and Naomi Zigmond (1991). These researchers have designed a system for observing remediation in progress so as to appraise what is taking place, or failing to take place. The system, called SORIN (System for Observing Reading Instruction), is based on earlier unpublished work by Bean, Lazar, and Zigmond (1987). The categories in the SORIN system are instructive in themselves in terms of what we, as teachers, can be doing, the direction a lesson may take, and what students might be experiencing (see Figure 6.6).

The researchers who developed SORIN used it in two phases of a recent study that compared teacher behavior, student behavior, and lesson focus in remedial "in-class" and "pull-out" settings. In the first phase, they observed each child for 5 seconds, then coded the teacher behavior experienced by that child during the next 5 seconds, for a total of 7 teacher behavior codings during each observation. In the second phase, data were collected on other aspects of the lesson: lesson focus, types of materials used, and difficulty level of materials.

FIGURE 6.5

Guidelines for Dynamic Assessment

Assessment Content (ANTICIPATED RESPONSE)	ALTERNATIVE INSTRUCTIONAL EPISODES
I. Word Recognition in Isolation (Rapid and Correct Identification)	display word for analysis present word in context (contextual analysis) divide word into syllables (phonic analysis) divide word into morphemes (structural analysis) compare word with a similar but easier item (initial phoneme substitution) identify word for student (direct instruction)
II. Word Recognition in Context	preteach low frequency vocabulary (Unrehearsed Fluent Reading) provide opportunity for rehearsal model passage for student
III. Comprehension—Oral and Silent Reading (Correct Response to Comprehension Questions)	*Prereading Activities* preteach low frequency vocabulary activate appropriate prior knowledge preteach difficult concepts provide direction for reading identify organizing principles *Postreading Activities* provide forced-choice responses ask student to find answers direct student to key section of the text

Carney and Cioffi (1990)

The setting in which the lessons occurred proved to have a great impact on how teachers organized and conducted lessons (Bean, et.al., 1991). The researchers plan to move on to try to determine how these differences affect student learning outcomes.

We shall return now to the topic of observing students, though in a different setting. The topic is interviewing. It falls somewhere between passive and improvisational observing, in that it requires a considerable amount of mental agility to probe and listen at the same time. It seems comparable to the task of metacognitive processing that we expect students to engage in while reading.

Interviewing

Just as testing, observation, and portfolio analyses provide the data bases for supporting or refuting suppositions about students, interviewing offers the best

BOX 6.4

Example of Dynamic Assessment of Word Recognition

In this example, Carney and Cioffi illustrate how to understand the nature of a poor reader's pattern of errors better, in this case on a standardized test, by seeing just what kind of teaching must be done to overcome specific word analysis and recognition problems. The process is based on progressively "slicing," or simplifying, component parts of the task until the student can handle it.

Gary, whose total reading score on the Stanford Achievement Test is at the 12th percentile, begins by reading preprimer and primer lists with no errors. On the grade two list, Gary makes one error, reading the word "scarecrow" as "scarcrow." When the examiner presents the word structurally (scare crow), Gary responds correctly. At grade three, Gary corrects two errors made on the initial flash presentation when the words are placed in context. The third word (though) is taught using several strategies, but Gary does not respond appropriately. The examiner then tells Gary what the word is. At both levels four and five, Gary makes five initial errors on the ten word samples. He corrects all five errors at the grade four level as a result of dynamic intervention and four of five errors at grade five. One instructional episode will illustrate the dynamic procedure. Gary reads the word "rough" as "rush," then "ranch." He does, however, recognize the word "tough" in context; the examiner then uses initial consonant substitution to move Gary from "tough" to "rough."

An analysis of Gary's performance under the two conditions—static, as measured by the initial response to the word, and dynamic—provides two very different profiles, particularly as Gary approaches his present grade/age placement. At the grade four and five levels, Gary's initial responses are incorrect in half the cases. Yet his performance with the instructional support provided in the dynamic assessment reaches levels that are age and grade appropriate (10/10—grade four; 9/10—grade five). In addition to these quantitative results, the analysis of the instructional episodes that constitute the dynamic assessment provides a pattern of behaviors that are a rich source of information for remedial intervention. In Gary's case, for example, it was found that most of his incorrect responses were graphically similar to the target word. In all cases, the examiner was able to elicit an appropriate phonic generalization, either by presenting a similar word or by dividing the stimulus word into syllables or morphemes. This suggests that Gary has appropriate phonic skills to identify words at grade level, but that he does not use phonic generalizations spontaneously. When cued to do so, Gary responds appropriately.

Carney and Cioffi (1990)

FIGURE 6.6

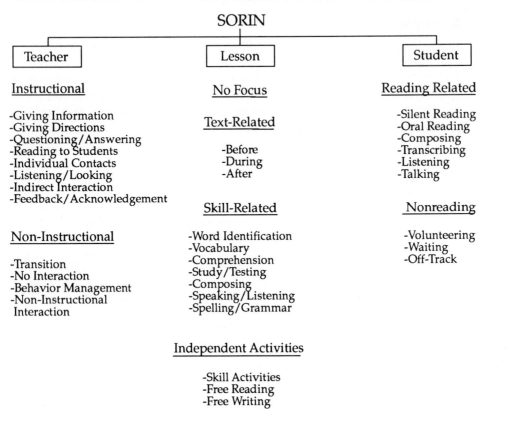

SORIN

| Teacher | Lesson | Student |

Instructional · No Focus · Reading Related

Teacher — Instructional:
-Giving Information
-Giving Directions
-Questioning/Answering
-Reading to Students
-Individual Contacts
-Listening/Looking
-Indirect Interaction
-Feedback/Acknowledgement

Teacher — Non-Instructional:
-Transition
-No Interaction
-Behavior Management
-Non-Instructional Interaction

Lesson — Text-Related:
-Before
-During
-After

Lesson — Skill-Related:
-Word Identification
-Vocabulary
-Comprehension
-Study/Testing
-Composing
-Speaking/Listening
-Spelling/Grammar

Lesson — Independent Activities:
-Skill Activities
-Free Reading
-Free Writing

Student — Reading Related:
-Silent Reading
-Oral Reading
-Composing
-Transcribing
-Listening
-Talking

Student — Nonreading:
-Volunteering
-Waiting
-Off-Track

Bean, Cooley, Eichelberger, Lazar, and Zigmond (1991)

means of raising hypotheses. Interviews with parents, children, and other teachers also are the most efficient means of learning about all aspects of a student's difficulties in learning, including deficiencies, defects, disruptions, and differences. An "in-take" interview can be so productive that it may be in order even for youngsters that you may think you know well. Get ready for an interview by thinking of yourself as preparing a student's biography.

Interview as Biography

An interview is access to a student's on-going life story with you as the biographer. When properly conducted, the interview can be a powerful heuristic leading to insights for both the interviewer and even the person interviewed. In this sense, it can be therapeutic in itself since it is a formal beginning to accepting and dealing with a problem.

In the chapters ahead, there also are incidental classroom-based strategies for eliciting biographical information related to reading, learning, and study skills (see especially the Problem-Solving Approach to Study Skills and Dialogue Journals). For the moment, however, let's consider some standard pointers for conducting an effective interview.

Guidelines for Diagnostic Interviewing:

As previously noted, there are three kinds of overt instructional dialogue that one needs to develop expertise in to be a master teacher. They are the Diagnostic Dialogue, Instructional Conversations, and the Therapeutic Dialogue. The latter two are developed elsewhere in the text, but consider now how to convert an initial in-take interview into a rich diagnostic dialogue.

1. Enter the interview with a genuine interest in the student, the protagonist in the story that you are assembling.
2. Be sure the child understands who you are and what is being undertaken.
3. When possible, interview the student, both parents, and acquire available anecdotal reports from teachers and former child-care providers.
4. Follow an interview schedule, but don't ignore potentially useful information that might emerge, merely to get through each item on an interview form.
5. Ask for permission to tape record the interview as well as to take notes.
6. Keep a neutral attitude by avoiding approving or rejecting remarks, or even by intermittently taking notes. (Try to write about the same amount throughout the interview.)
7. Ask, intermittently, if there is anything else that the child or parent might wish to add even to simple biographical questions, and then remember to *pause* for a response.
8. Ask, intermittently, "why" they think something is as they report (e.g. "*Why is it, do you think, that you don't like math?*")
9. Remember to ask some open-ended questions: "Tell me about your reading"; "Do you think her reading problem is affecting other aspects of her school or personal life?"
10. Avoid unnecessary technical terms in questions ("Is he an *introvert?*")
11. Be on guard against the tendency to become overly occupied with yourself in an interview. Self-consciousness and insecurity can cause subconscious ego defense on your part, such as talking too much, speaking in an affected manner, being overly apologetic, or simply appearing too nervous.
12. Listen not only to what youngsters and parents say, but to what they mean.

Figures 6.7 and 6.8 offer examples of two interview schedules that, with slight wording changes, may be used with a child or with parents. Figure 6.8 offers an interview schedule that is better directed at parents or guardians. First, however, consider the careful wording offered by Roselmina Indrisano (1982) as a means of initiating an empathetic diagnostic conversation:

> Today we'll try to discover more about you and the ways you learn. We'll need two kinds of experts, one expert on learning and one expert on you. I've studied about learning. You've been making discoveries about yourself all of

FIGURE 6.7

Basic Interview Schedule

Interviewer Information

Date: _____

Examiner: _____

Person being interviewed (if other than the student): _____

Relationship to the student: _____

$$$

Student Information

Name: _____   Birthdate:

Address: _____   Age: _____

_____

_____   Telephone: _____

Siblings: Name	Sex	Age	Grade
_____	_____	_____	_____
_____	_____	_____	_____
_____	_____	_____	_____
_____	_____	_____	_____

$$$

1. The Reading Problem: Do you think it is severe? Do others in the family have a similar problem?

_____

2. Describe home life to me:

_____

3. Tell me about interests and activities, outdoors and indoors: _____

_____

4. About your friends: Who are they? What are they like? _____

_____

5. Home Relationships: Who do you get along best with at home? Who don't you get along with? How is a living earned? Do you have pets? _____

_____

_____

6. Home Responsibilities: Do you have regular chores? What are they? Do you tend to them as you should? _____

_____

7. School: What is the name of your school? Where is it located? What is/are your teacher's name(s)? What grade are you in? How do you feel about school and teachers? What is your favorite and least favorite subject? Why? How do you feel when you are in school (hot/cold; healthy/sickly; comfortable/restless)?

_____

_____

FIGURE 6.7

Basic Interview Schedule (*continued*)

8. What would you most like teachers to change about school? _____
_____

9. What would you most like your parents to change about your home life? _____
_____

10. What would you most like to change about yourself? _____
_____

11. If you had 3 wishes, what would they be: _____
_____
_____

12. What would you like to do for a living when you grow up? _____
_____
_____

your life while you've been living there inside you. If we work together, we will
have the information we need to help you. I'll begin by asking a few questions.
(p. 13)

The interview schedules that follow try to get at five areas that Indrisano
pursues: what the youngster does well; what he/she does not do well; what
coping strategies he/she is using; which coping or learning strategies he/she
isnot using; and what the youngster would most like parents and teachers to
know about him/her so that they can best help him/her to achieve.

This last item is especially important, since it can help the troubled student
see the examiner as his or her agent, and possible means of rescue from further
failure. This, again, is a good example of a diagnostic dialogue that can be
inherently therapeutic as well.

FIGURE 6.8

Parent/Teacher Interview Schedule

Examiner _____
Date _____

General Student Data

Child's Name _____ Birthdate _____ Age _____
Home Address _____ Telephone Number _____
School _____ Grade _____
School Address _____ Telephone Number _____
Person Being Interviewed: _____
(address and phone, if different): _____
_____

SSSSSSSSSSSSSSSSSSSSSSSSSSSSSSSSSSSSSSSSSSSSSSSSSSSSSSSSSSSSSSSSSSSSSSSSSSSSSSSSSSSSSSSSS

FIGURE 6.8

Parent/Teacher Interview Schedule (*continued*)

I. Home Background

Father's Name: _____ Occupation: _____

Mother's Name: _____ Occupation: _____

Siblings: Name   Sex   Age   Grade

_____ _____ _____ _____

_____ _____ _____ _____

_____ _____ _____ _____

Other persons living in the home: _____

Marital status of parents: _____

With whom does child live? _____

Child's relationships with other family members (close to; at odds with):

_____

Language spoken in the home: _____

Examples of reading matter in the home: _____

_____

Parent's attitude toward reading difficulties: _____

_____

§§

II. Physical Status

General health (poor, good, excellent) _____

Date of last complete physical examination: _____

Doctor's name and address: _____

Major chronic illnesses, operations, accidents, and allergies: _____

_____

_____

Physical handicaps: _____

Present height: _____   Present weight: _____

Vision: _____   Hearing: _____

Speech: _____   Motor coordination: _____

Preferred hand: _____

Rest and sleep habits: _____

Energy and strength levels: _____

Eating habits; appetite: _____

Tensions: _____

Outdoor activities: _____

Other: _____

_____

§§

FIGURE 6.8

Parent/Teacher Interview Schedule (*continued*)

III. Emotional Factors

Indicate behavior patterns observed on a 1 to 5 scale, with 1 = lowest and 5 = highest:

___ aggressive	___ hyperactive	___ overly dependent
___ anxiety	___ hypoactive	___ poor self-control
___ apathetic	___ immature	___ sense of humor
___ curious	___ impulsive	___ sensitivity
___ daydreams	___ infantile behavior	___ social success
___ defensive	___ inferiority complex	___ talkative
___ fearful	___ nail biting	___ thumb sucking
___ hostile	___ obsessive	___ withdrawn

Comments on personal-social adjustment: _____

_____

_____

§§§

IV. School History

Day care/preschool experiences: _____

Kindergarten experience: _____

Age at entrance to first grade: _____

Schools attended: _____

Has attendance been regular? _____

Grades skipped or repeated: _____

Approximate report card grades or yearly grade level achievement (disregard if cumulative record is attached):

Grade:	1	2	3	4	5	6	7	8	9	10	11	12
Reading												
Language Arts												
Handwriting												
Spelling												
Arithmetic												
Social Studies												
Science												
Other:												

FIGURE 6.8

Parent/Teacher Interview Schedule (*continued*)

Recent test results: _____

Date   Test   Score

_____   _____   _____

_____   _____   _____

_____   _____   _____

_____   _____   _____

Favorite subject: _____ Least favorite subject: _____

Special abilities: _____

Comments on schooling: _____

_____

_____

§§§

V. Reading Progress

Type of initial reading instruction: _____

Child's attitude toward reading: _____

Reading interests: _____

When were reading difficulties first noticed? _____

_____

Type of difficulties noted: _____

_____

Remedial effort of any type to date: _____

_____

Present status in reading: _____

_____

Are there any other facts in the child's reading or academic history that you think
might help to explain present difficulties in reading and learning?

_____

_____

While the interview system provides a perspective and a backdrop for
initiating an intensive diagnosis, it is through the analogous system of conferencing that diagnostic information is shared and the groundwork for remediation is firmly lain.

Conferencing

A conference, in this context, is an assessment debriefing that attempts to pull
together all that has been learned from referral, observation, interviewing, and

testing. It is a dynamic report that involves the child, parents, and other professionals who may have participated in the diagnosis.

Typically, the report is addressed to the parents, but much of the conference can and should be addressed to the youngster. The conference may take place within 30 minutes of final testing, or scheduled for another time, though preferably not more than a few days later.

Youngsters usually find themselves flattered by all the attention and tend to behave quite maturely. Parents typically are touched by the interest and concern shown for the child.

A conference tends to serve an important healing role for a youngster who may be feeling a bit overexamined and overscrutinized. Every debriefing is a little bit different, but all are an education for those concerned. (See Chapter 11 for another form of debriefing following remediation suggested by Nancy Lee Cecil [1990].)

In a team-based assessment, it is best to have each team member report on areas relevant to their expertise, or at least on the tests and the roles they play. The team leader should keep the discussion going and ensure that each team member's presentation is concise and to the point. The best way to begin a conference is by addressing a question to the youngster who was diagnosed: "Can you tell us your idea of why you were here to be tested today?" Questions such as this one can set the stage for some very easy and straightforward reporting of results. On occasion, it also will open up a line of discussion and revelations that you could not have anticipated. These insights may even cause all previous information to be seen in a different light.

This and related questions and test results lead to some remarkably instructive interactions. In such situations, we have seen things like:

- a remedial level child who was surprisingly masterful at manipulating his parents
- parents whose excessive concern about the child's "reading problem" came to be recognized as a substitute for a more serious problem that they seemed on the brink of disclosing but never quite disclosed (we recommended family counseling)
- parents who wished to use the conferencing period as an opportunity to punish the child for failures, or as a vehicle for seeking help with their own interpersonal problems
- comments that revealed a family history of reading problems similar to those the child was displaying.

In general, conferences tend to serve as an effective form of "reality therapy." They tend to confirm what everyone has been thinking and feeling, to establish more realistic expectations, and to raise hope, since the child's problems now are being labelled and addressed.

It is wise to begin collecting actual verbal protocols for talking with students and parents, much as Indrisano (1982) offered for initiating the diagnostic workup. When you have collected and tried a few repeatedly, you might hold a workshop for other teachers on how they have handled parent-teacher conferences and how you do so. Here are some examples of specific findings and the phrasing that generally is most appropriate for post-test conferencing situations.

Finding:	Charles scored in the 37th percentile on a standardized reading test.
Phrasing:	In reading, Charles' scores indicate that he reads as well as or better than about 37 children out of 100 children in his age and grade.
Finding:	Thomas has an IQ score of 97.
Phrasing:	Thomas' general intelligence is within the range classified as "average." With some effort and help, he should be able to improve his reading to near grade level.
Finding:	David selected "dog" as his favorite animal on the MBI.
Phrasing:	Testing suggests that David's reading will likely improve with individual or small group tutoring. He feels most comfortable in these situations, and probably would be most responsive to this friendly, personal touch.
Finding:	Brenda selected "hog" and "alligator" as her favorite animals on the MBI.
Phrasing:	Our tests and observations support what you and her teachers report: Brenda seems to have a poor self-image and probably is more angry and difficult to deal with than she really wants to be. She does not need to be taught *what* to answer as much as *how* to answer. She needs guided practice in responding in ways that improve her confidence in herself, and everyone else's confidence in her as well.
Finding:	Mark's score on a standardized vocabulary test is in the 20th percentile.
Phrasing:	Mark, what do you think of your vocabulary? (Wait for response) Well, you're right. It could be a lot better. Do you have any ideas about how to help make it better?
	(In a case such as this one, it is sometimes best to begin to focus attention on the chief area of weakness immediately, rather than dwelling on the entire array of low scores. The conferencing session then can become a briefing session on how to improve vocabulary. When the parents are present, they are likely to express interest in helping with this need. You might then make these suggestions: 1. use a more upscaled vocabulary at home; 2. watch at least a half hour a day of informational television; and 3. subscribe to some magazines that they and the child might be interested in.)
Finding:	Mike, a 7th grader, has an IQ of 117, but is reading almost 2 years below grade level.
Phrasing:	Mike's general intelligence score is within the range classified as "high average." We believe his actual intelligence level may be even higher than the test score indicates. As you suspected, his

reading and academic work are considerably beneath grade level. To investigate the possible causes for the difference between Mike's achievement and ability level, we asked him to complete several different types of learning tasks. Our observations suggested two possibilities. (Turning to address Mike and his parents) Tell us what you think of these:

1. Mike has a tough time accepting corrections or criticisms; as soon as he hears criticism coming, he tightens up and doesn't hear much of anything afterwards.
2. Mike is susceptible to distraction. When reading silently, his attention to words and meanings seems to be interrupted by his own thoughts, which appear to drift pretty far from the task at hand.

Does this sound accurate, Mike? (This can be followed with: "How else do these two problems trouble you in school; among your friends; with your family?")

Conferencing has a way of putting reading problems into a larger perspective. In so doing, it often manages to lend assistance to parents, teachers, and children in a more far-reaching way than does a report itemizing the mere particulars of a child's reading deficiencies.

Reporting

There are several different ways to make a report. Two options are described here: the basic reading "Report of Testing," and the more elaborate "Reading Evaluation." Before examining these, here are some general tips on report writing:

1. Be sure all basic facts are current and accurate (age, grade, gender, etc.).
2. State the full name of every test employed, and what the test is designed to measure.
3. Use simple declarative sentences. Keep verb tense parallel within sections of the report.
4. Avoid unnecessary technical language, but don't shy away from appropriate professional language if the context fully supports it and makes its meaning clear to an intelligent lay reader.
5. Write to your "audience"—usually parents and other teachers.
6. Write as if your audience could become: a newspaper, a court, a child, an antagonist.
7. Use phrases and words that indicate degrees of reasonable probability but not certainty (e.g., "it seems," "it appears," "in all probability," etc.)
8. For the sake of brevity, describe and explain the full nature of tests or testing protocols only as it may be necessary to understand the significance of a certain finding.
9. Use standard English, avoiding colloquialisms, contractions, and other unnecessary signs of informality.

10. Avoid value-laden comments.
11. When reporting test results, report scores with interpretative value, such as scaled scores, percentiles, or age or grade equivalents; do not report raw scores.
12. Do not try to paint either a rosy or a dark picture; let the facts speak for themselves.
13. Be sure to edit carefully, spell-check, and revise your report before going public with it.

Report of Testing

Now let's consider two of the most popular means of reporting. The first and most basic could be called a *Report of Testing*. It tends to concentrate on reading and related tests. Figure 6.9 is an example format for a Report of Testing. This format has been modified from one used by Warren Wheelock, at the University of Missouri–Kansas City.

FIGURE 6.9

Format for Report of Testing (With Sample Phrases)

Name: _____   Grade: _____

Age: _____   School: _____

Birthdate: _____   Date Tested: _____

Gender: _____   Examined by: _____

Reason for Referral:

_____ was referred for testing and evaluation by his mother, who feels that he is not achieving in reading, possibly due to a learning disability.

Tests Administered: (List titles of tests used)

1. Wechsler Intelligence Scale for Children – Revised
2. Keystone Visual Survey Tests
3. Maico Audiometric Sweep Check Test
4. Wepman Auditory Discrimination Test (Form ___)
5. Betts Visual Discrimination Tests
6. Harris Test of Lateral Dominance
7. Bender Visual-Motor Gestalt Test
8. Silvaroli Informal Reading Inventory
   a. Word Recognition
   b. Oral Reading – Word Recognition and Comprehension
9. Silvaroli Informal Spelling Survey

FIGURE 6.9

Format for Report of Testing (With Sample Phrases) (*continued*)

Observations: (Describe physical features and demeanor of child, such as appearance
and general behavior and attitude during testing.)
_____ was a youngster of average build, who appeared to be well cared for. He was
somewhat shy at first; however, rapport was established. _____ seemed verbal, articulate, and well-oriented to time and place. He worked well and with sustained interest throughout the testing. _____ wears glasses and writes with his right hand.

Tests Results: (List the name and type of each test, and the results of testing.)

1. On the Wechsler Intelligence Scales for Children—Revised, _____ had a Full Scale
   IQ, which is classified as _____ according to the Wechsler norms for his age group.
   His Verbal Scale Score also is classified as _____. His Performance Scale Score is
   within the range classified as _____. There was some unevenness of functioning. . .
2. The results of the Keystone Visual Survey Tests indicate. . .
3. The results of the Maico Audiometric Sweep Check indicate. . .
4. The results of the Wepman Auditory Discrimination Test (form ___) indicate. . .
5. The results of the Betts Visual Discrimination Tests indicate. . .
6. On the Harris Test of Lateral Dominance, the protocol is suggestive of. . .
7. On the Bender Visual-Motor Gestalt Test, the protocol is suggestive of. . .
8. On the Silvaroli Informal Word Recognition Survey, _____ achieved the following
   scores at the levels indicated:

Level Untimed	Untimed
Preprimer	100%
Primer	95%
First	80%
Second	65%

_____'s phonetic and structural analysis skills are inadequate for his level of devel-
opment. He has particular difficulty with short vowel sounds, dipthongs, and other irregular vowel combinations, and the analysis and synthesis of polysyllabic words.

On the Silvaroli Informal Reading inventory, the following levels were established:

Independent	First
Instructional	Second
Frustration	Third
Hearing Capacity	Fifth

_____'s oral reading in context at sight was characterized by. . .
9. On the Silvaroli Informal Spelling Survey, the following scores were obtained:

Level	Score
First	80%
Second	40%

_____ seems well able to transfer his word attack skills to a spelling situation. Those
errors he did record were usually phonetically correct; e.g., wrote *rase* for *raise*, *lurn* for
learn.

FIGURE 6.9

Format for Report of Testing (With Sample Phrases) (*continued*)

Case Typing: (Summarize the test results)

_____ reading difficulties are characterized by the following factors:
1.
2.
3.
4.
The results of the measures used in this diagnosis are commonly associated with the type of case referred to as_____

Discussion: (Elaboration on the meaning of the above)

_____ is a youngster of at least average intellectual capacity who appears to be re-tarded approximately two years in the development of his phonetic and structural analysis skills. His comprehension skills, however, appear to be adequate for his level of development.
It appears that _____ . . .

Recommendations: (Specific instructional suggestions)

1. _____'s corrective reading program should be initiated at about a second grade difficulty level. His program should. . .

_____
Clinician's signature

Reading Evaluation

The second format, which we shall call a *Reading Evaluation*, implies a broader look at the child. It generally amounts to adding a brief psychoeducational evaluation of personal-social adjustment to the Report of Testing. It attempts to show how reading, schooling, and living are being affected. The Reading Evaluation format is offered as an alternative, rather than a simple extension of the Report of Testing, since some states and school districts openly discourage this type of evaluation at this time. Figure 6.10 illustrates how the MBI might be added to the above and used in such an appraisal to draw up appropriate instructional recommendations. The wording could differ considerably depend-ing upon which instruments were used for this appraisal, but the qualitative dimension added will not go unnoticed. Findings and interview information from the Difference Inventory presented in the previous chapter can also be used alone or in combination with the Incomplete Sentence or other projective information in this section.

FIGURE 6.10

Sample Reading Evaluation (Charles, Age 10)

Test Administered

The Manzo Bestiary Inventory (MBI) was used to help understand Charles's state of personal-social adjustment. This can be vital information in helping a youngster reach academic and emotional maturity. The MBI uses a student's expressed identifications with 33 animals to arrive at this appraisal.

Results

first and second choices: lion, moose
third and fourth choices: falcon, wolf
fifth and sixth choices: fox, tiger
least preferred: dove, swan

Interpretation

Results of the MBI are interpreted on four levels: 1. the first and second choices indicate the way a child wishes to appear; 2. the third and fourth choices indicate the way the child typically feels and behaves; 3. the fifth and sixth choices indicate personal resources or reserves that the child can call on in difficult situations; and 4. the least preferred choices indicate the way the child would *least* like to be or appear.

Charles's first order of identifications, lion and moose, indicate that he wishes to appear stable, strong, "male," in control, and self-directed. His second choices, falcon and wolf, suggest that he typically shows himself to be bold, emotionally aloof, sometimes sociable, but also occasionally tough or threatening. His third level of choices, fox and tiger, generally indicate that when placed in a challenging situation, he likely will first try to be clever and evasive, and then possibly become angry and aggressive. The choices he least prefers, dove and swan, are very often preferred by females, and in this context are interpreted to mean that Charles probably is going through a normal gender identity stage, or that he has an exaggerated fear of appearing passive, accommodating, or vulnerable.

In general, this profile descirbes a strong-willed child who sees his current life and circumstances as requiring defensive attitudes and behaviors. This profile may well explain Charles's weakness in accurate literal comprehension and in spelling and grammar, since these skills are likely to be viewed as requiring attention to details and passive conduct. Charles seems to have acquired good critical reading and divergent thinking skills. These, too, are compatible with his fundamentally more aggressive and clever approach to life, school, and reading. It may be this very attitude and characteristic type of behavior that explains Charles' generally poor grades and the consistent underestimations of his reading and academic abilities by his teachers, as compared with his uneven but generally higher scores on standardized tests.

Recommendations

Appropriate instructional approaches for Charles would be instruction that offers opportunities for him to: 1. assert himself gently, rather than to feel as if he is being led around; 2. interact with someone who can model competent and serene behavior; 3.

FIGURE 6.10

Sample Reading Evaluation (Charles, Age 10) *(continued)*

permit him to express and learn about himself through reading and writing; and 4. follow a program that permits a higher level of activity. The Reciprocal Questioning Procedure, story writing, and an interactive computer program for reading and writing are examples of three practices that together help meet some of these requirements.

> ➤   **LOOKING BACK**   ◄

The chapter provided guidelines and sample material designed to heighten your ability to make observations. It further suggested means to heighten your craft in conferring and reporting findings. The chapter stressed portfolio analysis and other means of finding strengths and reasons for hope, as well as weaknesses and reasons for concern.

> ➤ *LOOKING AHEAD*

The next chapter presents the essence of remedial instruction as distilled from extensive reviews of the literature on reading, learning, and related theories. These largely research-based findings are informed by suggestions drawn from clinical, classroom, and teacher-training experiences. Answers are provided to a range of questions, from "Does remediation work?" to "How can you make quality distinctions among the various methods and materials available?"

PRINCIPLES AND PRACTICES OF REMEDIATION

Principles and Practices for Guiding Remediation

7

"*Children are always ready to learn; they're just not always ready to be taught.***"**
ANONYMOUS

➤ LOOK FOR IT

This chapter primarily addresses four integrated questions:
- What is remedial instruction?
- Does it work?
- How is it best conducted, organized, and environmentally supported?
- How can we informally assess and select appropriate materials and methods?

What is Remedial Instruction and Does it Work?

What is Remedial Instruction?

Remediation is a well-thought-out form of helping for whatever is hurt or underdeveloped. Generally, it is provided by a well-informed professional, and delivered with care, concern, and sensitivity to meet individual needs and differences. It often is thought of as rehabilitative, but in education, it is largely habilitative—helping with the initial developmental process. The basic issue of whether remediation even works periodically needs to be thought through and sometimes defended just as was the policy question, in a previous chapter, of whether diagnosis is necessary. However, the answer to this question must be preceded by a more elaborate explanation of just what is meant by "remedial reading instruction."

In minimal terms, remedial instruction is supplemental to regular instruction, and should not supplant it. This is the goal, for example, of the federally funded, school-based "Chapter I" programs for at-risk children.

Remedial instruction can be much more, depending on need and resources. It can be based on a system of referral whereby a classroom teacher requests the reading specialist to take a closer look at a student and to prescribe a plan of assistance. A "referral" typically is taken to mean that the student should see the reading specialist on a pull-out basis, in addition to regular classroom reading instruction, and that remediation should be terminated when the student can better keep pace with the class. Referrals should, but seldom do, include students who are reading at grade level, but who are far beneath their measured capacity levels. Referrals also should, but almost never do, include students with various kinds of higher-order literacy needs, such as are detailed in a chapter ahead.

Actual instruction can vary from simply more of whatever the child receives in class, to some array of methods that the remedial instructor has come to master and believe in. Careful matching of student needs to appropriate methodology is ideal but also is seldom found, largely because it can be a tedious task, fraught with tricky questions such as, "Should we have them do more of what they clearly can not do well, or have them do more of what they can already do?" The short answer, of course, is—both, and more. However, the "more" often adds to the problem, since it can involve providing rather exotic, in the sense of not well-known, forms of remedial therapy. Some of these methods might seldom be called for in a given school, but more than likely are needed with some regularity on a districtwide basis. For that reason, progressive school districts operate a clinic program staffed by highly trained specialists, who may regularly confer with one another and with university-based specialists in a variety of related disciplines. Initially, this may involve some additional expense, but it is wise, and it can be very cost effective on the longer term. This is one place where the political approach taken by LD supporters has proven to be most appropriate. The state of Missouri, for example, operates a technical resource center (at the University of Missouri–Kansas City School of Education) providing technical assistance to individuals, businesses, and schools, on the rules, laws, and procedures for working with LD students and the developmentally disabled. There is, to our knowledge, no such service available in reading anywhere in the country. (Great interest was shown in developing a similar capability on a computer bulletin board that would be part of a clinical network by 200 participants in a "Clinic Update" symposium of the International Reading Association conference in 1988. You may add your name to the list of this group by writing to the authors for an update on this effort.)

A final factor implicit in remedial instruction is the requirement that the specialist provide a plan that can be employed both by the student and the classroom teacher to reinforce and support out-of-class remedial efforts within the regular classroom, and potentially from other sources and agencies. This can be the most important duty provided, yet it is the one that often receives the least attention and follow-through.

Does Remediation Work?

The most popular thing to say about remediation is that its effectiveness is "mixed" (Harris & Sipay, 1985; Johnston & Allington, 1991). This view stems from the fact that some studies have shown that a few programs and practices do not have immediate impact (Raim, 1983; Spreen, 1982), that the effect is not long-lasting (Balow & Blomquist, 1965; Carroll, 1972), or that the outlook is not rosy for children who come from low SES families and/or whose instruction did not rely on a program of intensive treatment (Schonhaut & Satz, 1983).

Some writers are just plain sour on remedial reading. Peter Johnston and Richard Allington (1991) have identified several (e.g., Bowles & Gintis, 1976; Giroux, 1981; Fraatz, 1987) who essentially believe that "...remedial instruction is simply a lavishly concealed way of maintaining a classed society..." (p. 1006). Our conclusion is that remedial efforts tend to be soundly and predictably effective, and, more than that, they represent a humane and demonstrably effective means of dismantling class-based societies. This conviction is strengthened when consideration is given to the odds against which remedial efforts are provided, and when the incidental findings from empirical studies are added to the explicit ones.

Consider first the issue of odds. Remedial programs, by definition, address the needs of those who are failing or have failed. Reasons for failure, as already noted, can come from a confluence of sources—constitutional defects, emotionally disruptive thinking patterns, as well as from learning, thinking, cultural and lifestyle differences (Cazden, 1988). Most of these causes are outside the realm of school operations, and reversing them constitutes a great challenge to our collective ingenuity and resourcefulness. Nonetheless, schools—and, specifically, remedial programs—have tackled many of these problems, and have been able to affect change and growth in many pupils. Consider the hard evidence.

In a review of some forty earlier studies, George Spache (1981) concluded that students make about two months of progress for each month of remediation. More recent studies have also found significant improvement due to remediation (Gittelman & Feingold, 1983; Ito, 1980). In another study, 95 percent of *dyslexics* studied made significant gains as a result of remediation (Kline & Kline,

1975). To these findings can be added hundreds of studies in which researchers comparing specific remedial approaches report gains for disabled readers that surpass average gains for average students. Many of these studies are cited in the chapters ahead that cover specific remedial methods. In any case, the conclusion that remediation, in general, works and is worthwhile seems solidly supported by research, ecological evidence, and intuition.

There are, of course, circumstances and conditions that tend to increase or decrease the effectiveness of remediation. Joan Coley and Dianne Hoffman (1990), for example, identified a group of six youngsters who exhibited signs of "learned helplessness and inadequate self-esteem." The teacher-researchers modified these students' program to include elements such as teaching children how to use question response cues, double entry response journals, and self-evaluation. As a result, *all* subjects began to view themselves more positively. John Guthrie, Mary Seifert, and Lloyd W. Kline (1978) did a masterful job of identifying several other factors that result in increased effectiveness. They considered 15 studies that met fairly stringent standards for research design in field work. What they found was that:

- remedially tutored groups had greater improvements in reading than non-treatment groups
- a learning rate double that of normal children was obtained in several studies
- several studies reported gains that were discernible two years following initial remediation
- elementary and secondary students both made solid gains, although the secondary students tended to require more time
- middle-class students and students with IQ's over 90 tend to do better than low SES's with IQ's below 90.
- remediation was most effective when it continued for 50 hours or more and was delivered by certified and experienced teachers or supervised tutors.

Findings from three other studies contribute to our understanding of how to sustain gains. Long-term gains were sustained when:

- the remedial reading teacher maintained some contact with the students after terminating routine lessons (Balow & Blomquist, 1965).
- students were encouraged to read *and write* extensively (Rennie, Braun, & Gordon, 1986).
- the remedy was provided within one year of identification of the problem (Clay, 1985).

Let us look now at some specific precepts and practices that can be relied upon to produce high-quality remediation. Many of these would be of value to consider by anyone who teaches at any level.

Principles of Remediation

Most theories of learning and instruction have implications for remediation. Therefore, the information covered in this chapter can not pretend to cover

> ## Reflective Activity Box 1
>
> To achieve personal mastery of these principles, try using the learning process known as "subjective association." As you read ahead, try to identify an experience or story from your life or personal thoughts that can be associated with each principle discussed. This type of constructive-associative reading tends to heighten comprehension, enhance meaning, and aid recall in problem-solving situations.

all that might apply, or that one would ever need to know. Nonetheless, you should find this collection of principles useful and relevant to guiding remediation in both classroom and clinical situations. (See Reflective Activity Box 1.)

Naturally, these principles will also grow more meaningful as you encounter and see them applied throughout the book. For example, the very notion offered in Reflective Activity Box 1 for your learning is offered as a means of teaching vocabulary in another chapter. Further, several of the principles described are used in this chapter in discussions of structuring and designing remedial sessions, building conducive environments, and selecting appropriate materials and methods.

When a listing becomes as extensive as this one, it is natural to ask something like, "Is it realistic to expect practitioners to take all of this into consideration in planning each strand of instruction?" No matter how sheepishly it is delivered, the answer is, "yes." However, the longer answer would add these points. First, these principles represent the factors that have been found to influence learning outcomes most, and can not really be deleted simply to make a more manageable list. Second, from a practical point of view, you probably already are inclined to tend to most of these based on prior training and personal disposition. Third, not all of these principles need to be employed in each and every segment of teaching, but they probably do need to be part of each strand or larger segment of instructional planning, if patterns of non-achievement are to be reversed. Fourth, we must have greater capacity to learn and internalize complex rules from instruction and experience than we realize, or else how could anyone ever learn to be a "strategic reader." Finally, academic courses and texts can only set one on the path to professional competence: becoming a "strategic teacher" is a life-long process.

1. Use a "Diagnostic-Teaching" Paradigm. All teaching, like all diagnosis, must be provisional. It should be done with an eye toward collecting information on how students learn, what obstacles they tend to encounter, and what provisions need to be made to attempt to overcome these. To this end, Jeanne Paratore and Roselmina Indrisano (1987) recommend that the diagnostic teacher develop a set of methods and materials (passages, tasks, and prompts) that they routinely use to teach each student experiencing difficulty in learning. Using these, the teacher then can note student patterns of success and difficulty with passages of various subject type and difficulty, with different types of tasks (from unaided retelling to multiple choice recognition), and with different levels of prompts or supports. Principle number 9 ahead, which emphasizes the importance of "reciprocity," offers another means of becoming a more effective diagnostic teacher. Diagnostic teaching has other facets and names that you will encounter. These include "clinical diagnosis" (Chall & Curtis, 1987); "intervention assessment" (Paratore & Indrisano, 1987); "trial teaching" (Harris & Sipay, 1985); "alternative methods" (Lipson & Wixson, 1991); "dynamic assessment" (Cioffi & Carney, 1983); and "responsive teaching" and "instructional conversations" (Tharp & Gallimore, 1989a; 1989b); "reflective teaching" (Duffy & Roehler, 1987); and "reciprocal teaching" (Palincsar & Brown, 1984; Manzo, 1969a,b). Reflective Activity Box 2 explains more about how the instructional

---

Reflective Activity Box 2
The Reflective-Strategic Teacher

To develop your ability to learn from on-line teaching experience further, try following these guidelines as an instructional episode unfolds:

1. Mentally put yourself in "Stage I Standby-Alert" when you are teaching to notice a possible problem or solution that has unfolded. To aid in this process, picture yourself carrying some brackets ([ ]) with you that you install at the moment the dialogue or scenario begins to reveal something of instructional interest or value.
2. Once you have installed an initial bracket, you will automatically go to "Stage II Alert," where you will now begin to pay close attention to what is occurring, and how you are intuitively thinking you should handle or facilitate it.
3. Next go to "Stage III Full Alert", as you see the episode playing itself out. At that point, close the brackets, and try to label it so it can be compressed and recalled in a more tranquil moment.
4. Soon afterward, try to recall what you experienced, by reopening the brackets containing the images, words, and labels. Now try to highlight the relevant interactions by removing the extraneous ones and carefully relabelling or languaging through your experience and the lessons learned.

To enhance this process further, a) intentionally use teaching procedures that have rich heuristic value — that is, that tend to ignite experimentation and self-discovery; b) talk your experience through with a friend or colleague, and, ideally, c) write it out.

For some vivid examples of this process, see "Clinical Lessons Learned from ReQuest Interactions" in Chapter 10 on comprehension methods, and what Carol Kirk (1990) learned from "Mitch" in the previous chapter.

episode can be used as a "schoolroom" for developing the clinical intuition necessary for becoming a "strategic teacher."

2. Establish Initial Rapport, Mindset, and Motivation to Learn. The first five minutes of every instructional hour usually determines what, if anything, of value will occur thereafter. Give considerable thought to what you will do or say, or have students do or say to win their attention and commitment. It need not be dramatic, and it is best when it is diagnostically suited to the student's area of greatest need. For some youngsters, it may be as simple as a self-starting, self-pacing activity to orient them to the printed page; for others, a few moments of eye contact and congenial conversation. Begin now to collect a set of starters and motivators that are suitable to you and that seem appropriate for your students. Doing so will also help to raise your own enthusiasm and readiness for your next remedial group. This bit of simple wisdom is part of most every culture's experience, as is attested to by the old French proverb that says: "A good meal ought to begin with hunger." The next point continues this simple wisdom to a slightly deeper level of significance.

3. Make Sure Students are Engaged During Instruction. "Academic engaged time" is one of the best predictors of achievement in reading and learning in school (Fisher, et.al., 1978a). Academic engaged time is another name for attention, or situational motivation (Anderson, Evertson, & Brophy, 1979; Chall & Feldman, 1966; Cobb, 1972; Luce & Hoge, 1978). Academic engaged time can be improved through direct training or through mastery learning techniques that incidentally increase attention and commitment to learn (Anderson, 1975). Dixie Lee Spiegel (1980a) stresses the importance of providing time and opportunity *before* reading for students to orient and familiarize themselves with the content of the new material. Studies of advance organizers (Ausubel, 1964), discussed more fully in another chapter, and research on schema theory (Anderson, et.al., 1977) have shown a strong and consistent effect of prereading orientation on subsequent reading effectiveness. Prereading and purpose setting strategies are the most prized by reading specialists (Gee & Raskow, 1987). Michael Kirby (1989) validated a related notion called the "focus of attention" hypothesis. He was able to show that engagement can be achieved by focusing student attention on a target task by intentionally minimizing other important but potentially distracting tasks at that time. Accordingly, he showed that the rate of words learned per minute of instruction was twice as great when students were trained in visual word recognition under a minimal context condition as compared with one emphasizing context, meaning, and usage. This study also tends to support the reasonability of the traditional notion of isolating and focusing instruction on areas of diagnosed need. Of course, it should not be taken to mean that context usage and practice should not follow closely. The next point relates to another means of heightening attention and engagement.

4. Quicken the Pace and the Amount Covered. Slower coverage of less material is a perceived cornerstone of remedial instruction. This is a fallacy probably based upon an incorrect inference that *rate*—or the amount of time that it takes a pupil to learn—is synonymous with the *pace*—or speed of presentation of information. While the precise reasons are not yet fully understood, it seems that rate of learning increases with pace of teaching. In other words, it is better to cover more material faster. The principle of quick pacing with more content is supported by many studies covering material from number of words learned to books covered (Anderson, Evertson, & Brophy, 1979; Barr, 1973-74; Beez, 1968) Contrary to common intuition, this same finding seems to hold true in mathematics and science (Comber & Keeves, 1973; Good, Grouws, & Beckerman, 1978; Walker & Schaffarzick, 1974), and irrespective of the typical learning rate of the pupils (Carroll, 1963; 1977; Chang & Raths, 1971; Paulsen & Macken, 1978). In quickening the pace, or covering more in less time, you also must be sure that other principles are met, especially the next one calling for frequent, spaced repetitions, or distributed practice.

5. Provide Frequent and Spaced Practice to Ensure Deep and Effective Learning. The simple strategy of providing students with "distributed," or frequent, short, and spaced practice, as opposed to "massed" or long duration teaching and practice, has been called "one of the most remarkable phenomena to emerge from laboratory research on learning" (Dempster & Farris, 1990, p. 97). Despite over a hundred years of research to support this effect, remedial sessions still tend to be conducted once or twice per week for one hour, when more and shorter sessions clearly would be more beneficial. If scheduling forces a one-hour slot, then the hour should be arranged so that the critical feature of the lesson is spaced and repeated two to four times during the hour. Distributed practice also will tend to incidentally quicken the pace of instruction, hence adding some of the benefits of the previous principle.

6. Build Self-Efficacy—It Will Build Self-Concept. Attempts to build self-concept as a means of prompting effective learning tend to rely on verbal suasion, encouragement, and other praising comments. These have a positive, though relatively weak, effect on improving learning and belief in self (Bandura, 1977a). On the other hand, self-efficacy, or actual effectiveness as a student, is a key component of self-concept that is based on performance accomplishments, real experiences, and personal mastery. Self-efficacy, or evidence of progress, routinely leads to increased academic success and feelings of self-worth (Campbell & Hackett, 1986). Self-efficacy, according to social learning theorists, is raised or lowered by a combination of factors based on past performance, observations of others successfully modeling a task, verbal encouragement, and the level of emotional arousal (not enough or too much) that is experienced in doing a certain task (Gorrell, 1990). In other words, the cornerstone of all remedial efforts must include having students experience greater success and less anxiety in reading, before they can be brought to believe that they will be able to persist in mastering reading. Since it sounds circular to say "success breeds success," four quick examples of how to do this are in order. One is to provide pupils with a manageable, self-correcting, and self-pacing task on which they can chart their own day-to-day progress. Another is to use portfolios to collect and represent progress over longer time frames. A third is not to shy from mixing *correction* with *encouragement*—gratuitous encouragement turns kids into dependent "praise junkies," whereas the philosopher Goethe observed, "Encouragement after censure is as the sun after a shower." Finally, remember to ask questions that have more than one right answer (Spiegel, 1980a). This decreases the likelihood that a pupil will be completely wrong when answering. (See Reflective Activity Box 4 at the end of this chapter for an example.)

7. Use a Fair Amount of Teacher-Directed Instruction. Direct instruction typically is recognizable by the fact that the teacher generally tells students what they are going to learn, how they are going to learn it, why they are going to learn it, when they are going to learn it (Pearson & Fielding, 1991), and even when they have learned it. It can sound rather authoritarian, but it has been consistently found that learning takes place best (at least short term) when the teacher takes charge and reduces extraneous choices (Rosenshine & Stevens, 1984). This has been found to be true at every socioeconomic level, in every grade, and for bright as well as for remedial students (Soar, 1973; Stallings & Kaskowitz, 1974; Solomon & Kendall, 1979). Permissiveness, "spontaneity," and lack of control have even been found to be *negatively* correlated to growth in creativity, inquiry, writing ability, and self-esteem as well (Rosenshine & Stevens, 1984). Too many choices left to students seem to reduce academic engaged time and to leave students and teacher distracted and feeling uncertain. It has sometimes been suggested that "direct instruction" is the antithesis of reflective teaching (Kameenui & Shannon, 1988). However, as Edward Kameenui (in Kameenui & Shannon) points out, "Direct instruction is not the whole of education nor should it be. Neither, I suspect, is reflective teaching" (p. 41). See the next guideline for a means of achieving a balance between teacher and student control.

8. Use Heuristic Instructional Strategies. The last 20 years have produced some very carefully designed and robust methods of teaching in remedial situations. Rely upon these carefully crafted and proven methods to anchor your craft as an instructor. Many of these strategies also have a naturally heuristic value that tends to evoke appropriate responses from students and self-explorations and discoveries in you in how to be a more reflective, flexible , and strategic teacher. In other words, additional to following your subjective judgements, permit your instincts to come to be better informed by the practices that are the foundations of your profession. As an additional advantage, heuristic methods tend to encourage the teacher to become a co-learner with the student. The next point helps in the selection of appropriate strategies.

9. Select Methods that Contain the Rudiments of Quality Instruction, Particularly Modeling and Reciprocity. The rudiments of quality instruction include: a predictable sequence of statements of objective, guided practice, feedback and corrections, and independent practice (Rosenshine & Stevens, 1984), as well as demonstration, or cognitive modeling and reciprocity (Manzo, 1969a,b; Palincsar & Brown, 1986). Reciprocity, the often overlooked cornerstone of effective cognitive modeling, means providing opportunities for students to "pokeback" and influence the direction of the lesson in a conversational way that does not cause the teacher to relinquish responsibility or control over lesson objectives and means (Manzo & Manzo, 1990a). Reciprocity is a seamless form of diagnostic teaching that permits teacher and student to home in on what has been called the "zone of proximal development" (Vygotsky, 1978), or the "region of greatest sensitivity to instruction" (Wood & Middleton, 1975, in Baker & Brown, 1984, p. 382). Reciprocity also provides a dynamic means for students to interject needed breaks, repetitions, and clarifications in the instructional conversation (Tharp & Gallimore, 1989a, b). See especially the ReQuest procedure in the chapter on comprehension for a vivid example of how this tactic can pay off in instruction.

10. Build Students' Metacognitive Awareness and Sense of Personal Responsibility. Help students articulate what they are learning, why they are learning, the extent to which they have learned, and in some measure, what more they may need to learn (Brown, Campion, & Day, 1981; Sanacore, 1984). Self-questioning and self-appraisal of the level of effort required to do a task are critical elements in achieving this goal (Good, 1987). See especially the Guided Reading Procedure as a tangible example of how to impart the skill of self-appraising the level of effort required to achieve effective recall of a passage.

11. Build Students' Schemata as well as their "Skills." All new learning is built, in some way, on prior knowledge and experience. Building students' fund of background knowledge and concepts prepares them to comprehend new information and ideas better. Topical knowledge improves one's schema and capacity to comprehend (Vygotsky, 1962; Manzo, Manzo, & Smith, in preparation); therefore, be sure to hold students accountable for learning (remembering and internalizing) a certain percentage of what they read. This is the reciprocal side of the content area reading movement that says that the reading teacher must learn to value topical knowledge as much as he or she would have the content teacher value reading and language arts objectives.

12. Teach the Whole Person. Instruction tends to be addressed chiefly to the cognitive domain, to a lesser degree to the affective domain, and rarely, if at all, to the sensorimotor (physical) domain (Ceprano, 1981; Manzo, & Manzo, 1990a). See Motor Imaging, a vocabulary building strategy, for a particularly vivid example of this point. The full significance of involving all domains in learning is further realized in the next point addressing the behavioral aspects of learning.

13. Provide for Behavioral Reconditioning. Failure has biological consequences. It changes the chemistry of human functioning so that failure becomes a "habit" of body as well as of mind. To build success where habits of failure have become embedded, it often is necessary to employ methods that neutralize negative chemistry and inappropriate coping systems. One means of aiding in this is by behavioral reconditioning; that is, where students are led to engage in and practice more appropriate coping strategies that countercondition the chemistry of failure with the feel and chemistry of success (Bandura & Walters, 1963; Oldrige, 1982; Manzo, 1977a). This point could be called the behavioral dimension of self-efficacy training, principle 5.

14. Reduce Distractions. For many years, a standard rule of remediation was that children with reading and learning problems should be taught in a physical setting that had a greatly reduced level of extraneous stimuli (Strauss & Lehtinen, 1947). This rule lost favor when evidence mounted to show that remedial reading and LD kids are not any more hyperactive than normals. However, the general rule should still be followed, not because there are more remedial readers who are hyperactive and highly distractible, but because those who *are* need more help in focusing on the reading task than do normals, and hence will be more adversely affected by a distracting environment. In practical terms, this may mean exercising reasonable controls over the remedial environment by closing the door to the hallway, turning youngsters' seats away from overly distracting bulletin boards, and perhaps from one another. It does not and should not result in the creation of a sterile cell, but one with a sharp "focus of attention" as validated by Kirby's (1989) work cited in principle 3 above.

15. Phase Yourself Out. All learning is built on the expectation that the student is working toward independence. This is *the* most basic principle of teaching. Design instruction so as to fade out supports, or "gradually release responsibility" (Pearson, 1985) and encourage ever greater self-reliance. Bruner (1978) first referred to this as the principle of "scaffolding." It can take the form of verbal directions and support (Roehler, Duffy, & Warren, 1987), or of combined physical and verbal support (Manzo & Manzo, 1990b; Scardamalia, Bereiter & Steinbach, 1984). See the Note Cue comprehension and participation training strategy as an example of this principle in operation.

16. Provide Materials and Offer Tasks that are Challenging but Manageable. Failure often leads to "learned helplessness," or the sense that effort does not make a difference (Dweck & Goetz, 1978; Dweck & Repucci, 1973). Students of any age and level are more likely to take active control of their own cognitive endeavors when they are faced with tasks and materials of intermediate difficulty (Baker & Brown, 1984). This assumption underlies many theories of achievement motivation as well as most theories of learning and instruction. It is, for example, the root notion in Vygotsky's (1978) "zone of proximal development"—that "zone" is the distance between a student's performance with and without instructional aid. This notion also underlies the distinctions between independent, instructional, and frustration levels in reading. It should be noted that there are individual differences with respect to tolerance for challenge and frustration, and this is one of the chief objectives of a differential diagnosis that includes assessment of affect.

17. Provide for Students' Basic Needs Before Attempting Instruction. Whenever possible, try at least situationally to provide for students' basic human needs since these are necessary requisites to expecting students to be responsive to cognitive development—a higher order need. This point also is a fundamental and inescapable aspect of human motivation. It was best described by Abraham Maslow (1954), and is illustrated in the triangle seen in Figure 7.1. In very practical terms, this needs hierarchy is meant to remind us of such things as when a child is too hot/cold, hungry, or needs to go to the restroom before he or she is ready to engage and learn. Our colleague, John George, reports a telling story of how easy it is as instructors to become preoccupied with our own needs to the detriment of the child's. He had teachers in a tutoring situation pointedly ask students questions like, "Are you too hot or cold?" "Would you like to go to the restroom first?", etc. Later, he observed a lesson in which a student responded "yes" to three such questions, after which the teacher absentmindedly

FIGURE 7.1

Maslow's Hierarchy of Needs

This theory of motivation assumes that human needs are arranged along a hierarchy of potency. Lower level needs that have not been met take on the strongest priority, and must be satisfied before the next level of needs can emerge and press for satisfaction. Triggered by the satisfaction of more basic needs, those from the next level of the pyramid then may surface, but not before. This need structure is represented by the pyramid shown below.

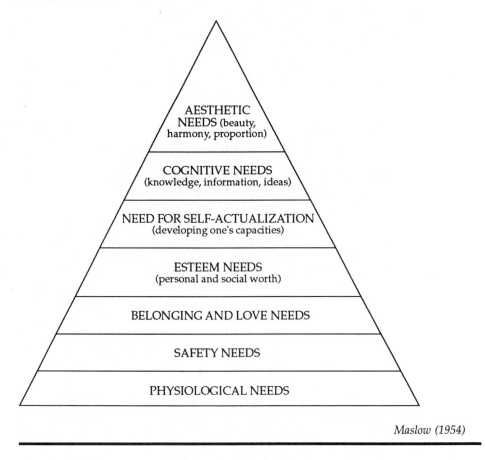

AESTHETIC NEEDS (beauty, harmony, proportion)

COGNITIVE NEEDS (knowledge, information, ideas)

NEED FOR SELF-ACTUALIZATION (developing one's capacities)

ESTEEM NEEDS (personal and social worth)

BELONGING AND LOVE NEEDS

SAFETY NEEDS

PHYSIOLOGICAL NEEDS

Maslow (1954)

said, "Good, OK, now let's begin to learn" (George, personal communication). For further illustrations of how to provide for basic needs in a seamless manner, see the discussion of bibliotherapy in this text.

18. Avoid Confounding Elements. Teachers often attempt to support and enrich instruction by introducing ideas or concepts *similar* to the one being taught. The problem with this is that students tend to learn all similar ideas together in a confused lump of interrelated details. A simple way to avoid this problem is to identify new concepts to be taught in each lesson and introduce related concepts only after the target concept has been thoroughly learned. For example, don't teach "**p**," "**b**," and "**d**" at the same time, but one at a time until each is separately mastered. This is technically known as problems of "proactive inhibition," where new learnings interfere with immediately subsequent ones, and "retroactive inhibitions," where subsequent learnings undo or interfere with things previously learned (Manzo & Manzo, 1990a).

19. Use Concurrent Teaching Methods. Concurrent teaching methods are designed to serve more than one objective simultaneously (Manzo & Manzo, 1990a; Rubin, 1984). Typically, such methods tend to focus on one conventional objective (Rubin, 1984), such as comprehension, and one or more collateral objectives, such as student questioning skill (Yopp, 1988) or selected aspects of personal-social adjustment.

20. Let Students Read! Reading alone, as Carver (1991) eventually discovered, will not appreciably improve reading. However, the absence of ample opportunity to read both orally and silently does impede reading progress (Allington, 1977). During silent reading, children have opportunity to control their own pace, review material, and formulate personal reactions (Richek, List, & Lerner, 1989). Nonetheless, it has been found that poor readers are given only a third as many opportunities to read as are good readers. In one study, the low achieving group in a first grade averaged only five words of silent reading per day (Allington, 1984). Furthermore, during oral reading, better readers tend to be encouraged to figure a word out for themselves, while low achieving readers tend to be supplied the word too quickly by the teacher (Allington, 1980; Hoffman, et.al., 1984). The need for selective and supported practice in independent reading is made clearer in the next principle.

21. Provide Environmental Support. In order for reading, writing, and thinking skills to take hold and flourish, there must be an ecologically conducive, or literate, environment (Morrow, 1989). Each school must create an environment that consciously, though largely incidentally, supports literacy. This can be done in a variety of ways, ranging from regular classroom teachers using literacy nurturing strategies to the skillful use of support personnel and community resources. Several such support systems are described ahead in this chapter.

22. Exercise Student Minds in Areas Often Left to Atrophy. Several studies, as well as good sense, now confirm that remedial level students genuinely benefit from engagement with activities and mental operation that they frequently are deprived of during conventional remedial and even normal school instruction. These include higher-literacy questions (Beck, 1989; Spiegel 1980a), and activities to stir inventive thinking (Haggard, 1976), and other overlooked aspects of literacy, dictionary usage, and spelling. The chapters ahead further explain and illustrate how each of these neglected areas can profitably be attended to within the framework of remedial reading instruction.

23. Do Something Joyful! There is no research of which we are aware that has explicitly tested this proposition, but that may be because it is so obvious, and, we suspect, because there would seem to be little agreement on just what may be "joyful." Nonetheless, each child has some things that cause him/her to feel better, happier, and more optimistic. The good teacher should begin to collect a treasure chest of these and use them on a trial and error basis. A few examples will suffice for now; others are mentioned throughout the text:

- Read a rousing tale or sentimental piece to your students each session. This may be a continuing story or a series of short stories.
- Open your eyes wide, engage the students in a conversation about something that they wish to talk about, and listen with real and observable interest. (Several studies by social psychologists have shown that persons with the pupils of their eyes dilated are immediately perceived as warm and caring.)
- Help the child read about and better understand some personally selected goal (anything from weight loss to a pressing assignment).
- Use a teaching method that the child clearly enjoys.
- Read joke books and humorous tales.

24. Connections and Carryouts. In order for learning to reach a generative state, it is necessary not only to conjure and bring relevant prior knowledge and experience to the classroom, but to engage in activities and discourse (Hall, 1979) that cause students to conjure and bring home learning from the classroom. This is "homework" at its best. One example: consider the recommendation of Sigrid Renner and Joan Carter (1991) to have youngsters learn more about the folkways of their families by collecting examples of family sayings, recipes, jokes, and songs (see proverbs study in the chapter on comprehension for elaboration).

These twenty-four principles of teaching and learning, as well as others, are concretely represented ahead in individual teaching methods and other recommended practices. The remainder of this chapter is dedicated to describing some basic remedial lesson structures, providing examples of how to foster a literate environment, and providing guidelines for the selection and skillful use of remedial materials.

Organizing the Remedial Session

School-based remedial sessions tend to involve 3 to 10 youngsters, and typically last between 30 and 50 minutes, depending on whether they are in an elementary or secondary school. A plan to maximize the utilization of that time should be a high priority.

There has been relatively little research on the various possible ways to organize and use remedial time. There is ample research, however, to indicate that the more that remedial time is spent as academic engaged time, the greater will be the gains in learning (Rosenshine & Stevens, 1984). Achieving this in real circumstances often involves attention to a variety of logistical and human needs, including the needs of teachers and remedial therapists.

One of the best means of using remedial time effectively is to have a clear grasp of the activities or components of an *ideal* remedial program. Six components of an ideal remedial reading program are described here primarily from the perspective of a single remedial session. These components tend to follow the master plan inherent in the Directed-Reading Thinking Activity, a lesson structure described in Chapter 10. The actual order of these and the extent to which they may blend into one another may vary with circumstances. Initially, it is advisable to take these in the order shown, since it will ensure that you attend to and develop expertise in each, and the child will get to experience each.

1. The Orientation Component. The orientation component provides continuity and focus to the remedial session. It may be an engaging question or statement related to local or national news, or even school life. Ironically, this works best when it is served on a plate that is structured and fairly routine. This should include an agenda for the day written on the chalkboard. Part of the routine can be based on a task that the student is expected to do independently immediately upon entering class. Often, this is in an ongoing, auto-instructional material that also provides a reasonable level of corrective feedback. Most instructional "kits" and computer assisted instruction (CAI) programs are suitable for this purpose. Free reading is not recommended at this time; free reading is something that is better done once attention is oriented and fixed. This 5–10 minute activity period is a good time to take roll and otherwise tend to "housekeeping" functions.

2. Direct Instructional Component. During this segment of the period, it is best to conduct a hard-hitting and robust type of lesson activity. This is the instructional heart of the remedial session, and should never be traded away, even for one period, without some compelling reason. Many of the methods described in the chapters ahead meet this requirement.

3. Reinforcement and Extension Component. This period of time, ideally, should build on the direct instructional period and be spent in empowered reading, writing, and discussion of what was read. Writing activities may vary from simply listing key words to summarizing and reacting.

4. Schema-Enhancement Component. This unit of time should be spent in building a knowledge base for further reading and independent thinking. It is an ideal time to teach study skills such as outlining, notetaking, and memory training. Ideally, it should flow from or precede Component 3.

5. Personal-Emotional Growth Component. There is little learning of any consequence that can occur without the learner involved and anticipating personal progress.

This unit of time can be built into any of the other components in a variety of ways, including doing reading that is akin to one's interests and emotional concerns (bibliotherapy), writing for self-exploration or toward some authentic objective (a letter to someone), and through attempting to identify and develop strategies for dealing with personal study and learning needs. (See the Problem-Solving Approach to Study Skills in a later chapter.)

This component should serve as a reminder to the teacher to have students pause to hear, record, and then state what they learn each day (Poostay, 1982). It also is a good time to have students say what they might be doing or thinking to help themselves outside of class, and in preparation for the next remedial session. The latter function comprises a metacognitive thread that continues in the next component.

6. Cognitive Development Component. This component should contain an attempt to enhance basic thinking operations such as:

- inference
- abstract verbal reasoning
- analogical reasoning
- constructive-critical/creative reading
- convergent and divergent analysis
- problem solving
- metacognition

Most of these forms of thinking can be taught concurrently as a routine part of vocabulary, comprehension, and study skills instruction. However, they may be pursued individually, or as a separate component to draw further attention and amplitude to them.

Collectively, these overlapping components, as illustrated in Figure 7.2, should help students build the interests, habits, language skills, knowledge base, self-discipline, and cognitive abilities needed to become more effective readers, writers, and thinkers. The size of each component should vary for individuals and groups according to diagnostically established need. However, all components will fall under the influence of the life-space, or personal environment, in which students are nurtured—a realm over which schools can exert greater control and influence than we have tended to realize.

Consider now some conducive environmental support systems that could

FIGURE 7.2

Overlapping Components of Remediation

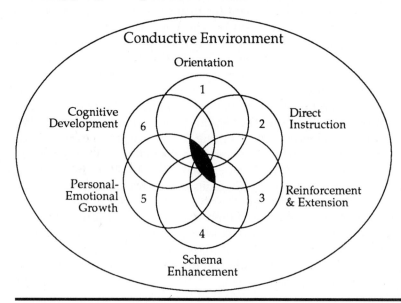

serve as a seventh Component of Remedial Instruction. To exert influence over these larger systems further epitomizes what is meant by a holistic approach to remedial education.

Creating an Authentic and Literate Environment

The value of creating a literate environment is best illustrated with a metaphor. It is easier to heat and cool a home to 70 degrees when the ambient (outdoor) temperature is 60 degrees than when it is 20 degrees or 90 degrees. So, too, is this true with building literacy. It is not easy to build a conducive ambient temperature for effective reading, writing, and thinking, but it can be done, and it can be very efficient to do so. Here now are some operations that can be undertaken to create a more conducive environment for learning within the school, and possibly even to transfer some of that ambient effect to home and community. Think of these as environmental, or ecological, strategies. Most require considerable cooperation with and support from others. Several of these are ideal projects for grant proposals to special sources of state or private funding designated for innovative educational programming.

1. Enriched Community of Language. All teachers and support staff in a school or clinic situation are given a list of 100 words that all try to use in a variety of situations and circumstances. In this way, youngsters come to learn new, slightly elevated vocabulary in much the same way that all other language learning occurs—naturally and in authentic contexts.

A plan such as this one can have effects far beyond the classroom. When students learn new words in this naturalistic fashion, they are much more likely to use them with each other and at home. Consequently, the students themselves become models of a richer language in their communities and a source of influence on the language of siblings and parents (Manzo & Manzo, 1990a, 1994, in press).

2. Student Advocates. This is a simple plan to try to prevent students from "falling between the cracks" of whatever organizational scheme or curricula that comes to dominate a school (Manzo & Manzo, 1990). In brief, each student in the school is assigned to a teacher-ombudsman who should make every reasonable effort to get to know that student in personal terms, and be ready to hear him/her out and even represent his/her interests on thorny issues or problems arising in school. The idea is to serve as a student's personal counselor and advocate, not merely as an agent of the school. Playing this role can raise the empathy of the teacher for the student, and the student's respect for and sense of responsibility to the teacher. Some schools have attempted to do this in group fashion through the "Homeroom" plan. Under this arrangement, pupils come to a designated room for about 20 minutes first thing each day. Following general school announcements, the "homeroom teacher" tries to make human contact with students by expressing interest in their other classes and encouraging them to do better, or asking about their report cards. Students often are quite touched by such simple gestures. It has been wisely observed that everyone needs "someone to show their report card to" throughout life. Another practical means of accomplishing this end is to have someone openly represent any child who is the subject of a "staffing," or conference to assess a child's placement and instructional program. The act of serving as a student's advocate can be a powerful heuristic in guiding remedial specialists to represent them in a more holistic manner. Schooling, for example, is particularly harsh to youngsters with artistic temperaments and "off-beat" views, a fact verified each day on talk shows as actors and comedians recount a litany of demoralizing experiences in school.

3. ThemedSchool. A ThemedSchool is little more than a focus that a school adopts for a given year. It can range from "artistic expressions" to "inventive thinking." Ideally, the theme ought to culminate in a fair or display such as an Invention Convention (for more information on the latter contact Invent America! 510 King Street, Suite 42, Alexandria, VA 22314; Weekly Reader, 245 Long Hill Road, Middletown, CT 06457; Venture, 140 E. Monument Ave, Dayton, OH 45402; or Foundation for Better Ideas, Education Building, University of Missouri-Kansas City, 64110). ThemedSchool tends to bring the community into the school and school learning out to the community. The broad, cross-disciplinary nature of the project also tends to create authentic opportunities for cooperative work and learning.

4. A Living Library. A Living Library (Manzo, 1973; Manzo & Manzo, 1990a) is one that encourages the active participation of users in a variety of ways that collectively tends to encourage constructive, reactive reading and incidentally builds aids and encouragements to students to read, write, and think in a more literate or constructive way. Four examples are presented here.

a. WeWriters—this is a section of the library designed to house student, faculty, and community essays, plays, poetry, books, and other literary productions. Desk-top publishing systems now help to have these printed, bound, and cataloged for circulation as part of the library's regular collection.

b. Inquiry Books—these are books of interesting questions that refer the student to precisely the book and page where an answer might be found. These can be accumulated from the reading and writing of students, teachers, and community members.

Examples:
Which animals that grow larger than people are born smaller than a hand? [World Book, Vol. 2, p. 36 (panda bears and kangaroos)]
In what way are humans more powerful than most animals? [*The Human Ape*, p. 12 (We have more lung power for our size and can travel farther in a day than most animals).]

There are two books that we have found especially useful in teaching students how to construct questions of this type: *Can Elephants Swim?* (Robert Fores, Time Life Books, 1969); and *Fabulous Fallacies* (Thaddeus Tuleja, 1982).

c. Certified Independent Study—It has been noted that selective study on most any topic for just fifteen minutes a day will make one a specialist in that subject within just four years. Focused study of most anything, as Vygotsky

(1962) has noted, greatly enhances schema, prior knowledge (a key to successful comprehension), vocabulary, and a sense of the structure of all knowledge. The reading specialist and school librarian can aid in this goal by instigating and certifying planned independent study. Several software programs are available for printing some very impressive looking certificates. Teachers, students, and even community members can be brought together monthly to share questions, knowledge, and related interests and hobbies (Manzo, Sherk, Leibert, & Mocker, 1977).

d. Exchange Reading System (Manzo, 1973). Dialectical, or back and forth discussion and thinking, is the basis for all learning and a strong source of motivation to read, think, and write further (Manzo & Manzo, 1990a; Riegel, 1979). The Exchange Reading Program, which is more fully developed in the chapter on higher order literacy, offers a means for better readers and thinkers to share their thoughts and insights with each other and with less capable readers. This system also invites participation from teachers and community members alike.

5. Cross-Age and Peer Reading. Under this plan, below average readers from grades 4–8 serve as readers of children's books to kindergarten and first grade children. This simple weekly program can help poor readers gain practice and self-esteem, as well as adding to the overall sense that books and reading are prized activities. Labbo and Teale (1990) report reading gains and improvements in self-concept from just such a program. There was a further incidental benefit in that the tutors became much more open and willing to learn how to read effectively to the kindergarteners. These fifth graders were taught how to improve their own fluency and to focus on comprehension through "repeated readings" and "mental modeling" (Duffy, Roehler, & Hermann, 1988). The mental modeling was limited to relating personal experiences to the stories read, a strategy proven valuable to active text processing by Mason and Au (1986). Susan

---

Reflective Activity Box 3
When in Doubt

The greatest asset in planning and providing instruction to reading and learning disabled youngsters is our personal capacity to call up an appropriately empathetic sense of what will get the job done. When you are in doubt about what you should do, picture yourself trying to help an uncoordinated child to hit a ball with a bat.*

Try this right now and list some things you might try to do. Compare your thoughts with those of others in training. You may wish to use this same activity with students in "Doer-Helper."

*move closer; tell the child to swing while you literally try to hit the bat with the ball; get a bigger ball; get a "t-ball" holder.

Coleman (1990) reports similar results from a three-year cross-age tutoring program called "Doer–Helper," in which middle school Chapter I students have planned and conducted reading and writing sessions with kindergarten and second grade students. The middle schoolers developed greater self-confidence, library skills, leadership skills, as well as their own reading and writing skills (Coleman, 1990). In addition, by stepping into the teacher's shoes, these youngsters have developed more understanding and positive attitudes toward teachers and school in general. To help yourself to self-discover many of the attributes of an effective remedial teacher, try the heuristic in Reflective Activity Box 3.

Materials: Types, Appraisal, Use

Materials are the teacher's silent partner in instruction. The effective teacher uses a wide variety of materials, including the dictated and written stories of students themselves to enhance reading, language, and thinking.

Generally speaking, the first thing the remedial specialist looks for is high-interest, controlled vocabulary material. This permits the teacher to control the level of difficulty that the pupil encounters in the early, tender stages of recovery from reading disability. Several means of matching students to materials of appropriate level of difficulty are discussed in other portions of the book (see readability estimation, Degrees of Reading Power, and cloze procedure).

The next thing the remedial teacher often looks for are materials designated for teaching specific skills. These often vary in quality and in the relative merit of what they ask students to do in order to learn. There are three concepts that are helpful in evaluating the tasks that materials ask students to do. A system for assessing tasks in materials was devised by Eanet, Condon, and Manzo (1974). The initial system, designed for secondary and college materials, was built on three concept-terms: perfunctory, assumptive, and generative. We have modified and expanded these to cover a broader range of concerns and levels. These concept-terms are described below.

Some Concept-Terms for Thinking about Instructional Tasks and Materials

The terms offered here should serve as useful guides, or heuristics, for thinking about and appraising most any instructional plan or methodology under consideration. Of course, the value of any material or program can be enhanced or diminished by the purpose for which it is used and how it actually is presented and employed. An illustration is presented further ahead in the chapter for how a mediocre material and task are enhanced by thoughtful usage.

Counterproductive

There are tasks and exercises found in materials and in teachers' guides which, while well-intended, can induce defensive reactions that result in "avoidance," and negative learning outcomes. It is difficult to give examples of this category since it is the context, or the way that it is presented, that pretty much determines whether it will be productive or counterproductive. However, here are some examples of practices that generally are at risk of becoming counterproductive:

- Whole class spelling bees and other such highly competitive systems can breed more fear and anxiety about spelling than interest and learning.
- Materials that ask students who are poor readers to rely largely on standard dictionaries to learn new words can be counterproductive, since such students rarely can read and abstract appropriate meanings without some further assistance.
- Textual materials that are "inconsiderate," or assume knowledge that students don't have, or simply are too dense, can be counterproductive (math and science materials are notorious for this, but novels with huge casts of characters can be equally inaccessible).
- Materials that make little instructional sense can be counterproductive (e.g., "underline the letters of the alphabet in order as you find them on this page of print until you reach 'z' ").

Generally, relatively few tasks and materials are counterproductive *in and of themselves*. The worst that most materials and practices get is described by the next category.

Perfunctory

These are tasks and activities that are superficial, though largely innocuous, except that they may waste valuable instructional time. Many "visual-perceptual" training programs contain tasks that fit in this category. They have students draw lines connecting one thing to another, to improve "eye-hand-motor coordination," an operation that has no proven bearing on reading, thinking, or learning (Leibert & Sherk, 1970).

Perfunctory tasks are rather like running in place: much activity, lots of sweat, but no progress to speak of. But again, if diagnosis suggests a possible benefit for running in place, and the teacher realizes this, then the task is no longer perfunctory, it is a prescription mapped into a diagnosed need. Put another way, when a match can be found between a task or material and a need, go ahead and light it, no matter how inconsequential the task or material may appear without that context. This is the prerogative of the reflective teacher.

The next concept-term refers to a category that is a considerable step above this and is characteristic of most materials and school learning tasks.

Incremental

These are tasks and materials that tend to result in average increments of learning. That is, increments that tend to be small, but do achieve competence in a fashion. There are many remedial reading methods and materials that fit this description. They plug along, but fail to engage students to think about and otherwise practice desired skills or objectives outside of the strictly instructional setting. They tend to lead students through repetitive exercises in a mind-numbing way. They make a one-hour trip feel like two.

Remedial students are characteristically incremental learners to begin with. This is their greatest problem. They usually learn what they are taught each period, but do not reach independence. There are several reasons why they remain "suboptimal-incremental" learners:

1. they fail to learn something deeply enough to begin with,
2. they do not think about it any further outside of class time,
3. they live in a nonreinforcing environment, and/or
4. it just isn't high on their personal agenda.

Whatever the reason, their learning, in effect, remains summative, when learning, to become secure, must be synergistic and generative.

Generative Learning

In one stage theory of reading, Gray (1925) identified a "stage 3" progression (occurring between second and third grades) that he called a period or stage of "unusually rapid development" (p. 100) in word recognition, rate, silent and oral reading, comprehension, and ability to read for different purposes (as cited in Chall, 1983c). Such obvious leaps in learning must be preceded by periods of knowledge-seeking and consolidation. There are certain tasks that greatly spur these periods of apparent growth. These we have labelled generative tasks. As a general rule, such tasks tend to occupy the student's mind beyond as well as in the classroom, and also tend to result in inner rehearsals that build strategies for learning more so than just new increments of knowledge. Generative learning, in the language of Louise Rosenblatt (1969), is more transactional (process oriented) than transmissional (product oriented).

Tasks that are generative tend to be epistemological in the sense that they engender active mental play with the concepts and skills in a variety of contexts and cause further and deeper learning to occur. They raise a teaching episode from a merely summative, or incremental level, to a synergistic one—that is, the amount learned is greater than the simple sum of the increments of instruction. This, of course, is the ideal purpose of all instruction, and it is assumed to be part of schooling, whether we realize it or not. It is impossible, for example, to teach students all the possible combinations of ways letters can be pronounced in every possible word; therefore, the implicit expectation is that they must leave the classroom and in some way engage letters, words, and print on signs, in names, and on labels in ways that ultimately results in synergistic leaps that lead to mastery. Ironically, the strongest criticism that can be made of many "mastery learning" programs is that they try to accomplish all learning through these incremental units, with little reference to authenticity and inspiration.

The remedial specialist actively needs to seek methods and materials that can combine to induce generative learning. It simply is not enough to offer up tasks and materials that tend to produce incremental outcomes. Reflective Ac-

Reflective Activity Box 4
Converting an Incremental Activity to a Generative One

Presume that a small group of seventh grade students are doing comprehension practice work in SRA's *Reading for Understanding* Kit (Thelma Thurstone, 1969). The instructional task is to select the best word or phrase to complete a sentence or brief paragraph.

> Sample (card 08, #5)
>
> Fixed stars actually move about in space, but the ancients who first saw and named them were unable to discern their:
>
> a. arrangement   b. size   c. motion   d. light

(Correct answer is *c. motion,* the key words in the sentence are "move about")

While students do such exercises and self-correct them, the teacher usually supervises by walking about and monitoring their work. This, typically, involves pausing when a student is making errors and helping the student puzzle out the correct answer.

As described, this is a solid incremental learning activity involving close knit analytical reading, self-pacing, self-scoring, and teacher monitoring. It is not generative, however, since feedback is shallow, there is no incentive to think deeply, and whenever the teacher stops at a desk there is the implicit suggestion that the student has erred. This causes most students to become distracted and to terminate thinking in order to solve the new social problem created by the impression that the teacher only stops to talk to those who are weak and wrong. To overcome this, students typically will quickly (and mindlessly) select another answer so that, if correct, the teacher will keep moving.

This incremental lesson can become somewhat more generative by a little fine tuning. In this case, the teacher need only be sure that when stopping at a desk, that she should ask a student to explain some answers that are correct as well as incorrect.

This slight adjustment can result in several positive and generative outcomes. First, it releases the impression that the teacher stops only when errors are being made. Second, it gives a student an opportunity occasionally to demonstrate competent thinking. Third, it gives the teacher a chance to reinforce and refine solid thinking. Fourth, it develops a stronger sense of self-examination of one's own thinking and responding.

tivity Box 4 offers an example of how a greater level of generativeness often can be achieved even with a simple auto-instructional task.

In brief, a low-impact exercise can be upgraded to a more robust interaction when the student is given a chance to acquire a strategy for how to think and talk about—or language through—a learning problem. For an example of an inherently generative task, see the section on Dialogue Journals in Chapter 12, Remedies for Defects, Disruptions, and Differences.

The "Pill" Analogy

There is another way to think about methodology that is more metaphoric than explicit. Consider the "pill analogy" as another self-guiding way of characterizing and understanding the value of certain methods. A pill has essentially three components: 1) an active ingredient that actually causes change to occur; 2) a facilitating ingredient that allows the active agent to work or be absorbed; and 3) an inert ingredient that holds the other ingredients together in the convenient form of a pill.

Like a pill, instruction can have several ingredients. Tasks that require students to translate or transform information can be compared to the active ingredients in a pill. Tasks that generate interactions among students, call up background knowledge, or raise motivation could be considered facilitative ingredients. Tasks that require only practice-type writing, reading, speaking, or listening could be considered as inert bonding ingredients.

While analogies are, by definition, only imperfect comparisons, we think you will find this one useful in several ways. It causes one to realize that a good program requires all three types of ingredients. It gives one a means of determining when a program or method is over or under weighted with some ingredients. And, it can be a useful means of communicating the essential character and purpose of elements within instructional methods and approaches.

By this analogy, remedial principle #7, Teacher-Directed Instruction, would tend to be an "active ingredient." Remedial principle #1, "Diagnostic Teaching," would tend to serve as a facilitative ingredient. Finally, remedial principle #20, "Student Reading," would tend, despite its importance, to be almost an inert ingredient, with little force unto itself without the support provided by other components such as an engaging instructional conversation. The potential value of the analogue will be made more vivid in some of the more contextualized examples presented in the chapters ahead. Remember, the purpose of the analogy is not to be persuasive of one point of view or another, as much as to clarify and communicate perspectives that deserve your consideration, and for you to be able to respond in kind.

LOOKING BACK

The chapter built a structure for understanding and planning successful remediation. It did so by pointing up the sometimes overlooked values in remediation, and by developing several related ideas. These included: principles to guide remediation, ways to organize a remedial session, means of building a supportive environment, and means of guiding selection of methods and materials. The chapter concluded with an analogy that can serve as a guide, of sorts, in evaluating the appropriateness of instructional methods and materials.

➤ LOOKING AHEAD

The next chapter puts the principles and precepts of remediation into motion in the most basic area of reading instruction—word decoding. The chapter treats word analysis and recognition separately and together in considerable detail.

8

Remedies for Decoding and Word Recognition Deficits

"*Decoding is a comprehension skill.*"
NANCY LEWKOWICZ
(1987)

➤ *LOOK FOR IT*

Surely the most painful and vivid part of being a poor reader is the feeling of apprehension that grips a person each time he or she must decipher print symbols in some public way. There are only 26 symbols and 44 sounds, as the "Hooked on Phonics" advertisements are fond of saying. Nonetheless, there is a certain perversity to the English alphabetic system. George Bernard Shaw used to enjoy asking people to read this word: Ghoti. The word, he would say, is fish, as anyone who can "read" should know: "gh" pronounced as in enou*gh* (f); "o" as in "w*o*men" (i); and "ti" as in "defini*ti*on" (sh)

    The challenge of teaching decoding in the face of such perversity has attracted many honest efforts, no little dissension, and a good deal of confusion. The chapter opens with a word on philosophical considerations underlying decoding instruction in general, then provides relevant background information on the decoding process as it relates to remedial readers. The remainder, and largest portion, of the chapter is a catalog of means and methods for remedying deficits in word analysis and recognition.

Considerations in Teaching Decoding

Three considerations have a direct bearing on remedial instruction in decoding:

- the general design of the remedial decoding *program*
- what needs to be done for *students*
- what needs to be done to optimize the effectiveness of *teachers*

The Decoding Program

Regarding the overall remedial decoding *program*, the view is that there is no real difference in purpose in teaching a child to decode a word, to learn its meaning, or to comprehend it in written text. Each of these is a part of the unifying objective of teaching children to read for meaning. For most specialists, this means that each portion of the instructional program benefits from both incidental and explicit instruction. Some, however, such as whole language enthusiasts, are less certain of the proportion of need for explicit instruction in any of these realms. They tend to believe, for example, that deciphering can largely be learned incidentally through repeated encounters with words in context, through language experience stories, through variations on cloze exercises that encourage speculating on which word might best fit a certain context, and by reading in linguistically controlled but meaningful materials (Y. Goodman, 1975). The methods offered ahead are less self-conscious about appearing to be segmented or explicit. While the overall reading program has a rich concern for language, meaning, and children's needs, the methods offered here for remedial readers contain a rather clear focus on identifying and treating specific aspects of need in word recognition and analysis.

Student and Teacher Needs

Where students are concerned, the objective is to find or develop some compelling ways to keep their attention focused on words and word parts. A variety of means for doing this are offered throughout the text. Where teachers are concerned, one objective is to use methods that help them sustain their *own* interest and will to work with remedial students through the many repetitions they require. Another teacher-related objective is to make the student's learning style, rather than the teacher's teaching style, the priority. This may mean mastering and using methods that are less personally favored. From this brief overview, let us now develop some deeper understandings of how word analysis and recognition might best be understood and remediated in those with apparent deficits.

Reflective Teaching is a Must

As noted in a previous chapter, there is a persistent controversy regarding whether word recognition and analysis, which must *become* nearly seamless, should be *taught* seamlessly (the whole language view), componentially (the traditional emphasis), or almost atomistically—one tiny step at a time (the mastery learning view). The remedial child's needs, in practical terms, often require a special combination of approaches, since, by definition, the previous program was inadequate and a problem needs to be solved. This requires flexibility and reflective teaching.

The methods described ahead are largely compatible with the principles of remediation detailed in the previous chapter. Collectively, those principles support a reflective and interlocking holistic view designed to meet the needs of students more so than merely their reading "skills." The poor reader, having already lapsed into a dysfunctional state, must, according to Maslow's hierarchy of needs, have his or her damaged ego needs bolstered in order to be able to tackle higher cognitive objectives. Helping students who are failing requires a very pragmatic and flexible approach that is unencumbered by philosophies that are rejecting of anything that may prove to be worthwhile in a given case. The objective is simply to build self-efficacy, and for some children this is best accomplished in a highly structured, almost lock-step program, while for others it may require a more incidental, almost sidling-up-to-literacy approach.

The professional remedial specialist can seldom afford the luxury of believing in and practicing one approach or another. He or she must be prepared to deliver that which is most likely to get the job done—and that often requires differential diagnosis, knowledge of a variety of approaches to each area of need, and the realization that every instructional decision likely will require fine tuning, at best, and an occasional inversion of tactics for achieving the same goal with different students. (For a dramatic example of this kind of inversion of tactics, see the section on Implosive Therapy and Antithetical Role Play in Chapter 11.) Now consider what is known about the process and concepts of word recognition and analysis. This will provide you with much of the knowledge base for selecting and adapting strategies that are best suited to your students.

The Decoding Process

Word Recognition and Phonetic Analysis

There are essentially two interacting processes used in the decoding aspect of reading. In one, popularly called *word recognition*, the reader attempts to identify a word rapidly, with little attention to letter-to-sound relationships. This process relies heavily on eidetic imagery—the ability to hold an image in short-term memory while physically moving past it to other words or images, to test to see whether the word should be called one thing or another (e.g. Is this word *their* or *then*?). In word recognition, the reader depends on two additional aids: the most distinguishing features of the word (Gibson & Levin, 1975), and the context in which it is used. Every word has special distinguishing features, including its configuration, or shape (Marchbanks & Levin, 1965). The word recognition process is especially crucial in the learning of phonetically irregular words that are used frequently in everyday speech and writing.

In the second process, called *phonetic analysis*, the reader applies knowledge of letter-to-sound relationships until a hypothesis can be made as to what the word probably is. That hypothesis is tested against the context in which the word is used. This read-predict-read process occurs hundreds of times in reading even relatively easy material. A key component of phonetic analysis is the "distinguishing of boundaries of linguistic elements within the sound stream" (Clark, 1988, p. 8). This has been referred to as *phonemic awareness* and *phonemic segmentation.* (For a program explicitly addressing this need, see Hallie Yopp, 1992).

Boder's Classification System

Problems can arise with either or both of these functions. Elena Boder (1971a, b), as noted in a previous chapter, offers a classification system for severe decoding and related spelling problems that is useful in addressing the needs of most mildly remedial and corrective readers. Boder's system describes three types of problems, as detailed below.

The *dysphonetic* condition is a severe deficit in letter-sound integration with a resulting inability to learn phonetic word-analysis skills. Reading, for these youngsters, is global and based almost wholly on sight recognition. Spelling, even of known words, seems to be based more on the look of the word than its sound units (*letter* for *little; wet* for *was*). According to an earlier account by Boder (1970), spelling of unknown words tends to be totally nonphonetic (*arefl* for *story; alley* for *almost; rsty* for *guess*). The most striking errors, however, are semantic substitution errors, as in reading *funny* for *laugh, chicken* for *duck,* and *answer* for *ask* (p. 289).

The *dyseidetic* condition is an inability to recognize words easily on sight, with a resulting overreliance on phonetic analysis, even for frequently encountered words.

The *combined dysphonetic/dyseidetic* condition is characterized by poor phonetic and poor eidetic reading and spelling. It is the most severe form of reading disorder.

Of students with severe reading problems, about 10% are dyseidetic, 59% are dysphonetic, and about 25% are combined dysphonetic/dyseidetic. About 6% have patterns of errors that can not be classified in any of these three ways (Boder & Jarrico, 1982).

These same types of disorders have been found to a lesser extent in those with less severe reading disabilities. For example, simple phonemic awareness tasks such as asking children merely to repeat a part of a word, have been found to predict successfully which children will have difficulty in learning to read (Fox & Routh, 1980; Liberman, Sankweiler, Liberman, Fowler, & Fischer, 1977; Rosner, 1974; Rosner & Simon, 1971). Importantly, those who were taught to read also improved their phonemic awareness (Morais, Cary, Algeria, & Bertelson, 1979).

It is not totally clear just how much phonetic awareness is necessary to learn how to read since some pupils seem to learn how to read despite poor aptitudes, and even constitutional weaknesses in this regard. However, they do seem to rely to a great degree on some form of whole-word learning that seems to parallel the eidetic means used by the Chinese to master ideographs. The question is whether it is worth the bother to raise phonemic awareness and teach speech-to-print and print-to-speech sounds. Teachers who believe in its worth seem to be influenced by at least one conscious and one subconscious motive. At a conscious level, they believe that it is essential to effective reading and that it will help students who would have chronic spelling problems for much of their lives without such training. At a subconscious level, they seem to gravitate toward it because it is the way *they* learn best and, therefore, like to teach. Since this helps these teachers to take pride in providing direct and sustained instruction in phonics, it tends to have beneficial effects for all but a few students. In general, all such decisions are more professionally acceptable when they are made more consciously. When made consciously, such decisions tend to be less doctrinaire, and easier to put aside when they don't work.

To help in this complex decision-making process, consider now what is currently known about decoding instruction, more so than just the decoding process. This section is followed by general recommendations for a decoding program, and then by specific teaching methods.

Research on Decoding Instruction

In a thorough review of the early stages of learning to read, Connie Juel (1991) reached several conclusions that are pertinent to understanding and providing instruction in the decoding process. Those conclusions that are most relevant to remedial instruction are summarized here.

- Word analysis and recognition skills are neither "easy" (Gibson & Levin, 1975, p. 265) nor "natural" (Gough & Hillinger, 1980, p. 180). Further, they may actually impair or stifle a child's interest in learning to read. Nonetheless, they must be taught and learned, since early success in these is a solid predictor of eventual growth in decoding (Lundberg, 1984), comprehension (Lesgold & Resnick, 1982), and subsequent exposure to words—good decoders encounter roughly twice as many words as poor ones in the earliest stages of reading (Juel, 1988).
- There is little evidence to suggest that good readers use context clues more than poor readers. On the contrary, good readers decode words using word-analysis techniques that then strengthen their understanding of the context. Readers can only predict about one out of four words from context (Gough, Alford, & Holly-Wilcox, 1981).
- Reading errors tend to be made in inverse proportion to the number of times a word has been previously exposed in print (Gough, Juel, & Roper-Schneider, 1983).
- Most poor readers have a "strategy imbalance"—they tend to rely excessively on one tactic to the exclusion of others (e.g., context but not sounding, or glued-to-print, laborious sounding to the exclusion of visual imprinting and context) (Sulzby, 1985).
- Several studies and theories have led to the belief that there are essentially three stages to developing decoding skills:
  1. *The selective-cue (predecoding) stage.* At this stage, the child initially tends to rely upon three categories of cues in roughly this order:
     a. random cues—most any visual clue that is present is used to remember what a word might mean, even a thumb print (Gough, 1991);

      b. environmental cues—such as where the word is located on the page;

      c. distinctive letters (the "y" in "pony").

2. *The spelling-sound stage.* At this stage, the child tends to recognize some words by a combination of visual recall of their spelling and a beginning sense of sounds of some of the letters. The pinnacle of this stage is sounding out and plausibly decoding most words.

3. *The automatic response stage.* At this stage, a fair-sized vocabulary of frequently occurring words are recognized automatically. Juel (1991, p. 783) notes that "we do not know exactly what it is about word recognition that becomes automatic"—recognition of whole words due to frequent exposure to a small number of words, or letter-sound relations due to exposure to letter-sound patterns in many different words.

- A little bit of phonics can go a long way. It takes a fairly minimal amount of explicit phonics instruction to induce the learning and use of even untaught spelling-sound relationships when the text children are exposed to contains a number of regular decodable words (Juel & Roper-Schneider, 1985).

- The least time should be spent teaching specific phonic rules per se, and the most time actually reading (Juel, 1991).

- Other simple practices that seem, in combination, to build strategic cue use best include the following:

  1. labeling of objects with printed cards;

  2. language experience activities where students dictate words, sentences, or stories;

  3. use of "big books" where children can see the words the teacher is reading (Holdaway, 1979);

  4. use of patterned, predictable chart stories (Bridge, 1986; Bridge, Winograd, & Haley, 1983).

- When a child asks the question "What's this word?" this gives the strongest evidence that he or she is thinking about reading and print decoding, and hence is on the way to becoming a generative learner (Clark, 1976; Durkin, 1966).

Research-Based Program Components

Taken together with the research on disabled readers, and with individual diagnostic findings, it seems that most students tend to need a decoding program that addresses six aspects of word analysis and recognition. These include:

- interest in and knowledge of language and literacy
- an optimal level of phonemic awareness (such as the ability to hear and segment sounds in words)
- phonetic decoding of words in isolation
- use of context to aid decoding
- instant recognition of phonetically irregular words
- connection of decoding to the other language arts, especially writing and spelling

Read ahead now to learn more about the choices that are available to the reflective teacher of reading. You will see most of the principles and research findings previously discussed represented in these methods. The first set of methods addresses the needs of students who are to a greater or lesser degree dyseidetic; that is, they have difficulty learning whole words by sight.

Teaching Eidetic Imagery and Sight Words

Overview of Sight Word Instruction

About 85% of the words in the English language are phonetically regular; however, the 15-20% that are not regular appear with the greatest frequency in print, or about 80% of the time (Hanna, Hodges, Hanna, & Rudolph, 1966). This happens neither by conspiracy nor by accident. It is in the nature of language: the more a word is used, the more its sounds tend to become relaxed, clipped, or otherwise suitable to oral use, while its print characteristics remain fairly constant. This is especially the case with "function words." These are words that do not convey much meaning in themselves, but aid in sentence building, or syntactical construction (*and, but, then, if, however*). These words traditionally are taught as sight words—you say the word when you see the letters, but you don't pay much attention to the sounds of the letters or complex phonetic rules. The reader is taught to practice "selective inattention," as in saying *nite* for *night* rather than a guttural pronunciation of the **gh**—or an **f** sound pronunciation of the **gh,** as in *rough*—*night* becoming *nift*!

Teaching sight words is appropriate since the objective is that eventually all words will become "sight words" in the sense that they must be recognized quickly and automatically in order for meaningful and fluent reading to occur; that is, they must reach what LaBerge and Samuels have called "automaticity" (1974). The basic principles behind teaching sight words are fairly simple: get the student to *see* words and their distinguishing features, orally *say* those words, and look for and silently *practice* saying these words wherever they might be encountered until they are learned to 100% accuracy.

Following is a collection of ways to enhance eidetic imaging, or short-term memory, as well as to improve long-term memory for sight words. While it can not be firmly established just how many repetitions it takes to learn words, Arthur Gates is said to have estimated that it takes between 20 and 44. This, in any case, is more than most teachers tend to provide. (For additional information on teaching sight words, see George W. McNinch's Intensive Sight Word Routine, and Edward Dwyer and Rona Flippo's [1983] Multisensory Approach in Chapter 12 on treating severe reading disabilities or dyslexia.)

Flash Card Approaches to Eidetic Imagery and Sight Words

There are many variations on this approach. The one described here is a synthesis of several methods, based largely on those described by Patricia Cunningham (1980) and by Eldon E. Ekwall and James L. Shanker (1988). It uses voice variations and questions about the word to provide necessary repetitions and attention to its distinguishing features, and to building eidetic imagery. Since it incorporates several techniques, we have referred to it as an "omnibus strategy."

Omnibus Strategy to Sight Word Automaticity

This strategy can be done with one or more students. The teacher holds up a flash card or writes a word on the chalk board:

Teacher: See this word? The word is *and*. Everyone look at this word, and say it together.

Students: *And.*

Teacher: That's correct. Now say it five times while looking at it.

S's: *And, and, and, and, and.*

T: Good. Now say it louder.

S's: **And**!

T: Come on, you can say it louder than that!

S's: **AND!**

T: OK, I have three other cards here (again, answer, arrange). When I show a card that is not *and*, say "No!" in a loud voice. But when you see *and,* say it in a whisper.

S's: No!

S's: No!

S's: (whisper) *And.*

T: Great. Look at it carefully, and when I remove it, close your eyes and try to picture the word under your eyelids. Do you see it? Good. Now say it in a whisper again.

S's: *And.*

T: Good. Now spell it.

S's: A...N...D.

T: Now pretend to write it in the air in front of you with your finger while saying each letter.

S's: A...N...D.

T: Good. Now describe the word. The way you would describe a new kid to a friend who hasn't seen him yet.

S1:   It's small.

S2:   It has a witch's hat in the beginning.

S3:   It has a belly at the end.

T: What's its name again?

S's: *AND!*

T: Let's search for *and*'s throughout the day and even after you go home tonight. We'll ask you later if you found any in school and again tomorrow morning if you found any at home.

In the morning, have on the board, "**Did you find any *and*'s last night?**" Over the next few lessons, ask if the student has seen an *and*.

Up to three words a day usually can be taught in this general way. Be sure that the target words do not *look* at all alike. Words that are shown in context with the object word and that do look like the object word should not be overstressed. These often will be learned incidentally, as the student sets about distinguishing them.

The most traditional source of high frequency sight words was compiled by Edward Dolch (1951), and is found in Figure 8.1. Two more recent sight word lists, by Edward Fry (1980) and Marilyn Eeds (1985), are found in Figures 8.2 and 8.3. Fry's list is based on the frequency of occurrence of words in more recent school texts and trade books. Eeds's list is shorter, containing 227 words, also in order of frequency of occurrence, but in 400 storybooks for beginning readers, and therefore is more suitable for a "literature-based" reading program. The Dolch, Fry, and Eeds lists can be used for diagnostic testing and teaching of sight word vocabulary.

Other Flash Card Activities

To reinforce targeted sight words further, try these traditional methods:

1. Put the words on oak tag and place them around the room.
2. Have the child put the words on a ring that can be carried about for self-review.
3. Create a buddy system that has students checking and helping one another to learn the words.
4. Distribute word cards to students and have them sort them into known and unknown words. Have them say all the words (they think) they know. Next, begin to use the look-alike words by asking them to try to figure out what each of them say. Note the letters and sounds that give trouble and teach the student how to decode these using the cluster of methods ahead under word analysis.
5. Have children practice eidetic imaging techniques with spelling words. Gerald Glass (personal communication), a veteran diagnostician and clinician at Adelphi University, maintains that this also is a formidable means of teaching children how to spell correctly.
6. Have students try to construct sentences from their flash cards. Tell them that you will help them add any words they wish, but that the words added then become part of their personal word card file, and they must learn to read them at sight.
7. Use media-assisted reinforcement devices. There is an excellent (older) device called a Language Master (product of Bell & Howell Corporation) that was designed for training in sight word recognition. It is a card with a piece of magnetic tape across the bottom of both sides. The student pushes it through a tape recorder while saying what he thinks the word is. The card then is reversed and put through with a prerecorded voice saying the word correctly. There also are computer programs that now do essentially the same thing. Robert Cutler and Carrol Truss (1989) have designed one that

FIGURE 8.1

Dolch Sight Word List

a	come	grow	many	run	too
about	could	had	may	said	try
after	cut	has	me	saw	two
again		have	much	say	
all	did	he	must	see	under
always	do	help	my	seven	up
am	does	her	myself	shall	upon
an	done	here		she	us
and	don't	him	never	show	use
any	down	his	new	sing	
are	draw	hold	no	sit	very
around	drink	hot	not	six	
as		how	now	sleep	walk
ask	eat	hurt		small	want
at	eight		of	so	warm
ate	every	I	off	some	was
away		if	old	soon	wash
	fall	in	on	start	we
be	far	into	once	stop	well
because	fast	is	one		went
been	find	it	only	take	were
before	first	its	open	tell	what
best	five		or	ten	when
bring	fly	jump	our	thank	where
big	for	just	out	that	which
black	found		over	the	white
blue	four	keep	own	their	who
both	from	kind		them	why
bring	full	know	pick	then	will
brown	funny		play	there	wish
but		laugh	please	these	with
buy	gave	let	pretty	they	work
by	get	light	pull	think	would
	give	like	put	this	write
call	go	little		those	
came	goes	live	ran	three	yellow
can	going	long	read	to	yes
carry	good	look	red	today	you
clean	got		ride	together	your
cold	green	made	right		
		make	round		

Dolch (1951)

FIGURE 8.2

Fry's "The New Instant Word List"

FIRST HUNDRED

First 25 Group 1a	Second 25 Group 1b	Third 25 Group 1c	Fourth 25 Group 1d
the	or	will	number
of	one	up	no
and	had	other	way
a	by	about	could
to	word	out	people
in	but	many	my
is	not	then	than
you	what	them	first
that	all	these	water
it	were	so	been
he	we	some	call
was	when	her	who
for	your	would	oil
on	can	make	now
are	said	like	find
as	there	him	long
with	use	into	down
his	an	time	day
they	each	has	did
I	which	look	get
at	she	two	come
be	do	more	made
this	how	write	may
have	their	go	part
from	if	see	over

SECOND HUNDRED

First 25 Group 2a	Second 25 Group 2b	Third 25 Group 2c	Fourth 25 Group 2d
new	great	put	kind
sound	where	end	hand
take	help	does	picture
only	through	another	again
little	much	well	change
work	before	large	off
know	line	must	play
place	right	big	spell
year	too	even	air
live	mean	such	away
me	old	because	animal
back	any	turn	house
give	same	here	pint

FIGURE 8.2

Fry's "The New Instant Word List" (continued)

SECOND HUNDRED

First 25 Group 2a	Second 25 Group 2b	Third 25 Group 2c	Fourth 25 Group 2d
most	tell	why	page
very	boy	ask	letter
after	follow	went	mother
thing	came	men	answer
our	want	read	found
just	show	need	study
name	also	land	still
good	around	different	learn
sentence	form	home	should
man	three	us	America
think	small	move	world
say	set	try	high

THIRD HUNDRED

First 25 Group 3a	Second 25 Group 3b	Third 25 Group 3c	Fourth 25 Group 3d
every	left	until	idea
near	don't	children	enough
add	few	side	eat
food	while	feet	face
between	along	car	watch
own	might	mile	far
below	close	night	Indian
country	something	walk	real
plant	seem	white	almost
last	next	sea	let
school	hard	began	above
father	open	grow	girl
keep	example	took	sometimes
tree	begin	river	mountain
never	life	four	cut
start	always	carry	young
city	those	state	talk
earth	both	once	soon
eye	paper	book	list
light	together	hear	song
thought	got	stop	leave
head	group	without	family
under	often	second	body
story	run	late	music
saw	important	miss	color

Fry (1980)

FIGURE 8.3

High Frequency Words from Children's Literature
Final Core 227 Word List Based on 400 Storybooks for Beginning Readers

the	1314	good	90	think	47	next	28
and	985	this	90	new	46	only	28
a	831	don't	89	know	46	am	27
I	757	little	89	help	46	began	27
to	746	if	87	grand	46	head	27
said	688	just	87	boy	46	keep	27
you	638	baby	86	take	45	teacher	27
he	488	way	85	cat	44	sure	27
it	345	there	83	body	43	says	27
in	311	every	83	school	43	ride	27
was	294	went	82	house	42	pet	27
she	250	father	80	morning	42	hurry	26
for	235	had	79	yes	41	hand	26
that	232	see	79	after	41	hard	26
is	230	dog	78	never	41	push	26
his	226	home	77	or	40	our	26
but	224	down	76	self	40	their	26
they	218	got	73	try	40	watch	26
my	214	would	73	has	38	because	25
of	204	time	71	always	38	door	25
on	192	love	70	over	38	us	25
me	187	walk	70	again	37	should	25
all	179	came	69	side	37	room	25
be	176	were	68	thank	37	pull	25
go	171	ask	67	why	37	great	24
can	162	back	67	who	36	gave	24
with	158	now	66	saw	36	does	24
one	157	friend	65	mom	35	car	24
her	156	cry	64	kid	35	ball	24
what	152	oh	64	give	35	sat	24
we	151	Mr.	63	around	34	stay	24
him	144	bed	63	by	34	each	23
no	143	an	62	Mrs.	34	ever	23
so	141	very	62	off	33	until	23
out	140	where	60	sister	33	shout	23
up	137	play	59	find	32	mama	22
are	133	let	59	fun	32	use	22
will	127	long	58	more	32	turn	22
look	126	here	58	while	32	thought	22
some	123	how	57	tell	32	papa	22
day	123	make	57	sleep	32	lot	21
at	122	big	56	made	31	blue	21
have	121	from	55	first	31	bath	21

FIGURE 8.3

High Frequency Words from Children's Literature

Final Core 227 Word List Based on 400 Storybooks for Beginning Readers *(continued)*

your	121	put	55	say	31	mean	21
mother	119	read	55	took	31	sit	21
come	118	them	55	dad	30	together	21
not	115	as	54	found	30	best	20
like	112	Miss	53	lady	30	brother	20
then	108	any	52	soon	30	feel	20
get	103	right	52	ran	30	floor	20
when	101	nice	50	dear	29	wait	20
thing	100	other	50	man	29	tomorrow	20
do	99	well	48	better	29	surprise	20
too	91	old	48	through	29	shop	20
want	91	night	48	stop	29	run	20
did	91	may	48	still	29	own	20
could	90	about	47	fast	28		

Eeds (1985)

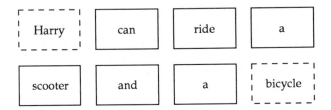

pronounces and gives meanings for targeted words in popular teenage novels.

8. Connect sight words to meaningful contexts by grouping new words in categories, such as words associated with activities and tools used in the classroom (chalkboard, eraser, desk, etc.).

9. Connect sight words to authentic experiences with "Postcard" and other Language Experience activities—have students write brief postcard letters to friends and family. Mention the weather, what they are doing, how they are feeling, and some special salutation and closing (Dear cousin. . . Your grandson). Similarly, have students tell a story or relate an experience. Write it out for them on oak tag or on the chalkboard as they tell it. Have them indicate which words they have seen before. Underline these and have them try to read them in the story context.

10. Use word games—commercial and teacher-made (word bingo, consonant lotto, word dominoes, crossword puzzles, word wheels). Hangman, one of

the oldest, can be used with little preparation, and can be used as a large group, small group, or paired activity.

11. Have students try to act out with their hands and/or body what they think a certain word "looks" like. Select one of the pantomimes offered by the students and have everyone do it while saying the word. For example, for *church,* the pantomime might be hands in steeple shape. This step adds an encoding, or recoding, step to word recognition learning as well as a certain degree of motor learning. This method was suggested to us by a primary school teacher who modeled it after Motor Imaging, a meaning vocabulary strategy detailed in the vocabulary chapter ahead. Word analysis, or deciphering, should be taught alongside word recognition. They can be combined or taught separately.

Teaching the Phonetic Analysis Aspects of Decoding

There are four basic approaches to teaching the word analysis aspects of decoding unknown words: analytic, synthetic, tactile-kinesthetic, and contextual. Most word analysis programs combine the contextual element with one or more of the others.

Overview of Approaches to Analytic Phonics
Analytic Phonics Approaches

Analytic phonics, also sometimes known as *implicit phonics*, is based on beginning with a known word, and studying its parts. Analytic phonics methods tend to teach the sounds of the alphabet, then sight words, then regular consonants, and then irregular consonants and vowels. Students are taught to rely on initial and final consonants to get a rough idea of what a word says. In general, students are encouraged to see and hear certain targeted letters and then to continue to analyze a word until they recognize it as a word they know. The assumption is that the students will internalize this process and apply it, by analogy, to decode other familiar and eventually unfamiliar words. The importance of analogical thinking in phonics instruction was demonstrated in a study in which dyslexic fifth graders were taught to decode nonsense words, their nemesis, by giving them extensive training in generalizing and analogy strategies (Wolff, Desberg, & Marsh, 1985). For the most part, however, analytical phonics programs tend to avoid nonsense words. Students are taught to rely on context as an additional clue in recognizing familiar words and making predictions about the pronunciation of newer ones.

Synthetic Phonics Approaches

Synthetic phonics is based on beginning with an unknown word and building, or synthesizing, it into a meaningful whole. Synthetic phonics approaches usually begin with teaching the names of the letters of the alphabet, then teaching vowel sounds, then consonant and consonant blend sounds. The student is taught to rely on linear, phonetic analysis to "synthesize" each new word (i.e., sound them out). Nonsense words are often used in instruction, since emphasis is placed on the phonetic elements of words rather than on context and meaning. Context and meaning, in fact, are viewed as distractions that actually can sabotage progress toward independent word decoding. Synthetic phonics programs tend to begin with highly controlled, phonetically regular reading, and then leap to high "quality" literature. Several of these programs were born in a deeply religious context, and therefore are seen as the best means of quickly preparing youngsters for the rigors of Bible study. The synthetic phonics approach sometimes is known as *intensive* or *explicit phonics,* or the *alphabet approach.*

Tactile-Kinesthetic Approaches

Tactile-kinesthetic approaches encourage the learner to examine new words through a combination of senses or modalities: visual, auditory, tactile (touch), and kinesthetic (hand or body movement). These approaches, long dormant, have begun regaining popularity due to the learning styles research indicating that sensorimotor learning provides an important foundation for higher level verbal learning (Casale & Manzo, 1983). Learning styles research also provides abundant evidence that children seem to prefer multimodality learning (Carbo, 1988), although it is not as clear that they actually learn better in this way. In a broad sense, this general approach also can be said to include certain "mastery learning" programs since these emphasize the saying-doing or associative aspects of word learning. "Associative learning" has a certain physical cadence and rhythm to it that broadly qualifies it in this category.

Contextual Approaches

Contextual approaches emphasize reading for meaning. These are the methods of choice in whole language teaching. Children are encouraged to use pictures and context as clues to help in decoding unfamiliar words. Cloze passage exercises are encouraged (Y. Goodman, 1975). The use of quality children's literature also is emphasized, particularly stories with repetitions and other predictable elements that support children's early efforts to associate meaning with printed words. Reading to children is seen as an essential means of sparking and extending children's interest in reading. Words tend to be taught as "wholes," and phonic elements are taught incidentally. When this approach is combined with the analytical approach described earlier, it sometimes may be called a *functional, intrinsic,* or *incidental approach* to phonics.

As a rule, most initial reading programs rely on some combination of the approaches described above. Remedial programs, however, have tended to rely primarily on the first three only. Synthetic phonics is the most popularly known, though not necessarily used, form of treatment for severe reading disorders. When combined with the tactile-kinesthetic, it is offered as a multimodality tactic that some hold to be an ideal treatment for dyslexia and related learning disabilities. Analytic phonics clearly is the most frequently used approach to initially teaching the decoding aspects of reading both in the classroom and in remedial situations.

In the next section, basic strategies are outlined for each of the four major approaches to teaching phonetic analysis: analytic, synthetic, kinesthetic, and contextual.

Strategies for Decoding Instruction

Gray's Paradigm: An Analytic Phonics Approach

William S. Gray is sometimes called the "founder of modern reading instruction." Gray's paradigm (1948), a model for analytical phonics instruction, probably was assembled from the work of many researchers and practitioners. It represents the earliest and most complete articulation of this approach to reading instruction, and remains the basis for most all subsequent forms of word analysis training. The paradigm is explained and illustrated below using the **squ** blend.

Steps in Gray's Paradigm

Step 1 *Visual and Aural "Fixing"*

a. *Recognizing visual similarities*: Words are written on the board. The student circles the part(s) that all the words have in common:
   squirrel squeeze squeak square squaw
b. *Recognizing aural similarities:* Using the same list as above, the teacher reads each word from the board, giving only slight emphasis to the **squ** sound. The students try to identify the sound that these words have in common. The auditory step may precede the visual step if the students tend to have an auditory orientation.

Step 2 *Visual and Aural Discrimination*

a. *Visual discrimination:* Presenting words in groups of three, the student first underlines **squ** in each word in which he or she finds it. Next, the student attempts to say only those words containing the **squ** sound:

queen	retire	squirrel	shrimp
squat	squirt	squirm	spring
whom	whenever	sprint	squeaky

b. *Auditory discrimination:* The teacher says three (3) words. Without seeing the words, the student identifies the word(s) containing the **squ** sound:

squeal	squash	shield	squelch
spur	squid	square	squeak
dig	send	squash	squat

Step 3 *Blending (Substitution)*

The teacher shows the student how to blend and substitute sounds to form new words.

*Example: Substitute the **squ** sound for the existing sound at the beginning of each word:*

$$ball - b = all + squ = squall \quad wire - w = ire + squ = squire$$
$$what - w = at + squ = squat \quad tint - t = int = squ = squint$$

Step 4 *Contextual Application*
The student underlines words containing the **squ** sound, which are embedded in sentences:
1. *He led a **squad** of men into battle.*
2. *He leads a **squadron** in the army.*
3. *Try not to **squash** it, please.*

There are three ways to select which letters and sounds to teach using this paradigm:

- Based on diagnostic need as revealed on informal inventories and by casual observation
- By referring to frequency as a guide to predictable phonics rules and elements (See Figure 8.4 for data from two studies of frequency of occurrence of phonics rules, and Figure 8.5 for data from five studies of frequency of occurrence of phonic elements.)
- By referring to the most frequently used letter clusters identified by Glass (See Figure 8.6 ahead following a description of Glass Analysis.)

Figures 8.4 and 8.5 also serve as something of a primer on phonics. You may wish to read through it to get a better grounding in these rules yourself.

Alphabetic Phonics: A Synthetic Phonics Approach

Alphabetic phonics is clearly the most traditional form of phonics instruction. The alphabet is taught in sequence; names of the letters are taught first and then the sounds. Alphabetic phonics is almost a synonym for synthetic or intensive phonics, but for the fact that some synthetic phonics programs teach the sounds of the letters before their names. The method taken up next is one of the oldest still in use with only minor updates and revisions.

Orton-Gillingham.

The synthetic phonics approach is well represented by the Orton-Gillingham (Orton, 1937) approach to teaching severely reading disabled, or dyslexic, children. The program is the work of Sally Childs (a neuropediatrician trained by Anna Gillingham), Lucius Waites, and Aylett Cox (Clark, 1988). Cox, a teacher at the Scottish Rite Hospital in Dallas, Texas, drew up the curriculum described below. She further modernized the Orton method, which primarily is multisensory, by adding two features: one stressing discovery principles and the other putting a greater emphasis on verbal and oral expression.

A typical lesson, according to Cox (1985), is one hour long and includes about five to eight *fast-paced* activities lasting from 1 to 10 minutes. Typical activities include:

1. "meta-language" training—students are taught the language necessary to talk about how to learn reading, language, and phonics (e.g., medial sound, morpheme, modality)
2. flashcard training in letter names

FIGURE 8.4

Predictable Phonics Rules
Identified by Moore (1951) and Black (1961)

[Note: Moore's count is based on the number of times a given phonics rule *worked* in a basic 3,000 word vocabulary bank. Black's count is based on 1,300 words, and is adjusted (multiplied by 30/13ths) so that it could be directly compared with Moore's count. Note that the two counts are fairly similar in most of their findings.

Vowels: Major Rules	Moore	Black
1. **SHORT VOWEL RULE.** Teach short sounds of vowels first.		
A as in **cat**	379	347
E as in **pet**	428	412
I as in **pin**	598	499
O as in **hot**	168	117
U as in **cup**	98	102
2. **FINAL E RULE.** The letter E at the end of a word is often silent and it frequently makes the preceding vowel long.		
Long A as in **age**	114	97
E as in **here**	8	7
I as in **ice**	98	106
O as in **hope**	49	50
U as in **use**	32	32
3. **LONG VOWEL DIGRAPHS.** At its simplest, this rule states "When two vowels are together, the first is long and the second is silent," but this oversimplification has too many exceptions, as pointed out by Clymer (1963). Therefore, teachers should teach these as vowel digraphs.		
Long A AI as in **aid**	58	48
AY as in **day**	29	37
Long E EA as in **eat**	83	108
EE as in **beef**	69	64
Long O OW as in **own**	38	37
OA as in **oak**	26	35
Long U UE as in **due**	15	12
4. **SYLLABLE-ENDING RULE.** If the syllable is open (ends in a vowel) the vowel is long. Irrespective of this rule, E at the end of a word is nearly always silent, for example, *come*, except in one vowel-letter words like *me*.		
A as in **baby**	70	58
E as in **he**	33	106
I as in **tiny**	55	73
O as in **go**	87	71
U as in **pupil**	50	23
Silent E as in **come**	577	206
5. **SCHWA RULE.** A, E, and O sometimes make a sound similar to the short U sound when there is another accented vowel in the word.		
A as in **about**	180	242
O as in **lemon**	128	177
E as in **taken**	92	200

	Moore	Black
6. **VOWEL PLUS R RULE**. The basic rule is that R after a vowel makes a new vowel sound. *ER, UR, and IR all make the same sound.*		
ER in **verb**	46	327
UR in **urge**	34	32
IR in **bird**	28	25
AR makes the sound of AR in **arm** *or the sound of AR in* **vary**	23	
OR makes the sound of OR in **for**	49	23
7. **THE Y RULE**. Y at the end of a long word (another vowel present) has the sound of		
Long E in **baby**	186	168
Y at the end of a short word or in the middle of a word has the sound of		
Long I in **my, cycle**	25	25
Y at the beginning of a word has the consonant sound		
Y in **yes**	10	23

Vowels: Minor Rules

	Moore	Black
8. **OW, OU RULE**. OW and OU both have the same dipthong sound, **out** *and* **owl**.		
OU in **out**	48	17
OW in **owl**	27	19
(note that we have already seen an OW as a Vowel Digraph also)		
9. **DOUBLE O RULE**. Two O's have the sound of OO, as in book, and OO as in choose about an equal percentage of times.	17	21
10. **BROAD O RULE**. Broad O sound is made by AU, AW, A followed by L and O in some words such as *off*.		
AU in **auto**	26	12
AW in **jaw**	13	9
A in **ball**	29	28
O in **off**	27	41
11. **OI, OY RULE**. OI and OY both have the same sound as:		
OI in **oil**	21	18
OY in **boy**	9	12
12. **VOWEL EXCEPTIONS**. There are only two exceptions to the forgoing rules with a high enough frequency to be worth teaching beginning readers.		
EA sometimes has a short E sound as in **head**	39	41
E is silent at the end of a word as in **come**	577	206

Consonants: Major Rules

	Moore	Black
RULE 1. SINGLE CONSONANTS are quite consistent in making the same sound. They should be taught in the following order:		
Group 1		
T	667	416
N	627	413
R	487	260
M	450	185
D	418	274

	MOORE	BLACK
Group 2		
S *(sat)*	343	288
L	342	340
C *(cat)*	338	156
P	332	118
S	279	288
F	220	132
Group 3		
V	179	74
G *(got)*	120	93
H	114	67
W	100	81
K	78	68
J	47	13
Z	24	5
Y	10	10

RULE 2. SECOND CONSONANTS have a surprisingly high frequency and should not be neglected

	MOORE	BLACK
C *makes the S sound as in cent before I,E,Y*	128	42
S *makes the Z sound as in* **has**	107	53
G makes the J sound as in gem before I and E	67	33

Note that S makes the Z sound four times more often than the letter Z, and G makes the J sound twice as often as the letter J.

RULE 3. CONSONANT DIGRAPHS must be taught as digraphs because they make a unique sound (phoneme) like a single consonant. They are not blends. For example, the TH in *thing* does not sound like a blend of T and H.

	MOORE	BLACK
CH *in* **chair**	83	37
TH *in* **thing** *(voiceless)*	82	40
SH *in* **she**	72	30
TH *in* **they** *(voiced)*	45	28
WH *in* **which**	19	12

Note that there are two sounds for TH. Since the voiceless TH has the highest frequency it should be taught first.

RULE 4. DIFFICULT CONSONANTS do not have any sound of their own but instead make the sound of a blend of two other consonants. X is usually found at the end of a word or syllable where it makes the KS sound as in **box** — 32 / 18

Q almost always appears in combination with U, and QU makes the sound of KW and in **queen.** — 27 / 8

CONSONANTS: MINOR RULES (using Moore's count only)

RULE 5. INITIAL CONSONANT BLENDS have a high degree of consistency. They should be taught in the following order:

Group 1	MOORE
ST	151
PR	75
TR	55
GR	40
BR	40

*and Y—gym, gypsy

Group 2

PL	35
SP	34
CR	33
CL	31
DR	27
FR	24

Group 3

SC	20
BL	17
FL	16
SK	15
SL	14
SW	12

Group 4

SM	8
GL	7
SN	4
TW	6

Consonant blends are classed in the Minor Rules for two reasons: frequency and necessity. From the standpoint of frequency, they are generally behind the single consonants and digraphs. In fact, from a standpoint of frequency, it is hardly worthwhile to teach Group 4 to beginning readers except for the fact that in teaching phonics one of the easiest to apply, and consequently most helpful principles of phonics, is the initial sound of the word. From the standpoint of necessity, blends can be "figured out" if the child knows the sound of each of the consonants, but teaching the letters as blends saves several mediating steps. We might also note that with the exception of TW, all the initial blends fall into only three families: S family—ST, SP, SC, SK, SL, SW, SN, and SM; R family—PR, TR, GR, BR, CR, DR, and FR; L family—PL, CL, BL, FL, and GL. Teaching the blends in families might be helpful to the teacher.

RULE 6. FINAL CONSONANT BLENDS. From the standpoint of necessity, these blends are not as useful as initial sounds, but some teachers might find them worthwhile (NG is really a digraph)

Group 1

ND *hand*	61
NT *dent*	44
CT *tract*	32
NG *along*	20

Group 2

LD *bold*	15
NK *bank*	13
RT *part*	13
MP *bump*	11
PT *kept*	10

RULE 7. DOUBLED CONSONANTS usually make the sound of a single consonant. Some common examples are as follows:

LL *all*	54
RR *arrow*	36

PP *apple*	26
TT *attic*	34
RULE 8. PH ALWAYS SOUNDS LIKE F as in phone	27

RULE 9. SILENT CONSONANTS are rather uncommon. The only ones worth mentioning are as follows:

C *before K as in* **back**	54
K *before N as in* **know**	11
W *before R as in* **write**	9

Since KN and WR occur at the beginning of some common words, they have a little greater importance than their frequency indicates. There is one so-called silent blend, GH as in the phonograms **ought** (10) or **right** (20), but it is usually taught as part of the phonogram in which it appears.

in Fry (1964)

3. flashcard training in letter sounding and then letter writing from sounds
4. 10 minutes of practice in reading and spelling
5. handwriting practice
6. practice in verbal expression, including speaking and writing ideas in sequence and on creative expression
7. listening to literature and discussing it, while reading instruction focuses on actually reading phonetically regular linguistic materials such as *Let's Read* (Bloomfield, Barnhart, & Barnhart, 1965)
8. discovery learning experiences to introduce new decoding concepts

In the latter case, students might be told to say a certain sound (long e = eeee), and then through a series of questions are led to discover the voice and feeling properties of that sound: "What are you doing with your mouth?"; "Is it open or closed?"; "Put your hand on your throat. What do you feel?" (Clark, 1988, p. 128). This latter step is the basis for another intensive phonics approach called Auditory Discrimination in Depth.

Auditory Discrimination in Depth (ADD).

This program, founded by Charles and Pat Lindamood (1975), uses nonsense words to train students to feel and label the various mouth and vocal forms associated with the major sounds of the English language. B's and P's, for example, are "lip poppers"; T's are "tip toppers"; M's and N's are "nose sounds"; S's are "skinny sounds"; G's are "scrapers"; and F's are "lip coolers." Students and teacher then talk about, or engage themselves in, phonics by talking about how words sound. The teacher might ask: "How does the sound of ZAB differ from ZAF?" And the student, by thinking and feeling while he or she speaks the two, would answer, "The lip popper, B, has been replaced by the lip cooler, F."

Most of these programs require extensive teacher training, and are surrounded by a good deal of orthodoxy, but generally do produce sound results

FIGURE 8.5

5 Counts of Frequency of Occurrence of Phonic Elements in Counts by Moore (1951), Cordts (1925), Fry (1957), Black (1961), and Kottmeyer (1954)

Letter Sound	Moore	Cordts	Fry	Black	Kottmeyer
B (bat)	279	238	21	123	56
C-K sound (cat)	338	187	18	156	36
C-S sound (city)	128	37	2	42	10
D (dog)	418	514	42	274	99
E—silent (come, late)	577		45	206	
E—short (bed)	428	366	26	179	44
E—long spelled EA (meat)	83	106	11	47	11
E—long spelled EE (meet)	69	93	7	28	18
E—schwa (enough)	92	216	1	87	
E—spelled ER (her)	46	10	18	142	1
E—short spelled EA (bread)	39		0	18	2
E—long open syllable (be)	33	17	8	46	5
E—long final E rule (here)	8	1	1	3	2
F (fat)	220	167	25	132	54
G (got)	120	102	13	93	38
G—J sound (gem)	67	43	0	33	
H (hat)	114	160	22	67	36
I—short (pin)	598	512	25	217	45
I—long final E rule (fine)	98	63	9	46	19
I—long open syllable (tiny)	55	95	6	16	3
I—IR (fir)	23	39	3	11	4
J (Jack)	47	22	2	13	2
K (kick)	78	101	16	68	24
L (love)	342	477	44	340	78
M (main)	450	261	31	185	56
N (no)	627	476	67	413	33
O—short (hot)	168	156	7	51	11
O—schwa (lemon)	128	38	9	77	
O—long open syllable (go)	87	88	17	31	14
O—long spelled OW (know)	38	71	5	16	8
O—long spelled OA (goat)	26	31	1	15	7
O—long final E rule (note)	49	47	4	21	0
O—broad (off)	27	7	6	18	6
O—OI dipthong (boil)	21	12	0	8	0
O—OY dipthong (boy)	9	8	1	5	2
O—OU dipthong (out)	48	40	7	17	8
O—OW dipthong (owl)	27	33	5	19	6
O—OO long (food)	42	40	3	18	8
O—OO short (look)	17	12	4	9	8
O—OR (for)	49	28	6	40	8
P (pin)	332	247	18	181	49
Q—QU equals KW (queen)	27	11	0	8	

Letter Sound	Moore	Cordts	Fry	Black	Kottmeyer
R (rat)	487	447	30	260	178
S (sat)	343	411	41	288	92
S–Z sound (has)	107	340	14	288	92
T (teacher)	667	454	63	416	166
U–short (hut)	148	153	14	59	20
U–long open syllable (pupil)	50	5	0	10	
U–long final E rule (use)	32	13	1	14	1
U–long spelled UE (due)	15		0	5	1
U–UR (fur)	34	46	3	14	3
V (very)	179	105	10	74	18
W (we)	100	147	18	81	36
X–KS (fox)	32	13	3	18	3
Y–long E (funny)	185	148	12	73	
Y–long I (fry)	25	18	7	11	6
Y (yes)	10	23	5	10	8
Z (zero)	24	4	0	5	0
Digraphs					
CH (chair)	83	69	4	37	8
SH (show)	72	88	6	30	11
TH–voiceless (thing)	82	66	29	40	21
TH–voiced (they)	45	52	14	28	19
WH–(when)	19	28	8	12	6
NG (long)	20	206	8	33	16
PH–F sound (phone)	27	2	0	4	
GH silent (right)	43			17	

in Fry (1964)

(Vickery, Reynolds & Cochran, 1987; Calfee, 1976; Howard, 1986). However, some of these findings are questionable. For example, the Calfee study, previously noted, is referenced as a letter to the Lindamoods (in Clark, 1988), with no other indication that it has been published or reported elsewhere.

Slingerland/Recipe for Reading.

Other variations on the Orton-Gillingham method include Beth Slingerland's (1971) approach that begins with learning to write in manuscript, and Nina Traub's (1982) "Recipe for Reading"—a spelling-precedes-reading approach that also places a heavy emphasis on early preventative training.

In considerable contrast to most other intensive phonics systems, the next one does not require extensive teacher training, nor does it teach either phonics rules or any other labels for language. It is more a decoding training program than a phonics teaching program.

Glass Analysis: A No-Rules Phonics Approach

Gerald G. Glass (1973) developed a simple method for teaching the decoding aspects of reading. The method, called Glass Analysis, is a form of analytic

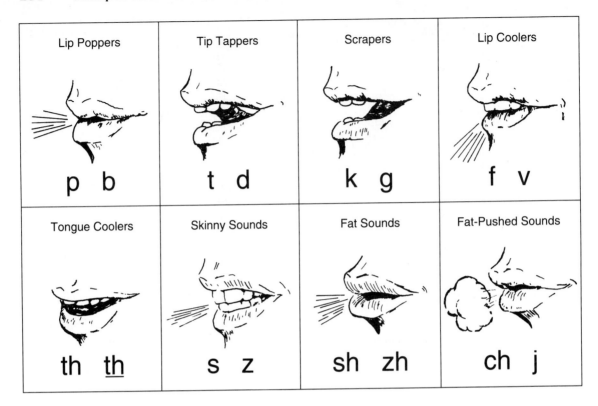

phonics, and is compatible with the strategies used by successful decoders (Glass & Burton, 1973).

In Glass Analysis, the act of decoding is isolated from comprehension and word meaning in order to maximize the student's attention and focus on the target word and word elements. Two verbal "scripts" are used to question students and encourage word analysis. One script is to ask what *sound* a given letter or letter cluster makes; the other script is to ask what *letter* or *letter cluster* makes a given sound.

Glass has identified 119 letter clusters by their frequency of occurrence in initial reading material and, therefore, their utility in helping children to decode more rapidly. These letter clusters (listed in Figure 8.6) can be used to develop word lists for Glass Analysis instruction. Glass also has marketed boxed word cards, arranged by letter cluster, to facilitate use of the Glass Analysis decoding approach. These inexpensive materials also include a quick program for teaching the alphabet.

The Glass Analysis method emphasizes the following basic ideas:

- Students should look at the target word throughout the lesson.
- Avoid undue attention to word meaning during the initial emphasis on sound decoding and word recognition.
- Keep a very brisk pace.

FIGURE 8.6

Letter Clusters (by Difficulty Level) for Use With Glass Analysis

STARTERS	MEDIUM ONE	MEDIUM TWO	HARDER ONE	HARDER TWO
1. at	1. ed	1. all	1. fowl	1. er
2. ing	2. ig	2. aw	2. us	2. air
3. et	3. ip	3. el(l)	3. il(l)	3. al
4. it	4. ud	4. eck	4. ite	4. ied
5. ot	5. id	5. ice	5. es(s)	5. ew
6. im	6. en	6. ick	6. om	6. ire
7. op	7. ug	7. if(f)	7. oke	7. ear
8. an	8. ut	8. ink	8. ore	8. eal
9. ay	9. ar	9. ob	9. *tow*	9. *tea*
10. ed	10. em	10. od	10. ast	10. ee
11. am	11. up	11. og	11. ane	11. *care*
12. un	12. ate	12. ub	12. eat	12. *deaf*
13. in	13. ent	13. uf(f)	13. as(s)	13. oat
14. ap	14. est	14. ush	14. ev	14. ue
15. and	15. ake	15. able	15. ind	15. oo
16. act	16. ide	16. ight	16. oss	16. ou
17. um	17. ock	17. is(s)	17. oem	17. ound
18. ab	18. ade	18. on	18. ost	18. ure
19. ag	19. ame	19. or	19. *rol(l)*	19. ture
20. old	20. ape	20. ul(l)	20. one	20. ur
21. ash	21. ace	21. ac	21. ate	21. ir
22. ish	22. any	22. af(f)	22. ave	22. ai
	23. enk	23. ook	23. ove	23. au
	24. ong	24. tion	24. *folly*	24. oi
			25. age	

Glass (1973)

- Avoid discussion of phonic rules, such as dropping the final "e" before adding a suffix.
- Avoid breaking up units that logically belong together (e.g., th, wr, ing, st).
- Reinforce correct responses, and do not punish incorrect ones. If a student can not answer a question, merely state the answer and return to it again before leaving that word.

Steps in Glass Analysis

Step 1   Check to make sure the student knows the alphabet and most of the letter sounds.

Step 2   Pick a set of word cards that teach a particular letter cluster.
*Example: the letter cluster **eck***

Step 3   Seat the student beside you, and show the first word card. Ask if the student can pronounce it; if not, pronounce it and have the student repeat it.
Example: What is the word? [pecking]

Step 4   Starting with the letter cluster of the packet, focus on as many letters and letter clusters as is reasonable, asking what *letters* make a given sound.

*Example: What letters make the **eck** sound?*
*What letters make the **ing** sound?*
*What letters make the **p** sound?*

For words that contain only the teaching cluster plus an initial letter (e.g., cat), treat the initial letter as you would a cluster so that the student has been exposed to all the letter sounds in the word.

Step 5   Focus on sounds next, asking what *sound* is made by a given letter cluster or letter.

*Example: What sound does the letter **p** make?*
*What sound do the letters **p-e-c-k** make?*
*What sound do the letters **e-c-k** make?*
*What sound do the letters **i-n-g** make?*

The ease and rapid pace of Glass Analysis seems to offer two special advantages for combating functional illiteracy at any level. The first is that paraprofessionals and volunteer workers can be easily trained to use the method with children or adults. The second is that schools can set up "decoding stations" (just two desks facing one another in a quiet place) where students with word analysis and recognition problems can be scheduled to make stops for 5 to 15 minute training sessions as often as several times a day until they become proficient (Manzo & Manzo, 1990a).

Syllabication: A Backup Phonics Approach

Ability to syllabicate is another form of phonic awareness, and those who do it well tend to learn to read well. It is arguable, however, whether teaching syllabication results in significant improvement in their word recognition and word analysis skills.

Some phonics rules are based on syllabication (see Figure 8.8 for the most

FIGURE 8.7

Rules for Dividing Words into Syllables

These are roughly in the order that a student would find them most dependable in syllabicating a word.

1. Two identical consonants are divided to form two syllables: *lit/tle; bet/ter.*
2. The number of vowel *sounds* in a word indicates the number of syllables: *"cave"* (one vowel sound - "a" - one syllable); *"caboose"* (four vowels but only two vowel sounds - therefore two syllables—*ca/boose*).
3. Two unlike consonants generally also are divided to form syllables: *mar/ket* (exceptions: do not divide between blends and digraphs—*be/tween,* not *bet/ween;* "s" family blends do separate: whis/per, whis/key, aus/tere
4. Each small word in a compound word usually is a syllable (*cow/poke; horse/fly*).

FIGURE 8.8

Rules for Pronouncing Words Based on Syllables

1. *"Le"* is pronounced as *"ul"* when it appears at the end of a word, as in *little* and *battle*.
2. A syllable ending in a vowel often has a long vowel sound (*be/tween*).
3. When a vowel does not complete a syllable and is followed by two consonants, it has a short sound (*ap/ple*; *pic/nic*).

predictable syllable-based pronunciation rules). For those students who find syllabication easy and natural, these syllable-based phonics rules may be useful. Students who do not syllabicate easily, however, must rely on syllabication rules rather than the sounds they "hear" (see Figure 8.7 for the most predictable rules for dividing words into syllables). It is not very reasonable to expect children to be able first to recall and apply one rule to determine syllable breaks, and then to use that information to recall and apply a second rule to determine pronunciation of the word.

These factors, however, do not completely argue against teaching syllabication. The primary means of teaching word decoding skills, you will recall, is to keep the word in front of the student long enough for him/her to identify its distinguishing features, and to internalize the subtle ways that words can be divided and sounded. In this way, students subconsciously learn to recognize regularities and to recognize when they have come upon an irregularity in how a word might be pronounced.

Syllabication Rules.

In general, the idea is to teach students to recognize word patterns, in almost a conditioned response manner, rather than have them memorize complex rules. Specialists who believe in teaching to a weakness argue that there is a certain merit in teaching at least a few guiding rules that can shore up a pupil's constitutional sound-symbol weakness. This must be done very judiciously, however, since rules can appear very abstract and, as noted earlier, have many exceptions. This tends to make learning from rules quite difficult for the remedial student since he/she can not fall back on the phonemic sense that others intuitively draw upon to remind them of a rule. Remedial reading students who are "sequential processors" do seem to profit from such rule-based instruction. Conversely, those with more artistic temperaments, who tend to be "simultaneous processors", have an especially difficult time learning and applying explicit rules.

Teaching Syllabication.

Here are some ways to raise syllabic awareness:

1. Teach syllabication through known words, and preferably in context.
2. Use a deductive approach—cite one appropriate rule and have students apply it to several words until they see how it applies.

3. Alternate this with an inductive approach—show the student several words that have the same syllabication rule in common; ask them to try to state the rule (little, battle, carried—divide between double consonants).
4. Teach students to use this sequence in syllabication:
   a. Look for prefixes, then suffixes, then familiar root words (these are all syllables).
   b. Try applying the rules itemized above (these can be recorded on a cue card for easy reference).
   c. Check the dictionary—it is the final arbiter, and every word listed in it is syllabicated.

The latter means that a student, a list of words, and a dictionary can be an "auto-instructional system" for practicing syllabication in a self-pacing and self-correcting way. Students should be encouraged to read the rest of the dictionary definition even of words that they "know." In addition to building knowledge of multiple meanings of familiar words, the definitions often suggest conceptual aids to syllabication and spelling of a word. Most importantly, students develop familiarity and comfort with using the dictionary in a relatively unthreatening way. This can be a good orientation activity for the first few minutes of each remedial session.

Patricia Cunningham (1975–76) devised a method of teaching word identification through syllabication. The method, which she called Syllabary, proved to be more effective than traditional phonics instruction. Nonetheless, the method did not catch on, largely for the reasons previously cited, plus the fact that "dialectic differences in readers make for differences in syllable pronunciation" (Tierney, Readence, & Dishner, 1990, p. 413). This is a difficult obstacle to overcome in a mobile and multicultural society.

Kinesthetic and Proprioceptive Training Schemes: VAKT, DISTAR

VAKT.

The Fernald Visual-Auditory-Kinesthetic-Tactile (VAKT) technique probably is the best-known clinical training method of its type. Since it is almost exclusively a clinical practice, and the archetype of other such methods, it is discussed fully in Chapter 12 on severe reading disabilities.

DISTAR.

DISTAR is a commercial program (Engleman & Brener, 1983) that takes a lock-step, direct instructional approach. It is said to epitomize the "mastery learning" approaches frequently recommended for disadvantaged youngsters (Becker, 1977). In point of fact, it more properly represents a shift from concern about a child's weaknesses, strengths, or the etiology of a problem to the tasks a child simply must learn in order to read (Haring, Bateman, & Carnine, 1977). DISTAR provides actual scripts that cause teachers and students to act out the basic behaviors of good remedial teaching and effective reading and learning. It is, in effect, a form of associative learning that relies on cadence, quick pacing, repetition, and behavioral, or proprioceptive (nerve and motor) conditioning.

Many instructors find the scripted program tedious, since they feel that they are reduced to "teaching machines." The program was, in fact, designed to be "teacher proof," and it has proven to be quite effective in helping disadvantaged youngsters to experience success (Beck & McCaslin, 1978). It also has been around for over 15 years, attaining a certain degree of staying power (Meyer, Gersten, & Gutkin, 1983) that lends it a further degree of credibility.

The acronym DISTAR only partially describes the breadth and tack of the program: Direct Instructional System of Teaching Arithmetic and Reading. There is, in fact, a language portion of the program that aligns with the reading portion. The language program has three levels. The first level focuses on teaching the language of instruction, building vocabulary, developing oral language, and laying in a foundation for logical thinking. This preschool and early primary segment is followed by one that stresses the language foundation for reading comprehension. It does this by emphasizing the meanings of words and sentences, following directions, and only then by addressing more advanced reasoning skills. The third level reemphasizes sentence analysis—both spoken and written, builds familiarity with the mechanics of language, and lays the foundation for content area reading by stressing topical information. The actual Reading Mastery portion of the program has six levels. Both decoding and comprehension are taught from the outset. The decoding program starts with letter names, then goes to pronunciations of letter sounds. Diagrams, games, teacher hand signals, rhyming activities, and unison responding are all used to quicken the pace and (apparently) to tap into associative learning, more so than higher-order cognitive learning domains. To this extent, the initial approach is not unlike the manner of teaching used in many East Asian countries.

The DISTAR program tries to remove as many obstacles as possible to early learning success. It even uses a slightly modified orthography in the initial stages. Silent letters, for example, are printed smaller, to signal the student not to try to say these, and all long vowel sounds are marked to help students distinguish them instantly from saying a short sound or a schwa sound. The DISTAR program also teaches handwriting and spelling.

Where word decoding and spelling are concerned, DISTAR gets the job done. It has been shown that students moved on average from the 18th to the 84th percentile in word recognition and analysis, and from the 8th to the 49th in spelling (Becker, 1977). Comprehension lagged behind at the 40th percentile, but this was still much higher than at non-DISTAR schools. Even more interesting was a longitudinal study indicating that this advantage persisted to the 9th grade level and beyond: the dropout rate for DISTAR students was half that of the control groups, and their acceptance rate to college was twice that of the non-DISTAR students (Meyer, 1984).

There are some crucial confounding elements in some of the studies reported. DISTAR programs have tended to include a high degree of parental involvement and extensive inservice teacher training, supervision, and hands-on technical assistance when needed (Meyer, Gersten, & Gutkin, 1983). These factors do not negate the impressive results, but they do suggest that future comparison studies will need to take these effects into consideration.

The chapters ahead on comprehension enrichment and on higher-order literacy offer several means and methods for complementing this associative learning approach rather than dismissing it. The next approach offers a softer, gentler, and less teacher-directed tack in building language and reading skills.

Contextual Approaches to Decoding

Dictated Story.

This approach is not teacher-directed, nor does it attempt to be "teacher-proof." It relies instead on teacher sensitivity and agility in making the most of language experiences to teach word learning and writing. The approach has been known and used for generations as Language Experience Stories (Allen, 1976; Hall, 1981; Stauffer, 1980), but now is more familiarly referred to as a "whole language" approach.

The basic assumption of the contextual approach to word learning is that word recognition and analysis skills can largely be learned incidentally from contact — being read to, writing, and reading. There are several variations on the basic approach. A strategy called the Dictated Story is the one most often recommended for use with remedial level readers. The Dictated Story is described here as it might be used with a small group. Only slight and obvious adjustments are necessary for one-on-one use.

Steps in the Dictated Story Approach

Step 1   A discussion is generated around a question, event, or some concrete object.

Step 2   Youngsters are asked to compose a story or set of thoughts and reactions in response to the question, event, or object.

Step 3   The teacher records the story as told by the students, saying back what is being printed (50 to 250 words).

Step 4   The teacher reads the story back to the group, asking if there is anything that they would like to change or correct.

Step 5   Corrections and changes are made.

Step 6   The story is reread and individual words are stressed in a variety of possible ways:

   a. Have students attempt to read the story while you underline every word they know (rather than marking those they do not) — tell them the words they miss, but first have them try to use context, letter, and syntactic clues to decode the words not recognized.

   b. Have students reread the story, again underlining for a second time those they now know with a double line and those they figured out with a single line. Do not underline words they previously got correct, but missed the second time — have them make a list of the words underlined once or not at all, and convert these to flash cards for further practice as described earlier.

c. Have students attempt to read some sentences that you compose using essentially the same words, and ideally along the same story line. When thoughtfully conducted, these "writings" can become a therapeutic dialogue as well as a lesson in word recognition. See the example in Figure 8.9 of how a teacher might respond orally or in writing to a student's story. For other examples of such interactions, see Dialogue Journals in Chapter 9 on vocabulary, and in Chapter 13 on higher-order literacy.

FIGURE 8.9

Students' Dictated Story

Stimulus: What do you suppose the tiger is thinking as he is being caged? (tiger was this female student's feared-self, or rejection, on the MBI)

Student's Story:
The tiger knows that he did the wrong thing by scaring the children. He shouldn't have tried to escape from the zoo. Animals don't really belong in zoos, I guess. But once they are in one, they must be kept locked up. They also can be sent back to the jungle. But if they were in the zoo for a long time, they wouldn't know how to get food and could die.

Teacher's addition for student to read and think about:
Tigers don't really do right or wrong things. They do what their nature tells them to do.

An important word of caution related to using the Dictated Story Approach has been offered by Sandra McCormick, based on research with nonreaders at the Ohio State reading clinic. Severely disabled readers, McCormick notes, tend to dictate stories that, reflecting their oral language, have too many words, and too few repetitions of words for these nonreaders to learn and remember (1990). This can result in lessons that are more frustrating than they are empowering. McCormick has developed an alternate strategy for nonreaders, discussed next, that introduces new words gradually, and provides intensive practice with these words in a variety of contexts.

Multiple-Exposure/Multiple-Context.

The M-E/M-C strategy (McCormick, 1990) was developed for severely disabled readers. It provides frequent practice with new words (multiple exposures), but without isolated drill (multiple contexts).

Steps in Multiple-Exposure/Multiple-Context

Step 1   Select a high-interest/difficulty-controlled book series.

Step 2   In the first remedial session, have the student read orally, as a pre-test, the first chapter of the preprimer of the selected series. Make note of all words the student does *not* recognize on sight. These words are the instructional content for the next sessions.

Step 3   Beginning with the second session, for the first 5–10 minutes, read aloud *to* the student from good children's literature. This provides exposure to connected text that nonreaders are not yet able to access themselves. The remaining 50 minutes are devoted to exposure to the set of words identified from the chapter. The objective is to expose the student to these words in a variety of contexts, involving:
- games and manipulatives
- contextual activities to promote transfer to real text
- attention to internal features of words

During this process, the teacher visually demonstrates progress by having the student count words learned and record these on a graph or chart. The chapter itself is *not* referred to again until all the words have been mastered.

Step 4   When all the words have been mastered, the student rereads the first chapter of the preprimer. At this point, the student should have his or her first experience in successfully reading a complete text.

Step 5   The student reads the second chapter as a pretest to target the next set of unknown words. The teacher proceeds with Steps 3 and 4; that is, teaching words to the automatic stage and only then having the student reread the chapter. Steps 2, 3, and 4 are followed with every chapter in the book.

Step 6   The student rereads the first book in one sitting—again, a first-time occurrence for nonreaders.

Subsequent Steps: The student progresses through other books in the series in a manner consistent with the previous steps. Learning *rate* should increase as the student moves through the program, until it begins to approximate the norm. At that time, the M-E/M-C strategy is abandoned, and the student participates in a more typical program of instruction.

Positive Oral Reading (POR).

POR is the name we have given to several methodologies that have evolved over some time and have several possible variations. It is based on the principles of high positive reinforcement, frequent and distributed practice, and transfer of control and responsibility for the job of monitoring word recognition from the teacher to the student. It is similar to the Repeated Readings method (see more ahead), which Samuels (1979) and others have developed to promote fluency and "automaticity" in word recognition.

Positive Oral Reading is a one-on-one tutorial method. It teaches words both in context and in isolation. It has an A and a B form. Materials needed include a copy of a selection that can be written on and 3 or 4 different colored pencils.

Steps in Positive Oral Reading, Form A:

Step 1   The teacher identifies a piece to be read orally—either a student's language experience story or a selection of appropriate length and difficulty level. (Ideally, the passage would have been prepared with triple spacing between the lines.)

Step 2   The student reads the selection aloud while the teacher underlines each word read correctly with a single straight line. The word is supplied by the teacher if it is not known or the student pauses for too long.

Step 3   The teacher points to an equal number of previously correct and incorrect words to be read without context. Words read correctly are underlined in a different color. If missed, more elaborate help is given (e.g., "That word is *bite*. The silent "e" at the end of the word reminds us to say a long sound for the previous vowel. The word, again, is *bite*. What is the word?")

Step 4   The passage is read once more. All words read correctly are again underlined in a third color.

Step 5   The teacher checks comprehension with four or five questions that prompt retelling more so than short answers. The teacher again points to an equal number of words previously decoded correctly and incorrectly. These are underlined in a fourth color (or back to the first color).

Step 6   The student copies an equal number of previously missed words and words of his or her choosing onto a list. The teacher draws further attention to the troublesome words, such as by using one of the Glass Analysis verbal protocols with the words (e.g., "That word is *bite*. Which letter makes the **buh** sound? Which letters make the **ite** sound? What letter makes the **i** sound? What sound do the letters **i-t-e** make? What sound do the letters **b-i** make? What is the word?") This portion of POR should continue until every word is underlined three times.

Step 7   The underlined passage and word list are saved and used again by the student for study and rereading, ideally the same day. Help with pronunciation may be given during study, if requested.

Passages marked in POR may be saved in the student's portfolio for further analysis and progress reports.

Steps in Positive Oral Reading, Form B:

Step 1   The student is permitted first to read the selection silently, underlining all known words.

Step 2   The teacher then gives help with unknown words (those not underlined).

Step 3   The student rereads the passage orally while the teacher underlines again.

Step 4   The teacher checks student comprehension.

Step 5   The teacher points to individual words again, checking for proper reading, but also giving attention to word meaning.

Form B is more appropriate for use with content-based material. The remedial teacher can use this with reproduced passages from the student's own textbooks. Also, old or damaged books may be used, even if these are not identical to one being used in the student's class.

Positive Oral Reading also lends itself well to use by volunteer helpers and paraprofessionals. The teacher may wish to streamline it for such uses. This can be done by reducing colors, reducing rereadings to two, and/or by eliminating or providing written questions for the comprehension check.

Providing Reading Opportunities for Those with Decoding Deficits

Some methods are needed by the reading specialist and classroom teachers that permit pupils to engage in effective reading despite decoding deficits (Allington, 1977). Discussion here will focus on a particular class of compensatory methods that are categorically known as Repeated Readings methods. Research evidence tends to suggest that poor readers with decoding problems benefit the most from repeated readings methods (Carver & Hoffman, 1981).

Repeated Readings Methods

In this context, "repeated readings" refers to a cluster of methods that have a student do one or any combination of the following:

1. Read the same material more than once.
2. Listen to it before reading.
3. Read it with immediate support from another on first or second reading.

These methods are held to be especially valuable since they provide review and further exposure to new words, pacing with rate and fluency, and an opportunity to continue to enjoy the three major benefits of reading: pleasure, knowledge growth, and opportunity to understand self and surroundings better.

The version of repeated readings described here is fashioned largely from the work of Allington (1983), but also of Samuels (1979), Ballard (1978), Topping (1987), and Koskinen and Blum (1986).

Repeated Readings: Steps and Pointers:

1. Help a child select an interesting portion of a selection (100 to 200 words) at the student's instructional level, and set a goal for an appropriate oral reading rate, in words-per-minute.
2. Time the student's initial, unrehearsed oral reading of the passage.
3. Instruct the student to practice in pairs and at home.
4. Time and graph reading rate again.
5. Continue oral rereadings, timing, and graphing of times at intervals of several days.
6. When the preset goal is reached, begin a new passage or continue the remainder of the same passage.

7. Option 1: The teacher, buddy, or parent can serve as a "talking dictionary," providing any word the student calls for with the phrase "word please." (Ballard, 1978; Topping, 1987).

Option 2: The teacher, buddy, or parent can give the reader feedback, and have the reader self-evaluate progress (see Figure 8.10 for guidelines from Koskinen & Blum, 1986).

Teachers and parents report that this simple method is highly motivating and results in increased word recognition and fluency. It also improves rate and confidence in reading new passages, not merely those used in repeated practice.

To heighten these effects further, the teacher can read portions of the selection, pausing to discuss the first few paragraphs with students. This approach, called the Oral Reading Strategy in content area reading (Manzo, 1980), also is an easy way to get youngsters started on silent reading with good cadence, and while providing incidental help with unknown words and initial concepts. To this extent, it parallels the "readiness" step of the Directed Reading-Thinking Activity, an important comprehension strategy developed further in the next chapters.

Mark Aulls and Michael Graves provide a handy chart (see Figure 8.11) and excellent commercial material (from Scholastic, Inc.) for practicing and visualizing progress from repeated readings.

FIGURE 8.10

Self-Evaluation of Reading 1, Reading 2, and Reading 3

Reading 1 (Self-evaluation)
How well did you read? (Circle one)

Reading 2 (Peer Evaluation)
How did your partner's reading get better? (Check *all* that apply.)
__ He or she read more smoothly.
__ He or she knew more words.
__ He or she read with more expression.
** Tell your partner one thing that was better about his or her reading.

Reading 3 (Peer Evaluation)
How did your partner's reading get better? (Check *all* that apply.)
__ He or she read more smoothly.
__ He or she knew more words.
__ He or she read with more expression.
** Tell your partner one thing that was better about his or her reading.

Drawings from IR-TI © Anthony and Ula Manzo
Inventory from Koskinen and Blum (1986)

Other Methods for Empowering Readers with Decoding Deficits

Other methods for engaging pupils in the act of reading despite decoding deficits are covered in various other sections of the text. These include: the Neurological Impress method (Hecklemann, 1966, 1969), Echo Reading (B. Anderson, 1981), Listening-Reading Transfer Lesson (P. Cunningham, 1975), the Listen-Read-Discuss Heuristic (Manzo & Casale, 1985), and the Structured Listening Activity (Choate & Rakes, 1987).

FIGURE 8.11

Repeated Reading Chart

If you repeatedly read the same passage, you will soon read it smoothly and easily. This sheet will help to record your progress in reading

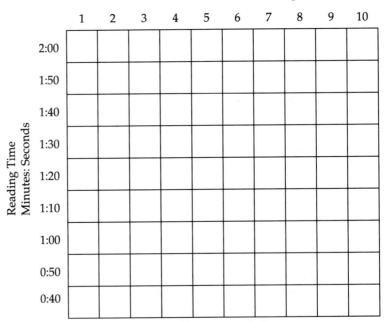

Number of Times I Read the Same Passage

Number of Miscues Each Time

1st Time ___   3th Time ___   5th Time ___   7th Time ___   9th Time ___

2nd Time___   4th Time ___   6th Time ___   8th Time ___   10th Time ___

Aulls and Graves (1985)

➤ *LOOKING BACK* ➤

This chapter provided a catalog of means and methods for improving word recognition and analysis. It also discussed the "perversity" of the English phonemic system, and how this interacts with the process of learning to decipher words and constructing a sensible, research-based program for doing so. The chapter stressed the need to be a reflective teacher in order to meet the needs of students, the demands of the task, and, to a lesser extent, your own inclinations—a factor that can be of some importance in remedial education where the teacher's enthusiasm for what he or she is doing is essential to getting the student engaged and keeping oneself engaged.

➤ *LOOKING AHEAD*

Earlier in the chapter, it was noted that there is no real difference in purpose in teaching a child to decode a word, to learn its meaning, or to comprehend it in written text, since each is part of the unifying objective to teach children to read for meaning. This same philosophy is apparent in the next chapter. It stresses meaning vocabulary, which is central to comprehension, and two lesser but potentially valuable contributors to full literacy: spelling and handwriting. Read ahead to discover the values of each of these in a remedial reading program.

9

Remedies for Vocabulary, Spelling, and Handwriting Deficiencies

---

> ➤ *LOOK FOR IT*
> _____
>
> This chapter reflects the Russian psychologist Vygotsky's (1962) sentiment that remedial level students have an even greater need for a concentrated program of vocabulary and concept enrichment than other students (Camperell, 1982). The chapter also addresses aspects of writing, spelling, and handwriting.

Vocabulary and Remediation

Words are food for the brain. Nonetheless, remedial programs tend to deprive reading-deficient students of this source of academic nourishment, much as hospitals have been known to overlook good nutrition, rest, and exercise in helping cure patients. In principle, most people agree that remedial students should be taught new words. In practice, however, there is a sense that there is no rush to do so since remedial students presumably have a more dramatic need to learn how to read known words. This sentiment tends to deprive remedial students of one of the main sources of normal concept and vocabulary growth.

A holistic remedial reading perspective is based on three major considerations. First, each of the language arts further nourishes reading. Second, the proper goal of a remedial reading program is not merely to promote gains in reading, but to improve overall literacy. And, third, the long-term interests of the *whole* child are served by being careful not to overlook or otherwise deny nourishment to one part of their development while attending too narrowly to more apparent deficiencies. These sentiments have also been expressed by Wayne Otto, Richard McMenemy, and Richard Smith (1973), in an earlier language arts-based approach to remedial reading, and further supported more recently by Kenneth Goodman, Lois Bird, and Yetta Goodman (1991) in a collection of anecdotal reports on Whole Language teaching, and by Jana Mason, Patricia Herman, and Kathryn Au (1991) in a review of children's developing knowledge of words. Let us now consider some other possible benefits for promoting vocabulary development in remedial level students. Many of the same arguments could be made for giving greater attention to vocabulary in working with average and above average students as well.

Benefits of Vocabulary Instruction

A rich vocabulary enhances "inner speech," or the mediational system (Manzo & Sherk, 1971–72; Graves & Hammond, 1980; Vygotsky, 1962) by which we process information, reflect, and feel. Most concepts are given specific names in the language. These words and their public meanings hence become the operational bases for thinking and communicating. According to findings by Lane Roy Gauthier (1992, in press), Steven Stahl and Barbara Kapinus (1991), and David O'Brien (1986), enlarging the range of words available for improving this inner speech tends to improve:

- comprehension of what is read and heard
- accuracy and clarity of thinking
- school and real life problem solving
- access to concepts, allusions, and other new words
- access to and comprehension of one's own feelings and experiences
- one's sense of self-efficacy and self-worth

In a word, words tend to be empowering. Size of vocabulary is the best single predictor of IQ and intellectual prowess (Manzo & Sherk, 1971–72). Curiously, words are more easily learned than is commonly recognized: students learn about 3,000 words a year, and the *average* high school senior knows about 40,000 words (Nagy & Herman, 1984).

How is Vocabulary Naturally Acquired?

Vocabulary is initially acquired in basically four ways:

- Incidentally, through reading and conversation
- Through direct instruction, as when a teacher or auto-instructional program is used to intentionally build vocabulary power
- Through self-instruction, as when words are looked up in a dictionary, or their meanings are sought from others in a conscious manner
- Through mental manipulation while thinking, speaking, and writing

Each of these functions, as shown in the illustration below, is set in motion by an appropriate social climate and conducive community of language (Vygotsky, 1962; Manzo & Manzo, 1990a). It has been further noted that words, as illustrated below, generally are acquired in five stages, or levels: incidentally, through direct instruction, through self-instruction, through use, and through a social climate or community of language that tends to amplify and impel each of these.

Isabelle Beck, Margaret McKeown, and Richard Omanson (1987) characterize these levels of knowledge of word meanings as follows:

- no knowledge
- general informational level
- narrow recognition (usually context-bound)
- need to hesitate to remember a meaning
- easy recognition and full knowledge

Vocabulary study, essentially, is a process of moving words through each of these stages. It especially involves taking steps to keep a healthy number of words flowing into the general informational or awareness level and into the full knowledge, or permanence stage.

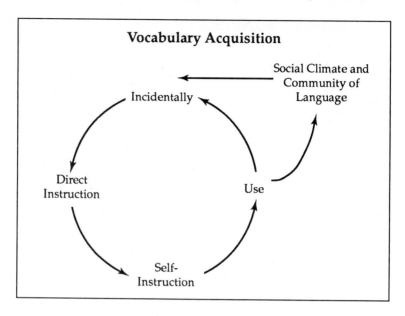

Considerations in Remedial Vocabulary Instruction

Several comprehensive reviews of the literature on vocabulary acquisition, the most recent by James Baumann and Edward Kameenui (1991), make it possible to summarize research-supported findings related to remedial readers. Three considerations emerge: connecting instruction to the process of vocabulary learning; the need to impart a disposition to acquire words; and overcoming a paradox between incidental and direct teaching. Each of these is discussed below, and followed by teaching methods that translate these considerations into practice.

Teach the Phases

To connect vocabulary instruction to the natural processes of word learning, the literature on vocabulary acquisition tends to divide the teaching of vocabulary into five phases. These are:

- *Disposition* — opening the student's mind and will to engage new words.
- *Integration* — establishing ties between the meaning of a new word and the student's existing knowledge.
- *Repetition* — provisions for practice distributed over time, as well as opportunities for frequent encounters with the word in similar and differing contexts.
- *Interaction and meaningful use* — social situations conducive to using new words in interactions with others and, thus, mentally referencing new words in listening, reading, writing, and speaking.
- *Self-instruction* — maintaining an awareness of new words outside the classroom.

Impart Disposition

Since disposition and self-instruction are essential qualities of effective word learning, remedial teachers need to do at least three things in teaching vocabulary. One is to view *every* instructional episode as an opportunity to model interest in new words and strategies for learning word meanings. Second, it is important for lessons to be varied and engaging. Vocabulary instruction should be more than dictionary worksheets. Use methods that exploit all domains of language learning—cognitive, affective, and sensorimotor. Third, increase student involvement by asking students to select some methods that they feel to be most profitable and using these more frequently. It is not a good idea, however, to surrender the right and responsibility to use less preferred methods. Occasionally, a less popular method may be related to considerations that the student may not understand, such as the one described next.

The Paradox of Incidental Versus Direct Teaching

No matter which methods are chosen to provide instruction in vocabulary, there is a paradox reported in the research literature that needs to be anticipated and planned for. The paradox is as follows: Direct instructional approaches are almost always more effective than wide reading and other incidental means of promoting word learning (Nagy & Herman, 1984; Nelson-Herber, 1986). Nonetheless, most knowledge of word meanings, as noted above, seems to be acquired incidentally and through wide reading (Harris & Sipay, 1990, p. 533), and potentially in television viewing (Newman & Koskinen, 1992). The reason, William Nagy speculates (1988), is the "sheer volume" of new words encountered in reading, and again, in viewing. Consequently, it seems fairly obvious that a solid vocabulary development program needs to involve both direct and indirect methods of promoting vocabulary acquisition.

Let's look now at some specific methodologies that embody these considerations. See Appendix B for handy lists of words for conducting vocabulary diagnosis and instruction. As mentioned in a previous chapter, these were selected from over 43,000 words that Edgar Dale and Joseph O'Rourke (1976, 1981) administered to students at a variety of grade levels in order to establish the relative level of difficulty of each.

Vocabulary Procedures for Classroom and Clinic

The initial two vocabulary strategies address the matter of student disposition toward words. They are extensions of the idea of "organic words," a means used by Sylvia Ashton-Warner (1959) to describe her chief method of encouraging the Maori children of New Zealand to become literate. They would tell her what they wished to know, she would show them how to spell it out, and they then would own the word. However, they were expected to read it anytime she asked. If they missed their own word three times, they would lose it. The methods presented next extend this organic, or "words as an extension of self and environment," approach from the word recognition to word meaning level.

Vocabulary Self-Collection (VSC)

VSC (Haggard, 1982) is more than a vocabulary teaching strategy; it is a fundamental way of reopening students' minds to the wealth of words that they encounter in print and that surround them each day. Essentially, VSC emphasizes teaching new words following initial reading. It requires the students to search their viewing, reading, and home environments for words and to bring them to the classroom or remedial situation.

For regular classroom use, Martha Haggard-Ruddell would have students write their words on the chalkboard upon entering the classroom, then have the youngster(s) who submitted a word define it. The teacher and class then would comment on its features and try to extend or further clarify its meaning. Words and meanings are recorded in a vocabulary journal. Ideally, word exercises that further embed their meanings should follow. These can be of the type found in conventional vocabulary workbooks, or through one of the word manipulation or embellishment methods described ahead.

In a more remedial situation, the teacher should expect to help the youngsters with the definition of the word. Initially, it is more important that they be willing to identify words that they wish to learn than it is that they look them up. The next method has the same premise, but it is based on a slightly larger definition of vocabulary building.

Cultural Academic Trivia (Treasures)

The CAT game (Manzo, 1970; 1985) is designed to build "prior knowledge" or schemata, as well as just vocabulary. It says to the student: be attentive to your environment for anything that you don't know, make a note of it on a 3x5 card (given to students once a week), and bring it as your admission ticket to class. The card is intended to serve as a constant reminder to be thinking about words, facts, and ideas in and outside of the school situation.

When students bring their CAT cards to class, the teacher is obliged to tell whatever she/he knows about the word, fact, or idea. This information is written on the back of the card, which can then be used to play the "trivia" game. If the teacher is uncertain about an item, the teacher and student together try to clear it up by checking appropriate sources—dictionary, almanac, encyclopedia, other teachers.

The CAT game can be played noncompetitively and individually by simply keeping count of the number correct out of 10 each time the game is played, or it can be played competitively for points. It also can be tied to a random factor to make it more game-like; for example, each time a correct answer is given, the student gets to roll a die and the number shown is recorded and added until a winner is declared (25 points or more to a game).

CAT is an especially good means of helping youngsters learn the many allusions or referents that are used by others in speaking and writing. To that extent, it helps with schema building and comprehension (e.g., to teach students who Freud is and to help them understand what ideas people are referencing when they use his name). The same could be said for Ghandi, Malcolm X, and Gallileo. Students quickly learn that there is no such thing as trivia, only minds that lack sufficient knowledge to give meaning to the referents that surround us. The students who first played the game came eventually to suggest that it should be called "Cultural Academic Treasures" (Manzo, 1970) because they realized that "trivia" is in the eye of the beholder.

A variation on CAT, called a Friday "Quiz Bowl Competition" is a major component in the most successful programs in the country at preparing black minority youngsters for medical school. The other major components of this Xavier University of New Orleans program are practice in analytical reasoning and "think alouds" (Whimbey & Lochhead, 1980), both of which are further developed in the chapters ahead.

As a further means of converting facts and information into something richer, consider the next idea. It draws on an ancient notion called "Loci," a memory training idea developed more fully in the chapter on study skills.

Vocabulary Classmates

Developed by the authors, this child-centered, whole-language approach to vocabulary seats a child in a classroom, imaginary or real, made up of "classmates" named from a list of new words. The teacher aids students in getting to know their new "vocabulary classmates" by asking questions and encouraging activities that build increasingly greater empathy and understanding with their newfound word friends. Sample questions and activities include the following:

- How does this person say his/her name (pointing to a seat and word)?
- Let's check the dictionary to find out what this person's name means. (A good lead-up to this is to illustrate that many popular names, first and last, have meanings—the library might have a book of these.)
- Let's check the dictionary to learn where this person is from. (Check the derivation of the word.)
- Let's check the dictionary to learn about this person's family heritage. (Check the dictionary for the word's "parentage"—meaningful affixes and morphemes brought together to form the word.)
- Who is this person related to? (synonyms)
- Who is this person most different from? (antonyms)
- What is this person's usual job? (noun, verb, etc.)
- Tell a story about these three classmates on the playground (e.g., glorious, pageant, and pale): what are they doing(?), what are they saying(?)
- Who would you like to have sit near you? (The teacher should find a reason to

move a "classmate" near the child who he or she is having trouble learning about—proximity, in this case, breeds familiarity.)

- Which classmates do you think are likely to be friends? Why?
- Draw or describe the clothing each would wear and what each might look like physically (see Figure 9.1).
- Have each classmate say something he/she might have on his/her mind. The teacher can provide some statements that may stimulate deeper understandings, associations, and further word study (see Figure 9.1).

Classmates is designed to stimulate deeper learning than typically occurs with vocabulary instruction. To evaluate progress in word learning:

- Look for compatibility between word meanings and story lines developed.

FIGURE 9.1

Illustrations from Vocabulary Classmates as Assembled with "Mandy" (age 10)

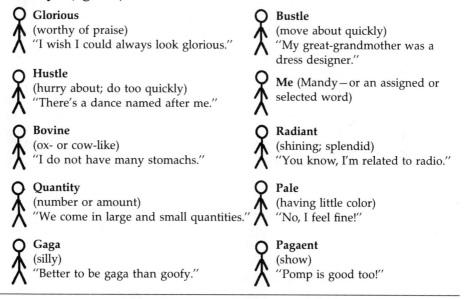

Glorious
(worthy of praise)
"I wish I could always look glorious."

Hustle
(hurry about; do too quickly)
"There's a dance named after me."

Bovine
(ox- or cow-like)
"I do not have many stomachs."

Quantity
(number or amount)
"We come in large and small quantities."

Gaga
(silly)
"Better to be gaga than goofy."

Bustle
(move about quickly)
"My great-grandmother was a dress designer."

Me (Mandy—or an assigned or selected word)

Radiant
(shining; splendid)
"You know, I'm related to radio."

Pale
(having little color)
"No, I feel fine!"

Pagaent
(show)
"Pomp is good too!"

Glorious' story*
Glorious is English and French.
She wears wonderful clothes.
Her best friend is Radiant, and
she also likes Pale, even though
Pale has poor color. Maybe
that's why Glorious is so
worthy of praise.

*Mandy looked up the word "glorious" in the dictionary.

- Ask leading questions that can best be answered with word names: do you have classmates who you think could be film star material? (glorious and radiant) Why?
- Select the original words to be learned from a book of crossword puzzles and other vocabulary exercises; then give the puzzles as tests of knowledge.
- Administer conventional matching, recall, and multiple choice tests on the new words.

Other activities and considerations:

- Have youngsters fill about a third of the seats in the room with words of their own self-collection. Also, have them fill other rooms at upper and lower grade levels with words they think to be easier and more difficult.
- When using an actual classroom, be careful not to select names for the children that may have derisive meanings or connotations. Have students select their own middle and last names and nicknames from word lists (see Appendix B for a helpful word list).
- Have youngsters create "autobiographical notes" for new words, complete with illustrations. Have youngsters add places they subsequently find the word in context. (See Figure 9.2.)

The next method is similar to Classmates in that it too links knowns to unknowns.

FIGURE 9.2

Autobiography of Pale Hustle

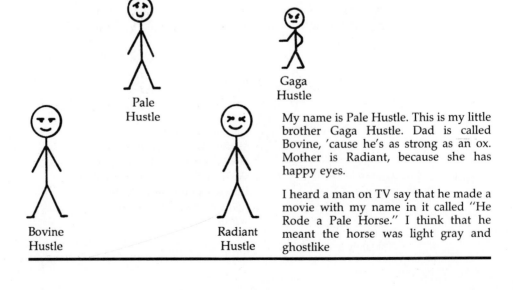

Pale Hustle

Gaga Hustle

Bovine Hustle

Radiant Hustle

My name is Pale Hustle. This is my little brother Gaga Hustle. Dad is called Bovine, 'cause he's as strong as an ox. Mother is Radiant, because she has happy eyes.

I heard a man on TV say that he made a movie with my name in it called "He Rode a Pale Horse." I think that he meant the horse was light gray and ghostlike

The Keyword Method

The Keyword Method is akin to an ancient method for improving memory. It links relatively unfamiliar things to familiar things that are similar in some way, and then combines the two in some thematic way into an odd and therefore memorable mental image. For example, to remember the meaning of the word "plateau," it could be combined with "plate," with a plate pictured or drawn as a raised flatland.

This method has been reported as effective with LD students (Gutherie, 1984; Condus, Marshall, & Miller, 1986), and in learning content material (Levin, et.al., 1986, Konopak & William, 1988). Michael Pressley and associates, who have studied Keyword extensively, maintain that it helps pupils learn how to form connections and to develop elaborations on concepts (Pressley, Levin, & Miller, 1981; Pressley, Johnson, & Symons, 1987; Pressley, Levin, & McDaniel, 1987).

The Keyword method can be especially demanding for youngsters under 11 years old. They tend to require several explicit examples (Pressley, Levin, & Miller, 1981). This has led some critics to maintain that it is cumbersome and artificial (Moore, 1987).

Keyword does create an interesting instructional conversation in which the teacher and students come to the workbench together, and it inculcates a potentially useful memory training device (see Chapter 13 for additional memory devices). The Keyword Method also tends incidentally to reveal students' thought processes.

The next method is more of a paradigm, or essential system, for teaching words and ideas. Its components can be found in several methodologies, including the one just described.

Concept-Based Approach to Vocabulary Building

Words can be taught by a concept-based approach to aid students further in converting words into concepts and concepts into richer and more precise words. Several writers have offered guidelines for teaching concepts (Rentel, 1971) and words as concepts (Frayer, Fredrick, & Klausmeir, 1969; Graves & Prenn, 1986). The concept-based approach to teaching meaning vocabulary has much in common with Gray's paradigm for teaching phonics, or word elements. The model for teaching meaning vocabulary essentially is as follows:

Steps in the Concept-Based Approach

Step 1   Identify the relevant and irrelevant features of the concept in question (see Semantic Feature Analysis ahead as a technique that does this especially well). For example, a relevant attribute or feature of the concept of "globe" is that it is roundish, or spherical, and three dimensional. It is *not* a circle, and it is *not* flat or two dimensional.

Step 2   Provide examples of the concept. For example, a classroom globe— pointing out that it is more rounded than the actual globe.

Step 3	Provide examples of irrelevant but loosely related concepts with which it might be compared, such as a two-dimensional drawing of a circle.
Step 4	Relate the concept by some possible smaller, or subordinating concepts, such as a ball, an egg, or the moon.
Step 5	Relate or categorize the concept by some possible larger, or superordinating concepts, such as "spherical objects" and stars (which are not really star-shaped but only appear that way due to the effect of viewing them through the atmosphere which causes their light to disperse and appear to twinkle).
Step 6	Relate or categorize the concept alongside equal, or coordinating, terms, such as other planets.

This approach leaves little to chance. It covers most possible areas in which a youngster's grasp of a word's meaning might go astray; hence, it tends to be a bit arduous. Nevertheless, it is an effective way to help youngsters with serious reading or language disabilities, and particularly those who are developmentally disabled, or mildly retarded.

The next method can be added to this one to reduce the heavy cognitive emphasis of this conceptual approach. It relies more on a student's personal schema, and can be much more lighthearted.

Subjective Approach to Vocabulary (SAV)

The SAV procedure (Manzo, 1983) builds on students' personal views and associations with a word. It uses these "knowns" to anchor fleeting word meanings, keeping them from drifting off and being forgotten. The method imparts a self-instructional strategy, since students learn how to use their own prior knowledge and experiences to build word knowledge.

The teacher, using a "talk-through" technique, simply helps students tie their lives and experiences to new words. Thus, the biographies of individual lives become part of the ongoing biography of a word, much as in Classmates. When used in a group situation, the method offers keen diagnostic opportunities for discovering how a youngster thinks and what he or she might be saying to him/herself. It also gives students a chance to hear the views of others. In this way, multicultural learnings and insights can occur in a very natural and authentic manner. (See Rational-Emotional therapy in Chapter 12 for further ideas on how to use this process to advance personal-social growth and adjustment.)

SAV has another important characteristic. It tends to speed up transfer of learning and application because the associations drawn on to understand the word arise from the context of the students' lives and, therefore, are easily applicable to both school and life outside school. (See Figures 9.3 and 9.4).

Steps in the SAV Group Remedial Form

Step 1	The teacher identifies two to four words to be taught, or "pretaught" if SAV is used as a prereading activity. If a word list

FIGURE 9.3

Subjective Approach to Vocabulary

THE WORD IS "MAGNETIC"

Teacher: Do you know what a *magnet* is?

Student: Yeah, you have one on your desk with paperclips stuck to it.

Teacher: Well, the word *magnetic* comes from *magnet*, and, according to the dictionary, it means two things: 1. having the properties of a magnet — that is, doing what magnets do; and, 2. being attractive and charming, and therefore drawing people to you, such as having a "magnetic personality." Let's write these meanings down in your Word Study Journal. [Pause to record meanings.]

Teacher: What comes to mind when you hear the word *magnetic*?

Student: My brother Billy. Mr. Ablomp, our neighbor, is a grump. But he gave Billy some of his old golf clubs. Everyone likes Billy, and they give him things.

Teacher: I guess you'd say that he had a "magnetic personality?"

Student: He has a *lot* of "magnetic personality."

Teacher: Another way to say that is, "He has a great deal of *personal magnetism.*"

Student: He's got it, whatever you call it.

Teacher: Do you think that you'll mention Billy's magnetic personality to anyone at home? It's good to use new words.

Student: Yeah, I guess I'll tell my dad. He says that being pleasant is important in selling stuff.

Teacher: Being *magnetic*?

Student: Right.

Teacher: Let's write out your personal association with magnetic to help you to remember it. See if you can illustrate the word with a drawing.

Student: OK.

---

is used, be sure to include as many words as possible that impart concepts and feelings that you would wish students to learn.

Step 2   The teacher tells the student the full meaning of a word, much as it might be found in a dictionary. It is recorded in a Word Study Journal as the "objective," or dictionary, meaning.

Step 3   The teacher asks the student(s), "What does this word remind you of?" or "What do you picture or think of when you hear this word?" (Explain that discussion of a personal association with a word can be very helpful in remembering and clarifying its meaning.)

Step 4   The teacher talks the student through this personal search for meaning by asking further clarifying questions, and in group situations by pointing out those images suggested that seem most vivid. The teacher may add his or her own images, especially when student images appear vague. Students are then directed to write some "subjective," or personal, associations for the new word under the previously written dictionary definition in their Journals. Drawings can be added (see Figure 9.3 and 9.4).

FIGURE 9.4

The New Word
Magnetic

Dictionary Meaning
1. having the properties of a magnet
2. charming, powerfully attractive

(Linking words to one's autobiography)

Personal Association
My brother Billy has
a magnetic personal-
ity. People just take
to him. They give
him things.

Illustration

Bill

Gee, thanks!

Step 5   Silent reading follows next when SAV is used for prereading vocabulary development. When it is being used for general vocabulary development, students are given 5 to 10 minutes to study and rehearse the new and previously recorded words.

Step 6   The teacher has students close their Word Study Journals and asks them the meanings of the words studied that day and a few others from previous days. This step can be tied to seat exercises in conventional workbooks such as crossword puzzles, category games, etc. This manipulation and reinforcement step can be made easier by selecting the words to be taught from the exercise material.

The next strategy makes further and deeper use of personal associations. It taps into a seldom-used domain of learning.

Motor Imaging (MI)

Motor Imaging (Casale-Manzo, 1985) involves the physical-sensory, as well as affective and cognitive, domains. There has been little recognition even of the existence of this domain; it certainly was not acknowledged by Bloom, et al (1956) nor by Krathwohl, et.al. (1964), the chief architects of the handbooks of the cognitive, affective, and attitudinal domains. MI relies on a form of learning that incorporates muscle movements to supplement conventional means of word learning. It sometimes is known as proprioceptive learning—learning that comes to reside within the nervous system.

The basic idea is very old, though generally overlooked in the design of instruction for all but seriously disabled readers with basic word recognition problems (see the Visual-Auditory-Kinesthetic-Tactile technique in Chapter 13). Developmental psychologists, such as Jean Piaget, have observed that young children first respond to a stimulus with gross motor movements. Over time, these motor responses are "abbreviated" into more subtle motor responses, and eventually are interiorized (Piaget, 1963). To test the effect of linking new word meanings to interiorized motor meanings, a study was conducted that compared three approaches to vocabulary learning: one relying heavily on cognitive train-ing—a dictionary-based technique; one based on the affective domain—a sub-jective association method similar to SAV; and a motor-based method—Motor Imaging described ahead. Fifth and sixth grade students were rotated through each of these three treatments in different orders. The words they were exposed to had been shown to be equally difficult. The study showed that the motor and subjective approaches were superior to the dictionary method, and that the motor was superior to both on four of five possible measures. This was true across ability levels (Casale & Manzo, 1983).

It appears that even the highest forms of vocabulary and concept learning have psychomotor foundations, or equivalents. Hence, motor movements asso-ciated with certain stimuli can become interiorized as a "symbolic meaning" (Piaget 1963). There are three considerable advantages to knowing this where remediation is concerned:

1. First, since physical-sensory, or proprioceptive, learnings can be interiorized, they also can be self-stimulating and; as such, they are easier to rehearse and recall with the slightest mental reminder, as well as from external stimulation.
2. Second, proprioceptive learning is so basic to human learning that it is common to all learners, fast and slow, and hence, ideal for heterogeneously grouped classes.
3. Third, the act of identifying and acting out a word becomes a life experience in itself with the word—a value that Frederick Duffelmeyer (1980a) demon-strated when he successfully taught youngsters words by an "experiential" approach.

Steps in Motor Imaging

Step 1   The teacher takes a difficult word from the text, writes it on the chalkboard, pronounces it, and tells what it means.

Step 2   The teacher asks students to imagine a simple pantomime for the word meaning ("How could you show someone what this word means with just your hands or a gesture?").

Step 3   When the teacher gives a signal, students do their gesture panto-mimes simultaneously.

Step 4   The teacher selects the most common pantomime observed. The teacher then demonstrates it to all the students, who then say the word while doing the pantomime.

Step 5   The teacher repeats each new word, this time directing the class to

FIGURE 9.5

Motor Imaging Examples

New Word	Language Meaning	Motor Meaning
appropriate	right or fit for a certain purpose	both palms together, matching perfectly
convey	take or carry from one place to another	both hands together, palms upward, moving from one side to the other
woe	great sadness or trouble	one or both hands over the eyes, head slanted forward
dazzle	shine or reflect brightly	palms close together, facing outward, fingers spread
utmost	the very highest or most	one or both hands reaching up as far as possible
abode	place where you live	hands meeting above the head in a triangular "roof" shape

	do the pantomime while saying a brief meaning or simple synonym.
Step 6	The students' next encounter with the word is in the assigned reading material.
Step 7	The teacher should try to use the pantomime casually whenever the new word is used for a short time thereafter.

Figure 9.5 presents some examples from a Motor Imaging lesson.

Several teachers and specialists have reported that they have successfully used this same basic approach in teaching youngsters letter sounds: a hand gesture or expression is selected for a troublesome sound; the same gesture then is used each time the sound occurs, no matter what grapheme is present (e.g., a finger pointing to the eye for the long sound of "i" whether in **sigh**, **lie**, or by; a hand compressing any vowel forming a schwa—the neutral vowel sound of most unstressed syllables in English, as of "a" in a**go** or in cobr**a**.

The next method makes use of structural analysis of words to teach their meanings more so than to promote effective word decoding and spelling—although the latter two benefit as well.

Incidental Morpheme Analysis (IMA)

IMA (Manzo & Manzo, 1990a) was developed to give on-the-spot supplemental assistance in word learning during content class and basal reading instruction. It also is a useful means of teaching morphemes without excessive reference to rules and issues in syllabication. The method is designed to appear to be incidental to the student; however, it can require careful thought by the teacher, as does most successful incidental teaching.

The term *morpheme* is almost synonymous in practice with teaching prefixes, suffixes, and roots. A morpheme is the smallest possible unit of meaning in a word. Some morphemes have meaning only when attached to other word parts. Examples of such "bound morphemes" include *-ed, -ing, tele-,* and *-cide.* Other morphemes, such as *cover, graph,* and *stand,* called "free morphemes," can stand alone as words in themselves.

Most expert readers and language users use morphemes to make sense out of and remember new words. The Incidental Morpheme Analysis strategy teaches students to apply knowledge of morphemes to "doping-out" plausible meanings of new words encountered in reading. It is a further aid to using context effectively. Remember, however, that both morpheme analysis and context clues are "in-flight" maneuvers that can be misleading.

Steps in Incidental Morpheme Analysis

Identify words in a reading selection that probably are unfamiliar to students but have familiar word parts, or morphemes. Using the following steps, pre-teach and/or reinforce these terms. See the example below of a difficult word found in a middle grade's newsmagazine article.

Step 1   Write the term on the chalkboard and underline the meaningful word parts, or morphemic elements, that might help students understand the word's concept base.

Example: *seis   mo   graph*

Step 2   Ask students if they can use the underlined parts to grasp the word meaning, and why. If the word meaning is predicted correctly, write it under the word and proceed with steps 3 and 4 as reinforcement.

Step 3   Tell students you will give them additional clues for predicting (or remembering) the word meaning. Beneath the underlined word parts, write "level one" clues which are other, easier, words using those morphemes. If students have not yet correctly predicted the word meaning, continue to ask for predictions.

Step 4   Beneath the "level one" clues, write "level two" clues, which are the word part meanings, and continue to ask for predictions until the correct definition is reached and written below the clues.

Example:	*seis*	*mo*	*graph*
Level one clues: familiar word containing the underlined morphemes	seizure		telegraph graphic
Level two clues: word part meanings	to shake		written
Definition:		An instrument that records the direction, time, and intensity of earthquakes	

See Chapter 11 for a partial list of frequently used Latin and Greek morphemes and a rationale for teaching these to remedial readers as an exercise in memory training. The next method relies on teacher-focused analytical reasoning as a form of cognitive enrichment.

Semantic Feature Analysis (SFA)

SFA originally was developed by Dale P. Johnson and P. David Pearson (1984). It is a method designed to teach students how to think systematically about words in terms of their relevant and irrelevant features. It resembles the paradigm, previously described, by which concepts are learned. The method has been shown by Patricia Anders and Candace Bos (1986) to be especially effective in improving content area reading vocabulary and comprehension. The version described and illustrated below was refined by Charles and Ezra Stieglitz (1981) for use with content material, and, thus, to build a fund of information and schema. They call it SAVOR, for Subject Area Vocabulary Reinforcement.

Steps in SAVOR

Step 1   The teacher identifies a category of words highly familiar to students. For a fun example, try "monsters," a category within the interest range of many students (see Figure 9.6). The teacher first elicits words from the pupils that fit in this category (King Kong, Hulk, Dracula, Cookie Monster, Godzilla) and has the students list these examples in a column on their own paper.

Step 2   The students list some features of these monsters (hairy, huge, strong, mean, transforming) across the top of the page. Following this, they fill in the matrix by using plus (+) or minus (-) signs to indicate whether a monster has a particular feature.

Step 3   After the matrix is filled in, the teacher leads students to study the different patterns of pluses and minuses and to discover the uniqueness of each word (or, in this case, creature).

Johnson and Pearson (1984) state that as pupils gain more experience with Semantic Feature Analysis, the teacher may wish to switch from a plus/minus

FIGURE 9.6

Sample SAVOR Worksheet

	MONSTERS				
	HAIRY	HUGE	STRONG	MEAN	TRANSFORMING
King Kong	+	+	+	+	−
Hulk	−	+	+	−	+
Dracula	−	−	−	+	+
Cookie Monster	+	−	−	−	−
Godzilla	−	+	+	+	−

Johnson and Pearson (1984)

system to a graduated numerical system (0 = none, 1 = some, 2 = much, 3 = all). The method is particularly suitable for helping remedial students clarify frequently confused terms (see Figure 9.7 on Semantic Feature Analysis in Mathematics).

Learning outcomes can be amplified by tying concept-based learning to subjective and motor-based equivalents. The next method offers another means of noting the distinctive features of words from an even broader concept base.

Themed Vocabulary Study (TVS)

One of the best and oldest means of vocabulary enrichment is based on theme studies, also called Semantic Clusters by Robert and Jana Marzano (1988). This is another method that draws strength from the paradigm for teaching concepts. Themed Vocabulary Study permits students to take well-known, partially known, and barely recognized words and link them together into a semantic web able to catch and hold entirely new words and unusual nuances of meaning for familiar words. It also builds precision in thinking and writing and causes knowledge of words to continue to accumulate. Ironically, continued word study is necessary because many words do not always have precise, distinct, and unchanging meanings—a point well developed in a recent review of the literature on word meanings (Anderson & Nagy, 1991).

Steps in Themed Vocabulary Study

Step 1 Identify a theme.

Step 2 Ask students to state those words they think to be related to the designated theme, and to say what they think those words mean.

Step 3 Use dictionaries to check word meanings and to find synonyms, antonyms, and nuances of meaning.

Step 4 Link the relevant words to one another (with brief definitions) in the form of a semantic map (see illustration below).

FIGURE 9.7

SAVOR Worksheet with Mathematics

	SHAPES				
	Four Sided	Curved or Rounded Lines	Line Segment	All Sides Equal in Length	Right Angles
Triangle	−	−	+	+	−
Rectangle	+	−	+	−	+
Parallelogram	+	−	+	+	−
Circle	−	+	−	−	−
Trapezoid	+	−	+	−	−
Semicircle	−	+	+	−	−
Square	+	−	+	+	+

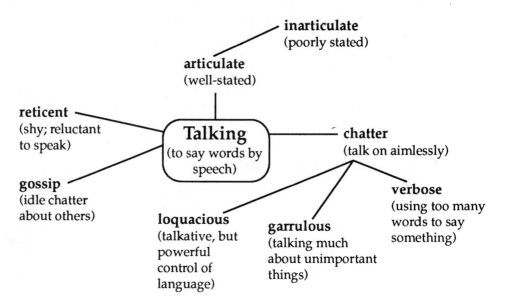

Step 5   Reinforce and evaluate by testing students' recall and by having them write sentences or descriptive pieces designed to use the new words. Note: The once traditional practice of having students write a sentence or two containing a new word still makes sense. It has the diagnostic advantage of revealing whther the students' knowledge of the word includes the often context-specific way in which a given word is used. Anderson and Nagy (1991) give the example of the word *correlate*. The dictionary definition says *"to be related one to the other."* This led a student to write "Me and my parents *correlate*, because without them I wouldn't be here" (p. 719). In a diagnostic-teaching situation, this would immediately reveal that the term *correlate* is not yet within the student's grasp.

Other themes to consider in word study:

- Noncomplimentary terms but nonvulgar terms (pesky, brusk, prissy, antsy, baudy, addlebrained)
- Behavior-related terms (manners, comportment, deportment, inappropriate, maladaptive, poised, irascible)
- Character traits (endurance, restraint, perseverance, reflection, tolerance)
- Thinking terms (abstract, concrete, rational, irrational, creative, critical, cognition, diffusive, coherent)
- Temperament labels (sanguine, industrious, hyper, choleric, mercurial, pensive)
- Attitudes (positive, negative, hostile, aggressive, assertive, constructive)

(See Marzano & Marzano [1988] for further recommendations.)

Vocabulary learning from themed study can be greatly amplified when combined with Semantic Feature Analysis, Subjective/Objective Vocabulary recording, and/or Motor Imaging. Coupling student reactions to the words in themes such as those described above also provides excellent opportunities for diagnosing aspects of personal-social adjustment and getting a fix on a student's "world view"—or the way in which he/she is experiencing reality.

The next method inherently contains this same opportunity, as it has students create sentences based on anticipating word meanings that will be developed in text. It also contributes to writing, comprehension, concept formation, and acquisition of a greater fund of information.

Possible Sentences

Steven Stahl and Barbara Kapinus (1991) recently revisited and tested the value of a method first developed by David and Sharon Moore (1986), and showed it to be a valuable and easy-to-use approach to vocabulary development in a content class or a remedial setting.

Steps in Possible Sentences

Step 1   The teacher lists several key concept words from a selection, pronounces them, and elicits and/or gives meanings for them.

Step 2   Students are encouraged to predict sentences that could possibly appear in the textual material containing these words.

Step 3   Students read the textual material to check the relative accuracy of their sentences, in the sense that their sentences seem to be compatible with, though not identical to, those in the text.

Step 4   The students' sentences are then analyzed, evaluated, and corrected as needed.

Step 5   New sentences are invited that reflect the sum of learnings from the prediction, reading, and sentence analysis steps.

When used in this way, Possible Sentences significantly improved vocabulary acquisition and recall of text (Stahl & Karpinus, 1991). Again, as Stahl and associates also have pointed out in numerous articles, it appears to be the discussion—the pointed instructional conversation—that seems to make Possible Sentences really work (Stahl, 1986; Stahl & Vancil, 1986; Stahl & Kapinus, 1991).

Word Games

Word games can help build motivation for vocabulary study. James Bowman (1991) suggests that two classes of games based on word pairs, "Wordy Gurdy Puzzles" and "Oxymorons," are especially useful because they are based on cues within words and word relationships. By providing practice in attending to these types of cues, these games reinforce comprehension processes as well as contextual vocabulary processes.

Wordy Gurdy

Develop a list of definitions that could be associated with two rhyming words—each of the rhyming words having the same number of syllables. Give the definitions to students, indicating the number of syllables in each word of the "answer":

principal plumbing outlet [1]	*(main drain)*
Henry's practical jokes [1]	*(Hank's pranks)*
comical rabbit [2]	*(funny bunny)*

Once students have provided the "answers" to several Wordy Gurdy Puzzles, challenge them to make up their own "definitions" and trade puzzles.

Oxymorons

An oxymoron is a word pair in which one word contradicts the other, such as *jumbo shrimp, cruel kindness,* and *eternal moment.* Introduce several such oxymorons to students, pointing out their contradictory nature. Have students compose definitions for oxymorons. Then furnish definitions and have students create an oxymoron for each.

Dictionary Usage

Use of the dictionary is another thing that remedial students desperately need, but which they can not get in most remedial programs. The impression seems to be that remedial students have more pressing needs. There also is the frequent finding of vocabulary studies that direct teaching methods are better than dictionary methods that amount to "looking up words" (Gipe, 1978-79; Casale & Manzo, 1983). Such results must be interpreted with caution, however, since the studies rarely involved explicit and extensive teaching of the use of the dictionary, and often did not account for possible long-term effects. Further, and most importantly, the dictionary is a vital piece of a total literacy program. It really is not an approach to vocabulary instruction, as much as an essential component of it.

A review of the parts and functions of the dictionary reveals its intrinsic worth. It can be a pass-key that opens most every lock on the entry door to full literacy.

Much of what is described ahead on how to promote dictionary study is derived from two classical sources: William S. Gray's text, *On Their Own in Reading* (1948, 1960), and Clyde Roberts's *Teacher's Guide to Word Attack* (1956). These exercises can be done independently or in cooperative learning pairs.

1. A good place to begin dictionary study is to show that it can be a fun book to browse through. One way to do this is to use it to learn what certain unusual things are, or what some very usual things are called, or are also called. Gray (1960) recommends uncommon animals for the first category (e.g., *rhea, marten, pelican*). The second category would be covered by words such as: *hinge* (as on a door), and *mucilage* (another name for common sticky glue).

2. Write adjectives such as *agile*, *smug*, and *arrogant* with appropriate page numbers after each and ask students to decide whether they would like to have these words used to describe them.

3. Make a point of showing how words in the dictionary are arranged in alphabetical order, and how this can be used to help spell words correctly as well as to look up their meanings. Illustrate how to look up the spelling of a word by considering several possible ways it might be spelled other than the way it immediately sounds (e.g., the word *mucilage* sounds like musilage, but is spelled mucilage). Take this point a bit further and show how the dictionary can be used to discover, more or less, how to pronounce words encountered in print (e.g., rhea = rē·ə). Give students a great deal of practice in doing this with known words and then less known and finally unknown words. Have them study and create pictorial representations of key sounds (see Figure 9.8). In this way, a student could conceivably learn how to decode most any word in the language. The effort spent doing this also increases time on task in acquiring basic word analysis and recognition skills.

4. The dictionary contains a wealth of etymological information on the origins of words. This activity which often is considered an additional burden for the remedial student, can be a very helpful way to remember meanings and spellings. When it's combined with Vocabulary Classmates, it can be like learning about the background of a new acquaintance. Teach students to look at the information between the brackets—[ ]—when these are available, to find out about the origins and special features of a word (e.g., **horology** [< Gr. *hora*, hour + logy]–the science or art of measuring time; **bonfire** [literally, *bone fire*, fire for burning corpses]–a fire built outdoors).

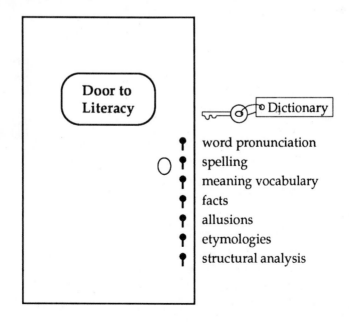

FIGURE 9.8

VOWEL

A	E	I	O	U
ā āpe	ē ēagle	ī īce	ō ōak	ū ūkulele
ă ăpple	ĕ ĕgg	ĭ ĭgloo	ŏ ŏx	ŭ ŭmbrella
ä arm	ẽ pẽrcolator	ĩ bĩrd	ô ôrgan	û tûrtle
à sofà			o͞o bo͞ot	
â châir			o͝o fo͝ot	

FIGURE 9.8 (continued)

CONSONANTS

b boy   j jug   p pan   w watch

d dog   k kite   r rat   y yoke

f fan   l leaf   s snake   z zebra

g goat   m man   t toad

h hat   n nose   v vase

FIGURE 9.8 (continued)

COMBINATIONS

oi coins   oy oyster   ou house

ow owl   ch church   th teeth   du educate   ng wing

sh sheep   th teeth   tu picture   zh treasure

Roberts (1956)

5. Familiarize students with any additional informational values the particular dictionary available may have (e.g., geographical and biographical information). Older dictionaries—which often can be acquired inexpensively at garage sales—can be expected to contain any number of other bits of fascinating information (e.g., flags of nations, military uniforms, the dress of various countries).

If dictionary study, and for that matter all word study, is combined at every opportunity with authentic experiences in reading, writing, and further understanding a student's environment, it will be engaging, satisfying, and empowering. At an anecdotal level, we are always surprised at how enthusiastic youngsters are about writing a letter to a grandparent, or other relative, requesting that they consider giving them a dictionary, even an old one, for a birthday or holiday present.

To reiterate and summarize, children without skill or natural aptitude for language need vocabulary training, conducive language environments, and dictionary study more, not less, than other achieving youngsters. Metaphorically speaking, if children lived on boats and didn't take to the water immediately, we would put "floogies" on their arms to keep them afloat and build confidence until they learned how to swim. It seems wise to do the same with children who don't take to the sea of printed and spoken language we are immersed in each day. The dictionary can be a life raft until they get their literacy "sea-legs."

At the risk of mixing metaphors, if vocabulary development is a frequently overlooked child of remedial reading instruction, the next two sections of the chapter on spelling and handwriting are more like step-children and foster children respectively. If you are not now inclined to be concerned about either of these, we hope that you will consider them now with an open mind, since they too are time-tested traditions in education and, therefore, deserving of every consideration.

Spelling

Spelling Assessment System

Gable, Hendrickson, and Meeks (1988) have assembled a dynamic five-step system of collecting, analyzing, and remedying spelling errors. It can be used along with other reading and language arts activities or used as a separate, intensive training program. It can be used as a whole-class activity, or in small groups or individual tutoring settings. The five-step system is largely based on the work of Anderson (1985), Henderson (1985), and others on "invented spellings"—where students experiment with language while writing—as well as Gentry's (1982) stage model of progression that builds on the relationship of language skills to spelling. Gentry's self-defining stages are referred to as:

- precommunicative (little resemblance to the target word)
- semiphonetic (partially resembling the target word, usually accurate in the initial sounds)
- phonetic (having accurate sound representations despite incorrect spelling)
- transitional (marked by good phonetic and configurational representation but still containing some inaccuracies)
- correct (accurate spelling)

First graders typically approach spelling strictly letter-by-letter, left-to-right. By the end of first grade, children begin to recognize patterns such as the final silent letter in single syllable words. Later, they begin to recognize patterns in multisyllabic words, and the connections between (seeming) irregular spellings and word meanings. These stages are useful, too, for understanding and categorizing remedial readers.

The Spelling Assessment System is designed to help identify a student's spelling stage and to assist the student in advancing to the next stage. The five steps in this process are described below.

Steps in The Spelling Assessment System

Step 1   *Sample and Identify*

       a) Obtain a sample of student spellings of approximately 50 words in any reasonable way, as by dictating a conventional word list or by dictating a paragraph roughly at a student's independent reading level. (This can be done either way because students' spelling errors on paragraphs are quite consistent with those on word lists—DeMaster, Crossland, & Hasselbring, 1986.)

       b) Use the words missed to replenish a 5–10 word flow list of test-teach-test items, where a word is moved off the list and replaced when it is spelled correctly five consecutive times.

Step 2   *Interview Students*

       Talk to students about their spelling to establish instructional priorities. Ask: "Are there any words you hate to spell? What confuses you about spelling that word? Tell me another word you tend to have trouble spelling." Also ask: "Which part of this word (pointing to several, one at a time) do you tend to have trouble spelling?" Finally, ask: "What difficult words can you spell correctly? How did you learn these words? How do you remember these words?" This introspective approach can have a very generative payoff if it leads remedial students to realize and correct a serious strategy flaw that permeates their spelling and reading: they tend to invert the most productive order for decoding and spelling words, using a visual, whole-word approach to *reading* words, and a phonetic approach to *spelling* them (Clark, 1988).

Step 3   *Analyze and Classify Errors*

       Errors, or invented spellings, can be analyzed in several possible ways. The letters-in-place method is recommended. With this method, strengths as well as patterns of errors become apparent; for example, the word is *bucket*, and the student writes *b-a-c-c-e-t*. Letters-in-place reveals only two errors in this strange word. Errors can be categorized further as regular, predictable, or irregular (see Figures 9.9 and 9.10).

Step 4   *Select a Corrective Strategy*

       The GHM approach recommends ten basic teaching strategies for spelling instruction. These have been grouped into three major diagnostic categories as shown below:

       Corrective Spelling Strategies

       For *regular* words
- Stress letter-sound correspondence
- Stress application rather than memorization

       For *predictable* words
- Emphasize spelling rules
- Use mnemonic devices
- Teach rhyming words
- Teach word families

FIGURE 9.9

Teacher's Analysis Chart for a Student's Spelling Errors

Student _____   Date _____

Material/level _____

Word source: Word list ( )   Paragraph ( )   Other _____

Type of analysis/scoring: Word ( )   Syllables ( )   Clusters ( )   Letters ( )

Words Types:

	Regular	Predictable	Irregular	Instructional Priority
Error type				
Rules/patterns				
Consonants				
Vowels				
Error tendency				
Order				
Substitution				
Insertion				
Omission				

Beginning time _____   Ending time _____   Number of minutes _____

Correct _____   Errors _____

*from Gable, Hendrickson, and Meeks (1988), adapted from
DeMaster, Crossland, and Hasselbring (1986) and
Hendrickson, Gable, and Hasselbring (1988)*

FIGURE 9.10

Types of Spelling Words

WORD TYPE	DESCRIPTION	EXAMPLES
Regular	Word contains exact phoneme-grapheme correspondence	pig, nap, set, see
Predictable	Word contains orthographic patterns or generalizations without strict phoneme-grapheme correspondence; spelled by applying rules of sound-letter correspondence	receive, may, day, sweet, soap
Irregular	Word does not conform to sound-letter or orthographic regularities; several graphemic clues exist	melon, through, might, laughing

*Based on Hasselbring and Owens (1982) (in
Gable, Hendrickson, and Meeks, 1988)*

For *irregular* words
- Use flash cards
- Use look-cover-copy-compare
- Use multisensory VAKT approaches (detailed in Chapter 12)
- Use visual memory experiences (see ahead)

Note: For single errors associated with carelessness or inattention, simple corrective feedback is advised. For repeated mistakes, strategies such as modeling correct spellings or discriminating correct from incorrect spellings (verbal or written) are recommended.

Step 5   *Evaluate the Strategy*
To evaluate the effectiveness of the spelling program, GHM recommends repeated testing with conventional or free-flow dictation. The traditional criteria for a set of words is 80%. To arrive at some valid standards for remedial and exceptional children, collect scores of proficient and low-achieving youngsters and establish a band within which reasonable levels of success can be expected.

Adapted from Hendrickson, Gable, and Hasselbring (1988)

This approach to spelling instruction is suitable for conventional classroom as well as remedial use. The next four methods were designed primarily for use with reading and language disabled students.

Simultaneous Oral Spelling (SOS)

SOS is part of the Orton-Gillingham reading system (Orton, 1966). Very simply, the child pronounces a word, spells it orally, and then writes the word while saying the letter names. With SOS, inconsistent and irregular spellings are not taught until the student can successfully spell most words that are phonetically regular. With SOS, there is a good deal of emphasis placed on syllabication. Inflectional endings, prefixes, and suffixes, on the other hand, are treated as morphemes and taught by rules.

Bannatyne's Method

Alexander Bannatyne's (1974) technique is a multisensory approach that has students: first pronounce the spelling word slowly (listening for its phonemic parts); second, pronounce it while trying to separate it into its phonemic parts; third, study the word visually in print (while attempting to separate and identify the graphemes that make each phonemic sound); fourth, pronounce each phoneme as the teacher points to each grapheme; and fifth, say the sounds and write the letters repeatedly until each word is learned.

Auditory Discrimination in Depth (ADD)

ADD is the Charles and Pat Lindamood (1975) approach previously described in the chapter on decoding. ADD is almost purely an auditory and proprioceptive (physical feedback) system. Students are taught to feel and label each type of sound as it passes between their lips. The sounds, which the Lindamoods have named with terms like "lip popper" (p and b), "lip cooler" (f and v), and skinny sounds (s and z), are known in classical linguistics by more technical names (explosives, fricatives, and continuents, respectively). This method requires extensive inservice training (approximately two weeks).

Eidetic Imaging (EI)

EI is an approach fashioned by the writers from several sources, most notably Slingerland (1971), Fernald (1943), and personal communications from Gerald Glass (of Adelphi University). The method places heavy emphasis on the natural ability of most youngsters, with a little refresher training, to be able to hold a mental image before them for several seconds after a stimulus has been removed. EI follows these steps:

1. A word is written or printed in large letters and held before the student.
2. The student indicates when he or she has inspected it long enough to have a good image of it.
3. The word then is removed and the student attempts to continue to see it before them while writing and spelling it in the space in which they "see" it (should they begin to err, the word card is raised again to be studied and reimaged) — the word should be correctly spelled and written in space three times, one under another.
4. The student tries to copy the word from "space" onto the top of a sheet of paper.
5. When this is done correctly, the paper is folded to conceal the first effort and it is written again from memory, and then once more after folding and covering the second effort.

EI has students use their own imaging powers to sizeup and write a word under decreasing, or fading, levels of support. It also provides metacognitive training as students come to monitor and understand better how much effort, exposure time, and trial and error it takes them to learn how to spell a word. This method is especially suitable to paired learning situations and as an independent strategy for learning to spell difficult words any time the need arises. The method also provides an opportunity for incidentally teaching handwriting.

Handwriting

Why Handwriting?

There are several reasons to work to improve the handwriting of remedial readers and learning disabled students. These include the following:

- Poor handwriting, according to Gable, Hendrickson, and Meeks (1988), is responsible for over 20% of spelling errors.

- Handwriting is something manageable that most students can learn to do better, and is, therefore, an ideal skill for building self-efficacy.
- Individuals who write hastily tend to be highly impulsive and inattentive to details. Handwriting can be used as a self-monitoring device by which to gauge when one is becoming too hasty, and possibly negligent of important details in school and in life in general.
- Well-crafted handwriting has an aesthetic dimension that many societies value. Hence, taking the time to teach the poor reader and LD student to write neatly and distinctively is to show a raised sense of expectation for their role in society and to make them part of an established tradition.
- The process of teaching someone to write legibly can be an intimate and caring exchange that builds a beneficial reserve of good will and trust between teacher and student.

Put another way, it isn't wise to abandon this educational tradition. How one writes is not as important as what one writes, but it is not unimportant either. It is the clothing that our thoughts wear in a variety of circumstances. It is the means by which class notes and tests are taken in school, and the way in which most memos, notes, and letters are written in personal communications to everyone from the mail carrier to family members to our employers. Legibility is a sign of maturity and respect for others.

To get a sense of empathy with the student who has poor handwriting, and an idea of why instruction in handwriting is important, just write your name with your "other" hand (your left hand if right-handed, your right hand if left-handed). To make the writing legible, you practically have to "draw" the letters. Anyone would tend to avoid such an awkward, painstaking process. The only way to master legible and effortless handwriting is through practice and good instruction.

Reginia Cicci (1983) has identified seven forms of handwriting difficulty that tend to accompany poor reading: pencil grasp, excessive tension, incorrect paper position, inappropriate spacing of letters or between words, poor visual memory of letters, slow rate, and poor fine motor skills (as cited by Clark 1988). Cox (1984) further notes that handwriting training for undiagnosed dyslexic children can be as time-consuming as teaching them to read. It also can be stigmatizing as they begin to write in school and in other life situations.

How to Proceed: Some Guiding Principles

Handwriting instruction begins with posture and pen grip. One should sit back comfortably, with shoulders relaxed, both feet on the floor, and the elbow of the writing hand *not* resting on the desk. The grip should also be relaxed: one should be able to hold a small wad of paper in the writing hand without crushing it. A common cause of poor handwriting is the "death grip"—holding the pen or pencil so tightly that it is impossible to exercise fine motor control necessary for smooth writing. For children with poor psycho-motor skills, it sometimes is helpful to have them hold the pen or pencil between the first and second fingers, instead of resting it on top of the first (index) finger.

Having established comfortable posture and pen grip, students can be guided in regular practice of the basic strokes. It may be helpful to guard against some common misconceptions about handwriting instruction:

- *"There's no time to teach handwriting."* We tend to *make* time for what we see as important. Even so, a handwriting lesson shouldn't take longer than 15 minutes. Further, "squeezing it in" may increase the pace of all other instruction, and therefore may heighten attention and learning outcomes in all areas, rather than diminish them.
- *"I can't really make a difference."* The teacher's attitude toward handwriting does make a difference. If the teacher returns illegible papers for rewriting, children will attend more carefully to their handwriting. In so doing, they will develop habits that contribute to comfortable, easy, and legible handwriting.
- *"Poor handwriting is a sign of intelligence."* False. Handwriting is purely a psycho-motor skill. It can only be improved through practice and good instruction, and yes, academically gifted students and future doctors need it too. For remedial students, as previously noted, it can be an area where they can succeed and build self-efficacy and faith in personal effort.
- *"Teaching handwriting is boring."* Means of teaching handwriting can be as varied as the teacher's own imagination. One thing to avoid is the copybook approach: if writing something 7 times is good practice, it does not follow that writing it 100 times is excellent practice. After more than just a few repetitions in isolation, the value of handwriting practice diminishes sharply, and can thereafter even become counterproductive. Handwriting exercises should be varied and students' best products should be showcased. Have students select some of their best works for inclusion in their portfolios.

There are essentially five ways to teach the mechanics of handwriting. Each can be done with cursive or print. They are: explaining, tracing, copying, matching, and framing.

In *explaining* or commanding, the teacher individualizes instruction by talking the pupil through the process, much as a coach might. There are four key

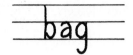

terms for doing this: the approach stroke, drop stroke, the anchor down stroke (made on the base line), and release stroke.

In *tracing,* pupils write over letters that are formed, on tracing paper or exercises sheets.

In *copying,* the pupil reproduces, or transliterates, print into cursive.

In *matching,* the pupil reproduces precisely the form shown.

In *framing,* a second line is drawn about halfway down across the writing line, and pupils are reminded to have all lowercase letters and bulbous parts of other letters confined within the lower two lines.

Which are the Better Approaches?

Copying serves to promote better learning than tracing (Askov & Greff 1975; Williams, 1975). However, when compared to explaining and copying, copying alone was less effective (Kirk, 1981). Our conclusion is that any combination of explaining, copying, and framing seems to be the most effective method of teaching handwriting.

For youngsters who seem to be excessively tense or diagnosed as having dysgraphia (very poor writing), there also are prewriting warm-up exercises to consider. King (1985) recommends the "windshield wiper"—making arching lines back and forth, and "windtunnels"—circular scribbles. These can be done with eyes closed to develop relaxation and rhythm. Cox (1984) and Slingerland (1971) also have pupils do skywriting—a technique similar to that recommended in this chapter for Eidetic Imagery Spelling. The whole arm movements are believed to be a relaxing and attention-raising activity.

Finally, handwriting should be practiced in a variety of situations. This can be done through simulations. Simulate essay tests, dictation of short passages, or notetaking of brief 5 to 10 minute lectures. Also have students fill some authentic needs, such as writing a "thank you" note to grandparents for a recent gift, or a note to a teacher explaining absent or late work. The pupil who otherwise would shy from criticism or direction often welcomes both when his or her work is going public to family, teachers, or friends.

> ## LOOKING BACK <

The chapter addressed three aspects of literacy that tend to be undervalued or totally ignored where remedial readers are concerned: vocabulary, spelling, and handwriting. The greatest concentration was given to a variety of methods for igniting attention to and concern for words and precision in thought. Methods ranged from attention to word parts (morphemes) to a variety of means for connecting new words to concepts, personal experiences, and even interiorized muscle movements.

Spelling and handwriting were presented as frequently ignored collateral goals of remedial instruction. It was argued that these are more easily improved than reading, and, thus, can be a means of raising student self-efficacy and optimism about learning. These "skills" also are part of a student's persona; hence, paying attention to them tells students that the instructor cares about them and their public image. It also reminds them to show respect for others by writing to them in a legible and accurate way, despite the extra effort required.

> ## LOOKING AHEAD

Word meanings vary greatly with the context in which they are used. But, too, words establish "context" that suggests meanings. The next chapter addresses the paradox of how to use words to get meaning and yet to build or reconstruct meaning from textual material. This complex process is otherwise known as *reading comprehension.*

10

Remedies for Comprehension Deficits

> "Comprehension is inherently reconstructive."
> ROBERT CALFEE & ELFRIEDA HIEBERT

IV. Complementary Comprehension Techniques
   A. *Humor: Or, Do Something Uplifting!*
   B. *Lookbacks*
   C. *Paraphrasing*
   D. *Summarizing*
   E. *Text Structure: Outlining, Paragraph Pattern Analysis, and Grammars/Maps/Guides*
      1. *Outlining*
      2. *Paragraph Patterns*
      3. *Grammars/Maps/Guides*
   F. *Knowledge Activation and Integration Techniques*
      1. *K-W-L Plus*
      2. *PreP*
      3. *Inferencing*
      4. *Sustained Silent Reading*
      5. *Cuing Systems*
         a. *Monitoring Cards*
         b. *Note Cue*
         c. *Chunking Cues*
   G. *Imaging*
   H. *Parallel Lessons*
   I. *Dramatization*
   J. *Following Directions*

> ➤ *LOOK FOR IT*

Look for a discussion of comprehension process that is based on an interactive model that gives appropriate attention to both its reconstructive and constructive aspects. Notice how this chapter focuses on reconstructive comprehension by including a helpful listing of traditional factors and skills involved in comprehension, but relies on contemporary findings that support the importance of instructional conversations that permit readers to influence as well as be influenced by lesson activity. Notice too that many of these methods serve a variety of collateral human needs as well as traditional reading comprehension objectives.

Fixing Comprehension: Understanding the Comprehension Process

To fix comprehension, it is necessary to know what might be broken. Stated briefly, effective comprehension is dependent on effective decoding, relevant vocabulary, appropriate purpose, motivation, perception, memory, and prior knowledge. Each of these interact in a fluid way in the overall process of comprehending. The section that follows lays the conceptual foundation for these points.

Reading comprehension, according to Robert Wilson and Linda Gambrell (1988), is "the process of using one's own experiences and text clues to infer the author's intended meaning" (p.12). This view of reading has been called interactive, in the sense that the reader constructs meaning from experience, perceptions, and prior knowledge. The written words of the author are said to serve largely as a stimulus and catalyst for understanding. However, to say that readers construct meaning can be a bit misleading since it implies that one may choose to build one meaning versus another. In fact, the reader is obliged, in Wilson and Gambrell's words, to make every effort to comprehend the author's "intended meaning," even to seeing beyond unintentional ambiguities, and to construct further meanings or significance from that point forward. Hereafter, for the sake of clarity, we shall use the term *reconstructive* to refer to the act of "constructing" meaning from the combination of the author's words and the reader's prior knowledge and experience. The term *constructive*, as previously stated, will be used to address the other (though not necessarily second) interactive process of building meanings, connections, and applications beyond the author and the page. The term "interactive" should be thought of more along the lines of the dialogue that the reader has within him/herself about what the author might be saying, whether it is accurate, and its possible implications. In so doing, the reader may, and in fact should, represent the author in this "inner conversation" and to that extent, all efforts to read and comprehend can be called an "interactive process."

Since this chapter is intended to guide in the remediation of basic comprehension processes, it tends to focus on the reconstructive aspects of comprehension. However, it can not do so without some reference to the constructive aspects of the reading process, since the two are complementary pieces of the same quest for immediate and deeper understanding of life's many questions. Let's review the reconstructive-constructive relationship a bit more closely because it contains some important implications for the diagnosis and remediation model.

Even a cursory listing of factors and functions involved in the comprehension process serves to illustrate why the remedial specialist or teacher needs to be a high-level problem solver. This list also supports the need for differential diagnosis. The chief factors and functions related to comprehension dysfunction are listed below, in roughly the order of their frequency of occurrence. See if you agree with the order in which they are listed.

1. Orientation and motivation to read (Mason, Herman, & Au, 1991)
2. Word recognition and analysis (Chall, 1983a; Holmes & Singer, 1961; LaBerge & Samuels, 1974; Lewkowicz, 1987)
3. Knowledge of word meanings and ability to infer meanings from context (Graves, 1986)

4. Prior knowledge and experience (schema) (Bartlett, 1932; Gray, 1948; Lar 1981; Rumelhart, 1980; Meeks, 1991)

5. Adequate mental aptitude and basic thinking skills such as identifying a main idea, seeing details, and being able to make logical inferences (Marzano, 1991)

6. Fundamental curiosity and the ability to ask appropriate questions (Baker, 1979a, b; Maw & Maw, 1967; Manzo, 1969a)

7. Familiarity with the language patterns in prose, and hence with the syntactic and semantic clues used to anticipate meaning (Mason, Herman, & Au, 1991)

8. Adequate social-psychological maturity to respond empathetically and objectively to information and story narratives (Mason, Herman, & Au, 1991; Rumelhart, 1980)

9. Continuously developing metacognitive skills that permit the self-monitoring and self-fixing of comprehension problems as they arise (Paris, 1986)

10. Ability and willingness to see and find *larger* structures and organizational patterns in print (Meyer, 1975)

11. Ongoing development of higher mental processes, such as the ability to reason analytically and think metaphorically, evaluatively, and constructively (Gaskins & Elliot, 1991; Manzo & Manzo, 1990a)

12. Ability and skill in taking notes, summarizing, and critiquing (Bromley & McKeveny, 1986)

13. Ability and skill to write reflectively in response to what one has read and thought (D. Anderson & Hidi, 1988-89; Graves, 1983; Eanet & Manzo, 1976)

14. Continuing evolution of a "world view" (Chall, 1983b), or of appropriate values (Hoffman, 1977; Schell, 1980), interests, and understandings of how things are and ought best to be (Knafle, Legenza-Wescott, & Passcarella, 1988)

Consider now how researchers and practitioners have sifted through these factors and translated them into some principles to guide reflective teaching and methods for teaching comprehension. You undoubtedly will wish to add to this list in time, if not immediately.

Principles to Guide Successful Comprehension Instruction

The principles stated here are essentially comprehension-specific elaborations of the principles of remediation described in Chapter 7. These are taken largely from reviews of the literature by Levin and Pressley (1981), Pearson and Fielding (1991), Pearson and Gallagher (1983), Santa and Hayes (1981), and Tierney and Cunningham (1984). Additional information was drawn from chapters and critiques of methodologies by Duffy, et.al. (1987), Gaskins (1981), Manzo and Manzo (1990a), and Maria (1990). Elements of consistently effective comprehension teaching methods include:

1. Front-loading. This term refers to attempts to empower pupils before they read. Such techniques tend to reduce potential vocabulary obstacles to comprehension, activate relevant prior knowledge, and provide specific information on text structure and actual facts covered in the text. It could be argued that such methods enable students to engage a reading selection as if they had elevated IQ's, skill, and knowledge.

2. Transformations. Readers are made more alert, active, and engaged by a requirement to transform the text from our ideas to those of the reader. Reconstructive transformations, the focus of this chapter, include tasks such as:

a. translating, or retelling what one has read, with the text available
b. recalling and retelling, without looking back at the text
c. rewriting, or summarizing, with the text available
d. summarizing, without consulting the text
e. outlining with and without available text
f. representing the text in a student-constructed graphic overview or illustration, with the text available for reference

Additional types of constructive transformations for remedial readers are discussed in the chapter on higher-order literacy. These include compressing and categorizing information for long-term memory (study skills), and various means of writing, reflecting, and connecting.

3. Authentic Text and Tasks. There are many possible ways to achieve some level of authenticity. None, however, is perfect, since schools are designed to teach about and simulate life conditions in some systematic and controlled manner. Nonetheless, teaching methods and materials need to be selected that come closer to the ways that real interests are built and language is used and learned. This is exemplified in the next point.

4. Instructional Conversations. Known by several other names, such as *responsive teaching, reciprocity,* and *cognitive apprenticeship,* this notion simply means that the teaching method is built on a relatively authentic interaction between teacher and students, and students with one another. Such interactions tend to rouse minds to life (Tharp & Gallimore, 1989a) and provide opportunities for effective thinking to be modeled, or made public, and for ineffective thinking to be detected and fixed in an "on-line" way.

5. Teach Strategies, Not Skills. Each lesson should be crafted so as to impart possible strategies for dealing with reading and learning needs. Accordingly, it is important to focus on teaching students to use strategies such as self-monitoring and self-fixing, and to plan for the gradual fading out of teacher direction with a corresponding increase of student responsibility. Skills instruction is not a way of teaching—it is an objective that comes from student commitment and practice in effectively using personal learning strategies until these become automatic, or habitual.

Examples of these and several other principles and elements of comprehension instruction are developed in the pages ahead. The remainder of this chapter is a compendium of reading comprehension teaching methods. The term "strategies," as used hereafter, refers to methods that promote reflective, or strategic, teaching; that is, using the most appropriate approaches, methods, and techniques to meet students' reading-learning needs.

Reading Comprehension Improvement Strategies

Some methods described ahead contain a great deal of detail and anecdotal information to illustrate some of the rich empirical and/or clinical base that can emerge from reflective use. Such in-depth information on at least a few methods also reveals a good deal about the structure of knowledge and how it can increase with use and experience.

The first method, the Directed Reading-Thinking Activity (DR-TA), is based on the Directed Reading Activity that Betts (1946) developed by synthesizing instructional guidelines from the teachers' manuals of basal reading programs dating back to the 1920s. The DR-TA has been called a "master plan" for teaching reading (Estes, 1991). Everyone who teaches, at any level and on any subject, should be familiar with this model lesson design. Notice that it embodies several of the elements found in successful comprehension teaching methods, and more importantly, that it is built to incorporate many more.

Directed Reading-Thinking Activity

Russell Stauffer's Directed Reading-Thinking Activity (DR-TA) proceeds through three instructional phases: prereading, active reading, and post-reading (1975). It can be used profitably with narrative or expository materials of most any length (Gill & Bear, 1988); however, it is best suited to narrative material, having been developed to be used with basal reader stories.

Steps in the DR-TA
Step 1   *Prereading: Relate, Reduce, Anticipate*
   a. Discuss and expand students' background experience and knowledge related to the selection.
   b. Reduce obstacles to comprehension by preteaching difficult words and concepts. (Note: Stauffer advises *not* to preteach vocabulary if the material is at the student's *instructional or independent reading level.* It is better, he believes, to have the child try to figure such words out for him/herself, much as any effective reader needs to do while reading.)
   c. Preview the reading material (look at title, pictures, summaries, etc).
   d. Help students to anticipate what the remainder of the selection is likely to be about.
Step 2   *Active Reading: Predict, Read, Prove*
   a. Guide thinking by interrupting reading to ask for predictions for what the selection will say next.

       b. Have pupils read silently to test their hypothesis (which may differ from student to student).

       c. Ask for proof, or verification from the material, that they predicted correctly, or if incorrectly, why(?).

Step 3   *Post-Reading: Check, Refine, Relate, Reanticipate*

       a. Check comprehension by discussing answers to a general purpose setting question and by additional recognition, recall, inferential, explanatory, and evaluative questions.

       b. Refine understanding by seeking verifications for comprehension questions that require silent and oral rereading and citing of the material.

       c. Relate the story or information covered to other materials read, or to common experience or mass media events.

       d. Build fresh anticipation of something to be read at a later time by connecting it to some relevant aspect of the post-reading discussion.

When properly orchestrated, the DR-TA has an attractive symmetry that begins and ends with anticipation, hence creating an impelling reason to read immediately, and again on the same topic thereafter. Classroom, as opposed to remedial, versions tend to put additional emphasis on a follow-up phase that may involve any number of things, from writing activities to dramatization of the story line (Tierney, Readence, Dishner, 1990).

Research Related to the DR-TA

The overall strategy has been shown to be quite effective for teaching reading comprehension and improving classroom interactions (Bear & Invernizzi, 1984; Davidson, 1970; Grobler, 1971; Petre, 1970). The DR-TA also offers a practical and effective means of improving critical thinking (Haggard-Ruddell, 1988) and content area applications (Shepherd, 1978). Under certain conditions, the DR-TA also can build remarkable levels of independence. Meribeth Schmitt (1988) showed this rather dramatically with third grade students who were trained to activate their own prior knowledge, set their own purposes for reading, raise and answer their own questions, verify or reject their own predictions, and to monitor their own successes. This was done merely by the teacher-experimenter gradually releasing greater responsibility to pupils for each of these key strategic reading functions. This focus resulted in students in the experimental group scoring higher than the control group on all post-test measures. They effectively learned how to conduct their own Self-Directed Reading-Thinking Activity (Schmitt & Baumann, 1986b).

The next method also attempts to build independence and release of responsibility, though in a manner based more squarely on the notions of "responsive teaching" (Duffy & Roehler, 1987), "instructional conversations" (Tharp & Gallimore, 1989a,b), and "modeling" (Duffy, Roehler, & Hermann, 1988; Manzo & Manzo, 1990a).

The Reciprocal Questioning (ReQuest) Procedure

Background and Rationale

The Reciprocal Questioning (or, ReQuest) procedure was designed to teach students how to set their own purpose for reading through self-directed inquiry (Manzo, 1969a, b; 1985). Originally developed in a clinical setting, ReQuest represents a form of apprenticeship training that might be called *mental modeling*. Prior to ReQuest, modeling was used exclusively for teaching external or visible behaviors. However, the modeling process, as structured by the ReQuest procedure, proved to be an effective means of externalizing and teaching the internal mental processes, as well as related attitudes and behaviors, involved in reading. In the ReQuest procedure, the teacher engages in "reciprocal interactions" or "instructional conversations" with students. This interactive sharing of "cognitive secrets" (Pearson & Fielding, 1991) tends to sharpen the student's attention to the teacher as a model of effective thinking and related conduct. The teacher also gains a great deal of diagnostic information about the student's thinking, as this is externalized in the questions the student chooses to ask, as well as in the responses to the teacher's questions.

ReQuest can also be characterized as a psychoeducational, whole-student procedure, since it concurrently attends to several reading, language, thinking, and personal-social adjustment needs. Meeting "collateral" objectives has been found to be a key feature of effective cognitive and affective education (Rubin, 1984). While most modern-day strategies have their theoretical basis in cognitive psychology, ReQuest's can also be found in the influence of social context on learning. Accordingly, it is equally related to the work of the Russian psychologist, Lev Vygotsky (1978), and to its American branch, *social and imitation learning theory*, as espoused by Miller and Dollard (1941) and by Albert Bandura (1987). This is significant in dealing with remedial readers since much of their inability to make progress in reading can be traced to a variety of social and emotional inhibitions, such as fearing further failure, and other social consequences for appearing incompetent.

From a broader theoretical perspective, the union of cognitive and social-imitation learning theory recasts the teacher as a facilitator of learning, and as more of a co-equal with students in a literacy community. This has led P. David Pearson and Linda Fielding (1991) to conclude that methods employing such cognitive apprenticeships and responsive teaching modes "may be the bridge that spans the chasm" (p. 850) that exists between explicit, and largely teacher-directed forms of teaching, and more student-centered approaches such as those associated with the Whole Language movement. Dorothy Watson, a well-known whole language supporter, made a similar observation (personal communication, 1977).

Steps in the ReQuest Procedure

Step 1   Both teacher and students read the *title and first sentence* only of the first paragraph of a selection, and look at any pictures or graphics that are part of the introduction.

Step 2   The teacher tells students to ask as many questions as they wish about the first sentence, the title and/or pictures or graphics. The teacher turns his/her copy of the selection face down, but students may continue to look at their copies. Students are told that they should ask the kinds of questions that they think a teacher might ask. (This permits students to ask "ego-protective" questions since they need not reveal whether *they* know the answers to the questions they ask.)

Step 3   When all student questions have been fully and politely answered, the teacher turns his/her book face *up* while students are instructed to turn theirs face *down*. The teacher then asks as many additional questions (about the title, first sentence, and illustrations) as seems appropriate to bring about a sense of focus and purpose for reading the selection. The last of these questions (over the first sentence, and then in subsequent question sets on following sentences) should simply be, "What do you suppose the remainder of this selection will be about?"

Step 4   The next sentences are handled in the same way, with the student again leading off the questioning, followed by teacher questioning, and concluding with the question, "What do you suppose the remainder of this selection will be about?". The number of sentences covered should be based on teacher judgment: the ReQuest activity should conclude as soon as a plausible purpose for reading has been evolved, but should not last *more* than about ten minutes.

Step 5   At the conclusion of the ReQuest activity, the student is encouraged to continue reading the selection silently for the purpose that has been developed.

Step 6   Following silent reading, the teacher should *first ask the evaluative question*: "Did we read for the right purpose?"

This final question is asked before the purpose-setting question for three reasons. First, it helps to overcome what has been called "confirmation bias" (Garrison & Hoskisson, 1989), or the tendency to conclude only what has been predicted. Second, it helps to keep the focus of instruction on the development of effective strategies for independent reading and learning more so than merely on comprehending a given selection. Third, it further develops the important metacognitive habit of monitoring one's own comprehension and use of strategies while reading.

The ReQuest procedure can be used across subject areas and grade levels. Use of ReQuest over time, and in a variety of settings, helps the student proceed, in stages, from explicit questioning to a greater awareness of the implicit questions that surround us, and finally, to the development of a characteristically curious and probing nature.

ReQuest has a strong body of research and clinical trials to support it. It has been shown to be successful in individual and group settings in the improvement of comprehension and questioning of students (Larking, 1984), and incidentally improving the questioning skills of teachers (Manzo, 1969a; Helfeldt & Lalike, 1979). It also has been used effectively with juvenile delinquents (Kay, Young, & Mottley, 1986); in accommodating learning disabled youngsters who have been "mainstreamed" (Alley and Deshler, 1980; Hori, 1977); with second-language students (McKenzie, Ericson, & Hunter, 1988); in content area reading (Gaskins, 1981); and to teach general purpose-setting to elementary school students (Spiegel, 1980b). Additionally, ReQuest provided the basis for a more encompassing and well-validated strategy called Reciprocal Teaching (Palincsar and Brown, 1984), a method that relies more on peer teaching, and adds certain other features, such as summarizing.

The value of ReQuest-induced "instructional conversations" as a heuristic for enhancing teaching is further illustrated in some anecdotal accounts of things that teachers have discovered by using it in clinic and classroom situations. You may wish to consult this rather extensive section before, during, and after you have tried this methodology in your teaching practicum. Think of this section as a textual example of clinical apprenticeship, a sharing of some of the finer points of reflective teaching.

Anecdotal Insights from ReQuest Interactions

The Impact of Modeling Can be Broad.

One of the earliest lessons learned from ReQuest use was how to get the students to select and home-in on the teacher as an effective model of questioning behavior. Thomas Estes (now a professor at the University of Virginia) raised a very clever question to a 14-year-old boy who flatly stated that he had no questions to ask, and sat silently defying of Estes to ask anything he could not easily answer about a first short sentence. The question Estes asked was, "What was the fifth word in the sentence?" Startled, the boy fumbled around. Tom then told him that he could turn his book over to check which was the fifth word. When it again was the boy's turn, he quickly asked Tom a similar question about the next sentence that was much longer. The student waited for Tom to cringe, but instead he remained composed and said, "Gee, I thought you might ask me a question like that, but I knew that if I tried to remember all those words in sequence that I'd miss the whole point of this sentence. So I guess I don't know." The student was stunned by this response and commented that he felt like a fool for not being able to answer this question, yet Tom looked collected, and sounded smart when he missed the same kind of question.

The same reciprocal interaction that caused the young man to first see Tom Estes as a model of *questioning behavior,* caused him then to take note of him as a model of *question answering behavior.* This clever question couldn't have worked better in communicating to this frightened and socially failing student (he had been expelled from school for being "incorrigible") that here was a master of this environment worth watching and emulating. As is frequently the case according to social and imitation learning theory, the boy began to emulate many more aspects of Tom's thinking and language than the initial behaviors and skills that were targeted.

It is important to further note that following the clever question that caused this student to select Tom as a possible model, Tom then asked several conventional questions to settle the student down and turn him more to the task of analyzing the text: "What was the name mentioned in this sentence?", "What happened to this person?", "What do you suppose happens next?", and finally "What do you suppose the remainder of this story will be about?" A failure to return to a more expected pattern of questioning here could have resulted in the slippage of the lesson into a game of who could ask the quirkiest questions.

Larger Segments, Forced Responding, and Teacher Training.

Several users of ReQuest have reported that under some circumstances they prefer to have students read and analyze more than one sentence at a time. They also prefer to force attention and responding by alternating the role of questioner after each question (Tierney, Readence, & Dishner, 1990).

To be certain that the teacher learns to use the procedure effectively from the outset, and that students are being appropriately responsive, Robert Tierney, John Readence, and Ernest Dishner (1990) also recommend the use of what they call a ReQuest Evaluation Form. See their excellent compendium of reading strategies for details, or begin to construct your own.

Content Material That is "Lexically Dense."

Katherine Maria (1990), in an in-depth text on comprehension methods, offers this advise from her use of ReQuest:

> I used the ReQuest technique to help fifth grade remedial readers understand one section of a narrative text. The story, *The Mystery of Moon Guiter* (Niemeyer, 1976), was an excerpt from a book. The part of the book that preceded the excerpt was summarized on the first page. If the children did not understand the background information from this page, they would not understand the excerpt. Since the first page was a summary, it was more *lexically dense* than a regular story and thus more like expository text. Reading this page sentence by sentence and asking questions about each sentence was helpful to children in this situation. (p. 168)

The effectiveness of ReQuest with lexically dense material was first brought to our attention by a professor of English literature who used it to prepare college students for reading difficult selections that they were assigned to complete outside of class. ReQuest has proven useful at lower levels for teaching certain decoding aspects of reading as well.

ReQuest in Teaching Decoding.

Once the teacher and student have established an apprenticeship relationship, the teacher can easily shift from modeling comprehension processes to "think alouds" (Davey, 1983) that model decoding processes. This shifting can be seamlessly achieved in regular classrooms as well as in clinical settings.

One way to step into this more basic function is to ask questions that use either of the two scripts of the Glass Analysis system covered in a prior chapter. For example, after showing and pronouncing the word *lakefront*, one script would go: "Which letters make the **ache** sound in *lakefront*?; Which letters the **fr** sound?; Which make the **ont** sound?" The second script reverses the process: "What sound do the letters **a-k-e** make?; What sound do the letters **l-a-k-e** make?; What about **f-r**?; **o-n-t**?"

In using this approach, the teacher typically engages in a great deal of inner speech (e.g., "Let's see now, where should this word first be divided? What are the regular sounds? Which are irregular?"). To gain much of the effect of the procedure, the teacher has only to externalize some of this inner speech. It is important not to try to be so smooth that one never considers asking about a cluster of letters that don't go together very well (e.g., "Should I ask what sound the letters **e-f** makes in this word(?). No, the **e** clearly belongs to the **l-a-k** part of the word."). Oddly, even these misses can turn out to be informative. We watched a teacher engaged in this instructional conversation who then looked up at the student, as if to let her in on her thinking, and said, "You'd know that too easily, wouldn't you?" Of course, the student wouldn't have easily known that, but the teacher nonetheless retaught the concepts of compound words and silent "e" in a stage aside that further familiarized the student with the "psycholinguistic guessing game" of decoding, as Goodman aptly called it (1967).

Peer Modeling.

A sixth grader named Clarence taught us a valuable way to bring about effective peer modeling during a ReQuest interaction. The second author had been leading a demonstration lesson of ReQuest based on a passage from a sixth-grade social studies text.

Students first were given some background information about the three "Estates" that comprised the Estates General of Paris. Once the reciprocal questioning portion of the lesson began, Clarence proceeded to ask five to six unusual questions about each sentence. The other students noticed the unique nature of Clarence's questions and tended to follow with similar ones. So, when he asked "What does *watched* mean here?," someone else would say, "What does *turns to* mean here?" And, when he asked, "Did the king think that he was a hero?," others asked, "Did the clergy think they were heros?"

From this simple heuristic experience, we learned that whenever a student asks an interesting or potentially generative question, the teacher can shift the class's attention toward appropriate peer models by responding, "Can anyone ask another question like that one?" (Manzo & Manzo, 1990a).

ReQuest with Pictures and Objects.

Several experiences with younger children have shown how the inquiry and comprehension aspects of emergent literacy, or nontext based literacy, can be taught with pictures and objects as well as with text. In developing the ReQuest Picture Procedure (Manzo & Legenza, 1975), for example, Alice Legenza asked youngsters to study a picture and then ask some "good" questions about it. She would point out that she would ask some questions back, to see how carefully the students had studied the picture.

In this context, it is possible to impart much of the formula for story analysis even to youngsters who can hardly read:

"What is the main thing shown in this picture?"—the main idea question
"What do you suppose came just before?"—the inference question
"What do you think will happen next?"—the conjecture question
"If these people/objects could speak, what do you suppose they would say?"—the language and personal connection question
"How do you feel about what is pictured?"—the evaluative and transfer question.

A student viewing a picture of a little girl teetering on a step stool to reach a cookie jar said sheepishly that he never realized how dangerous this was until he really looked at this picture.

Strategic Parroting.

In another situation with kindergartners, Alice Legenza found one student who seemed to be totally devoid of all curiosity (Manzo & Legenza, 1975). The child was very attractive and attentive, yet seemed to be intent on standing idly by in neutral. In desperation, Alice said to the child, "Here is a question that you could ask, repeat it after me.... Now ask me that question." Legenza then proceeded to answer the question fully and thoughtfully as if the child had thought of it herself. After just a few such parroted questions, the child began to initiate her own twists on the strategic questions, and thereafter to ask many of her own.

Annemaria Palincsar, Ann Brown, and Suzanne Martin (1987) report equally remarkable success with Reciprocal Teaching episodes. They couldn't seem to impart the idea of a student leading a discussion until they had one student "mimic" the teacher's discussion-leading statements. Thereafter, the discussion began to flow rather naturally.

There is a strategy for promoting classroom participation, called Note Cue (Manzo & Manzo, 1990b), that is based on this discovery. It is described ahead in the chapter under "cuing techniques."

Incidental Teaching Value.

The story reported here is from Susan Mandel Glazer, Director of the Reading/Language Arts Clinic at Rider College in Lawrenceville, New Jersey (personal correspondence, January 1992). Teachers at the Clinic are expected to facilitate children's learning by tapping into their interests and "jumping in" to provide guidance at what they judge to be a "teachable moment." Glazer felt that the moment reported here demonstrated both the incidental and concurrent teaching value of ReQuest.

A clinic teacher, Denise Nugent, had been working with a group of four 11-year-old boys who had been classified as reading disabled and had little motivation for the prescribed school curriculum. A teachable moment occurred during a fire drill. Being out of doors in 20 degree weather without coats caused the boys to exercise as if warming up for a football game. The teacher began a dialogue on something of immediate interest to the boys and continued it back in the classroom with a connection to the spirit of ReQuest inquiry training—namely, to realize that you have questions, that appropriate print contains lots of answers, and that personal power grows as one makes the effort to connect the two.

Teacher: You guys look like you're warming up for the Giants game.

Scott: I wish I were. It's Sunday, ya' know. It's at the Meadowlands and that's so close.

Teacher: Yeah? Do you think there's a possibility of getting tickets?

Kyle: My Mom wouldn't let me go if I could. She hates football.

Teacher: My Mom does too, but I'd go with you.

Michael: Hey, Mrs. Nugent, do you really think we could get tickets to the Super Bowl game?

Teacher: Good question. There are several newspapers in the principal's office. After the fire drill, I'll get them, and you guys can look for the answer to your question.

Michael: What question?

Teacher: The one you just asked, Michael.

Michael: What's that?

Teacher: You know, "Do you think we can get tickets for the Giants game?"

Michael: Oh yeah, I forgot I asked it.

Teacher: Maybe we should write the question down so you remember it. By the way, fellas, if we can get tickets, there are lots of other questions that need to be asked before we go.

[Once they returned to the classroom, the following happened.]

Michael: Here it is! Here it is!

Glen: Let me see. What is it?

Michael: It's the ad for tickets to the game.

Teacher: Does it say how to get them?

Michael: How should I know!

Teacher: Well, Michael, if you want to go, you'd better get some answers to these questions.

Michael: What questions?

Teacher: Fellas—Michael, Glen, Kyle, and Scott—come over here. (Teacher moves to an area in the classroom where there is an easel and marker. The boys follow.) Pretend we are doing ReQuest. What questions do we need to ask to go to the game?

Glen: How much are the tickets?

Scott: Yeah, and how will we get there?

Teacher: Wait a minute. I need to write these down, and you're talking too fast! (As she begins to write . . .) What did you ask, Glen?

Glen: (Slows down his language to match the teacher's writing) How much are the tickets?

Teacher: Here's the newspaper. Glen, you can read to find out the answer to that question.

> *Scott:* I asked, "How will we get there?"
> *Teacher:* You and Kyle might want to write a plan of action for that.
> *Scott:* What do you mean?
> *Teacher:* Well, make a list of all of the possibilities for getting to the stadium.
> *Scott:* You mean, like my Mom taking us?
> *Teacher:* Yes, and others too.
> *Scott:* OK, come on, Kyle, let's do it.
> *Glen:* Mrs. Nugent, what about you, do *you* have any questions?
> *Teacher:* Well, yes, I guess I do. Does it say anything in the paper about student discounts or transportation?

Guiding the youngsters to "ReQuest" information about their favorite pastime in this incidental way helped to collapse some of their inhibitions about reading and writing. It also caused at least one to remember to invite a question from a "mentor," a sign of social sensitivity and emotional growth.

ReQuest in Teaching Underlining.

Edward T. Poostay (1984) combines training in underlining with the ReQuest strategy. He has teachers read and underline 5–7 concepts within the first 150 words of a larger selection. He then photocopies that page and distributes it to youngsters. Next, they study the page with underlines and are encouraged to ask as many questions as they care to about how one or two of these are connected to the story and to one another. The teacher then does the same. This Reciprocal interaction continues until all underlines are suitably discussed. Silent reading follows as students attempt to determine whether they have adequately inferred what the selection is about from the underlines. Poostay urges that the teacher *not* force students into a common set of predictions, but rather let them read to discover which actually turn out to be the most accurate, and which portions probably should have been underlined and were not.

Translation and Evaluation Questions.

ReQuest-based instructional conversations tend to promote two educationally valuable though infrequently asked question types: translation and evaluation. A translation question simply requires that something be expressed in a different way or in another symbolic form: "What did Jack just say?" "What, in your own words, did this paragraph say?" "What does this picture say?" "What picture could you draw to show what the author is saying?" Translation questions tend to be in the middle level, between literal and higher-order level questions, of most hierarchies of question types (Bloom, 1956; Aschner, et.al., 1962). As such, they frequently act as bridges, permitting students to more comfortably cross over to sound higher-order thinking. Despite the value of this type of translation question, studies indicate that teachers tend to ask these questions less than *one percent* of the time (Guszak, 1967; Manzo, 1969a,b). Teachers using the ReQuest Procedure, however, were shown to naturally ask this type of question about 10 times as frequently as teachers using more conventional practices such as the Directed Reading Activity (Manzo, 1969a).

This was found to be similarly so for the highest order of question, the evaluative type, in which students are asked to pull together all they know, feel, and value, to render a defensible judgment. More importantly, students taught with the ReQuest Procedure asked significantly more questions than those who were not; and in roughly the same type and proportions as did their teachers (Manzo, 1968; Manzo & Manzo, 1990a).

It appears that ReQuest-based instructional conversations generate a mature and respectful give and take among teachers and students. Some exceptions and solutions are worth noting from other classroom and clinical experiences.

Exceptions and Solutions.

While mature conversation between teacher and students is a frequent incidental benefit of the Reciprocal Questioning interaction, there are two factors that sometimes have tended to turn a teacher away from its use.

One factor is the tendency of students to reflect back the initial types of questions teachers ask, or some emotionally convoluted form of them. This can be disconcerting to a teacher since some of our less thoughtful questions also can come back to haunt us when we put ourselves up as models. The best way to deal with this problem is to listen carefully to the convoluted questions that students may be asking, assume that there is something that you are doing or saying that is evoking those questions, and then try to ask better questions. Here are two useful guidelines that have emerged from "debriefings" for improving questioning: 1) try to ask the types of questions that you would hope someone might ask you; and 2) try to ask questions that reflect the highest objectives of your teaching as well as more literal or reconstructive ones. It was in the latter context that we came to ask the reflective question, "Why do you suppose the author put a comma after the fourth word in that sentence?" After a student tries to read a sentence with the comma in two other locations in the sentence, it will become abundantly clear that there is an important relationship between punctuation and communication, and that these other markings and signal words such as "also," "but," and "moreover" should be consulted in building meaning (Stevens, 1982). Such attention to text signals also helps students to "read like a writer," and hence incidentally acquire some of the complex craft of successful writing.

Finally, the reciprocal interaction has led some teachers to become so overwhelmed by the flood of diagnostic information they have received back that they have felt immobilized by what some students didn't seem to know. To our pleasant surprise, we have found that students in group situations tend to be quite patient while the teacher tries to help those who do not understand the simplest of things: they seem to sense that they might require the same courtesy another time.

In conclusion, the greatest strength of ReQuest seems to be in that it gets students to overcome some of the subtle liabilities that tend to inhibit questioning—such as having to admit ignorance, and not knowing how to frame questions, and simply not realizing what it is that they don't know. To this extent, it is a valuable clinical and classroom practice that generally can be counted on to generate an instructional conversation that improves reading comprehension, oral language, poise, and an inclination to become more inquiring.

Structured Comprehension

Background and Rationale

This technique is similar to the ReQuest Procedure in several respects. Most notably, it creates an intimate instructional conversation between the teacher and a student, and builds meaning by micro-analysis of one sentence at a time. Marvin Cohn, creator of Structured Comprehension (1969), and the author of the ReQuest procedure, worked alongside one another in a university reading clinic some time ago, and appear to have influenced one another's thinking in several ways that were not apparent to either at the time (see also Proverbs Study ahead).

Steps in Structured Comprehension

Step 1   The pupil reads the first sentence and actively asks and answers the question: "Do I know what this sentence means?"

Step 2   If the readers feel that they do not understand something, they are expected to raise questions to the teacher, or a peer.

Step 3   Once a student has had his or her questions answered, the teacher asks one or more questions about the sentence, and the student is obliged to *write out* the answers. (In a group situation, this is a good way to ensure that *every* student participates in the prereading activity.)

Step 4   Student answers to the teacher's question(s) are checked and discussed.

Cohn recommends that the teacher ask literal questions at first, rather than relational questions, and that the reading selection be kept available during questioning. In working with remedial readers, he particularly recommends questions that ask for the antecedent of pronouns, interpretation of figurative language, and the meanings of key vocabulary terms. The student is expected to ask the same kinds of questions that the teacher has asked.

The next method moves smartly from concrete to abstract thinking.

Proverbs Study

Background and Rationale

Proverbs can be a stimulating source and means of working with remedial students. Discussion of proverbs has been an established clinical practice in psychology (Gorham, 1956), intelligence testing (proverbs items are included in both the Stanford-Binet and Wechsler IQ tests), and a mainstay of education, off and on, for several hundreds of years. Clinicians Marvin Cohn and Michael

McKenna have found proverbs-based discussions to be a valuable instructional tool for use with children in remedial situations (personal communications). More recently, we have adapted and developed the notion of proverbs study as described here.

A proverb is like a small book. It is the condensed wisdom of the ages. Efforts made to grasp and understand proverbs provide several far-reaching benefits. Skill in interpreting proverbs has been found to be significantly related to a number of language, thinking, and comprehension factors (Manzo & Casale, 1981). Because they tend to be value-laden, proverbs are an excellent medium for picking up diagnostic information about a student, while simultaneously carrying out an authentic and potentially therapeutic dialogue on a broad range of human experiences, values, and thoughts.

Proverbs study is useful with a broad range of students. It is appropriate for treating certain higher-order thinking deficits, such as failing to see the deeper meanings in literature and human experience, as well as for remedying a variety of conventional remedial conditions, such as overly concrete thinking and weak vocabulary. Consider now this adaptation of the original elementary classroom version of the Proverbs Mastery Paradigm (Manzo, 1981b; Manzo & Manzo, 1987b) for use with remedial readers. Notice that it links remedial sessions one to another, as well as offering a "carry-out" and "carry-home" capability.

Proverbs Study for Remedial Students

Step 1   Present a proverb at the students' reading level and commensurate with age and grade development (see Box 10.1 for a starter list).

Step 2   Establish the surface, or concrete, meaning of the proverb by helping the students to *translate* the proverb into his or her own words, or a picture.

Step 3   Ask students to suggest a possible deeper, or more abstract, meaning.

Step 4   Ask the students whether the proverb seems to relate to anything in their own experience, reading, or viewing (such as movies or television).

Step 5   Discuss and help students clarify any misconceptions or misunderstandings.

Step 6   Provide "carry-out": Give students a proverb on an index card, and with little other help, simply ask that they carry it with them until the next class session when you will discuss it. (You will be pleasantly surprised at how such a proverb serves as a magnet, drawing insights out of common experiences.)

For another interesting "carry-out" and "back-in" activity, consider this suggestion from Sigrid Renner and JoAnn Carter (1991): have students collect "family sayings" in the tradition of *Poor Richard's Almanac*. (These need not be famous sayings.) Then, have them match a collection of famous and family sayings for similarities. The often-heated discussions about matches involve the kind of analysis and transformations that spurt growth in abstract thinking, critical thinking, and schema enhancement.

BOX 10.1

Sample Proverbs, Adages, and Quotations

Coding Key	
LANGUAGE DIFFICULTY	AGE LEVEL DIFFICULTY
1. primary 2. intermediate 3. secondary 4. archaic or otherwise unusual language form	A. 5 to 7 years old B. 8 to 12 years old C. 13 to 16 years old D. 17 to 21 years old E. adult life

PROVERB (DIFFICULTY CODE): MEANING	COMPARISON PROVERB (DIFFICULTY CODE)
HE WHO MAKES NO MISTAKES MAKES NOTHING. (1 D): The person who is afraid of making mistakes never does anything of value.	Same: A BURNED CHILD DREADS THE FIRE. (2 C)
A MISS IS AS GOOD AS A MILE. (2 C): Failure by however little is still failure.	Opposite: OMELETS ARE NOT MADE WITHOUT BREAKING EGGS. (3 C)
MONEY BEGETS MONEY. (4 E). Money that's put to use earns more money	Opposite: A PENNY SAVED IS A PENNY EARNED. (2 B)
THE LOVE OF MONEY IS THE ROOT OF ALL EVIL. (2 D): People's drive to acquire money and things causes them to do evil things.	Same: POVERTY IS THE ROOT OF ALL EVILS. (2 D) Same: MONEY IS A GOOD SERVANT BUT A BAD MASTER. (3 C)
REVENGE IS SWEET. (2 D): It feels good to get back at someone who has wronged you.	Opposite: TWO WRONGS DON'T MAKE A RIGHT. (2 B)
THERE IS NO ROSE WITHOUT A THORN. (2 C): There is nothing good that doesn't have negative aspects as well.	Opposite: EVERY CLOUD HAS A SILVER LINING. (2 C)
WHAT IS SAUCE FOR THE GOOSE IS SAUCE FOR THE GANDER. (4 A): What applies to one person applies equally to another.	Opposite: CIRCUMSTANCES ALTER CASES. (3 D)
OUT OF SIGHT, OUT OF MIND. (1 A): When someone or something is not immediately present, our thoughts turn to other things.	Opposite: ABSENCE MAKES THE HEART GROW FONDER. (2 C)
SILENCE GIVES CONSENT. (2 E): Have the courage of your convictions, or live with the consequences.	Opposite: THERE IS TIME TO SPEAK AND TIME TO BE SILENT. (2 D) Opposite: SPEECH IS SILVER BUT SILENCE IS GOLDEN. (2 D) Opposite: DISCRETION IS THE BETTER PART OF VALOR. (4 D)
SPARE THE ROD AND SPOIL THE CHILD. (1 A): Love means being critical, at times, of the ones you love.	Contrast: BOYS WILL BE BOYS. (1 A)

BOX 10.1

Sample Proverbs, Adages, and Quotations *(continued)*

Proverb (difficulty code): Meaning	Comparison Proverb (difficulty code)
THREATENED FOLK LIVE LONG. (2 E): People who must struggle learn how to survive.	Same: A CREAKING GATE HANGS LONG ON ITS HINGES. (2 E)
NEVER TROUBLE TROUBLE TILL TROUBLE TROUBLES YOU. (3 C): Don't spend your time imagining difficulties that may never come about.	Same: DO NOT CROSS THE BRIDGE TILL YOU COME TO IT. (2 C) Opposite: PREVENTION IS BETTER THAN CURE. (2 C) Opposite: FOREWARNED IS FOREARMED. (3 D)
IT IS BETTER TO WAR OUT THAN TO RUST OUT. (1 C): It is better to act than to live in fear.	Opposite: A LIVING DOG IS BETTER THAN A DEAD LION. (1 C) Opposite: IT'S BETTER TO BE SAFE THAN SORRY. (1 C)
WHERE THERE'S A WILL THERE'S A WAY. (2 C): If you are determined to do something, you will find a way to do it no matter how difficult this might be.	Same: NECESSITY IS THE MOTHER OF INVENTION. (2 C) Opposite: WHAT CAN'T BE CURED MUST BE ENDURED. (3 D).

Renner and Carter cast their advocacy of proverbs study in the larger multicultural context of folklore. "Folklore," they point out, "is concerned with recurring traditional beliefs such as art, customs, stories, songs, sayings, charms, speech, jokes, proverbs, and riddles" (1991, p. 602).

There are many other variations and options on this basic read, translate, delve into, and discuss model for teaching proverbs. Most will arise naturally as teachers and students engage in instructional conversations that reference other proverbs and maxims that are similar and opposing.

In our judgement, the value of proverbs study reaches beyond reading comprehension to "social comprehension," of the type measured by the Comprehension subtest of the WISC. This type of comprehension helps one begin to build a rational "worldview," and a rich schema for understanding the "universal truths" found in longer books. See Appendix **C** for a list of proverbs with multiple choice alternatives that can be used for teaching or testing progress in reading, and toward higher levels of abstract thinking. This exercise also can be used for identifying pupils with a propensity toward hyper-emotionality. This is revealed by their tendency to select emotive responses over other possible choices, as illustrated in the example below:

Look Before You Leap.

(Abstract)	1. Do not act in haste.
(Literal)	2. Watch before you step down
(Emotive)	3. Do not leap, just look.
(Error)	4. We see further in leap year.

The multiple choice proverb interpretation format can be followed with discussion, to better determine if a response was an honest error, or was prompted by emotionally disruptive thinking. This is a good opportunity to use Carney and Cioffi's "dynamic assessment" approach, previously described, to determine whether there is a consistent pattern of choices. (Write to the authors for an AppleWorks computer program that automatically collects and classifies student responses.)

Another way to use proverbs is simply to present some as incomplete sentences, and have students create their own endings. Students' endings can be playful, revealing, or just grounds for an interesting and sometimes therapeutic dialogue. Here are a few responses that we have found to be representative:

If you can't beat them. . .
("call Mom!")
A stitch in time. . .
("can put you back in line.")
Do unto others. . .
("as they have to you.")

The next three methods presented are especially effective for improving the reconstructive, or "get-the-facts," level of comprehension. The first two rely heavily on listening, and the third can be converted into a listening activity.

Listening-Reading Transfer Lesson

Background and Rationale

Patricia Cunningham (1975) designed this "front-loading" method to teach students to first find the main idea by listening to a passage, and then to transfer the same task to a different passage that is read.

Steps in the Listening-Reading Transfer Lesson

Step 1   Prepare three sentences related to a passage that the student will listen to, with one of the three being the best representation of the main idea.

Step 2   Tell pupils that the main idea of the selection that they will listen to is stated in one of three sentences that you will present to them (either as a handout, on the board, or on an overhead).

Step 3   Following listening, have youngsters indicate which sentence best captures the chief ideas.

Step 4   Repeat the same process with a passage that is read.

For a variation on this, try the Listen-Read-Discuss Heuristic (Manzo & Manzo, 1985) when the material is especially content-laden and/or the same book must be read in a content class by students of diverse ability levels. The L-R-D uses the same passage for listening and reading, and has the teacher present the information in a conventional lecture format rather than by orally reading it to students. Further, the comprehension check and discussion may focus upon important details and concepts as well as main ideas.

The L-R-D is a good transfer method for teachers as well as students. It is recommended as a heuristic for helping content teachers become involved in an instructional conversation that tends to more naturally infuse reading instruction into content-based classroom instruction (Manzo & Manzo 1990a).

Several writers and researchers have offered support for the basic idea underlying the Listening-Reading-Transfer and the Listen-Read-Discuss lesson approaches. Key among these are Joseph Moore and John Readence (1980), Thomas Sticht, et.al.(1974), and Hal Seaton and O. Paul Weilan (1979). The latter study by Seaton and Weilan is especially notable since it demonstrated that higher order comprehension, such as interpretation and appreciation, surprisingly, were the most significantly improved. In a critique of this study, Rona F. Flippo (1981) adds this valuable point: "Children enjoy being read to and it is possible that this enjoyment factor could be a concomitant variable positively affecting their comprehension of the intricacies of the story" (1981, p.108).

There are several other excellent means of relying on the listening ability of remedial level students to compensate for, or otherwise enhance, comprehension. J. S. Choate and Thomas A. Rakes (1987), for example, offer the Structured Listening Activity, which essentially is a Directed Reading-Thinking Activity with the focus on listening instead of reading. Similarly, there are the Guided Lecture (Kelly & Holmes, 1979) and Guided Listening (Cunningham, Cunningham, & Arthur 1981) procedures, which are modeled after the Guided Reading Procedure, described next.

The Guided Reading Procedure

Background and Rationale

The Guided Reading Procedure (GRP) was first developed to demonstrate to low-achieving students that they could greatly increase their reading comprehension through simple self-determination (Manzo, 1975a). It does this by having students experience a learning activity in which, by self-monitoring their level of attention, concentration, and commitment, they actually do comprehend and remember more information than they typically are able to handle. This effect is accomplished as a result of the redundant nature of the GRP lesson, in which the facts and ideas in the selection are stated, repeated, and reviewed in various forms. Students, even those who were not willing or able to read the selection initially, acquire a firm grounding in the reconstructive-level information in the selection.

In analyzing the steps of the GRP, notice that it guides students toward greater independence by stressing some of the most frequent but least taught requirements of school: factual reading, notetaking, organizing, and test preparation. Notice, too, how steps 4 and 8 reinforce metacognitive development. When used in a remedial situation to help students prepare for conventional content area tests, the method tends to validate the remedial sessions by building self-efficacy in students who might never have faced a test better prepared.

The method is presented here as it would be used with a group or class. It can be similarly done with individuals by using shorter passages and having the teacher provide slightly more help with the initial recall portion of the lesson.

Steps in the Guided Reading Procedure

Step 1   *Teacher Preparation*
Identify a selection, to be read or listened to, of moderate to high difficulty, and not exceeding 2,000 words for a senior high class, 900 words for a junior high class, 600 words for an intermediate class, and 100-250 words for a remedial or LD class. Prepare a 10 to 20 item test on the material to be given at the end of the class period. A recognition type test, such as a multiple choice test, tends to ensure early success.

Step 2   *Student Preparation*
Solicit background knowledge on the topic, then explain to students that they are to "Read to remember *all that you can*, because after you have read, I will record what you remember on the chalkboard just as you restate it to me."

Step 3   *Reading and Recalling*
Following silent reading, begin asking for free recalls. Record all information on the chalkboard until students have retold all that they can remember. Difficulties in remembering and differences in what students do remember form the implicit questions that set up the next steps.

Step 4   *Self-Monitoring/Self-Correcting*
Instruct students to review the material read and self-correct inconsistencies and information overlooked in their initial attempts to retell. Note changes and additions on the chalkboard.

Step 5   *Restructuring*
Encourage students to organize their retellings into outline form. It gives a sense of authenticity and purpose to this effort if pupils are encouraged to record this information in their notebooks. The outline can be as simple or elaborate as ability level permits. You may ask nonspecific questions at this time, such as "What was discussed first?"; "What details followed?"; "What was brought up next?"; and "What seems to be the main idea?" Avoid questions that are too specific or leading if you wish to keep them focused on the text cues rather than the teacher's clues.

Step 6   *Teacher Monitoring and Correction*
If it appears that students have overlooked any important ideas, raise focusing questions about these points, such as "What do you suppose is the most important of the five points made by the author?"; "How do you suppose this information relates to what we talked about last week in the selection, 'Man and the Moon?' "

Step 7   *Evaluation*
Give the test prepared in step 1. A score of 70% to 80% should be required for a "pass." Students see this as a fair "pass" level due to

the extraordinary level of empowerment they have received. They also tend to look forward to the test as an opportunity to show what they have learned.

Step 8   *Introspection*

Discuss any insights students may have reached about their own learning processes as a result of the GRP experience. The chief point to be made is that accuracy in comprehension and recall can be improved to a great degree by an act of will to do so.

Step 9   *Optional But Important Study Step*

Several days later, give a second test on the same material. Allow students about 15 minutes prior to the test to review material from their notes. The exam can be half the items from the original multiple choice test or another unaided recall test. This step also can serve to establish the "teachable moment" for further study skills training of the type presented in the chapter on study, writing, and higher-order thinking.

The GRP teaches an aspect of metacognition that has been called "executive control" (Paris, Cross, & Lipson, 1984), in which the reader takes conscious control of his/her own learning process. The GRP empowers poor readers to master reconstructive-level comprehension, an important step on the road to constructive concept-formation and analysis (Dempster, 1991).

The GRP has been supported by several experimental and field studies testing its use from fourth grade through high school levels (Ankney & McClurg,1981; Bean & Pardi, 1979; Culver, 1975) as well as by anecdotal accounts at the elementary level (Gaskins, 1981) and at the secondary level (Maring & Furman, 1985; Tierney, Readence, & Dishner, 1990). The basic paradigm also has been used to develop a variety of other teaching methods such as writing (Eanet, 1983; Hayes, 1988), science knowledge acquisition (Spiegel, 1980b), and, as previously mentioned, listening (Cunningham, Cunningham, & Arthur, 1981; Kelly & Holmes, 1979).

The next method described has been evolving for decades due to the work of many more researchers than can be listed. It now can be used to concurrently teach familiarity with the subtle language patterns needed to anticipate the next word in print, as well as inferential thinking and comprehension.

Cloze Procedure Training

Background and Rationale

Patricia Cousin (1991), writing in a recent issue of *Reading Today*, reminds us of the challenge to help remedial readers, who almost by definition do not have adequate experience with written language, learn to deal with the "complex linguistic structures used in both literature and expository text" (p.9).

Using a factor analysis technique, Wendell Weaver and Albert Kingston (1963) established that cloze procedure, or the fixed deletion of every fifth to ninth word, essentially is a measure of a student's familiarity with the "language redundancy" patterns of prose. James Bowman (1991) notes that "Redundancy helps readers predict, thereby increasing their odds in favor of suitable comprehension" (p. 66). Its value as a testing and teaching method in reading comprehension has been called into question by Victor Culver and associates (1972), and more recently by Timothy Shanahan and Michael Kamil (1983). These researchers have questioned the value of cloze training as a means of improving reading comprehension primarily because of its low level of relationship to certain key comprehension factors such as background knowledge, connections between sentences, rate of reading, and reading vocabulary. There also is the fact that insignificant gains were shown in several early studies relying on cloze training (Cf. E. Jongsma, 1980).

Recently, however, several researchers have found some rather inventive ways to use cloze passage exercises in ways that take advantage of their value in improving familiarity with linguistic patterns in prose while overcoming their dubious value to the meaning side of comprehension (Schell, 1972; Jongsma, 1980; Guthrie, Barnham, Caplan, & Seifert, 1974; Guice, 1969; Cunningham & Tierney, 1977; Meeks, 1980).

The Inferential (Cloze) Training Technique described below was developed from these earlier works by Peter Dewitz, Eileen Carr, and Judith P. Patberg (1987). The technique has been shown to improve general inferring ability, reading comprehension, self-monitoring, and, implicitly, 'linguistic awareness'—the area which Weaver and Kingston (1963) initially found cloze to be most significantly related. The "active ingredient" in the Inferential (Cloze) Training Technique seems to be the instructional conversation it generates, more so than any inherent value in cloze exercises.

Steps in the Inferential (Cloze) Training Technique

Step 1   Begin with a cloze passage with 5 to 25 words deleted—every fifth to ninth word, depending on the level of difficulty you wish for the pupil to encounter.

Step 2   Preteach students essential vocabulary from the passage.

Step 3   Beginning first with one sentence and increasing progressively to paragraphs, demonstrate to students, by sample talk-throughs, how to infer a correct word replacement by using semantic (context) clues, syntactic (grammatical structure) clues, and background knowledge. This can be done with the teacher and then the students alternately talking through each deletion or sentence units containing more than one deletion.

Step 4   During the talk-through, try to use these self-monitoring guidelines (Cambourne, 1977):
a. Does the replacement make sense?
b. Does the replacement cause the sentence to make sense?
c. Does the replacement combine prior knowledge with clues in the passage?

  d. Is there a forward clue in the same sentence paragraph, or passage?

  e. Is there a backward clue in the same sentence, paragraph, or passage?

  f. Did the clue cause you to change your replacement?

Step 5 The teacher expresses him or herself by explaining why a certain replacement seems correct, and then helps the student do the same thing by asking the student questions that aid in inferring why certain replacements are more correct than others.

Step 6 The teacher asks students to read a second intact (usually continuing) sentence, paragraph, or passage.

Step 7 The teacher checks overall comprehension with typical main idea, detail, and inferential questions.

This same cloze task can be made even more accessible by offering choices for the words that are deleted. This "Maze" format (Gutherie, et.al., 1974) is used in several major comprehension tests such as the Gates-MacGinitie tests (MacGinitie & MacGinitie, 1989), and has been shown to much more closely resemble conventional reading comprehension.

In general, the absence of choices tends to put the emphasis on language pattern training, and the presences of choices tends to shift the task to comprehension, or meaning seeking. Select the emphasis that best meets the students language and comprehension needs.

As an uplifting activity, Lane Roy Gauthier (1990a) has devised Inverse Cloze: delete *all but* every fifth word of a passage and ask students to try to write in a connected story of their own making. Have students share their creations. Students seem to really enjoy this unlikely looking task.

Complementary Comprehension Techniques

Until fairly recently, there were not more than a handful of strategies for teaching reading comprehension. The popular textbook, *Reading Strategies and Practices: A Compendium*, contained only four in its first edition (Tierney, Readence, & Dishner, 1985, 1990). The pages that follow attempt to represent a fair sampling of recent and alternative approaches and strategies that deserve particular attention. Most of these, however, could be called techniques. Techniques are smaller adjustments that tend to either fit nicely into the overall structure of a total lesson design such as the Directed Reading-Thinking Activity, or serve well as fine-tunings to support a more general approach, such as whole language, instructional conversation, or strategy mastery. Most of the techniques described here have been designed to build reconstructive comprehension. Most also have roots deep in the history of remediation, and have evolved and continue to evolve with use.

Humor: Or, Do Something Uplifting!

> "Why shouldn't the number 288 ever be mentioned in polite company? It's *two gross.*"

Humor can provide a very agreeable means of engaging in reading, writing, speaking, and listening about many aspects of human emotion, culture, and just plain factual information. Here are some simple means of using this inherently therapeutic device to entice students to read and think effectively, and simply feel better about school and life.

1. Read and analyze puns for their meanings (see Figure 10.1 for a popular list).
2. Get a book of jokes from the library—they typically have many at different levels of reading and sophistication. Read jokes orally with different pauses to explore the value of good timing. Then have youngsters read one aloud—or silently read it and then "retell" it. Urge students to modify and write new jokes in a similar vein.
3. Build a collection of various types of humor, from comic strips to the wry wit of Mark Twain and local newspaper columnists.
4. Collect tales of funny things youngsters have experienced or observed in church, at school, at home, or wherever.

Jokes often prompt students to look back to see if they have missed some subtlety. There is an entire category of remedial techniques to further encourage looking back.

Lookbacks

The idea of "lookbacks," very simply, is to get students to *re*read certain material in an effort to independently clarify comprehension by self-fixing misapprehensions or by figuring out word meanings from context. Successful "lookback" procedures have been described by Diane August, John H. Flavell, and Renee Clift (1984), and by Ruth Garner, Victoria Hare, Patricia Alexander, Jacqueline Haynes, and Peter Winograd (1984). Good readers tend to do it, and poor readers do not (Garner & Reis, 1981; Garner & Kraus, 1981-82)—except, we have noticed, with jokes.

Joseph Sanacore (1984) has suggested interspersing questions during reading, either orally or in written form, to require lookbacks. The questions that he recommends also tend to reveal text structure, e.g., "Who is the leading character? What is the leading character trying to accomplish in the story? What stands in the way?" (Sanacore, 1984, p. 710).

For related methodology that emphasizes the decoding aspects of reading comprehension, see Repeated Reading Approaches in the chapter on decoding. The next method also urges lookbacks.

Paraphrasing

Several leading authorities in the field believe strongly in the value of orally paraphrasing as one reads, starting at the sentence level, and building up to

FIGURE 10.1

Puns for Remedial Readers

1. The Eskimo stabbed himself with an icicle. He died of cold cuts.
2. In his dessert list, a San Antonio restaurateur suggests, "Remember the a la mode."
3. There was an advice-to-the-lovelorn editor who insisted, "If at first you don't succeed, try a little ardor."
4. The commuter's Volkswagen broke down once too often. So he consigned it to the Old Volks Home.
5. When a fire chief responded to a call from a lingerie shop, he found no trace of a blaze. His official report read, "Falsie alarm."
6. The wise old crow perched himself on a telephone wire. He wanted to make a long-distance caw.
7. A talkative musician couldn't hold a job. Every time he opened his mouth, he put his flute in it.
8. A farmer with relatives in East Germany heard that a food package he had sent had never arrived. Optimistically, he reassured them, "Cheer up! The wurst is yet to come!"
9. When the promoter of a big flower show was told that a postponement was necessary because the exhibits could not be installed on time, he explained to his backers, "We were simply caught with our plants down."
10. There was an unscheduled event in a Baghdad harem. The sultan barged in unexpectedly — and his 62 wives let out a terrified sheikh!
11. A critic declared that he always praised the first show of a new theatrical season. "Who am I," he asked, "to stone the first cast?"
12. Egotist: a man who's always me-deep in conversation.
13. A hen stopped right in the middle of the highway. She wanted to lay it on the line.
14. The husband of a talkative wife sighed, "I've given that woman the best ears of my life."
15. "It's raining cats and dogs," one man remarked. "I know," said another, "I just stepped into a poodle."
16. In Peru, a gallant cavalier fished a drowning maiden out of a lake — and married her before the Inca was dry.
17. An eccentric bachelor passed away and left a nephew nothing but 392 clocks. The nephew is now busy winding up the estate.
18. The baseball pitcher with a sore arm was in the throws of agony.
19. A Turkish salesman promoted an audience with an old-time sultan. "I don't recall your name," said the sultan pleasantly, "but your fez is familiar."

From *The Book of Lists* #2, by I. Wallace and D. Wallechinsky (1980)

paragraphs and passages (Haynes & Fillmer, 1984; Kalmbach, 1986; and Shugarman & Hurst, 1986). Paraphrasing also is known as translating, transforming, and encoding, or recoding in another form. This technique can be used comfortably in the ReQuest procedure as a question type ("Can you tell me in your own words what this sentence says?"), and in the verification step of the DR-TA ("Explain how the text supports your prediction.").

This technique, as suggested above, tends to externalize misapprehension in reading, and hence, naturally encourages lookbacks. In so doing, it builds the routine comprehension of main idea and supporting details, and metacognition.

Summarizing

When the practice of paraphrasing is extended, without the text to refer to, it is known as "retelling," or free recall (see Chapter 4 for details). When the text may be referred to, it generally is known as summary or precis writing. It has been studied and recommended by several authorities for its positive influence on building knowledge and writing as well as reading (Bromley, 1985; Cunningham, 1982; Eanet & Manzo, 1976; Hayes, 1988; and Simpson & Nist, 1990).

Summary writing is part of a rich tradition in England and most of Europe. Only in the U.S.A. is it not taught routinely from the earliest grades. The absence of such an emphasis would seem, in itself, to explain much of the difficulty experienced by students in reconstructive reading, and specifically in unaided recall. Summarizing, also known as encoding process, tends to increase demand for active, reconstructive reading of the type that results in effective and organized retelling.

The fact that many remedial level and at-risk readers can not do summarizing should not discourage teachers from teaching it. Rather, the teacher should make it more manageable by slicing the task into more manageable parts and drawing pupil attention to the "Rules for Summarizing," one rule at a time:

1. Delete trivial or irrelevant information.
2. Delete redundant information.
3. Provide a *super*-ordinate term for classes of things (e.g., "flowers" for roses, petunias, daisies).
4. Identify and *restate* any main idea expressed in the selection.
5. Create your own main idea statement when the author has not provided one.

(Brown & Day, 1983; Simpson & Nist, 1990)

The deletion rules usually can be taught successfully by fourth to fifth reader level; the other rules take longer to acquire. The rules can be given to students on a "cue card" (McNeil & Donant, 1982). See Cuing Techniques ahead.

In contrast to these rule-guided approaches to summarizing, James Cunningham (1982) advocates a self-discovery approach that urges students to simply get the "GIST"—*G*enerating *I*nteractions between *S*chemata and *T*ext— by writing 15-word summaries. A comparison of McNeil and Donant's rule-governed approach with Cunningham's more intuitive approach found them to be equally effective (Bean & Steenwyck, 1984).

Other studies on summarizing provide these additional pointers for promoting effective summarizing:

1. Focus on main idea searching. (Baumann, 1984)
2. Teach summarizing initially from familiar patterns such as those following a chronology rather than a logical order. (Hill, 1991)

3. Provide frequent and extensive feedback about the general effectiveness of strategy use, especially to remedial students. (Schunk & Rice, 1987)
4. Combine and integrate summarizing with questioning, clarifying, and predicting. (Palincsar, Brown & Martin, 1987)
5. Provide a lead-in sentence (Cassidy, as cited in Gaskins, 1981) or key words for constructing one.
6. Provide a simple grammar to follow, such as: First this happened... Then... Then... and Finally... (Pincus, Geller, & Stover, 1986)
7. Give students an outline of a story that has been read, or elicit one from them, and then have them reconnect it into a summary. (Eanet, 1983; Hayes, 1988).

There are several other effective lead-ins to effective retelling and summarizing that follow in the chapter. See Chapter 13 on Higher-Literacy for three other methods of improving summary writing following reading, and especially for methods of promoting writing beyond summarizing.

Text Structure: Outlining, Paragraph Pattern Analysis, and Grammars/Maps/Guides

The ability to see and follow the larger organization of a selection is one of the most durable operations isolated in factor analytic and "good reader vs. poor reader" studies of reading comprehension (Davis, 1944, McGee, 1982, Meyer, 1975). While no single method has yet proven to be very beneficial in teaching both text organization and also improving general comprehension, several have proven useful in heightening awareness of text organization, and to that extent can be said to contribute to reading comprehension proficiency. One study showed reading specialists to have ranked text structure instruction 14th out of 23 teaching practices for comprehension improvement (Gee & Raskow, 1987). Nonetheless, attention to organizational patterns, especially when it is made a part of more inclusive operation, tends to improve story and content comprehension and recall (McGee, 1982). (For an in-depth treatment of text structure, see Pearson & Camperell, 1985, and Manzo & Manzo, 1990a.) Several popular practices for drawing attention to text structure include outlining, paragraph pattern analysis, and various uses of grammars/maps/guides.

Outlining

The simplest method of teaching outlining is to provide students with incomplete outlines to be completed while reading. For additional support, offer students a guiding graphic containing portions of the outline. One popular graphic calls for a wagon wheel with the main idea to be written on the rim, and the supporting details on the spokes. This is best done, initially, one paragraph at a time.

Another popular graphic, shown below, is called "pyramiding" (Clewell & Haidemenos, 1983, in Maring & Furman, 1985). When these are fully constructed by the teacher to guide reading, they are referred to as structured overviews, an idea more fully developed ahead.

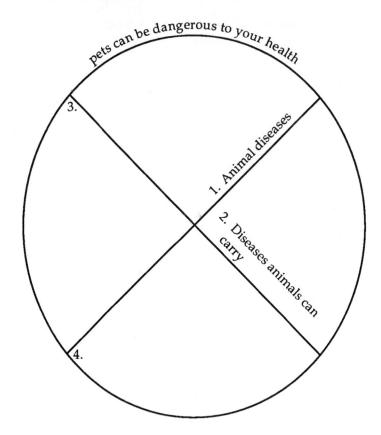

Paragraph Patterns

Several means and methods have been offered to describe patterns or structures in individual paragraphs. One of the more popular clinical practices has students cut up paragraphs and put them in envelopes according to paragraph pattern. Discussion of students' reasons for how they have categorized the paragraphs is the active ingredient in this method. Marion Tonjes and Miles Zintz (1987) list 12 traditional paragraph patterns that can be used for this type of activity, recommending that a limited number of pattern types be used, with the category "other" representing the types that have not yet been taught. Most of these are self-explanatory.

1. Introductory
2. Definition
3. Transactional (shift attention from a previous pattern)
4. Illustrative
5. Summary
6. Main idea and/or supporting details

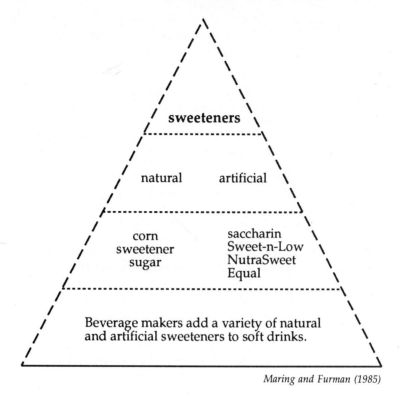

Maring and Furman (1985)

7. Chronological ordering (See Pincus, Seller, & Steven, 1986, on summarizing in the section above)
8. Comparison/contrast
9. Cause and effect
10. Problem/solution
11. Descriptive (attempting to evoke a mental picture)
12. Narrative (containing a sequence of story-like events)

Recent findings and insights by modern theorists and practitioners have added new value to teaching structures and patterns. L. M. McGee and Donald Richgels (1986) offer three helpful guidelines for successfully teaching text structure: 1) the teacher should thoroughly analyze the text to learn its structure; 2) the teacher should be sure that the passages used for instruction clearly represent the targeted pattern or structure; 3) students must be actively involved in using the structure to gain information.

Several methods have been devised in an attempt to achieve these ends (Readence, Bean, & Baldwin, 1985, 1989; Flood, Lapp, & Farnan, 1986; Miller & George, 1992; Muth, 1987). Most of these methods base their approaches on steps such as: a) read and discuss model text structures; b) recognize these in another

FIGURE 10.2

Text Connection Questions

Compare-Contrast

People who want to buy a horse for pleasure riding usually choose between the Quarter horse and the Saddle horse. The Quarter horse has a thick mane and tail. It is strong and is able to carry heavy riders over rough trails for several miles. It is also very healthy and does not catch diseases easily. However, the Quarter horse is not comfortable to ride. It has a jerky walk. which bumps its rider up and down. Also, it is nervous and is hard to control when something unexpected happens.

The Saddle horse is usually brown with dark eyes. It has a steady walk, which is comfortable for riding. It is also easy to control; it responds instantly to commands and is always ready for unexpected things that might lie in its path. The Saddle horse is not very healthy though, and tends to catch diseases easily from other horses. Also, it is not strong enough to carry heavy loads.

The teacher's questions should focus on helping students understand the author's purpose for using the compare-contrast structure and on the relationships among the ideas in the passages. Here are some questions (and possible student answers) which could help students build "internal connections" among the ideas in the passage.

1. What is the author comparing and contrasting? (the Saddle horse and the Quarter horse)
2. Why is the author comparing and contrasting these two types of horses? (so we can decide which horse is best for pleasure riding)
3. Why did the author use the compare-contrast structure in this particular passage? (to show us that each type of horse has advantages and disadvantages for pleasure riding)
4. What are the advantages of the Quarter horse for pleasure riding? (strong and healthy)
5. What are the advantages of the Saddle horse? (comfortable and easy to control)
6. What are the disadvantages of the Quarter horse for pleasure riding? (uncomfortable and hard to control)
7. What are the disadvantages of the Saddle horse? (not healthy or strong)
8. What other characteristic of the two horses does the author include in the passage? (physical appearance)
9. Is the appearance of the horses important in determining which horse is best for pleasure riding? (no)
10. According to the passage, which of the two types of horses is best for pleasure riding? (there is no clear-cut answer)
11. How would someone decide which of the horses to buy based on what he or she read in this passage? (they would have to decide which horse is best for their particular needs)

context or mode, such as by listening; and c) write or speak some illustrative examples of selected patterns.

K. Denise Muth offers a means of teaching text structure incidentally. She suggests that the teacher merely construct "Connection Questions" that follow the format of the text. To ensure that the point of the lesson is not missed, Muth

FIGURE 10-2

Text Connection Questions *(continued)*

Here are some questions which could help students build "external connections":

1. Which of the two horses would you pick, and why? (I'd pick the Saddle horse because I'm light and wouldn't be carrying heavy loads; also, I don't have any other horses, so it would be hard for my Saddle horse to catch a disease if there aren't any other horses around.)
2. Do you know anyone who might be concerned with the appearance of the horses? (My aunt would. She participates in horse shows, and appearance is very important for show horses.)

CAUSE-EFFECT

Why do some things become rusty? Perhaps you found out if you left a shovel or rake out overnight. When you picked it up a few days later, you might have seen rough, brown spots of rust on it. Air is composed partly of oxygen. Oxygen combines with iron to make rust. Moisture or water helps to bring about the change. Tools like rakes and shovels are made of iron, and they rust quickly if they are left out in wet or damp air. If you left them out long enough, they would rust completely and crumble away.

Again, teacher's questions should focus on helping students understand why the author used the cause-effect structure and how the ideas in the passage are related to each other.

Here are some questions which could help students build "internal connections" among the ideas:

1. Why did the author use the cause-effect structure for this passage? (to describe a process; to give an example of one thing causing something else to happen)
2. What is the cause-effect process that the author is describing? (how things rust)
3. Describe the process of how some things rust. (oxygen and moisture in the air combine with the iron in the objects to cause rust)
4. What causes the process? (the oxygen and the moisture combining with the iron)
5. What is the effect of this combination? (rust)
6. What are the three necessary "ingredients" for rusting? (oxygen, moisture, iron)

These questions could help students build "external connections":

1. Why don't most things usually rust inside your house? (there's not enough moisture)
2. When do you think things might rust in your house? (when the humidity is very high)
3. Can you think of some things that might rust in your house? (the scale in the bathroom, the pipes in the basement)
4. Can you think of some things that you own that might rust if you left them outdoors long enough? (bicycle, wheelbarrow, car)
5. Can you think of some things that you own that won't rust if you leave them outdoors? (basketball, book, sweatshirt)

Muth (1987)

advises that the teacher comment on how a certain question parallels the comparison-contrast or cause and effect nature of the expository (see Figure 10.2).

The next cluster of techniques tend to rely on deducing or following text structure to achieve comprehension. Some, such as grammars and mapping, do so to a great degree.

Grammars/Maps/Guides

The theory underlying grammars, maps, and guides simply is that students will be better able to follow a story, or line of exposition, if they have a set of categories to help them properly anticipate and recognize information or story parts when they see them, and from which an outline can be constructed. The most common story grammar categories are: setting, problem, goal, action, and outcome. Results of studies on story grammar instruction have been mixed. However, two studies are especially worth noting. In one study (Idol, 1987), when story grammar information was provided to guide reading, learning disabled and low-achieving readers in a heterogeneously grouped class were shown to be able to better participate and follow materials up to a year or more above their level. In a second study, it was shown that story grammar instruction of very low-achieving fourth graders resulted in their producing much more complex and fully formed stories than did a control group (Spiegel & Fitzgerald, 1986). This finding is consistent with many other anecdotal reports of the value of various means and methods of structuring, mapping, and charting which are described next.

Story Mapping is one means of teaching story grammar. The technique has the teacher explain and demonstrate how a story can be reduced to a series of frames detailing factors such as setting, characters, time, place, problem, action, and resolution or outcome. Students then are led through several stories as the teacher gradually fades support, and urges students to complete these for themselves and begin to make maps that others might use to follow or complete. (See Figure 10.3 for a teacher-generated example.)

Joan E. Heimlich and Susan D. Pittelman (1986) compiled an entire monograph that details several classroom applications of a related technique called Semantic Mapping (see Figure 10.4 for an example).

These graphic methods and approaches appear to have begun with the pioneering research of Richard Barron (1969) on Structured Overviews, and M.B. Hanf (1971) on mapping, per se. The general objective of structuring is to help students become more sensitive to the conceptual basis of a piece. This also is the role of reading guides, which are textual rather than graphic organizations of a piece (Clewell & Heidemenos, 1983).

"Reading Guides" is a collective name for several forms of efforts to relieve readers of possible obstructions to comprehension by focusing their attention to particular points, and to induce higher levels of thinking in some sequential way. The guide can be in the form of a few sheets that look like old-fashioned work sheets, but which are completed during pauses in reading, rather than

FIGURE 10.3

Story Grammar

My Story Map

Name _____ Date _____

Characters:	Time:	Place:
Bessie and friends	*now*	*Antarctica*

The Problem:

The other penguins made fun of her because she was always so messy.

Action:

She ran away to find a skin that would not get messy. She met a monkey, a porcupine, a bear, a deer, and a wise old owl that told Bessie that she had just the right skin for a penguin. So Bessie went home.

Resolution/Outcome:

Bessie went back home and her friends had made her a bib to keep her clean.

Courtesy of Debbie Fidler and Maryann Spears, Kansas City Public School District, 1989

FIGURE 10.4

A Classroom Map (for Kate and the Zoo)

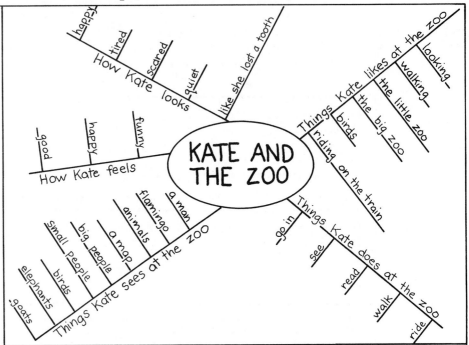

Heimlich and Pittelman (1986)

after reading a long passage. Daniel Tutolo (1977) explained the value of guides as coming from their proximity to the reader and the text at the point of greatest felt need. Harold Herber (1978) developed three specific types of guides to serve different focuses, which he called "reading guides," "study guides," and "thinking guides."

In general, guides tend to be of two types: those that are advice-giving, and those that explicitly deal with the content. In the advice category, the teacher might prepare a sheet with page numbers on it corresponding to the page numbers in the reading material containing prompts to the student for what to read for, or how to read that page. One version, called Guide-O-Rama (Cunningham & Shablak, 1975), prompts such as the following might be seen:

pp. 242–243 Try to figure out what Pip is *really* up to on these pages.

pp. 244–245 Reread the paragraph that begins on p. 244 and continues onto p. 245. It contains an important clue to the rest of the plot.

pp. 246–250 To more easily follow this complex section, *first* skip to p. 251, and read the second and third paragraphs. These paragraphs pretty much summarize what happens up to that point.

In the second type of guide, dealing directly with content, the reader is guided by questions and activities more so than statements (Herber, 1978). These might be as follows:

pp. 242–243 Who is the main character?
What is he doing?
What does he hope to accomplish?
pp. 244–245 What problem, or conflict, arises between Pip and his Aunt Sally?
What leads Aunt Sally to question Pip's loyalty to her?
pp. 246–250 Complete the list of events on pps. 246-250 beginning with:
a. Pip drops the jar of coins
b. _____
c. _____
d. _____
e. _____

Many studies have attempted to demonstrate the effectiveness of reading guides, but results tend to vary in relation to the quality of the particular collection of guides constructed. In general, however, they do seem to facilitate comprehension according to several research reviews (Vaughan, 1982; Cunningham, 1984; Wood & Mateja, 1983; and Wood, 1988).

There is another variation on guides that is worth noting for its promise, more so than availability or ease of construction. This type builds the needed assistance into the textbook. This work may be found under the titles "adjunct aids" (cf. Jonassen, 1985a,b), "imbedded aids" (Manzo 1979), and "marginal gloss" (Otto & Hayes, 1982; Dana, 1982; Witte, 1982; Richgels & Hansen, 1982; Richgels & Mateja, 1984). By any name, the hope is the same: that books might someday be constructed to teach rather than just tell. "Teach" here means more than it does in reading guides. It includes side comments by someone other than the first author. This potential already exists in computers with software called "hypertext." There is one other form of supporting device for silent reading discussed ahead in the chapter under the title, "Cuing Systems." However, the next method discussed returns to the concept of front-loading, but with greater emphasis on calling up relevant prior knowledge.

Knowledge Activation and Integration Techniques

The general rule to activate relevant prior knowledge and experiences has been part of reading instruction from the earliest days. As you will recall, Emmett Betts (1946) included front-loading as the first phase of the Directed Reading Activity. The methods that follow describe recent efforts to activate relevant prior knowledge and experience.

K-W-L Plus

K-W-L Plus was developed by Eileen Carr and Donna Ogle (1987). It can be used as a total lesson plan since it has prereading, guided silent reading, and post-reading components. Its most significant contribution, however, is in activating prior knowledge in such a way that it stirs students to be able to say what they **Know (K)**, realize what it is they **Want (W)** to know from the textual material, and then what they have **Learned (L)** following reading. The **Plus** refers to the mapping or summarizing step that seemed to provide the additional active ingredient that an earlier version of this method needed to bring about more predictable benefits.

Steps in K-W-L Plus

Before Reading

Step 1   Students "brainstorm" and note on individual worksheets what they think they know about a topic. More recently, Ogle (1989) suggested that the best way to direct this step is to ask, "How is/ should this content be structured?"

Step 2   Students categorize information they have generated and anticipate categories of information that they may find in the selection.

Step 3   The teacher models categorizing by "thinking aloud" while combining and classifying information.

Step 4   Students generate a list of questions they want answered as they read.

Silent Reading

Step 5   During reading, students pause to answer the questions raised in the "want to know" list. (New questions can be added as they read.)

Step 6   Students list things they have learned while reading.

Post-reading

Step 7   Discussion of what was learned takes place, and questions raised before reading are reviewed to determine whether they were resolved.

Follow-up

Step 8   Students are encouraged to map and/or summarize the information from their "learned" list.

For an interesting variation on K-W-L Plus, see Mary Heller's (1986) metacognitive method in the chapter on higher-order literacy. The next method also is a good way to get kids talking—constructively.

PreP

The PreP, or Prereading Plan, was developed by Judith Langer (1981) to simultaneously provide opportunity for assessing the adequacy of students' prior knowledge while raising and focusing topic awareness. It is primarily a small group method. This 3-phase process has the teacher first identify key terms, then the teacher:

1. asks students for their associations with the terms;
2. builds a discussion around the question, "What made you think of that association?"; and then,
3. prompts further discussion and focus by asking, "Now that we have discussed this, have you any new ideas before we read?"

PreP tends to get students talking very freely. However, it does not seem to convert easily into "instructional conversation," since it often calls up too much irrelevant information that is difficult to channel back into analysis of the textual material. Studies of PreP indicate that the quality and quantity of the information it calls up are predictive of reading comprehension, but not necessarily related to improvement of comprehension (Langer & Nicholich, 1981). PreP needs to be thought of as a component of a more inclusive method, as in the previous and the next method.

Inferencing

Inferencing, a technique developed by Jane Hansen (1981), attempts to improve on the PreP model with story material. With Hansen's approach, there are three critical phases—two are front-loading. The first step has the teacher explain why the group will try to relate new information to old. The second leads students into a prereading discussion based on having them express what they think the story characters might do based on their own experiences. The third and amplifying phase has the teacher ask a steady diet of inferential story questions that require the integration of student experiences (as related to three selected concepts in the story) to events that might occur in the story.

Katherine Maria (1990) gives the example of a teacher leading children to discuss the central concept of "boredom," in preparation for reading Krasilvosky's story, *Cow Who Fell in the Canal*. The teacher then asks the text-related question, "Henduka, the cow in the story we are going to read, is bored. What do you think she will do so that she won't be bored anymore?" (p. 106) [She wanders off, falls in a canal, and floats into many adventures.]

This strategy had relatively little impact on good readers. However, it helped poor readers perform about as well as good readers who received traditional basal instruction on the same stories (Hansen, 1981; Hansen & Pearson, 1983).

For two other front-loading techniques that rely on writing, you may wish to consult Jay Blanchard's (1988) Plausible Stories technique and Karen Wood's (1984) Probable Passages. Consider now a popular method to keep reading going.

Sustained Silent Reading

Reading instruction with remedial readers and young children usually involves oral reading (Allington, 1984). The essence of reading power is to read silently and to keep going with ideas in print. From this perspective, Lyman Hunt (1970) and Robert McCracken (1971) created the notion of Uninterrupted Sustained Silent Reading (USSR). Recent name variations on USSR include Sustained Quiet Reading Time (SQUIRT), and DEAR (Drop Everything and Read) (Lipson & Wixson, 1991).

By any name, the purposes are clear: to provide opportunity, during the school day, for students to read connected text, to provide adult reading models, and to increase the duration of reading from a few minutes up to an hour or more. Ted Mork (1972), also a pioneer of USSR, reminds us to begin with a period of time that is so brief that it is no serious challenge. Robert McCracken and Marlene McCracken (1978) further advise that the rules be made clear, and that the teacher and anyone else in view also obey the basic rules of being *silent and reading*. Other helpful features of USSR include "book floods," in which reading areas are equipped with paperback book libraries (Elley & Mangubhai, 1983; Ingham, 1982), and where the reading area is regularly spruced up to be attractive (Morrow & Weinstein, 1986).

USSR can be a valuable means of starting a session or even a school day. In our experience, the ritual of silent and focused reading the first thing in the morning proved comforting to inner city students in schools that were otherwise disruptive and appeared unmanageable. Importantly, the entire staff of the schools were welcomed to participate, including clerical, cafeteria, and janitorial workers.

The success of USSR can be further ensured by giving considerable attention to explaining to students what they are doing and why, and by helping them select appropriate material. USSR now tends to be linked to a second period of time for recreational reading (Morrow, 1989), direct remedial instruction, or buddy-type reading (Koskinen & Blum, 1986).

The evidence supporting USSR is mixed. Several studies have shown outcomes related to better attitudes toward school, (Cline & Kretke, 1980) and faster movement through basals (Collins, 1980), but only two studies seemed to offer a link to achievement, and each of these studies contained an additional ingredient. One study was accompanied by peer and teacher interaction about books (Manning & Manning, 1984), and the other had poor readers spend a good deal of time writing as well as reading (Holt & O'Tuel, 1989).

Since no one seems to doubt that sustained silent reading ought to be a serious goal and practice in most every reading program, it is our inclination to think of it as the "inert substance" in a pill; that is, as a significant bonding agent, but generally in need of an active agent to promote more careful encoding, or just plain conversation, to ensure at least a minimum level of manipulation and transformation of text. Here now are three systems for getting such conversations going, even among the most reticent of students.

Cuing Systems

There are few methods that rely heavily on a *behavioral training* model to help inculcate certain desirable reading, language, and even thinking behaviors. Two are presented here; two others are developed in the last chapter under "Metacognition and Executive Control." When used judiciously, this general approach can be a powerful pump-primer in developing the physical and emotional experience base that sometimes is necessary to get a certain type of thought process and action flowing naturally. To this extent, cuing is similar to the "strategic parroting" technique described under "Anecdotal Lessons from ReQuest." Three such methods are described here. The first is something of a reading-study method based on providing direct, explicit instruction in *how*, *when*, and *why* to employ specific reading strategies. The second tends to gloss over the *why*, relying more on the act of participating to generate active involvement with ideas and text. The third attempts to alter the text to focus attention on idea units.

Monitoring Cards.

Patricia Babbs's (1983) method first has students actually taught about the reading process over several sessions. The discussion, she says, should center around five questions related to a reader's strategic planning:

1. What is reading?
2. What is my goal?
3. How difficult is the text?
4. How can I accomplish my goal?
5. How can I check on whether I have achieved my goal?

Once students reach reasonable proficiency in handling these questions, they are trained in the use of nine prompt cards that can be employed in silent reading in class or at home. The cards are used in the following manner:

After silently reading the first sentence, students should consider the first two cards—

1. *clink* — "I understand"
2. *clunk* — "I don't understand"

If a *clunk* is raised, the student first attempts to classify it as a word or a sentence problem. Then, the student reviews the cards in order until the problem is resolved with the help of one of the other cards that say—

3. Read on.
4. Reread the sentence.
5. Go back and reread the paragraph.
6. Look in the glossary.
7. Ask someone (such as the tutor in a remedial session).
8. What did it say at the paragraph level?
9. What do I remember at the end of the page?

Using this method, Babbs found that fourth graders in an experimental group spent more time on the reading task and had more than twice as many recalls of important ideas (Babbs, 1983). However, strategy use did not transfer as well as was hoped when the cards were not used with these fourth graders. You will need to think about how you might help along an effective transfer of these strategies in new material. The next method attempts to add some additional facilitating ingredients to this mix.

Note Cue (Manzo & Manzo, 1987a, 1990b).

This method is designed to increase student participation in class discussion, and to induce the social reinforcement that comes naturally from such instructional conversations. It attempts to build strength in *asking* questions and *commenting* on reading as well as in *answering* questions. It does this by initially relieving students of the complex burden of having to think what to say, how to say it, and leaving them only to think about *when* to say it. Note Cue is ideal for small group remedial sessions as well as whole-class use.

Steps in Note Cue:

Prereading

Step 1   Students are instructed to survey the reading material to try to predict what it will be about. They are told that a brief written test will follow reading and discussion of the selection.

Step 2   While students are surveying, the teacher places one or more random or selected prereading cards on each student's desk.

Step 3   Students are instructed to read their card(s) silently, and think about when they should read it (them) and about whether they wish to add anything else.

Step 4   Students with blank cards are instructed to think of a Question. Answer, or Comment and, if time permits, write it on their cards.

Step 5   The teacher begins the prereading, or prediction, stage of the discussion by asking who has a Question or Comment that seems to provide a good idea of what the selection will be about. If a Question is read, the teacher asks who has an Answer that seems to fit it. This process continues until the teacher feels that students have a sense of what the passage will be about. (This step should take no more than 10 minutes. The brisk pace and aura of evolving a purpose for reading will convey to students that not all cards need to be read to establish a reasonable purpose for reading.)

Step 6   The teacher instructs students to read the selection silently to test their predictions. The teacher also reminds them to read their post-reading cards, which will be placed on their desks while they are reading. (The teacher announces that he or she will come to the desk of any student who raises a hand for assistance.)

Post-reading Discussion

Step 7   The teacher asks, "Who has a good Question to check comprehension of this selection?"; then "Who has a good Answer to that Question?"; then "Who has a Comment that seems right to state?"; and finally, "Who has reaction(s) or personal Comment(s)?" The last question is intended to encourage extemporaneous statements as well as statements read from cards.

Follow-up

Step 8   Within the same class period, or later if preferred, the teacher gives a test of 5 to 10 questions that require brief written responses. Most questions should be taken directly from the cards to build an appreciation of the cooperative value in reading a cue card for all to hear and profit from.

The next cuing system also involves some additional teacher preparation time. However, the exercises are cumulative, and hence the workload is easier each year. While no empirical evidence has been collected on Note Cue, several field studies have yielded support for its use by some formerly skeptical teachers (Manzo & Manzo, 1988).

Chunking Cues.

This notion, also sometimes known as phrase training, attempts to focus students' attention on meaningful units of language by breaking sentences up into phrases, or ideational chunks. For example, the sentence below would be "chunked" as indicated by the slash marks:

Watch out, / Henry, / the cabinet door is opened above you, / and the floor is slippery, too.

Training in reading prechunked material, and in chunking material with slashes (/) can draw attention to wording, ideas, and sequencing, but it also needs to be accompanied by a good deal of discussion about meaning, which really is the chief dictate of phrasing. Asking students to indicate where they would place phrase markers evokes discussion about meaning in a close-knit, analytical way.

Kathleen Stevens (1981) found such chunking procedures to be of considerable value to 10th grade boys. Similarly, William Brozo and associates concluded that while such training helps poor readers, few studies have been able to show similar effects for competent readers (Brozo, Schmlzer, & Spires, 1983). This suggests that phrase training and related activities is best saved for remedial classes and tutoring sessions. Most competent readers have already, incidentally, learned all that they need to know about phrasing.

At an anecdotal level, several specialists have noted that phrase training can be effectively used to teach the use and connection between punctuation and communication. They have done this by stressing the role of clause markers such as "but," "and," "if," etc. Subtleties of language such as these can also be taught incidentally in a ReQuest conversation with questions like: "What does the word *but* signal to you about what will come next?" and "Why do you suppose it is preceded by a comma?"

Consider now those techniques that make use of the mind's eye to image and follow analogies. Imaging is something that proficient readers do naturally, but poor readers do not.

Imaging

It has been shown that attempting to construct mental images can help remedial readers to better integrate (Pressley, 1977), and detect inconsistencies (Gambrell & Bales, 1986) in textual material. Mark Sadoski (1983; 1985) found that those pupils who were able to image the climax of the story were also those who comprehended it best. This is not conclusive proof that imaging improves comprehension, but it does require a personalized transformation of textual material, and hence is a good bet to activate appropriate prior knowledge and comprehension strategies.

Following is a model for guided imagery instruction, liberally interpreted from a volume called *200 Ways of Using Imagery in the Classroom* (Bagley & Hess, 1982), and from specific recommendations (steps 2 and 6) by Mark Aulls (1978) and Katherine Maria (1990).

1. Have children relax and attempt to concentrate.
2. Demonstrate (model) for them what you mean by imaging, using a very brief piece.
3. Have them try to form images of the concrete objects mentioned in a second piece.
4. Have them attempt to broaden the pictures of the objects into pictures of large settings.
5. Ask students to think and say what else they see, smell, hear, and might feel. (Connect this step to building a vocabulary of the senses.)
6. Have students record or represent by stick figure drawings what they are imaging before it is spoken aloud by anyone. (This is done in order to permit them to first find their own images before being unduly influenced, and perhaps distracted by those of others.)

Maria (1990) notes that visual images can be so powerful as to be potentially disquieting emotionally to some children. We concur, but also feel that the quality of the information received from the youngsters on what they may be experiencing tends to outweigh the risks. Further, teachers and reading specialists are professionals who must be trusted to use certain potentially dangerous techniques judiciously. Most things that are powerful also are potentially dangerous when used inappropriately or in excess.

Related to imaging, either as a preparatory or support technique, is the notion of parallel lessons. This next form of comprehension treatment also contributes to cognitive development.

Parallel Lessons

There are basically two forms of parallel lessons: concrete parallels and dramatizations. Each is developed separately.

Concrete parallels, as suggested by David Moore and John Readence (1980), have the teacher progressively develop comprehension skills by beginning with pictures. In this strategy, the student is encouraged to locate the main idea of a picture and its supporting details. The teacher first models the task, then offers the student some supportive practice with similar pictures, accompanied by multiple choice options for main idea and details. The teacher then does the same with textual material, having students read aloud with the teacher.

Stephen Elliot and James Carroll (1980) report a similar procedure in which students are asked to manipulate objects on a story board following reading, in ways that retell or otherwise reflect, in concrete terms, that they understand what the story is about and what characters are saying or could be saying to one another. The "could be saying" portion can provide some powerful insights into the child's hopes, fears, and aspirations.

Dramatizations of parallels occurs by translating the main concepts of difficult textual material into more familiar terms. In the "dramatization" version, illustrated in Figure 10.5, Manzo (1977b) showed how minority group youngsters, who first acted out a fairly difficult piece of textual material, could then achieve rich comprehension of material that otherwise would have been too remote for them to handle.

Thomas Bean and associates (1987) showed that this approach was much more difficult, and not productive, where youngsters were asked to come up with their own analogies. Apparently, providing a parallel is helpful; asking for one is a further burden at this tender point in the reading-learning process.

Dramatization

Dramatics are activities in which students translate ideas from text into action. Mary Shoop (1985; 1986) offers an "interview" technique that covers the value of the simulation side of the extended analogy approach offered by Manzo (1977b), but which also offers help in achieving the purpose suggested by Thomas Bean and associates (1987), namely, that students be more actively engaged in developing the analogy. This method is better structured and requires a lot less preparation than Manzo's parallel form strategy.

Shoop's strategy, called Investigative Questioning, or "InQuest," involves the reader or listener with narrative text through student questioning and spontaneous drama techniques. As a precondition, students are led through a discussion and practice of the techniques involved in journalistic interviewing. The following points are made to students in the discussion:

1. Questions that get longer responses are more desirable.
2. Yes/no questions should be followed by a "why?"
3. Interview questions should try to elicit reflections and evaluations as well as simple information.
4. It is best to use a variety of question types.

Students may also have had experience using the ReQuest procedure, previously described, to develop further incidental knowledge about questioning types and strategies.

Subsequent steps in InQuest include:

1. The teacher selects an interesting story that is read by the teacher or students up to a critical point or incident.
2. The teacher suggests to students that they try to think of questions that they would like to ask a character as the story unfolds.
3. Students role-play a news conference in which someone plays the character, and everyone else assumes the roles of investigative reporters. (The teacher may model role-play either of these parts initially.)
4. Students are directed to read on to a next point, and repeat the interview process with a different or the same character.

FIGURE 10.5

Dramatizations of Parallels

The class was asked to pretend they were sixth graders attending a progressive elementary school that held an annual prom for its graduates. (There was such a school nearby.) An attractive new girl in class was said to have two boys vying for her attention. Their names were written on the proverbial love triangle: Alpha at the top, Donnie Ray and Osceola at either angle of the base. A situation was provided to stir the pot: Donnie Ray's father owned a florist shop, and Osceola's father was a candy maker.

The simulated scene was a schoolyard at recess some days before the prom. Donnie Ray's friends, the teacher said, were gathered about him demanding, "How will you win a date with Alpha?" To which he responded, "First I've got to let her know I exist." Suiting action to words, he proposed to dash past her several times to display his blazing speed.

Osceola was asked to suggest a countermove. He got on the athletic high bar and began to chin as his friends loudly counted, proclaiming his awesome strength to all within earshot.

Not very subtle, but it stirred Donnie Ray to suggest a persuasive countergesture: "In the morning, I will send Alpha a single rose" (by emissary).

Osceola immediately countered, "I will send candy" (in the same manner). "Tomorrow," Donnie Ray returned, "I will bring a bouquet."

But Osceola matched and surpassed his rival: "And I'll bring a box of candy and a cozy sack lunch for two."

The vying continued, to the cheers and jeers of the class, until Alpha was asked to choose her date. "Couldn't I wait another day or two?" she coyly asked.

"No way!" Donnie Ray snapped. "In fact, you're not deciding nothing!"

"Right," Osceola volunteered. "Me and this turkey are going to settle this thing right here and now!"

While the class was still laughing and jabbering at that macho proposal, the teacher began to slowly erase each name from the triangle and write in new ones. The class grew quiet and perplexed as they observed these changes on the chalkboard:

India
(Neutral Bloc)

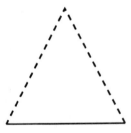

(Free World Bloc)   (Communist Bloc)

"You won't believe this," they were told, "but if you read pages 29 to 36 in your current events books, you will find a story very much like the one you 'sixth graders' just made up." This was true enough. Between 1955 and 1961, the United States and the Soviet Union were wining and dining India and the neutral nations to get their support in the General Assembly of the United Nations. When the giveaway programs appeared to be faltering, both countries began to test bigger and bigger hydrogen bombs while seemingly chanting the macabre refrain "My bomb's bigger than your bomb." In fact, the kids had anticipated, by a few months, the near catastrophe at the Berlin Wall, where the world learned a new word: brinkmanship.

From Manzo and Manzo, 1990a

5. Have students evaluate which questions proved most interesting, in the sense of bringing characters to life.

InQuest, a story-based method, can be followed with the Question-Only Procedure (Manzo, 1980), a content-based strategy. In Question-Only:

1. The teacher announces a topic before reading.
2. Students ask all the questions they think are relevant about it.
3. They then either read a content-based selection on the topic, or listen to a lecture on it.
4. Finally, a teacher-prepared test follows to help them evaluate how effectively they anticipated and asked topic-relevant questions.

This can be a "joyful" and highly active inversion of conventional reading practices. See the section on Enabling Questions in the chapter on higher-order literacy for a compatible method. Use this too, following Note Cue, previously discussed in this chapter, as an opportunity to quickly use what was learned about participation, but in a more meaning-driven format. For additional information on dramatization technique, look into Duffelmeyer and Duffelmeyer's Vocabulary Skits (1979) and see Antithetical, or Empowered, Role Play in the next chapter on treating deficits, differences, and disruptions. The next methodology used to be rather sedentary, but it now too contains some simulation, dramatization, and a raised activity level.

Following Directions

The ability to follow written directions is an important key to independent learning and functioning. It has been aptly said that, "At various points in almost every schoolday, students are expected to follow some form of written directions," and that life outside school is full of "basic life demands that require them to follow written instructions" (Henk & King, 1984, p. 62).

Some of the earliest "specific skills series" materials included practice in "Following Directions." These were not well received by students, largely because they were difficult to do and seldom engaging.

However, when materials involve more activity and are designed by teachers as well as by students, they can be quite engaging and a good deal of fun. They also can lead to improvements in comprehension, and in the ability to follow directions (Calder & Zalatimo, 1970).

Maring and Ritson (1980) offer this example of an activity that can be done in physical education class, at recess, or to break up the overly sedentary nature of schools and tutorials.

Read and Do Sheets

Prepare "Read and Do" instruction sheets so that students will learn required content, and at the same time improve their ability to follow written directions. Example: Motor Development Exercise

Single-heel click: Jump into the air, click your heels together once, and land with your feet apart (any distance).

This can be turned into an amusing exercise in which students try to write out totally unambiguous expository directions for their peers to follow.

Other popular "read and do" activities for classroom include:

1. having students write out explicit directions for others to follow on how to get from one place in the school to another
2. having students read and follow directions for drawing a certain graphic, or folding paper
3. having students work to assemble a something from directions, such as inexpensive model cars or planes

Such "real-life" directions often pose too great a challenge for poor readers. William Henk and Glynn King (1984) offer these suggestions for rewriting directions to provide practice activities for these students:

1. Use one sentence per direction.
2. Substitute simple synonyms for difficult words.
3. Avoid taking background information for granted.
4. Ensure that essential intermediate steps have not been omitted or just implied.
5. Avoid using lengthy or complex sentence structures.
6. Avoid ambiguous statements.
7. Omit irrelevant information.
8. Use numbers to mark the steps to follow (1984, p. 63).

To add another bit of mental manipulation to this task, have students try to anticipate and record a pretrial note on where they think another student will have trouble understanding or following the directions given. For a more controversial approach to teaching students to follow directions, see the section on Implosive Therapy in the next chapter on remedies for defects, differences, and disruptions. It tells of a bold, clinical use of following directions that is accompanied by feigned, though harsh-sounding criticism of students while they are attempting to read and follow directions in an atmosphere that is intentionally distracting.

➤ *LOOKING BACK* ➤

This chapter covered the improvement of comprehension and collateral aspects of oral language, thinking, and social-emotional adjustment. It attempted to impart a sense of how "clinical intuition" is acquired and enhanced by giving focus to the lessons that have been learned as well as those taught with a variety of methods, particularly ReQuest procedure. In all, over 35 procedures and techniques were presented for improving comprehension through the stages of prereading, guided silent reading, and post-reading. Most methods stressed that effective comprehension teaching tends to include: an engaging instructional conversation, modeling, practice, collateral objectives, and a planned fade-out of support to eventual student independence.

➤ *LOOKING AHEAD*

The "fade to independence," the objective of strategic reading, is more explicitly continued in the last chapter on higher-order literacy. That chapter also addresses three complementary themes related to effective comprehension: study skills, writing, and cognitive enrichment. The next chapter focuses on alleviating the differences and emotional disruptions that tend to prevent remedial readers from naturally linking reconstructive and constructive reading into one seamless capacity to respond appropriately to text.

UNATTENDED AND SEVERE LITERACY DISORDERS

Remedies for Defects, Disruptions, and Differences

Most of us will never do great things, but we can do small things in a great way.
ANONYMOUS

> ## ➤ *LOOK FOR IT*

Classroom teachers and reading-learning disability specialists are neither physicians, physical therapists, nor psychologists. Nonetheless, they are expected to know and do more than the average classroom teacher to alleviate the burden and complications associated with physical defects, social-emotional disruptions, and sociocultural and temperamental differences. This chapter provides some of the knowledge base and means by which to begin accumulating the wisdom to address such needs in whatever small ways we can. Disruptions and differences are given the most attention since these can be alleviated with strategic selection of conventional teaching methods and/or more intensive routines.

Defects

The explicit treatment of constitutional problems such as chronic illness, allergies, hyperkinesis, and minimal brain damage are largely beyond the scope of this text. However, methods are suggested to help alleviate or circumvent several of these problems in both clinical and classroom situations.

Allergies

Despite the fact that allergic reactions can cause enormous disruption to normal functioning, schools do a poor job of helping the many youngsters who suffer from common "hay fever" and other airborne allergies. Buildings are neither air-conditioned nor air-filtered, despite blazing temperatures in many parts of the country from late April to June and from August to early October. It is not at all uncommon to find windows opened wide and school lawns being mowed or nearby fields being cut in many suburban and rural settings. In most city schools, noise pollution and other types of airborne allergens are equally common.

The best a teacher can do at this time is to urge parents to have the child see a physician. There now are several reasonably effective "nondrowsy" antihistamines that can be taken once a day to relieve most symptoms. The second thing we can do is to remind school boards and communities that teachers and children are the only ones in this country still being packed 30-plus to a room in unair-conditioned buildings. Air cooling and air cleaning could easily add thirty to sixty more *productive* days to the school year without changing the school calendar or adding to labor costs. Over one student's thirteen years of schooling, this can conservatively add as much as two full years of reading and instruction.

Hyperkinesis

Hyperkinesis, also called Attention Deficit Disorder (ADD), now is largely treated by physicians with stimulant drugs such as ritalin and dexadrine. These stimulants, which also include caffeine, seem to make the mind more alert, thereby reducing the need for the body to try to stay alert through directionless activity that resembles the behavior of a tired, cranky child. Problems of this type have been shown to be relatively unrelated to severe reading disorders, but clearly compound any learning disorders. See ahead in the chapter for some behavioral means of alleviating this problem with methods such as relaxation exercises and antithetical role play. See also Appendix D and the chapter on severe reading disability for more information on related brain functions and birth disorders that have implications for reading and language learning.

Vision and Hearing

Vision and hearing problems remain part of the reading teacher's diagnostic battery, and to some measure, part of our treatment domain. However, most treatment is done through simple referral, and usually results in the simple prescription of corrective lenses and hearing aids. Orthooptic training, or eye exercises, also are offered by some optometrists (vision specialists) and ophthalmologists (eye doctors). The next chapter, on severe reading disabilities (dyslexia), reports on some of the more popular forms of treatment that directly involve vision and visual perception such as the reduction of reversals, eye tracking and drug treatment, and "scoptic sensitivity" training.

In general, attempts to improve reading through orthooptic and visual perceptual training have not proven to be durable and dependable solutions to reading problems (Leibert & Sherk, 1970). The results claimed for such treatments have tended to collapse into nonsignificance when the studies were conducted with controls for placebo effects, such as special attention to the child.

Autism

The withdrawal of a child into a noncommunicative state, sometimes including self-abusive behavior, has been categorically known as autism. The belief has been that these children could not be taught to read or write, since they clearly could not or would not communicate verbally, or even with normal body language that suggested awareness of those around them. As we prepare this book to go to press, we have just learned of a new treatment for autism (as reported on "Prime Time", ABC, January 25, 1992). We expect to be better informed about it soon. In the meantime, we thought you might wish to be alerted to it.

Basically, persons called "facilitators" are trained to help autistic children, who can not seem to communicate in other ways, to type messages. The facilitator lightly holds the child's hand or arm in front of an electronic keyboard, providing just enough stabilization for the child to touch the letters he or she intends.

In this way, many children are showing remarkable capacity with language and mathematics.

This treatment procedure, which originated in Australia, is being popularized by Douglas Biklen of Syracuse University (c.f. Biklen, 1990).[1] There is an increasing number of skeptics, even in Australia, who are saying that the facilitators are doing the writing. Advocates argue that this is not possible since eight hundred facilitators in the United States alone are having comparable experiences. Further, there are other clinical signs of progress in the communication and socialization of persons who have not shown much response to other treatments.

These findings are being offered as further evidence to those who may still have doubted it, that autism is a physical problem, and not an emotional or affective one.

Sources of Disruptions and Differences

Disruptions, or emotional interferences, and to a lesser degree, differences, or language, cultural, and learning-style variables, are more clearly within the reading teacher's realm and can be addressed in a variety of incidental and quasi-direct ways. This, however, is not the chief argument for attention to affect. Affect is part of the "hidden curriculum" (Beane, 1990, p. 8). Failure to attend to it blindsides other efforts (Giroux & Purpel, 1983). Most importantly, however, it puts education outside its obligation to educate the "whole" person (Beane, 1990).

The sources of problems in both reading and life that face all students, remedial or otherwise, can be quite varied in type and intensity. Difficulties may include cultural and linguistic differences, family relationships, gender confusions, moving, divorce, peer pressure, physical handicaps or differences, racial prejudices, death of loved ones, and even abuse.

It should be clearly understood that not everyone who has a reading problem or entanglement in an emotionally difficult situation has either a causative or even secondary emotional problem. Many people can withstand fairly serious physical and emotional trauma without any apparent emotional side effects. Nonetheless, it is natural to suspect that the incidence of emotional complications would be higher among remedial readers.

When observation and individual diagnosis reveal such a need, there are essentially four things that the professional reading or learning disability specialist can opt to do:

1. Not address it specifically, but rather work to build self-efficacy in reading and learning, hoping that this would also reduce the impact and complications from emotional distress.

[1]For more information, call (315) 443-9657, Syracuse University, Division of Special Education and Rehabilitation

2. Refer the child to a school counselor or psychologist for complementary assistance.
3. Suggest to the parents that the child might need psychological services beyond that which is available in the schools.
4. Take some of the responsibility on yourself to work with the counselor and/or to collaterally provide psychoeducational assistance incidentally through the remedial methods you employ.

The most popular option, where it is available, is to refer the child to a cooperating school counselor. Group counseling in conjunction with remedial instruction has shown to be quite effective (Lewis, 1984).

The focus of the remainder of this chapter will be on psychoeducational practices that are mostly incidental, and a few that are more explicit. Let us now illustrate the strong tie-in of reading and affect by momentarily considering what is involved in reading comprehension. An even stronger tie-in, in the form of an unconscious wish *not* to learn to read, is discussed in the next chapter (see the case for psychologically induced dyslexia).

Reconstructive and Constructive Processes

Comprehension occurs on two planes, both of which must involve active engagement of the textual material. One, however, tends to require that the reader should interact with the page in a largely receptive, or assimilative, mode to take in the author's intended words and meaning. This intentional reconstructive mode requires a great deal of effort and practice while the reader attempts to activate attention and appropriate background knowledge, experience, and resolve to permit the author's meaning to be heard through a bevy of possible obstacles: unknown words, the ambiguities inherent in all language, the author's peculiar way of structuring and writing, and the static from one's own emotional bent, personal needs, and values. Once this process is under way, and words are being converted to tentative understandings, the reader can afford the luxury of permitting greater levels of affective responding and further cognitive relating to occur more fully (Beck, Omanson, & McKeown, 1982). Again, however, this process often can and should be inverted to overcome the need for an extended period of patience and attention before responding. For example, at-risk children in Hawaii have successfully been taught by opening with higher-level questions and then using these as probes to lead them back to more detail-oriented information (Au & Kawakami, 1984). This more constructive phase involves correlating ideas to sentiments, and the interaction of the two to personally felt needs and values. If any combination of these cognitive or personal matters does not reconcile with the message, *assimilation* (or reception) can be impaired and *accommodations* (or adjustments) must be made. Accommodations, ideally, are made by further reflection, rereading, rethinking, schema building (making new slots to receive new information and ideas), and objective critical analysis (challenging the material). Of course, this process is not quite as sequential and linear as these words would make it appear. For example, when there is a poor match between what the author has said and what the reader may think, the first tendency is to disqualify it casually, rather than build an accommodation, or new structure, for it. In truth, what one reads, or whether in fact one will read at all, depends in large measure on what one wishes to construct. One's constructions tend to be most strongly influenced by perceptions, priorities, and personal agenda. Marjorie Lipson (1983) showed this to be the case in a study in which she showed how Jewish children's recall and interpretation of a piece on the holocaust was significantly less accurate than their recall of less emotionally charged material. Disruptive thinking problems such as these occur frequently in remedial readers, but it is not as predictable as to just what the elements are that will cause the disruptions to occur. However, it is known that problems arising from internal disruptive thinking patterns do tend to be strongly influenced by motivational factors such as the ability to reconcile personal needs with task demands. There are essentially two approaches to motivation: generic and specific. The remedial specialist and classroom teacher must consciously use both approaches to build and enhance the student's internal motivation.

Motivation

Generic Motivation Approaches

Common experience suggests that if a student has a keen interest in cars, he or she will be more inclined to read and learn about cars. To the student who has in mind to learn about cars, an otherwise wonderful, but "car-less," article or story may appear irrelevant simply because it is not on that student's personal agenda or priority list. That is not to say that the student will not or can not be induced to read the article or story. But the selection will need to be "sold" — that is, introduced in such a way as to move it onto the student's agenda and up his/her priority list before it will command the pupil's will and life energies. In other words, the student will need to be motivated to read and engage the notion as well as the text. One of the seemingly more efficient ways to approach this requirement is to sell the student on the idea that it is in his/her best interest to learn how to read effectively. This is the *generic motivation* approach. When it is done convincingly, it has students saying to themselves, "I want to be a competent, independent reader; therefore, I will attempt to read most anything put before me to strengthen my skills."

Intuitively, every parent and teacher tries to promote generic motivation because it unburdens them from having to deduce the best way to sell each and every reading and learning task we would have students undertake. When generic motivation to read does takes hold, the effect tends to be synergistic — greater than the sum of its parts. What is done in class carries over into out-of-class activities such as trying to read signs and just plain thinking about and imaging letters and words. This is almost a definition of what is meant by "generative learning"—learning that naturally grows and multiplies outside classroom instruction. Sensing this, parents and teachers find themselves "preaching" the simple wisdoms: "pay attention," "read," "study harder," and the like.

The remedial teacher also takes this approach, but with less preaching and more teaching and illustrating. The teacher realizes that reading can be used both to inform and to transform youngsters into individuals with the will and the skill to think and to read objectively and effectively. So, then, the basic tool of the remedial reading teacher is reading itself. The simple act of doing it and discussing it unhurriedly from different perspectives is both a means and an end in itself. However, there are some special problems in following the simple dictate to have youngsters read. First, there is competition in raising their will to read, and secondly, they must be led to read in ways that are active and engaging.

Competition for Will to Read

It has always been hard to sell some youngsters on reading, but it is now much harder than ever. Books, which once had a nearly exclusive market on stories, recreation, and information, have lost much of their luster to television, a medium that brought "Desert Storm" and the breakup of the Soviet Union as information and *"entertainment"* right into our kitchens and living rooms. There also are other sources of competition for what once was the subtle titillation and diversion provided through reading. Put bluntly, the "new" competitors are, among other things, easily available sex and drugs. Bodies and minds that are occupied with these pursuits at an early age have little left for the simpler pleasures of reading and imagining. More pointedly, reading must seem a quaint leftover from another time to youngsters who now are part of a second generation who have never known it to be otherwise. It has also prompted researchers to begin to study the values imparted in recent children's books (Knafle, Legenza-Wescott, & Passcarella, 1988). Additionally, youngsters now come to school representing a greater variety of problems than have ever been faced in such proportions. These aspects of teaching are part of a larger social evolution that also must be considered by the remedial specialist when designing remedial programs, and by parents, boards, and government in their demands for improvement and their willingness to support education.

The broad nature of the causes of "reading failure" has influenced the emphasis you will find in several sections of this text on methods that attempt to deal with authentic human problems and to offer promise of environmental impact on the student's home, community, and overall value system. Teachers ranked as most influential by their students later in life were those who were inclined to raise student internal motivation largely by appealing to their aesthetic sense, raising their intellectual curiosity, and implementing problem-solving approaches (Ruddell, 1990). Let's look now at some specific forms of motivation to read and comprehend effectively.

Specific Motivation to Read

There are several possible ways to induce a student to read. These are most effective when they are grounded in the slightly larger context of motivating uninterested learners. Stephanie Hewett (1991) offers guidelines for four such basic approaches, with a fifth added from Marlow Ediger (1991) that might apply to all levels:

- Know the students' interests, hobbies, leisure time activities, etc.
- Wherever possible, relate assignments and learning tasks to meaningful events and interests in the students' lives.
- Write positive comments on papers and generally try to *catch them being good!*
- Let students know that you care about them by talking to them as people as well as pupils.
- Casually indicate when an activity or assignment might offer help with one of the five puzzling questions that most occupy youngsters, if not all of us: What are my strengths and weaknesses?; Which beliefs are vital to possess in school and society?; Which purposes in life should I pursue?; What is ultimately good in life?; and, Who am I and what should I do in life?

Consider now some more specific reading motivators that teachers and researchers have tended to rely upon most. Some shortcomings also are noted.

READING MOTIVATORS

1. Identify and match students to materials based on compelling interests. Possible shortcomings: the things students claim interest in may be entirely too difficult or technical to read about (e.g., auto mechanics). But, let them try, and be there to help.
2. Cultivate a specific interest through discussion, and lead students into reading and writing in that area of interest.
3. Use newspapers, magazines, and television to explore interests and to stimulate reading and discussion. Several commercial publications, such as the *Reader's Digest*, *Scholastic Magazine*, and *Weekly Reader* are especially well designed and appropriately written for this purpose, and cable TV offers programming on virtually every topic and area of literature.
4. Share interests that you may have, and about which you may be contagiously enthusiastic. You're at your best as a teacher when you feel that you yourself are a life-long learner.
5. Appeal to students' desire to be powerful and effective, such as to have a more powerful vocabulary or ability to recall and remember information. (See the chapter on higher-order literacy for specific recommendations along these lines.)
6. Hook them on a story by telling a portion of it and having them learn the rest through reading. This process also tends to empower students to read more effectively by giving them a sense of story, plot, characters, and selection-specific words. (See Cunningham's Listening-Reading Transfer Lesson in the chapter on comprehension.)
7. Simply tell what *question* a piece answers; for instance, "Is there really a 'Big Foot' in the northern U.S. forests? This selection answers this question pretty convincingly." Work with students to make books of interesting questions and answers. (For fun, do a parody of the *Enquirer*: "Inquiring Minds Want to Know.")
8. Appeal to students' desire to overcome poor reading by using methods that

greatly reduce the risk of failure. (See especially the Repeated Readings techniques in the chapter on comprehension.)

9. Use methods that permit students to analyze and participate actively in what they read. (See especially the InQuest, Dramatization of Parallel, and Note Cue procedures in the previous chapter.)

10. Use materials and methods that are relevant to students' lives and concerns. (See especially proverbs study in the previous chapter, and "valuing," dialogue journals, and bibliotherapy in this chapter.)

11. Remember to ask students frequently what they feel and think about what they read. These "constructive" questions, when asked regularly, impart a sense of worth to the student that can profoundly impel the will and effort to read "reconstructively" — or accurately and effectively. (See especially the "valuing process" in this chapter.)

12. Read things that are joyful and uplifting. (See the section on humor in the previous chapter, and on homilies in this chapter.)

Having discussed motivation, the remainder of the chapter is an account of practical teaching methods and related recommendations that the reading teacher, and to a degree, the classroom teacher, can depend upon to inculcate motivation to read and to reduce, if not totally alleviate, internal disruptions and differences that weaken learning. Most of these methods rely upon an instructional conversation that evokes a natural therapeutic dialogue.

Easing the Impact of Disruptions and Differences

The Therapeutic Dialogue

A therapeutic dialogue is one that simply brings a more mature perspective to individuals whose situation has been narrowed by emotional pressures. It is straight talk and clear thinking presented in an empathetic way, and an invitation to the student to participate in his or her own educational life and betterment in individual settings (Garcia, 1988) or in groups (Morawski, 1991).

A therapeutic dialogue is *not* nonprofessionals practicing psychotherapy. Psychologists, in truth, adopted the idea of the "therapeutic dialogue" from caring laymen, giving each other advice and counsel. The greatest difference between what psychologists do and what teachers and parents do is the context in which it is done. Psychologists try to take someone aside who they do not know, and with whom they have no emotional attachment, and to build the knowledge base and the insights to help them to deal with their problems. Teachers, parents, as well as other relatives and friends already know the individual and his or her context, and try to offer counsel and guiding information as they walk and work alongside them through life and school. This has been the fundamental formula by which emotional maturity and wisdom have been imparted since our earliest beginnings. It is the basis for the rich oral language tradition and wisdom that is cultivated and transferred from one generation to another through proverbs, maxims, and famous sayings. This type of therapeutic dialogue may seem haphazard, but it is more workable and effective than we tend to realize. Further, it does not require the filling out of forms, nor the exchange of dollars, and it is delivered at the most appropriate moment.

The approaches to treating and alleviating emotional disruptions and differences presented here are largely teaching methods that simply contain the potential to promote greater self-knowledge and social-emotional maturity. They are, quite simply, based on a quaint old term that Sheldon Russell (1991) reminds us of when he urges all reading teachers to readapt "contemplation." Only a few of the methods described give even the appearance of being fundamentally psychological in nature. Collectively, they could be called psychoeducational methods and strategies.

Rules of Affective Teaching

The first rule for effectively remediating disruptive emotionality is to teach well; that is, to provide instruction that is so effective that it builds self-efficacy, self-worth, and willingness to continue to try to overcome reading difficulties (Cecil, 1990a). The second rule of affective teaching is to provide "encouragement rather than praise" (Werner & Strother, 1987, p. 542). Encouragement is realistic feedback, whereas praise can be patronizing and misleading. The third rule is to "exhibit respect for the child" (Werner & Strother, 1987, p. 543). The fourth rule is to "maintain a complex level of interaction with students when asking questions" (Guzzetti & Marzano, 1984, p. 757). This is the essential meaning in the terms instructional conversations, therapeutic dialogue, and reciprocity as these are used in this text.

Consider, too, some "don'ts," as suggested for classroom and remedial teachers by Barbara Guzzetti and Robert Marzano:

- Don't seat slow students far from yourself or in a group, as this makes it harder to monitor them.
- Don't pay less attention to lows in academic situations (smiling less often or maintaining less eye contact).
- Don't call on lows less often to answer classroom questions or make public demonstrations.
- Don't wait less time for lows to answer questions.
- Don't abandon lows in failure situations; instead ask follow-up questions.
- Don't criticize lows more frequently than highs for incorrect public responses.
- Don't praise lows less frequently than highs after successful public responses.
- Don't praise lows more frequently than highs for marginal or inadequate public responses.
- Don't give low-achieving students less accurate and less detailed feedback than highs.
- Don't give lows less frequent feedback than highs.
- Don't demand less work and effort from lows than from highs.

- Don't interrupt the performance of low achievers more frequently than that of high achievers.

(Guzzetti & Marzano, 1984)

Now let's consider some actual practices and teaching methods that contain high regard for affect. The first one is a fresh idea that we think you will find very worthy.

The Exit Interview

Nancy Lee Cecil (1990a) discovered from earlier research that remedial readers, even those who become successful afterwards, carry some of their embarrassment with them long after the remediation sessions have been completed. Her research further suggested that they had a great need to "vent" their lingering feelings. Accordingly, she has developed the 12-question format below that she recommends to be used in a debriefing session "to create a clear line of demarcation in the child's mind between the past time of being a disabled reader and the future time of being an adequate reader" (1990, p. 31).

1. How did you feel about being a remedial reader?
2. How did you feel when you realized you were having problems with reading?
3. Were you told what the problem was? What was your reaction?
4. Have your feelings toward reading changed as a result of being in a special reading class? If so, how?
5. What do you think might have made your experience in remedial reading more pleasant and your problem easier to overcome?
6. What activities, if any, caused you to feel more positive about reading?
7. What things have people said or done to you that made you feel you could not become a successful reader?
8. What advice would you like to give to a teacher who is working with a student who has a reading problem?
9. What advice would you like to give to a child who is experiencing a problem with reading?
10. How can your classroom teacher and reading teacher make your return to the regular classroom more pleasant?
11. How can your parents best help you with your reading?
12. How do you feel about yourself as a reader now?

The Valuing Process

There have been some very viable methods developed for integrating the "valuing process" (Raths, Harmon, & Simon, 1978) into regular classroom reading. The "valuing process" very simply is a means of helping youngsters better come to grips with the forces, or values, that are subconsciously driving their behavior. It is an ideal treatment for emotional dependency and "personal agenda correction," two critical deficiencies in conventional remedial readers, as well as in proficient readers who demonstrate poor evaluative thinking. "Valuing" is an example of a higher-order literacy approach to improving basic literacy from the top down. In this vein, James Hoffman (1977) offers Intra-Act, described in Figure 11.1.

Leo Schell (1980) developed several other variations on the valuing process that can be used in conjunction with Intra-Act. Two of these are illustrated here: "Value Voting" (Figure 11.2), and the "Valuing Sheet" (Figure 11.3).

Homilies, Proverbs, and Fables

It may sound a little corny, but we all need an occasional word of wisdom to strengthen our motivation and clarify our values. Every teacher should have a collection of homilies, proverbs, adages, anecdotes, or fables of deep personal meaning, and encourage students to begin their own personal collections.

Homilies, proverbs, and fables can help reduce emotionally disruptive thought patterns and heighten common sense. They are brief forms of the universal truths often sought in great literature. They provide a powerful way to communicate basic values and life management skills, especially when verbalized at a needed and, therefore, "teachable" moment. They can reset our "emotional clocks" when they become erratic from the effects of stress or ennui (the complacency that comes with the feeling that all is meaningless). They are to

FIGURE 11.1

Intra-Act Post-Reading Exercise Sheet

Directions: Now that you have discussed the reading selection with the members of your group, read each statement and circle "A" if *you* agree, or "D" if *you* disagree. *Do not discuss your answers* yet with your group members. Then, write the names of the other members of your group in the blanks at the top of each column, and, for each group member, circle "A" if you think *he or she* would agree, or "D" if you think he or she would disagree with each statement.

	Your Name:	Group Members: (write the names of your group members in the spaces below)		
1. Women probably don't make as good legislators as men.	A/D	A/D	A/D	A/D
2. A person should vote according to the wishes of the people he or she represents, not according to personal feelings.	A/D	A/D	A/D	A/D
3. I would have voted the same as *Rankin* both times.	A/D	A/D	A/D	A/D
4. The writer seems to approve of what *Rankin* did.	A/D	A/D	A/D	A/D

Hoffman (1977)

FIGURE 11.2

Values Voting

[Based on "The Black Stallion and the Red Mark" in *Moments*, grade 5(3)]

A stallion heads a band of wild horses which "steals" horses from surrounding farms. The farmers band together and capture the herd. The stallion stays with his blind mare rather than running to freedom.

After reading the story, students are told: "Listen to the following statements. If you agree, raise your hand; if you disagree, turn thumbs down; and if you are undecided, fold your arms."

1. Donald was wrong to tell his father where the wild horses were.
2. The stallion was dumb to stay with the mare and be caught.
3. Donald's father showed good judgement in letting the stallion and the mare stay together in captivity.

Schell (1980)

FIGURE 11.3

Value Sheet

[Based on "The Endless Steppe," *Racing Stripes*, grade 6(5)]

A ten-year-old girl and her family live in exile in a labor camp in Siberia in the 1940s. She and her grandmother take a few of the family's belongings to a village market to trade for food.

The teacher has students write responses to the following questions. Then the teacher instructs them to discuss their responses in small groups, or reads selected student responses without revealing who wrote them and without comment.

1. If exiled to a labor camp, what five personal belongings (other than clothes) would you take with you?
2. Which would you be willing to trade for food as Esther did?
3. After being on a restricted diet for several weeks like Esther was, what are two or three kinds of food you would trade your belongings for?
4. Is it right for a whole family to be sent to a labor camp when only the father was "guilty"? Why or why not?

Schell (1980)

mental health what vitamin supplements are to diet: great when you need them and harmless otherwise. The value of the following little homilies and proverbs to mental hygiene is obvious:

> Friendship is like a bank account. You can't continue to draw on it without making deposits.

The value of courage, persistence, and perseverance has rarely been illustrated more convincingly than in the life story of this man (his age appears in the column on the right):

Failed in business	22
Ran for Legislature — defeated	23
Again failed in business	24
Elected to Legislature	25
Sweetheart died	26
Had a nervous breakdown	27
Defeated for Speaker	29
Defeated for Elector	31
Defeated for Congress	34
Elected to Congress	37
Defeated for Congress	39
Defeated for Senate	46
Defeated for Vice President	47
Defeated for Senate	49
Elected President of the United States	51

That's the record of Abraham Lincoln.

Occasional failure is the price of improvement.

You may be disappointed if you fail, but you are doomed if you don't try.

(Beverly Sills)

Good sources for such homilies are Unity Village (Colbern Road, Lees Summit, MO 64063) and *Bits and Pieces* (a tiny monthly magazine from The Economics Press, Inc., Dept. BBS; 12 Daniel Road; Fairfield, NJ 07004).

Bibliotherapy and Dialogue Journals

Bibliotherapy requires a teacher who loves to read, knows books, and knows kids. It is a means of emotionally and intellectually "empowering" students to deal with personal-social adjustment dilemmas of a variety of types. The simple act of matching a student with a book or selection that deals with the situation he or she is facing can trigger three processes: empathy, catharsis, and insight. *Empathy* is the act of associating some real or fictional character in literature with oneself. *Catharsis* occurs when the reader observes the empathetic character working through a problem to a successful release of emotional tension. Through empathy and catharsis, comes further *insight:* the sense of self-discovery that comes with recognizing aspects of oneself and one's situation in a written tale. This alone often lends a sense of dignity to one's woes. Literary critics refer to this as the difference between a tragedy — the failing of great people, and pathos — the problems of the weak and pathetic.

Whenever possible, the teacher, librarian, or specialist who recommends a book to a student should invite the student to retell the story, highlighting incidents and feelings that are relevant to the central situation. Changes in behavior, feelings, and relationships should be looked at closely to permit vivid identification and empathy with the characters. Most important, the reader should have an opportunity to form a conclusion about the consequences of certain behaviors or feelings to determine whether or not these behaviors or feelings improve human relationships and happiness (Heaton & Lewis, 1955).

Bibliotherapy may be used in one of two ways. First, it can be used to help a student solve an *existing* emotional problem or anxiety by recommending a book that recounts an experience or situation similar to the student's own. By recognizing the problem and its solution in literature, the student may gain new insights about his or her own problem and then can take steps to solve it. Second, bibliotherapy may be used for *preventive* assistance. A student who has experienced a situation through literature may be better able to deal with similar situations encountered in real life. This technique can be compared to the process of inoculation against contagious diseases. Use of an instrument such as the Luscher Color Test (Luscher, 1969) or the Manzo Bestiary Inventory (Manzo, 1975b) can help students and teacher to better know kids, and thus more accurately pinpoint the kinds of problems they could be encountering.

Bibliotherapy can be enhanced by the addition of a writing component. The easiest way to do this is to have students keep personal journals in which they write brief reactions—at least one sentence—to whatever they read. These can be stored and, with the student's prior approval, the teacher may read through them and write back personal notes and thoughts. Of course, notes and dialog need not be limited to textual material; they can be extended to anything a student wishes to write. The idea of *dialogue journals* (Staton, 1980), as this process has come to be called, is as old as conversation between caring friends. Teachers who use this approach regularly report touching insights revealed and warm relationships formed with students who at first appeared apathetic, hostile, or otherwise reluctant to learn (Kirby & Liner, 1981). Barbara Bode (1989) added an even more interesting dimension to dialogue journals when she extended their use to include small children and their parents. For slight, but potentially significant, variations on journal writing, see the discussions about communicating with students through letters (Isakson, 1991) in Chapter 9 on vocabulary, spelling, and handwriting, and the use of such journals to improve writing and thinking in Chapter 13 on higher-order literacy.

Bibliotherapy and dialogue journals offer students help in adjustment and progress toward reading, language, thinking, and personal-social adjustment by:

1. Teaching students to think positively.
2. Encouraging students to talk freely to appropriate adults about their problems.
3. Helping students analyze their attitudes and modes of behavior.
4. Pointing out that there are alternative and constructive ways to solve most adjustment problems.
5. Helping students compare their problems with those of others as a means of lessening internal tension and conflicts in a society that sometimes can appear quite uncaring.

(Rongione, 1972, as cited in Edwards & Simpson, 1986)

Certain cautions should be followed in the use of bibliotherapy and dialogue journals. They must be employed carefully and sensitively since for some students it could make a bad situation worse. This can occur when:

1. A student's problem is constitutional (such as obesity) and the child would like a respite from thinking about it rather than to be more fully emersed in it.
2. The student is already receiving some form of emotional therapy, and you have not been called upon to participate and, hence, may be interfering or acting counter to the therapist's objectives.
3. You yourself are dealing with weighty emotional problems that may tend to be projected onto those of the child.

In general, bibliotherapy is best used to provide *better information* to a child striving to cope with life problems. Knowledge increases freedom and power. Teacher guides and bibliographies are available on a variety of themes that can be used in bibliotherapy and journal exchanges: divorce (Monteith, 1981), teenage problems (Halpern, 1978; Tillman, 1984), school adjustment (Jalongo & Renck, 1987). See a school librarian for other suggestions, and for collections of related fables and children's books (Spicola, Griffin, & Stephens, 1990). The school librarian often is quite skilled in matching students to relevant themes in their lives and in contemporary society—such as understanding and relating to minorities, to those who are handicapped, and to environmental issues. Occasionally, the best form of bibliotherapy is to intentionally turn a student away from himself/herself and toward the problems of others or those of the society and environment. This approach also is a form of bibliotherapy; it merely has the objective of using books to divert the student from excessive introspection and personal worry.

Finally, bibliotherapy need not be heavy-handed. It can, in fact, work together in a seamless way with uplifting and self-righting themes. Bonnie Stephens (1989), for example, offers an extensive list of children's books that provide what she calls "self-righting" literary experiences. Literature, she argues, has as its first purpose to delight, and second to teach. That is, "to help the reader grow into a healthy, strong, cheerful, contributing member of society" (p. 584). We agree with her intent, but would invert the order to justify the role of literature in the curriculum and in remedial situations.

Explicit Psychoeducational Practices

Drawing on fifty-plus years of reading and psychological research, Lance Gentile and Myrna McMillan (1984; 1987) have concluded that it is no longer acceptable to generate more studies that repeat what is known about the relationship between reading and emotions, nor, they add, is it reasonable simply to catalog children by their combined emotional and reading problems. We must, they argue, provide workable solutions.

Throughout this text, concurrent means and methods have been described that collaterally or incidentally advanced literacy objectives and features of affect and attitude. The ideas and methods presented here are more intentionally designed to foster literacy gains by using vehicles borrowed from the literature on psychology. They are not, as presented, psychological therapies, but models taken from psychology to attain educational goals and objectives that have proven resistant to conventional educational treatments. These approaches are based on two propositions that must be spoken honestly:

1. They are exceptional and, therefore, do require a good deal of additional effort and thought.
2. They should gradually be withdrawn, beginning at the earliest possible time, and replaced with more conventional or incidental approaches.

This is not to say that all of the ideas presented here are too novel for more routine use. On the contrary, they tend to tap into the everyday needs of students and can be adapted in some seamless ways even into conventional classroom practices.

Whether you actually use any of these methods is not as important as coming to understand better their availability and the theorems that underlie them. Most are based on simple human wisdom given a technological name, and "strategized" into a set of guidelines, or steps. It also should be noted that several of the methods discussed in this chapter are equally appropriate, if not essential, in treating the severe reading disabilities and higher-order thinking deficits discussed in the chapters ahead.

Relaxation Approaches

Fear and anxiety typically are spoken of in terms of their psychological impact. However, they have a physical side that can intensify their impact or, with proper training, can be used to reduce their effect. The physiological changes that take place in a state of fear or anxiety can be devastating to learning, especially where there is a history of failure.

Fear and anxiety tend to raise blood pressure, alter regular breathing, constrict the pupils of the eyes, and tighten muscles, among several other physical changes. This has the general effect of narrowing the person's focus and ability to be receptive. The simple idea underlying relaxation approaches is:

• To reduce the negative impact of this rigidity at the moment of instruction.
• To countercondition their overall reaction to whatever sets anxiety in motion.
• To teach students how to self-monitor and regulate these feelings when they begin to arise. (In this sense, relaxation approaches are little more than an extension of the concept of metacognitive training to include monitoring of internal feelings that disrupt attention and learning.)

The use of gradual tension release was well-delineated as early as 1924 by Mary C. Jones (as cited in Manzo, 1977a). It has been popularized again in contemporary times by Joseph Wolpe (1958) and Wolpe and Lazarus (1966). While it now is known by more esoteric names such as *desensitization* and *relaxation therapy*, the paradigm for doing it is familiar and natural.

We watched a seven-year-old, "Maria," intuitively create and use the approach with a four-year-old, "Sara." Realizing that Sara was terrified of Buffie, Maria's dog, and therefore would not come to play in Maria's yard, she devised and carried out this simple plan. Maria would tell Sara, while they were in the front yard, about the cute things Buffie had done in the back yard. Then, while having Sara lick an ice cream cone, she would walk her down the driveway a little farther over several days to see Buffie from a closer distance, though still from behind a picket fence. She would giggle with Sara and even hold her as they edged closer. Soon, they were petting Buffie through the fence, and very soon thereafter, entering the yard where Buffie first was tethered to a pole and later left to roam as they played.

Wolpe would refer to what Maria had done as drawing upon the principle of reciprocal inhibition, which states that "if a response antagonistic to anxiety can be made to occur in the presence of anxiety-evoking stimuli so that it is accompanied by a complete or partial suppression of the anxiety responses, the bond between these stimuli and the anxiety responses will be weakened" (Wolpe, 1958, p. 71). Maria's explanation for what she did was more empathetically stated, "I wanted to show Sara that Buffie wouldn't hurt her, and that Buffie was fun to play with."

Relaxation approaches tend to be equally useful in reducing stress reactions that lead to avoidance ("flight"), or to aggression ("fight"). Should you wish to distinguish whether "flight" or "fight" is the predominating condition, you can use Gentile and McMillan's Stress Reaction Scale for Reading (see Figure 11.4) alone or along with the instruments recommended in the chapter on diagnosing disruption.

Explicit relaxation training generally begins with practice in achieving complete physical relaxation, so that the individual is able to relax at will each of his major muscle groups. Next, the leader helps the student identify situations that cause anxiety, and constructs an anxiety hierarchy, beginning with the most terrifying condition and ending with a condition that produces no fear. Therapy then consists of combining the relaxed state with imaginary progression up the hierarchy, from the least anxiety-producing situation to the most. The client remains at each level until that situation can be imagined without anxiety as a reaction. The final payoff occurs when the event itself can be experienced without fear. A relaxation training script for children is provided in Figure 11.5.

As far as treatment is concerned, an advanced degree student gives an account, in Figure 11.6, of how she combined the relaxation (desensitization) program above with an attention-improving, or counterconditioning, program—a topic discussed more fully ahead.

David Wark, of the University of Minnesota, has developed a widely used audiotape that excellently presents the steps for relaxation. He also conducted a study that demonstrates the efficacy of this technique with high-test-anxiety college students. He had students visualize a TV set that showed the progression of events in a test situation. Any event that evoked anxiety was "turned off" and then re-viewed until it was no longer anxiety producing. Eventually, the

FIGURE 11.4

Stress Reaction Scale for Reading

For each of the following phrases, circle the letter, **a** or **b**, that most accurately describes the student's reactions when asked to read or during reading. If *neither one* applies, write *N/O* on the blank to the right of each pair.

When asked to read during reading, this student:

1. a. exhibits hostility or rage.
   b. becomes anxious or apprehensive.   _____

2. a. becomes sullen or exhibits aggressive acting out behavior.
   b. appears indifferent, insecure, or fearful.   _____

3. a. responds impulsively to requests or questions, blurts out answers, and
      offers information that is irrelevant or inaccurate.
   b. appears subdued, overly withdrawn, and depressed.   _____

4. a. throws temper tantrums, cries, or becomes verbally abusive.
   b. seeks an escape or runs and hides.   _____

5. a. clenches fists, becomes rigid, defiant, and angry.
   b. appears despondent, passive, and unable to concentrate.   _____

6. a. becomes defensive and resistive, verbalizes or expresses an attiude of
      "I don't want to."
   b. lacks confidence, appears timid, verbalizes or expresses an attitude of
      "I can't, it's too hard."   _____

7. a. demands entertaining, easy, or expedient activities; shows no tolerance
      for difficulty or challenge.
   b. takes no risks in challenging situations; constantly answers, "I don't
      know," even when answers are obvious.   _____

8. a. refuses to comply, does not follow directions or complete assignments.
   b. appears embarrassed, daydreams, or frets over lack of ability.   _____

9. a. becomes upset with change in routine, manipulates the situation to
      satisfy personal needs or whims.
   b. requires constant assurance, frequently checks with teacher by asking,
      "Did I get that right?" or "Was that good?"   _____

10. a. seeks to disrupt the teacher, the lesson, or other students.
    b. expresses fear of rejection by parents, teachers, or peers for reading
       weaknesses.   _____

11. a. uses any excuse for not being able to participate; temporizes until parent
       or teacher gives up.
    b. skips over material, ignores punctuation, inserts or deletes words or
       phrases, unable to follow structure or order.   _____

12. a. demands constant supervision, attention, or guidance; refuses to do
       any independent reading.
    b. will try as long as parent or teacher closely monitors situation, appears
       helpless when left to work independently.   _____

13. a. provides sarcastic, bizarre, or nonsensical answers to teachers' questions,
       makes weird sounds, sings, or bursts into loud, raucous laughter.
    b. becomes excessively self-critical, says things like, "I'm dumb," "I never
       get anything right," or "I'm not a good reader."   _____

FIGURE 11.4

Stress Reaction Scale for Reading *(continued)*

14. a. declares reading is "boring," "no fun," "hard work," refuses to cooperate.
    b. tries too hard, is immobilized by perceived failure.   _____
15. a. makes little or no effort to succeed, shows disdain for activities, voices
       anger or displeasure at parents, teachers, and students who offer assistance.
    b. verbalizes or expresses an attitude of apathy, shows no willingness to try. _____

Interpretation

To determine *fight* reactions, count the number of "a's" circled. For the flight reactions, count the number of "b's." Typically, one pattern will dominate. It is not unusual for a student to have some "a's" and some "b's" circled or to have some *N/O*'s recorded. Even if one reaction is not dominant, the information still can be used to help design individualized intervention.

Gentile and McMillan (1987)

students were able to view, without fear, the situation itself (personal communication from David Wark).

Positive Suggestion

Several researchers have shown that hypnosis can be a very effective tool in treating some cases of reading and learning disabilities (Fillmer, Nist, & Scott, 1983; Fillmer & Parkay, 1985; Oldridge, 1982). "Buff" Oldridge (1982), for example, reported that through hypnotic suggestion he was able to convince a twelve-year-old student to stop reversing *d* and *b*, although five years of previous efforts to correct the problem by conventional training had failed. Other studies have reported equally impressive success in increasing speed of reading (McCord, 1962) and even reading comprehension (Mutke, 1967).

Aware both of the potential value of hypnosis, but also of its apparent exotic nature and misunderstood premises, Oldridge tried to devise a roughly comparable method that could be used in school-like situations. He did so with marginal success.

In a comparison study with remedial level youngsters receiving either conventional reading, regular hypnosis, or nonhypnotic suggestion, there were no statistically significant differences in outcomes. However, there was a clear trend in favor of the hypnotic and nonhypnotic groups who scored higher on four of five of the variables measured. Clearly, more research is needed before these methods can be endorsed for whole-scale use. The Oldridge study contained one serious flaw from the point of view of the field of remedial reading: There was no attempt to determine diagnostically who might best benefit from the treatments offered. The notion, however, seems an appropriate area for discussion and further field evaluation by professional practitioners, and certainly for further empirical investigation.

FIGURE 11.5

Relaxation Scripts for Children

Hands and Arms

Pretend you have a whole lemon in your left hand. Now squeeze it hard. Try to squeeze all the juice out. Feel the tightness in your hand and arm as you squeeze. Now drop the lemon. Notice how your muscles feel when they are relaxed. Take another lemon and squeeze it. Try to squeeze this one harder than you did the first one. That's right. Real hard. Now drop your lemon and relax. See how much better your hand and arm feel when they are relaxed. Once again, take a lemon in your left hand and squeeze all the juice out. Don't leave a single drop. Squeeze hard. Good. Now relax and let the lemon fall from your hand. [Repeat the process for the right hand and arm.]

Arms and Shoulders

Pretend you are a furry, lazy cat. You want to stretch. Stretch your arms out in front of you. Raise them up high over your head. Way back. Feel the pull in your shoulders. Stretch higher. Now just let your arms drop back to your side. Okay, cats, let's stretch again. Stretch your arms out in front of you. Raise them over your head. Pull them back, way back. Pull hard. Now let them drop quickly. Good. Notice how your shoulders feel more relaxed. This time, let's have a great big stretch. Try to touch the ceiling. Stretch your arms way out in front of you. Raise them way up high over your head. Push them way, way back. Notice the tension and pull in your arms and shoulders. Hold tight, now. Great. Let them drop very quickly and feel how good it is to be relaxed. It feels good and warm and lazy.

Shoulder and Neck

Now pretend you are a turtle. You're sitting out on a rock by a nice, peaceful pond, just relaxing in the warm sun. It feels nice and warm and safe here. Oh-oh! You sense danger. Pull your head into your house. Try to pull your shoulders up to your ears and push your head down into your shoulders. Hold in tight. It isn't easy to be a turtle in a shell. The danger is past now. You can come out into the warm sunshine. Watch out now! More danger. Hurry, pull your head back into your house and hold it tight. You have to be closed in tight to protect yourself. Okay, you can relax now. Bring your head out and let your shoulders relax. Notice how much better it feels to be relaxed than to be all tight. One more time, now. Danger! Pull your head in. Push your shoulders way up to your ears and hold tight. Don't let even a tiny piece of your head show outside your shell. Hold it. Feel the tension in your neck and shoulders. Okay. You can come out now. It's safe again. Relax and feel comfortable in your safety. There's no more danger. Nothing to worry about. Nothing to be afraid of. You feel good.

Jaw

You have a giant piece of jawbreaker bubble gum in your mouth. It's very hard to chew. Bite down on it. Hard! Let your neck muscles help you. Now relax. Just let your jaw hang loose. Notice how good it feels just to let your jaw drop. Okay, let's tackle that jawbreaker again now. Bite down. Hard! Try to squeeze it out between your teeth. That's good. You're really tearing that gum up. Now relax again. Just let your jaw drop off your face. It feels so good just to let go and not have to fight that bubble gum. Okay, one more time. We're really going to tear it up this time. Bite down. Hard as you can. Harder. Oh, you're really working hard. Good. Now relax. Try to relax your whole body. You've beaten the bubble gum. Let yourself go as loose as you can.

Face and Nose

Here comes a pesky old fly. He has landed on your nose. Try to get him off without using your hands. That's right, wrinkle up your nose. Make as many wrinkles in your nose as you can. Scrunch your nose up real hard. Good. You've chased him away. Now you can relax your nose. Oops, here he comes back again. Right back in the middle of your nose. Wrinkle up your nose again. Shoo him off.

FIGURE 11.5

Relaxation Scripts for Children *(continued)*

Wrinkle it up hard. Hold it just as tight as you can. Okay, he flew away. You can relax your face. Notice that when you scrunch up your nose your cheeks and mouth and forehead and eyes all help you, and they get tight, too. So when you relax your nose, your whole face relaxes too, and that feels good. Uh-oh! That old fly has come back, but this time he's on your forehead. Makes lots of wrinkles. Try to catch him between all those wrinkles. Hold it tight now. Okay, you can let go. He's gone for good. Now you can just relax. Let your face go smooth, no wrinkles anywhere. Your face feels nice and smooth and relaxed.

Stomach

Hey! Here comes a cute baby elephant. But he's not watching where he's going. He doesn't see you lying there in the grass, and he's about to step on your stomach. Don't move. You don't have time to get out of the way. Just get ready for him. Make your stomach very hard. Tighten up your stomach muscles real tight. Hold it. It looks like he is going the other way. You can relax now. Let your stomach go soft. Let it be as relaxed as you can. That feels so much better. Oops, he's coming this way again. Get ready. Tighten up your stomach. Real hard. If he steps on you when your stomach is hard, it won't hurt. Make your stomach into a rock. Okay, he's moving away again. You can relax now. Kind of settle down, get comfortable, and relax. Notice the difference between a tight stomach and a relaxed one. That's how we want it to feel—nice and loose and relaxed. You won't believe this, but this time he's really coming your way and no turning around. He's headed straight for you. Tighten up. Tighten hard. Here he comes. This is really it. You've got to hold on tight. He's stepping on you. He's stepped over you. Now he's gone for good. You can relax completely. You're safe. Everything is okay, and you can feel nice and relaxed.

This time imagine that you want to squeeze through a narrow fence and the boards have splinters on them. You'll have to make yourself very skinny if you're going to make it through. Suck your stomach in. Try to squeeze it up or against your backbone. Try to be as skinny as you can. You've got to get through. Now relax. You don't have to be skinny now. Just relax and feel your stomach being warm and loose. Okay, let's try to get through that fence now. Squeeze up your stomach. Make it touch your backbone. Get it real small and tight. Get as skinny as you can. Hold tight now. You've got to squeeze through. You got through that skinny little fence and no splinters. You can relax now. Settle back and let your stomach come back out where it belongs. You can feel really good now. You've done fine.

Legs and Feet

Now pretend that you are standing barefoot in a big, fat mud puddle. Squish your toes down deep into the mud. Try to get your feet down to the bottom of the mud puddle. You'll probably need your legs to help you push. Push down, spread your toes apart, and feel the mud squish up between your toes. Now step out of the mud puddle. Relax your feet. Let your toes go loose and feel how nice that is. It feels good to be relaxed. Back into the mud puddle. Squish your toes down. Let your leg muscles help push your feet down. Push your feet. Hard. Try to squeeze that mud puddle dry. Okay. Come back out now. Relax your feet, relax your legs, relax your toes. It feels so good to be relaxed. No tension anywhere. You feel kind of warm and tingly.

Koeppen (1974)

FIGURE 11.6

Professional-in-Training's Report of Use of Relaxation Attention Exercises

The exercise period took 16 to 18 minutes of a 50-minute reading period. The boys seemed to look forward to the activity, often asking as they entered the room, "Are we going to get to do our exercises today?" As the days progressed, the boys were able to complete as much work in the time left after exercises as they were able to accomplish in the full 50 minutes before we started them. I felt that they were more settled and ready for work than they had been previously. I observed less inappropriate, " aimless" behavior as the exercise period lengthened.

In the beginning, I questioned the value of the attention exercises and substituted a physical activity instead for days 4 through 8. I went back to the attention exercises on day 9, however, and continued them through the 38th day. The boys have learned the principles related to the attention exercises, and perhaps these have contributed as much to the change in behavior as the relaxation exercises.

Jackie Humpert, course project, Education 650, UMKC, 1977

Hypnosis (employed by a trained professional) is recommended as a primary treatment for the psychological condition known as Conversion Reaction Syndrome. It has been hypothesized that this syndrome is one source of dyslexia (Manzo, 1977a). Based on this hypothesis, Manzo successfully used a nonhypnotic form of suggestion to treat two dyslexic students. Nonhypnotic, in this context, means persuasive points made at a responsive moment. Treatment of this form of psychologically induced dyslexia is discussed in further detail in the next chapter.

Following are some tips on the use of nonhypnotic suggestion, taken largely from Oldridge.

1. Suggestions must be based on facts. It is most effective if the student is aware that the facts come from tests he or she has taken.
2. Suggestions based on facts are most effective when made by an authority figure. The higher the authority, the more effective the suggestion.
3. Suggestions must be made in a direct, no-nonsense manner.
4. Suggestions should be directed toward expanding the positive, not toward eliminating the negative.
5. Those making the suggestions must be absolutely consistent in their behavioral support of their suggestions. Contradictory behavior makes future suggestions less effective.
6. Suggestions should be directed toward improving the student's self-concept. The effect will spill over into the learning area. A child behaves according to the way he believes himself to be perceived by the important people in his life.
7. Suggestions are usually most effective for both individuals and groups when they are made during times of physical relaxation. (Oldridge, 1982, p. 285)

The next method combines aspects of proprioceptive training with nonhypnotic suggestion and a very novel notion called *implosive therapy*, which deserves a parenthetical account of its own.

Implosive Therapy

Implosive therapy (Stampfl & Lewis, 1965) is based on the proposition that one way to overcome fears and anxieties is to be confronted with them in a dramatic way, and to discover that one's worst fears usually are wildly overblown. Ironically, the term *implosive* comes from phonics: the abrupt cutting-off of the breath stream in producing consonants such as *p, t,* and *k.*

There was a full-scale reading program based on this approach, although the founder, S. Willard Footlik, didn't acknowledge it in these terms. The program, operated by Chicago's Reading Research Foundation, won a good deal of national attention for a while that included an account in *Time* magazine (November 3, 1967, pp. 57-58). Many people were impressed with the effectiveness of some of its shock techniques, which attempted to jar failing youngsters into accepting greater responsibility for their inability to achieve. However, this notion also seemed to flounder, not because it was cruel or irascible—from personal observation we can assure you that it was not—but due to the indiscriminate use of the method without differential diagnosis. With this background, see if the next clinical practice does not seem to use some of this same "hard line" approach, though in balance with certain other notions (such as building self-efficacy, and with a proper period of differential diagnosis).

Consider now the next method, which is akin to implosive therapy, though more empowering. It grew out of a personal clinical experience that caused the author to put aside standard teaching practices in an effort to reach a child who had given up on himself.

Antithetical Role Play

Antithetical Role Play is a clinical device developed by Manzo (1977) in much the same intuitive way that led Maria to be able to help Sara overcome her fear of the family dog. This time, Sara was a "David" who was said to be brain damaged, mildly retarded, and unable to read a word. After several frustrating weeks of remedial reading instruction, it was decided that the least of David's problems was the fact that he could not read. Manifesting a full array of odd behaviors, including strange, worm-like movements said to be involuntary and related to this brain damage, twelve-year-old David was a picture of distress. The treatment devised had David assume the role of a West Point cadet, his tutor that of a lieutenant-instructor, while other clinicians who were willing to play along enacted roles of military personnel. David became immersed in a military atmosphere. He marched to his tutoring room accompanied by cadence calls from the instructor. He stood inspection and suffered the type of "tough-love" verbal abuse that is typical of military shaping. All communication was directed to David in the form of commands, and all commands had to be carried out in accordance with military precision and form. Within one hour, David brought many of his "involuntary" motor movements under control and began to learn and think according to military regimen. David was prepared to accept this role by a combination of open discussion of his disheveled appearance along with expression of the fact that he looked mightily like a archetypical cadet in his basic physical features: crewcut hair, square jaw, sharp blue eyes. Before initiating the role play, David and the first author studied cadet behavior. Availability in the Media Center of an old movie on cadet life proved most useful.

Several factors combine as a possible explanation for the potency of this therapy. First, antithetical role play forces the breakup of inappropriate behaviors in the habituated, subcortical areas in which they reside, and apparently much more quickly than by traditional behavior modification. Second, since the instructor and all other clinic personnel also assumed similar roles, the student had before him several models of more appropriate behavior. Third, teaching and learning were conducted when David was in his "empowered" role. Fourth, David could try new behaviors as the "Empowered David" that would have been too far a stretch for "Disabled David" (Manzo, 1977a).

Antithetical or Empowered Role Play is similar to play therapy as outlined by Virginia Axeline in 1946, and the psychodrama therapy discussed by J.L. Moreno in 1947. However, there are critical differences. In Antithetical Role Play, the therapist does *not* use a nondirective approach. Suggestions are freely given while choosing and shaping the roles, and even after the roles are assumed. Also, the roles assumed by both therapist and child are deliberately chosen to be diametrically opposite to the child's typical patterns of behavior. This is based on the belief that we have greater awareness of our *opposite* condition than of shades in-between. This may be due to the fact that a particular behavioral pattern is often developed in reaction to an opposite possessed by a parent or sibling. (David's father was a highly disciplined scientist.) However, role playing can be just as valuable, though a bit more difficult, for youngsters who have not previously been significantly exposed to a model of their opposite, or reciprocal, state.

Talk Therapies

There are several forms of talk therapies that combine nicely with most reading and language arts activities. The most popularly known form is called Freudian psychoanalysis. Freud offered some reasonable ideas for understanding and talking about human problems. However, Freudian-type therapy has some serious drawbacks as a treatment procedure: it takes too long; it is too subjective; it requires too much probing into past events and times; and there is no way to know whether the things reported are true or part of the illusions of the person reporting them. It didn't occur to Freud until late in his career that his clients may not have been seduced by their parents, as several reported, but felt or came to believe that they had. This is a story being told again today as it is revealed that occasionally an entire group of children can come to believe that something has happened that has not.

In contrast, there is the interesting and more applicable work of William Glasser (1965) called Reality Therapy, and Ellis and Harper (1967) called Rational-Emotional Therapy. The premise of Reality Therapy is that knowledge, understanding, or insight into the past are not necessary or sufficient for effecting behavioral change. Rather, it is more important to understand the reality of the here and now, and to accept personal responsibility for one's own behavior. Glasser observes that each person must feel the love and commitment of at least one other human being and return that love. In this way, that person is able to feel his/her own worth as he functions in the world. The reading and LD specialist can assist the student in an incidental way in identifying these significant others and moving toward them.

A game where students list how they see themselves and how they think others see them, with the addition of the reading teacher's perceptions, can be done with a dialogue journal, for example. As the students and teacher compare and contrast their lists, a clearer sense of "reality" begins to emerge for the student. Consider also the IntraAct Procedure (Hoffman, 1977) and Schell's (1980) valuing activities, both described earlier in this chapter, as ways to promote similar insights incidentally.

Glasser's work received an extraordinary amount of publicity for use in the schools. Many have been critical of both the publicity and his popularization of reality therapy in *Schools Without Failure*, a book with some rather simplistic solutions to complex problems. In contrast to the overblown reports of the value of Glasser's work, there has been the slower-growing and more stable development of Rational-Emotional Therapy.

Rational-Emotional Therapy, as conceived by Albert Ellis and Robert Harper (1967), also deals with the present. This procedure, however, is based on identifying the irrational beliefs and messages an individual is sending to himself/ herself that preclude success. They maintain that when a highly charged emotional consequence (C) follows a significant Activating Event (A), A may seem to, but actually does not, cause C. Instead, emotional consequences are created largely by B—the individual's Belief system. When the student verbalizes such thoughts, the language used can be examined and can then become the tool for modifying irrational perceptions.

There are several activities adaptable to this approach, any of which a reading or LD specialist could use. One variation that has proven effective is combining rational-emotional therapy with language experience stories. A student may be given a carefully selected picture as a stimulus or be asked to recall a specific situation. Students' responses reveal the sentences that they are subconsciously saying to themselves, which both reflect and determine feelings. Once the irrational messages are identified, various means can be used to defuse their power and employ students' rational thought processes for their elimination. This procedure is very likely at the heart of human interest in literature. Few would argue that we have learned as much about human feelings and foibles from the artist who introspectively searches for himself/herself through literary expression than by even the most sophisticated of psychological studies. This principle underlies the Subjective Approach to Vocabulary (described in Chapter 9).

Should you wish to build your psychological-mindedness further, you may wish to examine this last section. It offers a primer on maladjustment problems in children, and a minicourse in much of the Freudian concepts that have become part of everyday language.

Primer on Maladjustment in Children

Boxes 11.1 and 11.2 provide a handy primer on maladjustment in children. Box 11.1 describes Defense Mechanisms of the Ego. These constitute the most fre-

---

BOX 11.1

Defense Mechanisms of the Ego

1. **SUBLIMATION:** A socially unacceptable form of gratification of an instinctive drive is given up for a somewhat more socially accepted type of satisfaction. Also called *rechannelization.*
   Example: Thumb-sucking finds substitution in placing other objects such as pencils in the mouth, smoking, or some other form of oral satisfaction like excessive talking.
2. **DENIAL:** Refusal to acknowledge disturbing facts.
   Example: Never "knowing" what one's grades are.
3. **REPRESSION:** Purposeful but subconscious denial of inner impulses or external realities that pose possible punishments or temptations.
   Example: Denial of inner drives and interests, such as of sexual awakenings and the conflicts and anxieties that often accompany these.
4. **REACTION-FORMATION:** Unconsciously repressed feelings and wishes are converted into a more socially acceptable form.
   Example: Lack of willingness to think about something personally troublesome is converted into socially acceptable means of avoiding thinking. This might take the form of excessive reading or even the inability to read, as in dyslexic syndrome. (Both conditions are elaborated upon in chapters ahead.)
5. **PROJECTION:** Avoiding blame or responsibility by attributing unacceptable motives, feelings, or attitudes to someone or something else.
   Example: Accusing an envied classmate of acting envious of you or others.
6. **RATIONALIZATION:** An over-intellectualized explanation for actions or behaviors that are not acceptable to ourselves or others.

quent maladaptive means employed to protect an ego that feels under assault from any of the several challenges that face us, whether it be pressure to read when we can not, or fear that we have done something socially unacceptable or have a hidden desire to do so. These behaviors often have a subtly distorting effect on comprehension, writing, effective thinking, sensible classroom participation, and overall personal-social adjustment. Box 11.2 describes more serious types of of maladjustments that may be observed in children and that are also frequently found to correlate with literacy disorders. See especially the section on Reaction-Formation (#4 in Box 11.1), since it is developed further in the next chapter.

In general, the earmarks of maladjustment are not whether someone ever or occasionally does things such as are described, but whether these actions become excessive and frequent, that is, part of one's characteristic way of coping and behaving.

BOX 11.1

Defense Mechanisms of the Ego (continued)

Example: A student maintains that there is no sense in studying and trying, since school is a racist/impractical/boring place.

7. **DISPLACEMENT:** A transfer of feelings from one person or situation to another. *Example*: A child who misdirects excessive feelings of love or hate for a parent onto a teacher or other authority figure.

8. **COMPENSATION:** Seeking gratifications that can not be achieved in one phase of life in another phase. *Example*: A child who spends an excessive amount of energy and time on sports to make up for shortcomings in school, or one who buries himself/herself in schoolwork to compensate for a failed social life.

9. **REGRESSION:** Tendency to fall back on earlier, usually more infantile modes of behavior. *Example*: Most conduct disorders, such as tantrums, acting out, stealing, and lying fit into this category.

10. **OBSESSIVE-COMPULSIVE ACTIVITY:** An inner drive to perform certain acts, usually as a way of coping with internal and external demands and conflicts. *Example:* Perfectionistically kept notebooks, to the point of recopying them merely so they appear totally neat and orderly, while all the time feeling near hysteria inside.

*Note: Several of these behaviors, especially obsessive-compulsive activities, may have biochemical or constitutional components.

adapted from a class handout of Warren Wheelock (1990),
University of Missouri–Kansas City.

BOX 11.2

Classification of Maladjustment in Children*

1. **Primary Behavior Disorders** (chiefly made up of sublimations, displacements, compensations, and regression):
   a. Habit Disorders: feeding disorders, sucking, biting, vomiting, scratching, masturbation, enuresis (involuntary urine secretion), rocking, and head banging. Forms of autoerotic activity.
   b. Conduct Disorders: tantrums, defiance, destructiveness, cruelty, lying, stealing, and deviant sexual behavior. Various types of deviant behavior.
   c. Mild Neurotic Traits: inhibition of play and aggression; sleep disorders; night terrors; sleep walking; enuresis; excessive fear of animals, darkness, thunder, height, etc.
2. **Psychoneurotic Disorders** (chiefly made up of denials, reaction-formations, compensations, and obsessive-compulsive behaviors). The conflict is largely internalized, and the child is in conflict with himself/herself. Mild neuroses are converted into phobias: fixations and regressions; considerable anxiety marked by difficulty in functioning at capacity level; rigid and repetitive behavior; hypersensitivity; egocentricity; immaturity; varied physical complaints and fatigue; dissatisfaction and unhappiness; limited insight into one's behavior; and inability to test reality effectively.
3. **Psychosomatic Disorders** (chiefly made up of reaction-formations, and repressions). In children: colic, vomiting, constipation, diarrhea, breath holding, asthma. Any of the organ systems may be affected.
4. **Psychosis** (chiefly induced by psychological trauma or chemical imbalances). Extreme personality disorganization, defensive compensation and loss of contact with reality. Marked disturbances in memory, attention, and imagination; bizarre thought processes; extremely inappropriate affect; hallucinations. Significant repression and poor orientation.

*Note: Several of these disturbances may have biochemical or constitutional origins.

LOOKING BACK

This chapter offered practical advice on dealing with some common physical, emotional, and stylistic factors that affect reading and learning. Some of these recommendations played up the importance of overlooked problems, such as allergies, while others played *down* the importance of other factors that may be given too much attention, such as orthoptic or visual training.

The chapter attempted to serve as an invitation to consider, or reconsider, the role of affect in reading and learning. It did so by providing the information base to conceptualize such problems more clearly, and both incidental and direct means of tackling such difficult but inescapable aspects of teaching the whole child.

The greatest attention was given to those aspects of affect and reading that reading and learning disability specialists have traditionally been most responsive to: raising motivation to read, using the valuing process, informal bibliotherapy, and journal writing. Additionally, a strong advocacy was expressed for building one's capacity to engage in a natural "therapeutic dialogue" and to add an "exit interview" to the remedial process.

Explicit psychoeducational practices also were detailed for their general informational value and for those who find comfort in this area of personal interpretation. The chapter closed with a primer on the concepts and terms that often are used to describe and talk about maladjustments in children.

➤ *LOOKING AHEAD*

The next chapter addresses severe reading disorders or dyslexia. It fleshes out and gives further particulars to many of the topics dealt with in this chapter. Chapter 12 provides extensive information on neurophysiological and some specific psychological factors that have been linked to severe reading disorders. It also provides a handy catalog of traditional and "exotic" treatments that have been or are now being offered for dyslexia.

12

Remedies for Severe Reading Disorders (Dyslexia)

> *In all science, error precedes truth, and it is better it should go first than last.*
> WALPOLE

➤ *LOOK FOR IT*

This chapter provides a comprehensive treatment of severe reading disorders, or *dyslexia*. It is divided into three parts, with an appendix on related brain functions. The first part focuses on origins, definitions, and traditional treatments. The second part reports emerging neurolinguistic and psychological research and theories. The third part provides a review of popular theories and related treatments for dyslexia that one might encounter. The chapter concludes with a summary and evaluation of the more frequently cited indicators and treatments of dyslexia. You may wish to scan this summary before reading the chapter.

Part I: Treatments for Severe Reading Disability/Dyslexia

Many issues come into play in trying to understand and treat severe reading disorders (SRD). There are so many, in fact, that some obvious and manageable aspects of understanding and treating it become obscured. In an effort to disentangle some of these confounding elements, Part I of this chapter attempts to define and address SRD, or dyslexia, in relatively clear-cut terms, and to show how it can be treated by both classroom teachers and reading specialists. The most important point to keep in mind in reading this chapter is that *dyslexia is treatable* (Rosenberger, 1992).

Severe Reading Disability: Origin, Frequency, Definition

It's not the kind of thing that can be known for certain, but it appears that the word dyslexia first appeared as a means of describing severe reading disability in an article by Berlin in 1887 in a German-language journal, *Eine besondere Art der Wortblindheit (Dyslexie)*. Approximately 3% to 6% of the population are said to suffer from one form or another of this disability.

Let's take a little closer look at "nongenerative" learning and at the "naming rate" indicators, since these are rapidly becoming critical concepts in defense of use of the term *dyslexia* in educational circles.

Nongenerative Learning and Naming Rate Indicator

Dyslexic readers generally are most distinguishable from other remedial readers by a marked tendency to be nongenerative learners. That is, their learning rarely becomes self-propelled and organic, in the sense of growing and filling in gaps on its own. Generative learners know more than they have been taught over a few tutoring sessions. Facts may be forgotten, but skill and will are evident in broader applications of things taught and in statements suggesting that the student is learning incidentally outside of class. This is essential, since it is not possible to teach someone all that they will need to know in order to learn how to read the various ways the letters can be clustered into words. Accordingly, a task measuring effectiveness in handling nonwords (like *groph* or *proke*) as well as familiar words offers a good means of measuring generative learning in reading. Dyslexic children's performance on nonword tasks has *not* been found to change as a function of age, despite age-related increases in performance with familiar words (Rack & Snowling, 1992; Snowling, 1980; Olson, 1985). Findings such as these suggest that dyslexic children approach "leveling-off" in certain areas of functioning at an early age. While these findings tend to support the proposition that dyslexia is best defined as an acute form of nongenerative learning (Manzo, 1977a; 1987), arguments have persisted against the use of the term dyslexia.

One important argument against the use of the term dyslexia has been based on the alternate proposition that it is an entirely hypothetical condition with no basis in reality. In fact, until recently, several studies have been unable to show a clear difference in educational terms between dyslexics and other remedial readers (Gough & Tunmer, 1986; Seidenberg, Bruck, Fornarolo, & Backman, 1985). However, there is one behavioral task that now is showing a rather consistent difference between dyslexics and other remedial readers (Bowers, Steffy, & Tate, 1988; Denckla & Ruddell, 1974; Wolf, 1986). This task, called "naming-rate," involves the rapid recall of names of colors, numbers, or objects in pictures. One study of naming-rate has even shown this difference to hold up between dyslexics and children with attention-deficit disorder (Felton, et.al., 1987), another seemingly related type of learning disability.

The relationship between rapid and continuous naming tasks and dyslexia has stimulated a considerable amount of speculation as to the meaning and implications of these findings. For example, it has been offered as further evidence for the automaticity model of reading (LaBerge & Samuels, 1974), discussed in an earlier chapter. Further, the rapid naming of pictures, as opposed to colors or numbers, has been shown to be significantly correlated to comprehension as well as decoding performance up to fourth grade level (Wolf, 1991).

This empirically established difference between dyslexics and other remedial readers has failed to take strong hold, however, because it is difficult to use this naming task convincingly at this time; there are no normed tests available, and the task has varied greatly in format and procedure from study to study. The one instrument that has convincing norms (the controlled word-association subtest of the Multilingual Aphasia Examination, Benton & Hamsher, 1983) requires great oral fluency in naming words beginning with six different letters. Any test relying heavily on letters for the positive diagnosis of dyslexia must at least be held to be suspect of being circular in its findings. Importantly, Ronald Carver (1991) has shown that speed of letter-naming can be used more broadly as a measure of a new and potentially significant factor that he calls "cognitive speed," or rate of thinking.

Again, with respect to dyslexics, there are neuroanatomical findings to indicate that they do not have the slightly larger left brain hemisphere that is common in normal readers. Robert Rickelman and William Henk (1990b) cite several studies from the early 1980s in which it is claimed that it is possible to identify dyslexics with 80% accuracy in this way. However, these studies have been challenged on several methodological grounds. In general, most brain lateralization theories seem to have been overextended (Segalowitz, 1983). Nonetheless, there are newer findings in neuroanatomy and neurophysiology discussed ahead in this chapter that do now lend stronger support to the theory of a dyslexic state.

For now, let us conclude by saying that the term dyslexia probably *should* be preserved since it seems to represent a real condition. Further, it serves several professional purposes such as sustaining a dialogue among reading specialists, LD specialists, neuropsychologists, and neuroscientists, and it clearly (should) signal the need for continuous and intense help to the nonreading or chronically weak reading student.

One of the reasons that the terms SRD and dyslexia are used synonymously throughout this chapter is to indicate that it is a problem that is well within the jurisdiction of the remedial reading teacher. This assumes that the reading teacher is able to work with the child in a one-on-one situation as well as in small groups and can expect support from the regular classroom teacher. The teaching methods recommended in this section have tended to grow out of special attempts to treat this highly resistant form of reading difficulty. The previous chapter on remedies for deficits, disruptions, and differences offered some bold notions for empowering readers that can be combined with those presented here. You should find these combinations to be especially useful in trying to overcome stubborn cases of nongenerative learning.

A brief review of previously mentioned methods of subtyping severe reading disorders follows. This should provide a useful schema for following the match-ups that can be made between diagnostically established needs and available treatments.

Subtypes Review

Most severe problems, as indicated in an earlier chapter, are word learning problems that can be categorized as:

- dysphonetic—weak or twisted connections between letters (graphemes) and corresponding sounds (phonemes)
- dyseidetic—weak ability to recognize even familiar words
- dysphonetic-dyseidetic—the inability to do either of these two basic operations adequately

Categorizing a reader as one or the other would seem to be a fairly simple matter of observing and recording their responses to word lists and looking for a pattern of either or both types of errors. In fact, these patterns are often blurred or change from one testing situation to another. The percentage of students who remain characteristically one way or another can generally be treated much more easily than those whose profiles vary from time to time. We estimate that of those with SRD, about 60% have fairly stable profiles that can be determined by use of a conventional IRI (and word list), and by analyses such as have been suggested by Boder and Jerrico (1982), and detailed in Chapter 4. In general, all cases can be divided so that the fewest, about 10%, tend to be dyseidetic alone (Boder & Jarrico, 1982), while the remainder tend to be equally divided between the dysphonetic and dyseidetic-dysphonetic condition.

Subtypes Ahead

More recent information on subtyping, as derived from neurological testing, is found ahead in this chapter. Importantly, these findings seem to support Boder's categories strongly—those which, you will recall, were inferred by studying the spelling patterns of severely disabled readers.

Passing and Durable Practices for SRD (Dyslexia)

Much of the material covered in previous chapters provides the basis for treating most cases of severe reading disability. For example, several methods were presented for treating dyseidetic (rapid word recognition) problems in Chapter 8. Similarly, other methods were offered for treating the dysphonetic condition; namely, Glass Analysis (1976; 1978a; 1978b), Gray's Paradigm for Teaching Phonic Elements, and Lindamood's and Lindamood's (1975) and other aural approaches. Additionally, there is a summary of methods recommended by Connie Juel (1991) that provide environmental and contextual support to these essentially phonics-based programs. The methods offered in this chapter follow the same pattern, but for the fact that they typically were conceived in a clinical setting and were designed with disabled readers in mind. Some have endured while others, often containing useful elements, have failed to do so.

Passing Methods

The methods presented in most any contemporary book reflect those that have won popular support, as opposed to others that may have appeared viable for a while but, for reasons not necessarily related to their efficacy, were not sustainable. Two examples of such short-lived, though not necessarily ineffective, treatments are especially worthy of note. One, the Initial Teaching Alphabet (*i/t/a*), was an attempt by the Englishman Sir James Pitman to create a teaching alphabet with 44 symbols to match the language's 44 sounds. Research and development efforts by Harold Tanyzer and Albert Mazurkiewiez (c.f., Mazurkiewiez, 1966), among others, generally were supportive of the notion, but it simply did not take a firm hold. A second effort along this line was undertaken by three psychologists: Paul Rozin, Susan Poritsky, and Raina Sotsky (1971). They easily taught several inner-city children with severe reading disabilities to read English to grade level equivalency with material written as 30 Chinese characters. This eliminated the need to rely on phonological skill entirely. The success of the program, they acknowledged, probably stemmed from two sources: the novelty of the Chinese orthography, and the fact that Chinese characters map into speech at the level of words rather than phonemes.

In considering the implications of their findings, they stop short of recommending that all English words be taught by a whole-word or "look-say" approach. However, they felt that something like a syllabication approach might be useful for such students since syllables are pronounceable, whereas many phonemes can hardly be pronounced (Rozin, Poritsky, & Sotsky, 1971). Even this conclusion is not supportable from current research, but it is interesting to think about the potential value if all nations were to adopt the ideographic system of the Chinese as one means of permitting all educated people to be able to communicate with one another, to some degree, no matter what language they speak.

The presentation of durable practices begins with VAKT, a method that has ties deep in American lore. It developed out of efforts to teach Helen Keller, the scion of a wealthy and influential family at the turn of the 20th century, who grew up sightless, deaf, and mute.

Durable Practices

Visual-Auditory-Kinesthetic-Tactile (VAKT) Method.

The roots of this method were developed by Helen Keller and her teacher, Anne Sullivan. Sullivan taught Keller to communicate by tapping letters out on her hand. Years later, Keller was able to refine the method with the help of Grace Fernald (Fernald, 1943) into its current form.

The real benefit to dyslexic children of either VAKT, or its often abbreviated form, V-A-K, remains unsettled despite a good deal of research. Some of the reasons for the uncertainty of its value are discussed following a description of this one-on-one tutorial method.

VAKT Steps (freely adopted from Fernald, 1943)

Step 1   Ask the learner to suggest a word that he/she wishes to learn.

Step 2   The teacher then writes the word in large handwriting, speaking the word in a natural way as it is written. Use a black magic marker or grease pencil.

Step 3   The learner traces the word with his/her finger while speaking the *whole* word (not being permitted to say the individual letters of the word) and being careful to begin and end speech and writing at the same time.

Step 4   The learner does this as often as is needed, until he/she feels certain that he/she has learned it.

Step 5   The learner then visualizes it and traces it in the air with his/her finger.

Step 6   The learner turns the word card over, takes another piece of paper, and tries to write the word from memory, writing and speaking at the same time.

Step 7   The learner compares this production with the original model.

Step 8   In extraordinary cases, a tray may be filled with moist sand, and the child may be urged to trace the word in the sand.

Step 9   The words taught in this way should be reviewed daily in a short list with other words.

Through these steps, the learner processes the new word through four sensory modalities: *visual* (when the learner is shown the word, written in large letters), *auditory* (when the teacher pronounces the word, and when the learner says the word while tracing and writing it), *kinesthetic* (when the learner uses large and small muscle sets to trace the word in the air, and to write it from memory), and *tactile* (when the learner touches the word by tracing it with a finger, on a printed card or in a sand tray).

Additional notes from Fernald:

- At any point that an error is noted, the incorrect word is simply crossed out and the learner begins again at Step 3. The error may be noticed during the attempted writing of the word or during the comparing of the production and the model. In any case, it is important to maintain the unity of the word being learned. *Do not* erase or correct parts of the word, or else the word is no longer a unit. Simply draw a single line through the error and return to Step 3.

- There is little relation between the sound of the word and the sound made by the names of the letters. The auditory stimulation desired is the sound of the word as near to normal speech as possible. There is a great temptation to call off the names of the letters rather than to say the word. Watch carefully at Step 3 and Step 6 for this problem. The learner needs to say the word, not the letter names.

- Connect word study to writing, using the "normal experience story approach" (Fernald, 1943, p. 48).

Steps in the Normal Experience Story Approach

Step 1   Ask learners about their interests, and have them tell you a related experience or story. Say, "We will write a story together. If you don't know how to spell a word, we will learn it together."

Step 2   The student then begins to write the story. As each unfamiliar word appears, the teacher goes through the same procedure as outlined above.

Step 3   When the story is finished, it is typed immediately and the learner attempts to reread it from the typed copy.

Step 4   At the start of each subsequent session, the student is asked to reread the latest story.

VAKT is a powerful procedure, but it loses much of its impact when it is overdone. The "T" (tactile) step usually is only necessary with a few students who have proven to be responsive; a "VAK" approach can be used with most students by simply deleting the tracing steps. This modified version can be used in group settings when students are learning the same words. The teacher also should watch for signs that students are ready to go "V-A," deleting the "K" (kinesthetic) step as well, for some words.

It is recommended that systematic phonics and structural analysis be taught as soon as reading skill begins to emerge (Cooper, 1947; 1964). Most clinicians have found no additional benefit in the tactile step, the place from which it all got started, and simply use a V-A-K procedure. Edward Dwyer and Rona Flippo (1983) have offered a similarly abbreviated form for teaching spelling as well as sight words. It has the following steps:

1. Look at the word carefully.
2. Discuss the word to note its pronunciation and meaning further.
3. Close your eyes, mentally visualize the word, and write it in the air.
4. Write the word on paper without looking at it.
5. Check its spelling, and write it again from memory.
6. Write the word in a sentence.

Sources of Confusion. There are at least three main reasons for confusion regarding the value of VAKT:

- Most studies fail to differentiate diagnostically the type of dyslexic condition being treated. Therefore, it is difficult to determine if the approach may cause sensory overload for some students, while providing appropriate sensory stimulation for others.
- The procedure often is employed as a technique, or part of some other methodology, further confounding study outcomes. (It is, for example, part of two popular methods known as the Orton-Gillingham and Slingerland Approaches.)
- The procedure rarely is used in the comprehensive context that Fernald and Keller intended. The language experience, or whole-language, component often is missing from research evaluations of the method.

Of these, the failure to differentiate student need diagnostically seems to be the most troublesome problem. It has led, for example, to contradictory findings such as those reported by Bryant (1979) and Hulme (1981a, b). Susan Bryant found no differences between VAK and VAKT on reading or spelling, whereas

Charles Hulme found that the tracing step significantly benefits disabled—but not normal—readers. It will take some very careful research to determine where this strategy works best. Our own guess on this issue draws on the neurolinguistic model discussed more fully ahead. In brief, however, we believe that VAKT fails to achieve its intended goals in those cases where the spleenum (anterior portion of the corpus callosum) is implicated—damage to this bundle of nerves that is responsible for the crossover communication between the left and right hemispheres of the brain could easily add to the problem of reading where a "multisensory" approach is used.

Trial Teaching Determinant.

There is a tradition in clinical practice, that predates the Mills Word Learning Test, that makes it possible to dynamically assess which approach to teaching words is best for a given student. It is done simply by identifying a set of words and "trial teaching" the student by several methods. For each method you wish to try, compile a list of words in which half are abstract words and half are concrete words. Teach the student a different set of words by each method. Note time on task in each case. Compare learning outcomes for each method, and by the proportion of abstract and concrete words learned with each method.

If results are inconclusive, take all the words *not* learned by either method, and reteach these using still another method. Reassess learning outcomes in the same way on these more "difficult" words.

The next method also is widely known and frequently cited.

Neurological Impress Method (NIM).

The Neurological Impress Method (Heckleman, 1966, 1969) is a technique in which the teacher and student read aloud simultaneously from the same material. R.G. Heckleman, a psychologist more than an educator, hypothesized that such reading together would result in "neurological traces" being formed that would be beneficial to learning. This idea, which seemed rather exotic for its time, is regaining some stature due to the work of neurophysiologists who are reporting that physical webbings are observable in the brain in response to "optimal" levels of stimulation (Diamond, 1989). The word "optimal" here roughly translates as at one's instructional and interest level. Ironically, the idea underlying NIM has been traced back by Peter Pelosi (1982) to E.B. Huey, who called it "imitation reading" in his 1908 text.

Steps in the Neurological Impress Method:

Step 1   The teacher sits slightly behind the student.

Step 2   The teacher reads into the student's preferred ear. (This is usually the right: it has stronger connections to the left hemisphere, and does not have to cross the sometimes fragile corpus callosum—the hemisphere-connecting fibers—as does sound to the left ear. However, sound to either ear should cross the corpus callosum and give the sensation of the sound to the other ear. If it does not, this can be taken as an indication of a possible neurophysiological problem requiring a referral.)

Step 3   The teacher slides a finger under each word being read.

Step 4   The teacher first reads in a slightly louder and slightly faster voice than the student, and, with time, lower and slower, and with the student's finger setting the pace.

Step 5   The teacher does not attempt to teach word analysis skills at this time.

Step 6   The teacher attempts to provide words in advance of the student's need when it is believed that it will slow the student down, even after the shift to student control of pacing and louder oral reading.

Echo reading (Anderson, 1981), a variation on NIM, has the teacher first read segments of the material to establish cadence and comprehension. On re-reading, the student reads in a lower voice, echoing the material.

NIM was designed to improve word recognition and analysis. It seems best suited, however, to increasing fluency and automaticity in response to known words. It probably is best used with students who are dyseidetic rather than dysphonetic dyslexics. It can be used somewhat profitably with the dysphonetics, as well, though merely as a means of keeping a youngster who otherwise would not be reading at all immersed in print. William Henk (1983) makes essentially this point when he suggests that it be used to replace the guided silent reading portion of the directed reading activity, or by inference, any method requiring silent reading.

Although the NIM has much to recommend it as a clinical practice, the evidence supporting it is somewhat equivocal (Bos, 1982; Kann, 1983). Following are some helpful hints for detecting problems that may diminish the usefulness of NIM. Chief among these are:

- The teacher tends to go too fast or too slow.
- The story is too long, and therefore so is the activity.
- The story language is too difficult.
- The pupil attends more to the teachers voice than the print (Kemp, 1987).

See the Paired Reading techniques suggested by Samuels (1979), Koskinen and Blum (1986), and Topping (1987, 1989) in the chapter on decoding for classroom based strategies to support the NIM. As previously noted, repeated reading programs offer the greatest benefit to students with decoding problems (Carver & Hoffman, 1981).

McNinch's Intensive Sight Word Routine.

George McNinch (1981) drew from several different sources to assemble a procedure that classroom teachers could use more easily than the Fernald Technique to teach sight words to severely disabled readers. This intensive routine for teaching sight words relies heavily on direct instruction, demonstration, frequent responding, and a brisk pace. It should be part of any program to treat dyseidetic-dyslexia.

Steps in the Intensive Sight Word Routine

Step 1   The teacher selects a word of particular value or interest to the student and introduces it (as Gray's paradigm would suggest) as an aural unit in a simple oral context.

Step 2   The teacher presents the word in a textual context with other known sight words. The new word then is read and highlighted or underlined when read in context.

Step 3   The new word is lifted out of context and students are asked to note its distinguishing characteristics (what the first letter is, how many letters are in it, if there are any blends or other letter combinations that they recognize, what other words it might look like, and how it is different).

Step 4   The word is read again in a novel sentence containing no other unknown words. (This is also a good time to have them try to write and spell the word until they can do so correctly several consecutive times.)

Step 5   Provide additional contextual practices in other materials. (Since it is difficult to find such materials, where all other words are known, it is reasonable to use NIM up to the new word.)

Step 6   Further practice should be provided in the form of word games such as "hangman."

Whole language advocate Constance Weaver (1988) holds that steps such as these should be conducted as brief pauses in a larger context of interesting story reading. Her notion is that when reading is driven by meaning, and multiple exposures to words in silent reading, that even dyslexia can be prevented, and reduced "to a mere one percent of the school-age population" (Weaver, 1988, p. 407). Of course, even this low estimate still would leave approximately 500,000 children in need of some form of intensive instruction.

An Organizational Paradigm for Treating Dyslexia and Severe Learning Disabilities

Teaching a dyslexic child to read has been likened to trying to teach someone to hit a ball by trying to throw the ball at the bat. With so many possible causes and remedies to consider, the treatment of dyslexia can appear to be an overwhelming problem. This section is offered as a means of helping you parcel out and relate many of these points to one another and into a manageable remedial package. Several elements of the package ought to appear quite familiar from discussions in previous chapters.

1. Do some of what the student can do (60%) and some of what they can't do (40%). Alter the proportions to keep motivation high.
2. Try something *different* from what the student has previously experienced. The mere fact that instructional tack is different usually produces some initial

placebo effects that can build the student's motivation and self-esteem. It also should increase the probability of hitting upon a particular learning or cognitive style need that had not been considered or had been underutilized with the student. Examples of such include: antithetical (or empowered) role play; Lindamood or some other aural-auditory approach; an alternate orthography (see McKee's contrived "letter" system in the next chapter, or the Initial Teaching Alphabet); Creative Reading-Thinking Activities (described in the last chapter).

3. Teach something tangible that can be mastered and self-charted. This should tap into the benefits noted by psychologists in behavioral engineering studies, and by more contemporary theorists who have identified the importance of self-efficacy—or *real* power and worth—to *feelings* of power and worth. Examples of this include: teaching a list of "difficult" vocabulary words ("difficult" in the sense of unusual, but with high graphemic-phonemic correspondence); teaching a list of "odd" and interesting facts; teaching students to use memory devices to learn and recall interesting facts. Memory, as you will see in the next chapter, is easy to improve.

4. Carefully and repeatedly explain how 1, 2 and 3 will combine to bring about greater and more enduring power and effectiveness. This taps into the potentialities in nonhypnotic suggestion, and further strengthens self-healing, or placebo effect. This might begin with either relaxation exercises or a sharp confrontation, the implosive approach.

5. Give special attention to training in higher-literacy operations. This is to uplift the mind, reassert belief in the worth of the student as a thinking and feeling person, and inculcate the critical and creative mental attitude that makes one wish to read, write, and think effectively. Examples of this include answering evaluative questions; being asked to write reactions, as opposed to mere summary pieces; and, again, memory training and critical reading-thinking activities (see the next chapter for details).

6. Provide incidental and, where possible, direct assistance with approachable aspects of personal-social adjustment. This tends to reduce disruptive thinking patterns, raises hope and increases available mental and emotional energy for dealing with one's reading and learning needs. Examples of such approaches are described in the previous chapter.

7. Provide opportunities to experience competence in the area of their greatest weakness. This is to countercondition patterns of inappropriate behaviors with appropriate ones. Examples here might include coaching students on how to ask the kinds of questions they most need to have answered in order to benefit from regular classroom experiences (e.g., Note Cue and Enabling Questions) and, again, antithetical or empowered role play.

8. Work with the classroom teacher to avoid showing favoritism; encourage self-competition rather than peer competition; use previous performance as a gauge to success; and avoid forcing the weak reader to perform a reading task in front of an audience without adequate preparation. (Harriet Light, as cited by Ness, 1991)

Consider now, for its informational value, how investigations of dyslexia also are stimulating more sophisticated neurolinguistic models of reading and psychological insights into reading and learning disabilities. The latter includes a vivid example of why it is difficult to deny the influence of affect in reading disability, despite our collective desire to do so.

Part II: Emerging Neurolinguistic and Psychological Theories of Dyslexia and Related Learning Disabilities

Modern Neurolinguistics: Neurophysiological Dyslexia

A primer on the brain and brain functions is available in Appendix D. You may wish to refer to it as you read this section. The prevailing view today of the role of brain functions in dyslexia might best be called the "discrete zones" perspective (Luria, 1980). It is part of what is coming to be known generally as the *neurolinguistic model of reading*. Much of what is known is due to recent breakthroughs in medical technology. Where once researchers were forced to rely on autopsies, they have now moved well beyond even EEG's (electroencephalograms) on living subjects at rest. The charting of brain activity now is done in several ways:

- Computerized Tomographic (CT) scanning and Magnetic Resonance Imaging (MRI)—both forms of sound imaging that use computers to create pictures of the living brain.
- Positron Emission Tomography (PET)—a way to read brain functioning by tracking an injection of radioactive material (Xenon) in the bloodstream (not recommended for children).
- Regional Cerebral Blood Flow (rCBF)—a method that also maps blood flow by monitoring expansion and contractions of blood vessels.

This type of charting has further strengthened the discrete zones perspective. This perspective falls between two previously opposing positions.

Discrete Zones Perspective

This perspective counters the position that there is *one* discrete "reading center" in the brain, as well as the position that the entire brain is involved in the act of reading, a view that was quite popular as late as the 1950s. It says instead that there are several, though quite discrete, areas of the brain involved in the act of reading, and that each of these plays a specific role. The implication of this is that trouble in any given region can result in a variety of different types of dyslexia or, at the least, a diminished ability to engage in certain reading acts of the several anatomical components of the brain that appear to be involved in the act of reading; the largest in size are the right and left hemispheres. Then there are lobes (loaf-like portions of the brain of which there are five in each hemisphere). There are still smaller anatomical components (called sylvi—singular form, sylvius); and, finally, there are components that are mere minute etchings on the surface of the brain (called gyri—singular form, gyrus). Each marking on the cortex—the wrinkled surface of the brain—seems to have particularly intense powers. However, there is research to suggest that there also are subcortical structures (below the thinking portion of the brain) that have been implicated in cases of dyslexia. Albert Galaburda and associates (1982) for example, find such evidence for the thalamus. The thalamus is located in the diencephalon—the huge "primitive" white area under the cortex—and is responsible for most life support functions.

Information follows on neurolinguistic elements of decoding and comprehension. This information moves us much closer to a neurological model of reading, something first attempted by Holmes in 1948.

Neurolinguistic Elements of Decoding

There have been several discrete zones of the brain posited to be involved in learning to read. Those described here are part of an emerging neurolinguistic model of reading (see Figure 12.1). Various types of neurolinguistic difficulty are possible. Each component of the neurolinguistic model, shown in Figure 12.1, is detailed here as to location and function. There are relatively few specific areas to know about, and a basic knowledge of these will help you follow this line of research as it continues to unfold in future years.

Broca's Area

This is an area of the left hemisphere between the left eyebrow and the temple named for Paul Broca, who first identified its purpose in 1861. This has been called the language area of the brain. Recent research has shown that it also is a general motor-programming region that controls a variety of coordinated movements of the mouth and the entire body. It is heavily involved in oral reading, and has even been shown to "light up" computer screens attached by electrodes to the skull with evidence of use when subjects were asked even to *imagine* movements (Montgomery, 1989). This fact seems to lend further support to the potential value of kinesthetic (body motion) teaching strategies such as VAKT and imaging—both described in previous chapters. Damage to Broca's area alone might result in a more generalized form of language disability, called an *aphasia*. All language-related brain dysfunctions are called aphasias; those involving the senses are called *agnosias*. Those involving body movements (see Frank & Levinson, 1975-76, ahead) are called *praxias*. Both agnosias and praxias have been thought to be involved in dyslexia. Of the two, the agnosias seem more credible. Individuals with certain agnosias might actually be able to write their names but then not recognize them as their names. The next area discussed appears to be heavily implicated in this and related neurolinguistic functions.

Side and Top Views of Brain Areas Important for Reading and Their Interrelationships

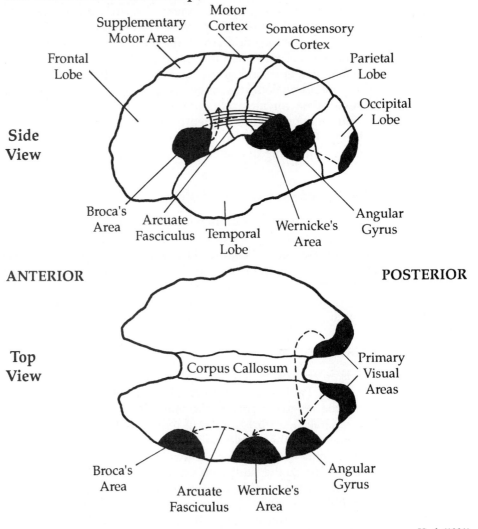

Henk (1991)

Wernicke's Area

This area of the brain also is language-related; it seems to play an important and highly specific role in recognition of meaning (Wernicke, 1874). It is especially-critical in the visual-spatial functions involved in whole word recognition. Damage to it tends to result in poor recognition of whole words, but not necessarily to phonological or sounding out skills. The next portion of the brain involved in

FIGURE 12.1

Neurolinguistic Model of Normal Decoding

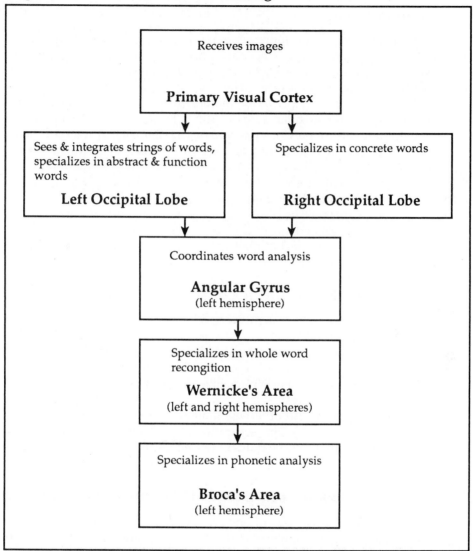

Modified from Hynd and Hynd (1984)

Note: This model does not show multiple transfers of information back and forth across the spleenum (rear portion) of the corpus callosum, a bundle of nerves that ties the cerebral hemispheres together, and held by some to be implicated in certain cases of dyslexia.

reading represents one of the smallest "cytoarchitectural," or cellular structural, areas referenced in neurolinguistic research.

Angular Gyrus

The angular gyrus, in evolutionary terms, is a very recently developed cluster of cells on the brain that is only found in humans. It has nerve connections to Wernicke's area and appears to reinforce the ability of the brain to recognize words when spoken or written. The angular gyrus is also connected to Broca's area, which is concerned with the motor function of speech, and therefore oral reading. When the angular gyrus of the left hemisphere suffers a lesion (scar tissue resulting from previous physical or viral damage), it can result in alexia— the loss of the mature ability to read due to a shut-down of transmission between Wernicke's and Broca's areas. It has been found that injury or incomplete development of the angular gyrus disrupts the ability of the brain to convert graphemes (Wernicke's job) to phonemes (Broca's job) (Geschwind, 1979). The angular gyrus also appears to have important connections to the occipital lobe discussed next (Geschwind, 1979). To that extent, the angular gyrus may be the very seat of the latent ability in humans to be able to read and record spoken language.

Left and Right Occipital Lobes

The occipital lobes are just slightly above and behind the ears and generally are responsible for visual functions. The portion on each side where words are registered, or consciously seen, is called the primary visual cortex. Slightly above it is a seemingly distinct seeing center. The left occipital sees and integrates strings of words, with a specialized ability to handle abstract words and function words ("democracy," "fear," "and,") while the right occipital lobe amplifies and backs up this process, but otherwise limits itself to dealing with concrete words ("car," "brick," "house"). This separation of functions tends to be the case in all individuals, whether they be right- or left-hemisphere dominant (Hynd & Hynd, 1984).

Corpus Callosum (not part of this neurolinguistic model)

A four-inch-long, thick body of nerves, also known as the "cerebral commisure," the corpus callosum connects and permits communication between the two hemispheres of the brain so that each may do what it does best. The posterior section, called the spleenum, handles transfers related to several aspects of reading. Lesions to the spleenum of the corpus callosum continue to be implicated in post mortems on patients with acquired dyslexia (Duane & Gray, 1991; Goldberg, Shiffman, & Bender, 1983). Ironically, many individuals who have had this connective nerve mass surgically severed eventually are able to resume most normal functions, including reading, with either one or the other sides of the brain. (This surgery sometimes is done to reduce the severity of epileptic seizures.) The popular explanation for this paradox is that each half of the brain can do all that the other can do, but that when both are available, the brain organizes itself in an optimally efficient manner using the side that is most suitable for each specific job (Segalowitz, 1983).

Neurolinguistic Elements of Dyslexic Comprehension

Recent research is revealing that there are quite specific areas of the brain that are heavily involved in meaning building, or comprehension. Among these are:

1. The right cerebellum—a lower back portion of the brain previously believed to have been exclusively involved in spatial orientation and body coordination functions.
2. The arcuate fasciculus—a cluster of areas in and around the left frontal and temporal lobes.
3. The anterior cingulate—a region in the middle of the frontal cortex (Montgomery, 1989).

The anterior cingulate (a gyrus on the front of the limbic lobe) comes closest today to being called the center of volition (will). Persons with lesions or scars from previous damage to this area can understand and talk, but seem to lose their will to do so. The movie *Awakenings* with Robin Williams and Robert DeNiro was based on several clinical accounts by Oliver Sacks of cases of individuals so damaged (Sacks, 1987). The damage became fully evident twenty years after they had survived a virus that had caused encephalitis—or cerebro-spinal fluid inflammation. These individuals seemed to have the abilities intact to do most anything but to be self-directed. They could not will themselves to do anything, but could be induced to reach out and grab at an object thrown their way, as if the object, by its motion, became a command to their neutral minds to catch it.

Most comprehension-related research to date has been based on the use of classical word-association type experiments more so than reading to comprehend complex ideas. However, in one study where a longer narrative passage was used, there was evidence of a great deal more bilateral blood flow between the right and left hemispheres of the brain during reading than had been anticipated (Hynd, Hynd, Sullivan, & Kingsbury, 1987). The right brain, which has shown relatively little activity in word recognition tasks, showed a great deal of activity in narrative reading. We suspect that this is due to two factors: 1) that the right brain is a center for emotions and beliefs, and hence that these play a significant role in comprehension; and, 2) that comprehension involves a dialectic—or interaction within itself between the left hemisphere which tends to be "pro" and rather blithe-spirited, whereas the right tends to be a little more "con" and negativistic. In possible contradiction to this, individuals who have had the two halves of the brain severed from one another in *adult* life do not seem to have their comprehension processes seriously impaired. It appears, as suggested above, that one or the other half of the brain comes to serve as the major integrator of information (usually the left), and therefore, by adult life it may contain and have shared with the right, most of the knowledge, values, and wisdom that are required to handle most comprehension tasks (Segalowitz, 1983).

Comprehension processes will be an especially intriguing area of study as researchers begin to search for evidence of what is meant by "schema activation," "metacognitive functioning," and critical and creative processing. It appears that the latter two should show a high degree of bilateral activity, with the right brain slightly more dominant in critical reading, and the left more so in creative reading and constructive problem solving. While the by-play between the two clearly appears to be essential to these aspects of higher-order literacy, the subject of the next chapter, it could be some time before anyone figures out how to activate and sustain these functions in those who are not inclined to do this kind of thinking for physiological or psychological reasons; assuming that these should prove to be different.

Neurological Dyslexia Subtypes

With so many brain elements involved in reading, there obviously are several possible causes of dyslexia. In general, reading is like a chain; it can only be as strong as its weakest link. Having said that, it is equally notable, again, that the brain is highly adaptable and that alternative substrata (as Holmes called these "neurological working systems" over forty years ago) can be mobilized to get the job done.

Previously, in Chapter 8 on decoding, we discussed the classification system offered by Boder (1972). This system has proven sound. Significant electro-physiological differences have indeed been found between dysphonetic dyslexics (great difficulty with graphemic-phonemic aspects of reading) and dyseidetic dyslexics (characterized by visual-spatial, or whole-word, blindness) (Pirozzolo, 1979; Fried, Tanguay, Boder, Doubleday, & Greensite, 1981). They also found the third subtype, dysphonetic-dyseidetics, or near total alexics, to have both significant deficits in both visual and linguistic domains.

The Boder system, however, is largely based on spelling rather than reading patterns. While the two systems may be near synonymous, the absence of certainty in this area, where slight differences can have major implications, has led others to attempt to generate a classification system based on a neurolinguistic model of reading. There are other dyslexic subtypes based on "genetics, behavior, and brain imaging " (Lubs, et.al., 1991).

Neurolinguistic Models of Surface, Phonological, and Deep Dyslexia

Three subtypes of dyslexia are described here. These are based on the combined work of several investigators (Sevush, 1983; Marshall & Newcombe, 1973, 1980; Hynd & Hynd, 1984; Hynd, Hynd, Sullivan, & Kingsbury, 1987). See Figure 12.2 ahead for a comparison of each of these subtypes with each other and with "normal" reading functioning.

Surface dyslexia

has three main characteristics:

1. A seemingly ironic ability to read nonwords more easily than meaningful words.
2. A tendency to process short words better than long words.
3. A tendency to read by well-established phonological rules. (Deloche, Andreewsky, & Desi 1982)

The surface dyslexic also, as a result of these tendencies, is likely to be unable to respond to words as wholes (poor flash-word reading; having particular difficulty with nonphonetic words); make disproportionately more visual confusion, or paralexic (word and letter confusion) errors (i.e., *hug* for *bug*); have a poor semantic (word meaning) access to what is read, and therefore also to be weak in reading comprehension, especially at higher levels of abstraction. As a result of their auditory-linguistic strength, surface dyslexics also are likely to read better orally than silently.

Surface dyslexics are likely to have damaged or inadequate development in Wernicke's area where words and meanings are associated; whereas, Broca's area (oral language) is likely to be fully functional. This same basic condition also has been called visual dyslexia (Marshall & Newcombe, 1973), visual-spatial dyslexia (Pirozzolo, 1979), and dyseidetic-dyslexia (Boder, 1971a,b).

From the information reported by Boder and Jarrico (1982) on the proportion of dyseidetic-dyslexics, it seems safe to speculate that this type of disorder has the lowest frequency of occurrence as an isolated condition free from other complications—probably less than 10% of dyslexics.

Phonological dyslexia

is the inverse of surface dyslexia. This condition is characterized by:

1. The ability to read *familiar* words well, but extreme difficulty with unfamiliar words, such as nonwords and function words.
2. Poor phonemic awareness and lack of word analysis skills beyond initial consonant sounds.
3. Poor oral reading, although comprehension of what is read appears to be fairly good.

(Marshall, 1973, Marshall & Newcombe, 1980).

Phonological dyslexics tend to rely on whole word reading to compensate for their weak phonetic skills They are comparable to Boder's dysphonetic-dyslexics, and as such can expect to have neurological impairments in Broca's oral language area, and/or to the angular gyrus that connects it to Wernicke's area where there usually is adequacy, or even strength.

Deep dyslexia

is comparable in several ways to Boder's dyseidetic-dysphonetic condition, but has been better detailed as to its neurological and behavioral traits.

The condition of deep dyslexia is characterized by George and Cynthia Hynd (1984) as:

1. An ability to read most familiar words and nouns well.
2. A tendency to make many semantic paralexic (or substitution and convolution) errors—saying *glove* for *mitten,* or seeing *mitten,* thinking *mutton,* and saying *sheep.*
3. A tendency to have particular trouble with nonwords, verbs, and abstract nouns (love, honor).

Neurologically speaking, deep dyslexics seem to take words into the primary visual cortex (the starting placing for all seeing), but the image then seems to go to the right occipital lobe, and not at all to the left (which handles more abstract words), and then to Wernicke's area, skipping again the angular gyrus where grapheme-phoneme conversion occurs. Figure 12.2 shows the paths of each type of dyslexia in terms of this neurological model. The figure is a modification and amplification of one developed by Hynd and Hynd (1984).

Very Different Minds

One reason that remedial readers are worth everyone's attention is because they often do odd things that challenge our understandings of normal functions. They represent the anomalies that challenge our rules and classification systems. Hence, it seems appropriate in a text on remediation to note some of these anomalies, or oddities that do not fit neatly into expectations. These exceptions will surely prompt intriguing hypotheses that will come to shape future research, understandings, and practices.

One such hypothesis, raised by several researchers, says that there is *not* a significant difference between phonological and deep dyslexia. Those who have claimed that there is a difference (Hynd et al., 1987) have not been able to offer such evidence with case study reports using the regional Cerebral Blood Flow (rCBF) method. Nonetheless, the search led them to discover unusual right hemisphere activity. They did not speculate as to what this might mean. However, we suspect that it suggests an elevated level of negativistic thinking that is characteristic of the right hemisphere, and arising from apprehensions about having to engage in a task that can be belittling for those who can not do it.

An equally puzzling anomaly, called *concrete word dyslexia*, has been discovered (Warrington, 1971). The patient with this very specific form of disability had difficulty recognizing concrete rather than abstract words. There also are several reports of what has been called *spelling dyslexia*. The term has nothing to do with whether the students can spell or not, but with the need to say (spell out) each letter of a word before it can be processed as a whole (as reported by Hynd & Hynd, 1984).

There are two other reading-related anomalies that stand out: hyperlexia and Williams syndrome. Each represents levels of exceptional ability in a sea of disability.

FIGURE 12.2

Neurolinguistic Model: Dyslexic Subtypes

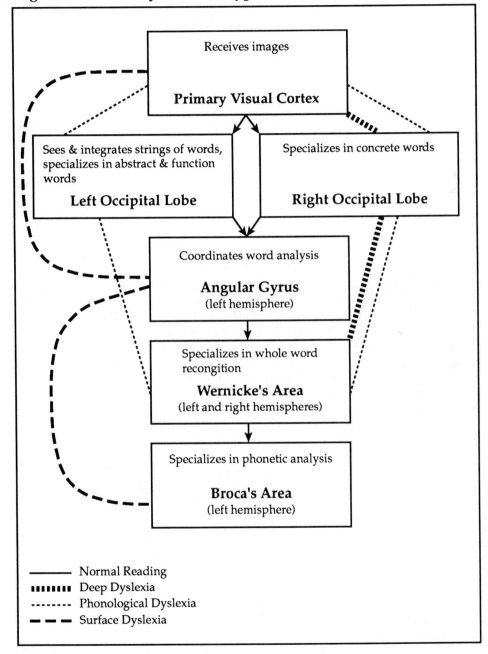

Hynd and Hynd (1984)

Hyperlexia is the name given to a rare condition wherein a child with diminished mental capacity will learn to read, in the sense of decode, at a very precocious level, but with very little comprehension. Peter and Janellen Huttenlocher (1973) report one case of a boy who had been previously diagnosed as having "infantile autism." He scored below the three-year-old level on the Peabody Picture Vocabulary Test when he was seven years old, yet he could sound out words that were upside down and backwards (even saying them backwards). He also was an excellent speller. While he greatly enjoyed this skill and wanted to read everything in sight, he could hardly follow simple oral or written directions, and in the characteristic way of autistic children was socially withdrawn, living largely within himself.

Children with *Williams Syndrome*, on the other hand, tend to be very sociable. In fact, because of the friendliness and characteristic appearance of people with this rare genetic disorder, they are sometimes called "pixie people." They have narrow faces, broad foreheads with widely spaced eyes, and narrow, pointed chins. They always seem to be smiling. Their intellectual development, however, is a maze of incongruities. They typically begin speaking at a much later age than other children, but often begin speaking in sentences rather than words and phrases. Subsequent language development tends to be accelerated, and their vocabularies are peculiarly rich. One Williams Syndrome child, when asked to name all the animals he could think of, reeled off the names of about 20 animals, including "brontosaurus, tyranadon, whale, yak, koala, and ibex" (Finn, 1991). Yet the IQ range of Williams Syndrome people tends to be between 50 and 70. They have difficulty following simple directions, and have poor motor control. Despite their extensive vocabulary and language facility, they often miss the underlying meaning of conversations. There seems to be a disconnection between these people's linguistic ability and their understanding. They comprehend parts, but not the whole; they see each tree, but not the forest. As with Down's Syndrome, another group marked by a facial similarity, Williams Syndrome also is accompanied by characteristic medical problems, particularly heart and gastrointestinal disorders (Finn, 1991).

In general, "idiot-savants," as this class of retarded yet specific-area geniuses are known, prove in dramatic fashion just how discrete certain brain functions are. They also help us understand better the many individuals who are gradients away but on the same continuum.

As promising as neurological research has been in defining and describing patterns of dyslexia, it still leaves many cases showing similar symptoms, but with no distinctive evidence of these differences apparent with current neurological mapping instruments. This fact leaves the door open for alternative explanations for some cases of dyslexia and related learning disabilities, such as the one described next.

Psychologically Induced Dyslexia

Some years ago, in a yearly seminar on dyslexia and related learning disabilities, the first author concluded that in some cases this mystifying reading disability could be a form of psychological defense known for many years in the literature of psychiatry as Hysteria Conversion, and more recently called Conversion Reaction Syndrome (CRS) (Manzo, 1977a; 1987).

Support for this proposition is drawn primarily from compelling parallels that have been found between the conversion reaction and dyslexia syndromes. A brief critique of CRS and a clinical test with two cases are presented to support and clarify further how these two conditions can sometimes be linked.

Conversion Reaction Syndrome (CRS)

CRS is said to be a subconscious process by which deep emotional conflicts or fears that otherwise would give rise to considerable anxiety are disowned or put aside by converting them into an external expression of some type. This results in a feeling of detachment, which may appear as relaxed indifference — or la belle indifference, as it sometimes is called in psychiatric literature. This condition has been found in some dyslexics and in some persons with specific neurological damage. Denckla (1972), for example, identified a sub-type of dyslexics that she called a "dyscontrol" group because they were "sweet, sloppy, and silly." Satz and Morris (1981), and Lyon and Watson (1981) also have identified subgroups of dyslexics that have related "motivational and emotional" problems. Curiously, a similar form of indifference has been found in patients with right-hemisphere damage: they seem indifferent to the point of denial of other severe symptoms of physical illness (Segalowitz, 1983, p. 215).

Similarly, the CRS condition seems to arise when a deep conflict is converted to a form that symbolically represents the repressed ideas or repressing forces, whatever these might be. Examples of some typical child-centered fears and conflicts would include:

- Fear of the parents' learning of the child's "intellectual inadequacy" relative to their expectations
- Fears related to revelations about premature sexual interests, activity, abuse, or gender confusion
- Fear that a family might break up without some crisis to hold it together

Consider now the symbolic meaning of reading. Reading symbolizes growing up and being responsible. The knowledge, insights, and universal truths it brings are supposed to help one face complex issues. But what if a child is facing an issue that appears bigger than life, one so insurmountable that it seems best to deny it? In order for denial to be complete, and for life to go on, the problem must be converted or restructured into something less intrusive and more acceptable.

Conversion tends to take either of two forms, one called *somatic*, the other *physiologic*. Somatic conversions typically result in the apparent loss of control over fundamental voluntary muscles (Laughlin, 1967). One example is the conflict experienced by the soldier who wishes to be brave and yet fears dying. Repression of his fear leads to a heightened anxiety level. Sensing that he is near hysteria, the soldier subconsciously converts the repressed desire to run away into a psychologically saving illness or incapacitation, such as loss of control of the muscles in the legs that carry one to battle.

A similar condition can occur physiologically to *involuntary* muscles and functions. In these cases, so called organ (or vegetative) difficulties occur. These tend to incapacitate or delimit sensory awareness, resulting in apparent losses or distortions of vision, hearing, speech, and the like. These incapacities sound remarkably like the word reversals, semantic paralaxis (word distortions), auditory discrimination problems, speech impediments, WISC profile irregularities, and even the "scotopic" visual problems (see ahead in the chapter), that have been found to be associated with some reading and learning disabilities. The possible connection between these two sets of conditions is made clearer when the next two ideas are considered.

Substitution and Endogain

Both somatic and physiologic conversion conditions become an alternate expression of the deeper repressed conflict or problem. This substitution can serve several useful purposes for the person who is disabled.

The student who is diagnosed as dyslexic, particularly the preteen whose life is largely influenced by parental rather than peer pressures, can win considerable attention from his parents while reducing his or her preoccupation with the true emotional conflict (whatever it might be), and do so at the relatively small inconvenience of simply not being able to read. This is known as an *endogain*. That is, a net gain arising from an apparent liability.

In the case of dyslexia, the parents also are inconvenienced and made to feel guilty. In this way, the child's problem is passed on to the parents, who not only bear the student's pain but must wonder what in them may have created the disorder—even to the point of feeling guilt about whether they have transmitted damaging genes.

Further, the child not only gains the attention of his parents but the outside assistance and empathy of teachers, doctors, and other specialists in resolving the symbolic problem. More importantly, hope of resolving the real problem is kept alive by those pressed into service to work on its symbolic representation.

In brief, a learning disability such as dyslexia can provide several possible endogains for a troubled child:

- It can sharply reduce anxiety and pressure to resolve a difficult personal problem.
- It can win the assistance and empathy of many adults.
- It offers the hope of resolving the real, or repressed, problem.

Figure 12.3 gives six diagnostic indicators of psychologically induced dyslexia or learning disability.

Clinical Evidence

Working from the premise that a reading dysfunction could be a symbolic representation for a deeper conflict, we developed a simple test of this proposi-

FIGURE 12.3

Diagnostic Indicators of CRS Dyslexia and Learning Disability

Three or more signs indicate possible Conversion Reaction Syndrome:

1. Considerable emotional gain from an apparent liability.
2. Evidence of generative learning in most areas other than reading, or whatever the specific disability might happen to be.
3. A logically inconsistent or unreliable pattern of errors on an IRI or miscue analysis.
4. A reversal of subtest scores on the WISC, or other such test, from one testing to the next (e.g., high Verbal/low Performance one time, low Performance/high Verbal another).
5. A look of relaxed, resigned indifference to the disability (la belle indifference condition).
6. Learning can be greatly accelerated with an essentially placebo treatment.

tion. We would try to teach dyslexic students to read using a system that was identical to conventional reading but the students would be told that the program was recently invented for children who had problems like theirs. They also would be told that no one could really be sure that they ever would be able to read regular print, even if they learned the alternate system.

If they could be taught to read by this system, it was reasoned, then it would not be logical to attribute their disability to a neurological impairment, but to some psychological phenomenon. Employing an alternate alphabet (Paul McKee's funny squiggles [1948] that he used to show parents how difficult it is to learn how to read), Manzo and associates attempted to teach a boy of 12 and a girl of 11 to "read" (see Figure 12.4 for a sample story). Both youngsters had been in clinic programs for several continuous semesters and tested at primer levels. They were by all indications "severe dyslexics."

Exceeding every expectation, the two children learned the new code more rapidly than their tutors, who had to work as a team to keep abreast of their rate of learning. In about 15 hours, they were reading at about third to fourth grade reading level. Time did not permit the teaching team to devise a plan for gradually substituting the alternate orthography for the conventional alphabet, nor for isolating the deeper emotional conflicts. Nevertheless, the clinical studies gave strong reason to believe that the children could be taught to read, and rather easily, once they became remotivated to do so with such "non-hypnotic" suggestion.

Raising Awareness

Obviously, there is much more to be said about Conversion Reaction Syndrome and about these two cases. But, it seems fair to say that some forms of dyslexia, and possibly other forms of learning disability, can be induced by psychologically damaging circumstances as well as by neurophysical impairments, or poor teaching.

It seems reasonable that with all that has been written on Conversion Reaction Syndrome—it has been called the most common and oldest of syn-

FIGURE 12.4

Sample Story in McKee Orthography

⊔┼◊   ┼◊⊔   ∧⊏⊗   ⊔≠Ⲙ

⊔┼◊ ⅂┼◊ ∧≠ ✕┼∨∨ ∧⊏⊗ ⊔≠Ⲙ. ∧⊏⊗

⊔≠Ⲙ ⅂┼◊ ∧≠ ⊔┼◊. ⊔┼◊ ┼◊⊔ ∧⊏⊗ ⊔≠Ⲙ

⅂┼◊ ∧≠ ∧⊏⊗ -◦┼∨∨. ⊔┼◊ ⊓⊗┼∧ ∧⊏⊗

⊔≠Ⲙ. ⊔┼◊ ┼◊⊔ ∧⊏⊗ ⊔≠Ⲙ ⅂┼◊ ∧≠ ∧⊏⊗

∨┼⅂⊗. ∧⊏⊗ ⊔≠Ⲙ ⊓⊗┼∧ ⊔┼◊ ∧≠ ∧⊏⊗

∨┼⅂⊗. ⊥⊏⊗ ✕┼◊ ⊗┼∧ ∧⊏⊗ ∧⅂⊗┼∧ △⅂≠◊

⊔┼◊'⊥ ⊏┼◊⊔. ⊔┼◊ ∨≠Ⲙ⊗⊥ ∧⊏⊗   ⊔≠Ⲙ

┼◊⊔ ⊥⊏⊗ ∨≠Ⲙ⊗⊥ ⊔┼◊.

Translated Story

Dan and the Dog

    Dan ran to call the dog. The dog ran to Dan. Dan and the dog ran to the wall. Dan beat the dog. Dan and the dog ran to the lake. The dog beat Dan to the lake. She can eat the treat from Dan's hand. Dan loves the dog and she loves Dan.

McKee (1948)

dromes—that we should be finding some proportion of reading and learning disabled students who fall into this subtype. None, however, are ever reported.

    Now let's consider some of the most frequently cited corollaries of dyslexia that may compound or complicate diagnosis and remediation, but generally should be considered as more associative than causative. Some of these conditions are the basis (probably false) for large-scale volunteer and commercial efforts. The professional educator will no doubt find it necessary and useful to refer to this catalog of dyslexia indicators and practices for quick information and reference. One or the other can be expected to raise interest in your community at some time. You surely will find some of these extremely interesting, if not mystifying.

Part III: Review of Theories and Treatments of Dyslexia

This part might also be called "Everything that has ever been said about dyslexia." These are grouped into nine categories. It was difficult to group these treatments and symptoms into categories since often a similar condition "discovered" by different researchers may be differently named by each discoverer. Sometimes, too, a novel condition is suggested with a common, and therefore misleading, label. The greatest source of difficulty, however, comes from the fact that each discovery of cause or treatment has a unique set of circumstances surrounding it, making each something of a story unto itself. Nonetheless, since the mind craves order, the "stories" are reported in the following categories:

- visual perceptual
- vision problems (eyesight)
- sensorimotor clumsiness (or dyspraxia)
- sound-related types
- laterality, or mixed dominance issues
- irregular neurological development
- evolutionary considerations
- biochemical (circuit malfunction)
- related learning disabilities and soft signs

Notwithstanding their popularity, most of these conditions tend to be "false-positives"; that is, they have not proven to be significant factors in the diagnosis or remediation of dyslexia. Graduate students in the first author's yearly Seminar on Dyslexia (1990) attempted to summarize their appraisals of the relative merit of these and most other indicators considered in this chapter on both accounts for their own study purposes. (See Figure 12.5 on pp. 414–416 for a graphic critique of their appraisals of each.) The first category, the visual-perceptive, represents one of the most frequently recurring themes in the literature on dyslexia.

Visual-Perceptual Condition and Dyslexia

The primary and longest standing beliefs regarding dyslexia are those proposed by Samuel Orton (1937). The chief notion in this package is that dyslexia is related to paralexia (word distortions), and can be most easily diagnosed in the tendency of students to make "reversals." There are several classifications of "reversals." These include rotations (b-p); mirror images (b-d); inversions (u-n), and even reversals of words in sentences ("Jim jumped over Bob" for "Bob jumped over Jim"). Despite all the study and specificity, the general impression is that this syndrome simply is *not* significant in the diagnosis or understanding of dyslexia for several reasons.

Reason 1   *Lack of consistency of error.* Simply put, why would someone see *some* things backwards and not *others*? If they see *everything* backwards, wouldn't they simply habituate to that, and cope with it as we do with the fact that the retina sees things upside down, but we don't perceive things this way?

Reason 2   *Misunderstanding.* In the earliest stages of reading, children will appear to be "seeing" a word backwards because they are relying on

FIGURE 12.5

Dyslexia: Confidence Ratings for Indicators and/or Treatments

Coding symbols:
- − − very weak
- − + weak
- + − strong
- + + very strong

INDICATORS & TREATMENTS	CONFIDENCE RATING
Nongenerative Learning (characterized by learning increments that level off and fail to become synergistic)	+ +
Performance on Timed Naming Tasks (such as naming letters, colors, numbers, and pictured objects)	+ +
Hemispheric Imbalance (characterized by a larger right than left hemisphere, or two of the same size)	− +
Neurophysiological Functions	
The "discrete zones perspective" indicates that specific parts of the brain function differently during varied reading tasks	+ +
Broca's Area—area of the left hemisphere that is heavily involved in oral reading	+ −
Wernicke's Area—area of the brain that is important in word recognition	+ +
Angular Gyrus—a cellular structure that coordinates the ability of the brain to recognize words when spoken or written	+ +
Left and Right Occipital Lobes—the parts of the brain responsible for visual functions; they see and integrate abstract and concrete words	+ +
Corpus Callosum—(specifically, the spleenum or posterior section of the Corpus Callosum)—the bundle of nerves tying the cortical hemispheres together and permitting rapid communication between one side of the brain and the other	+ −
Neurolinguistic Elements of Dyslexic Comprehension	
Right Cerebellum	+ −
Arcuate Fasciculus	+ −
Anterior Cingulate	+ −
Conversion Reaction Syndrome	
Inability to read as a form of the psychological defense mechanism known as "conversion reaction," accompanied by:	
a) nongenerative acquisition of reading skill	+ +
b) indifference to reading problem (*la belle* indifference)	− +
c) highly inconsistent WISC patterns from one testing to another	+ +
d) highly unreliable oral reading error patterns	+ −
e) accelerated learning with a placebo treatment	+ +
Genetic Predisposition	
High incidence of dyslexia in family tree.	+ −
Visual-Perception (reversals)	
Orton's theory that some people perceive images (letters, words, numbers, etc.) in *reverse*.	− +

INDICATORS & TREATMENTS	CONFIDENCE RATING

Vision problems (eyesight)

Nearsightedness, farsightedness, and other visual problems.   — —

Scotopic Sensitivity

Irlen's theory that ordinary light causes discomfort for some people when   — +
reading; specifically, words on a page appear to crowd together, or wiggle about,
or even disappear. This discomfort is thought to be eliminated by determining a
comfortable "wavelength," or color of light that can be provided for the person
via eyeglasses with a specific lens color. (They really felt this hypothesis to be
"unlikely," but felt obliged to defer to the literature, which says that it is
"possible.")

Dysmetric Dyslexia and Dyspraxia

Frank and Levinson's theory that dyslexia is related to "steering and spatial ori-   — —
entation disturbances," also known as cerebellar-vestibular dysfunction. The condition is thought to be diagnosable from visual tracking tasks and evidence of
mild vertigo and nystagmus.

Sound Treatment for Testosterone Deficiency

Based on Volf's finding that "many" males who experience reading difficulties   — —
have an undescended testicle that inhibits normal testosterone production.
Johansen has used a tuning fork test to diagnose dyslexia, and audio therapy to
induce the testicle to descend, normalizing testosterone production, and ameliorating attending conditions.

Laterality, or Mixed Dominance

A widely held theory that if one hemisphere is not clearly dominant, as evi-   — +
denced by one's preferred hand, eye, foot, etc., then one's brain functions and
learning will likely be confused as well. The proportion of people with mixed or
crossed dominance has sometimes been found to be significantly higher among
remedial readers than in the general population. The proportion of left-handed
people also is higher among remedial readers than in the general population.

Irregular Neurological Development

Dolman and Delacato developed this theory based on the idea that if one does   — +
not follow the phylogenetic sequence in one's own ontogenetic development,
reading and communication disorders can result.

Evolutionary Theory

Calanchini and Trout's theory that human differences in ability to acquire certain   + —
higher learing skills are related to the recency of their evolutionary development.

Biochemical or Circut Malfunction

Smith and Carrigan's theory that effective reading is determined by the efficacy   — +
of synaptic transmission in the nervous system. Early research addressed the balance of two chemicals (ACh and ChE) involved in this transmission; more recently, it has been found that synaptic transmission is even more complex, involving as many as 38 different chemicals.

Dietary Deficiency

Recent studies have attempted to connect biochemical imbalances, and related   — +
reading and learning problems, with improperly balanced diet, and/or possible
effects of additives.

INDICATORS & TREATMENTS	CONFIDENCE RATING
Gerstmann's Syndrome	
Also known as *finger agnosia*, this condition renders one unable to determine which finger is being touched when the head is turned the other way, and unable to move a specific finger on command. The condition occasionally accompanies dyslexia, though it is not thought to be a *causal* factor.	− +
Synergism Syndrome	
A condition described by Kinsbourne that sometimes accompanies dyslexia, and which is characterized by an involuntary motor reflex following a previous movement.	− +
Perseveration	
The inclination to repeat sensorimotor tasks involuntarily, or to remain conceptually fixed on something when change is in order.	− +

prior training that says a thing is what it is no matter what direction it is pointed. A child, for example, is expected to say *chair* whether the chair faces frontward, backward, is turned over, or even is missing certain parts.

Reasonably, then, when taught the word *saw*, the child will try to recognize it in its varied forms, even when it might be pointed in some other direction.

Reason 3   *Developmental learning lag.* Studies of children's emerging literacy indicate that these confusions about print are not uncommon (Clay, 1985). Some children may not even have internalized the left-to-right relationship of English orthography.

There are other factors that may cause children to be confused about *p* and *q* or the direction of *w* up until the fourth grade. Reversals and inversions will persist, for example, in children who:

1. are slower to learn how to read and, therefore, make more of the type of errors characteristic of early learners (Bruck, 1988);
2. do not receive adequate instruction and practice; and
3. may have confounding problems (such as being left-handed), and therefore have general directional problems in early reading.

Another form of visual-perceptual deficit and training is epitomized in the once great popularity of the Marianne Frostig Perceptual Test and Training Program (1964). Several researchers attempted to establish whether there was a meaningful relationship between reading and such training. John K. Sherk Jr. (1967) proved rather conclusively that there is not. Further, in his study with remedial readers, those receiving such training failed even to make greater progress on the Frostig visual-perceptual tests than did a control group receiving conventional remedial reading training. Robert Leibert and John Sherk (1970) found similar results in a replication study.

 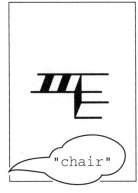 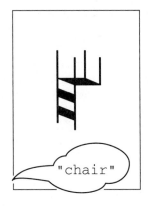 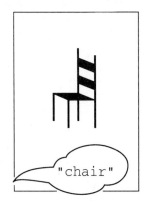

Curiously, adults who suffer brain injury and lose the ability to distinguish direction are likely to have a tougher time overcoming reversal problems than would children. Young brains have greater "plasticity"—they can learn most any given operation in a number of different ways. This should not be confused with the general ability to learn, which remains great at every age level, though for different reasons. Next, consider a very current explanation for a form of dyslexia that has been initially called "vision" related, although very recently has been suggested to be "visual-perceptually" related.

Also see ahead the section on laterality, or right-left dominance, which also is said to be involved in producing certain types of reversals.

Scotopic Sensitivity: A Cure with No Apparent Cause

Scotopic sensitivity is the name given by Helen Irlen to discomfort in reading caused by certain "wavelengths" of light. Some readers, according to Irlen (1983), see the words crowded together, or look at a word and have it disappear on the page—or have it move all over the page.

Irlen collected these reports from students in her capacity as an educational psychologist at the California State University at Long Beach where she served between 1980 and 1985 as director of an adult learning disability program. The discovery of scotopic sensitivity came about simultaneous with its treatment. Irlen says that she was working one day with color plastic overlays and a client reported that the words had stopped moving on the page. According to a Knight-Ridder news story (*Kansas City Star*, Walt Murray, Nov. 5, 1989, P. 2E), Irlen went to the store and bought every possible color of plastic overlay. Using the overlays, all 35 students could read somewhat better. Next, she had colors created so as to individualize color combinations. The color codings, according to Irlen, are so specific to each individual that even two yellows that look the same to the eye can make the difference between being able to read comfortably for ten minutes or for two hours. Further, no color is most common, nor is there any apparent commonality among persons of the same family in their responsiveness to a particular color.

Since the overlays were inconvenient for taking tests or writing, Irlen developed specialized visual tests and colored lenses that are sold as part of a larger program at any one of 41 centers that she now operates across the country. She has applied for, and by one account received, patents on 155 color combinations.

Several studies have now been done on "vision dyslexia" with the Irlen lenses (Rickelman & Henk, 1990a). One, from Australia, reports spectacular results over a 12-month period (Robinson & Conway, 1990). The subjects, ages 9 to 16, showed significant improvement in attitude toward school, in reading comprehension and accuracy, but surprisingly not in rate—the area that Irlen suggested would be most strongly influenced (Solan, 1990). A more recent Australian study showed equally dramatic improvements over a control group in which subjects used clear filters or filters other than the ones they preferred (O'Connor, Sofo, Kendall, & Olsen, 1990). A third study by American optometrists found no statistically significant changes in oral reading or oral comprehension (Blaskey, et.al., 1990). These researchers further asserted that "scotopic sensitivity" was not a new entity, but little more than "undetected vision problems" (p. 610), and that poor readers responded just as favorably to conventional vision therapy. In a summary of these studies, it has been pointed out that each has certain design problems that threaten the validity of the findings (Parker, 1990). Recently, Helen Irlen has suggested that "Scotopic Sensitivity Syndrome" may not be a vision problem, since there is no physical evidence that such exists, but rather that the term "perceptual dysfunction" might be more appropriate (Weiderholdt, 1990, p. 588). We are further reminded that the claims made by Irlen conjure images of Pons and Fleishmann's reports of successful cold fusion, another bit of wonder that no one has yet been able to replicate. To date, however, over 15,000 people have taken the Irlen treatment and franchises continue to open around the world.[1]

---

[1]One franchise now is offering "10 pairs of different tinted overlays with instant results" for $95.00. The mail flier further advertises "Instant Help for 90% of all Reading Problems" (National Reading Service, P.O. Box 1445, Peoria, IL 61655).

Next, consider a form of dyslexia that could be classified as either visual or neurological, depending on how far one goes back in classifying point of origin. This form also introduces a new term, "dyspraxia."

Dysmetric Dyslexia and Dyspraxia

The terms "dysmetric" and "dyspraxia" refer to a form of dyslexia that has been proposed by Jan Frank and Harold Levinson (1975-76; 1976; 1977), and similarly by Jean Ayres (1978). This form of dyslexia relates to "steering and spatial orientation disturbances noted in the writing and drawings of dysmetric dyslexic children" (Frank & Levinson). It also is known as *cerebellar-vestibular dysfunction*. The root problem is believed to be located roughly in the inner ear and possibly in the cerebellum—the lower back region of the brain responsible for balance and orientation. It is said to result in, and therefore be diagnosable from, difficulty in visual tracking tasks and mild vertigo and nystagmus (a rapid involuntary rolling of the eyeballs as from dizziness). Nystagmus generally can be induced, and therefore diagnosed, by having the subject rotate the head or the body, or perform other related balancing tasks. The role of the vestibular was first suggested by Orton and therefore accepted by Frank and Levinson, also physicians, as virtually an operational definition of dyslexia.

This factor has been shown, however, not to distinguish dyslexics from normals (Brown, et.al., 1985). Further, the drugs (Cyclizine and Ritalin) and elaborate training systems which they recommend to counter the poor visual tracking and vertigo, that ostensibly cause reading disability, have been found to be unrelated to reading, and unnecessary even to the treatment of the "poor refractory responses" that they have noted. It is notable, too, that the effects of the prescription drug treatment that they offer can be achieved just as easily with over-the-counter medication available for motion sickness (e.g., Dramamine).

The next explanation and treatment for dyslexia can only be called exotic. It is not one you shall soon forget.

Dyslexia and Sound Treatment

Kjeld Johansen (1984) has reported that he has been able to diagnose dyslexia with tuning forks, and to treat it with sounds played through earphones. The tuning forks are used, we presume, to determine whether there is damage to the air conduction system of hearing, part of the vestibular system that Frank and Levinson (above) associated with dyslexia. This is done by striking the tuning fork and raising it to the patient's ear. When the patient says that he/she no longer hears sound, the still vibrating fork is touched to the bone behind the ear to see if he/she then again "hears" the sound due to direct conduction along bone and nerves. This is known in the United States as the Weber-Renee test. Johansen's work is based on an odd and possibly legitimate finding by a Charles Volf (who died in 1967) that many males who experience reading difficulty have an undescended testicle that hampers testosterone production and results in "headaches, nailbiting, bedwetting, and *reading* and spelling problems" (1984, p. 33).

Through the use of audio therapy, the testicle ostensibly is (somehow) induced to descend from the groin into the scrotum, thereby normalizing testosterone production and greatly ameliorating each of the above mentioned conditions. Johansen's study, like other studies by Danes before him, has shown a statistically significant correlation between children's abilities to read and spell and their tuning fork audiogram tests. However, no evidence has been presented to support the treatment, or the theoretical relationship of male hormones and reading ability. Despite the absence of evidence of efficacy, the diagnostic and treatment system first described by Volf continues to be popular in several major clinics in Scandinavia, where thousands of people have been so treated.

We have been told by our consultants at the UMKC Medical School that the relationship between selected sounds and the endocrine gland system, and specifically the sex glands, has previously been established to be true in several studies of animals, particularly birds, but they are not aware of any such established connection in human beings. Furthermore, the physicians we consulted say that it is at least ironic that Johansen should attribute dyslexia to low testosterone development when an excess of it during pregnancy has been implicated as a cause of dyslexia. The suspicion is that excess testosterone slows down the formation of strong connections between the two hemispheres of the brain, thereby weakening some of the cross-communication necessary for learning to read efficiently.

There is yet another sound-based system that involves listening to simulations of the sounds a child might hear in the womb, and claims on equally great impact on reading and learning disabilities. It has been described in many lectures and presentations in Canada and much of the English-speaking world by a Dr. Alfred Tomatis, who has not himself written about either his theory or treatment.

Laterality, or the preference for use of the right or left hand, foot, eye, etc., has often been studied as a correlate of dyslexia, and according to some authorities is a frequently cited but false-positive sign.

Laterality, or Mixed Dominance

It has been suspected and suggested for some time that if one hemisphere is not clearly dominant, as evidenced by one's preferred hand, eye, foot, etc., then one's other brain functions and learning also will be "mixed up." An early study, for example, reported that there was evidence of either mixed or confused and unsettled dominance in 37% of remedial readers and crossed, or settled but different, dominances for eyes, hands, and/or feet, in almost 40% of them (Harris & Chesni as reported by Critchley, 1964). Another study of 500 dyslexics revealed similar findings (Klasen, 1972). It is interesting to note some of the other conceptual and historical origins of this belief.

The conceptual origins of this belief again seem to be with Samuel Orton who seemed to be correctly aware that at least in some cases of stammering, the right hemisphere of the brain could pick up a typically left-side language task and actually compete with the left and interfere with smooth speech execution. From this, he must have concluded that similar competition would occur between the hemispheres in learning to read (Segalowitz, 1983, p. 201). The literature from Germany, where there has been a long-standing historical interest in laterality, includes a report by Leiser-Eggert in which she shows that mixed and cross dominance is found in fairly high proportions in other segments of the population as well: 30% in emotionally disturbed children; 15% in highly stable children; and 13% in college students (reported in Klasen, 1972).

In general, quantitative estimates of mixed or crossed dominance have been found to lie between 13% and 27% in normals, and between 37% to 44% in retarded readers. Norman Geschwind, a leading authority on dyslexia, further affirms that there is a disproportionately high incidence of left-handedness among dyslexics and their families, and that this tendency (and the right-brain competition for language dominance that it suggests) causes confusion in acquiring reading proficiency, an essentially left-brain function (Geschwind, 1982, 1972). From such information it has been concluded that crossed dominance, or the developmental delay of laterality, certainly beyond age 9, probably is *associated with* lack of clear hemispheric dominance and, therefore, with reading retardation in some way. However, this probably is not a significant factor, since many persons with this condition learn to read quite well. More to the point, mixed and crossed dominance clearly are not strong enough factors to *cause* reading retardation independently. Nonetheless, several programs and institutions have made it a matter of policy to diagnose and provide treatment for such conditions, usually as a collateral or incidental part of their remedial reading therapy. The thinking seems to be that even a potentially mildly causative factor is worth noting and possibly treating. There also have been recent reports in the public news media (April 1990) that left-handed persons have a 9-year shorter life span. This highly suspect, unconfirmed and probably erroneous information certainly will continue to attract attention to handedness and cross-dominance, though just *what* treatment might follow is still in question.

One other aspect of laterality suggests that it should continue to be studied. It relates to a surprising difference between the sexes. Males tend to be more lateralized than females, meaning that their brain functions, including reading, may tend to be more centered in the left hemisphere than in females. Since females have a more symmetrical pattern of development and distribution of functions, the belief is that they are less likely to be rendered dysfunctional in tasks such as reading where the left hemisphere might be damaged (Bradshaw & Nettleton, 1983, p. 2201). The tendency of the left hemisphere to be very orderly and logical and of the right to be more comfortable with visual-spatial matters may help to explain our perception that most males tend to prefer nonfiction to fiction.

It is notable that there now is a clear, although highly intrusive, means of determining left-brain language dominance. It is called the Wada test, developed by John Wada of the University of British Columbia. In the Wada test, the anesthetic sodium amytal is injected into the left carotid artery. The patient is then asked to count aloud. He or she should stop within moments as soon as the drug reaches the left hemisphere. This test has confirmed Orton's suspicions about stammers. It has been shown that when they are injected on the left side, they begin to count, hesitate when the drug reaches the left hemisphere, and then continue with the right hemisphere obviously quickly ready to take over. This suggests that the right probably is quite active and competing with the left in conventional speech, thus producing the stammering effect (Segalowitz, 1983).

Irregular Neurological Development

This condition is best explained within the context of the story of Glenn Dolman and Carl Delacato. The Dolman-Delacato story symbolizes several different notions that have sprung up over the years for diagnosing and treating dyslexia and related learning disabilities. As with notions of this ilk, it contains some interesting ideas, but it also is laced with disproven ideas and idiosyncratic features that can only be called "quirky." Glen Dolman, a physical therapist, and Carl Delacato, an educational psychologist, founded the Institute for the Achievement of Human Potential in Philadelphia to foster their ideas and offer their brand of treatment. (Dolman now is promoting methods to raise the IQ levels of young children.)

The theory, as first proposed by Delacato (1959, 1963) rests on four basic tenets:

1. Individual human development (or ontogeny) repeats the pattern of humankind's evolutionary development (phylogeny). In their terms, "ontogeny recapitulates phylogeny."
2. If one does not follow the phylogenetic sequence in one's own ontogenetic development, there will be problems in mobility and communication (including reading).
3. The neurological consequences of this can largely be remediated, though never fully rectified, since neurological systems do not regenerate, but alternate systems can be trained.
4. "Patterning" is one of the best systems of remediation since it helps to complete "cortical dominance wherein one side of the cortex controls the skills in which man outdistances lower forms of animals" (Delacato, 1959, p. 21).

An area that Dolman and Delacato frequently have found deficient has been the cross-pattern movements used in "creeping." This they view as a midbrain function typical of reptiles and characteristic of infants of 10 months old. Accordingly, creeping exercises would then be prescribed that would complete the link between "crawling," a means of movement characterized by both the right arm and leg moving in unison and then the left arm and leg doing the same. Crawling is the movement characteristic of amphibians who are closer to fish; it also is characteristic of the movements of 4-month-old infants. Crude walking, the step after creeping, would resemble the movements of primates and children of about 1 to 4 years old.

This treatment is coupled, in the Dolman-Delacato regime, with an array of other conventional and unconventional prescriptions and inhibitions. For example, parents and neighbors must work with the child for up to 13 hours per day; regular reading instruction is provided; children may not listen to music if they are at the cortical level, but have not yet established unilateral dominance, whereas primitive, heavy beat music is beneficial if the child is at the midbrain level of development.

A careful study of the effectiveness of this approach failed to support the theory or the practices (Glass & Robbins, 1967). The *Journal of the American Medical Association* (1967) also published these objections that are worth noting for their generalizability to similar operations and ideas:

1. It is wrong for some Institutes to assume that their methods treat the brain itself, whereas other methods merely treat symptoms.
2. Policies that make parents therapists are ill-advised.
3. It is not defensible to prevent children forcefully from engaging in self-motivated functions (such as listening to music).
4. It is countereffective to make assertions that increase parental anxiety and concern, especially where almost universal child-rearing practices are called into question.

A similar statement followed from the National Health and Medical Research Council of Australia where this odd system also had taken hold. It is worth noting that several very prominent American families and foundations had once been supporters of the Dolman-Delacato Institute.

Next, consider an "evolutionary" theory that is similar to Dolman and Delacato's, but by some accounts more plausible.

Evolutionary Theory

Evolutionary Theory (Calanchini & Trout, 1971) is based on a general hypothesis that applies to many learning disabilities. It simply says that since all higher functions are cortical, and the cortex is the most recent phylogenetic (or species) development, that it stands to reason that there would be greater variability among individuals in these areas on the basis of embryonic (or ontogenetic) development as well. This effectively means that some differences in human ability to acquire certain higher learning skills may be related more to "an imperfection of nature than a result of actual insult to the brain" (in Tarnopol & Tarnopol, 1977, p. 14).

This theory is seldom discussed, even in academic circles, for fear that it will be adopted by racists to argue for the inferiority of those populations with the largest numbers of youngsters with reading and learning disabilities. The theory also is impossible to test except with post hoc, or after-the-fact, data. Some specialists do find the theory tenable, however, and think that it can be used to strengthen arguments for early intervention for any and all youngsters who might be having early and detectable problems in learning to read. Their position is that evolutionary theory would not be used to exclude anyone from instruction and opportunity, but to focus our efforts to bring it to them. Central to this position is the belief that reading not only *requires* brain power, but that it *builds* brain power.

Biochemical or Circuit Malfunction Dyslexia

Some time ago, Donald E.P. Smith and Patricia Carrigan (1959) posited a biochemical basis for reading retardation. The researchers came to believe that effective reading was determined by the levels of two interacting chemicals involved in "synaptic transmission." Synapses are the tiny spaces that exist between one neuron, or nerve, and another. Contrary to intuition, and even casual inspection, nerves are not continuous strands like wires. Rather, they are a mesh of thousands of tightly woven neurons. Messages are transmitted across each tiny chasm by electro-chemical activity.

Acetylcholine (ACh) is released by the endocrine system (glands) to make an electrical circuit (transmission) to the next neuron. The firing continues as long as the ACh remains present. Upon the introduction of cholinesterase (ChE), the circuit is broken. Thus, in a normally perceptive person, ACh and ChE are in some delicate balance. If there is more ACh than ChE, then firing continues and the subject is unable to *change* fixation/attention. This, Smith and Carrigan hypothesized, would be typical of slow readers. In the alternate condition, where ChE exceeded ACh, the circuit would be continuously interrupted, and the subject would be unable to maintain fixation/attention. This, Smith and Carrigan hypothesized, would typify the fast, but inaccurate, reader.

Clinical studies revealed that this was not an adequate model. This initially led to the conclusion that it was necessary not only to account for the amount of ACh and ChE, but also its concentration at a particular point. It was also learned that these chemicals were extremely sensitive to a subject's anxiety level. The Smith and Carrigan study was further muddled, and the ideas abandoned, when it was discovered that there were many, perhaps as many as 38, chemical current makers and breakers other than ACh and ChE. So it remains questionable as to whether the endocrine system is or is not significant to chemical regulators in neural transmission during reading.

There have been more recent attempts to connect biochemistry to reading and learning disabilities through issues in diet and the possible negative effects of food additives, etc. None of these have yet *proven* to have a profound effect on reading or learning. As with scotopic sensitivity training, there also are clinical reports of children who presumably have been helped by correcting dietary deficiencies. One, for example, reports that a dyslexic boy "responded positively to a biochemical approach that corrected deficiencies in iron, zinc, vitamin B-16, and an imbalance in fatty acids" (Baker, 1985). This study further reported that "[h]is hair and skin improved, as did his reading" (p. 6). Most researchers hold these outcomes to be placebo effects that vanish in controlled experimental studies.

Related Learning Disabilities and Soft Signs of Dyslexia

There are several learning disabilities and "soft signs," or observable behaviors, that are taken as indications of neurophysiological problems and thought by some to be common or even causative of dyslexia. Most of these are only coincidentally related. Some of these symptoms are similar to behaviors found in certain forms of emotional distress, and can not easily be distinguished as being one or the other, or both. Three syndromes illustrate this point: Attention Deficit Disorder, Gerstmann's Syndrome, and "Synergism."

- Attention-Deficit Disorder (ADD), as stated in a previous chapter, is the modern name for hyperactivity. It tends to be treated with powerful drugs, frequently is misdiagnosed, and is only occasionally related to reading disorders. Walter E. Sawyer (1989) calls it "a wolf in sheep's clothing" because on those occasions where it is accompanied by a reading disorder, the label and drug treatment are given quickly, but needed remedial instruction often is not provided. In any case, it is not related to dyslexia, even though it may be found in some dyslexics as a compounding, and from the point of view of diagnosis, a *confounding* factor.
- Gerstmann's syndrome is an unusual condition characterized by tactile-sensory localization deficit, also known as "finger agnosia." This is the inability either to determine which finger is being touched when the hand is open and the head is turned the other way, or being unable to move a specific finger on command. Gerstmann children also tend to have right-left orientation problems, and dyscalculia (extremely poor ability to do simple calculations). Their Performance Quotients tend to be significantly lower than their Verbal Quotients on the Wechsler IQ test (as reported by Hynd & Semrud-Clikeman, 1989). Dyslexic children showing this neurological sign "have shown less improvement from instruction than those without it" (Silver & Hagin, 1964, in Thomson, 1984, p 63). Many of these soft signs of neurological impairment tend to disappear beyond 10 years of age even in very poor readers (Finlaysen & Reitan, 1976, in Thomson, 1984).
- "Synergism" (Kinsbourne, 1973, 1989) is another neurological soft sign that has sometimes been thought to be a concomitant of dyslexia. This is an involuntary motor reflex following a previous movement. There might be difficulty, for example, in releasing something once it is grasped. The first grasping move is, in effect, followed by another involuntary one. This condition may be akin to another related condition called *perseveration* — the inclination to involuntarily repeat sensorimotor tasks, or persistently go back over previously covered ground. It also resembles the kind of condition posited by Smith and Carrigan (1959) in which there is a good "circuit maker," but a poor "circuit breaker."

In recent years, it has been learned that many of these conditions, while troublesome and deserving of attention, are not related to dyslexia. Several of them, particularly perseveration, do influence aspects of reading behavior, but do not seem to be limited to poor readers.

Now that we have laid out a catalog of "indicators and treatments" of dyslexia, let's summarize.

Summary of Indicators and/or Treatments

As mentioned earlier, several graduate students carefully reviewed both literature and lecture material of this chapter to organize a chart of the relative confidence that, in their judgement, could be placed in the various indicators of and/or treatments offered for dyslexia in the chapter. The chart in Figure 12.5 (see pp. 414–416) also serves as a chapter summary. You may wish to use this as a Reflection Box, and see how your understandings and judgements compare with theirs.

> ## LOOKING BACK

The chapter provided a detailed account of how teachers and reading specialists can conceptualize, diagnose, and treat severe reading disabilities in fairly traditional ways. It also provided a thorough look at the state of current knowledge from a neurolinguistic and psychological perspective. This included sections on unusual brain syndromes related to reading disorders.

The chapter then provided a comprehensive review of indicators and treatments of dyslexia that have won wide attention here and abroad. It included a chart (see pp. 414–416) summarizing and evaluating much of the information presented.

> ## LOOKING AHEAD

The next chapter completes the structural presentation of reading disability by taking up issues at the other end of the spectrum—higher-order literacy. As you read ahead, you will see interesting relationships drawn between severe reading disorders and certain forms of higher-order literacy deficits. Some of these relationships are indicating that there are comparable, though largely undetected, deficits to be found in certain "proficient" readers, and that many methods and objectives that tend to be reserved for proficient readers may serve traditional remedial readers in some surprisingly fruitful ways.

Remedies for Higher-Order Literacy Deficits: Studying, Thinking, and Writing

Teach up. You'll often get performance at a higher level than you would have thought possible.

PARAPHRASE FROM
THOMAS H. ESTES

> ## ➤ *LOOK FOR IT*
>
> Look for the unfolding story of how higher-order literacy approaches are helping meet the needs of conventional remedial readers. See how further to improve "strategic reading" by explicit attention to studying, thinking (including metacognitive thinking), and writing. Learn how to educate yourself better in detecting and treating higher-order literacy needs with an Informal Reading-*Thinking* Inventory. Finally, note how new forms of reading deficiencies are being detected even among "proficient" readers.

Higher-Order Literacy

What Is It?

Simply put, higher-order literacy is the ability to read and think between and beyond the lines; that is, to monitor one's own thinking, analyze critically, respond constructively, and be transformed as well as informed by relevant information from credible sources. The essayist John Locke expressed the interplay of reading and higher-order thinking when he said, "Reading furnishes the mind only with materials of knowledge; it is thinking that makes what we read ours" (1706). Specific attributes of higher-order thinking have been identified by several researchers (Gentile & McMillan, 1991; Manzo & Manzo, 1990a; Marzano, 1991; Resnick, 1987). Five attributes are particularly relevant here:

- It is *dispositional*, or driven by orientation and will as much as ability.
- It is the mediational system, or method of inner speech by which we are able to impose meaning and find structure in apparent disorder.
- It involves aspects of self-examination and "strategic reading" that have come to be known as study skills and metacognitive functioning.
- It implies effective memory and the acquisition of a rich fund of information.
- It suggests command of the related language arts, particularly of writing, a means by which to mediate as well as communicate.
- It probably has anatomical and physiological correlaries

Interestingly, higher-order literacy does *not* appear to be simply an upward extension of reading comprehension. Disorders are almost as likely to be found among proficient readers as among remedial readers, and *strengths* are almost as likely to be found among average and below average readers as among proficient readers (Casale, 1982; Manzo & Manzo, 1990a). This branch of the field of diagnosis and remediation is uncovering tangible evidence of previously undetected reading problems. An experimental instrument, the Informal Reading-Thinking Inventory, described ahead in this chapter, has been developed as a means of gathering diagnostic information about students' ability and inclination to read between and beyond the lines, to self-evaluate, and to use writing as a tool for thinking.

In due course, it may not be uncommon for reading specialists to diagnose and treat conditions such as "excessive literalness" — characterized by proficient literal comprehension and weak applied and critical level reading; and the neglected problem of those who "read too much" — those whose reading is not merely diversion and entertainment, but a means of escape. These points are developed further ahead in the chapter.

Can It Be Taught?

Lance Gentile and Myrna McMillan (1991) point out that: "Higher order thinking is not developed using lock-step methods and materials" (p. 76). Some educators, such as Frank Smith (1990), even contend that higher-order thinking can not be taught because it is temperamental and dispositional. Nonetheless, evidence continues to mount that it *can* be taught easily and profitably. Recently, for example, Cathy Collins (1991) showed that simply by infusing explicit thinking training into the reading-language arts curriculum, experimental groups of middle school students outperformed comparable youngsters who received a traditional curriculum. This improved performance was evident on a variety of measures, including the "Reading Comprehension" and "Vocabulary" subtests of the *Iowa Test of Basic Skills* and the *Harter Self-Perception Profile for Children*—a measure of self-esteem. In addition, and most importantly, they transferred their training to writing samples—experimental group students' writing reflected 13 divisions of higher-order thinking, as opposed to those in the control group, who could muster only 3. See the "Caboose Theory" (Cooter & Flynt, 1986) ahead for further evidence of the how attention to higher-order thinking can aid remedial readers.

Part of the rationale for any new commitment must include evidence of need. Since no one really doubts that higher-order thinking should be a central objective of schooling, the issue of commitment becomes one of degree.

How Great is the Need?

The 1990 *Reading Report Card* indicated that there have been large gains by African-Americans and Hispanics in reading comprehension, thus narrowing the gap between these minorities and White and Asian students. The "down side" is that the performance of White students had not improved significantly over a comparable 17-year period (1971-1988), and that such gains as have been made were at the literal-reconstructive levels. No gains were evident at the higher levels of reading ability as defined by adept use of advanced skills and strategies (Mullis & Jenkins, 1990).

This chapter, beginning in the section below, first addresses the building of strategic reading, continuing the discussion of this topic that was begun in an earlier chapter. The theme of higher-order literacy is then followed through study skills applications, and means of improving a variety of cognitive abilities, including metacognition and writing, both for remedial level and proficient readers.

Strategic Reading

The term *strategic reading* can refer to the highly skilled and self-directed act of flexible, mature reading, or to a stage of progress toward that end. Since the subjects of this text are forming readers, strategic reading, in this context, will refer to those slightly more conscious acts of self-direction that have not yet become completely internalized skills. Others have referred to strategic reading as "skills under consideration" (Paris, Wasik, & Turner, 1991, p. 611); "unrefined skills" that haven't yet "gone underground" (c.f., Vygotsky, 1978); skills that have not reached automaticity (c.f. Samuels & LaBerge, 1983); "substrata" mental operations that have not yet been fully subsumed into a higher worker system"

FIGURE 13.1

Profile of a Strategic Reader

The Strategic Reader:
- Understands how different reading goals and various kinds of texts require particular strategies (analyzes)
- Identifies task and sets purpose (discriminates between reading to study for a test and reading for pleasure)
- Chooses appropriate strategies for the reading situation (plans)
  –Reading, skimming, summarizing
  –Paraphrasing
  –Looking for important ideas
  –Testing understanding
  –Identifying pattern of text
  –Sequencing the events
  –Looking for relationships
  –Reading ahead for clarification
  –Mentally executing the directions
  –Relating new knowledge to prior knowledge
  –Summarizing
  –Questioning
  –Clarifying
  –Predicting
- Monitors comprehension, which involves
  –Knowing that comprehension is occurring (monitors)
  –Knowing what is being comprehended
  –Knowing how to repair comprehension (regulates)
- Develops a positive attitude toward reading

Monahan (1990)

(c.f. Holmes, 1965); and nascent "reading-study-writing skills" (c.f. Nila Banton Smith, 1964). To get a clearer sense of the target, Joy Monahan (1990) has compiled a list of skills that eventually need to be mastered in order to become a strategic reader (see Figure 13.1).

Consider now some further examples of means and methods of promoting effective reading-study practices. The first method is based on imparting a proper disposition to the reader, and involving the reader in the decision-making process. The second method offers a more explicit approach to teaching. Together, they offer general guidelines for how to approach most higher-order literacy teaching.

Reading-Study Strategies

The reading-study strategies discussed here are rather more like paradigms, or models, that need to be adapted to use with remedial students. Be creative, think about how you might adapt them to use with a middle school child with apparent reading-study problems.

PASS: A Guiding Principle

The Problem-Solving Approach to Study Skills, abbreviated as PASS (Manzo & Casale, 1980), is based on an underlying philosophy that each student should be intimately involved in the process of diagnosing and treating their own reading-study needs in some age-appropriate way. Active involvement in the pursuit of personal competence has the value, in and of itself, of imparting personal responsibility, self-efficacy, and a proper disposition toward problem recognition and problem solving. PASS is an example of an instructional conversation that contains elements of both the diagnostic and the therapeutic dialogues.

Steps in PASS

Step 1   *Count.* The teacher presents students with a list of common study skills problems and asks them to check those that apply to them (see Figure 13.2).

Step 2   *Characterize.* The teacher guides students in defining selected problems, and themselves, in specific terms. The teacher helps students to think about what they are like and what they do well. With older students, this can be done with inventories of learning style, temperament, skills, abilities, and attitudes.

Step 3   *Consider.* Students consider how they typically have dealt with their particular needs and problems and the possible merit in these intuitive self-management and coping strategies.

Step 4   *Collect.* Students discuss and judge standard techniques for dealing with reading/study problems on the basis of their compatibility with their personal styles and values. Where these appear incompatible, the procedures are dismissed as inappropriate, or set aside for reconsideration in the next step.

FIGURE 13.2

Common Study Skills Problems

Directions: Check *all* that are problem areas.

___ 1. Accurate and complete class notes	___ 10. Attention span while reading
___ 2. Basic reading comprehension	___ 11. Attention span while studying
___ 3. Identifying the main idea	___ 12. Vocabulary knowledge and strategies
___ 4. Noting important details	___ 13. Informational background
___ 5. Drawing inferences from facts	___ 14. Mathematical skills
___ 6. Memory	___ 15. Writing
___ 7. Test anxiety	___ 16. Test-taking techniques
___ 8. Concept formation	___ 17. Outlining/Text notetaking
___ 9. Attention span in class	___ 18. Library and reference skills
	___ 19. Classroom discussion skills

Step 5 *Create.* Students seek inventive modifications and alternatives that match their personal styles. This step can be handled initially in individual and small-group settings, and then in larger-group discussions from which all may benefit.

PASS was refined and tested in case study fashion by Casale and Kelly (1980), and was found to be an effective means of involving students in advancing their own competence. Next, consider Huhn's paradigm as a model for explicitly teaching needed reading, study, and thinking skills.

Huhn's Guidelines for Direct Teaching

Ralph H. Huhn (1982) offers a simpler formula for explicit teaching called "RSM2P" that comes very close to defining a set of general guidelines that could guide virtually all direct teaching. See how you would adapt this to use with remedial level students.

Rationale	Tell students what you are going to teach them and why.
Steps	Provide the steps of the strategy in writing as well as orally.
Model	The teacher demonstrates the strategy while thinking aloud.
Practice (aided)	The student uses the strategy while thinking aloud and with the teacher assisting in the process.
Practice (independent)	The student uses the strategy with similar materials, and is permitted to personalize or modify the strategy as long as production remains high.

See now how Dana (1989) and Vaughan (1984) have used the notions underlying PASS and Huhn's model to improve strategic reading and study.

Strategy Families

The previous chapter offered some "cuing" methods that could be prepared by a teacher to increase student success at different stages of the reading process, particularly the initial steps. Carol Dana (1989) has taken this a significant step further. She has designed a few cuing systems, the purpose of which is to get disabled readers to use and internalize various strategies—a goal that was demonstrably achieved, when they began to invent their own. Dana describes four major cuing strategies—or "families," as she calls them—that she initially offered to students. These fall into the three stages of reading as follows:

Before reading: as preparation for reading	**RAM** <u>R</u>elax <u>A</u>ctivate your purpose <u>M</u>otivate yourself
During reading: to focus on the content	**SIPS** <u>S</u>ummarize natural sections <u>I</u>mage—visualize the contents <u>P</u>redict what's coming

OR

to make repairs   **RIPS**
Read further/read again
Image — visualize the content
Paraphrase the troublesome section
Speed up/slow down/seek help

After reading: **EEEZ**
to set your   Explain what it all means to you
memory   Explore other versions
Expand with related material

Creative involvement often becomes playful as well as practical. Dana reports that one group of boys created a strategy family called "BURP":

*B*reath
*U*nderstand
*R*eread
*P*redict

Dana (1989) reports that in a 5-week summer reading program with 42 remedial readers (aged 7 to 15), 10 teachers worked with small groups of students. The teachers were trained to provide direct instruction in strategy families, using fiction and nonfiction materials. These remedial readers made significant gains in reading comprehension on the Gates-MacGinitie Reading Tests (1978), a standardized measure that is not easily influenced by surface-level gains.

Dana attributes her initial strategy suggestions to the work of several researchers (Frey, 1980; Duffy, et.al., 1987; Gambrell, Kapinus, & Wilson, 1987; Lapp & Flood, 1984; Levin & Pressley, 1981; Pressley, 1976; and Zenker & Frey, 1985). The next method takes a somewhat greater conceptual approach, and is more text-based. How would you adapt it for remedial use?

ConStruct

Joseph Vaughan's (1984) ConStruct, or Conceptual Structuring Procedure, essentially has students read and reread material, each time attempting to construct a graphic representation of it, following Victor Rentel's advice of some time ago (1971) to make the representation as "concept-centered" as possible. ConStruct adds another level of thought manipulation to simple outlining. It also adds the opportunity to personalize information in a manner that need not duplicate the author's structure. A subordinate point, for example, can be made the featured portion of the graphic. Transforming the information in this way tends to spark a lively discussion, and to make the information more life-connected and memorable. Remedial students should be given the opportunity to see and compare their renditions with the teacher's and those of peers. Graphics can be displayed, discussed, and revised any number of times over a unit of study. Students should be encouraged to include their best graphics in their portfolios. This method is especially suitable to youngsters with an artistic bent. See Postay's underlining method and the Guided Reading Procedure as useful presteps to "ConStructing."

Now consider one of the most widely used of all reading-study strategies. It too may require careful thought and adaptation for remedial level students.

SQ3R

The Survey-Question-Read-Recite-Review (SQ3R) technique is the acknowledged granddaddy of study formulas; however, it appears to have a faulty gene or two. The plain truth is that it does not work quite as well as its billing would suggest. This section should help you form a personal critical judgement of the relative value of SQ3R and determine if, when, and how it might properly be used in its present form or whether it can be fine tuned to produce better and more consistent results with remedial readers.

SQ3R was developed by Francis Robinson (1946), who traced its roots back to 1923. Robinson developed it in response to a need expressed by the U.S. Department of Defense during World War II (Stahl & Henk, 1986). American troops had much to learn and little time in which to learn it. They needed a rigorous, *self-guided* Directed Reading Activity that they could use with minimal instruction in field training situations. SQ3R stresses meticulous, self-guided, step-by-step analysis of text, followed by repeated efforts to "overlearn" the material to the point where key information can be recalled and recited with minimal cuing under stressful circumstances, such as tests and classroom recitations.

Steps in SQ3R

1. *Survey.*   Survey a chapter before reading it closely:
   a. Read the title and think about what it says or implies.
   b. Read the headings and subheadings.
   c. Read the summary if there is one.
   d. Read the captions under the pictures, charts, graphs, or other illustrations.
   e. See if there is a bibliography or a list of books related to the content of the chapter.
2. *Question.*   Ask yourself questions about what you are going to read:
   a. What does the title of the chapter mean?
   b. What do I already know about the subject?
   c. What did my instructor say about this chapter when it was assigned?
   d. What questions can be stated from the headings and sub-headings to guide reading?
3. *Read.*   Read actively:
   a. Read to answer the questions you raised while doing the survey/question routine.
   b. Read all the added attractions in the chapter (maps, graphs, tables, and other illustrations).

        c. Read all the underlined, italicized, or boldface words or phrases extra carefully.

4. *Recite.*   Go over what you read in step 3 by either mumbling to yourself what you just read or making notes of some type.

5. *Review.*   Periodically survey what you read and learned:
        a. Use your notes or markings to refresh your memory.
        b. Review immediately after reading.
        c. Review again periodically.
        d. Review again before taking an exam on the subject.

The consensus among specialists regarding the efficacy of SQ3R as a total formula is positive, though not always enthusiastic. Studies reported by Wooster (1958), Willmore (1967), Donald (1967), Diggs (1973), Gurrola (1975), and McNamara (1977) found no significant differences between SQ3R and control (i.e., placebo) treatments. In a widely cited review of the literature on SQ3R, Wark (1964) undertook a point-by-point analysis of each step of the strategy. Only the Recite, or the "mumbling to yourself" (McIntyre, 1991), step was supported in this analysis. Wark aptly concluded: "There is no body of data to demonstrate that any other integrated package of skills could not work just as well. Like the legal age for marriage, SQ3R seems to be supported by tradition, rather than a rigorous consideration of the data on productivity" (p. 168).

The fact is, despite the popularity of SQ3R, its actual effectiveness as a self-guided reading-study formula still is uncertain. We believe there are at least two reasons why SQ3R does not appear to work. First, many of the students who need it most are too impulsive and undisciplined to implement it fully. Second, there is a lack of effective training and thorough follow-through. Francis Robinson himself observed that SQ3R can not possibly be effective until it becomes "automatic" and "subordinate to the task of reading" (1946, p. 21). For these reasons, we continue to endorse SQ3R as long as each step is practiced under *teacher guidance,* and with a gradual transfer of responsibility from teacher to student.

Study Skills Methods for Older Students

Several study strategies have been developed and well-researched, though most at the college level. These basic models can be easily adapted for use at high school, middle, and even elementary levels. They also will be of value to the many elementary school teachers who often find themselves needing to teach study strategies to older remedial students, and to those who teach in high school equivalency and vocational education programs.

PLAE

Michele Simpson and Sherrie Nist (1984) developed the PLAE model as a means of involving students in planning, monitoring, and controlling their own study. The acronym reminds students to follow these basic steps:

Preplanning	Find out about the test, and answer a series of questions to set performance goals.
Listing	Make a list of the most appropriate study strategies to use, and set time limits and goals for each study session.
Activating	Put the study plan into action, making adjustments where necessary.
Evaluation	After test scores have been received, have students engage in a self-guided form of "dynamic assessment" (Carney & Cioffi, 1990) by diagnosing errors, looking for patterns of strengths and weaknesses, and incorporating these findings into future study plans.

Three studies of the effectiveness of PLAE led to the following conclusions: planning is significantly related to test performance (Nist, Simpson, Olejnik, & Mealey, 1989); use of PLAE has a measurable effect on both test performance and metacognitive abilities (Nist & Simpson, 1989); and, students trained to use PLAE outperformed students trained in traditional time management on four content area examinations (Nist & Simpson, 1990).

PORPE

Michele Simpson (1986) also developed PORPE as an integrated study system for improving achievement on essay tests. The title of the strategy reminds students of the following procedure:

Predict	what essay questions will be asked. This should be done *before* beginning to read and study the material, in order to focus and direct reading.
Organize	the information in answer to predicted questions, using graphic organizers or conventional outline form.
Rehearse	through verbal recitation of the key ideas recorded in the maps or outlines.
Practice	by writing answers from memory (a significant step beyond the "recite" step of SQ3R).
Evaluate	written practice answers, using a checklist aimed at assessing completeness, accuracy, and appropriateness of the product as a response to the self-predicted essay question.

Two research studies found that students trained to use PORPE had significantly higher achievement on both essay and multiple choice examinations than students trained in a traditional question-answer format (Simpson, Stahl, & Hayes, 1989). The PORPE students' essays had superior content, organization, and cohesion, both on initial testing and on delayed testing two weeks later.

SPIN

SPIN (Aylward, 1990) is a new and interesting method that focuses on summarizing, predicting, inferencing, and notetaking, but in no routine, sequential order—except, of course, for reading before summarizing. This is a significant departure from methods based on a stage or sequence theory. The dissertation study that introduced this method (reported in Devine, 1991) claims impressive results for the eighth graders trained in its use. We look forward to learning more about it. (For an excellent coverage of other traditional and emerging methods for adults and underachieving high school and college students, see Volumes I and II of Flippo & Caverly, 1991a,b.)

Consider now a topic that is of clear value from fourth grade level onward, but seldom is explicitly taught—the topic of underlining and notetaking.

Underlining and Notetaking

The research on underlining has been mixed. Sometimes it helps with comprehension; other times it does not. It appears that there are two weaknesses to overcome with respect to teaching underlining. First, the strategy must be taught and routinely practiced until it is thoroughly learned. Second, everyone continues to need intermittent help in wading through material because there are at least three agendas that can become intermingled in determining just what is important and therefore should be underlined: the teacher's agenda, the author's agenda, and the student's personal interests, concerns, and occupations.

Poostay's Approach to Underlining

Edward Poostay (1982, 1984) offers a means of teaching underlining that he calls, simply "Show me your underlinings." Once a student has underlined, he has the child talk these through and compare them with the teacher's and with other students'. This not only provides training in underlining, but also offers experience in the "instructional conversations" that seem to be the active ingredient in most successful strategies for learning.

To further aid in this process, we have found it useful to add two features to Poostay's instructional conversation. One is to routinely ask youngsters to distinguish whether an underlined section is likely to be important to the *teacher*, the *author*, or the *student*. The second is to try to reduce an entire page to no more than a few key words, and then to highlight those in yellow or orange. This second transformation tends to compress information better for long-term recall and easier study. It also greatly aids in preparation for Vaughan's Construct, as noted above.

Notetaking can be guided in much the same manner. Of the several methods available, only one was designed to guide notetaking from lecture *and* reading. It was developed by Robert Palmatier (1973), who originally used this unified method as a control group treatment in an experimental study, but quickly realized its practical and theoretical significance.

Palmatier's Unified Notetaking System (PUNS)

Students need instruction in how to learn from listening as well as from text. Palmatier's Unified Notetaking System (PUNS) urges students to review lecture notes immediately after class and supplement them with text information. The notetaking format also provides a built-in study system by separating key words from the body of the notes. PUNS is one of the few notetaking methods that has been cross-validated in more than one study (Palmatier, 1971, 1973; Palmatier &

Bennett, 1974). The remedial reading teacher should expect to run regular simulation lectures to provide students with the practice necessary to transfer this strategy to regular classroom application.

Steps in PUNS

Step 1   *Record.* Use only one side of 8 1/2" x 11" notebook paper with a three-inch margin on the left side. (Many bookstores stock this type of paper for this purpose.) Record lecture notes to the right of the margin. Use a modified outline form to isolate main topics. Leave space where information seems to be missing. Number each page as you record the notes.

Step 2   *Organize.* As soon after the class as possible, add two sections to the notes. First, place labels inside the left margin. These should briefly describe the information in the recorded notes. Second, insert *important text information* directly into the recorded notes. If you need more space, you can use the back of the notebook paper.

Step 3   *Study.* Remove the notes from the looseleaf binder, and lay them out so that only the left margin of each page is visible. Use the labels as memory cues to recite as much of the information on the right as you can recall. The labels can be turned into questions stems: "What do I need to know about (insert label)?" Verify your recall immediately by lifting the page to read the information recorded to the right of the label. As you master the material on each page of notes, set that page aside in an "I already know" stack. For objective tests, the labels can be approached at random, simulating the format of multiple choice, true-false, and matching tests. For essay tests, group information into logical units, formulate predicted essay questions, and practice writing answers. See ahead, how students can be urged to process material to higher levels by exposing them to several different means of annotating, critiquing, and responding to what they read and hear.

One means of serving students as a resource for more effective learning is to know more about how it best occurs. Here, for your information, is a "state-of-the-art" summary of what is known about notetaking.

Take More Notes! Research Notes on Notetaking

Students often have the mistaken belief that the purpose of taking notes is to record key ideas briefly when, in fact, they need to be encouraged to write more, not less. This may be the chief value of PUNS: It requires students to review and otherwise supplement skimpy lecture notes with text-based information. PUNS also urges the purposeful use of text to supplement notes and thus is likely to result in more effective textbook reading.

A thorough review of the research on student notetaking (Kierwa, 1985) provides these additional points for your consideration:

• *Notetaking helps.* 35 out of 38 recent studies have demonstrated that taking notes increases attention and learning during lectures.

- *Review makes sense.* 24 out of 32 studies have found that students who review their notes learn and remember significantly more than those who do not.
- *Use the chalkboard.* 88% of students record information from the chalkboard but only 52% record even the critical ideas when these were *stated* (Locke, 1977).
- *Pause briefly.* Providing occasional pauses during a lecture enriches lecture notes and increases recall (Aiken, Thomas, & Shennum, 1975).
- *Take breaks.* There is a 17% decrease in notetaking in the *second* 20 minutes of a 40-minute class period (Locke, 1977).
- *Vary* test formats. Students who expect multiple choice examinations take notes of lower structural importance and recall more of the details recorded than students who expect an essay test. On the other hand, students who expect an essay exam take notes of higher structural importance and recall more concepts (Rickards & Friedman, 1978).

Additional research by Victoria Risko and Alice Patterson (1989) suggests the need to add three very important features to improving notetaking. They found that inner-city, remedial readers produced the best notes when they were given a fixed time to read, a strategy for personal reflection, and, most importantly, an opportunity for ten minutes of group rehearsal. The strategy suggested next was designed to encourage analysis and rehearsal in listening, but could easily be adapted to taking notes from reading.

Directed Notetaking Activity

Hiller A. Spires and P. Diane Stone (1989) added an emphasis on self-questioning to the split-page notetaking approach. In this Directed Notetaking Activity (DNA), students are encouraged to ask themselves questions before, during, and after listening, as follows:

BEFORE LISTENING:

- How interested am I in this topic?
- If my interest is low, how do I plan to increase interest?
- Do I feel motivated to pay attention?
- What is my purpose for listening to this lecture?

WHILE LISTENING:

- Am I maintaining a satisfactory level of concentration?
- Am I taking advantage of the fact that thought is faster than speech?
- Am I separating main concepts from supporting details?
- What am I doing when comprehension fails?
- What strategies am I using to deal with comprehension failure?

AFTER LISTENING:

- Did I achieve my purpose?
- Was I able to maintain satisfactory levels of concentration and motivation?
- Did I deal with comprehension failures adequately?
- Overall, do I feel that I understood the information to a satisfactory level?

Students who were trained in this type of self-questioning outperformed students who received other forms of notetaking training that did not include training in self-questioning (Spires & Stone, 1989).

Here is a handy list of 15 simple study skills that have been freely adapted from Gordon Friedel (1976). These may be rewritten for most any grade level student. It is especially beneficial to rewrite these *with* the students. Students seem to enjoy rewriting, personalizing, and even laminating these for easy access and review.

Simple Study Skills

To win student commitment to to becoming effective at reading and study, it is best to begin in an upbeat and optimistic way. The school-based reading specialist should urge the classroom teacher to post the instant study skills list for students to read and reread at their leisure. Of course, they are not instant for all students, so the teacher needs to allude to the list periodically and invite discussion of progress on and the relative merit of each skill in different situations.

1. *Come early to class and leave late.* Important guides to the material and tips on exams frequently are given in the first and last minutes of a class.
2. *Sit close to the front of the room.* Studies have shown that students who sit in the front of class make better grades. Perhaps this is true because those who choose to sit closer to the front are the more "motivated" students—but why not assume that a positive feedback loop is at work here: that is, proximity to the instructor increases concentration, which enhances motivation.
3. *Make class notes as complete as possible.* The most effective study time may be the actual hour of the class. Take extensive notes and concentrate during class, and you will have a good record for thought and home study.
4. *Review class notes as soon as possible.* Immediate review probably is the most powerful learning strategy known. Go over the material mentally as you walk to your next class. Make it a habit to review class notes briefly each school night, preferably at the same time and in the same place.
5. *Preread before reading a section in the textbook* This gives focus and purpose to reading and a built-in review mechanism.
6. *Underline after you have read a paragraph.* This focuses attention and concentration and avoids "automatic" reading or, worse, mindless reading.
7. *On exams, read slowly and answer quickly.* Focus on the question stem instead of the choices. This prevents the frequent and irritating problem of "misreading the question" due to the attractive wording of one of the foils.
8. *On exams, do the easy questions first.* Go through the test quickly. Skip and mark hard questions, and pick those up later. Attempting to do the difficult questions first can be emotionally disruptive, causing you to forget answers that you do know.
9. *Overlearn for exams.* Memorize as many things as you can. Research shows that over 90% of test anxiety can be reduced with better preparation.
10. *To make an A.* There is a relatively easy formula for making an A in any class.

Ask yourself, "What is the very most the teacher would expect someone to do to get an A on this paper/test/project?" Then do more!

11. *Hand pace to speed read.* To read faster and with better comprehension, take your hand and begin (right now!) to move it down the page. Gradually increase the speed of movement, and try to read along. "Hand pacing" has been proven to be an effective means of increasing reading rate.

12. *Spell with the mind's eye.* Spelling accuracy is in "the mind's eye," not in the rules of spelling. Study a word in print (such as business) for a moment. Then look up and try to envision the word before you. Try to write the word by copying it from this mental image. Compare your results with the correct spelling. Repeat the process until you have spelled the word correctly three times in a row.

13. *Think "back and forth."* Periodically, try to predict the complete opposite position of a view you now hold or have read about. Giving consideration to the opposite viewpoint often stimulates thought about reasonable compromise positions that might not otherwise have occurred to you. This back-and-forth inner conversation is called "dialectical thinking." It is the foundation of all logical and critical thinking.

14. *Learn the "right words."* According to some psychologists, if you are anxious and unhappy, there is a good chance that you're saying the wrong *words* to yourself. In your conversations with yourself, try using more understated words. Think of your arch-enemy as a "scoundrel" rather than a "&S##*@@%." You will be less emotional, more stable, and have greater constructive energy.

15. *Your past and present are your future.* It has been wisely observed that "We find little in a book but what we put there." That's because the knowledge one *has* is the best predictor of how well one will read and learn. Build your *fund of information* by reading an encyclopedia, almanac, or other nonfiction work for at least 15 minutes every day. You will be surprised at how quickly facts and ideas will begin to repeat themselves.

Higher-Literacy Approaches to Remediation

Cognitive Training Techniques

Robert B. Cooter and E. Sutton Flynt (1986) provided an interesting and poignant test of what they called the Cognitive Caboose Theory. According to this theory, if students were asked only inferential and higher-order questions, these might serve as the locomotive that pulled along a caboose of literal facts and skills. When they compared two groups, one being asked only higher-order questions and one asked a conventional blend that generally began with literal questions, they found that the experimental (higher-order) group performed significantly better on inferential comprehension questions, and just as well, actually slightly better, on literal and detail questions. While this study lends considerable credibility to the caboose theory, it does not prove it unequivocally, since many questions used tended to be more of a "between the lines," or inferential type than of a "beyond the lines," or applied, evaluative or constructive type. In other words, they did ask some foundational questions, since inferential questions tend to correlate most highly with factual questions. Further, their students were average third and fourth graders. However, when these findings are added to the research of Cathy Collins (1991), previously mentioned in the chapter, and that of Martha Haggard-Ruddell, described below, the caboose theory gains considerable credibility.

Martha Haggard-Ruddell (1976) provided strong evidence for the value of higher-order cognitive training for remedial readers. Haggard-Ruddell compared the reading gains and creative thinking scores of two groups of remedial readers, ages 7 to 17. The experimental group received regular reading instruction and about 15 minutes of "warm-up" creative thinking exercises prior to reading instruction. Examples of these activities are illustrated ahead under the heading Creative Thinking-Reading Activities (CT-RA's). The control group also had regular reading instruction, and about 15 minutes of reading games such as hangman, "consonant lotto," and the like. Post-test results showed that the creative thinking (experimental) group performed significantly better on all reading measures. This study used activities of the type described next.

Creative Thinking and Creative Reading Activities

Ideally, Creative Thinking-Reading Activities (CT-RA's), as Martha Haggard-Ruddell (1979) came to call them, tend to contain three elements: creative thinking, group interaction, and guided transfer. An intimate instructional conversation between the teacher and a student in a one-on-one tutorial can easily replace the group interaction component. There are many commercial materials to promote these activities. Most stem from the early research on the assessment of creativity by Guilford (1968) and those who came before him. (See Appendix E for a representative listing of commercially available critical and creative thinking materials.)

Here are some examples of commonly used creative thinking activities, and then of some practical means and methods of tying these to reading and writing tasks (Cecil, 1990b). Notice how these activities help to engender an atmosphere where learning is joyful and higher-order thinking becomes part of the instructional conversations between students and teacher and students with one another.

Unusual Uses
Have students try to think of as many unusual uses as they can for common objects. Objects may vary from "a red brick" to "watermelon seeds."
Circumstances and Consequences
What would happen if . . .
. . . school was on weekends and not during the week?
. . . water stuck like glue?
. . . all babies looked alike at birth?

Product Improvements

These *questions* require as much or more imagination than do the answers: How could school desks be improved? How could living room furniture be improved to provide better storage and even exercise while we watch television? How might tables be designed so that children would be less likely to spill and drop things off them? How can we better equip book carrying bags to handle lunches and other needs that you can think of?

Systems and Social Improvements

The major breakthroughs in world order, peace, and sanity are the result of the creative vision of a few individuals who have pictured social and systems changes such as democratic government, the post office, better teaching methods, and medical procedures. There is little incentive provided for this type of thinking. To encourage such thinking, pose questions and reward plausible solutions to questions such as: How can we get ourselves to be as courteous to people who aren't attractive as we are to people we think of as pretty? How can we help people who are not very bright, or are less able due to aging, to meet the complex obligations of modern life? (Name some examples: licensing, insuring, and getting plates and inspections for a car.) How can schools be made a more agreeable place without sacrificing learning? What problems do you see that others don't seem to notice?

Haggard-Ruddell (1980) offers these additional suggestions for using CT-RA's in group situations:

- *Pose a stimulating question* (such as those listed above).
- *Brainstorm.* Initial responses should be generated in small groups, following standard brainstorming groundrules: *all* responses are permitted, without criticism; as many ideas as possible are to be listed; unusual, even "wild" ideas are encouraged; and, new ideas can be formed by combining ideas already mentioned.
- *Compare ideas.* After brainstorming, each small group should share their ideas with the class, or in a tutoring situation with the teacher, for critical evaluation. Students may wish to choose the "funniest," or the "wildest," response generated by each small group. At this point also, ideas are are assessed for "plausibility" or practicality. It is important to point out that all creative solutions are at best just "possibles" until tried and proven.
- *Transfer to Reading.* The whole point of reading and thinking is to transfer new knowledge and power to solving life problems. This is most likely to occur when real problems such as stated above are allowed to surface and drive reading and thinking. However, this same mindset can be used to drive reading so that it connects to the creative thinking activities:

  Before we find out how Huck saved Jim, think of all the possible ways for him to do so. (Haggard, 1980, p. 2)

  Remember our CT-RA on new inventions? What new invention [or system] could you come up with that would change the end of this story? (Haggard, 1980, p. 2)

  (After reading Liang and the Magic Paintbrush) What would you paint if you had a magic paintbrush and whatever you painted would then come to life? (Gross, 1990)

Cathy Collins (1991) offers several transfer activities similar to those recommended by Haggard-Ruddell. One of these methods is especially relevant here. (See Cathy Collins & John Mangieri, *Thinking Development: An Agenda for the 21st Century*, in press, for several related methods.) Students were taught to ask certain clarifying questions of material presented to them in lecture or textual form. Seven questions were stressed:

Could you give me an example?
What do you mean by _____ ?
What is *not* an example, but similar to the idea that you are describing?
Is this what you mean: _____ ?
Would you say more about _____ ?
Why do you believe (feel or think) that _____ ?
What is the main point?

These questions were contextualized by first asking students to report times in their lives when they benefitted from asking clarification questions. Then they were urged to select books with vivid characters, and to write up incidents in the books where characters asked questions for clarification, and how it affected the plot. Finally, students practiced using the clarifying questions with one another in group discussions. (See Note Cue and Enabling Questions for related methods for inculcating these behaviors into the classroom environment.)

Creative Thinking-Reading Activities of the types described are probably valuable and useful to any educator who is willing to test it for themselves. It seems that the tendency of the mind to follow patterns that can become mind-numbing can be interrupted and reset on more imaginative paths rather easily. Experience suggests that even the most convergent thinking of individuals can be much more creative and imaginative if we just remember to "ask for it!" (Cecil, 1990; Manzo & Manzo, 1990a). However, heuristic methods are needed to help remind teachers and students to ask for inventive thinking. Thus far, no completely natural means has been developed for raising this pattern-interrupting question.

Behind all creative problem solving is a rich, internalized collection of facts and experience. Being able to store and recall these mentally at appropriate times is a skill that can be taught.

Memory Training

One of the cornerstone purposes of schooling is to impart and have students learn and remember a wide array of facts. Nonetheless, little thought or effort goes into teaching students efficient and effective ways to recall under pressure. In a comprehensive review of formats for assessing reading comprehension, Samuel R. Matthews and Kaybeth Camperell (1981) concluded that the relationship between comprehension and memory is much more profound than instructional practices would seem to indicate. A brief look at the nature of memory reveals that this overlooked area of training for disabled readers may offer a relatively easy and hope-lifting means for improving content mastery and student achievement.

There are three types of memory. *Short-term memory* is good for about 30 seconds and is useful in doing simple computations. *Eidetic memory*, which often is forgotten about, is even shorter: It holds the mental image that the mind's eye needs to connect letters into words and words into sentences. Some reading specialists attribute one type of severe reading disability (dyseidetic-dyslexia) to weakness in eidetic memory. Finally, there is *long-term memory*, where the past resides. It has two functions: episodic and semantic memory. *Episodic memory* keeps track of our real experiences or autobiographies, while *semantic memory* stores vicarious and schooltype learnings.

There are several proven methods for improving semantic memory. These are particularly worthwhile because most people can achieve dramatic improvement in memory with relatively little training. More important, the impact of memory training on content mastery can be substantial and remarkably enduring; most things easily forgotten probably were poorly learned to begin with. Following are seven memory enhancing devices that date back centuries, to when there were few books and fewer readers and memory was extremely important.

Imaging

David Meier, director of the Center for Accelerated Learning, claims that guided imaging can create greater "ownership" of study material. Working with a colleague, Owen Caskey, Meier devised an interesting and telling experiment to verify this claim (in Trotter, 1979). In the study, material on biology was shown to students in two different types of videotaped presentation. Half the students were taught via a lively lecture accompanied by attractive props and illustrations. The other half received the identical material on a videotape that guided them to an internal, multisensory experience of the material.

Students in the latter group first were presented with material describing the "elements of a typical brain neuron." Then they were told to imagine that they were floating around in the cytoplasm of a neuron. They were further instructed to conjure up a multisensory image of the cell, in which they would encounter a mild electrical charge, interact with various parts of the neuron, and even poke and play with the things they discovered. Most important, they were told to lock this in mind by realizing that they were inventing a vivid, memorable experience. The students in this group performed 12% better on immediate recall and 26% better on long-term retention. From this it has been concluded that: "There is no device for learning, no matter how sophisticated, that can equal the power, flexibility, and ease of the human imagination."

Loci Imaging

Loci imaging, a form of mental imaging, was well-known among Greek orators. The idea is to take a familiar location and associate words and ideas with precise locations, or loci points, along the way. Deborah Uttero (1988) suggests that youngsters select a familiar spatial layout, such as their homes. Then they are encouraged to place mentally a list of items to be remembered in various rooms. When the items are to be recalled, students need only retrace their steps and retrieve the images from where they deposited them.

Spatial Arrangements

The *spatial arrangements* technique has some of the same characteristics as loci imaging, is equally simple, and lends itself even better to notetaking and conventional study. Words and ideas to be remembered are laid out in any desired simple spatial arrangement, such as an X, a K, or a 2.

Bellezza (1984) reports that this simple technique proved more effective than another, also ancient form of visual imaging in which one tries to create an unusual mental picture. For example, in trying to remember "baby," "window," and "ship," one might first visualize a baby breaking a window and then sailing away in a ship. Apparently the risk in this latter system is the need to remember the unusual, whereas the familiar symbols are more easily recalled even in stressful circumstances. Nonetheless, this type of associative spatial arranging system has proven effective in the Keyword Method of vocabulary learning (Guthrie, 1984), described in a previous chapter.

Clustering

Clustering, or the progressive parts approach, involves breaking down longer items to be learned and reorganizing them into parts for individual mastery (e.g., part A, part B, etc.). There is a conventional element of this approach that should be avoided: the tendency to begin study from the same starting point each time. It is better to begin study at different points each time so as not only to learn the initial points, A and B, well but to be fresh and attentive when beginning elsewhere, such as with points C and D. Semantic maps and outlines are good aids for this type of partitioning, because, according to Uttero (1988), they are helpful when studying a middle section (such as C or D) with a sense of its conceptual place in the longer piece.

Acronyms

Acronyms—memory words constructed from the first letter of each word in a list of words to be memorized—can be invaluable aids for life. An example of an acronym that almost every student of geography would be pleased to learn is HOMES, to signify the names of the Great Lakes: Huron, Ontario, Michigan, Erie, and Superior (Uttero, 1988). Another familiar acronym is ROY G. BIV, which represents the colors of the spectrum: red, orange, yellow, green, blue, indigo, and violet.

Read and Recite

It has been said that those who have the best memories for fact-based tests spend 20% of their time *reading* and 80% *reciting* what they want to learn. In other words if you spend fifteen minutes reading and clarifying your notes, you will need to spend about one hour learning them (preferably in spaced practice sessions).

Overlearning

Overlearning is the key to remembering. Most forgetting occurs due to poor initial learning: the rest results from fear and interference, often between what one learned initially and what one learned subsequently. The easiest way to overcome all three of these problems is to "overlearn" each section of material before going on to the next. The power of overlearning was demonstrated by psychologists Paul Foos and Cherie Clark (1984) in a simple study that you can replicate with your own students. Students who were told to get ready for a multiple choice (or recognition-type test) did less well, even on multiple choice questions, than did those who were directed to prepare for an essay (or recall and integration) test. When preparing for unaided recall and recitation, memory will rise to the demand. This finding seems to lend further credence to the "caboose theory" (Cooter & Flynt, 1986) mentioned earlier.

In general, the thesis for this section simply is to teach remedial level students those things that address their wholeness, and that can be expected to have a counterbalancing and strengthening effect on their "basic" remedial deficits, much as doctors now prescribe stomach muscle exercises to support weak lower back disorders. This message, which has been implicit in previous chapters, now turns to some areas of learning that would have been considered out of sequence for remedial readers just a generation ago; namely, abstract thinking, evaluative thinking, metacognitive training, and creative thinking and writing.

Abstract Thinking

Abstract thinking is an operation that everyone has in some measure, or we would not be able to connect any symbol or representation with its concrete form. The task facing the remedial teacher, therefore, is to enrich this process further and to have it operate during reading.

There are essentially four explicit means of teaching and practicing this fundamental mental activity:

- The act of reading and interpreting proverbs (as discussed in the previous chapter) and provocative quotations is probably the most productive and manageable.
- Reading and discussing fables, homilies, and parables, which essentially are metaphoric, or abstract representations, can also be valuable, since they really are extended proverbs.
- Exercises in doing and creating simple analogies [Example: *dog* is to *wolf* as *cat* is to: a) moose; b) lion; c) canine; d) feline], as well as in seeing analogies in print and using them in explanations: "In this story, John and his mother seem very different, but how might the things that they do show that they may be a lot alike?"
- Categorization activities, which are the basis for all concept formation, can be done in a variety of ways. These include sorting words by some predetermined criterion (e.g., things that can swim); by placing items into as many different categories as are possible (e.g., things that swim, things that eat other living things, things that can live out of water); by grouping information under outline headings; by trying to create group or class names; and by methods that concurrently teach vocabulary, such as the Semantic Feature Analysis method (Pearson & Johnson, 1978), discussed in the previous chapter.

Donald Durrell and Helen Murphy were among the first to demonstrate the effectiveness of using categorization activities to teach word recognition, word meanings, and abstract thinking more than forty years ago (Durrell, 1956). These exercises can be made engaging or unproductive, depending upon the quality and extent of the instructional conversations that accompany their use. (See Readence & Searfoss' [1980] three-component categorization technique for further examples of how to teach categorization.)

Evaluative Thinking

The ability to evaluate has been called the highest act of reading-thinking by several writers. We see it as beneath creative thinking, but still as a necessary requisite to it. Evaluative thinking has been tied to affective and moral growth, and has come to be known as the "valuing process" (Raths, Harmon, & Simon, 1978). As such, it is further detailed in the chapter on defects, differences, and disruptions. Recall especially the work of James Hoffman (1977) and Leo Schell (1980) in weaving such training into reading comprehension and metacognitive instruction, the next area of concentration.

Metacognitive Techniques

Metacognition refers to introspective awareness of the factors that influence our ability to monitor and fix internal problems that arise in effective reading, language use, and thinking. It represents one of the highest orders of human functioning, and could be considered a logical extension of such traditional maxims as "know thyself," and of such high-minded objectives as the charge to lead an "examined life," as Aristotle simply phrased it.

In practical terms, Annemarie Palincsar and Kathryn Ransom (1988) observe that such training is important for poor readers since they especially need to be made aware of and party to efforts to take control of their lives and learning environments. They can and should be taught to be their own agents, advocates, and teachers, since it is impossible for any other individual or agency to do so for them completely.

Several well-thought-out means and methods have been designed to increase student self-monitoring and self-correction behaviors. It is good to keep in mind while using these that the intent is to teach and achieve insight and responsibility without causing students to divert attention from the printed page (Hayes, 1990), or to become excessively introspective or sullen. To an extent, metacognitive training is like bibliotherapy (described in a previous chapter), a potentially powerful curative, which if misused can be made dreary and even sabotage, rather than enhance, a child's own natural coping mechanisms. These cautions should not discourage use, however, since all respected professionals work with "controlled substances" that contain risks and must be used judiciously.

Most metacognitive techniques can be appended to other standard methods. Several operate at an implicit level in methods already described, such as the

Guided Reading and ReQuest Procedures. The methods described here typically were designed to promote this ability in a somewhat more explicit way.

Heller's Metacognitive Approach

Mary Heller (1986) offers a simple method, which is akin to K-W-L Plus (Carr & Ogle, 1987). Before students read content material, they are trained to set up three columns to guide their reading and post-reading reflections on their state of knowing:

Column A	Column B	Column C
What I Already Knew	*What I Now Know*	*What I Don't Know*

This is one of very few methods that places an emphasis on building knowledge of what one doesn't know, and presumably needs to learn about, as well as what has been learned. This seemingly slight adjustment, or collateral function, can be a highly valuable asset in building root elements of internal motivation, such as curiosity and commitment to one's own state of knowing.

Strategy Awareness

Suzanne Wade and associates (Wade & Reynolds, 1989; Wade & Trathen, 1989; Wade, Trathen, & Schraw, 1990) developed a list of metacognitive strategies based largely on research in which college students reported strategies they used naturally when reading textbook materials. They suggest the following process for guiding students toward greater awareness and use of metacognitive strategies:

1. Have students read a short text selection, and then ask what reading-study methods they were using. Record their suggestions on the board under one of these headings: "Observable Strategies" (e.g., underlining) or "In-the-Head Strategies" (e.g., relating to other knowns). Encourage students to elaborate on how they use strategies they suggest, and why they find them to be useful.
2. Give students the Strategy Definition Sheet (see Figure 13.3). Review each strategy on the list, asking students to think about whether, when, and how they use each.
3. Hand out the Strategy Record Chart (see Figure 13.4). Use passages of different types, over a period of time, and have students check which strategies they use when reading each passage.

Question-Answer Relationships

Taffy Raphael (1982; 1986) developed and tested a simple strategy that aids students in thinking about the state and source of information. Basically, the teacher trains students to understand and periodically to indicate how they

FIGURE 13.3

Strategy Definition Sheet

OBSERVABLE STUDY METHODS

Highlight or underline	Designate important key words and phrases.
Copy	Write down information either on note paper or in the margins exactly as it is written in the text.
Write down in your own words	Make notes on a separate sheet of paper or in the margins.
Outline	Organize ideas on paper in categories or under headings to show which are the main ideas and which are supporting ideas or examples.
Draw	Organize ideas on paper in diagrams that show how they relate to each other.

IN-THE-HEAD STUDY METHODS

Look over before reading	This is a very fast type of reading. It involves either reading for the main ideas in order to get an overview of the passage, or moving very quickly over unimportant information.
Read at your usual rate	This is right for some materials.
Read slowly	Slow down your reading for better comprehension or concentration.
Go back and read again	Read certain parts of the text a second time, usually when information is confusing or you want to understand it better.
Special attention!! Review or memorize	Concentrate on specific information in order to remember it. This includes mentally reciting material, concentrating on specific information, memorizing, reading aloud, and going back over notes or underlinings.
Put together in ideas in your head	Stop to get the whole picture, to summarize the information in your head, or to connect ideas.
Relate ideas to what you already know	Create associations between a new idea and something you already know or have experienced.
Make a picture in your mind	Imagine a picture of a place, object, event.
Question or test yourself	Think of questions and answer them as you read along; test your comprehension.
Guess what will happen	Make predictions about what will happen next or what the reading will be about.
Other	Anything you do when reading or studying that is not listed above.

Wade and Reynolds (1989)

FIGURE 13.4

Strategy Record Chart

	PASSAGES							
OBSERVABLE STUDY METHODS	1ST	2ND	3RD	4TH	5TH	6TH	7TH	8TH
Highlight or underline	—	—	—	—	—	—	—	—
Copy	—	—	—	—	—	—	—	—
Write down in your own words	—	—	—	—	—	—	—	—
Outline	—	—	—	—	—	—	—	—
Draw	—	—	—	—	—	—	—	—
IN-THE-HEAD STUDY METHODS								
Look over before reading	—	—	—	—	—	—	—	—
Read at your usual rate	—	—	—	—	—	—	—	—
Read slowly	—	—	—	—	—	—	—	—
Go back and read again	—	—	—	—	—	—	—	—
Special attention!! Review or memorize	—	—	—	—	—	—	—	—
Put together in ideas in your head	—	—	—	—	—	—	—	—
Relate ideas to what you already know	—	—	—	—	—	—	—	—
Make a picture in your mind	—	—	—	—	—	—	—	—
Question or test yourself	—	—	—	—	—	—	—	—
Guess what will happen	—	—	—	—	—	—	—	—
Other	—	—	—	—	—	—	—	—

Wade and Reynolds (1989)

should have or have derived an answer to a question. Four phrases are taught to reference:

- *"Right There"* — explicitly stated in the text
- *"Think and Search"* — the answer is in the text, but must be inferred, or constructed from different parts of the text
- *"Author and You"* — the answer is not in the story; it must be constructed by prior knowledge and text information
- *"On my Own"* — the answer is almost exclusively from the student's experience and prior knowledge; the text was merely a convenient means of stimulating consideration of it.

This method has tended to prove effective in training students to increase their understanding of question-answer relationships, but less so at actually improving comprehension. It may tend to create the kind of diversion from thinking about the page that has caused David Hayes (1990) to become skeptical of such methods. For a further discussion of how similar categories are being piloted to raise the teacher's awareness of appropriate question types more so than student's, see the discussion ahead in the chapter of the Informal Reading-Thinking Inventory.

SMART

Joseph Vaughan and Thomas Estes (1986) offer this easily acquirable method for self-monitoring comprehension.

Steps in SMART

Step 1   Students keep track of their comprehension by using only two marginal notations:

> ✔ I understand
> ? I'm confused

Step 2   Students then attempt to express the concepts and ideas they have understood to themselves, a peer, or an inquiring teacher.

Step 3   Students are urged to try solutions to apparent lapses in comprehension (reread; more carefully identify the word or idea source of the problem; go for help).

The value of such metacognitive methods has not been adequately studied to say which work best. Susan Clark, a doctoral student at UMKC, currently is conducting doctoral research on this issue. Nonetheless, our experience suggests that SMART is smart because it is easily learned, and doesn't seem to add to the mental burden of the remedial reader by requiring complex thinking and notations. As with other such methods, the chief active ingredient in this prescription is likely to be the extent to which teachers regularly engage students in something resembling an instructional conversation about their efforts to reach for meaning.

Now consider the role of writing in remedial education. There are some surprises here.

Writing Ignites Reading

Despite a good deal of empirical support for a connection between reading and writing (Loban, 1963, 1964; Shanahan & Lomax, 1986), there also is recognition that reading and writing represent some "quite different patterns of cognitive behaviors" (Langer, 1986). Put another way, while one undoubtedly benefits from progress in the other, this is not the greatest justification for teaching both. Rather, the justification for teaching writing along with reading is that it contributes to the wholeness of an individual, and to their total literacy. From the perspective of remedial level students, there are two often overlooked values in teaching writing. First, writing to read creates an *alternative* means of building literacy. This can be especially useful with remedial students whose reading problems may stem from neurological irregularities specific to the reading process, or who have simply acquired a formidable backlog of negative experiences with reading, that hinders every new experience with the printed page. Secondly, there is growing evidence that where reading and writing are taught together, a *synergistic* outcome can be expected, that is, an educational outcome that is greater than the simple sum of the two parts. It is rather like combining aerobic exercise with good diet. It doesn't merely produce one who is stronger and lighter, but stronger, lighter, and physically and mentally healthier.

A recent research report provides strong support for this proposition. Rob Tierney and associates examined the nature of the thinking that students engaged in under a variety of treatments, such as reading with no writing; draft writing but no reading; and drafting, reading, and rewriting. Their findings lay the foundations for the modern advocacy of writing. They found that students who wrote prior to reading tended to read more critically, and that whenever reading and writing were combined in any way, students generally were more thoughtful in their treatment of ideas than they were if they had only read or only written. This was especially evident in the changes students made in their drafts, such as additions, deletions, and fresh points of view (Tierney, Soter, O'Flahavan, & McGinley, 1989).

It is of further significance to note that prior research has demonstrated that different types of writing affect thinking in different ways (Hayes, 1987; Copeland, 1987; Applebee, 1986; Applebee et al., 1987). This finding is especially relevant to the improvement of higher-order thinking as is illustrated in REAP, a reading-writing-study strategy covered in the final section of this chapter.

In general, writing can be expected to advance reading and full literacy in the following ways:

- Writing activates the reader's background knowledge before reading (Langer & Applebee, 1986).
- Writing builds anticipation of story events (Short, 1986).
- Writing raises the reader's level of intellectual arousal and activity (Newell, 1984).
- Writing encourages meaningful comparisons of the reader's perspective with that of the writer (Penrose, 1988).
- Writing helps the student appreciate the writer's craft, and therefore to think like a writer (Smith, 1984).
- Writing helps the reader to formulate a "worldview," or personally examined perspective on key issues (Gentile & McMillan, 1990; Hayes, 1987).
- Writing builds critical reading, since the thought processes involved in revision in writing and critical reading are highly related (Fitzgerald, 1989; Ericson, et al., 1987; Flower & Hayes, 1981; Colvin-Murphy, 1986).
- Writing builds metacognitive as well as cognitive abilities since writing forces deeper levels of introspection, analysis, and synthesis than any other mediational process (Gentile & McMillan, 1991; Flood & Lapp, 1987; Duffy, Roehler, & Hermann, 1988).

Principles to Guide Writing Instruction

Carol Hittleman (1984), in reviewing the literature on writing research, found support for guidelines which say that writing should be:

- Daily rather than infrequent
- Done for real audiences and purposes

- More student than teacher initiated
- Allotted sufficient time for stages of thought and editing to occur
- Set in a writing community environment
- Peer guided, reviewed, and supported
- Done with an initial emphasis on "reacting and responding" to the intended message rather than on "proofreading and editing"

Kenneth Goodman (1986, p. 8) expressed compatible guidelines, suggesting that language processes, in general, are best learned when:

- It's real and natural
- It's whole
- It's sensible
- It's interesting
- It's relevant
- It belongs to the learner
- It's part of a real event
- It has social utility
- It has purpose for the learner
- The learner chooses to use it
- It's accessible to the learner
- The learner has the power to use it

Let us look now at some means and methods of improving writing and reading that generally are compatible with these guidelines, as well as with some of the more acute needs of some remedial readers. Previous chapters have already introduced several methods that emphasize writing as well as reading. These included the Language Experience Story and Summary Writing. Four additional methods are described here: The Writing Process Approach, Sentence Combining, Reducing/Expanding Sentences, DeComposition/GRASP, and the Language Shaping Paradigm. One additional method, called Dialogue Journals, is covered in Chapter 12 and reviewed briefly below.

Writing Methods for Remedial Readers

Dialogue Journals/Study Journals

When students record their thoughts in brief notes and teachers pause to write back their responses, a dialogue journal is created. Dialogue journals map into some of literacy's most prized objectives. They are "written conversations between two persons on a functional, continued basis, about topics of individual (and even mutual) interest" (Staton, 1988, p. 312, as cited by Bode, 1989).

Good readers tend to read as if they were wide-eyed and attentively listening; good writers also tend to write as listeners (Witty, 1985). Dialogue journals offer an ongoing means for teachers and students to learn to write as naturally as youngsters learn to talk (Gambrell, 1985). Students also learn to think more clearly about what they are saying: written language invites reconsideration, or editing and critical review (Reid, 1990). The presence of a written record of a student's thoughts, along with the opportunity given the teacher to be informed by as well as to further inform those thoughts, could serve equally well as a definition of both whole language learning and diagnostic-teaching, two views that sometimes may seem oppositional. Here now are some accounts of how dialogue journals have been used to promote higher-order literacy.

- Julie E. Wollman-Bonilla (1989), a teacher turned researcher, writes that her greatest awakening came when she realized that conventional writing assignments failed to tap the heuristic potential of writing. Abandoning structured assignments dealing with analysis of plot, author's technique, and the like, she simply invited students to write about whatever thoughts were triggered by what they read. Curiously, their written responses revealed greater depth than had been evident in previous assigned writings and oral responses to conventional questions.
- Marne B. Isakson (1991) reports that students invited to exchange personal letters with her found voice for their interests and objections to certain stories and books. In this way, they were motivated to read a great deal more.
- Lane Roy Gauthier (1991) had content teachers offer student opportunities to comment on coursework. Invariably, they found statements from the students that directly influenced what they taught and how they taught it. Students, on the other hand, became increasingly aware of their own learning needs and ability to seek help.
- Barbara A. Bode (1989), an elementary and middle school principal, encouraged teachers to engage students in journal dialogues. The teachers learned simple and useful things from students. One teacher had a student point out that his class had been "doing" [studying] India for about a month and that now they were coming to hate it.

The Dialogue Journal has several of the same interactive features as the ReQuest Procedure. It is intimate, personal, empowering, and corrective. It also can point up flaws that send us, as teachers, running for cover. It is important to stay with the program and permit our sometimes delicate egos to continue learning from our experience as instructors.

The Writing Process

The Writing Process is a description of the stages that good writers tend to go through in producing a written piece—much as the Directed Reading Activity roughly parallels what a good reader does, moving from schema activation, to reading, to schema enhancement. (See Figure 13.5 for a description of how the teacher can guide students through the stages of the process.)

Sentence-Combining

Sentence-Combining is an instructional technique based on teaching students to combine two or more simple sentences into one. It has been shown to improve both writing fluency (Combs, 1975; Green, 1972; Mellon, 1967; O'Hare, 1973; Perron, 1974) and reading comprehension (Machie, 1982; Obenchain, 1971; Stotsky, 1975; Straw & Schreiner, 1982). This simple activity can be used with

FIGURE 13.5

Guiding Students Through the Steps in the Writing Process

PREWRITING: *"GETTING IT OUT"*

In this phase, the teacher helps students get ready to write by:

1. Raising motivation and interest.
2. Encouraging students to select and/or explore a topic.
3. Calling up relevant prior knowledge and experiences.
4. Laying out the basic expectations for the final product.
5. Assisting students in identifying an audience they can keep in mind to guide the form and character of the composition.

DRAFTING: *"GETTING IT DOWN"*

In this phase, the student attempts to channel the simultaneous din of ideas, purposes, facts, personal feelings, and biases into the linearity of words and structure. This includes finding out what you really think and then whether you can, or dare, say it. Typically, the teacher's role in this phase is to:

1. Help students express initial thoughts and ideas on paper.
2. Urge students to use prewriting notes and experiences.
3. Encourage the free flow of ideas, even where they seem to contradict one another.
4. Build personal conviction that learning and clear thinking are desirable and attainable goals.

REVISING: *"GETTING IT ORGANIZED"*

This is an evaluative phase that requires a good deal of introspection and willingness to critique oneself, to be critiqued, and to think like an editor and critique the work of others. In this phase, the teacher's role is to:

1. Set up peer editing teams: students read and evaluate their partner's paper, using a revision checklist.
2. Encourage students to reorder, rewrite, and revise for fluency and coherence as suggested by their peer editor.
3. Guide discussions that clarify and thereby point to specific areas of composition that require rewriting.
4. Encourage redrafting as needed with an eye toward initial purpose and audience.
5. Help students learn how well others have understood and interpreted their writing.

EDITING: *"GETTING IT RIGHT"*

In this phase, the composition is reviewed for correct mechanics such as spelling, grammatical usage, and punctuation. The teacher assists by:

1. Encouraging students to fine tune their work.
2. Noting common mechanical problems and providing class instruction in these areas.
3. Providing an editing checklist for peer editing teams.

PUBLISHING: *"GOING PUBLIC"*

1. Using methods that ensure that there will be readers for students' efforts.
2. Offering opportunities for the work to serve as a foundation for reading, discussion, or study.
3. Offering evaluative feedback based on the guidelines for the assignment.

students from primary grades through college to improve familiarity with written language patterns at increasing levels of syntactic complexity. Simple levels of sentence combining include insertion of modifiers, connecting subjects or predicates, or connecting two or more sentences in sequence.

INSERTION OF MODIFIERS

She sat behind a table.
The table was long.
The table was wooden.
[*She sat behind a long, wooden table.*]

CONNECTING SUBJECTS

Football is one of my two favorite sports.
Baseball is one of my two favorite sports.
[*Football and baseball are my two favorite sports.*]

CONNECTING PREDICATES

Marvin topped the pizza dough with sauce and cheese.
Marvin popped the pizza in the oven.
Marvin waited hungrily for his dinner.
[*Marvin topped the pizza dough with sauce and cheese, popped it into the oven, and waited for his dinner.*]

CONNECTING SENTENCES IN SEQUENCE

I had lost my passport
I did not worry about it
[*I had lost my passport, but I did not worry about it.*]

More complex sentence-combining exercises include inserting modifying clauses and phrases, and combining a list of short sentences into a fluent paragraph.

INSERTION OF MODIFYING CLAUSES AND PHRASES

My father was always worried about money.
My father wanted me to get a job.
[*My father, always worried about money, wanted me to get a job.*]

COMBINATION OF A LIST OF SHORT SENTENCES

Thomas Carlyle wrote an interesting analysis of what makes a "great man."
Thomas Carlyle had strong views on the the divinity of heroes.
It is hard to relate Thomas Carlyle's views to current thought.
There is a basic difference between Thomas Carlyle's time and ours.
Thomas Carlyle's ideas fit the mood of the Victorian era.
In the Victorian era, men agreed on certain values.
In the Victorian era, heroes could be measured by those principles.

Today, things are different.
Today, values are more a matter of individual choice.
Today, heroes are more a matter of individual choice.
Today, we each have our own heroes.
[*Thomas Carlyle's strong views on the divinity of heroes are hard to relate to current thought. There is a basic difference between his time and ours. Carlyle's ideas fit the mood of the Victorian era, when men agreed on certain values and heroes could be measured by those principles. Today, things are different. Values and heroes are more a matter of individual choice. Today, we each have our own heroes.*]

Sentence-combining activities lend themselves well to small group, whole class, or individual tutorial instructional settings. In any setting, the teacher should introduce the activity by offering an example and showing how the sample sentences might be combined. After students have tried their hand at combining sentences, instruction should focus on how well and why different combinations work. Students should not be discouraged from using any grammatical labels they might know to talk about the sentence-combining exercises. However, one of the values of sentence-combining, particularly as a remedial tool, is that it provides a way to provide focused, intensive language instruction *without* the need to use the cumbersome terminology of traditional grammar instruction. In brief, sentence-combining tends to induce productive and tangible instructional conversations.

Reducing/Expanding Sentences

Bill Martin, Jr., children's author and enthusiastic supporter of children's writing, suggests two variations on sentence-combining for improving writing: Reducing Sentences and Expanding Sentences.

Reducing/Expanding Sentences is especially useful when done as a whole-class activity using samples from students' own writing. It concentrates attention on the main ideas of sentences and the subtle changes of meaning evoked by slight changes of words and punctuation.

The process of reducing and expanding sentences helps students figure out how sentences work. To *reduce* a sentence, the student underlines all words, phrases, and clauses that are unnecessary to the essential meaning of the sentence. The danger in reducing a sentence is that one is apt to alter or destroy subtleties of sentence meaning or the author's style of writing. Let's reduce a few sentences and analyze the results.

A bird also has another way to help keep himself warm in winter.
By seeing to it that the birds near your home have plenty to eat, you can "keep their furnaces roaring" and their bodies warm in winter.
The bird's outer feathers are staggered like shingles on a roof to keep out the rain and snow.

> from *"How Birds Keep Warm in Winter,"*
> *Sounds of Mystery*

Discussion: In the first sentence, the reducing sharpened the sentence. The eliminated (underlined) words are truly unnecessary. In the second sentence, the meaning is preserved but the aesthetics seem to suffer. In the third sentence, the basic sentence is unchanged, but an important conceptual detail is eliminated.

Source: Bill Martin, Jr., lecture,
Kansas City, Missouri (July 1985)

Expanding Sentences is done by providing students with kernel sentences, such as the examples below.

The children heard a noise.
They ran to the window.
They could hardly believe their eyes.

Students are encouraged to add elaborative words and phrases—an activity that lends itself well to whole-class participation, cooperative learning groups, or individual work.

DeComposition and GRASP

Marilyn Eanet (1983) and David "Jack" Hayes (1989) have independently designed methodologies that expand the Guided Reading Procedure (GRP) into a method for teaching writing and reading in combination.

Eanet's DeComposition strategy uses the GRP to teach students how textual material is composed. The steps of the GRP are used to "decompose," or break the material into component parts. Then students are asked to use their notes to "recompose" the text in their own words. Hayes's Guided Reading And Summarizing Procedure (GRASP) also begins with the textual analysis generated from the Guided Reading Procedure. Students use their GRP notes as the basis for composing their own *summaries* of the material. The strategy described below is synthesized from these two methods.

Steps in DeComposition/GRASP

Step 1 *GRP lesson.* The teacher conducts a conventional Guided Reading Procedure lesson up through the outlining step.

Step 2 *Decomposing.* The teacher asks students, "Can you describe how the author put this information together?"

Step 3 *Recomposing.* The teacher asks the class, "Can you think of other logical ways by which this selection could have been composed?"

Step 4 *Summarizing.* The teacher has students write their own summaries, following these guidelines:

a. Include only important information (leave out unimportant details).

b. Where possible, compress information by combining it.

c. Add information needed to achieve coherence.

Note: Hayes suggests that the teacher demonstrate how the first cluster of information can be written into a single sentence, explaining why certain information is omitted, how other information can be combined, and the purpose(s) served by the changes. Then students are directed to write the next sentence while the teacher does the same on the chalkboard, preferably at the rear of the room. Students then share their sentences and comments about how their summary sentences compare with the teacher's. The teacher should be prepared to revise his or her sentence, writing changes above or below the original sentence to leave a visible record of the revision process. Students work individually (or in pairs) to compose additional sentences to complete the summary.

Step 5   (Optional) The teacher encourages students to write a brief reaction to the material read, analyzed, and summarized. Refer to the REAP Procedure (described ahead in this chapter) for examples of possible ways to react.

The Language Shaping Paradigm

The basic idea of the *Language Shaping Paradigm* (Manzo, 1981a) is to connect students to the printed page through their own writing. More important, the method urges students to value and profit from personal thoughts and experiences. In these respects, the Language Shaping Paradigm resembles two other methods: the traditional elementary-school-oriented Language Experience Story and a method well-described by its title, Read and Meet the Author, or RAMA (Santeusanio, 1967).

The efficacy of the Language Shaping Paradigm is inferred from a study of its parent, RAMA, and from experience and anecdotal accounts. RAMA was found to be significantly more effective than a control treatment in improving the reading comprehension and writing of college freshmen (Santeusanio, 1967). Our own experience with the Language Shaping Paradigm has tended to support and extend the generalizability of this approach to other levels, including functionally illiterate adult education students.

The basic teaching strategy entails having students read essays written (or dictated) by classmates. Each time the method is used, someone's essay is treated as an important work. The essay is edited (by both the teacher and the student-author) and reproduced with accompanying exercises designed (by the teacher) to improve reading comprehension, language usage, and creative writing.

Steps in the Language Shaping Paradigm

Step 1   The teacher begins with a *provocative discussion* to establish an authentic purpose for writing.

Step 2   Students *write themes* in a conventional way, or the teacher writes as the student dictates his or her essay.

Step 3   The teacher *selects a student story* or essay and edits it jointly with the student-author, informing the student that his or her work will be used for class study.

Step 4   The teacher prepares *comprehension questions* and language improvement exercises for the material.

FIGURE 13.6

Language Shaping Paradigm: Student Theme and Language Improvement Exercises

"I Dreamed I Was Green"
Author: Frank Fxxxxx, Age 31
Kansas City, Missouri

1   I fell asleep late last night on the couch in front of my TV. I
was watching an old movie called "Boy with the Green Hair." My body
ached from another long day. My stomach was now working on the
corned beef and cabbage, Dynamite! The combination made me dream a
5   strange dream. I dreamed that I woke up and had turned green. God,
it was so real! At first I thought it was the light. Then I thought
someone was playing a practical joke on me. But none of these things
made sense. The kids were fast asleep and my wife had not yet come
home from her part-time job. She is a ticket girl at the Waldo. I
10   called the doctor. The answering service wanted to know what was
wrong. I told them. He never called back. I went next door to my
neighbor, Bud. He was shocked. He brought me to the hospital. His
wife watched our kids.
        The doctors said there is nothing wrong with you that we can
15   tell, except that you are definitely green!
        Now the dream gets all crazy. All I know is that I find myself
planted in the backyard and beginning to look more and more like a
tree. Then a lot of time passes. An the house is old and my wife
and kids are gone, but I'm still in the backyard. No one seems to
20   notice me. I'm not unhappy. I'm not happy. I'm nothing. I'm just
there.
        Well, that's not really true, about my just being there, I mean.
There are moments when I'm very happy, like when squirrels and birds
are playing on my branches. And I really feel good when I turn
25   beautiful colors in the fall. And even though I don't like the
winter, it's kind of nice to be covered with blue-white snow.
        February is the worst. Dark and sad. But then in March I begin
to swell on the inside. I feel life stirring inside me, like a woman
does long before anyone even knows she is pregnant. Then April
30   showers and then in May I bust-out of myself and turn beautiful
green.
        I woke up at about that time. This may sound crazy, but I was
a little disappointed that I was not green.

Step 5   The teacher duplicates the theme and exercises for the *group to read and discuss*. The student-author is urged to maintain a "low profile" during the initial discussion.

Step 6   The teacher *invites the student-author to participate* more openly as the discussion moves to the language improvement exercises. This is the student-author's greatest learning opportunity in terms of writing, speaking, and learning to benefit from constructive criticism.

Level 1 Exercises: Choosing More Appropriate Words

Directions: Sometimes changing a few words in a paragraph can make an essay much sharper and clearer. Carefully study the paragraph below. Decide which of the underlined words you would replace from the list of words in the left column.

1
I called the doctor. The answer service wanted to know what was wrong. I told them.

3
He never called back. I went next door to my neighbor, Bud. He was shocked. He

2

4

5
brought me to the hospital. His wife watched our kids.

6

Replacement words	
spoke to	I (1) _____ the doctor. The answering
phoned	service (2) _____ what was wrong. I told
asked	them. (3) _____ never called back. I went
the doctor	next door to my neighbor, Bud. He was shocked. (4)
Bud	(5) _____ me to the hospital. His wife
drove	(6) _____ our kids.
looked after	
told	

Level 2 Exercises: Improving Style/Mood

Directions: "I Dreamed I was Green" is written in a half-humorous, half-serious vein; that is to say, the language is quite casual. Decide which of the sentences below best matches the *mood* of "I Dreamed I Was Green." Underline the words, phrases, and/or punctuations that seem to contribute to, or take away from, that mood. Write "I" for improved, "N" for not improved. (Number 1 is done as an example.)

_N_ 1. I asked the doctor's answering service if they might have <u>an opinion on why I was green.</u>

___ 2. I called the doctor. Naturally, I got some corny answering service.

___ 3. You got it! The doc never called back.

___ 4. I went next door to consult with my neighbor, Bud. He was shocked.

___ 5. Bud's wife, Martha, volunteered to look after the children while I was at the hospital.

The theme shown in Figure 13.6 is the product of a nearly illiterate adult who had enrolled in a basic education program. The story was stimulated by a discussion of dreams and their meanings. The instructor worked individually with "Frank," writing his story for him as he dictated it. The other class members wrote their own stories. Frank, working with the instructor, edited the theme until it was to his liking, and took editorial suggestions in good spirits. The forthcoming "publication" of the written piece seemed to offer its own justification for such straightforward editing and correcting of the more glaring grammatical and logical inconsistencies.

Frank's essay was reproduced for the other students. After an oral comprehension check, using a set of *who, what, where, when, why,* and *how*

Level 3 Exercises: Rewriting or Reorganizing
Directions: Do either A or B:

A. Pretend that you are the author of the article, and rewrite the paragraph between lines 16 and 21 in a way that you believe would improve it.

_____

_____

_____

_____

_____

B. Reorganize: Can you see any ways to reorder the story so that the basic story remains the same but the effect is more imaginative or stylish? (You may rewrite small sections, if necessary, to show what you mean.)

_____

_____

_____

_____

_____

questions, the students did the Language Improvement Exercises shown in Figure 13.6.

Further Detecting and Treating Higher-Order Literacy Problems and Needs

The most significant challenge to any field is to explain the things for which it is responsible. The study of higher-order literacy dysfunctions helps to complete a conceptual picture that will bring help to an overlooked group of youngsters, while simultaneously helping us understand better and treat lower-order, or more conventional, literacy disorders as well. In a well-designed comparison study, Victoria Purcell-Gates (1991) added considerable support to the higher-order literacy approach to remedial reading. In comparing effective and ineffective readers, she found that remedial readers were the weakest in three higher mental processes that need to be overcome as part of the remedial program: a) stepping in and out of plot line to "confer with oneself"; b) overcoming a general failure to construct wholes; and c) a struggle with the "language of literacy discourse" (1991, p. 242).

The practical value of pursuing higher-order literacy goals, as previously mentioned, has been strikingly demonstrated in a series of longitudinal studies by Robert Ruddell and associates (Ruddell, Draheim, & Barnes, 1990; Ruddell & Haggard, 1982; Ruddell & Harris, 1989; Ruddell & Kern, 1986). These studies looked at the behavior of "influential teachers" (as determined by surveys of students dating back 8 years) versus those not so nominated. What they discovered in actually observing these teachers was that the influential ones rely heavily in reading instruction on building internal reader motivations, a sense of aesthetics, intellectual curiosity, understanding of self, escape, and problem resolution (Ruddell, 1990). Moreover, influential teachers used higher-order thinking questions three times as often as did noninfluential teachers. In line with the "higher-thinking *can* go first" hypothesis, their students had significantly greater growth in conventional, or reconstructive, comprehension as well. Such hard evidence aside, there are problems in diagnosing and treating higher literacy disorders and in having these practices become more widespread.

There are three fundamental problems that stand in the way of launching a full scale effort to improve higher-order literacy. One is a set of agreed upon measures to stimulate teacher explorations and attention to such needs. Second is an interactive environment that values, encourages, and sets standards for higher-order thinking in students. The third is a clearer understanding of the nature and extent of problems that exist at this level.

The Informal Reading-Thinking Inventory: A Teacher-Heuristic to Higher-Order Literacy

To hasten and guide teachers in recognition of higher-order literacy needs, the writers and associates Robert Leibert, Siriwan Ratanakarn, and Fengfang Liu of the Center for Studies in Higher Order Literacy (University of Missouri-Kansas City), and Michael McKenna of Georgia Southern University, are attempting to develop a new formula to guide construction of Informal Reading Inventories that would pay more explicit attention to such needs. The simple expectation is that if continuing assessment in reading included this additional dimension, educators would become more sensitive to it, knowledgeable about it, and committed to teaching toward it. This impression is given a boost by findings that show that the simple act of altering teachers' questioning also alters their feedback and discussion practices, and that student behavior and learning soon follow (Ruddell, 1990; O'Flahaven, Hartman, & Pearson, 1988).

Emerging Rationale, Formula, and Criteria for IR-TI

The rationale for the IR-TI simply is to broaden attention to certain valued aspects of reading and literacy development that now tend to receive short shrift. The reasoning is that this can be partially achieved simply by enhancing current IRI formulas, such that teachers and schools begin to measure them better and, more likely, attend to these highly prized but under-attended features of full literacy.

The current Informal Reading-Thinking Inventory (IR-TI) is a diagnostic, evaluative, and research device that both assesses and highlights aspects of student progress in reading and thinking. It also is designed to elicit information relevant to assessing aspects of language proficiency and personal-social adjustment that may be implicated in comprehension and thinking. Quantitative and qualitative scoring systems are used toward these ends. Elements of the inventory are further explained here, along with indications of how it differs from a conventional IRI.

Construction of the inventory begins with two sets of passages. One set is used for assessment of the student's oral and silent reading, and the other set is used to assess capacity through listening comprehension. Each reading/listening passage is followed by a series of questions that can be grouped to yield nine scores:

- flash word level
- word analysis level
- oral reading time (rate)
- silent (rereading) reading time (rate)
- ability to read the lines—or literal, factual comprehension
- ability to read between the lines—or to make inferences
- ability to read beyond the lines—or to think in a variety of conjectural, critical, metacognitive, and constructive ways such are detailed ahead
- personal-social growth and adjustment (as inferred from metacognitive functioning and qualitative assessment of responses to open-ended questions and to the proportion of incongruent or irrelevant responses to questions)
- language functioning (as inferred from selected quantitative and qualitative measures of "congruency" and "details" of conversations and writing samples)

Differences

In general, the IR-TI should be structured as a diagnostic conversation between a teacher and a student. Anything that seriously detracts from this should be set aside, unless the information is crucial at that time. The IR-TI formula differs from most conventional IRI's in several additional ways:

1. Each selection is preceded by a motivating and schema-activating question or statement. Most published IRI's include purpose-setting statements to be used prior to the student's reading. The schema-activating component of the IR-TI is directed to eliciting *background* information the student may have, rather than directing attention to passage-specific information or ideas.
2. Following this brief discussion, students are asked to indicate, from the outset, whether they think they will enjoy reading or listening to the remainder of the selection. This permits the teacher and student to judge performance against likely level of interest and motivation.
3. Question types include literal, inferential, interpretative, and non-text specific, or beyond the lines questions. Questions are selected because they seem to fit the context of the selection or because of some reasonable connection that could or should be made. To this extent, the IR-TI attempts to be more meaning-driven than driven by the need to ask a certain kind of question.

4. Account is taken of two important qualitative features of learning: Incongruities and Details. Incongruity refers to the tendency to respond with an answer which is illogical, or "out-of-the ballpark," more so than just incorrect. This is a useful measure of whether the pupil was really engaged in the reading and subsequent diagnostic dialogue, and therefore whether the findings can be trusted to be valid. Current estimates suggest that when incongruent responses exceed one-third of the questions asked, it is an indication that engagement was weak and nonproductive. Detailed responses, on the other hand, are documented in the scoring system. Plus-marks (+) are given for responses that are especially full, fresh, or elaborated in some meaningful and appropriate way. Detailed responses may be prompted if none occur naturally with comments or questions, such as "Do you want to say more about that?" or, "Does this make you think of anything else that you have heard, seen, or done?" Our current data base suggests that anything more than one such elaboration per selection can be taken as evidence of an alert mind that is engaged and being driven by meaning. It is too soon to say if any significant meanings can be attached to the absence of elaborations, or how much of this can be expected with different types of questions and formats. It also needs to be determined whether this is related to personality variables more so than cognitive ones, per se. Nonetheless, detailed responses seem to be worth noting, since it only requires a simple recording system, and it tends to reveal inclination to be engaged and to naturally make connections.

5. Self-monitoring is assessed by a simple request to the student to self-appraise how well he or she has answered a prior set of questions. It is uncertain how predictive or good this format is for assessing this aspect of metacognition, but a study in progress is looking very supportive.

6. All responses, even to the "beyond the lines" questions, are totaled, and used with the typical Betts criteria for classifying reading levels. However, separate scores also are listed for reconstructive (literal and inferential) and constructive type (metacognitive, conjectural, critical-creative) questions. These two scores should not vary more than 20%. If it does, it should be taken as a greater or lesser degree of discrepancy, and therefore need, in the lower of the two categories.

7. Selections include excerpts from conventional story and nonfiction prose as well as brief but complete fables. Figure 13.7 provides an example of a portion of an IR-TI we have constructed for experimental work.[1]

8. A full IR-TI need not be given, nor need the full inventory be given in one sitting. It is okay to establish instructional level with another IRI, or with just the standard word lists, and conventional questions of the IR-TI, and then conduct a full inquiry with a passage at the student's instructional level. In other words, it can be used to gather further information on students you

---

[1]A complete set of these along with a test manual and sample responses is available upon request from the publishers or the author for use with this text.

suspect of being either *better* than their conventional IRI scores, or those you suspect of being mechanistic thinkers who are functionally *below* their otherwise proficient reading as indicated on a conventional IRI.

In any event, most informal reading inventories can be upscaled to include a "beyond the lines" component. The process of constructing higher level questions is, in itself, a valuable professional development experience. Should you choose to construct an IR-TI, or upscale an existing IRI, you might wish to add an unaided recall portion (see the example offered in the retelling portion of Chapter 4).

Overall, the IR-TI could be called a whole-language, whole-person inventory since it attempts to look at the reader as well as his or her reading; involves reading, listening, speaking, and writing; invites subjective as well as objective involvement and assessment; and attempts to connect teacher, students, textual material, and ideas at a workbench where each is given an opportunity to take a lead in influencing facets of the diagnostic conversation.

It is this by-play of parts and opportunities for each of these features to come into play that we believe will create a meaningful heuristic to guide professional interest and attention to the higher-literacy needs of remedial children. The broad adoption of such a formula could also bring about a more tangible and lasting interest in higher-order reading and thinking in the schools.

Consider now a further example of how to get the environment working to support full literacy. This example extends the suggestions made in Chapter 4.

FIGURE 13.7

Informal Reading-Thinking Inventory Excerpt

Grade 4
Number of words: 151
The Shepherd Boy and the Wolf
A shepherd boy was tending his flock near a village, and thought it would be great fun to trick the villagers by pretending that a wolf was attacking the sheep. He shouted out, "Wolf! Wolf!" and when the villagers came running up he laughed at them for being so easily tricked. He tried this hoax more than once. Every time the villagers ran to help the boy, they found that they had been tricked again, and there was no wolf at all.

At last, a wolf really did come, and the boy cried, "Wolf, Wolf!" as loud as he could, but the people were so used to hearing him call that they took no notice of his cries for help. So the wolf had it all his own way, and killed off many sheep.

The moral of this story is: no one believes a liar, even when he tells the truth.

The Shepherd Boy and the Wolf
(Grade 4)

MOTIVATION/SCHEMA ACTIVATION

What does a shepherd do?

_____

_____

Now you are going to listen to a story about a shepherd boy who got in the habit of telling lies. Then I will ask you some questions about what you have heard and what you thought about it.

1. How much did you enjoy this story? Point to the picture that is closest to the way you feel. (*Show student the "rating card" provided with the test materials, reproduced below. Briefly review the meaning of each choice, and circle the number of the student's choice. You may also indicate the "value" of responses by recording a "√" for any responses that are clearly incongruent or illogical, or a "+" for any that are exceptionally full or detailed.*)

Explanation (optional)

_____

_____

Value:_____

READING THE LINES

Guidelines for Recording Student Responses
In the "Score" column, record "0" for incorrect or "1" for correct answers. in the "Value" column, record a "✔" for any responses that are clearly incongruent or illogical, and record a "+" for any responses that are exceptionally full or detailed.

	Score	Value
2. What was the shepherd boy's job? (*taking care of the sheep*)		
3. What idea did he think of as a way to have fun? (*tricking the villagers by pretending that a wolf was attacking the sheep*)		
4. What did the villagers do when the boy first shouted "Wolf"? (*they came running to help*)		

	Score	Value

5. What does the word "hoax" mean in this passage?
(*a trick or a joke*)

_____   _____   _____

READING BETWEEN THE LINES   *Silent Reading Time:* ___ *min.,* ___ *sec.*

	Score	Value

6. Did the villagers think that a wolf might harm the sheep?
(*yes — that's why they came running when the boy called.*)

_____   _____   _____

7. Why didn't the villagers come when the wolf was really killing the sheep?
(*they couldn't believe the boy when he finally told the truth*)

_____   _____   _____

8. How well do you think you answered these factual and thought questions? Point to the picture that is closest to the way you think you answered. (*Show student the "rating card," reproduced below. Circle the number of the student's choice. You may also indicate the "value" of responses by recording a "√" for any responses that are clearly incongruent or illogical, or a "+" for any that are exceptionally full or detailed.*)

Explanation (optional)

_____

_____

Value:_____

READING BEYOND THE LINES

> *Guidelines for Recording Student Responses*
> In the "Score" column, record "0" for incorrect, "1" for correct answers, or "2" for answers that are correct *and* elaborated upon. In the "Value" column, record a "✔" for any responses that are clearly incongruent or illogical, and record a " +" for any responses that are exceptionally full or detailed.

9. Tell how much you agree with this statement — *"Trust is more important than fun."* — point to the picture that shows the way you feel: (*The student's explanation should indicate that fun is important, but trust is more so, and that it is possible to have fun without destroying trust.*)

Score   Value

10. Why is it important not to tell lies? (*Score any of the following answers correct, as well as any other reasonable answers the student gives.*)
___ People may not help you when you need it, because they won't
      know you really do.
___ People won't believe you.
___ People won't like you.
___ Nothing works well when we lose trust in each other.
___ Other _____

11. This fable is sometimes called "The Boy Who Cried Wolf." Can you see
    another possible meaning for the term "crying wolf," based on this fable?
    (*calling for help when it isn't really needed*)

    _____   _____   _____

    _____

12. How well do you think you answered these related questions? Point to the picture that is closest to the way you think you answered. (*Show student the "rating card," reproduced below. Circle the number of the student's choice. You may also indicate the "value" of responses by recording a "√" for any responses that are clearly incongruent or illogical, or a "+" for any that are exceptionally full or detailed.*)

Explanation (optional)

_____

_____

Value:_____

13. What might the shepherd boy do, now that no one believes him anymore? (*Build new trust by saying he is sorry, and then doing good deeds*)

    Score   Value

    Oral response notes: _____   _____

    _____

    _____

    _____

14. **Optional:** Following initial discussion of question #13, ask the student
    to write his/her answer on a separate sheet of paper.   _____   _____

    Original drawings by Manee Buranaburoostham
    © Anthony Manzo and Ula Manzo

Building a Literate Environment: Beyond Summary Writing

Building a conducive environment is one of the most durable ways of promoting full literacy. The proposal described next is offered as a means of facilitating improvement in literacy and thinking of both conventional remedial readers and students who have deficiencies in constructive—or critical, creative, and applied—thinking.

Simply put, the idea is to introduce students to a variety of means of responding to textual material beyond retelling and summarizing. David Hayes (1987) tested this idea by asking high school students to engage in a variety of writing tasks—paraphrasing, formulating questions, and developing compare-and-contrast statements. As he had hypothesized, students who wrote questions and compare-and-contrast statements had better recall of what they had read. More importantly, these students recalled more of the abstract and structuring information from what they read. Hayes concluded that the greater level of challenge resulted in greater and more profound levels of "integration of text information with learner knowledge" (as cited in Tierney & Shanahan, 1991). In other words, the writing tasks resulted in higher levels of *constructive* thinking and reading.

Manzo (1973) undertook a similar field-experiment with minority youngsters who had previously failed English at least once with similar results. Later, working with Marilyn Eanet, this effort was formalized into a reading-writing-study strategy called REAP (Eanet & Manzo, 1976). REAP has been aptly described as a "technique that actively involves readers in processing the ideas an author has set down in print, and in communicating in their own words an understanding of those ideas with others" (Tierney, Readence, & Dishner, 1990, p. 289).

REAP: A Reading-Study Strategy

Read-Encode-Annotate-Ponder, or REAP (Eanet & Manzo, 1976), uses writing as a means of improving thinking and reading. The basic process is summarized by the title of the strategy:

Read	to discern the writer's message.
Encode	the message in a personalized way, by translating it into your own language.
Annotate	the message in one or or more ways (see annotation forms ahead).
Ponder	what you have read and written, first introspectively and then by sharing or discussing it with others.

Students are introduced to a variety of annotation forms by which to capture and/or respond to the essence of a writer's message. Ten types of annotations are described in Figure 13.8. A sample passage from our experimental IR-TI is annotated in these ways in Figure 13.9.

How to teach REAP to Readers with Reconstructive and Constructive Deficits.

The following paradigm can be used to teach each type of annotation, using several short, interesting passages at students' independent to instructional

FIGURE 13.8

REAP Annotation Types

RECONSTRUCTIVE ANNOTATIONS

1. *Summary annotation*—condenses the selection into a concise form. In fiction, it is a synopsis of the plot and main characters; in nonfiction, it is an unelaborated statement of the key ideas.
2. *Precis annotation*—an incisive thesis statement of the author's primary proposition, with all unncessary words removed. The result is an uncluttered, telegram-like message.
3. *Provocative annotation*—a statement, usually in the author's words, that symbolically illustrates the central idea of the selection in a way that tends to provoke a response.
4. *Question annotation*—converts the author's main point into a question that the narrative is written to answer.

CONSTRUCTIVE ANNOTATIONS

5. *Personal view annotation*—answers the question "How do one's personal experiences, views, and feelings stack up against the author's main idea?"
6. *Critical annotation*—a supportive, rejecting, or questioning response to the main idea. The first sentence should restate the author's position. The next sentence should state the annotator's position. Additional sentences should explain how the two differ.
7. *Intention annotation*—states and briefly explains the annotator's impression of the author's intention, plan, and purpose in writing the selection. This is a variation of the critical annotation.
8. *Motivation annotation*—speculates on the author's likely experiences and motive(s) for having created or written the piece. This too is a form of critical annotation, with particular emphasis on searching inside oneself to discover what might be motivating the author.
9. *Probe annotation*—identifies practical questions that merit further attention before an evaluation of the author's points can be reached. This requires identifying supporting points and thinking about consequences.
10. *Creative annotation*—an attempt to come up with an alternative view or resolution. This annotation type usually requires a question or further bit of stimulation to get the creative juices flowing.

reading level. The same sample passages can be used to teach all annotation types. The steps below are worded for teaching constructive level annotations, but they demonstrate how each type can be similarly taught.

Step 1   *Responding.* Students read or listen to a selection. They are encouraged to express their initial, "gut level," responses to the piece. this can be structured by having them record their responses on a semantic differential scale such as is shown below:

Step 2   *Articulating.* Students attempt to explain their feelings about the piece in twenty-five words or less.

FIGURE 13.9

Sample REAP Annotations (written in response to an IR-TI selection)

"Travellers and the Plane-Tree"[1]

Two Travellers were walking along a bare and dusty road in the heat of a midsummer's day. Coming upon a large shade tree, they happily stopped to shelter themselves from the burning sun in the shade of its spreading branches. While they rested, looking up into the tree, one of them said to his companion, "What a useless tree this is! It makes no flowers and bears no fruit. Of what use is it to anyone?" The tree itself replied indignantly, "You ungrateful people! You take shelter under me from the scorching sun, and then, in the very act of enjoying the cool shade of my leaves, you abuse me and call me good for nothing!"

Moral: Many a service is met with ingratitude.

modified from *Aesop's Fables*

RECONSTRUCTIVE ANNOTATIONS:

1. *Summary annotation*
   Travellers take shelter from the sun under a large tree. They criticize the tree for not doing much but being there. The tree tells them that they take shelter under her leaves and say she's no good.
3. *Precis annotiation*
   Travellers stop to rest and get out of the sun when they come to a big tree. They criticize it for not making fruit. The tree takes offense and tells them so.
2. *Provocative annotation*
   This is a story about a tree that talks back to people. The tree says, "You ungrateful people! You come and take shelter under me. . . and then . . . abuse me and call me good for nothing!"
4. *Question annotation*
   What can happen when people begin to exploit everything around them without thought or gratitude?

CONSTRUCTIVE ANNOTATIONS

5. *Personal view annotation*
   a. We use material resources like coal without thinking. Then we criticize it for damaging our lungs and dirtying our air.
   b. We often use our own parents the way the travellers used the tree, and then criticize them without much thought about their feelings.
6. *Critical annotation*
   Not every word spoken in criticism is meant that way. The travellers were just making conversation. The tree is too sensitive.
7. *Intention annotation*
   The author of this fable intended for us to be more sensitive to those people and things that we rely on.

[1]a type of tree with one broad leaf.

8. *Motivation annotation*
   The author probably wrote this after having a bad experience with friends or family. He or she must have felt used.
9. *Probe annotation*
   I wonder how many of us know that we can be "users." We ought to take a secret poll to see how many people (class members) feel that they have been used and how many see themselves as users.
10. *Creative annotation*
    a. This fable reminds me of how Dobie Gillis uses and then abuses that nice, but plain girl who is always hanging around him.
    b. I think teachers are also used and then unfairly criticized for being only human when they make small mistakes.
    c. Maybe we should put this fable on the bulletin board where we can read it more often and remind ourselves not to be ungrateful "user types."
    d. [How would you retitle this fable if you were writing it?] I'd call it "Travellers in the *Dark*," to show that most of us go through life unaware of the many gifts that come to us.

Directions: Circle the number closest to your feelings about the piece you have just read (heard):

A. Boring						Exciting
1	2	3	4	5	6	7
B. Cold						Hot
1	2	3	4	5	6	7
C. Stale						Fresh
1	2	3	4	5	6	7
D. Lame						Interesting
1	2	3	4	5	6	7

Step 3   *Recognizing and defining.* The teacher provides students with a well-written example of a constructive annotation (see example ahead) and asks them how it parallels what they have read.

Step 4   *Discriminating.* Students read a second selection. This time, the teacher gives them four annotations to consider. One example should be a good constructive-type annotation and the others faulty in some way—too emotional, too narrow, not directly related to the idea(s) in the selection, and/or lacking sufficient justification. In class discussion, students choose the best annotation, logically defend their choice, and explain why the others are unsatisfactory.

Step 5   *Modeling the process.* Students read a third selection. This time, the teacher actually demonstrates to students how to write a constructive level annotation. This step is most effective when the teacher "thinks aloud," writing and rewriting as necessary to compose an honestly felt but balanced statement.

Step 6   *Practicing.* Students read a fourth selection and individually try writing their own constructive level annotations. A few of the students' productions are duplicated or put on the chalkboard and compared and evaluated by the teacher and class.

Step 7   *Sequencing.* After students have tried their hand at writing a few constructive level annotations, the teacher formally introduces the other annotations that could be written in response to text. Mastery of one type of annotation is not necessary before introducing other types: some students who have difficulty with constructive level annotations often produce quality annotations of other types.

Step 8   *Reinforcing.* The teacher has students exchange annotations and write annotations in response to one another's work. At this point, the teacher should introduce the idea of letters-to-the-editor from newspapers and magazines as examples of dialog centered on issues and text, and as models of effective writing from which students can learn incidentally each time they read a newspaper or magazine.

The annotation types listed and described in Figure 13.8 are roughly in order of difficulty: lower numbers tend to indicate more reconstructive and mechanistic thinking, and higher numbers more sophisticated and constructive patterns of responding. A good index of a student's general level of literacy development can be inferred by noting the kind of annotation he or she tends to prefer and to construct. Annotations are excellent candidates for portfolios and can be assembled to show progress over time. Most importantly, they give insight into reading, language, and thinking development.

Next, see how student annotations can be fashioned into a reader response system.

REAP: A Reader Response and Exchange System.

REAP can be used as the basis for creating a more literate and constructive reading environment for readers at all levels (Eanet, 1978; Manzo, 1985; Manzo & Manzo, 1990a). Simply put, the classroom or school-based Annotation Exchange, or AnX system, offers a means for readers to respond reconstructively and constructively to text and to share those responses with others. The sharing of summary-type annotations can serve to help others grasp the basic reconstructive message; critical-type annotations impart insight and deeper meanings that naturally teach constructive responding. Text-responders might include parents, grandparents, community members, and teachers, as well as other students. The creation of cross-age and cross-cultural conversations among these otherwise seldom interacting groups of individuals not only stirs higher-order thinking in the classroom, but carries this objective out into the community, enriching the writing and thinking of the larger environment in which school is conducted. Kathy Short's (1984) collaborative model of reading and writing, shown in Figure 13.10, particularly the "people" and "their texts," illustrates the key ingredients of this higher-order literacy exchange plan.

FIGURE 13.10

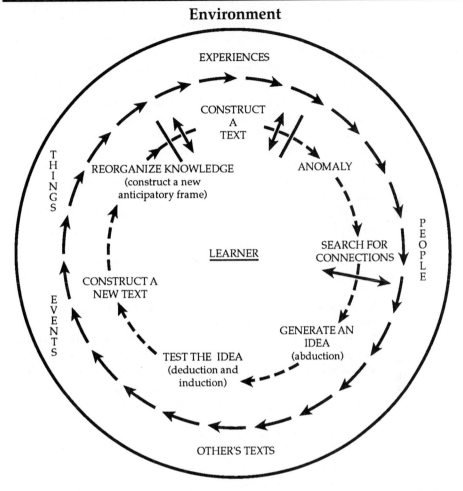

Environment

EXPERIENCES

CONSTRUCT A TEXT

ANOMALY

THINGS

REORGANIZE KNOWLEDGE
(construct a new
anticipatory frame)

PEOPLE

LEARNER

SEARCH FOR CONNECTIONS

CONSTRUCT A
NEW TEXT

EVENTS

GENERATE AN IDEA
(abduction)

TEST THE IDEA
(deduction and
induction)

OTHER'S TEXTS

Short (1984)

Three levels of such exchange are possible, each increasingly demanding to implement, but each also yielding higher returns. To establish a classroom, or resource room program, the teacher merely needs some large index cards and a file box. Students are first invited to write annotations, then assisted with editing their work for it to "go public." The best of these then is stored in the file box under the title of the book or selection to which it is a response or reaction. Other students then are free to read these to scan for books and selections they may wish to read, and to guide their pre-, during-, or post-reading of the material. They then may write an annotation of their own that is of the same type or different from those available, or in response to one that is on file.

Each file card should have an index number and be signed (optional) and dated by the reactor. Selections should be alphabetized, and reaction cards numbered. If a card is permanently removed or lost for any reason, merely invite students to use that card for the next new annotation. Reactions to previous cards should state this fact plainly: "Reaction to Card #15 by Maryann Jones."

The prospects of establishing a school or community-based library exchange program are greatly assisted by two new technical innovations. There now are inexpensive personal computers and text scanners (about $300 to $600) that make it possible to "download" an annotation, handwritten or typed, into the computer merely by scanning it with a hand-held or full-page device. If the original material is written, the scanner will enter the material as a graphic and reproduce it as such. If the original is in print form, it can be entered right into the system's word processing software and be further edited by the teacher and the student.

Material stored in this way can be turned into hard copy and made available as "reference book" material. It also can be called up on the computer and printed on an "as needed" basis.

The selections read and annotations written can also be reviewed periodically by classroom teachers in search of writing samples that can be used in class lessons for sharpening thinking and writing craft. Again, students can be encouraged to select from their earlier and then "best" works for their portfolios.

A committee can be formed to select the best annotations for the school or community-based library system. It should be composed of persons who represent different perspectives. The greatest contribution of an exchange reading, or response-to-text program is the creation of a literate community of readers and thinkers who are rewarded for their insightful thinking and writing, more so than for their ability merely to respond to "comprehension check" questions. In so doing, the system makes new "stars"; that is, it offers new models of thinking to admire and possibly emulate.

Social star shifting is a very important part of enhancing thinking and options. An Annotation Exchange, or AnX, System continues to provide meaningful opportunities beyond the classroom for individuals to think and respond constructively. It can become a natural reinforcer and ecological force for higher literacy within the school and the community. It also teaches responsibility of a new kind, as individuals come to see the importance of giving something back to the community of books and teachers and efforts to educate them. Christopher Lichtenberg (1764-99) put it this way: "To read means to borrow; to create out of one's reading is paying off one's debt."

The next section attempts to set out the current state of the effort to draw attention to higher-order literacy dysfunctions. Most such problems go undetected and untreated largely due to the paucity of information on this emerging area of professional interest.

Every book worthy of the name contains some small corner in which the author(s) "mumble to themselves" about some forming ideas, in the hope that

someone might overhear them and wish to join the
section tends to fit this billing.

Higher-Order Literacy Problems of Proficient

In this context, higher-order literacy dysfunction refers to
enced by those who read well at reconstructive levels, bu
comprehension to constructive levels. Francis Chase (1961)   ....uy described
one such group as "higher illiterates":

> The higher illiterate can absorb and repeat ideas found on the printed page but
> has not developed the ability to relate these ideas to the life around him. He does
> not engage in the kind of dialogue which will test the relevance of what he has
> read to his own personal experience, to the lives of those he meets, or to the
> behavior of individuals and social groups in general . . . . He can not entertain
> ideas which are at variance with his preconceptions of the "nature of things". . . .
> In short, for the higher illiterate reading is not an invitation to reflective thought.
> It does not arouse an active process of relating the abstractions of the printed page
> to persons, events, and institutions of the real world; it does not lead to an inter-
> nal reorganization of ideas previously received or the establishment of receptiv-
> ity to other ideas; and it does not become a seizing of the present moment to ex-
> tract from past experience insights into the future. (p. 11)

There are problems in addressing and treating reading disorders of this
type. The chief problems in diagnosing and treating higher-order literacy disorders are very pragmatic. The trouble begins with a general lack of acknowledg-
ment that such problems even exist, especially at the elementary to high school
levels. College professors often are the first ones to take serious note of such
problems. Not surprisingly, there is no system of referral for such deficiencies at
any level. Accordingly, other than the IR-TI, there are relatively few instruments
or protocols for assessing such dysfunctions in a timely way. The Watson-Glaser
Test of Critical Thinking (1964) is a notable exception, as are tests designed by
researchers to correspond to specific operational definitions in a particular study
(Patching, et.al., 1983). Topping this are two factors that add to the problem of
diagnosing and testing such deficiencies:

- The subjective level of responding that is a necessary element of assessing
higher-order thinking tends to invite controversy, and schools shy from controversy.

- The type of thinking required for higher-order operations (called "formal
operations" by Piaget) seem to be undeveloped in about 20%–30% of the general
population, irrespective of level of formal education (Karplus, 1974).

From these points it can be seen that it would naturally be an up-hill fight to
win fair consideration for higher-literacy disorders, despite the fact that such
concerns have been expressed from the time of Socrates to that of Dewey, and
now in recent NAEP reports as well. Here now are some additional general

recommendations of practices that concerned teachers and reading specialists can engage in that will help lift this area of concern into common practice.

Suggested Ways to Promote Higher-Order Literacy

- Become more conversant with such problems and related issues ourselves.
- Talk and write about these issues in curriculum meetings and teacher inservice situations.
- Form a cadre of fellow teachers who are interested in this issue (a higher-order literacy special interest group, as it were).
- Work to improve your own higher-order operations.
- Work to get students involved in this effort.
- Begin immediately to teach toward and respect such skills in your own class-room.

The next section is meant to share some of our current impressions on the nature of higher-order literacy dysfunctions. It does this by focusing on the specifics of one such disorder that we are attempting to understand and treat better, that of literalness.

The Diagnosis and Treatment of Literalness in Reading

Attempts to treat what we have come to call "literalness" are not merely on the forefront of the field of current practices in diagnoses and remediation, but the forefront of human development. Literary criticism, or the constructive reading of literature, is a form of higher-order literacy that was "invented" only 2,000 years ago by Aristotle (Source: Encyclopedia Britannica). This may seem a good deal of time ago, but it is a mere moment in social and evolutionary history. Furthermore, one must consider the fact that Aristotle was the student of Plato, who in turn was a student of Socrates, and it had not occurred to either of these two great minds to engage in this high art, despite the fact that the ancient world had already produced several great playwrights.

In lieu of this fact, it might be asked why the field of Diagnosis and Remediation should become involved in understanding and treating such higher-literacy disorders. To set the stage, it must first be said that we are not advocating that current specialists should necessarily become fully committed to such problems in their day to day practice, although they are encouraged to do so if their will and circumstances permit. Rather, we are saying that representatives from the field of literacy need to become involved in this newer direction since: a) no other established school "subject" or group is formally addressing the needs of this population; b) the problem fits our present model; and c) it can be quite enlightening to study the mirror image, or analog of a traditional problem that has become bogged down, as has the study of conventional remedial reading.

There also is the realization that "literalness" is a problem of poorer readers as well. Therefore, the study of it in better readers can help overcome the difficulty in identifying it in poorer readers whose overall levels of reading, thinking, and scholastic achievement are often too depressed to pick up this more subtle problem. The current effort, therefore, is to understand the effects of literalness in better readers so that we might identify and study the problem better wherever it is encountered. There are yet other advantages discussed ahead for beginning investigation at this level.

One traditional means of studying a presumed disorder is to ascertain its attending, or correlative, characteristics. This has been widely done, for example, with conventional remedial level readers, as illustrated in previous chapters. There has been much less research done with higher-level disabilities. Thus, by necessity, the characteristics of higher-literal level readers reported here are marshalled together from fewer empirical sources, and with a good deal more reliance on clinical experiences and speculations. Keep in mind as you read these that not all characteristics are said to be true of all who are overly literal, nor is "literalness" a state that one has or does not have. There are five levels of literalness that appear to us to be behaviorally discernible. With some prompting, most individuals can be helped to make this determination of themselves.

Levels of Literalness

1. Not literal
2. Tendency to be literal
3. Partial literalness (Several characteristics, but also some offsetting characteristics)
4. Predominantly literal (Many characteristics, a few off-setting)
5. Acute literalness (A clear trait characteristic reaching into several aspects of life)

The diagnostic indicators of persons who are likely to be overly literal are divided below into two general categories—those related to Reading, Writing, Thinking Behaviors; and Other (largely speculative) Personal, Behavioral, Personality, and Physical Characteristics.

Keep in mind as you study these that several will appear particularly biting. They appear this way because society, while giving lip service to placing a high value on deep and analytical reading and thinking, has been disinclined to study or address it in earnest; therefore, our language choices are few and probably not yet "politically correct." A related reason that this listing may appear biting is that it touches us and those we know in very personal terms. It is not about an unrepresented group of "have nots," such as "remedial readers," or even about our own failing children, who we prefer to call "learning disabled." Rather, it is about us, our friends, and some of our seemingly achieving children.

On the positive side, an investigation of this type could usher in a new era of educational research marked by greater honesty and incisiveness as the population under study will be among the first to be able to participate in the investigation on an equal footing. Consider now some of the diagnostic characteristics of literalness as we have assembled them from empirical evidence, clinical impressions, and suppositions as we now understand them. Collectively, these characteristics could be said to be a current working definition of this condition.

Reading-Writing-Thinking Behaviors Associated with Literalness

- Cognitive processing tends to be "successive" more so than "simultaneous."
- The reader perceives an inordinate number of ambiguities in even simple messages.
- The reader continues to enjoy reading predictable books (especially series) into and beyond teenage years.
- Word decoding is good, but there is a continued conscious reliance on rules and prompts long after these processes should have been internalized.
- Comprehension of details is solid, except when details are at odds with existing schema.
- Comprehension that involves inferencing, particularly to the level of conjecture, or speculation, is relatively weak.
- Inclination to form connections among stories and ideas read is weak (although the reader is apparently able to do so with prompting).
- Reading is not related to self-examination and self-understanding.
- Information and books are treated cursively; lack of reflection is apparent in a lack of textmarking or highlighting.
- The reader seldom raises questions beyond textual limits, such as the intentions or motivation of the writer.
- He/She is good at following print directions.
- He/She possesses high verbal aptitude; good at word games.
- The reader is easily seduced by good writing and can be gullible.
- The reader exhibits immature levels of criticism and writing, sometimes characterized by veiled "me-centered" propositions.
- He/She strongly prefers reading fiction to nonfiction.
- He/She has a tendency to write and say obvious things as if they were significant insights.
- This person likes to write, but is discouraged by a sense of "nothing to say."
- He/She is good at retellings and summary writing.
- Thinking generally is mechanistic, and marked by good internal logic but weak external validation.
- The reader does well on school subjects, with little improvement in related areas of thinking.
- When giving criticism, the tendency is to be too severe, indicating an underlying self-deprecating nature.
- The reader overgeneralizes despite frequently criticizing others for doing so.
- He/She often finds reason to say variations on "What do you mean?"

- Thinking tends to be either excessively "field dependent" (i.e., overly influenced by the context and people involved more so than the objective value of facts and ideas) or excessively "field independent" (i.e., lacking appropriate sense of context, and having little regard for the consequences of saying certain things).
- The reader exhibits weak mechanical aptitude; perhaps, more correctly, low mechanical orientation.

Other Personal Behavioral, Personality, and Physical Characteristics

The correlates noted in this category are of far less value currently to teachers than those stated above. However, they are part of our "working theory" and, to an extent, further exemplify our own efforts to look at the whole person whenever possible.

- Socially conforming, but often isolated
- Late emotional and often physical maturation
- Tendency to hold forth, and speak in a big and self-assured voice
- Tendency to be defensive and occasionally doctrinaire
- Inability to take criticism well
- Generally ill-informed on current events despite being well-read
- Tendency toward perfectionism, often with attendant difficulty in reaching closure (another way of avoiding exposure and personal criticism)
- Tendency to have mild emotional disorders, such as obsessive-compulsive or infantile behaviors
- Handwriting is typically neat, often small; often doesn't dot "i's" or cross "t's"; handwriting is occasionally infantile and unstructured
- Enjoys gatekeeping roles that permit one to say "no" to others
- Nonintrospective, with low body awareness; though generally enjoys good health
- Can be witty; arising from seeing the humor in his/her own literalness
- Achievements tend to come from a high fear of failure
- Can be trained in mathematics, but math reasoning remains relatively weak
- May appear reserved, but has poor impulse control once aroused
- Has good social skills, but tends to feel insecure nonetheless
- Tendencies toward retentiveness (rarely charitable)
- Likes routines and patterns, but also easily swayed by the exotic
- Problem solving tends, for the most part, to be uninspired and impractical
- Problem solving can be good to excellent when encouraged, and when under threat of open criticism (responds to fear of consequences)
- Primary coping mechanisms: denial and avoidance
- Responds well to praise
- Trouble seeing the "big picture"
- Tendency to be emotionally dependent
- Generally impractical and given to romantic notions

- Reads for escape more so than simple reprieve or pleasure
- Drawn more to form than to substance (more intrigued by how something is said or portrayed than by what was said or pictured)
- When facing a choice between fight or flight, tends to choose flight (though often into self)
- Uses "no response" as a preferred means of dealing with problems or challenges
- Takes comfort in group membership
- Tendency for males to be more androgynous than general population (less clearly given to stereotypic masculine behaviors)
- As workers, tendency to achieve "journeymen," but rarely "mastercraftmen" status, though nonetheless often emerging as surprise leaders
- Appearance of judiciousness offset by highly opinionated thinking
- Good with details, but tends to lack "vision"

Having listed some of the diagnostic indicators of literalness, let us now consider some possible means of reducing the nonproductive and increasing the productive aspects of this condition.

Remedies for Literalness

A problem such as this one which is nested in denial and fear is best treated with *exposure*. "Talk-therapy" or discussion can help such students acknowledge a diagnosis of literalness and to become a part of the remedy. Since literalness is as much a characteristic of thinking and acting as it is of reading, most students are not likely to be quick to connect their behaviors to matching traits. On the other hand, a student engaged in such denial sometimes can be very open to a well-intentioned professional assessment, since it can offer the prospect of a helping hand and possible relief from potentially crippling fears and insecurities. Such students can also find encouragement in the fact that they will be consulted and counseled all along the way; that is, that they will be acting on their fear rather than having it acting upon them. With such an approach, diagnosis may actually raise self-worth, rather than further diminishing it. So, then, for those with literalness and denial, revelation and acceptance alone can be therapeutic. In general, it offers them emotional support in dealing with their angst, reified (or overly concretized) thinking, fear, denial, and the unassertive, or defensive, living style that tends to dog them.

Other possible remedies for "literalness" include one from a whole-language perspective. It is to emerge the student in an environment which is more analytically literate, in the sense of exposing the student to higher levels of literary criticism. The Annotation Exchange system described in this chapter provides some clear guidelines for assessing and improving student responses to literature from several constructive perspectives. To this there can be added features such as explicit, rule-guided instructions in how to respond at higher levels of operation. Ironically, the literal learner can probably be taught higher-level responding most comfortably in this rule-guided manner. Another instructional option would be to have students write critiques of pieces of literature that have been previously critiqued by professional reviewers in newspapers and literary magazines. They, then, could compare their reviews to those of accomplished reviewers. Students also should be encouraged to compare views with their peers, including those who tend not to be interested in literature and who may have different perspectives to offer, such as those with mechanical or graphic arts orientations.

The chief means of treating literalness, however, is by imparting a more flexible, insightful, and constructive mindset. To help achieve this, students should be given practice in reading from prescribed perspectives tailored toward these ends. For example, to read . . .

- in order to write in support of or in opposition to what is printed
- to determine how well this same material, or set of ideas, might apply some-where else, or be used to argue an opposing conclusion
- in order to write about how a selection may relate to a real life situation
- from some divergent perspectives (e.g., a burglar; a magician; a highly creative mind)
- with an eye toward appraising the quality of the phrasing or other features of the writing ("reading like a writer")
- to connect the material to a larger category of information or literature
- to determine what the questions, or issues, are that underlie a particular body of information (thereby further grappling with the concepts that connect seemingly diverse fields of information)
- to answer practical questions that could raise curiosity by sensitizing them to the mechanical forces at work in our environment (e.g., why do you suppose all the water doesn't run down a toilet stool?)
- while using a text-marking system to help them realize the force of their values on their thought and comprehension processes
- to form larger conceptual categories for factual information

If you are picturing someone with this problem, or you believe it to be true of yourself, you probably are getting the sense that most of these suggestions would help, but that in all probability literalness might never be totally over-come. If you are concluding this, you are coming closer to understanding why some theorists have attributed reading and learning disabilities primarily to constitutional factors, and why this position probably will grow in popularity as scientific technology permits us to identify such factors better. For example, damage to the right hemisphere of the brain can result in highly accurate but very literal level thinking (Weaver, 1986). It also would be good to conclude from this that most of us, no matter what our area of weakness, should be able to find an empathetic ear in the schools, since none of us is born perfect and we probably all could use a little help in making long-term progress toward reading, language, thinking, and social-emotional maturity.

➤   **LOOKING BACK**   ◄

The chapter spoke to the role and promise in addressing the higher-order literacy needs of remedial level students. To this end, it provided incidental and explicit methods of improving various aspects of strategic reading, study, writing, and thinking. The latter included attention to metacognitive thinking and memory training. It also offered means for creating a more conducive environment for higher-order literacy. The chapter concluded with a discussion of an emerging area of diagnosis and remediation, that of detection and treating higher-order literacy deficits in both remedial and proficient readers.

➤ *LOOKING (WAY) AHEAD*

As textbooks for reading diagnosis and remediation are prepared in the future, it seems safe to expect that they will devote an increasing proportion of space to the higher-order thinking and language needs of conventional remedial readers. It is too early even to speculate about whether they also will include greater attention to the higher-order thinking and literacy needs of those currently called proficient readers.

APPENDICES

Appendix A

MBI Administration, Scoring, and Interpretation

Administration

The MBI can be given individually or in group form. The instrument calls for expression, on a one (low) to five (high) scale of the relative degree of identification a student might have with each animal on the inventory. It also calls for the selection of the six strongest and two weakest (most negative) identifications. This form can be administered orally or as a silent written inventory in about 15 minutes.

Scoring and Interpretation

Currently, there is no quantitative scoring system for the MBI, but one is being developed. The likely reliability of each test administration can be estimated by comparing the responses made on the three animals that are repeated: horse, squirrel, and pheasant. Ideally, responses should not differ by more than one point. If responses are found to vary more greatly, exercise even greater caution in drawing firm conclusions.

Several studies of the MBI have provided a rich data base for interpretation of test protocols for classroom and school use. There is a good deal known, for example, about the relationship of animal choices to several aspects of academic skills, interests, and abilities. These are listed ahead. First, however, consider the different levels of interpretation of the MBI. These parallel the Luscher Color Test from which it derives its construct validity.

Levels of Interpretation

An MBI protocol can be interpreted on several levels. In general, the order of preference of choices offers the most stable and predictive meanings. Here is a guideline for interpreting order of preference.

First Level Choices:	Describes the "Ideal Self," or what the student most wants to be or tries to be.
Second Level Choices:	Describes the "Typical Self," or the way the student usually behaves and expresses feelings.
Third Level Choices:	Describes the "Restrained Self," or behavior and feelings reserved for triggering occasions (such as stress, anger, or high ambition).
Rejections:	Describes the "Feared Self," or the way the student does not want, or fears to be (but may occasionally lapse into).

To further aid interpretation, this appendix includes key associations and information on school related and other factors also found to be associated with each animal identification. For example, youngsters who have strong identification with "dog" have been found to profit more readily from attention and remediation, but tend to lack self-initiative. Students who identify with "eagle" tend to have strong verbal comprehension and vocabulary, but also tend to be aloof, impractical, fragile, and somewhat cunning.

There also is a good deal known about the type and level of motivation associated with most of the animals on the inventory. *Aversive* motivation is an externally directed desire to avoid negative consequences. Some forms of fear of consequences, such as fear of failure, may lead to superficial levels of success, usually in the form of good grades but poor abstract and evaluative thinking. Strong identification with "chicken" is correlated to a high level of aversive motivation. *Appetitive* motivation is an internally directed desire to achieve personal goals, irrespective of external reward systems. Identification with "lion" is strongly correlated to high appetitive and low aversive motivation. Some identifications indicate high levels of both types of motivation ("eagle") or low levels of both ("moose"). Two animal identifications tend to be most indicative of hyper-emotionality and poor personal-social adjustment: "snake" and "alligator."

A word of caution: should you decide to talk to youngsters, their parents, or other teachers about your findings, be sure to stress that the MBI was used as an initial "eye-opening" tool to help in understanding the reader as well as his or her reading. Ultimately, you will need to verify, refute, or add to the findings from the inventory with specific examples of observed behavior and/or with information derived from other tests and other persons.

Selected Associations and Key Factors Significantly Correlated to MBI Animal Identifications

ANIMAL	ADJECTIVALS		OTHER FINDINGS
1. alligator	powerful	dangerous	male
	ruthless	mean	defensive
	cunning		hostile
			unstable
2. badger	aggressive	sneaky	male
	unfriendly	offensive	strong vocabulary
	stubborn		high aversive motivation
3. chicken	cackling	dumb	high cloze performance
	follower	flighty	high aversive motivation
	coward		
4. cow	slow	serene	emotionally dependent
	lazy	dumb	weak comprehension
	big		low appetitive and aversive motivation
5. coyote	howling	loner	
	scavenger	sneaky	
	cunning		
6. dog	loyal	lovable	benefit from remediation
	affectionate	frisky	high vocational aspirations
7. dove	peaceful	gentle	strong cloze performance
	graceful	quiet	female
	free		
8. duck	noisy	playful	weak writing skills
	follower	cute	
	foolish		
9. eagle	soaring	bold	strong comprehension
	proud	courageous	strong vocabulary
	alone		emotionally distant
			high aversive and appetitive motivation
10. elephant	big	strong	helpful
	powerful	awkward	well-behaved
	gentle		low aversive motivation
11. falcon	soaring	predatory	male
	fierce	aggressive	high appetitive motivation
	majestic		high aversive motivation
12. fox	sly	clever	strong vocabulary
	smart	sneaky	high aversive motivation
	fast		moderate appetitive motivation

Animal	Adjectivals		Other Findings
13. giraffe	tall quiet friendly	gentle passive	strong cloze performance weak comprehension female no benefit from remediation high aversive motivation moderate appetitive motivation
14. goat	smelly destructive	stubborn dumb	emotionally unstable high aversive motivation moderate appetitive motivation
15. hippopotamus	enormous homely dull	lazy dumb	no benefit from remediation high aversive motivation
16. hog	dirty gross unimaginative	fat dumb	emotionally unstable weak comprehension
17. horse	strong thoroughbred noble	spirited proud	female good comprehension high appetitive motivation
18. leopard	stalking sleek fearless	cunning silent	weak writing skills strong cloze performance high appetitive and aversive motivation
19. lion	majestic leader dominant	proud powerful	weak writing skills emotionally strong high appetitive motivation low aversive motivation
20. mink	furry scurrying elegant	small beautiful	female weak comprehension high aversive motivation
21. moose	big towering	powerful awkward	male low aversive motivation low appetitive motivation
22. owl	wise self-assured haughty	watchful silent	high aversive motivation
23. peacock	beautfiul arrogant vain	proud regal	female high aversive motivation moderate appetitive motivation
24. penguin	amusing friendly gregarious	cute distinguished	strong cloze performance female
25. pheasant	colorful proud alert	wild graceful	weak writing skills
26. porpoise	smart friendly helpful	playful gentle	strong comprehension strong cloze performance emotionally stable low aversive motivation

ANIMAL	ADJECTIVALS		OTHER FINDINGS
27. rooster	cocky aggressive leader	arrogant chauvinistic	high aversive motivation moderate appetitive
28. snake	slithering evil	deadly ugly	weak comprehension no benefit from remediation male emotionally unstable high aversive motivation
29. squirrel	frisky hoarder cute	industrious nervous	weak cloze performance no benefit from remediation high aversive motivation
30. swan	graceful dignified lovely	beautiful quiet	female high aversive motivation moderate appetitive motivation
31. tiger	fierce free dominant	proud brave	strong comprehension high aversive motivation high appetitive motivation
32. turtle	slow cautious quiet	steady patient	high aversive motivation
33. wolf	sly savage resourceful	wild fast	male weak cloze performance weak writing skills high aversive motivation moderate appetitive motivation

Appendix B

Sample Meaning Vocabulary by Grade Level

Words identified by the proportion of youngsters knowing the meaning shown below. Excerpted and extrapolated from *The Living Word Vocabulary**

GRADE 3	WORD — WORD MEANING
1.	accuse — to blame
2.	acrobatic — skilled in gym
3.	adventure — exciting happening
4.	balloon — kind of aircraft
5.	bargain — to discuss prices
6.	camel — humped desert animal
7.	camera — takes pictures
8.	check — an order for money
9.	discuss — talk over
10.	tender — loving and gentle
11.	snap — to break suddenly
12.	election — selection by vote
13.	Eskimo — lives in Arctic north
14.	ferry — a river-crossing boat
15.	fool — to play a trick on
16.	harbor — where ships unload
17.	hobby — favorite fun
18.	hurricane — bad storm
19.	inventor — the one who thought it up
20.	joyful — happy
21.	lazy — won't work
22.	lifeless — dead
23.	lonely — not visited much
24.	loudmouth — talks too much
25.	messy — not neat

*By Edgar Dale and Joseph O'Rourke (1981). Word Book–Childcraft International, Inc. By permission of World Book, Inc., 525 W. Monroe, Chicago, IL 60661.

GRADE 4	WORD — WORD MEANING
1.	ball — big dance
2.	band — musical group
3.	banquet — big, formal meal
4.	charcoal — fuel
5.	coffin — case for dead person
6.	collection — things brought together
7.	concert — musical program
8.	continent — land mass like Asia
9.	desert — very dry land
10.	diamond — expensive jewel
11.	dike — dam
12.	temple — place of worship
13.	treat — to entertain
14.	eagle — large, strong bird
15.	equator — map line dividing earth
16.	forbid — do not allow
17.	foreigner — from another country
18.	forgive — pardon
19.	grassland — pasture land
20.	industrious — hard-working
21.	innocent — free from wrong
22.	manufacture — makes things
23.	mask — to disguise
24.	mightier — more powerful
25.	nasty — not pleasant

GRADE 5	WORD — WORD MEANING
1.	abolish — get rid of
2.	abuse — treat badly
3.	blackmail — threat of harm
4.	darkroom — photo workshop
5.	daydream — unreal fancies
6.	debate — to discuss
7.	empire — countries under one ruler
8.	enthusiastic — very eager
9.	flexible — adapts easily
10.	flutist — a flute player
11.	fragile — easily broken
12.	furious — very angry
13.	generous — unselfish
14.	heiress — woman inheriting money
15.	horrify — make afraid
16.	hostage — person held as pledge
17.	hourglass — measures time
18.	icebreaker — kind of ship
19.	ignore — pay no attention to
20.	initial — to mark with first letters of name
21.	inventive — creative
22.	juror — member of a jury
23.	kayak — Eskimo canoe
24.	kerosene — colorless oil
25.	sculpture — art of carving

GRADE 6	WORD — WORD MEANING
1.	acquaint — make familiar
2.	biographer — a writer of life stories
3.	boastful — bragging
4.	caesar — a dictator
5.	camouflage — disguise
6.	cancel — to destroy the force or effect
7.	canvas — oil painting
8.	caravan — traveling group
9.	dainty — fine and pretty
10.	dazzle — make very bright
11.	editor — corrects writing
12.	eliminate — get rid of
13.	embarrass — make uncomfortable
14.	emigrate — leave own country
15.	fragrant — sweet-smelling
16.	gambler — a person who takes chances
17.	generation — people about the same age
18.	headstone — marker for grave
19.	hilarious — very funny
20.	holiday — a religious holiday
21.	hospitable — friendly to guests
22.	hostage — person held as pledge
23.	hysterical — out of all control
24.	luxurious — rich and comfortable
25.	society — group of people

GRADE 7	WORD — WORD MEANING
1.	attack — start work on
2.	catch — get the disease
3.	laborious — requiring hard work
4.	majestic — impressive
5.	manual — book of instruction
6.	mariner — sailor
7.	memorandum — a reminder
8.	mint — money-coining agency
9.	misquote — use another's words incorrectly
10.	mission — church building
11.	mockery — making fun of
12.	nightmare — a horrid experience
13.	nuclear — atomic
14.	parson — minister
15.	reformatory — prison for youth
16.	regretfully — sadly
17.	scripture — sacred writing
18.	seafaring — traveling on the sea
19.	semicivilized — part savage
20.	sociology — study of society
21.	solar — of the sun
22.	stanza — verse of poem
23.	tender — young and immature
24.	treat — try to cure
25.	snap — to move quickly and smartly

GRADE 8	WORD — WORD MEANING

1. astound — surprise greatly
2. befuddle — to confuse
3. benumb — take away feeling
4. flourish — thrive
5. knighthood — rank of knight
6. legislator — a law maker
7. lyric — poem expressing feeling
8. microfilm — very small photograph
9. mischievous — harmful
10. navigation — steering a boat
11. notable — famous person
12. notorious — of bad reputation
13. obituary — death notice
14. pallbearer — carries coffin
15. palmist — sees future in hands
16. password — a pre-arranged sign
17. pavilion — shelter for short time
18. peeper — spies on people
19. Pentagon — Army headquarters
20. persuasive — convincing
21. pessimistic — gloomy
22. racist — believes own race best
23. radiate — shine brightly
24. reverent — worshipful
25. Satan — the Devil

GRADE 9	WORD — WORD MEANING

1. academician — scholar
2. adolescence — youth
3. bar — group of lawyers
4. battery — unlawful attack
5. campaign — war operation
6. candlepower — measure of light
7. cardinal — church officer
8. deduction — process of reasoning
9. defame — slander
10. depressed — lowered
11. descendants — children
12. elaborate — give more details
13. electrometer — measures electric potential
14. emissary — sent as an agent
15. formally — in customary manner
16. fortification — a defense building
17. forum — the Roman market
18. fossil — old-fashioned person
19. genetics — science of heredity
20. gorge — eat greedily
21. habitual — regular
22. hideous — very ugly
23. identify — to class in a group
24. illuminate — to explain, make clear
25. mandatory — compulsory

GRADE 10	WORD — WORD MEANING
1.	admirably — excellently
2.	adorn — decorate
3.	Advent — a holy period
4.	backslapper — an overly sociable person
5.	baroness — noblewoman
6.	capitalist — wealthy investor
7.	carnivorous — meat-eating
8.	desegregate — to open to all races
9.	devout — religious-feeling
10.	empress — woman ruler of an empire
11.	fiery — easily excited
12.	fiscal — about money
13.	flagship — commander's ship
14.	flowery — full of fancy words
15.	heartfelt — sincere
16.	heroine — main actress
17.	idolatry — worship of images
18.	leak — tell secret information
19.	limerick — nonsense verse
20.	linguist — has language skill
21.	lore — traditions and legends
22.	lynch — to hang unlawfully
23.	Magi — three wise men
24.	malcontent — dissatisfied
25.	matchmaker — helps people get married

GRADE 11	WORD — WORD MEANING
1.	abdicate — give up rights
2.	balance — harmony
3.	blaze — brilliant display
4.	bleed — take money by force
5.	cahoots — in partnership
6.	cakewalk — kind of dance
7.	calendar — things to do
8.	cantankerous — never agreeable
9.	debutante — girl entering society
10.	defamation — harming reputation
11.	effigy — image
12.	ego — the conscious self
13.	elaboration — to give more details about
14.	elite — upper class
15.	embark — begin a voyage
16.	fieldpiece — wheeled cannon
17.	flophouse — cheap hotel
18.	gaudy — showy
19.	highwayman — robber
20.	hosanna — a religious cry
21.	humble — not rich
22.	indifference — not caring
23.	ironical — means opposite of what it says
24.	irrelevant — having no relation
25.	jam — to spoil radio reception

GRADE 12	WORD — WORD MEANING
1.	abandon — reckless enthusiasm
2.	abbey — group of monks
3.	antagonistic — enemies to each other
4.	bar — legal profession
5.	blight — to frustrate
6.	cadence — rhythmical movement
7.	callous — not sensitive
8.	canticle — a hymn or chant
9.	cantilever — type of bridge
10.	dastard — a mean coward
11.	dauntless — brave
12.	egghead — a professor
13.	electric — exciting
14.	emancipate — set free
15.	fine — the end in music
16.	fishwife — a rough-talking woman
17.	focus — central point
18.	following — supporters
19.	gate — ticket money
20.	gawky — awkward
21.	high-hat — a snob
22.	hit — to criticize sharply
23.	homogenize — to make all parts the same
24.	intelligence — information
25.	invocation — an opening prayer

GRADE 13	WORD — WORD MEANING
1.	loguacious — talkative
2.	manna — food from heaven
3.	matricide — murders his mother
4.	medium — a means for doing
5.	mercurial — very changeable
6.	nihilist — believes in nothing
7.	nullify — make useless
8.	objective — led by facts
9.	oppressive — very severe
10.	outrage — a shocking offense
11.	predestination — fate
12.	railroad — to force through
13.	recant — withdraw statement
14.	refraction — deflection of light
15.	sector — military area
16.	seditious — stirs rebellion
17.	seismograph — earthquake recorder
18.	tit for tat — return in kind
19.	topflight — the best
20.	tribunal — court of justice
21.	tropic — circle 23½ degrees from equator
22.	ultra — extreme
23.	undercurrent — hidden tendency
24.	undermine — weaken gradually
25.	unfathomable — can't be understood

GRADE 14	WORD — WORD MEANING
1.	kernel — the essential part
2.	knave — tricky person
3.	larder — food storage place
4.	lethargy — lack of interest
5.	libretto — words of opera
6.	licentiate — holder of permit
7.	magnitude — star's brightness
8.	messianic — believing in future savior
9.	naturalism — represents everyday life
10.	omnivore — eats everything
11.	papacy — Pope's term of office
12.	passe — out of date
13.	perpetuate — to continue
14.	polyglot — has many languages
15.	precursor — forerunner
16.	recapitulation — a review by summary
17.	saucy — disrespectful
18.	schizophrenia — a personality disorder
19.	sectarian — narrow-minded
20.	teleprompter™ — shows speech
21.	tender — to offer
22.	theocracy — government by priests
23.	transcendental — beyond experience
24.	trauma — a damaging shock
25.	underground — non-commercial film

GRADE 15	WORD — WORD MEANING
1.	aboriginal — native
2.	absence — run away and hide
3.	adage — proverb
4.	basilica — early form of cathedral
5.	bereavement — loss by death
6.	bestial — very brutal
7.	charge — responsibility
8.	chastisement — punishment
9.	cockle — animal with shell
10.	codify — systematize laws
11.	desecrate — spoil sacred things
12.	differential — distinguishing factors
13.	disseminate — spread far and wide
14.	dissertation — formal discourse
15.	enclave — a surrounded section
16.	euphuism — flowery expression
17.	exploit — take advantage of
18.	Gestalt — structural form or pattern
19.	heliotherapy — sun treatment
20.	hexameter — line in poetry
21.	induction — way of reasoning
22.	inflection — variation in word form
23.	lacteal — milky
24.	licentious — not moral
25.	lithe — flexible

GRADE 16   *WORD — WORD MEANING*

1.	absolution — forgiveness
2.	abstractionism — modern art style
3.	adulation — excessive praise
4.	bile — ill humor
5.	bully — excellent
6.	chaise — lightweight carriage
7.	cherubim — child angels
8.	clairvoyant — fortune teller
9.	colloid — suspended matter
10.	degenerate — grow worse
11.	disrepute — bad reputation
12.	eureka — triumphant discovery
13.	exponent — believes strongly
14.	fire-eater — bold person
15.	French leave — depart without notice
16.	gladiator — slave fighter
17.	heady — exciting
18.	hydrotherapy — water treatment
19.	imagery — figurative language
20.	immemorial — very old
21.	infirm — weak
22.	lama — a Buddhist monk
23.	litigation — a lawsuit
24.	liturgy — the church service
25.	mandarin — Chinese official

Appendix C

Proverbs Exercises For Discussion or Assessment

PART I

Directions: Choose the one that best represents the idea stated. Be sure to read all choices before selecting one. Place an (X) in front of the letter of your choice.

> *Example:*
> **Look before you leap.**
> XA. Do not act in haste.
> B. Watch about you before you jump forward.
> C. Do not leap, just look.
> D. We see further in Leap Year due to the extra day.
> *Answer Key for Questions Below*
> A = Abstract
> C = Concrete
> E = Emotional
> M = Miscue

1. **Clothes make the man.**
   (A) A. A proper look brings out proper behavior.
   (E) B. Don't judge a book by its cover.
   (C) C. People who dress right tend to be successful.
   (M) D. A man is what he is no matter how he dresses.
2. **Many hands make light work.**
   (C) A. Six hands can often lift what four could not.
   (M) B. Many helpers lead to much confusion.
   (E) C. Light work requires many hands.
   (A) D. Cooperation brings relief.

3. **When the cat's away, the mice will play.**
   (C) A. When cats are not around, mice can have a good time.
   (E) B. Don't trust people who stare at you.
   (A) C. Some people can only be good when they are afraid to be bad.
   (M) D. Mice can play when cats are around.

4. **You can't have your cake and eat it too.**
   (C) A. You can't save money and spend it too.
   (M) B. It is better to eat cake than to save it.
   (A) C. Most every choice has its cost.
   (E) D. Don't risk the price—make no choice.

5. **If you can't stand the heat, get out of the kitchen.**
   (C) A. If the heat in a room bothers you go to another.
   (E) B. The kitchen is often the hottest room in a house.
   (M) C. Heat can make you sick, so get going.
   (A) D. If you want the best of something, expect to pay the price.

6. **It is no use crying over spilled milk.**
   (C) A. Do not cry when you spill your milk.
   (E) B. Avoid getting upset over little things.
   (A) C. Do not get upset over things you can not fix.
   (M) D. Crying is not good, but being careful is.

7. **Too many cooks can spoil the broth.**
   (M) A. Do not permit too many people into the kitchen.
   (C) B. Many things are done better by one person.
   (A) C. Work can be ruined by too many people and too many opinions.
   (E) D. Many hands make light work.

8. **When angry, count to ten.**
   (A) A. Delay is one remedy for anger.
   (C) B. If you are upset, then you should count to ten to calm down.
   (M) C. It is harmful to hold in your feelings.
   (E) D. Haste makes waste.

9. **East, West, home is best.**
   (A) A. There is no place like home.
   (M) B. There are many hurricanes on the east and west coasts.
   (C) C. Once you have been east and west, then you know that home is best.
   (E) D. When you can not go east or west, then home is best.

10. **The restless sleeper blames the couch.**
    (M) A. There is fault in every person.
    (A) B. Where fault is concerned, look first within.
    (C) C. The person who sleeps poorly says the couch was bad.
    (E) D. Couches make for restless sleep.

11. **Out of sight, out of mind.**
    (A) A. Immediate needs tend to get attention.
    (M) B. Old friends are soon forgotten.
    (C) C. The mind depends on sight for all it does.
    (E) D. Things not seen are things not thought of.

12. **You grow up the day you have the first real laugh — at yourself.**
    (C) A. Don't take yourself too seriously.
    (A) B. Maturity comes from recognizing acts of immaturity.
    (E) C. Laughing is emotional release.
    (M) D. Stop laughing and you will start crying.

13. **Don't bite off more than you can chew.**
    (C) A. It is difficult to chew when your mouth is stuffed.
    (M) B. Don't swallow without chewing.
    (E) C. Take risks, it is worth the price.
    (A) D. Stretch your feet as far as your sheet will cover.

14. **Give a boy a fish and feed him for a day. Teach him how to fish and feed him for life.**
    (C) A. Some one chopping wood can be better off than someone receiving it.
    (A) B. Giving spoils, helping strengthens.
    (E) C. The hungry are better left unfed.
    (M) D. Children must be taught how to eat fish.

15. **Barking dogs seldom bite.**
    (E) A. Don't do all the talking.
    (M) B. Someone who looks angry.
    (C) C. Those who yell, seldom hit.
    (A) D. Those who brag usually can't live up to it.

16. **Once bitten, twice shy.**
    (C) A. Once a child has learned that something might cause pain, he will avoid things like it in the future.
    (A) B. A person who has been tricked is more careful.
    (M) C. The child who likes to bite is always very shy.
    (E) D. People do not like to be faced with their problems.

17. **You do not teach the paths of the forest to an old gorilla.**
    (A) A. Experience can teach what words can hardly describe.
    (C) B. Animals know things by instinct, and instincts are best.
    (E) C. You can't teach an old dog new tricks.
    (M) D. The older animal certainly knows the forest.

18. **A prosperous fool is a great burden.**
    (C) A. Good fortune sometimes goes to fools and wrong-doers.
    (E) B. It is difficult to argue with those who have the look of success.
    (M) C. A prosperous person carries a fool's burden.
    (A) D. A fool with money can get away with a lot.

19. **All cruelty springs from weakness.**
    (E) A. Weakness makes for kindness.
    (A) B. He struck first because his fear was greater.
    (C) C. Beware of weakness.
    (M) D. Cruelty can be found in everyone.

20. **No author is a man of genius to his publisher.**
    (E) A. Publishers see errors and therefore weaknesses in the best of writers.
    (M) B. Those who can not are quick to find the flaws in those who can.
    (C) C. Mothers know weaknesses in children better than anyone else ever could.
    (A) D. Writing is a plunge into unknown; no one can do it perfectly.

21. **You can't lead anyone farther than you have gone yourself.**
    (C) A. You can't take others where you have not been.
    (C) B. Good leaders go farther.
    (A) C. Improve yourself first, and then others.
    (M) D. If you haven't been bad, you can't be good.

22. **Birds of a feather flock together.**
    (A) A. We tend to be friends with those who think as we do.
    (C) B. Birds of the same color stay together.
    (E) C. Beware of the bird that stands alone.
    (M) D. Birds that stay together are flocking.

23. **When life hands you a lemon make lemonade.**
    (C) A. In life, lemons can be used to make lemonade.
    (A) B. There's often a brighter side, if you look for it.
    (E) C. Life is more like a lemon than like lemonade.
    (M) D. In life you can make lemons or lemonade.

24. **There is nothing either good or bad, but thinking makes it so.**
    (A) A. Nature happens, mankind appraises.
    (M) B. It is written what is good or bad.
    (C) C. Behavior can not be judged without examination of motives.
    (E) D. What is good is what we value.

25. **Brevity is the soul of wit.**
    (M) A. Be brief and have wit.
    (C) B. Witty sayings use few words.
    (A) C. Where cleverness is concerned, less is more.
    (E) D. The heart of wit is cunning.

26. **Cast pearls before swine.**
    (E) A. Every form of life is worth something.
    (M) B. Offer something valuable to someone who is poor.
    (C) C. To throw pearls to a pig is foolish.
    (A) D. It is useless to say wise things to those who are not ready to hear.

27. **Rome was not built in a day.**
    (M) A. Important things often can not be done easily.
    (C) B. Great cities like Rome took workers years to build.
    (A) C. Do not try to do more than is possible in a limited amount of time.
    (E) D. You can not do anything all at once.

28. **When in Rome, do as the Romans do.**
    (E) A. Romans are warlike people. If you do not do things their way you
    will be in trouble.
    (C) B. When you go to Rome, eat, sleep and play like Romans.
    (M) C. If you go to Rome, try to blend in.
    (A) D. Adapt your conduct to the situation.

29. **You can lead a horse to water but you can't make him drink.**
    (M) A. You can show someone something but it doesn't mean they
    understand.
    (C) B. A horse does not have to drink just because you offer him water.
    (A) C. Giving someone an opportunity is no guarantee he will choose to try it.
    (E) D. There are many times when people will not do what you want, then you
    must force them to do so.

30. **The squeaking wheel gets the grease.**
    (E) A. Silence can be like a scream.
    (C) B. Loud children get the love and attention.
    (A) C. Non-complaint gets non-results.
    (M) D. The wheel that squeaks will get greased.

31. **All that glitters is not gold.**
    (E) A. Glitter is the downfall of mankind.
    (M) B. Not all gold glitters.
    (C) C. Things other than gold can glitter.
    (A) D. Looks can deceive.

32. **Where there's smoke, there's fire.**
    (E) A. Little lies sometimes are necessary in difficult situations.
    (C) B. With fire often is smoke.
    (A) C. Signs of wrong often mean that there is wrong.
    (M) D. Let sleeping dogs lie.

33. **Still waters run deep.**
    (C) A. When water is deep it does not easily move.
    (A) B. Lack of speech doesn't mean lack of thought.
    (M) D. Still waters are used in alcohol making.
    (E) C. Silence can be an indication of depression.

34. **Mediocre men often have the most acquired knowledge.**
    (E) A. "C" students are more practical than "A" students.
    (M) B. Facts change minds—not words.
    (A) C. Lesser minds can store but can not create new knowledge.
    (C) D. Mediocre women often have the most acquired knowledge.

35. **Better to die on your feet than live on your knees.**
    (C) A. It is better to die standing than live kneeling.
    (M) B. You shouldn't fight with your feet.
    (E) C. Feet or knees, we all must die.
    (A) D. Freedom can cost a lot.

36. **Happy is the man who can enjoy the scenery when he has to take a detour.**
    (M) A. Detours tend to have enjoyable scenery.
    (E) B. Be smart—avoid detours.
    (A) C. Difficulty must be expected—make the best of it.
    (C) D. Sometimes a detour can be more pleasant than the original route.

37. **He who will not where he may, when he will shall have nay.**
    (A) A. Strike while the iron is hot.
    (E) B. The chance to say no is a chance to grow.
    (C) C. If you do not do a thing when there is opportunity, you may not get to do it at all.
    (M) D. Act in haste, pay in leisure.

38. **Temper the wind to the shorn lamb.**
    (C) A. To a closely shorn lamb, give gentle winds.
    (M) B. Bad temper scares the meek.
    (E) C. Control sheep in a storm.
    (A) D. Adopt gentle methods to get things done.

39. **One should not wash one's dirty linen in public.**
    (A) A. Personal matters are best kept personal.
    (C) B. It is not right to wash in front of others.
    (E) C. Dirty linen should be forgotten.
    (M) D. Linen rarely needs to be washed after one public use.

40. **The grass is always greener on the other side of the fence.**
    (C) A. A neighbor's grass often looks better than yours because you can not see its flaws.
    (E) B. Your efforts will make your neighbor richer.
    (M) C. There are two sides to everything.
    (A) D. The things we see often look better than the things we have.

41. **He who laughs last laughs longest.**
    (C) A. If you are the last person to begin to laugh, you will be the last one to finish laughing.
    (M) B. If you want to laugh best, always laugh loud.
    (A) C. Be careful not to celebrate a victory until you are sure you have won.
    (E) D. Laughing is important; always have a sense of humor.

42. **You can catch more flies with honey than you can with vinegar.**
    (C) A. Flies are attracted to honey, not to vinegar.
    (E) B. To get what you want you sometimes have to be tricky.
    (M) C. People who are pleasant have more friends than those who are grouchy.
    (A) D. You can get further by being thoughtful than by being demanding.

43. **Out of the frying pan and into the fire.**
    (C) A. You no sooner solve one problem and another one come up. That's life!
    (M) B. If something falls out of the pan it will drop into the fire.
    (E) C. Trying to hide your mistakes can be dangerous.
    (A) D. Some bad situations can never be improved.

44. **The used key is always brightest.**
    (C) A. Metal gets shiny from being touched.
    (M) B. Something old is better than something new.
    (A) C. One who is always making himself useful usually amounts to something.
    (E) D. To be bright, you need the key.

45. **Improve yourself today, your friends tomorrow.**
    (C) A. Improve yourself before trying to improve your friends.
    (M) B. Pointing out the faults of your friends will strengthen them and you.
    (A) C. If someting is wrong, look within yourself first for a reason.
    (E) D. Friends don't improve.

PART II

Directions: Select the statement that is most nearly the *opposite* of the first stated idea. Place an (X) in front of the letter of your choice.

> *Example:*
> **Clothes make the man.**
>   A. Great bodies move slowly.
> XB. Don't judge a book by its cover.
>   C. The more cost, the more honor.
>   D. New things are fine to look at.

46. **Like to like.**
    (E) A. One must draw a line somewhere.
    (A) B. Opposites attract.
    (M) C. Live and let live.
    (M) D. Money makes money.

47. **Revenge is sweet.**
    (A) A. Two wrongs don't make a right.
    (E) B. One man's meat is another man's poison.
    (M) C. Don't cry over spilled milk.
    (M) D. There is no easy road to learning.

48. **Out of sight, out of mind.**
    (M) A. There is time to speak and time to be silent.
    (M) B. Silence gives consent.
    (M) C. A friend to all is a friend to none.
    (A) D. Absence makes the heart grow fonder.

49. **Spare the rod and spoil the child.**
    (A) A. Boys will be boys.
    (E) B. A stick is quickly found to beat a dog with.
    (E) C. Laugh before breakfast, and you'll cry before supper.
    (M) D. Better to be safe than sorry.

50. **Never trouble trouble, 'til trouble troubles you.**
    (M) A. Do not cross the bridge 'til you come to it.
    (M) B. Truth is stranger than fiction.
    (A) C. Forewarned is forearmed.
    (M) D. Don't let the sun go down on your anger.

Appendix D

Primer on the Brain

1. The cortex, or "gray bark" covering on the brain, is only ⅛ to ⅙ of an inch thick, yet it contains over 9 of the 12 billion neurons of the brain (75%). This gray matter actually is very pink in living subjects, since it is very well webbed with oxygen and nutrient-providing blood vessels; it merely appears gray in postmortems. The neurons of the brain are like computer chips; they are programmable and they permit communication with other neurons that in turn make other functions possible.

2. One of the reasons that there can be so many neurons in the cortex is due to the folds, ridges, and wrinkles on it. If it were flattened out, it would be much larger than it first appears. (It is these convolutions that permit a large brain to pass through a small birth canal).

3. The brain has three major parts. These correspond to the evolution of the human brain. Each division is a brain form that can be found in lower life forms. These are referred to as the forebrain, hindbrain, and mid- (or inside) brain. The forebrain includes the cerebrum (with two major thinking hemispheres) and the diencephalon (die-en-sef-uh-lon)—the large white area beneath the cerebrum and connecting consciousness to certain autonomic systems such as hunger, thirst, and temperature. The hindbrain lies toward the back and base of the skull. It is called the primitive brain because it was the first to develop and all animals have one (though not all insects). It includes the medulla oblongata (controlling basic life or autonomic functions such as breathing, swallowing, heartbeat, etc.) and the two hemispheres of the cerebellum, which regulates posture, balance, and movement. The midbrain is deep in the core of the brain. It is centered around the pons, and represents the next level of evolutionary development. It contains an important part of the *reticular system*—a relay station between the cerebrum and the cerebellum. As such, it regulates and

coordinates the basic life support and orientation functions of the hindbrain with the other life support systems of the diencephalon (or white brain). It also helps connect these to sensory data and the thought processes of the cerebral cortex.

The deep and well-protected nature of the hindbrain and portions of the mid-brain explains how patients can be called "brain-dead," that is, having no consciousness, and yet continue to breathe, swallow, and maintain normal temperature. They often can remain in this vegetative state for indefinite periods of time if put on life-support systems.

4. The reticular formation (a part of the medulla oblongata and reticular system deep within the brain) keeps the entire brain alert and regulates and coordinates most life-sustaining functions.

5. Each hemisphere of the cerebrum (or cerebral cortex and diencephalon) is divided into five lobes or major convolutions. Four are visible from a side view: the frontal, temporal, parietal, and occipital. The fifth, called the limbic lobe, is on top of the brain where the two hemispheres face one another.

6. The diencephalon, or white brain, under the cerebral cortex, contains the hypothalmus, the subthalamus, and the thalamus. It also contains the pituitary gland, the master gland that is largely responsible for growth. The hypothalamus controls temperature, sugar and fat metabolism, and secretions of the endocrine glands. The roles of the subthalamus and thalamus are not well-understood. They are believed to be relay and information centers for sensory impulses, and are increasingly found to be implicated in complex thinking functions.

7. All structures of the brain exist in a double form, except the pineal gland in the center of the brain. (This led Descartes to falsely conclude that it must be the seat of consciousness and the soul.) The pineal gland appears to work in concert with the hypothalamus, the subthalamus, and the thalamus in regulating sleep and waking cycles as well as influencing certain seasonal changes in the activity levels of the brain and body. It is very sensitive to changes in the amount of daylight. More light tends to increase arousal, alertness, and energy level, but it also tends to reduce tolerance for closeknit, analytical tasks. It also has been implicated in "spring fever" in humans and in migratory instincts in lower animals.

8. The vascular (vein and artery) system of the brain keeps it well-nourished and removes waste matter. Lesions, or scar tissue, usually result from some interruption or injury to the vascular system. Certain viruses carried by the vascular system can do serious damage to the brain, particularly when they affect the flow of the cerebrospinal fluids. The heavy reliance of the brain on the vascular system is leading physicians to suggest that it may benefit as much from good diet and cholesterol reduction as does the heart.

9. Cerebro-spinal fluids serve to cushion the brain. The fluids flow around the cranium and into several ventricles, or chambers, within the brain and down the spinal column. These fluids are a separate system, but they do have major exchanges with the blood system, which both supplies the basic material for

the fluids (manufactured in the fourth ventricle) and for carrying away its wastes.

Note: There are recent reports that a neuroscientist, Solomon Snyder, has led a team that has caused some neural brain tissue to reproduce itself, thus reversing the conventional wisdom that brain neurons can never reproduce. This may be an oddity however, since the neurons came from the brain of a child with a rare brain disease that caused rapid and uncontrolled growth of brain cells, and eventually resulted in death (Radetsky, 1991).

Appendix E

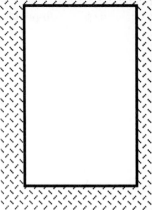

Selected Materials for Teaching Critical and Creative Reading and Thinking

The first four materials of this appendix are largely paraphrased from a review by Dixie Lee Spiegel (1990). Her review stressed the content validity of the material, its transfer potential, and the amount of reinforcement it provides.

1. *Critical Thinking: Reading, Thinking, and Reasoning Skills* Barnes, D., Burgdorf, A., & Wenck, L.S., Steck-Vaughn Co.; P.O. Box 260115; Austin, TX 78755; Teacher's editions, $5.95; student workbooks, $3.99-$4.47 if five or more are ordered

   A six-book program for Grades 1 through 6, these materials are organized around Bloom's taxonomy of thinking. The first four of Bloom's stages (knowledge, comprehension, application, and analysis) are emphasized in the materials for Grades 1 through 4. The higher level skills of synthesis and evaluation are introduced in Grade 3. For each stage, several different critical thinking skills are taught; e.g., the skills of judging completeness, determining relevance, differentiating between abstract and concrete, and identifying the logic of actions.

   What makes *Critical Thinking* stand out is the quality of its teachers' editions and the instructional format provided. A complete lesson plan is supplied for each new skill. This five-part plan includes defining the skill, identifying the steps of the thinking process to be taught, demonstrating the skill through teacher modeling, practicing the skill using the workbook pages, and providing feedback, a step that includes a metacognitive component asking the children to describe what they did to arrive at their answers. Last of all, a section called "Transfer the skill" suggests enrichment activity.

   Critical Thinking has strong content validity. Direct instruction focuses the learner on the processes of critical thinking. The importance of following a specific plan for thinking is emphasized through identification of the steps in the plan and teacher modeling. The workbook exercises vary in format and difficulty, and teachers who have used the workbooks with their students reported that the children really had to think!

The transfer potential of the material is also high, especially with the pervasive attention to the metacognitive aspects of critical thinking that involve exploring both right and wrong answers, explaining divergent answers, and identifying clue words. The extension activities at the end of each lesson promote transfer from workbook and class discussion exercises to other literacy activities such as examining magazine advertisements and writing stories.

2. *Building Thinking Skills* Edwards, R., & Hill, W.; Midwest Publications; P.O. Box 448, Dept. 17; Pacific Grove, CA 93950; Teacher's manuals/lesson plans $9.95 (primary level), $15.95 (Books 1-2); books of reproducible activity sheets $19.95 (all levels)

This is a set of teachers' manuals and separate reproducible activity sheets designed to develop the analysis skills of distinguishing similarities and differences, determining sequence, classifying, and thinking analogously. The primary level (K-2) focuses on the figural level and uses commercially available manipulatives such as pattern blocks and attribute blocks to help children learn these skills. (Such manipulatives are often already available in primary classrooms; they were for my teacher reviewers.) Book 1 (for Grades 2 through 4) and Book 2 (for Grades 4 through 7) make the transition from reasoning about figures to reasoning with verbal materials. Books 1 and 2 also expand the curriculum to include deductive reasoning, parts of a whole, and logical connectives, among other skills. The teachers' manuals for Books 1 and 2 provide transparency masters for the lessons.

The content validity of the *Building Thinking Skills* program is excellent. The skills selected are important aspects of critical thinking and the lesson plans in the teacher's manual are very detailed. Transfer potential is similarly high, with special emphasis on flexibility in thinking and on the importance of class discussion for aiding children to internalize the processes being taught. The amount of reinforcement is outstanding. For example, for teaching the skill of sequencing at the primary level, 30 lessons for 10- to 20-minute sessions are provided with 59 accompanying activity sheets.

3. *Primary Thinking Skills* (for Grades K through 2) Edwards, R., & Hill, W.; Midwest Publications; P.O. Box 448, Dept. 17; Pacific Grove, CA 93950; $10.95 each

This program is produced by the same publisher as *Building Thinking Skills* and is of the same high standard. However, *Primary Thinking Skills* is a teacher's resource manual only and does not provide worksheets. Rather, the detailed lessons involve the children in discussion, brainstorming, creative problem solving, and fun, physical activities such as drama and interviewing. For example, the children are asked to imagine what it would be like to be a chair or a particular animal. In a lesson on changing shapes, the children are asked to cut bananas into many different shapes by varying the angles and axis of their cuts.

The two A-level books require no reading or writing skills. The two B-level books require some literacy skills and are appropriate for Grades 1 through 3.

4. *Discover!* Tin Man Press; P.O. Box 219; Stanwood, WA 98292; $1.95 per set

These materials are sets of 4″ x 6″ activity cards designed to be used by an individual student in Grade 2 or higher. Each set has 20 cards that present "thinking challenges" to the student centered about one simple object. For example, the peanut set starts by asking the child to describe the color of the shelled peanut and to measure it. Quickly, the child is asked to move on to more interesting and divergent tasks such as using a magnifying glass to examine the peanut and making a list of everything observed, or telling how a peanut is like an egg. There are 24 different sets of cards, focusing on objects such as a spoon, a paper bag, or a shoelace.

5. *Breakthroughs: Strategies for Thinking* Jones, B.F., Tinzmann, M., & Thelen, J.; Zaner-Bloser; 1459 King Avenue; P.O. Box 16764; Columbus, OH 43216-6764; 800-421-3018; Teacher's editions and blackline masters available at no charge when ordering 10 or more books at $3.99 each

The most interesting aspect of this Grade 1-8 program is that it deals with authentic social and personal problems. In a series of short books, it simply introduces and teaches a certain thinking strategy and then follows it up with examination of a relevant issue. These include topics such as waste management, ecology, over-population, world economy, and substance abuse.

The topics do get a little heavy-handed, but they are real and important. The materials are recommended to be used with three methodological approaches: modeling, collaborative learning, and reciprocal teaching.

6. *Remarkable People!* Lewis, M., & Kudla, P.; Center for Applied Research in Education; West Nyack, NY; $27.95.

This ready-to-use collection of over 200 reproducible, biography-oriented projects, puzzles, and activity sheets is designed to teach research, writing, and critical thinking in Grades 4-8. Biographies include sports figures, artists, scientists, writers, inventors, naturalists, and world leaders.

[Spiegel, D.L. (1990). Critical reading materials: A review of three criteria. The Reading Teacher, 43, 6, 410-412.]

REFERENCES

Adam, M. J., & Collins, A. (1977). *A schema-theoretic view of reading comprehension.* Champaign: Center for the Study of Reading, University of Illinois.[4]

Afflerbach, P. P., & Johnston, P. H. (1986). What do expert readers do when the main idea is not explicit? In J. Baumann (Ed.), *Teaching main idea comprehension.* Newark, DE: International Reading Association. [4]

Aiken, E. G., Thomas, G. S., & Shennum, W. A. (1975). Memory for a lecture: Effects of notes, lecture rate, and information density. *Journal of Educational Psychology, 67,* 439-44. [12] [13]

Allen, R. V. (1976). *Language experiences in communication.* Boston: Houghton Mifflin. [8]

Alley, G., & Deshler, D. (1980). *Teaching the learning disabled adolescent: Strategies and methods.* Denver, CO: Love. [10]

Allington, R. L. (1977). If they don't read much how they ever gonna get good? *Journal of Reading, 21,* 57-61. [7] [8]

Allington, R. L. (1980). Teacher interruption behaviors during primary grade oral reading. *Journal of Educational Psychology, 72,* 371-77. [7]

Allington, R. L. (1983). Fluency: The neglected reading goal. *The Reading Teacher, 36,* 556-61. [8] [10]

Allington, R. L. (1984). Oral reading. In P. D. Pearson (Ed.), *Handbook of reading research* (pp. 829-64). New York: Longman. [7]

Alvermann, D., Bridge, C. A., Schmidt, B. A., Searfoss, L. W., & Winograd, P. (1988). *Strategy assessments.* Lexington, MA: D. C. Heath. [4]

Anders, P. L., Bos, C. S., & Filip, D. (1984). The effect of semantic feature analysis on the reading comprehension of learning-disabled students. In J. A. Niles & L. A. Harris (Eds.), *Changing perspectives on research in reading/language processing and instruction.* Thirty-third yearbook of the National Reading Conference (pp. 162-66). Rochester, NY: National Reading Conference. [9]

Anders, P. L., & Bos, C. S. (1986). Semantic feature analysis: An interactive strategy for vocabulary and text comprehension. *Journal of Reading, 29,* 610-16. [9]

Anderson, B. (1981). The missing ingredient: Fluent oral reading. *Elementary School Journal, 81,* 173-77. [8] [10]

Anderson, K. F. (1985). The development of spelling ability and linguistic strategies. *The Reading Teacher, 39,* 140-47. [9]

Anderson, L. M. (1981). Short-term student responses to classroom instruction. *Elementary School Journal, 82,* 97-108. [8] [12]

Anderson, L. M., Evertson, C. M., & Brophy, J. E. (1979). An experimental study of effective teaching in first-grade reading groups. *Elementary School Journal, 79,* 193-222. [7]

Anderson, R. C., & Nagy, W. E. (1991). Word meaning. In R. Barr, M. Kamil, P. Mosenthal, & P. D. Pearson (Eds.), *Handbook of reading research* (Vol. 2, pp. 690-724). New York: Longman. [9]

Anderson, R. C., Reynolds, R. E., Schallert, D. L., & Goetz, E. T. (1977). Frameworks for comprehending discourse. *American Educational Research Journal, 14,* 367-81. [7]

Anderson, R. C., Wilson, P., & Fielding, L. (1988). Growth in reading and how children spend their time outside of school. *Reading Research Quarterly, 23,* 285-303. [1]

Anderson, V., & Hidi, S. (1988-89). Teaching students to summarize. *Educational Leadership, 46,* 26-28. [10]

Anderson, W. W. (1975). Evaluation of college reading and study skills programs, problems and approaches. *Reading World, 14,* 191-97. [7]

Andrews, G. R., & Debus, R. L. (1978). Persistence and the causal perception of failure: Modifying cognitive attributions. *Journal of Educational Psychology, 70,* 154-166. [1]

Ankney, P., & McClurg, P. (1981). Testing Manzo's Guided Reading Procedure. *The Reading Teacher, 34,* 681-85. [10]

Applebee, A. N. (1986). Problems in process approaches: Toward a reconceptualization of process instruction. In A. R. Petrosky & D. Bartholomae (Eds.), *The teaching of writing.* Eighty-fifth yearbook of the National Society for the Study of Education, Part II. Chicago: University of Chicago Press. [13]

Applebee, A. N., Langer, J. A., & Mullis, I. (1987). *Learning to be literate in America.* Princeton, NJ: National Assessment of Educational Progress. [13]

Aschner, M. J., Gallager, J. J., Perry, J. M., Afsar, S. S., Jenné, W., & Farr, H. (1962). *A system for classifying thought processes in the context of classroom verbal interaction.* Champaign: University of Illinois, Institute for Research on Exceptional Children. [10]

Ashton-Warner, S. (1959). *Spinster.* New York: Simon and Schuster. [9]

Askov, E., & Greff, N. (1975). Handwriting: Copying versus tracing as the most effective type of practice. *Journal of Educational Research, 69,* 96-98. [9]

Athey, I. (1985). Reading research in the affective domain. In H. Singer and R. B. Ruddell (Eds.), *Theoretical models and processes of reading,* (3rd ed., pp. 527-57). Newark, DE: International Reading Association. [11]

Atwell, N. (1987). *In the middle.* Portsmouth, NH: Boynton/Cook [6]

Au, K. H., & Kawakami, A. J. (1984). Vygotskian perspectives on discussion processes in small-group reading lessons. In P. L. Peterson, L. C. Wilkinson, & M. Hallinan (Eds.), *The social context of instruction* (pp. 209-25). Orlando, FL: Academic Press. [10] [11]

Au, K. H., & Mason, J. M. (1981). Social organizational factors in learning to read: The balance of rights hypothesis. *Reading Research Quarterly, 17,* 115-52. [10]

Au, K. H., Scheu, J. A., Kawakami, A. J., & Herman, P. A. (1990). Assessment and accountability in a whole literacy curriculum. *The Reading Teacher, 43*(8), 574-78. [6]

August, D. L., Flavell, J. H., & Clift, R. (1984). Comparison of comprehension monitoring of skilled and less-skilled readers. *Reading Research Quarterly, 20,* 39-53. [10]

Aulls, M. W. (1978). *Developmental and remedial reading in the middle grades* (abridged ed.). Boston: Allyn & Bacon. [10]

Aulls, M. W., & Graves, M. F. (1985) Repeated reading chart. In *Quest, Desert Magic, Unit 1, Electric Butterfly and other Stories.* New York: Scholastic.

Ausubel, D. P. (1964). Some psychological aspects of the structure of knowledge. In S. Elam (Ed.), *Annual Phi Delta Kappa Symposium on Educational Research.* Chicago: Rand McNally. [7]

Axeline, V. M. (1946). *Play Therapy.* New York: Houghton Mifflin. [11]

Aylward, M. (1990). *The SPIN reading/study skills system.* Unpublished doctoral dissertation, University of Lowell, Lowell, MA. [13]

Ayres, A. J. (1978). Learning disabilities and the vestibular system. *Journal of Learning Disabilities, 11,* 30-41. [12]

Babbs, P. (1983). The effects of instruction in the use of a metacognitive monitoring strategy upon fourth graders' reading comprehension and recall performance (Doctoral dissertation, Perdue University, West Lafayette, IN). *Dissertation Abstract International, 5,* 44/06A. [10]

Bagley, M. T., & Hess, K. (1982). *200 ways of using imagery in the classroom.* Woodcliff Lake, NJ: New Dimensions of the 80's. [10]

Baker, L. (1979a). Comprehension monitoring: Identifying and coping with text confusion. *Journal of Reading Behavior, 11,* 365-74. [10]

Baker, L. (1979b). Do I understand or do I not understand: That is the question. (Reading Education Report No. 10). Washington, DC: National Institute of Education. (ERIC Document Reproduction Service No. EC174 948) [10]

Baker, L., & Brown, A. L. (1984). Metacognitive skills and reading. In P. D. Pearson, R. Barr, M. L. Kamil, & P. Mosenthal (Eds.), *Handbook of reading research* (pp. 333-94). New York: Longman. [7]

Baker, S. D. (1985). Biochemical approach to the problem of dyslexia. *Journal of Learning Disabilities, 18,* 581-84. [12]

Ballard, R. (1978). *Talking dictionary.* Ann Arbor, MI: Ulrich's Books. [8] [10]

Balow, B., & Blomquist, M. (1965). Young adults ten to fifteen years after severe reading disability. *Elementary School Journal, 66,* 44-48. [7]

Bandura, A. (1977a). Self-efficacy: Toward a unifying theory of behavioral change. *Psychological Review, 84,* 191-215. [7]

Bandura, A. (1977b). *Social learning theory.* Englewood Cliffs, NJ: Prentice-Hall.

Bandura, A. (1982). Self-efficiency mechanism in human agency. *American Psychologist, 37*(2), 122-47.

Bandura, A. (1987). Self-regulation of motivation and action through goal systems. In V. Hamilton, G. H. Bower, & N. H. Frijda (Eds.), *Cognition, motivation, and affect: A cognitive science view.* Dordrecht, Neth: Martinus Nijhoff. [10]

Bandura, A., & Walters, R. (1963). *Social learning and personality development.* New York: Holt, Rinehart and Winston. [7]

Bannatyne, A. (1971). *Language, reading, and learning disabilities.* Springfield, IL: Charles C. Thomas. [9]

Bannatyne, A. D. (1974). Diagnosis: A note on recategorization of the WISC scaled scores. *Journal of Learning Disabilities, 7,* 272-73. [5]

Barr, R. C. (1973-74). Instructional pace differences and their effect on reading acquisition. *Reading Research Quarterly, 9,* 526-54. [7]

Barr, R., Kamil, M. L., Mosenthal, P., & Pearson, P. D. (Eds.). (1991). *Handbook of reading research* (Vol. 2). New York: Longman. [3]

Barr, R., Sadow, M. W., & Blachowizc, C. L. Z. (1990). *Reading diagnosis for teachers: An instructional approach* (2nd ed.). White Plains, NY: Longman. [2] [6]

Barron, R. (1969). The use of vocabulary as an advance organizer. In H. L. Herber & P. L. Sanders (Eds)., *Research in reading in the content area: First report* (pp. 29-39). Syracuse, NY: Syracuse University Reading and Language Arts Center. [10]

Bartlett, F. C. (1932). *Remembering: A study in experimental and social psychology.* Cambridge, England: Cambridge University Press. [10]

Baumann, J. F. (1984). Implication for reading instruction from the research on teacher and school effectiveness. *Journal of Reading, 28,* 109-15. [10]

Baumann, J. F. (1986). Teaching third-grade students to comprehend anaphoric relationships: The application of a direct instruction model. *Reading Research Quarterly, 21,* 70-90. [4]

Baumann, J. F. (1988a). Direct instruction reconsidered. *Journal of Reading, 31,* 712-18. [4]

Baumann, J. F. (1988b). *Reading assessment.* Columbus, OH: Merrill. [4]

Baumann, J. F., & Kameenui, E. J. (1991). Research on vocabulary instruction: Ode to Voltaire. In J. Flood, J. M. Jensen, D. Lapp, & J. R. Squire (Eds.), *Handbook of research on teaching the English language arts* (pp. 604-32). New York: Macmillan. [9]

Baurgimeister, B. B., Blum, H., & Lorge, I. (1972). *Columbia Mental Maturity Scale.* New York: Harcourt, Brace & World. [5]

Bean, R. M., Cooley, W. W., Eichelberger, R. T., Lazar, M. K., & Zigmond, N. (1991). Inclass or pullout: Effects of setting on the remedial reading program. *Journal of Reading Behavior, 23*(4), 445-64. [6]

Bean, R. M., Lazar, M. K., & Zigmond, N. (1987). *System for observing reading instruction (SORIN).* Unpublished observation instrument, University of Pittsburgh, Institute for Practice and Research in Education, Pittsburgh, PA.

Bean, T. W. (1979). The miscue mini-form: Refining the informal reading inventory. *Reading World, 18*(4), 400-05. [4]

Bean, T. W., & Pardi, R. (1979). A field test of a guided reading strategy. *Journal of Reading, 23,* 144-47. [10]

Bean, T. W., Searles, D., Singer, H., & Cowen, S. (1987). *Acquiring concepts from biology text: A study of independent generation of procedural knowledge versus the use of text-based procedural knowledge.* Paper presented at the annual meeting of the National Reading Conference, St. Petersburg, FL. [10]

Bean, T. W., & Steenwyck, F. C. (1984). The effect of three forms of summarization instruction on sixth grades' summary writing and comprehension. *Journal of Reading Behavior, 16,* 297-306. [10]

Beane, J. A. (1990). *Affect in the curriculum: Toward democracy, dignity, and diversity.* New York: Teachers College Press. [5] [11]

Bear, D. R., & Invernizzi, M. (1984). Student directed reading groups. *Journal of Reading, 28,* 248-52. [10]

Beaven, M. H. (1977). Individualized goal setting, self-evaluation, and peer evaluation. In C. Cooper & L. Odell (Eds), *Evaluating writing: Describing, measuring, judging.* Urbana, IL: National Council of Teachers of English. [4]

Beck, I. L. (1989). Reading and reasoning. *The Reading Teacher, 42,* 676-82. [7]

Beck, I. L., & McCaslin, E. S. (1978). *An analysis of dimensions that effect the development of code-breaking ability in eight beginning reading programs.* Pittsburgh, PA: Learning Research and Development Center, University of Pittsburgh. (ERIC Document Reproduction Service No. ED155 585) [8]

Beck, I. L., McKeown, M. G., & Omanson, R.C. (1987). The effects and uses of diverse instructional techniques. In M. G. McKeown & M. E. Curtis (Eds.), *The nature of vocabulary acquisition.* Hillsdale, NJ: Erlbaum, 147-63. [9]

Beck, I. L., Omanson, R. C., & McKeown, M. G. (1982). An instructional redesign of reading lessons: Effects on comprehension. *Reading Research Quarterly, 17,* 462-81. [10] [11]

Becker, W. C. (1977). Teaching reading and language to the disadvantaged — What we have learned from field research. *Harvard Educational Review, 47,* 518-43. [8]

Beez, W. V. (1968). Influence of biased psychological reports on teacher behavior and pupil performance. In *Proceedings of the 76th Annual Convention of the American Psychological Association.* Washington, DC: American Psychological Associations. [7]

Beldin, H. O. (1970). Informal reading testing: Historical review and review of the research. In W. K. Durr (Ed.), *Reading difficulties: Diagnosis, correction and remediation* (pp. 67-84). Newark, DE: International Reading Association. [4]

Bellezza, F. (1984). The spatial-arrangement mnemonic. *Journal of Educational Psychology, 75,* 830-37. [12] [13]

Bender, L. (1936). *A Visual Motor Gestalt Test and its clinical use.* Research Monograph No. 3. New York: American Orthopsychiatric Association.

Bender, L. (1946). *Instructions for the use of the Visual Motor Gestalt Test.* New York: American Orthopsychiatric Association. [5]

Benton, A. L., & Hamsher, K. (1983). *Multilingual aphasia examination.* Iowa City, IA: AJA Associates. [12]

Berlin, D. (1987). *Eine besondere Art der Wortblindheit (Dyslexie).* Wiesbaden, Germany: J.F. Bergmann.

Betts, E. A. (1936). *The prevention and correction of reading difficulties.* Evanston, IL: Row Peterson. [4]

Betts, E.A. (1946). *Foundations of reading instruction.* New York: American Book.

Biklen, D. (1990). Communication unbound: Autism and praxis. *Harvard Educational Review.* 60:3, pp. 291-314.

Birch, H. G., & Belmont, L. (1964). Auditory-visual integration in normal and retarded readers. *American Journal of Orthopsychiatry, 34,* 852-61.

Bird, L. B. (1991). Anatomy of a student portfolio. In K. Goodman, L. B. Bird, & Y. Goodman, (Eds.), *The whole language catalog* (pp. 262). New York: American School Publishers, Macmillan/McGraw Hill. [6]

Black, Sister M. C., B.V.M. (1961). *Phonics rules verification by a thirteen hundred word count.* Unpublished master's thesis project, Loyola University of Los Angeles, July. [8]

Blanchard, J. S. (1983). A critique of Kenneth Goodman's: A linguistic study of cues and miscues in reading. In L. M. Gentile, M. Kamil, & J. S. Blanchard (Eds.), *Reading research revisited* (pp. 193-200). Columbus, OH: Charles E. Merrill. [2]

Blanchard, J.S. (1988). Plausible stories: A creative writing and story prediction activity. *Reading Research and Instruction, 28,* 60-65. [10]

Blanchard, J. S., & Rottenberg, C. J. (1990). Hypertext and hypermedia: Discovering and creating meaningful learning environment. *The Reading Teacher, 43*(9), 656-61. [3]

Blaskey, P., Scheiman, M., Parisi, M., Ciner, E. B., Gallaway, M., & Selznick, R. (1990). The effectiveness of Irlen filters for improving reading performance: A pilot study. *Journal of Learning Disabilities, 23*(10), 604-12. [12]

Bloom, B. S. (Ed.). (1956). *Taxonomy of educational objectives, Handbook I: Cognitive Domain.* New York: David McKay. [10]

Bloom, B. S., Hastings, J. T., & Madaus, G. F. (1971). *Handbook on formative and summative evaluation of student learning.* New York: McGraw-Hill. [3]

Bloomfield, L. (1955). *Language.* New York: H. Holt & Co. [8]

Bloomfield, L., & Barnhart, C. L. (1962). *Let's read.* Detroit: Wayne State University Press. [2]

Bloomfield, L., Barnhart, C. L., & Barnhart, R. K. (1965). *Let's read.* Cambridge, MA: Educators Publishing Service. [8]

Bode, B. (1989). Dialogue journal writing. *The Reading Teacher, 42*(8), 568-71. [10] [11] [13]

Boder, E. (1970). Developmental dyslexia: A new diagnostic approach based on identification of three subtypes. *Journal of School Health, 40,* 289-90.

Boder, E. (1971a). Developmental dyslexia: A diagnostic screening procedure based on three characteristic patterns of reading and spelling. In B. D. Bateman (Ed.), *Learning Disorders: Vol. 4* (pp. 298-342). Seattle, WA: Special Child Publications. [8] [12]

Boder, E. (1971b). Developmental dyslexia: Prevailing diagnostic concepts and a new diagnostic approach. In H. Myklebust (Ed.), *Progress in Learning Disabilities, Vol. II* (pp. 293-321). New York: Grune & Stratton. [8] [12]

Boder, E. (1972). Developmental dyslexia: A review of prevailing diagnostic criteria. In M. P. Douglass (Ed.), *Claremont Reading Conference 36th Yearbook* (pp. 114-25). Claremont, CA: Claremont University Center. [12]

Boder, E. (1973). Developmental dyslexia: A diagnostic approach based on three typical reading-spelling patterns. *Developmental Medicine and Child Neurology, 15,* 663-87. [3]

Boder, E., & Jarrico, S. (1982). *The Boder Test of reading-spelling patterns.* New York: Grune & Stratton. [8] [12]

Boder, L. A., & Wiesendanger, K. D. (1986). University based reading clinics: Practices and procedures. *The Reading Teacher, 39*(7), pp. 698-702. [1]

Bond, G. L., & Tinker, M. A. (1973). *Reading difficulties: Their diagnosis and correction* (3rd ed.). New York: Appleton-Century-Crofts. [3]

Bormuth, J. R. (1965). Validities of grammatical and semantic classifications of cloze test scores. In J. A. Figurel (Ed.), *Reading and inquiry.* International Reading Association Conference Proceedings, *10,* (pp. 283-86). Newark, DE: International Reading Association. [4]

Bos, C. S. (1982). Getting past decoding: Assisted and repeating readings as remedial methods for learning disabled students. *Topics in Learning and Learning Disabilities, 1,* 51-57. [12]

Bowers, P.G., Steffy, R., & Tate, E. (1988). Comparison of the effects of IQ control methods on memory and naming speed predictors of reading disability. *Reading Research Quarterly, 23,* 304-19. [12]

Bowles, S., & Gintis, H. (1976). *Schooling in capitalist America.* New York: Basic Books. [7]

Bowman, J. D. (1991). Vocabulary development by "twosies." *Arizona Reading Journal, 19*(2), 66. [9] [10]

Bradley, J. M., & Ames, W. S. (1977). Readability parameters of basal readers. *Journal of Reading Behavior, 9,* 175-183. [4]

Bradshaw, J., & Nettleton, N. C. (1983). *Human cerebral asymmetry.* Inglewood Cliffs, NJ: Prentice Hall. [12]

Brett, C., & Bereiter, C. (1989). A cognitive-adaptationist approach to remediating reading problems. *Journal of Reading, Writing, and Learning, 5,* 281-91. [2]

Brewster, C. (1988). *Dyslexia: Theory and practices of remedial instruction.* Parkton, MD: York Press. [8]

Bridge, C. A. (1986). Predictable books for beginning readers and writers. In M. R. Sampson (Ed.), *The pursuit of literacy.* Dubuque, IA: Kendall/Hunt Publishing Company. [8]

Bridge, C. A., Winograd, P. N., & Haley, D. (1983). Using predictable materials vs. pre-primers to teach beginning sight words. *The Reading Teacher, 36,* 884-91. [8]

Bristow, P. S., Pikulski, J. J., & Pelosi, P. S. (1983). A comparison of five estimates of reading instructional level. *The Reading Teacher, 37,* 273-79. [4]

Bromley, K. D. (1985). Précis writing and outlining enhance content learning. *The Reading Teacher, 38,* 406-11. [10]

Bromley, K. D., & McKeveny, L. (1986). Précis writing: Suggestion for instruction in summarizing. *Journal of Reading, 29*(5), 392-95. [10]

Brown, A. L. (1980). Metacognitive development and reading. In R. Spiro, B. Bruce, & W. F. Brewer, (Eds.), *Theoretical issues in reading comprehension* (pp. 453-81). Hillsdale, NJ: Erlbaum. [1]

Brown, A. L., Campione, J. C., & Day, J. D. (1981). Learning to learn: On training students to learn from texts. *Educational Researcher, 10*(2), 14-21. [4] [7]

Brown, A. L., & Day, J. D. (1983). Macrorules for summarizing texts: The development of expertise. *Journal of Verbal Learning and Verbal Behavior, 22*(1), 1-14. [10]

Brown, B., Haegerstrom-Portnoy, G., Herron, J., Galin, D., Yingling, C., & Marcus, M. (1985). Static postural stability is normal in dyslexic children. *Journal of Learning Disabilities, 18*(1), 31-34.

Brown, W. T., & Holtzman, W. H. (1967). *Survey of study habits and attitudes*. New York: The Psychological Corporation. [4]

Browning, N. F. (1986). Journal writing: One assignment does more than improve reading, writing, and thinking. *Journal of Reading, 30*(1), 39-40.

Brozo, W. G., Schmlzer, R. V., & Spires, H. A. (1983). The beneficial effect of chunking on good readers' comprehension of expository prose. *Journal of Reading, 26*, 442-45. [10]

Bruck, M. (1988). The word recognition and spelling of dyslexic children. *Reading Research Quarterly, 23*(1), 51-69. [12]

Bruner, J. S. (1978). The role of dialogue in language acquisition. In A. Sinclair, R.J. Jarvelle, & W. J. M. Leveet (Eds.), *The child's conception of language*. New York: Springer. [7 — scaffolding reference]

Bryant, S. (1979). *Relative effectiveness of visual-auditory versus-auditory-kinesthetic-tactile procedures for teaching sight words and letter sounds to young disabled readers*. Doctoral dissertation, Teacher College, New York. [12]

Buck, J. N., & Hammer, E. F. (1969). *Advances in the House-Tree-Person Technique: Variations and applications*. Los Angles, CA: Western Psychological Services. [5]

Buck, J. N., & Jolles, I. (1966). *H-T-P: House-Tree-Person projective technique*. Beverly Hills, CA: Western Psychological Services. [5]

Burke, H. R. (1958). Raven's Progressive Matrices: A review and critical evaluation. *Journal of Genetic Psychology, 93*, 199-228. [5]

Burnett, R. (1991). Empower: Responding to controversy. *The Missouri Reader, 15*(2), 12-13. [2]

Burns, P. C., & Roe, B. D. (1985). *Informal reading inventory* (2nd ed.). Boston: Houghton Mifflin. [3] [4]

Calanchini, P. R., & Trout, S. S. (1971). The neurology of learning disabilities. In L. Tarnopol (Ed.), *Learning disorders in children: Diagnosis, medication, education*. Boston: Little, Brown. [12]
(Also cited in Tarnopol, I., & Tarnopol, M. (Eds.). (1976). *Brain function and reading disabilities* (pp. 45). Baltimore, MD: University Park Press.)

Calder, C. R., & Zalatimo, S. D. (1970). Improving children's ability to follow directions. *The Reading Teacher, 24*, 227-31. [10]

Calfee, R. (1976). Letter addressed to Mr. and Mrs. Lindamood. Reported in D. B. Clark (1988). *Dyslexia: Theory practice of remedial instruction* (pp. 136). Parkton, MD: York. [8]

Calfee, R., & Hiebert, E. (1991). Classroom assessment of reading. In R. Barr, M. Kamil, P. Mosenthal, & P. D. Pearson (Eds.), *Handbook of reading research* (Vol. 2, pp. 281-309). New York: Longman. [10]

Cambourne, B. (1977, August). *Some psycholinguistic dimensions of the silent reading process: A pilot study*. Paper presented at the annual meeting of the Australian Reading Conference, Melbourne. [10]

Campbell, N. K., & Hackett, G. (1986). The effects of mathematics task performance on math self-efficacy and task interest. *Journal of Vocational Behavior, 28*(2), 149-62. [7]

Campbell, P. (1966). *Reading attitude inventory*. Livonia Public Schools, Livonia, Michigan. [8]

Camperell, K. (1982). Vygotsky's theory of intellectual development: The effect of subject-matter instruction on self-regulated cognitive processes. In G. H. McNich (Ed.), *Reading in the disciplines*. Second yearbook of the American Reading Forum (pp. 33-35). Athens, GA: University of Georgia. [2] [9]

Camperell, K. (1984). Equal educational opportunities and a core curriculum. In G. H. McNich (Ed.), *Comprehension computers communication*. Fifth yearbook of the American Reading Forum (pp. 15-19). Athens, GA: University of Georgia. [4]

Carbo, M. L. (1984a). Research in learning style and reading implications. *Theory Into Practice*, 23, 72-76. [5]

Carbo, M. L. (1984b). Reading styles: How principals can make a difference. *Principal*, 64, 20-26. [5]

Carbo, M. L. (1984c). You can identify reading styles and then design a super reading program. *Early Years, 14*, 80-83.

Carbo, M. (1988). The evident supporting reading styles: A response to Stahl. *Phi Delta Kappan*, 70, 323-27. [8]

Carlson, R. K. (1965). *Sparkling words: Two hundred practical and creative writing ideas.* Barkeley, CA: Wagner Printing Co. [4]

Carney J. J., & Cioffi, G. (1990). Extending traditional diagnosis: The dynamic assessment of reading abilities. *Reading Psychology, 11*, 177-92. [3] [4] [6]

Carr, E. M., Dewitz, P., & Patberg, J. P. (1989). Using cloze for inference training with expository text. *The Reading Teacher, 42*, 380-85. [10]

Carr, E., & Ogle, D. (1987). K-W-L Plus: A strategy for comprehension and summarization. *Journal of Reading, 30*, 628-29. [10] [13]

Carr, K., & William, W. (1991). Classroom research empowers teachers. *The Missouri Reader, 15*(2), 4-6. [2]

Carroll, H. C. M. (1972). The remedial teaching of reading: An evaluation. *Remedial Education, 7*, 10-15. [7]

Carroll, J. B. (1963). A model of school learning. *Teachers College Record, 64*, 723-32. [7]

Carroll, J. B. (1977). Developmental parameters of reading comprehension. In J. Guthrie (Ed.), *Cognition, curriculum, and comprehension.* Newark, DE: International Reading Association. [4] [7]

Carvell, R. L. (1980). Constructing your own textbook-specific study skills inventory. *Reading World, 19*(3), 239-45. [4]

Carver, R. P. (1982). Optimal rate of reading prose. *Reading Research Quarterly, 18*(1), 56-88. [4]

Carver, R. P. (1990). *Reading rate: A review of research and theory.* New York: Academic Press. [7]

Carver, R. P. (1991). Using letter-naming speed to diagnose reading disability. *Remedial and Special Education, 12*(5), 33-43. [7]

Carver, R. P., & Hoffman, J. V. (1981). The effect of practice through repeated reading in gains in reading ability using a computer-based instructional system. *Reading Research Quarterly, 16*(3), 374-90. [8] [10] [12]

Casale, U. P. (1982). Small group approach to the further validation and refinement of a battery for assessing "progress toward reading maturity" (Doctoral dissertation, University of Missouri-Kansas City). *Dissertation Abstract International, 43*, 770A. [1] [2] [13]

Casale, U. P. (1985). Motor imaging: A reading-vocabulary strategy. *Journal of Reading, 28*, 619-21.

Casale, U. P., & Kelly, B. W. (1980). Problem-solving approach to study skills (PASS) for students in professional schools. *Journal of Reading, 24*, 232-38. [12] [13]

Casale, U. P., & Manzo, A. V. (1983). Differential effects of cognitive affective, and proprioceptive approaches on vocabulary acquisition. In G. H. McNinch (Ed.), *Reading research to reading practice.* The third yearbook of the American Reading Forum (pp. 71-73). Athens, GA: American Reading Forum. [8] [9]

Cassidy, J. (1981, January). Lecture at Benchmark School, Media, PA. (As cited by I. W. Gaskins, 1981) [10]

Cazden, C. B. (1988). *Classroom discourse: The language of teaching and learning.* Portsmouth, NH: Heinemann. [7]

Cecil, N. L. (1990a). Diffusing the trauma: An exit interview for remediated readers. *Journal for Affective Reading Education, 10*, 27-32. [11]

Cecil, N. L. (1990b). Where have all the good questions gone? Encouraging creative expression in children. *Contemporary Issues in Reading, 5*(2), 49-53. [13]

Ceprano, M. A. (1981). A review of selected research on methods of teaching sight words. *The Reading Teacher, 35*, 314-22. [5] [7]

Chall, J. S. (1967). *Learning to read: The great debate.* New York: McGraw-Hill. [2]

Chall, J. S. (1983a). *Learning to read: The great debate* (updated edition). New York: McGraw-Hill. [10]

Chall, J. S. (1983b). Literacy: Trends and explanations. *Educational Researcher, 12*(9), 3-8. [10]

Chall, J. S. (1983c). *Stages of reading development.* New York: McGraw-Hill. [4] [5] [7]

Chall, J. S., & Curtis, M. E. (1987). What clinical diagnosis tells us about children's reading. *The Reading Teacher, 40*, 784-89. [7]

Chall, J. S., & Feldman, S. (1966). First-grade reading: An analysis of the interactions of professed methods, teacher implementation, and child background. *Reading Teacher, 19*, 569-75. [7]

Chang, S. S., & Raths, J. (1971). The schools' contribution to the cumulating deficit. *Journal of Educational Research, 64*, 272-76. [7]

Chapin, M., & Dyck, D. (1976). Persistence in children's reading behavior as a function of N length and attribution retraining. *Journal of Abnormal Psychology, 85*, 511-15. [1]

Chase, F. (1961). Demand on the reader in the next decade. *Controversial issues in reading and promising solutions,* Supplementary Educational Monographs, *91*, 7-18. Chicago: University of Chicago Press. [13]

Cheek, E. H., Jr., Flippo, R., & Linsey, J. D. (1989). *Reading for success in elementary schools.* Orlando, FL: Holt, Rinehart and Winston. [6]

Choate, J. S., & Rakes, T. A. (1987). The structured listening activity: A model for improving listening comprehension. *The Reading Teacher, 41*, 194-200. [8] [10]

Christie, J. F. (1979). The qualitative analysis system: Updating the IRI. *Reading World, 18*, 393-99. [4]

Cicci, R. (1983). Disorders of written language. In H. Myklebust (Ed.), *Progress in learning disabilities* (Vol. 5, pp. 207-32). New York: Grune & Stratton. [9]

Cioffi, G., & Carney, J. J. (1983). Dynamic assessment of reading disabilities. *The Reading Teacher, 36*, 764-68. [6] [7]

Clairborne, J. H. (1906). Types of congenital symbol amblyopia. *Journal of the American Medical Association, 47*, 1313-16. [12]

Claparide, L. (1916). Bradylexie bei einem sonst normalen Kinde, XI Meeting Swiss Neurological Society, May 13 & 14, Abs. *New.2161, 36*, 572. [12]

Clark, C. H. (1982). Assessing free recall. *The Reading Teacher, 35*, 764-68. [4]

Clark, D. (1988). *Dyslexia: Theory and practice of remedial instruction.* Parkton, MD: York Press. [8] [9]

Clark, M. (1976). *Young fluent readers.* London: Heinemann Educational Books. [8]

Clay, M. M. (1966). *Emergent reading behavior.* Doctoral dissertation, University of Auckland, Auckland, New Zealand. [2]

Clay, M. M. (1985). *The early detection of reading difficulties* (3rd ed.). Auckland, New Zealand: Heinemann. [2] [6] [7]

Clewell, S. F., & Haidemenos, J. (1983). Organizational strategies to increase comprehension. *Reading World, 22*, 312-14. [10]

Cline, R. K., & Kretke, G. L. (1980). An evaluation of long-term sustained silent reading in the junior high school. *Journal of Reading, 23*, 503-06. [10]

Clymer, T. (1963). The utility of phonic generalizations in the primary grades. *The Reading Teacher, 16,* 252-56. [8]

Cobb, J. A. (1972). Relationship of discrete classroom behavior to fourth grade academic achievement. *Journal of Educational Psychology, 63,* 74-80. [7]

Cohn, M. L. (1969). Structured comprehension. *The Reading Teacher, 22,* 440-44. [10]

Coleman, S. (1990). Middle school remedial readers serve as cross-grade tutors. *The Reading Teacher, 43,* 524-25. [7]

Coley, J. D., & Hoffman, D. M. (1990). Overcoming learned helplessness in at-risk readers. *Journal of Reading, 33*(7), 497-502. [7]

Collins, C. (1980). Sustained silent reading period: Effect on teacher's behaviors and students' achievement. *Elementary School Journal, 81,* 108-14. [10]

Collins, C. (1991). Reading instruction that increases thinking abilities. *Journal of Reading, 34*(7), 510-16. [13]

Collins, C., & Mangieri, J. (Eds.). (in press). *Thinking development: An agenda for the twenty-first century.* Hilldale, NJ: Erlbaum. [13]

Colvin-Murphy, C. (1986). *Enhancing critical comprehension of literacy texts through writing.* Paper presented at the National Reading Conference. [12] [13]

Comber, L., & Keeves, J. P. (1973). *Science education in nineteen countries.* New York: Wiley. [7]

Combs, W. E. (1975). *Some further effects and implications of sentence-combining exercises for the secondary language arts curriculum.* Unpublished doctoral dissertation, University of Minnesota. [13]

Condus, M. M., Marshall, K. J., & Miller, S. R. (1986). Effect of the key-word mnemonic strategy on vocabulary acquisition and maintenance by learning disabled children. *Journal of Learning Disabilities, 19,* 609-13. [9]

Cooper, C. R., & Odell, L. (1977). *Evaluating writing.* Urbana, IL: National Council of Teachers of English. [4]

Cooper, C. R., & Odell, L. (Eds.). (1978). *Research on composing, points of departure.* Urbana, IL: National Council of Teachers of English [4]

Cooper, J. L. (1947). A procedure for teaching non-readers. *Education, 67,* 494-99. [12]

Cooper, J. L. (1964). An adaptation of the Fernald-Keller approach to teach an initial reading vocabulary to children with severe reading disabilities. *The Australian Journal on the Education of Backward Children, 10,* 131-45. [12]

Cooter, R. B., & Flynt, E. S. (1986). *Reading comprehension: Out of the ivory tower and into the classroom.* Unpublished paper, Northwestern State University, Natchitoches, LA. [13]

Copeland, K. A. (1987). *Writing as a means to learn from prose.* Doctoral dissertation, University of Texas at Austin. [13]

Cordts, A. D. (1925). *Analysis and classification of the sounds of English words in the primary reading vocabulary.* Unpublished dissertation, University of Iowa. [8]

Cousins, P. T. (1991, April/May). Helping learners with special needs become strategic readers. *Reading Today, 8*(5), p. 9. [10]

Cox, A. R. (1985). Alphabetic Phonics: An organization and expansion of Orton-Gillingham. *Annals of Dyslexia, 35,* 187-98. [9]

Critchley, M. (1964). *Developmental dyslexia,* London: Wm. Heinemann Medical Books Limited. [12]

Cronbach, L. J., & Snow, R. E. (1977). *Aptitudes and instructional methods.* New York: Irvington. [5]

Crowder, R. G. (1982). *The psychology of reading.* New York: Oxford University Press. [2]

Culver, V. I. (1975). The guided reading procedure: An experimental analysis of its effectiveness as a technique for improving reading comprehension skills (Doctoral dissertation, University of Missouri-Kansas City). *Dissertation Abstracts International*, *36*, 7062A. [10]

Culver, V. I., Godfrey, H. C., & Manzo, A. V. (1972). A partial reanalysis of the validity of the cloze procedure as an appropriate measure of reading comprehension [Research report summary]. *Journal of Reading, 16*, 256-57. [10]

Cunningham, D., & Shablak, S. L. (1975). Selective reading guide-o-rama: The content teacher's best friend. *Journal of Reading, 18*, 380-82. [10]

Cunningham, J. W. (1982). Generating interactions between schemata and text. In J. A. Niles & L. A. Harris (Eds.), *New inquiries in reading research and instruction.* The 31st yearbook of the National Reading Conference (pp. 42-47). Washington, DC: National Reading Conference. [10]

Cunningham, J. W., Cunningham, P. M., & Arthur, S. V. (1981). Guided listening procedure. In J. W. Cunningham, P. M. Cunningham, & S. V. Arthur, *Middle and secondary school reading.* New York: Longman. [10]

Cunningham, J. W., & Tierney, R. J. (1977). *Comparative analysis of cloze and modified cloze procedures.* Paper presented at the National Reading Conference, New Orleans. [10]

Cunningham, P. M. (1975). Transferring comprehension from listening to reading. *The Reading Teacher, 29*, 169-72. [8] [10]

Cunningham, P. M. (1975-76). Investigating a synthesized theory of mediated word identification. *Reading Research Quarterly, 11*, 127-43. [8]

Cunningham, P. M. (1980). Teaching 'were,' 'with,' 'what,' and other 'four letter' words to slow readers. *The Reading Teacher, 34*, 160-63. [8]

Cunningham, P. (1984). Curriculum trends in reading. *Educational Leadership, 41*, 83-4. [4, 10]

Cunningham, P. (1990). The name test: A quick assessment of decoding ability. *The Reading Teacher, 44*(2), 124-29. [4]

Curry, L. (1990). A critique of the research on learning styles. *Educational Leadership, 48*(2), 50-56. [5]

Cutler, R. B., & Truss, C. V. (1989). Computer aided instruction as a reading motivator. *Reading Improvement, 26*(summer), 103-09. [3]

Dale, E., & O'Rourke, J. (1976). *The living word vocabulary.* Elgin, IL: Dome. [4]

Dale, E., & O'Rourke, J. (1981). *The living word vocabulary* (3rd ed). Chicago: World Book-Childcraft International. [4] [9]

Dana, C. (1982). Gloss in action: Gloss used in remedial reading classes to improve comprehension of expository text. In G. H. McNich (Ed.), *Reading in the disciplines.* Second yearbook of the American Reading Forum (pp.25-27). Athens, GA: American Reading Forum. [10]

Dana, C. (1989). Strategy families for disabled readers. *Journal of Reading, 33*(1), 30-35. [12] [13]

Davey, B. (1983). Think aloud—Modeling the cognitive processes of reading comprehension. *Journal of Reading, 27*, 44-47. [4] [10]

Davey, B. (1987). Postpassage questions: Task and reader effects on comprehension and metacomprehension processes. *Journal of Reading Behavior, 19*(3), 261-83. [4]

Davey, B. (1988a). Factor affecting the difficulty of reading comprehension items for successful and unsuccessful readers. *Journal of Experimental Education, 56*(2), 67-76. [4]

Davey, B. (1988b). The nature of response errors for good and poor readers when permitted to reinspect text during question-answering. *American Educational Research Journal, 25*(3), 399-414. [4]

Davey, B. (1989). Assessing comprehension: Selected interactions of task and reader. *The Reading Teacher, 42*(9), 694-97. [4]

Davey, B., & LaSasso, C. J. (1984). The interaction of reader and task factors in the assessment of reading comprehension. *Journal of Experimental Education, 52*(4), 199-206. [4]

Davidson, J. L. (1970). The relationship between teacher's questions and pupils' responses during a directed reading activity and a directed reading thinking activity (Doctoral dissertation, The University of Michigan, Ann Arbor). *Dissertation Abstracts International, 31,* G273A. [10]

Davis, F. B. (1944). Fundamental factors of comprehension in reading. *Psychometrika, 31,* 185-87. [10]

Davis, H., & Silverman, S. (Eds.). (1970). *Hearing and deafness.* New York: Holt, Rinehart and Winston. [5]

Dearborn, W. F. (1906). The psychology of reading. *Archives of Philosophy, Psychology and Scientific Methods, 1,* 71-132. [2]

Debes, J. A. (l962). A new look at seeing. *Media and Methods, 4,* 26-28. [4]

Dechant, E. (1968). *Diagnosis and remediation of reading disability.* West Nyack, NY: Parker. [5]

Degrees of reading power. (1981). Brewster, NY: Touchstone Applied Science Associates.

Delacato, C. H. (1959). *The treatment and prevention of reading problems.* Springfield, IL: Charles C. Thomas. [12]

Delacoto, C. H. (1963). *The diagnosis and treatment of speech and reading problems.* Springfield, IL: Charles C. Thomas. [12]

Deloche, G., Andreewsky, E., & Desi, M. (1982). Surface dyslexia: A case report. *Brain and Language, 15,* 12-31. [12]

DeMaster, V., Crossland, C., & Hasselbring, T. (1986). Consistency of learning disabled students' spelling performance. *Learning Disability Quarterly, 9,* 89-96. [9]

Dempster, F. K. (1991). Synthesis of research on review and tests. *Educational Leadership, 48*(7), 71-76. [10]

Dempster, F. N., & Farris, R. (1990). The spacing effect: Research and practice. *Journal of Research and Development in Education, 23*(2), 97-101. [7]

Denckla, M. B. (1972). Clinical syndromes in learning disabilities: The case for "splitting" versus "lumping." *Journal of Learning Disabilities, 5,* 401-06. [12]

Denckla, M. B., & Rudel, R. G. (1974). Rapid automized naming of pictured objects, colors, letters and numbers by normal children. *Cortex, 10,* 186-202. [12]

DeSanti, R. J., Casbergue, R. M., & Sullivan, V. G. (1986). *The DeSanti cloze reading inventories.* Newton, MA: Allyn & Bacon.

Devine, T. G. (1991). Studying: Skills, strategies, and systems. In J. Flood, J. M. Jensen, D. Lapp, & J. R. Squire (Eds.), *Handbook of research on teaching the English language arts* (pp. 743-53). New York: Macmillan. [12] [13]

Dewitz, P., Carr, E. M., & Patsberg, J. P. (1987). Effects of inference training on comprehension and comprehension monitoring. *Reading Research Quarterly, 22,* 99-121. [10]

Diamond, M. (1989, November). *The Brain* [Video tape]. University lecture Series #6, University of California-Berkeley: The Learning Channel. [12]

Diederich, P. B. (1974). *Measuring growth in English.* Urbana, IL: National Council of Teachers of English. [4]

Diener, C. I., & Dweck, C. (1978). An analysis of learned helplessness: II. The processing of success. *Journal of Personality and Social Psychology, 39,* 940-52. [1]

Diggs, V. M. (1973). The relative effectiveness of the SQ3R method, a mechanized approach, and a combination method for training remedial reading to college freshmen (Doctoral dissertation, West Virginia University, Morgantown, 1972). *Dissertation Abstracts International, 33,* 5964A. (University Microfilms No. 74-4, 786). [12] [13]

Dishner, E. K. (1974). *ReQuest evaluation form.* Unpublished paper, Arizona State University. [10]

Dishner, E. K., & Searfoss, L. W. (1977). Improving comprehension through the ReQuest Procedure. *Reading Education: A Journal for Australian Teachers, 2* (Autumn), 22-25. [10]

Dolch, E. W. (1951). *Psychology and teaching of reading.* Champaign, IL: The Gerrard Press. [8]

Donald, M., Sr. (1967). The SQ3R method in grade seven. *Journal of Reading, 11,* 33-35, 43. [13]

Dore-Boyce, K., Misner, M. S., & McGuire, L. D. (1975). Comparing reading expectancy formulas. *The Reading Teacher, 29,* 8-14. [3]

Dreher, M. J. (1990). The role of affect in the reading process. *Literacy: Issues and Practices, 7,* 20-24. [11]

Duane, D., & Gray, D. B. (Eds.). (1991). Commentary on dyslexia in neurodevelopmental pathology. *Journal of Learning Disabilities, 22*(4), 219-20. [12]

Duffelmeyer, F. (1980a). The influence of experience-based vocabulary instruction on learning word meanings. *Journal of Reading, 24,* 35-40. [10]

Duffelmeyer, F. (1980b). The passage independence of factual and inferential questions. *Journal of Reading, 24,* 131-34. [4]

Duffelmeyer, F. A., & Duffelmeyer, B. (1979). Developing vocabulary through dramatization. *Journal of Reading, 23,* 141-43. [4] [10]

Duffelmeyer, F. A., & Duffelmeyer, B. B. (1989). Are IRI passages suitable for assessing main idea comprehension? *The Reading Teacher, 42,* 358-63. [4]

Duffelmeyer, F., Long, J., & Kruse, A. (1987). The passage independence of comprehension question categories: Evidence of non-uniformity. *Reading Improvement, 24,* 101-06. [4]

Duffelmeyer, F., Robinson, S., & Squier, S. (1989). Vocabulary questions on informal reading inventories. *The Reading Teacher, 43,* 142-48. [4]

Duffy, G. G. (1985). Models of reading have direct implications for reading instruction: The negative position. In J. A. Niles & R. V. Lalik (Eds.), *Issues in literacy: A research perspective.* Thirty-fourth yearbook of the National Reading Conference (pp. 398-401). Rochester, NY: The National Reading Conference. [2]

Duffy, G., & Roehler, L. A. (1987). Improving reading instruction through the use of responsive elaboration. *The Reading Teacher, 40,* 514-20. [7] [10]

Duffy, G. G., Roehler, L. R., & Hermann, B. A. (1988). Modeling mental processes helps poor readers become strategic readers. *The Reading Teacher, 41,* 762-67. [7] [13]

Duffy, G. G., Roehler, L. R., Sivan, E., Rackliffe, G., Book, C., Meloth, M. S., Vavrus, L. G., Wesselman, R., Putnam, J., & Bassiri, D. (1987). The effects of explaining the reasoning associated with using reading strategies. *Reading Research Quarterly, 22,* 347-68. [10] [13]

Dunn, L. M. (l965, 1970). *Peabody Picture Vocabulary Test expanded manual.* Circle Pines, MN.: American Guidance Service. [5]

Dunn L. M., & Markwardt, F. C., Jr. (1970). *Peabody Individual Achievement Test.* Chicago: American Guidance Services. [4]

Durkin, D. (1966). *Children who read early.* New York: Teacher's College Press.

Durkin, D. (1978-79). What classroom observations reveal about reading comprehension instruction. *Reading Research Quarterly, 14*(4), 481-533. [4]

Durrell, D. D. (1937, 1955). *Durrell analysis of reading difficulty.* New York: Harcourt, Brace & World. [6]

Durrell, D. D. (1956). *Improving reading instruction.* Yonkers, NY: World Book. [13]

Durrell, D. D. (1969). Listening comprehension versus reading comprehension. *Journal of Reading, 12,* 455-60. [4]

Durrell, D. D. (1980). *Durrell Analysis of Reading Difficulty*. New York: The Psychological Corporation. [4]

Dweck, C. S., & Goetz, T. E. (1978). Attributions and learned helplessness. In J. H. Harvey, W. I. Ickes, & R. F. Kidd (Eds.), *New directions in attribution research* (Vol. 2). Hillsdale, NJ: Erlbaum. [7]

Dweck, C. S., & Repucci, N. D. (1973). Learned helplessness and reinforcement responsibility in children. *Journal of Personality and Social Psychology, 25*, 109-16. [7]

Dwyer, E. G., & Flippo, R. F. (1983). Multisensory approaches to teaching spelling. *Journal of Reading, 27*(2), 171-72. [12]

Dykstra, R. (1966). Auditory discrimination abilities and beginning reading achievement. *Reading Research Quarterly, 1*, 5-34. [5]

Eanet, M. G. (1978). An investigation of the REAP reading/study procedure: Its rationale and efficacy. In P. D. Pearson & J. Hansen (Eds.), *Reading: Disciplined inquiry in process and practice*. The twenty-seventh yearbook of the National Reading Conference (pp. 229-232). Clemson, SC: National Reading Conference. [13]

Eanet, M. G. (1983). Reading/writing: Finding and using the connection. *The Missouri Reader, 8*, 8-9. [10] [13]

Eanet, M. G., Condon, M. W. F., & Manzo, A. V. (1974). Subjective assessment of auto-instructional learning tasks in secondary and college reading materials. In G. H. McNinch & W. D. Miller (Eds.), *Reading convention and inquiry*. The twenty-fourth yearbook of National Reading Conference (pp. 94-99). Clemson, SC: National Reading Conference. [7]

Eanet, M. G., & Manzo, A. V. (1976). REAP—A strategy for improving reading/writing/study skills. *Journal of Reading, 19*, 647-52. [13]

Ediger, M. (1991). The affective dimension in middle school reading. *Journal for Affective Education, 11*(fall), 35-40. [11]

Edwards, P. A., & Simpson, L. (1986). Bibliotherapy: A strategy for communication between parents and their children. *Journal of Reading, 30*, 110-18. [10] [11]

Eeds, M. (1985). Bookwords: Using a beginning word list of high frequency words from children's literature K-3. *The Reading Teacher, 38*, 418-23. [8]

Ekwall, E. E. (1974). Should repetitions be counted as errors? *The Reading Teacher, 27*(4), 365-67. [4]

Ekwall, E. E., & Shanker, J. L. (1988). *Diagnosis and remediation of the disabled reader* (3rd ed.) Boston, MA: Allyn & Bacon. [3] [6] [5] [8]

Elkind, D. (1976). Cognitive development and reading. In H. Singer & R. Ruddell *Theoretical models and processes of reading*, 2nd ed. Newark, DE: International Reading Association.

Elley, W., & Mangubhai, F. (1983). The impact of reading on second language learning. *Reading Research Quarterly, 19*, 53-67. [10]

Elliott, S. N., & Carroll, J. L. (1980). Strategies to help children remember what they read. *Reading Improvement, 17*, 272-77. [10]

Ellis, A., & Harper, R. (1967). *A guide to rational living in an irrational world*. Englewood Cliffs, NJ: Prentice-Hall. [11]

Englemann, S., & Brener, E. C. (1983). *Reading Mastery I and II: DISTAR Reading*, Science Research Associates. [8]

Engler, B. U. (1917). Analplebetia Partialis: (kongenitale Wortblindheit) *Monat. Psych. News, 42*, 119-32. [12]

Erickson, L. G., & Krajenta, M. A. (1991). How fast should young readers read? *Illinois Reading Council Journal, 19*(2), 10-14. [4]

Ericson, B., Hubler, M., Bean, T. W., Smith, C. C., & McKenzie, J. V. (1987). Increasing critical reading in junior high classrooms. *Journal of Reading, 30,* 430-39. [13]

Ericsson, K. A., & Simon, H. A. (1980). Verbal reports as data. *Psychological Review, 87,* 215-51. [4]

Estes, T. H. (1991). In E. Fry (Ed.), *Ten best ideas for reading teachers* (pp. 59). New York: Addison Wesley. [10] [13]

Estes, T. H., & Vaughan, J. L., Jr. (1973). Reading interest and comprehension: implications. *The Reading Teacher, 27,* 149-53. [4]

Farnan, N. J. (1987). All the language arts for reading comprehension. *Journal of Reading, 31,* 274-75. [10]

Felton, R., Wood, F., Brown, I., Campell, S., & Harter, M. R. (1987). Separate verbal memory and naming deficits in attention deficit disorder and reading disability. *Brain and Language, 31,* 171-84. [12]

Fernald, G. M. (1943). *Remedial techniques in basic school subjects.* New York: McGraw Hill. [9] [12]

Feuerstein, R. (1979). *Instrumental enrichment.* Baltimore: University Park Press. [6]

Fillmer, H. T., Nist, S. L., & Scott, E. M. (1983). The use of hypnosis in improving reading performance. *Community College Review, 11,* 23-7. [11] [12]

Fillmer, H. T., & Parkay, F. W. (1985). How can hypnosis improve reading proficiency? *The Clearing House, 59,* 61-63. [11] [12]

Finlaysen, M. A. J., & Reitan, R. M. (1976). Tactile-perceptual functioning in relation in intellectual, cognitive and reading skills in younger and older normal children. *Developmental Medicine and Child Neurology, 18,* 442-46. [12]

Finn, R. (1991). Different minds. *Discover, 12*(6), 52-58. [12]

Fisher, C. W., Filby, N. W., Marliave, R., Cahen, L. S., Dishaw, M. M., Moore, J. E., & Berlner, D. C. (1978). *Teaching and learning in the elementary school: A summary of the beginning teacher evaluation study* (BTES Rep. VII-I). San Francisco: Far West Laboratory for Educational Research and Development. [7]

Fisher, J. H. (1905). A case of congenital word blindness. *Opthalmic Review, 24,* 315-18.

Fitzgerald, J. (1989). Enhancing two related thought processes: Revision in writing and critical reading. *The Reading Teacher, 43*(1), 42-48. [12] [13]

Flippo, R. F. (1981). Reaction: Effects of listening/reading transfer. In G. H. McNinch (Ed.), *Comprehension: Process and Product.* First yearbook of American Reading Forum (pp. 108-10). Athens, GA: University of Georgia. [10]

Flippo, R. F., & Caverly, D. C. (Eds.). (1991a). *College reading and study strategy programs.* Newark, DE: International Reading Association. [12] [13]

Flippo, R. F., & Caverly, D. C. (Eds.). (1991b). *Teaching reading and study strategies at the college level.* Newark, DE: International Reading Association. [12] [13]

Flood, J., & Lapp, D. (1987). Reading and writing relations: Assumptions and directions. In J. R. Squire (Ed.), *The dynamics of language learning: Research in reading and English.* Bloomington, IN: Eric/rcs, 9-26. [13]

Flood, J., & Lapp, D. (1989). Reporting reading progress: A comparison portfolio for parents. *The Reading Teacher, 42*(7), 508-14. [6]

Flood, J., Lapp, D., & Farnan, N. (1986). A reading-writing precedure that teaches expository paragraph structure. *The Reading Teacher, 29,* 556-62. [10]

Flower, L., & Hayes, J. R. (1981). A cognitive process theory of writing. *College Composition and Communication, 32,* 365-87. [13]

Foos, P. W., & Clark, C. (1984). Testing multiple study choices. *Human Learning, 2,* 86-94. [12] [13]

Fores, R. (1969). *Can elephants swim?* New York: Time Life Books. [7]

Fox, B., & Routh, D. K. (1980). Phonemic analysis and severe reading disability in children. *Journal of Psycholinguistic Research, 9,* 115-19. [8]

Fraatz, J. M. (1987). *The politics of reading: Power, opportunity, and prospects for change in America's public schools.* New York: Teachers College Press. [7]

Frank, J., & Levingson, H. N. (1975-1976). Dysmetric dyslexia and dyspraxia—synopsis of a continuing research project. *Academic Therapy, 11,* 133-43. [12]

Frank, J., & Levinson, H. (1976). Compensatory mechanisms in cerebellar-vestibular dysfunction, dysmetric dyslexia, and dyspraxia. *Academic Therapy, 12,* 5-28. [12]

Frank, J., & Levinson, H. (1977). Anti-motion sickness medications in dysmetric dyslexia and dyspraxia. *Academic Therapy, 12,* 411-24. [12]

Frayer, D. A., Fredrick, W. C., & Klausmeir, H. J. (1969). *A schema for testing the level of concept mastery* (Working Paper No. 16). Madison: University of Wisconsin, Wisconcin Research and Development Center for Cognitive Learning. [9]

Frey, H. (1980). Improving the performance of poor readers through autogenic relaxation. *The Reading Teacher, 33,* 928-32. [12] [13]

Fried, I., Tanguay, D. E., Boder, E., Doubleday, C., & Greensite, M. (1981). Developmental dyslexia: Electrophysiological evidence of clinical subgroups. *Brain and Language, 12,* 14-22. [12]

Friedel, G. (1976, September). *Instant study skills.* Workshop handout, University of Missouri-Kansas City. [12] [13]

Fries, C. C. (1963). *Linguistics and reading.* New York: Holt, Rinehart and Winston. [2]

Froese, V. (1974). IRI's at the Secondary level re-examined. In P. L. Nacke (Ed.), *Interaction: Research and practice for college-adult reading.* Twenty-third yearbook of the National Reading Conference (pp. 120-24). Clemson, SC: National Reading Conference. [4]

Frostig, M., & Horne, D. (1964). *The Frostig program for the development of visual perception.* Chicago: Follett. [13]

Fry, E. B. (1957). Developing a word list for remedial reading. *Elementary English, 34*(7), 456-58. [8]

Fry, E. B. (1964). A frequency approach to phonics. *Elementary English, 41* (7), 760-66. [8]

Fry, E. B. (1980). The new instant word list. *The Reading Teacher, 34,* 284-89. [8]

Fuchs, D., & Fuchs, L. S. (1986). Test procedure bias: A meta-analysis of examiner familiarity effects. *Review of Educational Research, 56,* 243-62. [3 — p. 243 cited in text]

Fuller, F. F. (1969). Concerns of teachers: Developmental conception. *American Education Research Journal, 6,* 207-26. [5]

Gable, R. A., Hendrickson, J. M., & Meeks, J. W. (1988). Assessing spelling errors of special needs students. *The Reading Teacher, 42*(2), 112-17. [9]

Gable, R. A., Hendrickson, J. M., Meeks, J. W., Evan, S. S., & Evans, W. H. (1990). Curriculum-based measurement of oral reading: Linking assessment and instruction. *Preventing School Failure, 35*(1), pp. 37-43. [2]

Galaburda, A. M., & Eidelburg, D. (1982). Symmetry and asymmetry in the human posterior thalamus: II. Thalamic lesions in a case of developmental dyslexia. *Archives of Neurology, 39,* 333-36. [12]

Gambrell, L. B. (1985). Dialogue journals: Reading-writing interaction. *The Reading Teacher, 38,* 512-15. [13]

Gambrell, L. B., & Bales, R. J. (1986). Mental image and the comprehension monitoring performance of fourth- and fifth-grade poor readers. *Reading Research Quarterly, 21,* 454-64. [10]

Gambrell, L. B., Kapinus, B. A., & Wilson, R. M. (1987). Using mental imagery and summarization to achieve independence in comprehension. *Journal of Reading, 30,* 638-41. [12] [13]

Gann, E. (1945). *Reading difficulty and personality organization.* New York: Kings Crown. [2]

Gans, R. (1941). *Guiding children's reading through experiences.* New York: Teachers College. [2]

Garcia, C. L. (1988). Working through emotional blocks to reading. *Journal of Affective Reading Education, 9*(1), 33-39. [11]

Garner, R., Hare, V. C., Alexander, P., Haynes, J., & Winograd, P. (1984). Inducing use of a text lookback strategy among unsuccessful readers. *American Educational Research Journal, 21,* 789-98. [10]

Garner, R., & Kraus, C. (1981-82). Good and poor comprehender differences in knowing and regulating reading behaviors. *Educational Research Quarterly, 6,* 5-12. [10]

Garner, R., & Reis, R. (1981). Monitoring and resolving comprehension obstacles: An investigation of spontaneous text lookbacks among upper-grade good and poor comprehenders. *Reading Research Quarterly, 16,* 569-82. [10]

Garrison, J. W., & Hoskisson, K. (1989). Confirmation bias in predictive reading. *The Reading Teacher, 42*(7), 482-86. [10]

Gaskins, I. W. (1981). Reading for learning: Going beyond basals in the elementary grades. *The Reading Teacher, 35,* 323-28. [10]

Gaskins, I., & Elliot, T. (1991). *Implementing cognitive strategy training across the school.* Media, PA: Brookline Books. [10]

Gates, A. (1941). The role of personality maladjustment and remedial reading. *Journal of Generic Psychology, 59,* 77-83. [2]

Gates-MacGinitie Reading Tests. (1978). Boston, MA: Houghton Mifflin. [4]

Gauthier, L. R. (1988). A study of listening comprehension as a predictor of reading gains. *Reading Improvement, 25,* 276-81. [5]

Gauthier, L. R. (1990). Five informal ways to assess students' reading comprehension. *Reading: Exploration and Discovery, 12,* 31-38. [4][10]

Gauthier, L. R. (1991). Using journals for content area comprehension. *Journal of Reading, 34*(6), 491-92. [13]

Gauthier, L. R. (1992, in press). The effects of vocabulary gain upon instructional reading level. *Reading Improvement.* [9]

Gee, T. C., & Raskow, S. J. (1987). Content reading specialists evaluate teaching practices. *Journal of Reading, 31,* 234-37. [10] [7]

Geissal, M. A., & Knafle, J. D. (1977). A linguistic view of auditory tests and exercises. *Reading Teacher, 31*(2), 134-41. [5]

Gentile, L. M., & McMillan, M. M. (1983). A commentary on Abrams' critique of Gann's study. In L. M. Gentile, M. L. Kamil, & J. S. Blanchard (Eds.), *Reading research revistied* (pp. 484). Columbus, OH: Charles C. Merrill. [12]

Gentile, L. M., & McMillan, M. M. (1984, December). *Stress as a factor in reading difficulties: From research to practice.* Paper presented at the American Reading Forum National Conference, Orlando, FL. [11]

Gentile, L. M., & McMillian, M. M. (1987). *Stress and reading difficulties: Research, assessment, intervention.* Newark, DE: International Reading Association. [2] [12]

Gentile, L. M., & McMillan, M. M. (1990). Literacy through literature: Motivating at-risk students to read and write. *Journal of Reading, Writing and Learning Disabilities International, 6,* 383-93. [13]

Gentile, L. M., & McMillan, M. M. (1991). Reading, writing and relationships: The challenge of teaching at risk students. *Reading Research and Instruction, 30*(4), 74-81. [13]

Gentry, R. (1982). An analysis of developmental spelling in GYNS at WRK. *The Reading Teacher, 36*(2), 192-200. [9]

George, J. E. (1975). *Reading Facilitating Experience.* Course handout, University of Missouri-Kansas City. [5]

George, J. E. (1990). *Incomplete Sentences Inventory*. Course handout, University of Missouri-Kansas City. [5]

Geschwind, N. (1972). Language and the brain. *Scientific American, 226*, 76-83. [12]

Geschwind, N. (1979). Anatomical foundations of language and dominance. In C. L. Ludlow & M. E. Doran-Quine (Eds.), *The neurological bases of language disorders in children: Methods and directions for research* (pp. 145-57). Bethesda, MD: U.S. Department of Health, Education, and Welfare. [12]

Geschwind, N. (1982). Why Orgon was right. *Annals of Dyslexia*, (reprint of the Rodin Remediation Foundation) *32*, 13-30. [12]

Gibson, E., & Levin, H. (1975). *The psychology of reading*. Cambridge, MA: MIT Press. [8]

Gill, J. T., & Bear, D. R. (1988). No book, whole book, and chapter CR-TAs. *Journal of Reading, 31*, 444-51. [10]

Gillet, J. W., & Temple, C. (1990). *Understanding reading problems: Assessment and instruction* (3rd ed.). Glenview, IL: Scott, Foresman/ Little, Brown Higher Education.

Gilmore, J. V., & Gilmore, E. C. (1968). *Gilmore oral reading test*. New York: The Psychological Corporation. [4]

Gipe, J. (1978-1979). Investigating techniques for teaching word meaning. *Reading Research Quarterly, 14*, 624-44. [9]

Giroux, H. (1981). *Ideology, cultural, and the process of schooling*. Philadelphia, PA: Temple University Press. [7]

Giroux, H., & Purpel, D. (Eds.). (1983). *The hidden curriculum and moral education*. Berkeley, CA: McCutchan. [11]

Gittelman, R., & Feingold, I. (1983). Children with reading disorders: Efficacy of reading remediation. *Journal of Child Psychology & Psychiatry & Allied Disciplines, 24*, 167-91. [7]

Glass, G. (1973). *Teaching decoding as separate from reading*. Garden City, NY: Adelphi University Press. [2] [12]

Glass, G. G., & Burton, E. H. (1973). How do they decode? Verbalization and observed behaviors of successful decoders. *Education, 94*, 58-64. [8]

Glass, G. G., & Glass, E. W. (1976). *Glass analysis for decoding only: Teachers guide*. Garden City, NY: Easier to Learn. [12]

Glass, G. G., & Glass, E. W. (1978a). *Glass analysis for decoding only: Easy starts kit*. Garden City, NY: Easier to Learn. [12]

Glass, G. G., & Glass, E. W. (1978b). *Glass analysis for decoding only: Quick and easy alphabet program*. Garden City, NY: Easier to Learn. [12]

Glass, G. V., & Robbins, M. P. (1967). A critique of experiments on the role of neurological organization in reading performance. *Reading Research Quarterly, 3*, 5-52. [12]

Glasser, W. (1965). *Reality therapy*. New York: Harper & Row. [11] [12]

Glazer, S. M. (1984). Liberating students to write. *Early years, 15*(1), 67-69. [4]

Glazer, S. M. (1992). Instructional apprenticeship and psychoeducational aspects of ReQuest: An anecdote. (personal communication).

Goldberg, H. K., Schiffman, G. B., & Bender, M. (1983). *Dyslexia: Interdisciplinary approaches to reading disabilities*. New York: Grune & Stratton. [5] [12]

Goldstein, K., & Scheerer, M. (1964). Abstract and concrete behavior: An experimental study with special tests. In J. F. Dashiell (Ed.), *Psycological Monographs*. Evanston, IL: American Psychological Association. [5]

Good, T. L. (1987). Teacher expectations. In D. C. Berliner & B. V. Roseshine (Eds.), *Talk to teachers* (pp. 67-79). New York: Random House. [7]

Good, T. L., Grouws, D. A., & Beckerman, T. M. (1978). Curriculum pacing: Some empirical data in mathematics. *Journal of Curriculum Studies, 10*, 75-82. [7]

Goodman, K. S. (1967). Reading: A psycholinguistic guessing game. *Journal of the Reading Specialist, 6*, 126-35. [2] [10]

Goodman, K. S. (1973). Miscues: Windows on the reading process. In K. S. Goodman (Ed.), *Miscue analysis: Applications to reading instruction* (pp. 3-14). Urbana, IL.: National Council of Teachers of English. [4]

Goodman, K. S. (1986). *What's whole in whole language?* Portsmouth, NH: Heinemann. [12] [13]

Goodman, K., Bird, L. B., & Goodman, Y. (Eds.). (1991). *The whole language catelog.* New York: American School Publishers, Macmillan/McGraw-Hill. [2] [3] [9]

Goodman, Y. M., & Burke, C. L. (1972). *Reading miscue inventory manual: Procedure for diagnosis and evaluation.* New York: Macmillan. [4]

Goodman, Y. M. (1975). Reading strategy lessons: Expanding reading effectiveness. In W. Page (Ed.), *Help for the reading teacher: New directions in research* (pp. 34-41). National Council of Teacher of English and Educational Resources Information Center. [8]

Goodman, Y. M. (1985). Kidwatching: Observing children in the classroom. In A. Jaggar & M. T. Smith-Burke (Eds.), *Observing the Language Learner* (pp. 9-18). Newark, DE: International Reading Association.

Goodman, Y. M. (1986). Children coming to know literacy. In W. H. Teale & E. Sulzby (Eds.), *Emergent literacy: Writing and reading* (pp. 1-14). Norwood, NJ: Ablex.

Goodman, Y. M. (1989). Roots of the whole-language movement. *Language Arts Journal, 90*(2), 113-27. [2]

Gorham, D. R. (1956). *Proverbs Test.* Missoula, MT: Psychological Test Specialists. [10]

Gorrell, J. (1990). Some contributions of self-efficacy research to self-concept. *Journal of Research and Development in Education, 23*(2), 73-81. [7]

Gough, H. G. (1975). *California Psychological Inventory.* Palo Alto, CA: Consulting Psychologist Press. [5]

Gough, P. B. (1991) (as cited by C. Juel). In R. Barr, M. L. Kamil, P. Mosenthal, & P. D. Pearson (Eds.), *Handbook of reading research - Volume II* (pp. 768-69). New York: Longman. [8]

Gough, P. B., Alford, J. A., Jr., & Holley-Wilcox, P. (1981). Words and contexts. In O. J. L. Tzeng & H. Singer (Eds.), *Perception of print* (pp. 85-102). Hillsdale, NJ: Erlbaum. [8]

Gough, P. B., & Cosky, M. J. (1977). One second of reading again. In N. J. Castellan, Jr., D. Pisoni, & G. Potts (Eds.), *Cognitive theory,* 2, (pp. 271-88). Hillsdale, NJ: Erlbaum Associates. [2]

Gough, P. B., & Hillinger, M. D. (1980). Learning to read: An unnatural act. *Bulletin of the Orton Society, 30,* 179-96. [8]

Gough, P. B., Juel, C., & Roper-Schneider, D. (1983). A two-stage model of initial reading acquisition. In J. A. Niles & L. A. Harris (Eds.), *Searches for meaning in reading/language processing and instruction* (pp. 207-11). Rochester, NY: National Reading Conference. [8]

Gough, P. B., & Tunmer, W. E. (1986). Decoding, reading, and reading disability. *Remedial and Special Education, 7,* 6-10. [12]

Graham, J. R., & Lilly, R. S. (1984). *Psychological Testing.* Englewood Cliffs, NJ: Prentice-Hall. [5]

Graves, D. H. (1983). *Writing: Teachers and children at work.* Portmouth, NH: Heinemann. [10]

Graves, M. F. (1986). Vocabulary learning and instruction. In E. Z. Rothkopf & L. C. Ehri (Eds.), *Review of research in education* (Vol. 13, pp. 49-89). Washington, DC: American Educational Research Association. [10]

Graves, M. F., & Hammond, H. (1980). A validated precedure for teaching prefixes and its effect on student's ability to assign meaning to novel words. In M. Kamil & A. Moe (Eds.), *Perspectives on reading research and instruction.* Twenty-ninth yearbook of the National Reading Conference (pp. 184-88). Washington, DC: National Reading Conference. [9]

Graves, M. F., & Prenn, M. C. (1986). Costs and benefits of various methods of teaching vocabulary. *Journal of Reading, 29*(7), 596-602. [9]

Gray, C. T. (1922). *Deficiencies in reading ability: Their diagnosis and remedies.* Boston: D. C. Health. [2]

Gray, W. S. (1925). *24th Yearbook of the NSSE, Part I — Report of the National Committee on Reading.* Bloomington, IL: Public School Publishing Co. [2]

Gray, W. S. (1948). *On their own in reading.* Glenview, IL: Scott, Foresman. [8] [9] [10]

Gray, W. S. (1960). Reading. In C. W. Harris (Ed.), *Encyclopedia of educational research* (2nd ed.) (pp. 1106). New York: Macmillan. [9]

Gray, W. S., & Rogers, B. (1956). *Maturity in reading.* Chicago: University of Chicago Press. [2]

Green, E. (1972). *An experimental study of sentence-combining to improve written syntactic fluency in fifth grade children.* Unpublished doctoral dissertation, Northern Illinois University. [12] [13]

Grobler, C. Van E. (1971). Methodology in reading instruction as a controlling variable in the constructive or destructive channeling of aggression. (Doctoral dissertation, University of Delaware, Newark, 1970). *Dissertation Abstracts International, 32*, 6197A. [10]

Groff, P. (1980). A critique of an oral reading miscues analysis. *Reading World, 19*(3), 254-64. [4]

Gross, D. (1990). *Unlocking and guiding creative potential in writing and problem-solving.* Unpublished Education Specialist Project, University of Missouri-Kansas City. [12] [13]

Guice, B. M. (1969). The use of the cloze procedure for improving reading comprehension of college students. *Journal of Reading Behavior, 1*, 81-92. [10]

Guilford, J. P. (1967). *The nature of human intelligence.* New York: McGraw-Hill. [5]

Guilford, J. P. (1968). Creativity: Yesterday, today and tomorrow. *Journal of Creative Behavior, 1*, 3-14. [13]

Gunning, R. (1979). Fog index of a passage. *Academic Therapy, 14*, 489-91. [4]

Gurrola, S. (1975). Determination of the relative effectiveness and efficiency of selected combinations of SQ3R study method components (Doctoral dissertation, New Mexico State University, 1974). *Dissertation Abstracts International, 35*, 6938A. (University Microfilms No. 75-10, 822) [13]

Guszak, F. J. (1967). Teacher questioning and reading. *The Reading Teacher, 21*, 227-34. [10]

Guthrie, J. T. (1984). Lexical learning. *The Reading Teacher, 37*, 660-62. [12] [9]

Guthrie, J. T., Barnham, N. A., Caplan, R. I., & Seifert, M. (1974). The maze technique to assess, monitor reading comprehension. *The Reading Teacher, 28*(2), 161-68. [10]

Guthrie, J. T., Seifert, M., & Kline, L. W. (1978). Clues from research on programs for poor readers. In S. J. Samuels (Ed.), *What research has to say about reading instruction* (pp.1-12). Newark, DE: International Reading Association. [7]

Guzzetti, B.J., & Marzano, R. J. (1984). Correlates of effective reading instruction. *The Reading Teacher, 37*(8), 754-58. [11]

Haggard, M. (Ruddell). (1976). *Creative Thinking-Reading Activities (CT-RA) as a means for improving comprehension.* Unpublished doctoral dissertation, University of Missouri-Kansas City, Kansas City, MO. [7] [13]

Haggard, M. R. (1979). Creative thinking-reading activities (CT-RA): Catalysts for creative reading. *Illinois Reading Council Journal, 7*, 5-8. [13]

Haggard, M. R. (1980). Creative thinking-reading activities (CT-RA): Bridging the gap between creative thinking and creative reading. *The Allyn & Bacon Reading Newsletter, 10*, 1-3. [13]

Haggard, M. R. (1982). The vocabulary self-collection strategy: An active approach to word learning. *Journal of Reading, 27*, 203-07. [9]

Haggard, M. R. (1988). Developing critical thinking with the Directed Reading-Thinking Activity. *The Reading Teacher, 41*, 526-35. [10]

Haggard-Ruddell, M. R. (1991). In E. Fry (Ed.), *Ten best ideas for reading teachers* (pp. 109-14). New York: Addison-Wesley. [10]

Hall, J. K. (1988). *Evaluating and improving written expression: A practical guide for teachers.* Boston: Allyn & Bacon. [4]

Hall, M. (1981). *Teacher reading as a language experience* (3rd ed.). Columbus, OH: Charles C. Merrill. [8]

Hall, M. A. (1979). Language-centered reading: Premises and recommendations. *Language Arts, 56*, 664-70. [7]

Halliday, M. A. K. (1975). *Learning how to mean: Explorations in the development of language.* London: Edward Arnold. [4]

Halpern, H. (1978). Contemporary realistic young adult fiction: An annotated bibliography. *Journal of Reading, 21*, 351-56. [10]

Hamilton, J. L. (1983). Measuring response to instruction as an assessment paradigm. *Advances in Learning and Behavioral Disabilities, 2*, 111-33. [6]

Hammill, D. D., & Larsen, S. C. (1983). *Test of written language (TOWL).* Austin, TX: Pro-Ed. [4]

Hanf, M. B. (1971). Mapping: A technique for translating reading into thinking. *Journal of Reading, 14*, 225-30, 270. [10]

Hanna, G. S., & Hanna, J. S. (1966). *Phoneme-grapheme correspondences as cues to spelling improvement.* OE-32008. Washington, DC: U.S. Government Printing Office. [8]

Hanna, P. R., Hodges, R. E., Hanna, J. L., & Rudolph, E. H. (1966). *Phoneme-grapheme correspondence as cues to spelling improvement.* Washington, DC: Department of Health, Education, and Welfare, Office of Education. [8]

Hansen, J. (1981). The effects of inference training and practice on young children's reading comprehension, *Reading Research Quarterly, 16*(3), 391-417. [10]

Hansen, J., & Pearson, P. D. (1983). An instructional study: Improving the inferential comprehension of good and poor fourth-grade readers. *Journal of Educational Psychology, 75*, 821-29. [10]

Haring, N. G., Bateman, B., & Carnine, D. (1977). Direct Instruction— DISTAR. In N. G. Haring & B. Bateman (Eds.), *Teaching the learning disabled child* (pp. 165-202). Englewood Cliffs, NJ: Prentice-Hall. [8]

Harman, S. (1982). Are reversals a symptom of dyslexia? *The Reading Teacher, 35*(4), 424-28. [4]

Harris, A. J. (1961). Perceptual difficulties in reading disability. In J. A. Figurel (Ed.), *Changing concepts in reading instruction* (pp. 281-90). Newark , DE: International Reading Association. [3]

Harris, A. J., & Jacobson, M. D. (1982). *Basic reading vocabularies.* New York: Macmillan. [4]

Harris, A. J., & Sipay, E. R. (1975). *How to increase reading ability* (6th ed.). New York: David McKay. [4]

Harris, A. J., & Sipay, E. R. (1980). *How to increase reading ability.* (7th ed.) New York: Longman. [4]

Harris, A. J., & Sipay, E. R. (1985). *How to increase reading ability* (8th ed.). New York: Longman. [3] [7]

Harris, A. J., & Sipay, E. R. (1990). *How to increase reading ability: A guide to developmental and remedial methods* (9th ed.). New York: Longman. [9]

Harste, J. C., Burke, C., & Woodward, V. A. (1982). Children's language and world: Initial encounters with print. In J. Langer & M. Smith-Burke (Eds.), *Reader meets author/ bridging the gap: A psycholinguistic and sociolinguistic perspective* (pp. 105-32). Newark, DE: International Reading Association. [2]

Hasselbring, T., & Owens, S. (1982). *A microcomputer-based system for the analysis of student spelling errors.* Unpublished manuscript, George Peabody College of Vanderbilt University, Nashville, TN. [9]

Hathaway, S. R., & McKinley, J. C. (1967). *Minnesota multiphasic personality inventory.* New York: Psychological Corporation. [5]

Hayes, D. A. (1987). The potential for directing study in combined reading and writing activity. *Journal of Reading Behavior, 19*(4), 333-52. [12] [13]

Hayes, D. A. (1988). *Guided reading and summarizing procedure.* Manuscript, University of Georgia, Athens. [10]

Hayes, D. A. (1989). Help students GRASP the knack of writing summaries. *Journal of Reading, 33*(2), 96-101. [12] [13]

Hayes, D. A. (1990). Thinking critically about reading. *Georgia Journal of Reading, 16*(2), 2-5. [2] [13]

Hayes, D. A. (1991). Passing the torch. *Georgia Journal of Reading, 16*(2), 2. [13]

Haynes, J. E., & Fillmer, H. T. (1983). Paraphrasing and reading comprehension. *Reading World, 24,* 76-79. [10]

Heaton, M. M., & Lewis, H. B. (1955). *Reading ladders for human relations* (3rd ed.). Washington, DC: American Council on Education. [11]

Hebb, D. O. (1949). *The organization of behavior.* New York: John Wiley & Sons. [3]

Hecklemann, R. G. (1966). Using the neurological impress remedial technique. *Academic Therapy Quarterly, 1,* 235-39. [8] [10] [12]

Hecklemann, R. G. (1969). Neurological impress method of remedial reading instruction. *Academic Therapy Quarterly, 4,* 277-82. [10] [12]

Heimlich, J. E., & Pittelman, S. D. (1986). *Semantic mapping: Classroom applications.* Newark, DE: International Reading Association. [10]

Held, D. (1976). *The effect of the Lozanov method for teaching word meaning to fifth and sixth graders.* Unpublished doctoral dissertation, Iowa State University. [9]

Helfeldt, J. P., & Lalik, R. (1979). Reciprocal student-teacher questioning. In C. Pennock (Ed.), *Reading comprehension at four linguistic levels* (pp. 74-99). Newark, DE: International Reading Association. [10]

Heller, M. F. (1986). How do you know what you know? Metacognitive modeling in the content areas. *Journal of Reading, 29*(5), 415-22. [10]

Henderson, E. (1985). *Teaching Spelling.* Boston, MA: Houghton Mifflin. [9]

Hendrickson, J. M., Gable, R. A., & Hasselbring, T. (1988). Pleez lit me pas spellin: Diagnosing and remediating errors in spelling. *Education and Treatment of Children, 11*(2), 166-78. [9]

Henk, W. A. (1983). Adapting the NIM to improve comprehension. *Academic Therapy, 19,* 97-101. [12]

Henk, W. A. (1991). Technological advances in the study of reading: An introduction. *Reading Research and Instruction, 30*(4), 1-19. [13]

Henk, W. A., & King, G. T. (1984). Helping students follow written directions. In G. H. McNinch (Ed.), *Reading teacher education.* Fourth yearbook of the American Reading Forum (pp. 62-64). Athens, GA: American Reading Forum. [10]

Henk, W. A., & Selders, M. L. (1984). A test of synonymic scoring of cloze passage. *The Reading Teacher, 38*(3), 282-87. [4]

Herber, H. L. (1978). *Teaching reading in content areas* (2nd ed.). Englewood Cliffs, NJ: Prentice-Hall. [10]

Hewett, S. (1991). Motivating a non-interested learner. *Journal for Affective Reading Education, 11*(fall), 21-22. [11]

Hieronymus, A. N., Hoover, H. D., & Lindquist, E. E. (1986). *Iowa Test of Basic Skills.* Chicago, IL: Riverside. [4]

Hill, M. (1991). Writing summaries promotes thinking and learning across the curriculum—but why are they so difficult to write? *Journal of Reading, 34*(7), 536-39. [10]

Hittleman, C. (1984, Spring/Summer). Peer response groups: The writing process in action. *Language Connections: Hofstra University Newsletter,* p. 4. [12] [13]

Hittleman, D. R. (1978). *Developmental reading: A psycholinguistic perspective.* Chicago: Rand McNally. [4]

Hoffman, J. V. (1977). Intra-Act: A language in the content areas teaching procedure (Doctoral dissertation, University of Missouri-Kansas City). *Dissertation Abstracts International, 38,* 3248A. [10] [11] [12] [13]

Hoffman, J. V., O'Neal, S. V., Kastler, L. A., Clements, R. D., Segal, K. W., & Nash, M. F. (1984). Guided oral reading and miscue focused feedback in second-grade classrooms. *Reading Research Quarterly, 14,* 367-84. [7]

Holdaway, D. (1979). *The foundations of literacy.* New York: Ashton Scholastic. [8]

Holmes, J. A. (1948). *Factors underlying major reading disabilities at the college level.* Unpublished doctoral dissertation, University of California, Berkeley. [12]

Holmes, J. A. (1965). Basic assumptions underlying the substrata-factor theory. *Reading Research Quarterly, 1*(1), 5-27. [13]

Holmes, J. A., & Singer, H. (1961). *The substrata-factor theory: Substrata-factor differences underlying reading ability in known groups.* (Final Report No. 538, SAE 8176) U.S. Office of Education. [2] [10]

Holt, S. B., & O'Tuel, F. S. (1989). The effect of sustained silent reading and writing on achievement and attitudes of 7- and 8- grade students reading two years below level. *Reading Improvement, 26*(winter), 290-97. [10]

Hood, J. (1975-76). Qualitative analysis of oral reading errors: The inter-judge reliability of scores. *Reading Research Quarterly, 11*(4), 577-98.[4]

Hori, A. K. O. (1977). *An investigation of the efficacy of a questioning training procedure on increasing the reading comprehension performance of junior high school learning disabled students.* Unpublished master's thesis, University of Kansas, Lawrence, Kansas. [10]

Howard, M. (1986). *Effects of pre-reading training in auditory conceptualization on subsequent reading achievement.* Doctoral Dissertation, Brigham Young Univeristy, Provo, UT. [8]

Hoyt, C. S., III. (1990). Irlen lenses and reading difficulties. *Journal of Learning Disabilities, 23*(10), 624-27.

Huey, E. B. (1908). *The psychology and pedagogy of reading.* New York: Macmillan. Reprinted Cambridge, MA: MIT Press, 1968. [4]

Huhn, R. H., Jr. (1982). RSM2P: A meta-cognitive approach for teaching cognitive strategies to facilitate learning. In G. H. McNinch (Ed.), *Reading in the discipline.* Second yearbook of the American Reading Forum (pp. 67-68). Athens, GA: University of Georgia. [13]

Hulme, C. (1981a). The effects of manual tracing on memory in normal and retarded readers: Some implications for multi-sensory teaching. *Psychological Research* (Developmental Dyslexia Issue), *43,* 179-91. [12]

Hulme, C. (1981b). *Reading retardation and multi-sensory teaching.* Boston: Routledge & Kegan Paul. [12]

Hunt, K. (1965). *Grammatical structures written at three grade levels.* Urbana, IL: National Council of Teachers of English. [4]

Hunt, L. (1970). The effect of self-selection, interest, and motivation upon independent, instructional and frustration levels. *The Reading Teacher, 24,* 146-51. [10]

Huttenlocher, R. R., & Huttenlocher, J. (1973). A study of children with hyperlexia. *Neurology, 23,* 1107-16. [1] [2] [12]

Hynd, G. W., & Hynd, C. R. (1984). Dyslexia: Neuroanatomical/ Neurolinguistic perspectives. *Reading Research Quarterly, 19,* 482-89. [12]

Hynd, G. W., Hynd, C. R., Sullivan, H. G., & Kingsbury, T. (1987). Retional cerebral blood flow (rCBF) in developmental dyslexia: Activation during reading in a surface and deep dsylexia. *Journal of Learning Disabilities, 20,* 294-300. [12]

Hynd, G. W., & Semrud-Clikeman, M. (1989). Dyslexia and neurodevelopmental pathology: Relationships to cognition, intelligence, and reading skill acquisition. *Journal of Learning Disabilities, 22*(4), 204-15. [12]

Idol, L. (1987). Group story mapping: A comprehension for both skilled and unskilled readers. *Journal of Learning Disabilities, 20,* 196-205. [10]

Indrisano, R. (1982). An ecological approach to learning. *Topics in Learning and Learning Disabilities, 1*(January), 11-15. [6]

Ingham, J. (1982). *Books and reading development: The Bradford book flood experiment* (2nd ed.). Exeter, NH: Heinemann. [10]

Irlen, H. (1983). *Successful treatment of learning disabilities.* Paper presented at the meeting of the 91st Annual Convention of the American Psychological Association, Anaheim, CA. [12]

Irwin, J. W. (Ed.). (1986). *Understanding and teaching cohesion comprehension.* Newark, DE: International Reading Association. [4]

Irwin, P., & Mitchell, J. N. (1983). A procedure for assessing the richness of retellings. *Journal of Reading, 26*(5), 391-96. [4]

Isakson, M. B. (1991). Learning about reluctant readers through their letters. *Journal of Reading, 34*(8), 632-37. [11] [13]

Ito, H. R. (1980). Long-term effects of resource room programs on learning disabled children's reading. *Journal of Learning Disablities, 13,* 322-26. [7]

Jacobs, D. H., & Searfoss, L. W. (1979). *Diagnostic reading inventory.* Dubuque, IA: Kendall/ Hunt. [4]

Jaggar, A. (1985). An observing the language learner: Introduction and overview. In A. Jaggar & M. T. Smith-Burke (Eds.), *Observing the language learner* (pp. 1-7). Newark, DE: International Reading Association. [6] [3]

Jagger, A. M., & Harwood, K. T. (1989). Suggested reading list: Whole language theory, practice, assessment. In G. S. Pinnel & M. L. Matlin (Eds.), *Teachers and research: Language learning in the classroom* (pp. 142-77). Newark, DE: International Reading Association. [2]

Jalongo, M. R., & Renck, M. A. (1987). Children's literature and the child's adjustment to school. *The Reading Teacher, 40,* 616-21. [10] [11]

Jastak, J., & Jastak, S. (1978). *Wide range achievement test.* Wilmington, DE: Jastak. [4]

Jensen, A. R. (1980). *Bias in mental testing.* New York: The Free Press. [5] [8]

Johansen, K. (1984, December). *Man laerer at laise ved at laese—maske (you learn to read by reading—maybe). On diagnosis and treatment of reading difficulties emphasizing some non-acknowledged methods.* Unpublished doctoral dissertation, Pacific Western University, Los Angeles, CA.
[Also issued as: Johansen, K. (1986). Dyslexia and sound therapy. *Research Abstracts, II*(Fall), 3.] [12]

Johnson, D. D., & Pearson, P. D. (1984). *Teaching reading vocabulary* (2nd ed.). New York: Holt, Rinehart and Winston. [9]

Johnston, P. H. (1985). Understanding reading disability: A case study approach. *Harvard Educational Review, 55,* 153-77. [2]

Johnston, P. H. (1987). Teachers as evaluation experts. *The Reading Teacher, 40,* 744-48. [6]

Johnston, P. H., & Allington, R. (1991). Remediation. In R. Barr, M. L. Kamil, P. B.

Mosenthal, & P. D. Pearson (Eds.), *Handbook of Reading Research, Vol. II* (pp. 984-1012). New York: Longman. [1] [7]

Johnston, P. H., & Winograd, P. N. (1985). Passive failure in reading. *Journal of Reading Behavior, 17*, 279-301. [1]

Jonassen, D. H. (1985a). Generative learning vs. mathemagenic control of text processing. In D. H. Jonassen (Ed.), *The technology of text: Principles for structuring, designing, and displaying text* (Vol. 2, pp. 9-45). Englewood Cliffs, NJ: Educational Technology Publications. [10]

Jonassen, D. H. (1985b). *The technology of text: Principles for structuring, designing, and displaying text* (Vol. 2). Englewood Cliffs, NJ: Educational Technology Publications. [10]

Jongsma, E. (1980). *Cloze instruction research: A second look.* Newark, DE: International Reading Association. [10]

Jongsma, K. S., & Jongsma, E.A. (1981). Test review: Commercial informal reading inventories. *The Reading Teacher, 34*(6), 697-705. [4]

Juel, C. (1988). Learning to read and write: A longitudinal study of fifty-four children from first through fourth grades. *Journal of Educational Psychology, 80*, 437-47. [1] [8]

Juel, C. (1991). Beginning reading. In R. Barr, M. L. Kamil, P. Mosenthal, & P. D. Pearson (Eds.), *Handbook of Reading Research, Volume II.* New York: Longman. [8] [12]

Juel, C., & Roper-Schneider, D. (1985). The influence of basal readers on first-grade reading. *Reading Research Quarterly, 20*, 134-52. [8]

Just, M. A., & Carpenter, P. A. (l980). A theory of reading: From eye fixations to comprehension. *Psychological Review, 87*, 329-54. [2]

Kalmbach, J. R. (1986). Getting at the point of retellings. *Journal of Reading, 29*, 326-33. [10]

Kameenui, E. J., & Shanon, P. (1988). Point/counterpoint: Direct instruction reconsidered. In J. E. Readence, R. S. Baldwin, J. P. Konopak, & P. R. O'Keefe (Eds.), *Dialogues in literacy research.* Thirty-seventh Yearbook of the National Reading Conference (pp. 35-43). Chicago: National Reading Conference. [7]

Kamhi, A. G., Catts, H. W., & Mauer, D. (1990). Explaining speech production deficits in poor readers. *Journal of Learning Disabilities, 23*(10), 632-36.

Kampwirth, T. J., & Bates, M. (1980). Modality preference and teaching method: A review of the research. *Academic Therapy, 5*, 597-605. [5]

Kann, R. (1983). The method of repeated readings: Expanding the neurological impress method for use with disabled readers. *Journal of Learning Disabilities, 16*, 90-92. [12]

Karplus, R. (1974). *The science curriculum improvement study.* Berkeley, CA: University of California Press. [13]

Kaufman, A. S., & Kaufman, N. L. (1983). *K-ABC Kaufman assessment battery for children: Interpretive manual.* Circle Pines, MN: American Guidance Services.

Kaufman, M. (1976). Comparison of achievement for DISTAR and conventional instruction with primary pupils. *Reading Improvement, 13*, 169-73. [5]

Kay, L., Young, J. L., & Mottley, R. R. (1986). Using Manzo's ReQuest model with delinquent adolescents. *Journal of Reading, 29*, 506-10. [10]

Kelly, B. W., & Holmes, J. (1979). The Guided Lecture Procedure. *Journal of Reading, 22*, 602-04. [10]

Kemp, F. (1987). The user-friendly fallacy. *College Composition and Communication, 38*, 32-39. [12]

Kierwa, K. A. (1985). Students' note-taking behaviors and the efficacy of providing the instructor's notes for review. *Contemporary Educational Psychology, 10*, 378-86. [12] [13]

Killgallon, P. A. (l942). *A study to determine the relationships among certain pupils' adjustments in language situations.* Unpublished doctoral dissertation, Pennsylvania State College, State College, PA. [4]

King, D. H. (1985). *Writing skills for the adolescent*. Cambridge, MA: Educators Publishing Services. [9]

Kinney, M. A., & Harry, A. L. (1991). An informal inventory for adolescents that assesses the reader, the text, and the task. *Journal of Reading, 34*(8), 643-47. [4]

Kinsbourne, M. (1973). Minimal brain dysfunction as a neurodevelopmental lag. *Annals of the New York Academy of Sciences, 205*, 268-73. [12]

Kinsbourne, M. (1989). Neuroanatomy of dyslexia. In D. J. Bakkar & H. Van der Vlagt (Eds.), *Learning disabilities, Vol. 1: Neuropsychological correlates and treatement* (pp. 105-22). Lisse, Netherlands: Swets & Zeitlinger. [12]

Kirby, D., & Liner, T. (1981). *Inside out: Developmental strategies for teaching*. Montclair, NJ: Boynton/Cook. [10] [11]

Kirby, J. R. (1988). Style, strategy, and skill in reading. In R. R. Schmeck (Ed.), *Learning strategies and learning styles* (pp. 229-74). New York: Plenum. [5]

Kirby, M. W. (1989). Teaching sight vocabulary with and without context before silent reading: A field test of the "focus of attention" hypothesis. *Journal of Reading Behavior, 21*(3), 261-78. [7]

Kirk, C. (1990). What Mitch taught me: A student at risk becomes a writer. *Wisconsin State Reading Association Journal, 34*(2), 11-14. [6] [7]

Kirk, S., & Elkins, J. (1975). Characteristics of children enrolled in child service demonstration centers. *Journal of Learning Disabilities, 8*, 630-37. [2]

Kirk, U. (1981). The development and use of rules in the acquisition of perceptual motor skills. *Child Development, 52*, 299-305. [9]

Klasen, E. (1972). *The syndrome of specific dyslexia: With special consideration of its physiological, psychological, test psychological and social correlates*. Baltimore: University Park Press. [12]

Kline, C. L., & Kline, C. L. (1975). Follow-up study of 216 dyslexic children. *Bulletin of the Orton Society, 25*, 127-44. [7]

Knafle, J. D., Legenza-Wescott, A., & Passcarella, E. T. (1988). Assessing values in children's books. *Reading Improvement, 25*(1), 71-81. [10] [11]

Koenke, K. (1978). A comparison of three auditory discrimination-perception tests. *Academic Therapy, 13*, 463-68. [5]

Koeppen, A. S. (1974). Relaxation training for children. *Elementary School Guidance and Counseling, 9*, 14-21. [11]

Konopak, B. C., & Williams, N. L. (1988). Using the key word method to help young readers learn content material. *The Reading Teacher, 41*, 682-87. [9] [13]

Koskinen, P. S., & Blum, I. H. (1986). Paired repeated reading: A classroom strategy for developing fluent reading. *The Reading Teacher, 40*(1), 70-75. [8] [10] 12]

Kottmeyer, W. A. (1954). Phonetic and structural generalizations for the teaching of a primary grade spelling vocabulary. Reported in *Webster Publishing Company Research File No. 528-S and 529-S*. St. Louis, MO: Webster. [8]

Krathwohl, D. R., Bloom, B. S., & Masia, B. B. (1964). *Taxomony of educational objectives; the classification of educational goals. Handbook 2: Affective domain*. New York: David McKay. [8]

Labbo, L. D., & Teale, W. H. (1990). Cross-age reading: A strategy for helping poor readers. *The Reading Teacher, 43*(6), 362-69. [7]

LaBerge, D., & Samuels, S. J. (1974). Toward a theory of automatic information processing in reading. *Cognitive Psychology, 6*(2), 293-323. [2, 8, 10, 12]

Langer, J. A. (1981). From theory to practice: A prereading plan. *Journal of Reading, 25*, 152-56. [10]

Langer, J. A. (1986). *Children reading and writing: Structure and strategies*. Norwood, NJ: Ablex. [13]

Langer, J. A., & Applebee, A. N. (1986). Reading and writing instruction: Toward a theory of teaching and learning. In E. Z. Rothkopf (Ed.), *Review Research in Education*, 13, 171-94. [13]

Langer, J. A., & Nicolich, M. (1981). Prior knowledge and its relationship to comprehension. *Journal of Reading Behavior*, 13, 373-79. [10]

Lapp, D., & Flood, J. (1984). Promoting reading comprehension: Instruction which ensures continuous reader growth. In J. Flood (Ed.), *Promoting reading comprehension* (pp. 273-88). Newark, DE: International Reading Association. [13]

LaPray, M., & Ross, R. (1969). The graded word list: Quick gauge of reading ability. *Journal of Reading*, 12(4), 305-07. [4]

Larking, L. (1984). ReQuest helps children comprehend: A study. *Australian Journal of Reading*, 7, 135-39. [10]

Laughlin, H. P. (1967). *The neuroses*. Washington, DC: Butterworths Press. [11] [12]

Legenza, A. (1974). *Questioning behavior of kindergarten children*. Paper presented at Nineteenth Annual Convention, International Reading Association. [10]

Legenza, A. (1978). Inquiry training for reading and learning improvement. *Reading Improvement*, 15, 309-16. [10]

Leibert, R. E. (1982). The IRI: Relating test performance to instruction — A concept. *Reading Horizons*, 22(2), 110-15. [4]

Leibert, R. E., & Sherk, J. K., Jr. (1970). Three Frostig visual perception sub-tests and specific reading tasks for kindergarten, first, and second grade children. *The Reading Teacher*, 24(2), 130-37. [7] [5] [11] [12]

Leong, C. K. (1980). Laterality and reading proficiency in children. *Reading Research Quarterly*, 15, 185-202. [2]

Leong, C. K., & Haines, C. F. (1978). Beginning readers' analysis of words and sentences. *Journal of Reading Behavior*, 10, 393-407. [2]

Lerner, J. W. (1975). Remedial reading and learning disabilities: Are they the same or different? *The Journal of Special Education*, 9, 119-31. [5]

Lesgold, A. M., & Resnick, L. B. (1982). How reading disabilities develop: Perspectives from a longitudinal study. In J. P. Das, R. Mulcahy, & A. E. Wall (Eds.), *Theory and research in learning disability*. New York: Plenum. [8]

Leslie, L., & Osol, P. (1978). Changes in oral reading strategies as a function of quantities of miscues. *Journal of Reading Behavior*, 10(4), 442-45. [4]

Levesque, J., & Prossor, T. (1991). Partnerships for tomorrow through knowledge and empowerment. *The Missouri Reader*, 15(2), 14-16. [2]

Levin, J. R., Morrison, C. R., McGivern, J. E., Mastropieri, M. A., & Scruggs, T. E. (1986). Mnemomic facilitation of text-embedded science facts. *American Educational Research Journal*, 23(3), 489-506. [9] [13]

Levin, J. R., & Pressley, M. (1981). Improving children's prose comprehension: Selected strategies that seem to succeed. In C. M. Santa & B. L. Hayes (Eds.), *Children's prose comprehension* (pp. 49-60). Newark, DE: International Reading Association. [13] [10]

Lewis, H. W. (1984). A structured group counseling program for reading disabled elementary students. *The School Counselor*, 31, 454-59. [11] [13] [12]

Lewkowicz, N. K. (1987). On the question of teaching decoding skills to older students. *Journal of Reading*, 31, 50-57. [10]

Liberman, I. Y., Shankweiler, D., Liberman, A. M., Fowler, C., & Fischer, F. W. (1977). Phonetic segmentation and recoding in the beginning reader. In A. S. Reber & D. L. Scarborough (Eds.), *Toward a psychology of reading*, (pp. 207-25). Hillsdale, NJ: Erlbaum. [8]

Liddell, H. G., & Scott, R. (1940). *A Greek-English lexicon*. Oxford, England: Clarendon Press. (Revised by H. S. Jones & R. McKenize.) [3]

Lindamood, C. H., & Lindamood, P. C. (1975). *The A.D.D. program, auditory discrimination in depth*. Books 1 and 2. Hingham, MA: Teaching Resources. [8] [9] [12]

Lipson, M. Y. (1982). Learning new information from text: The role of prior knowledge and reading ability. *Journal of Reading Behavior, 14*, 243-62. [5]

Lipson, M. Y. (1983). The influence of religious affiliations on children's memory for text information. *Reading Research Quarterly, 18*, 448-57. [5] [10] [11]

Lipson, M. Y., & Wixson, K. K. (1991). *Assessment and instruction of reading disability*. New York: HarperCollins. [2] [7] [10]

Loban, W. (1963). *The language of elementary school children*. Urbana, IL: National Council of Teachers of English. [13]

Loban, W. (1964). *Learning ability: Grades seven, eight, and nine*. Berkeley: University of California. (ERIC Document Reproduction Service No. ED 001 275) [13]

Locke, E. (1977). An empirical study of lecture note taking among college students. *Journal of Educational Research, 71*, 93-99. [13]

Locke, J. (1706). *Of the conduct of the understanding*. [As cited in Tripp, R. T. (1987). *The international thesarus of quotations*. New York: Harper & Row.] [13]

Lonberger, R. (1988). *Effects of training in a self-generated learning strategy on the prose processing abilities of 4th and 6th graders*. Paper presented at the annual meeting of the Eastern Education Association, Savannah, GA. [5]

Lubs, H. A., Duara, R., Levin, B., Jallad, B., Lubs, M., Rabin, M., Kushch, A., & Gross-Glenn, K. (1991). Dyslexia subtypes: Genetics, behavior, and brain imaging. In D. Duane & D. B. Gray (Eds.), *The reading brain: The biological basis of dyslexia* (pp. 89-117). Parkton, MD: York Press. [12]

Lucas, C. K. (1988). Toward ecological evaluation, part one and part two. *The Quarterly of the National Writing Project and the Center for the Study of Writing, 10*(1), 1-7; *10*(2), 4-10. [6]

Luce, S., & Hoge, R. (1978). Relations among teacher rankings, pupil-teacher interactions, and academic achievement. *American Educational Research Journal, 15*, 498-500. [7]

Lundberg, I. (1984, August). Learning to read. *School Research Newsletter*. Sweden: National Board of Education. [8]

Lundsteen, S. W. (1979). *Listening: Its impact at all levels on reading and other language arts* (rev. ed.). Urbana, IL: National Council of Teachers of English. [4]

Luria, A. R. (1980). *Higher cortical functions in man*. New York: Basic Books. [12]

Luscher, M. (1969). The Luscher color test (I.A. Scott, Ed. and Trans.). New York: Random House. (Original work published as *Psychologie der Farben*, first published as *Psychologie der Farben: Textband zum Luscher-Test*, 1949). [10] [11]

Lyon, G. R. (1985). Identification and remediation of learning disability subtypes: Preliminary findings. *Learning Disabilities Focus, 1*, 21-35. [2]

Lyon, R., & Watson, B. (1981). Empirical derived subgroups of learning disabled readers: Diagnostic characteristics. *Journal of Learning Disabilities, 14*, 256-61. [12]

MacGinitie, W. H., & MacGinitie, R. K. (1989). *Gates-MacGinities Reading Tests: Manual for scoring and interpretation—level 4* (3rd ed.). Chicago: Riverside. [3] [10]

Machie, B. C. (1982). *The effects of a sentence-combining program on the reading comprehension and written composition of fourth grade students*. Unpublished doctoral dissertation, Hofstra University. [13]

Malicky, G. V., & Norman, C. A. (1988). Reading processes subgroups in a clinical population. *The Alberta Journal of Educational Research, 34*(4), 344-54. [3]

Manning, G. L., & Manning, M. (1984). What models of recreational reading make a difference? *Reading World, 23,* 375-80. [10]

Manzo, A. V. (1969a). Improving reading comprehension through reciprocal questioning (Doctoral dissertation, Syracuse University, Syracuse, NY, 1968). *Dissertation Abstracts International, 30,* 5344A. [4] [7] [10]

Manzo, A. V. (1969b). The ReQuest procedure. *Journal of Reading, 13,* 123-26. [7] [10]

Manzo, A. V. (1970). CAT—A game for extending vocabulary and knowledge allusions. *Journal of Reading, 13,* 367-69. [9]

Manzo, A. V. (1973). CONPASS English: A demonstration project. *Journal of Reading, 16,* 539-45. [7] [12] [13]

Manzo, A. V. (1975a). Guided reading procedure. *Journal of Reading, 18,* 287-91. [10]

Manzo, A. V. (1975b). *Manzo's Bestiary Inventory.* Monograph of the Center for Resources Development in ABE, University of Missouri-Kansas City. [4] [5] [10] [11]

Manzo, A. V. (1977a). Dyslexia as specific psychoneurosis. *Journal of Reading Behavior, 19*(3), 305-08. [2,7,11] [12]

Manzo, A. V. (1977b). *Recent developments in content area reading.* Keynote address, Missouri Council of Teachers of English, Springfield, MO. [10]

Manzo, A. V. (1979). "Imbedded aids" to readers: Alternatives to traditional textual material. *The New England Reading Association Journal, 14*(11), 13-18. [10]

Manzo, A. V. (1980). Three "universal" strategies in content area reading and languaging. *Journal of Reading, 24,* 146-49. [4,8,10]

Manzo, A. V. (1981a). The Language Shaping Paradigm (LSP) for improving language, comprehension, and thought. In P.L. Anders (Ed.), *Research on reading in secondary schools: A semi-annual report* (Monograph No. 7, pp. 54-68). Tucson: University of Arizona, College of Education, Reading Department. [12] [13]

Manzo, A. V. (1981b). Using proverbs to teach reading and thinking; or, Com' faceva mia nonna (the way my grandmother did it). *The Reading Teacher, 34,* 411-16. [10]

Manzo, A. V. (1983). "Subjective approach to vocabulary" acquisition (Or "...I think my brother is arboreal!"). *Reading Psychology, 3,* 155-60. [9]

Manzo, A. V. (1985). Expansion modules for the ReQuest, CAT, GRP, and REAP reading/study procedures. *Journal of Reading, 28,* 498-502. [9, 10]

Manzo, A. V. (1987). Psychologically induced dyslexia and learning disabilities. *The Reading Teacher, 40*(4), 408-13. [2] [12]

Manzo, A. V., & Casale, U. P. (1980). The five c's: A problem-solving approach to study skills. *Reading Horizons, 20,* 281-84. [2] [12] [13]

Manzo, A. V., & Casale, U. P. (1981). A multivariate analysis of principle and trace elements in mature reading comprehension. In G. H. McNinch (Ed.), *Comprehension: Process and product.* First Yearbook of the American Reading Forum (pp. 76-81). Athens, GA: American Reading Forum. [2,5,10]

Manzo, A. V., & Casale, U. P. (1983). A preliminary description and factor analysis of a broad spectrum battery for assessing "progress toward reading maturity." *Reading Psychology, 4,* 181-91. [5]

Manzo, A. V., & Casale, U. P. (1985). Listen-read-discuss: A content reading heuristic. *Journal of Reading, 28*(8), 732-34. [8]

Manzo, A. V., Grey, L., & Haggard, M. R. (1977). Psychological approaches for the reading specialist: A reclamation project. *Reading World, 16*(3), pp. 188-95. [12]

Manzo, A. V., & Legenza, A. (1975). Inquiry training for kindergarten children. *Journal of Educational Leadership, 32,* 479-83. [10]

Manzo, A. V., Lorton, M., & Condon, M. (1975). *Personality characteristics and learning style preferences of adult basic education students.* Research monograph of Center for Resource Development in Adult Education University of Missouri-Kansas City. [5]

Manzo, A. V., & Manzo, U. C. (1985). Listen-read-discuss: A content reading heuristic. *Journal of Reading, 28*, 732-34. [10]

Manzo, A. V., & Manzo, U. C. (1987a). *Asking, answering, commenting: A participation training strategy.* Paper presented at the annual meeting of the International Reading Association, Anaheim, CA. [10]

Manzo, A. V., & Manzo, U. C. (1987b). Using proverbs to diagnose and treat comprehension dysfunctions. *Rhode Island Reading Review, 3*(2), 37-42. [4] [10]

Manzo, A. V., & Manzo U. C. (1990a). *Content area reading: A heuristic approach.* Columbus, OH: Merrill. [2] [10,8,9] [13] [7]

Manzo, A. V., & Manzo U. C. (1990b). Note cue: A comprehension and participation training strategy. *Journal of Reading, 33*(8), 608-11. [7]

Manzo, A. V., & Manzo, U. C. (1994, in press). *Teaching Children to be Literate: A Reflective Approach.* Fort Worth: Harcourt Brace Jovanovich. [7]

Manzo, A. V., & Sherk, J. K., Jr. (1971-72). Reading and "languaging in the content areas": A vocabulary acquisition. *Journal of Reading Behavior, 4*, 78-89. [9]

Manzo, A. V., Sherk, J. K., Jr., Leibert, R. E., & Mocker, D. W. (1977). *Re: Reading and the library* (Improvement of Learning Monograph Series No.1). Kansas City: University of Missouri-Kansas City, Reading Center. [7]

Manzo, A. V., Smith, W. M., & Manzo, U. C. (in preparation). *Effect of concept development training on the comprehension of at-risk 4th graders.* [2] [7]

Marchbanks, G., & Levin, H. (1965). Cues by which children recognize words. *Journal of Educational Research, 56*, 57-61. [8]

Maria, K. (1990). *Reading comprehension instruction: Issues and strategies.* Parkton, MD: York Press. [4, 10]

Maring, G. H., & Furman, G. (1985). Seven "whole class" strategies to help mainstreamed young people read and listen better in content area classes. *Journal of Reading, 28*, 694-700. [10]

Maring, G. H., & Ritson, R. (1980). Reading improvement in the gymnasium. *Journal of Reading, 24*, 27-31. [10]

Marshall, J. C., & Newcombe, F. (1973). Patterns of paralexia: A psycholinguistic approach. *Journal of Psycholinguistic Research, 2*, 175-99. [12]

Marshall, J. C., & Newcombe, F. (1980). The conceptual status of deep dyslexia: A historical perspective. In M. Coltheart, K. Patterson, & J. C. Marshall (Eds.), *Deep dyslexia* (pp. 1-21). Boston, MA: Routledge & Kegan Paul. [12]

Marshall, N. (1983). Using story grammar to assess reading comprehension. *The Reading Teacher, 36*, 616-21. [4]

Marzano, R. J. (1991). Language, the language arts, and thinking. In J. Flood, J. M. Jensen, D. Lapp, & J. R. Squire (Eds.), *Handbook of research on teaching the English language arts* (pp. 559-86). New York: Macmillan. [3, 10, 13]

Marzano, R. J., & Marzano, J. S. (1988). *A cluster approach to elementary vocabulary instruction.* Newark, DE: International Reading Association. [9]

Maslow, A. H. (1954). *Motivation and Personality.* New York: Harper Brothers. [7]

Mason, J., Herman, P., & Au, K. (1991). Children's developing knowledge of words. In J. Flood, J. M. Jensen, D. Lapp, & J. R. Squire (Eds.), *Handbook of research on teaching the English language arts* (pp. 721-31). New York: Macmillan. [9] [10]

Mason, J. M., & Au, K. H. (1986). *Reading instruction for today.* Glenview, IL: Scott, Foresman. [7]

Mastropieri, M. A. (1988). Using the keyboard [SIC] method. *Teaching Exceptional Children, 20*, 4-8. [12] [13]

Mathews, S. R., & Camperell, K. (1981). Comprehension research and diagnosis: Beyond single dependent measures. In G. H. McNinch (Ed.), *Comprehension: Process and product*. First Yearbook of the American Reading Forum (pp. 54-56). Athens, GA: The American Reading Forum. [13]

Matthewson, G. (1985). Toward a comprehensive model of affect in the reading process. In H. Singer and R. B. Ruddell (Eds.), *Theoretical models and processes of reading*, (3rd ed., pp. 841-56). Newark, DE: International Reading Association. [11]

Maw, W., & Maw, E. (1967). Children's curiosity as an aspect of reading comprehension. *The Reading Teacher, 15*(2), 236-40. [10]

Mazurkiewiez, A. J. (1966). *New perspectives in reading instruction: A book of readings*. New York: Pitman Publishing Corp. [12]

McCarthy, D. (1972). *McCarthy Scales of children's abilities*. San Antonio, TX: The Psychological Corporation. [4]

McClelland, D. C., Atkinson, J. W., Clark, R. A., & Lowell, E. L. (1976). *The achievement motive*. New York: Irvington. [5]

McConkie, G. W., & Zola, D. (1987). Two examples of computer-based research on reading: Eye movement monitoring and computer-aided reading. In D. Reinking (Ed.), *Reading and computers: Issues for theory and practice* (pp. 97-107). New York: Teachers College Press. [3]

McCord, H. (1962). Hypnosis as an aid to increasing adult reading efficiency. *Journal of Developmental Reading, 6*, 64-65. [11] [12]

McCormick, S. (1987). *Remedial and clinical reading instruction*. Columbus, OH: Merrill.

McCormick, S. (1990, December). *Multiple-exposure/multiple-context longitudinal study of Peter Parsons*. Paper presented at the National Reading Conference. [8]

McCracken, R. A. (1966). *Standard reading inventory*. Klamath Falls, OR: Klamath. [4]

McCracken, R. A. (1971). Initiating sustained silent reading. *Journal of Reading, 14*(8), 521-24, 582-83. [10]

McCracken, R. A., & McCracken, M. J. (1978). Modeling is the key to sustained silent reading. *The Reading Teacher, 31*(4), 406-08. [10]

McEneaney, J. E. (1992). Computer-assisted diagnosis in reading: An expert systems approach, *Journal of Reading, 36*, 36–47. [3]

McGee, L. M. (1982). Awareness of text structure: Effects on children's recall of expository text. *Reading Research Quarterly, 17*, 581-90. [10]

McGee, L. M., & Richgels, D. J. (1986). Attending to text structure: A comprehension strategy. In E. K. Dishner, T. W. Bean, J. E. Readence, & D. W. Moore (Eds.), *Reading in the content areas: Improving classroom instruction* (2nd ed.). Dubuque, IA: Kendall/ Hunt. [10]

McIntyre, J. (1991, June). *The developmental difference: "Skill and will": An investigation into the reported feelings of personal control and competency of community college developmental students*. Presentation to "ABD Club," University of Missouri-Kansas City. [12] [13]

McKee, P. (1948). *The teaching of reading in the elementary school*. Boston, MA: Houghton Mifflin. [12]

McKenna, M. C. (1976). Synonymic versus verbatim scoring in the cloze procedure. *Journal of Reading, 20*, 141-43. [4]

McKenna, M. C. (1983). Informal reading inventories: A review of the issues. *The Reading Teacher, 36*(7), 670-79. [4]

McKenna, M. C. (1986). CARA: New tool for reading assessment. *The Computing Teacher, 13*,(5), 16-19. [3]

McKenna, M. C. (1987). *Computer assisted reading assessment (CARA)* [computer program]. Burlington, NC: Southern MicroSystems. [3]

McKenna, M. C. (1991). Computerized reading assessment: Its emerging potential. *The Reading Teacher, 44*, 692-93. [3]

McKenna, M. C., & Layton, K. (1990). Concurrent validity of cloze as a measure of intersentential comprehension. *Journal of Educational Psychology, 82*, 372-77. [4]

McKenna, M. C., & Robinson, R. D. (1980). *An introduction to the cloze procedure: An annotated bibliography*. Newark, DE: International Reading Association. [4]

McKenna, M. C., Robinson, R. D., & Miller, J. W. (1990, April). *Whole language: A research agenda for the nineties*. Paper presented at the American Educational Research Association, Boston. [2]

McKenzie, J. V., Ericson, B., & Hunter, L. (1988). *Questions may be an answer*. Manuscript, California State University–Northridge. [10]

McLoughlin, J. A., & Lewis, R. B. (1990). Assessing special students. Columbus, OH: Merrill. [3]

McNamara, L. P. (1977). A study of the cloze procedure as an alternate group instructional strategy in secondary school American government classes (Doctoral dissertation, Northern Illinois University, DeKalb). *Dissertation Abstracts International, 39*, 216A. [13]

McNeil, J. D. (1987). *Reading comprehension: New directions for classroom practice* (2nd ed.). Glenview, IL: Scott, Foresman. [12] [13]

McNeil, J., & Donant, L. (1982). Summarization strategy for improving reading comprehension. In J. A. Niles & L. A. Harris (Eds.), *New inquiries in reading research and instruction* (pp. 215-19). Rochester, NY: National Reading Conference. [10]

McNinch, G. H. (1981). A method for teaching sight words to disabled readers. *The Reading Teacher, 35*, 269-72. [12]

McWilliams, L., & Rakes, T. A. (1979). *Content inventories: English, social studies, science*. Dubuque, IA: Kendall/Hunt. [4]

Meeks, J. W. (1980). Effects of imbedded aids on prose-related textual material. *Reading World, 19*, 345-51. [10]

Meeks, J. W. (1991). Prior knowledge and metacognitive processes of reading comprehension: Applications to mildly retarded readers. In *Advances in mental retardation and developmental disabilities, Vol. 4* (pp. 123-44). Lanhen, MD: Jessica Kingley. [10]

Meeks, J. W., Eanet, M., & Manzo, A. V. (1976). *'Difference' inventory: Construction, supporting data, implication*. Paper presented at the meeting of the National Reading Conference, Atlanta, GA. [4] [5]

Mellon, J. C. (1967). *Transformational sentence-combining: A method for enhancing the development of syntactic fluency in English composition*. Washington, DC: U.S. Office of Education Cooperative Research Project 5-8418. [13]

Mellon, J. C. (1969). *Transformational sentence-combining*. Urbana, IL: National Council of Teachers of English. [4]

Meyer, B. J. F. (1975). *The organization of prose and its effect on memory*. Amsterdam: North-Holland. [10]

Meyer, L. A. (1984). Long-term academic effects of the direct instruction project Follow-Through. *Elementary School Journal, 84*, 380-94. [8]

Meyer, L. A., Gersten, R. M., & Gutkin, J. (1983). Direct instruction: A Project Follow-Through success story in an inner-city school. *Elementary School Journal, 84*, 241-52. [8]

Mickulecky, L. J. (1987). Conquering aliteracy by increasing student motivation to read. *Reading Today, 4*, 14. [11]

Miller, S. D., & Smith, D. E. (1990). Relationships among oral reading, silent reading, and listening comprehension of students at different competency levels. *Reading Research and Instruction, 29*(Winter), 73-84. [4]

Miller, W. E., & Dollard, J. (1941). *Social learning and imitation*. New Haven, CT: Yale University Press. [10]

Mills, R. E. (1965). An evaluation of techniques for teaching word recognition. *Elementary School Journal, 56*, 221-25. [5]

Mills, R. E. (1970). *Learning methods test* (rev. ed.). Fort Lauderdale, FL: The Mills School. [5]

Mitchell, J. N., & Irwin, P. A. (1989). The reading retelling profile: Using retellings to make instructional decisions. In S. W. Valencia, W. McGinley, & P. D. Pearson (1990). Assessing reading and writing in G. G. Duffy (Ed.), *Reading in the Middle School* (2nd ed., pp. 147). Newark, DE: International Reading Association. [4]

Moe, I. L., & Nania, F. (1959). Reading deficiencies among abled pupils. *Developmental Reading.* Newark, DE: International Reading Association. (Reprinted in Lawrence E. Hafner (Ed.). (1974). *Improving reading in middle and secondary* (2nd ed.) (pp. 172-85). New York: Macmillan.) [12]

Monahan, J. N. (1990). Developing a strategic reading program. In G. G. Duffy (Ed.), *Reading in the Middle School* (2nd ed., pp. 179). Newark, DE: International Reading Association. [12] [13]

Monroe, E., Watson, A. R., & Tweddell, D. C. (1989). Relationships among communication apprehension, reading achievement, teacher perceived communication apprehension, and intelligence. *Journal of Reading Education, 15*, 10–20. [5]

Monteith, M. K. (1981). The magazine habit. *Language Arts, 58*, 965-69. [10] [11]

Montgomery, G. (1989, March). The mind in motion. *Discover*, 58-67. [12]

Moore, D. W. (1983). A case for naturalistic assessment of reading comprehension. *Language Arts, 60*, 957-69. [6]

Moore, D. W. (1987). Vocabulary. In D. E. Alvermann, D. W. Moore, & M. W. Conley (Eds.), *Research within reach: Secondary school reading* (pp. 64-79). Newark, DE: International Reading Association. [13]

Moore, D. W., & Moore, S. A. (1986). Possible sentences. In E. K. Dishner, T. W. Bean, J. E. Readence, & D. W. Moore (Eds.), *Reading in the content areas* (pp. 174-78). Dubuque, IA: Kendall-Hunt. [9]

Moore, D. W., & Readence, J. E. (1980). Processing main ideas through parallel lesson transfer. *Journal of Reading, 23*, 589-93. [10]

Moore, J. T. (1951). *Phonetic elements appearing in a 3000 word spelling vocabulary.* Unpublished doctoral dissertation, Stanford University. [8]

Morais, J., Cary, L., Algeria, J., & Bertelson, P. (1979). Does awareness of speech as a sequence of phonemes arise spontaneously? *Cognition, 7*, 323-31. [8]

Morawski, C. M. (1991). The class meeting for reading and writing remediation: An educational practice for holistic intervention. *Journal for Affective Reading Education, 11*(fall), 7-19. [11]

Moreno, J. L. (1947). *The theatre of spontaneity: An introduction to psychodrama.* New York: Beacon House. [11]

Morgan, C., & Murray, H. A. (1935). A method for investigating fantasies: The Thematic Apperception Test. *Archives of Neurology and Psychiatry, 34*, 289-306. [5]

Morgan, W. P. (1896). A case of congenital word blindness. *British Medical Journal, 2*, 1612-14. [2]

Mork, T. A. (1972). Sustained silent reading in the classroom. *The Reading Teacher, 25*, 438-41. [10]

Morphett, M., & Washburne, C. (1931). When should children begin to read? *Elementary School Journal, 31*, 496-503. [4]

Morrow, L. M. (1989). Creating a bridge to children's literature. In P. Winograd, K. Wixson, & M. Lipson (Eds.), *Improving basal reading instruction* (pp. 210-230). New York: Teacher College Press. [7, 10]

Morrow, L. M., & Weinstein, C. S. (1986). Encouraging voluntary reading: The impact of a literature program on children's use of library centers. *Reading Research Quarterly, 21,* 330-46. [10]

Mullis, I. V., & Jenkins, L. B. (1990). *The reading report card, 1971-1988, national assessment of educational progress.* Princeton, NJ: Educational Testing. [13]

Murray, H. A. (1938). *Explorations in personality.* New York: Oxford. [5]

Muth, K. D. (1987). Teachers' connection questions: Prompting students to organize text ideas. *Journal of Reading, 31,* 254-59. [10]

Mutke, P. H. (1967). Increased reading comprehension through hypnosis. *The American Journal of Clinical Hypnosis, 9,* 262-66. [11, 12]

Myklebust, H. R. (1965). *Development and disorders of written language, Volume One, Picture Story Language Test.* New York: Grune & Stratton. [4]

Myklebust, H. R. (1968a). Learning disabilities: Definition and overview. In H. R. Myklebust (Ed.), *Progress in learning disabilities* (Vol. 1). New York: Grune & Stratton. [3]

Myklebust, H. R. (1968b). *Progress in learning disabilities* (Vol. 1). New York: Grune & Stratton.

Myklebust, H. R. (1973). *Development and disorders of written language* (Vol. 2, Studies of Normal and Exceptional Children). New York: Grune and Stratton. [4]

Nagy, W. E. (1988). *Teaching vocabulary to improve reading comprehension.* Urbana, IL: National Council of Teachers of English. [9]

Nagy, W. E., & Herman, P. A. (1984). *Limitations of vocabulary instruction.* Technical Report No. 326. Champaign, IL: Center for the Study of Reading. University of Illinois, October. [9]

Nell. V. (1988). The psychology of reading for pleasure: Needs and gratificaions. *Reading Research Quarterly, 23,* 6-50. [4]

Nelson-Herber, J. (1986). Expanding and refining vocabulary in content areas. *Journal of Reading, 29,* 626-33. [9]

Ness, M. (1991, March). The relationship of emotional factors and reading ability. *North Dakota Reading Association News,* p. 4. [11] [12]

Newell, G. (1984). Learning from writing in two content areas: A case study/protocol analysis. *Research in the Teaching of English, 18,* 205-87. [12] [13]

Newman, S. B., & Koskinen, P. (1992). Captioned television as comprehensible input: Effects of incidental word learning from context for language monitoring students. *Reading Research Quarterly, 27*(1), 95-106. [9]

Niemeyer, M. (1976). The Mystery of the Moon Guiter. In W. K. Durr, V. O. Windley, & A. A. McCourt (Eds.), *Medley.* Boston: Houghton Mifflin. [10]

Nist, S. L., & Simpson, M. L. (1989). PLAE, a validated study strategy. *Journal of Reading, 33,* 182-86. [13]

Nist, S. L., & Simpson, M. L. (1990). The effects of PLAE upon students' test performance and metacognitive awareness. In J. Zutell & S. McCormick (Eds.), *Literacy Theory and Research: Analyses from Multiple Paradigms.* The Thirty-ninth Yearbook of the National Reading Conference (pp. 321-27). Chicago, IL: National Reading Conference. [12] [13]

Nist, S. L., Simpson, M. L., Olejnik, S., & Mealey, D. L. (1989). *The relation between self-selected text learning variables and test performance.* Manuscript submitted for publication. [13]

Obenchain, A. (1971). *Effectiveness of the precise essay question in programming the sequential development of written composition skills and the simultaneous development of critical reading skills.* Unpublished master's thesis, George Washington University. [13]

O'Brien, D. (1986). A test of three positions posed to explain the relation between word knowledge and comprehension. In J. A. Niles & R. V. Lalik (Eds.), *Solving problems in literacy: Learners, teachers, and researchers.* Thirty-fifth Yearbook of the National Reading Conference (pp. 81-91). Rochester, NY: National Reading Conference. [9]

O'Connor, P. D., Sofo, F., Kendall, L., & Olsen, G. (1990). Reading disabiliites and the effects of colored filters. *Journal of Learning Disabilities, 23*(10), 597-603.

O'Flahavan, J. (1989). *An exploration of the effects of participant structure upon literacy development in reading group discussion.* Doctoral dissertation, University of Illinois-Champaign. [10]

O'Flahaven, J. F., Hartman, D. K., & Pearson, P. D. (1988). Teacher questioning and feedback practices: A twenty year perspective. In J. E. Readence & R. S. Baldwin (Eds.), *Dialogue in literacy research.* The Thirty-seventh Yearbook of the National Reading Conference (pp.183-208). Chicago, IL: National Reading Conference. [12] [13]

Ogle, D. M. (1989). The know, what to know, learn strategy. In K. D. Muth (Ed.), *Children's comprehension of text* (pp. 205-23). Newark, DE: International Reading Association. [10] [13]

O'Hare, F. (1973). *Sentence combining: Improving student writing without formal grammar instruction.* Urbana, IL: National Council for Teachers of English. [12] [13]

Oka, E. R., & Paris, S. G. (1986). Patterns of motivation and reading skills in underachieving children. In S. J. Ceci (Ed.), *Handbook of cognitive, social, and neuropsychological aspects of learning disabilities* (Vol. 2, pp. 115-45). Hillsdale, NJ: Erlbaum. [2]

Oldridge, O. A. (1982). Positive suggestion: It helps LD students learn. *Academic Therapy, 17*(3), 279-87. [11] [7] [12]

Olson, R. K. (1985). Disabled reading processes and cognitive profiles. In D. Gray & J. Kavanagh (Eds.), *Behavioral measures of dyslexia* (pp. 215-67). Parkton, MD: York Press. [12]

Orton, J. (1966). The Orton-Gillingham approach. In J. Money (Ed.), *The Disabled Reader* (pp. 119-46). Baltimore: The Johns Hopkins University Press.

Orton, S. T. (1937). *Reading, writing, and speech problems in children.* New York: Norton. [8, 12]

O'Sullivan, P. J., Yseldyke, J. E., Christenson, S. L., & Thurlow, M. (1990). Mildly handicapped elementary students' opportunity to learn during reading instruction in mainstream and special education settings. *Reading Research Quarterly, 25*(2), 131-46. [2]

Otto, W., & Hayes, B. (1982). Glossing for improved comprehension: Progress and prospect. In G. H. McNinch (Ed.), *Reading in the disciplines.* Second Yearbook of the American Reading Forum (pp. 16-18). Athens, GA: American Reading Forum. [10]

Otto, W., McMenemy, R. A., & Smith, R. (1973). *Corrective and remedial teaching.* Boston, MA: Houghton Mifflin. [9]

Palincsar, A. S., & Brown, A. L. (1984). Reciprocal teaching of comprehension-fostering and comprehension-monitoring activities. *Cognition and Instruction, 2,* 117-75. [7] [10]

Palincsar, A. S., Brown, A. L., & Martin, S. M. (1987). Peer interaction in reading comprehension instruction. *Educational Psychologist, 22,* 231-53. [10]

Palinscar, A. S., & Ransom, K. (1988). From the mystery spot to the thoughtful spot: The instruction of metacognition strategies. *The Reading Teacher, 41*(8), 784-89. [13]

Palmatier, R. A. (1971). Comparison of four note-taking procedures. *Journal of Reading, 14,* 235-40, 258. [13]

Palmatier, R. A. (1973). A notetaking system for learning. *Journal of Reading, 17,* 36-39. [13]

Palmatier, R. A., & Bennett, J. M. (1974). Notetaking habits of college students. *Journal of Reading, 18,* 215-18. [13]

Paratore, J. R., & Indrisano, R. (1987). Intervention assessment of reading comprehension. *Reading Teacher, 40,* 778-83. [6, 7]

Paris, S. G. (1986). Teaching children to guide their reading and learning. In T. E. Raphael (Ed.), *The contexts of school-based literacy* (pp.115-30). New York: Random House. [10]

Paris, S. G., Cross, D. R., & Lipson, M. Y. (1984). Informed strategies for learning: A program to improve children's reading awareness and comprehension. *Journal of Educational Psychology, 76,* 1239-52.[10, 4] [5]

Paris, S. G., & Myers, M., II (1981). Comprehension monitoring, memory and study strategies of good and poor readers. *Journal of Reading Behavior, 13*(1) 5-22. [4]

Paris, S. G., Wasik, B. A., & Turner, J. C. (1991). The development of strategic readers. In R. Barr, M. L. Kamil, P. Mosenthal, & P. D. Pearson (Eds.), *Handbook of reading research* (Vol. 2, pp. 609-40). New York: Longman. [12] [13]

Paris, S. G., & Winograd, P. (1990). How metacognition can promote academic learning and instruction. In B. Jones & L. Idol (Eds.), *Dimension of thinking and cognitive Instruction.* Hilldale, NJ: Erlbaum. [13] [4]

Parker, R. M. (1990). Power, control, and validity in research. *Journal of Learning Disabilities.* 23:10, 613-20. [12]

Pask, G. (1988). Learning strategies, teaching strategies, and conceptual or learning style. In R. R. Schmeck (Ed.), *Learning strategies and learning styles* (pp. 83-100). New York: Plenum. [5]

Patching, W., Kameenui, E., Carnine, D., Gersten, R., & Colvin, G. (1983). Direct instruction in critical reading skills. *Reading Research Quarterly, 18*(4), 406-8. [13]

Paulsen, J., & Macken, M. (1978). *Report on the level of achievement in CAI reading programs.* Palo Alto, CA: Computer Curriculum Corporation. [7]

Peabody Picture Vocabulary Test. (1970). Circle Pines, MN: American Guidance Service. [4]

Pearson, P. D. (1985). Changing the face of reading comprehension instruction. *Reading Teacher, 38,* 724-38. [7]

Pearson, P. D., & Camperell, K. (1985). Comprehension of text structures. In H. Singer & R. B. Ruddell (Eds.), *Theoretical models and process of reading* (3rd ed., pp. 323-42). Newark, DE: International Reading Association. [10]

Pearson, P. D., & Fielding, L. (1991). Comprehension instruction. In R. Barr, M. L. Kamil, P. Mosenthal, & P. D. Pearson (Eds.), *Handbook of reading research* (Vol. 2, pp. 815-60). New York: Longman. [2] [7] [10]

Pearson, P. D., & Gallagher, M. C. (1983). The instruction of reading comprehension. *Contemporary Educational Psychology, 8,* 317-45. [10]

Pearson, P. D., & Johnson, D. D. (1978). *Teaching reading comprehension.* New York: Holt, Rinehart and Winston. [13]

Pelosi, P. L. (1982). A method for classifying remedial reading techniques. *Reading World, 22,* 119-28. [12]

Penrose, A. M. (1988). *Examining the role of writing in learning factual versus abstract material.* Paper presented at the American Educational Research Association, New Orleans, LA. [12] [13]

Perron, J. D. (1974). *An explanatory approach to extending the syntactic development of fourth grade students through the use of sentence-combining methods.* Unpublished doctoral dissertation, Indiana University. [13]

Petre, R. M. (1970). Quantity, quality and variety of pupil responses during an open-communication structured group directed-thinking activity and a closed-communication structured group directed reading activity (Doctoral dissertation, University of Delaware, Newark). *Dissertation Abstract International, 31,* 4630A. [10]

Pflaum, S. W. (1979). Diagnosis of oral reading. *The Reading Teacher, 33,* 278-84. [4]

Piaget, J. (1963). *The child's conception of the world.* Paterson, NJ: Littlefield Adams. [9]

Pichert, J. W., & Anderson, R. C. (1977). Taking different perspectives on a story. *Journal of Educational Psychology, 69,* 309-15. [5]

Pierce, K. M. (1991). Empowering readers and writers through knowledge and involvement. *The Missouri Reader, 15*(2), 2. [2]

Pikulski, J. J. (1974). A critical review: Informal reading inventories. *Reading Teacher, 28*(2), 141-51. [4]

Pikulski, J. J., & Shanahan, T. (1982). Informal reading inventories: a critical analysis. In J. J. Pikulski & T. Shanahan (Eds.), *Approaches to the informal evaluation of reading.* Newark, DE: International Reading Association. [4]

Pincus, A., Geller, E. B., & Stover, E. M. (1986). A technique for using the story schema as a transition to understanding and summarizing event-based magazine articles. *Journal of Reading, 30,* 152-58. [10]

Pirozzolo, F. J. (1979). The neuropsychology of developmental reading disorders. New York: Praeger. [12]

Poostay, E. J. (1982). Reading problems of children: The perspectives of reading specialists. *School Psychology Review, 11*(3), 251-56. [7] [13]

Poostay, E. J. (1984). Show me your underlines: A strategy to teach comprehension. *The Reading Teacher, 37*(9), 828-30. [10, 13]

Poostay, E. J., & Aaron, I.E. (1982). Reading problems of children: The perspectives of reading specialists. *School Psychology Review, 11*(3), 251-56. [5]

Porter, D. (1978). Cloze procedure and equivalence. *Language Learning, 28,* 333-41. [4]

Porteus, S. D. (1956). *The Maze Test and clinical psychology.* Palo Alto, CA: Pacific Books. [5]

Powell, W. R. (1978). *Measuring reading performance informally.* Paper presented at annual meeting of International Reading Association, Houston, TX. (ERIC Document Reproduction Service No. ED 155 589) [4]

Powell, W. R., & Dunkeld, C. G. (1971). Validity of informal reading inventory reading levels. *Elementary English, 48*(6), 637-42. [4]

Pressley, G. M. (1976). Mental imagery helps eight-year-olds remember what they read. *Journal of Educational Psychology, 68,* 355-59. [13]

Pressley, M. (1977). Imagery and children's learning: Putting the picture in developmental perspective. *Review of Educational Research, 47,* 585-622. [10]

Pressley, M., Johnson, C. J., & Symons, S. (1987). Elaborating to learn and learning to elaborate. *Journal of Learning Disabilities, 20,* 76-91. [13]

Pressley, M., Levin, J. R., & MacDaniel, M. A. (1987). Remembering versus inferring what a word means: Mnemonic and contextual approaches. In M. C. McKeown & M. E. Curtis (Eds.), *The nature of vocabulary acquisition* (pp. 107-29). Hillsdale, NJ: Erlbaum. [13]

Pressley, M., Levin, J. R., & Miller, G. E. (1981). How does the keyword method affect vocabulary comprehension and usage? *Reading Research Quarterly, 16*(2), 213-25. [9] [13]

Preston, R. C., & Botel, M. (1981). *Study Habits Checklist.* Chicago, IL: Science Research Associates. [4]

Purcell-Gates, V. (1991). On the outside looking in: A study of remedial reader's meaning-making while reading literature. *Journal of Reading Behavior, 23*(2). 235-53. [13]

Putnam, L. R. (1991). In E. Fry (Ed.), *Ten best ideas for reading teachers* (pp.100-101). Menlo Park, CA: Addison-Wesley. [2]

Quartz, J. O. (1897). Problems in the psychology of reading. *Psychological Review Monograph Supplements, 2,* 52.

Queens College Tests (1970) as cited in Harris, A. J., *Casebook on reading disability.* New York: David McKay. [4]

Rabin, A. T. (1991). In E. Fry (Ed.), *Ten best ideas for reading teachers* (pp. 102-103). Monlo Park, CA: Addison-Wesley. [2]

Rack, J. P., Snowling, M., & Olson, R. K. (1992). The non-word reading deficit in developmental dyslexia: A review. *Reading Research Quarterly, 27*(1), 29-53. [12]

Radetsky, P. (1991, April). The brainiest cells alive. *Discover, 12*(4), 83-90. [Appendix D]

Raim, J. (1983). Influence of the teacher-pupil interaction on disabled readers. *The Reader Teacher, 36,* 810-13. [7]

Rapaport, A. (1950). *Science and the goals of man.* New York: Harper & Brothers. [4]

Raphael, T. E. (1982). Question-answering strategies for children. *The Reading Teacher, 36,* 186-90. [13]

Raphael, T. E. (1986). Teaching questions-answers relationships, revisited. *The Reading Teacher, 39,* 516-22. [12] [13]

Raths, L. E., Harmon, M., & Simon, S. B. (1978). *Values and teaching* (2nd ed.). Columbus, OH: Merrill. [11] [13]

Raven, J. C. (1938). *Progressive Matrices: A perceptual test of intelligence, 1938, Individual Form.* London: H.K. Lewis [5]

Raven, J. C. (1960). *Guide to the Standard Progressive Matrices, Sets A, B, C, D, and E.* London: H. K. Lewis. [5]

Readence, J. R., Baldwin, S., & Bean, T. (1981). *Content area reading: An integrated approach.* Dubuque, IA: Kendall-Hunt. [4]

Readence, J. E., Bean, T. W., & Baldwin, R. S. (1985). *Content area reading: An integrated approach* (2nd ed.). Dubuque, IA: Kendall-Hunt. [10]

Readence, J. E., Bean, T. W., & Baldwin, R. S. (1989). *Content area reading: An integrated approach* (3rd ed.). Dubuque, IA: Kendall-Hunt. [10]

Readence, J. E., & Searfoss, L. W. (1980). Teaching strategies for vocabulary development. *English Journal, 69,* 43-46. [13]

Reid, E. R. (1990). Integrating the teaching of literature, comprehension, and composition. *Contemporary Issues in Reading, 5*(2), 61-67. [13]

Rennie, B. J., Braun, C., & Gordon, C. J. (1986). Long-term effects of clinical intervention: An in-depth study. *Reading Horizon, 27,* 12-18. [7]

Renner, S. M., & Carter, J. M. (1991). Comprehending text-appreciating diversity through folklore. *Journal of Reading, 34*(8), 602-04. [7] [10]

Rentel, V. M. (1971). Concept formation and reading. *Reading World, 11,* 111-19. [9] [13]

Resnick, L. B. (1987). *Education and learning to think* (Report). Washington, DC: National Academy Press. [13]

Reynolds, M., Wang, M., & Walberg, H. (1987). The necessary restructuring of special and regular education. *Exceptional Children, 53,* 391-98. [2]

Richardson, E., & DiBenedetto, B. (1985). *The Decoding Skills Test.* Parkton, MD: York Press.

Richardson, E., DiBenedetto, B., & Adler, A. (1982). Use of the Decoding Skills Test to study the differences between good and poor readers. In K. D. Gadow and I. Bialer (Eds.), *Advances in Learning and Behavioral Disabilities* (pp. 25-74). Greenwich, CT: JAI Press.

Richek, M. A., List, L. K., & Lerner, J. W. (1989). *Reading problems: Assessment and teaching strategies.* Englewood Cliffs, NJ: Prentice Hall. [7]

Richgels, D. J., & Hansen, R. (1982). Guidelines for writing gloss notations with a focus on comprehension skills and strategies. In G. H. McNinch (Ed.), *Reading in the disciplines. Second Yearbook of the American Reading Forum* (pp. 18-23). Athens, GA: American Reading Forum. [10]

Richgels, D. J., & Mateja, J. A. (1984). Gloss, II: Integrating context and process of independence. *Journal of Reading, 27,* 424-31. [10]

Rickards, J. P., & Friedman, F. (1978). The encoding versus the external storage hypothesis in note taking. *Contemporary Educational Psychology, 3,* 136-43. [13]

Rickelman, R. J., & Henk, W. A. (1990a). Colored overlays and tinted lens filters. *The Reading Teacher, 44*(2), 166-67. [12]

Rickelman, R. J., & Henk, W. A. (1990b). Reading technology and the brain. *The Reading Teacher, 43*(4), 334-36. [12]

Riegel, K. (1979). *The relational basis of language: Foundations of dialectical psychology.* New York: Academic. [7]

Ringler, L. H., & Weber, C. K. (1984). *A language-thinking approach to reading.* San Diego: Harcourt Brace Jovanovich. [4]

Rinsky, L. A., & deFossard, E. (1980). *The contemporary classroom reading inventory.* Dubuque, IA: Gorsuch Scarisbrick. [4]

Risko, V., & Patterson, A. (1989). Enhancing students independent learning and text comprehension with a verbally rehearsed composing strategy. In B. L. Hayes & K. Camperell (Eds.). *Reading researchers policymakers and practitioners.* The Yearbook of the American Reading Forum, Vol. IX (pp. 61-71). Logan, UT, Utah State University. **[13]**

Robert, C. (1956). *Teachers' guide to word attack: A way to better reading.* New York: Harcourt Brace & World. [9]

Roberts, J., & Kelly, N. (1985). The keyword method: An alternative vocabulary strategy for developmental college readers. *Reading World, 24*(3), 34-39. [9]

Robinson, F. (1946). *Effective study.* New York: Harper Brothers. [12] [13]

Robinson, H. M. (1946). *Why children fail in reading.* Chicago: University of Chicago Press. [2] [13]

Robinson, H. (1972). Visual and auditory modalities related to methods for beginning reading. *Reading Research Quarterly, 8,* 7-39. [12]

Robinson, H., Gregory L. W., & Conway, N. F. (1990). The effects of Irlen colored lenses on students' specific reading skills and their perception of ability: a 12-month validity study. *Journal of Learning Disabilities, 23*(10), 588-96. [12]

Roehler, L. R., Duffy, G. G., & Warren, S. (1987). Adaptive explanatory actions associated with effective teaching of reading strategies. In J. Readance & S. Baldwin (Eds.), *Dialogues in literacy research.* Thirty-seventh Yearbook of National Reading Conference (pp. 339-46). Chicago: National Reading Conference. [7]

Rogers, D. B. (1984). Assessing study skills. *Journal of Reading, 27*(4), 346-54. [4]

Rongione, L. A. (1972). Bibliotherapy: Its nature and uses. *Catholic Library World, 43,* 495-500. [10]

Rosenberger, P. B. (1992). Dyslexia—Is it a disease? *The New England Journal of Medicine, 326*(3), 192-93. [12]

Rosenblatt, L. M. (1969). Towards a transactional theory of reading. *Journal of Reading Behavior, 1*(1), 31-49. [7]

Rosenshine, B., & Stevens, R. (1984). Classroom instruction in reading. In P. D. Pearson (ed.), *Handbook of Reading Research* (pp. 745-98). New York: Longman. [7]

Rosner, J. (1974). Auditory analysis training with prereaders. *The Reading Teacher, 27*(4), 379-81. [8]

Rosner, J., & Simon, D. P. (1971). The auditory analysis test: An initial report. *Journal of Learning Disabilities, 4,* 384-92. [8]

Rozin, P., Poritsky, S., & Sotsky, R. (1971). American children with reading problems can easily learn to read English represented by Chinese characters. *Science, 171,* 1264-67. [12]

Rubin, L. J. (1984). *Artistry in teaching.* New York: Random House [7] [10]

Ruddell, R. B. (1990). *A study of the effect of reader motivation and comprehension development on students' reading comprehension achievement in influential and non-influential teachers' classrooms.* Paper presented at the annual meeting of the National Reading Conference, Miami, FL. [11] [13]

Ruddell, R. B., Draheim, M. E., & Barnes, J. (1990). A comparative study of the teaching effectiveness of influential and noninfluential teachers and reading comprehension development. In J. Zutell & S. McCormick (Eds.), *Literacy theory and research: Analyses from multiple paradigms.* The Thirty-ninth yearbook of the National Reading Conference (pp. 153-62). Chicago, IL: National Reading Conference. [13]

Ruddell, R. B., & Haggard, M. R. (1982). Influential teachers: Characteristics and classroom performance. In J. A. Niles & L. A. Harris (Eds.), *New inquiries in reading research and instruction* (pp. 227-31). Rochester, NY: National Reading Conference. [13]

Ruddell, R. B., & Harris, P. (1989). A study of the relationship between influential teachers' prior knowledge and beliefs and teaching effectiveness: Developing higher order thinking in content areas. In S. McCormick & J. Zutell (Eds.), *Cognitive and social perspectives for literacy research and instruction* (pp. 461-72). Chicago, IL: National Reading Conference. [13]

Ruddell, R. B. & Kern, R. B. (1986). The development of belief systems and teaching effectiveness of influential teachers. In M. P. Douglas (Ed.), *Reading: The quest for meaning* (pp. 133-50). Claremont, CA: Claremont Graduate School Yearbook. [13]

Rude, R. T., & Oehlkers, W. J. (1984). *Helping students with reading problems.* Englewood Cliffs, NJ: Prentice-Hall. [2] [3] [4]

Rumelhart, D. E. (1977). Toward an interactive model of reading. In S. Dornic (Ed.) *Attention and performance.* Hillsdale, NJ: Erlbaum. [2] [4]

Rumelhart, D. E. (1980). Schemata: The building blocks of cognition. In R. J. Spiro, B. C. Bruce, & W. F. Brewer (Eds.), *Theoretical issues in reading comprehension.* Hillsdale, NJ: Erlbaum. [10]

Russell, S. (1991). Thinking it over. *Journal for Affective Education, 11*(fall), 41-42. [11]

Sacks, O. (1987). *The man who mistook his wife for a hat, and other clinical tales.* New York: Simon & Schuster, Summitt Books. [12]

Sadoski, M. (1983). An exploratory study of the relationships between reported Simagery and the comprehension and recall of a story. *Reading Research Quarterly, 19,* 110-23. [10]

Sadoski, M. (1985). The natural use of imagery in story comprehension and recall: Replication and extension. *Reading Research Quarterly, 20,* 658-67. [10]

Samuels, S. J. (1979). The method of repeated readings. *The Reading Teacher, 32,* 403-08. [8] [10] [12]

Samuels, S. J. (1983). Diagnosing reading problems. *Topics in Learning Disabilities, 2,* 1-11. [2] [13]

Samuels, S. J., & LaBerge, D. (1983). A critique of, A theory of automaticity in reading: Looking back: A retrospective analysis of the LaBerge-Samuels reading model. In L. M. Gentile, M. L. Kamil, & J. S. Blanchard (Eds.), *Reading research revisited* (pp. 39-55). Columbus, OH: Charles C. Merrill. [12] [13]

Sanacore, J. (1984). Metacognition and the improvement of reading: Some important links. *Journal of Reading, 27,* 706-12. [4] [7] [10]

Santa, C. M., & Hayes, B. L. (Eds.). (1981). *Children's prose comprehension.* Newark, DE: International Reading Association. [10]

Santeusanio, R. (1967). RAMA: A supplement to the traditional college reading program. *Journal of Reading, 11,* 133-36. [12] [13]

Satz, P., & Morris, R. (1981). Learning disability subtypes: A review. In F. Pirozzolo & M. Wittrock (Eds.), *Neuropsychological and cognitive processes in reading* (pp. 109-41). New York: Academic Press. [12]

Sawyer, D. J. (1975). Linguistic and cognitive competencies in the middle grades. *Language Arts, 52*(8), 1075-79. [2]

Sawyer, D. J. (Ed.) (1980). *Disabled readers: Insight, assessment, instruction.* Newark, DE: International Reading Association.

Sawyer, W. E. (1989). Attention deficit disorder: A wolf in sheep's clothing...again. *The Reading Teacher, 42*(4), 310-12. [12]

Sawyer, W. E., & Wilson, B. A. (1979). Role clarification of remedial reading and learning disabilities teachers. *The Reading Teacher, 33,* 162-66. [2]

Scardamalia, M., Bereiter, C., & Steinbach, R. (1984). Teachability of reflective processes in written composition. *Cognitive Science, 8,* 173-90. [7]

Schell, L. M. (1972). Promising possibilities for improving comprehension. *Journal of Reading, 5,* 415-24. [10]

Schell, L. M. (1980). Value Clarification via Basal Readers. *Reading Horizons, 20,* 215-20. [10] [11] [13]

Schell, L. M. (1988). Dilemmas in assessing reading comprehension. *The Reading Teacher, 42,* 12-16. [2] [4]

Schell, L. M. (1991). In E. Fry (Ed.), *Ten best ideas for reading teachers* (pp. 115-16). Menlo Park, CA: Addison-Wesley. [4]

Schell, L. M., & Hanna, G. S. (1981). Can informal reading inventories reveal strengths and weaknesses in comprehension subskills? *The Reading Teacher, 34,* 263-68. [4]

Schmitt, M. C. (1988). The effects of an elaborated directed activity on the metacomprehension skills of third graders. In J. E. Readence & R. S. Baldwin (Eds.), *Dialogues in literacy research.* The Thirty-seventh Yearbook of the National Reading Conference (pp. 167-81). Chicago, IL: National Reading Conference. [5] [4] [10]

Schmitt, M. C. (1990). A questionnaire to measure children's awareness of strategic reading processes. *The Reading Teacher, 43*(7), 454-61. [5] [4]

Schmitt, M. C., & Baumann, J. F. (1986a, December). *Metacomprehension in basal reader instruction: Do teachers promote it?* Paper presented at the annual meeting of the National Reading Conference, Austin, TX. [10]

Schmitt, M. C., & Baumann, J. F. (1986b). How to incorporate comprehension monitoring strategies into basal reader instruction. *The Reading Teacher, 40,* 28-31. [10]

Schoelles, I. (1971). *Cloze as a predictor of reading group placement.* Paper presented at the International Reading Association annual convention, Atlantic City, NJ. [4]

Schonhaut, S., & Satz, P. (1983). Prognosis for children with learning disabilities: A review of the follow-up studies. In M. Rutter (Ed.), *Developmental neuropsychiatry* (pp. 542-63). New York: Guilford Press. [7]

Schunk, D. H., & Rice, J. M. (1987). Enhancing comprehension skill and self-efficacy with strategy value information. *Journal of Reading Behavior, 19,* 285-302. [10]

Searfoss, L. W., & Readence, J. E. (1989). *Helping children learn to read* (2nd ed.). Englewood Cliffs, NJ: Prentice-Hall. [2]

Seaton, H. W., & Weilan, O. P. (1979). *The effects of listening/reading transfer on four measures of reading comprehension.* Paper presented at the Annual Convention of the International Reading Association, Atlanta, GA. [10]

Segalowitz, S. J. (1983). *Two sides of the brain.* Englewood Cliffs, NJ: Prentice-Hall.

Seidenbert, M. S., Bruck, M., Fornarolo, G., & Backman, J. (1985). Word recognition processes of poor and disabled readers: Do they necessarily differ? *Applied Psycholinguistics, 6,* 161-80. [12]

Sevush, S. (1983, February). *The neurolinguistics of reading: Anatomic and neurologic correlates.* Paper presented at the Annual Conference of the International Neuropsychological Society, Mexico City. [12]

Shanahan, T. (1988). The reading-writing relationship: Seven instructional principles. *The Reading Teacher, 41,* 636-47. [7] [13]

Shanahan, T., & Kamil, M. L. (1983). A further investigation of sensitivity of cloze and recall to organization. In J. Niles & L. A. Harris (Eds.), *Search for meaning in reading/language processing instruction.* The Thirty-second Yearbook of the National Reading Conference (pp. 123-128). Rochester, NY: National Reading Conference. [10]

Shanahan, T., & Lomax, R. (1986). An analysis and comparison of theoretical models of the reading-writing relationship. *Journal of Educational Psychology, 78*, 116-23. [12] [13]

Shepherd, D. (1978). *Comprehensive high school reading methods* (3rd ed.). Columbus, OH: Merrill. [10]

Sherk, J. K., Jr. (1967). *A study of the effect of a program of visual perceptual training on the progress of retarded readers.* Unpublished doctoral dissertation, Syracuse University, Syracuse, NY. [12]

Shipe, D., Cromwell, R. L., & Dunn, L. M. (1964). Responses of emotionally disturbed and non-disturbed retardates to PPVT items of human vs non-human content. *Journal of Consulting Psychology* (submitted). (As cited in Dunn, 1965) [5]

Shoop, M. E. (1985). Oral language in the classroom: A foundation for literacy. *Kansas Journal of Reading, 1*, 7-12. [10]

Shoop, M. E. (1986). InQuest: A listening and reading comprehension strategy. *The Reading Teacher, 39*(7), 670-74. [10]

Short, K. (1984). *Literacy as a collaborative experience.* Doctoral dissertation, Indiana University. [12] [13]

Short, K. G. (1986). Literacy as collaborative: The role of intertextuality. In J. A. Niles & R. V. Lalik (Eds.), *Solving problems in literacy: Learners, teachers, and researchers.* Thirty-fifth Yearbook of the National Reading Conference (pp. 227-32). Rochester, NY: National Reading Conference. [12] [13]

Shugarman, S. L., & Hurst, J. B. (1986). Purposeful paraphrasing: Promoting non-trivial pursuit for meaning. *Journal of Reading, 29*, 396-99. [10]

Siegel, F. (1979). Adapted miscue analysis. *Reading World, 19*, 36-43. [4]

Siegel, L. S. (1988). A system for the early detection of learning disabilities. *Canadian Journal of Special Education, 4*(2), 115-22. [3]

Siegel, L. S. (1989). IQ is irrelevant to the definition of learning disabilities. *Journal of Learning Disabilities, 22*(8), 469-78, 486. [3]

Silvaroli, N. J. (1976). *Classroom Reading Inventory.* Dubuque, IA: William C. Brown. [3] [4]

Silver, A., & Hagin, R. (1964). Specific reading disability: Follow up studies. *American Journal of Orthopsychiatry, 34*, 95-102. [12]

Simpson, M. L. (1986). PORPE: A writing strategy for studying and learning in the content areas. *Journal of Reading, 29*, 407-14. [13]

Simpson, M. L., & Nist, S. L. (1984). PLAE: A model for planning successful independent learning. *Journal of Reading, 29*, 218-23. [13]

Simpson, M. L., & Nist, S. L. (1990). Textbook annotation: An effective and efficient study strategy for college students. *Journal of Reading, 34*(2), 122-29. [10]

Simpson, M. L., Stahl, N. A., & Hayes, C. G. (1989). PORPE: A research validation. *Journal of Reading, 33*, 22-28. [13]

Sinatra, G. M. (1990). Convergence of listening and reading processing. *Reading Research Quarterly, 25*(2), 115-30. [4]

Singer, H. (1985). Models of reading have direct implications for instruction: The affirmative position. In J. A. Niles & R. V. Lalik (Eds.), *Issues in literacy: A research perspective.* Thirty-fourth Yearbook of the National Reading Conference (pp. 402-413). Rochester, NY: The National Reading Conference. [2]

Slingerland, B. H. (1971). *A multi-sensory approach to language arts for specific language disability children: A guide for primary teachers, Books 1-3.* Cambridge, MA: Educators Publishing Service. [8] [9]

Slosson Intelligence Test. (1974). New York: Slosson Educational Publications [4] [5]

Slosson, R. L. (1963). *Slosson Oral Reading Test.* East Aurora, NY: Slosson Educational Publications. [4]

Slosson, R. L. (1982). *Slosson Intelligence Test* (2nd ed.). East Aurora, NY: Slosson Educational Publications. [5]

Smith, D. E., & Carrigan, P. M. (1959). *The nature of reading disability.* New York: Harcourt Brace and Co. [12]

Smith, F. (1973). Twelve easy ways to make learning to read difficult. In F. Smith (Ed.), *Psycholinguistics and Reading.* New York: Holt, Rinehart and Winston.

Smith, F. (1978). *Reading and nonsense.* New York: Teachers College Press.

Smith, F. (1979a). Conflicting approaches to reading research and instruction. In L. B. Resnick & P. A. Weaver (Eds.), *Theory and practice of early reading, vol. 2.* Hillsdale, NJ: Erlbaum.

Smith, F. (1979b). *Reading without nonsense.* New York: Teachers College Press. [4]

Smith, F. (1984). The creative achievement of literacy. In H. Goelamn, A. Oberg, & F. Smith (Eds.), *Awakening to literacy* (pp. 135-42). Portsmouth, NH: Heinemann. [12] [13]

Smith, F. (1990). *To think.* New York: Teachers College, Columbia University. [13]

Smith, N. B. (1964). Patterns of writing in different subject areas, part II. *Journal of Reading, 8,* 97-102. [13]

Smith, N. B. (1965). *American reading instruction.* Newark, DE: International Reading Association [1]

Smith, R. J., & Dauer, V. (1984). A comprehension-monitoring strategy for reading content area materials. *Journal of Reading, 28,* 144-47. [12] [13]

Snow, R. E., & Lohman, D. F. (1984). Towards a theory of cognitive aptitude for learning from instruction. *Journal of Educational Psychology, 76,* 347-76. [5]

Snowling, M. (1980). The developmental of grapheme-phoneme correspondence in normal and dyslexia readers. *Journal of Experimental Child Psychology, 29,* 294-305. [12]

Soar, R. S. (1973). *Follow-through classroom process measurement and pupil growth (1970-71): Final report.* Gainesville, FL: College of Education, University of Florida. [7]

Solan, H. A. (1990). An appraisal of the Irlen technique of correcting reading disorders using tinted overlays and tinted lenses. *Journal of Learning Disabilities, 23*(10), 621-23. [12]

Solomon, D., & Kendall, A. J. (1979). Children in classrooms. New York: Praeger. [7]

Spache, G. D. (1972). *Diagnostic reading scales.* Monterey, CA: CTB/McGraw-Hill. [4]

Spache, G. D. (1976). *Diagnosing and correcting reading disabilities.* Boston: Allyn & Bacon. [4]

Spache, G. D. (1981). *Diagnostic reading scales.* Monterey, CA: CTB/McGraw-Hill. [7]

Spicola, R., Griffin, M., & Stephens, C. (1990). Motivating reluctant readers through literature. *Reading Education in Texas: Yearbook of the Texas State Reading Association of the International Reading Association, 6,* 41-7. [11]

Spiegel, D. L. (1980a). Desirable teaching behaviors for effective instruction in reading. *The Reading Teacher, 34*(3), 324-30. [7]

Spiegel, D. L. (1980b). Adaptations of Manzo's Guided Reading Procedure. *Reading Horizons, 20,* 188-92. [10]

Spiegel, D. L. (1990). Critical reading materials: A review of three criteria. *The Reading Teacher, 43*(6), 410-12. [Appendix E]

Spiegel, D. L., & Fitzgerald, J. (1986). Improving reading comprehension through instruction about story parts. *The Reading Teacher, 39*(7), 676-82. [10]

Spires, H. A., & Stone, P. D. (1988, May). *Notetaking as a cognitive activity: Implications for the college reading class.* Paper presented at the annual convention of the International Reading Association, Toronto. [13]

Spires, H. A., & Stone, P. D. (1989). The directed notetaking activity: A self-questioning approach. *Journal of Reading, 33,* 36-39. [13]

Spreen, O. (1982). Adults outcomes of reading disorders. In R. Malatesha & P. Aaron (Eds.). *Reading disorders: Varieties and treatments* (pp. 473-98). New York: Academic Press. [7]

Stahl, N. A., Brozo, W. G., Smith, B. D., Henk, W. A., & Commander, N. (1991). Effects of teaching generative vocabulary strategies in the college developmental reading program. *Journal of Research and Development in Education, 24*(4), 24-31. [9]

Stahl, N. A., & Henk, W. A. (1986). Tracing the roots of textbook study systems: An extended historical perspective. In J. A. Niles & R. V. Lalik (Eds.), *Solving problems in literacy: Learners, teachers, and researchers*. The Thirty-fifth Yearbook of the National Reading Conference (pp. 366-374). Rochester, NY: National Reading Conference. [13]

Stahl, S. A. (1985). To teach a word well: A framework for vocabulary instruction. *Reading World, 24*(3), 16-27. [9]

Stahl, S. A. (1986). Three principles of effective vocabulary instruction. *Journal of Reading, 29*, 662-71. [9]

Stahl, S. A., & Clark, C. H. (1987). The effects of participatory expectations in classroom discussion on the learning of science vocabulary. *American Educational Research Journal, 24*, 541-56. [9]

Stahl, S., & Kapinus, B. (1991). Possible sentences: Predicting word meanings to teach content area vocabulary. *The Reading Teacher, 45*(1), 36-43. [9]

Stahl, S. A., & Vancil, S. J. (1986). Discussion is what makes semantic maps work in vocabulary instruction. *The Reading Teacher, 40*, 62-69. [9]

Stallings, J. A., & Kaskowitz, D. (1974). *Follow-through classroom observation evaluation, 1972-73*. Menlo Park, CA: Stanford Research Institute. [7]

Stampfl, T. G., & Lewis, D. J. (1965, November). *Implosive therapy: The theory, the subhuman analogue, the strategy and the technique*. Paper presented at the V.A. Hospital in Battle Creek, MI. [11]

Stanford-Binet Intelligence Scales. (1973). Boston: Houghton Mifflin [5]

Stanovich, K. E. (1980). Toward an interactive compensatory model of individual differences in the development of reading fluency. *Reading Research Quarterly, 16*(1), 32-71. [2]

Stanovich, K. E. (1986a). Cognitive processes and the reading problems of learning disabled children: Evaluating the assumption of specificity. In J. K. Torgesen & B. Y. L. Wong (Eds.), *Psychological and educational perspectives on learning disabilities* (pp. 87-131). NY: Academic Press. [2]

Stanovich, K. E. (1986b). Matthew effects in reading: Some consequences of individual differences in the acquisition of literacy. *Reading Research Quarterly, 21*, 360-407. [3]

Staton, J. (1980). Writing and counseling: Using a dialogue journal. *Language Arts, 57*, 514-18. [10] [11]

Stauffer, R. G. (1975). *Directing the reading-thinking process*. New York: Harper & Row. [10]

Stauffer, R. G. (1980). *The language-experience approach to the teaching of reading* (2nd ed). New York: Harper & Row. [8]

Stephens, B. (1989). Taking the second step in reading. *The Reading Teacher, 42*, 584-90. [10] [11]

Sternberg, R. J. (1987). Most vocabulary is learned from context. In M. G. McKeown & M. E. Curtis (Eds.), *The nature of vocabulary acquisition* (pp. 89-105). Hillsdale, NJ: Erlbaum. [13]

Stevens, K. C. (1981). Chunking material as an aid to reading comprehension. *Journal of Reading, 25*, 126-29. [10]

Stevens, K. C. (1982). Helping students understand complicated sentences. *Reading Horizons, 22*, 184-90. [10]

Sticht, T. G., Beck, L. J., Hauke, R. N., Kleiman, G. M., & James, J. H. (1974). *Auding and reading: A developmental model* (Air Force Contract No. F41609-73-C-0025, Project 1121). Alexandria, VA: Human Resources Research Organization. [4] [10]

Stieglitz, E. L., & Stieglitz, V. S. (1981). SAVOR the word to reinforce vocabulary in the content areas. *Journal of Reading, 25*, 46-51. [9]

Stotsky, S. L. (1975). Sentence-combining as a curricular activity: Its effect on written language development and reading comprehension. *Research in the Teaching of English, 9,* 30-71. [13]

Strang, R. (l964). *Diagnostic teaching of reading.* New York: McGraw-Hill. [3]

Strauss, A., & Lehtinen, L. (1947). *Psychopathology and education of the brain-injured children.* New York: Grune & Stratton. [7]

Straw, S. B., & Schreiner, R. (1982). The effect of sentence manipulation on subsequent measures of reading and listening. *Reading Research Quarterly, 17,* 339-52. [13]

Sulzby, E. (1985). Children's emergent reading of favorite storybooks: A developmental study. *Reading Research Quarterly, 20*(4), 458-81. [8]

Sunday, J. (1990). On defining learning and disability: Exploring the ecology. *Journal of Learning Disabilities, 23*(10), 628-31.

Swaby, B. E. R. (1989). *Diagnosis and correction of reading difficulties.* Needham Heights, MA: Allyn & Bacon.

Tarnopol, L., & Tarnopol, M. A. (1977). *Brain function and reading disabilities.* Baltimore, MD: University Park Press. [12]

Tarver, S. G., & Dawson, M. M. (1978). Modality preference and the teaching of reading: A review. *Journal of Learning Disabilities, 11,* 5-17. [5]

Taylor, W. (1953). "Cloze procedure": A new tool for measuring readability. *Journalism Quarterly, 30,* 415-33. [4]

Teale, W. H. (1986). Home background and young children's literacy development. In W. H. Teale & E. Sulzby (Eds.), *Emergent literacy: Writing and reading* (pp. 173-206). Norwood, NJ: Ablex. [7]

Tharp, R. G., & Gallimore, R. (1989a). *Rousing minds to life: Teaching, learning, and schooling in social context.* New York: Cambridge University Press. [10]

Tharp, R. G., & Gallimore, R. (1989b). Rousing schools to life. *American Educator, 13*(2), 20-25, 46-52. [10]

Thomas, C. J. (l905). Congenital word blindness and its treatment. *Opthalmoloscope, 3,* 380-85. [2]

Thomson, M. (1984). *Developmental dyslexia: Its nature, assessment and remediation.* Baltimore, MD: Edward Arnold. [12]

Thorndike, E. (1917). Reading as reasoning: A study of mistakes in paragraph reading. *Journal of Educational Psychology, 8*(6), 323-32. [2] [3]

Thorndike, E. L., & Lorge, I. (1944). *The teacher's word book of 30,000 words.* New York: Teachers College Press. [4]

Thurstone, T. (1969). *SRA reading for understanding.* Hempstead, NY: Science Research Associates. [7]

Tierney, R. J., & Cunningham, J. W. (1984). Research on teaching reading comprehension. In P. D. Pearson, R. Barr, M. L. Kamil, & P. Mosenthal (Eds.), *Handbook of reading research* (pp. 609-55). New York: Longman. [10]

Tierney, R. J., Readence, J. E., & Dishner, E. K. (1985). *Reading strategies and practices: A compendium* (2nd ed.). Boston: Allyn & Bacon. [10]

Tierney, R. J., Readence, J. E., & Disher, E. K. (1990). *Reading strategies and practices* (3rd ed.). Needham Heights, MA: Allyn & Bacon. [8] [10] [13]

Tierney, R. J., & Shanahan, T. (1991). Research on the reading-writing relationship: Interactions, transactions, and outcomes. In R. Barr, M. Kamil, P. Mosenthal, & P. D. Pearson (Eds.), *Handbook of reading research, Vol. 2* (pp. 246-80). New York: Longman. [12] [13]

Tierney, R. J., Soter, A., O'Flahavan, J. F., & McGinley, W. (1989). The effects of reading and writing upon thinking critically. *Reading Research Quarterly, 24,* 134-37. [13]

Tillman, C. E. (1984). Bibliotherapy for adolescents: An annotated research review. *Journal of Reading, 27*, 713-19. [11]

Tonjes, M. J., & Zintz, M. (1987). *Teaching reading, thinking and study skills in content classrooms.* Dubuque, IA: William C. Brown. [10]

Topping, K. (1987). Paired reading: A powerful technique for parent use. *The Reading Teacher, 40*, 608-14. [12]

Topping, K. (1989). Peer tutoring and paired reading: Combining two powerful techniques. *The Reading Teacher, 42*, 488-94. [8] [10] [12]

Torgesen, J. K. (1982). The learning-disabled child as an inactive learner. *Topics in Learning and Learning Disabilities, 2*, 45-52. [1]

Tortelli, J. P. (1976). Simplified psycholinguistic diagnosis. *The Reading Teacher, 29*(7), 637-39. [4]

Traub, N. (1982). Reading, spelling, handwriting: Traub Systematic Holistic Method. *Annals of Dyslexia, 32*, 135-45. [8]

Traub, N., & Bloom, F. (1975). *Recipe for reading.* Cambridge, MA: Educators Publishing Service. [8]

Trotter, R. J. (1979). Better learning: Imaging that. *Psychology Today, 19*(4), 22. [12] [13]

Tuleja, T. (1982). *Fabulous fallacies.* New York: Crown. [7]

Tutolo, D. (1977). The study guide—Types, purposes and value. *Journal of Reading, 20*, 503-07. [10]

Uttero, D. A. (1988). Activating comprehension through cooperative learning. *The Reading Teacher, 41*, 390-95. [13]

Valencia, S. (1990). A portfolio approach to classroom reading assessment: The ways, whats, and hows. *Reading Teacher, 43*(4), p 338-80. [6]

Valencia, S. W. (1991). Diagnostic teaching. *The Reading Teacher, 44*(6), 420-422. [2]

Valencia, S. W., McGinley, W., & Pearson, P. D. (1990). Assessing reading and writing. In G. Duffy (Ed.), *Reading in the middle school* (2nd ed., pp. 124-46). Newark, DE: International Reading Association. [4] [6]

Valmont, W. J. (1972). Creating questions for informal reading inventories. *The Reading Teacher, 25*, 509-12. [4]

Vaughan, J. L. (1982). Instructional strategies. In A. Berger & H. A. Robinson (Eds.), *Secondary school reading: What research reveals for classroom practice* (pp. 67-84). Urbana, IL: National Council of Teachers of English & ERIC/RCS. [10]

Vaughan, J. L. (1984). Concept structuring: The technique and empirical evidence. In C. D. Holley & D. F. Dansereau (Eds.), *Spatial learning strategies: Techniques applications, and related issues* (pp. 127-47). New York: Academic Press. [12] [13]

Vaughan, J. L., & Estes, T. H. (1986). *Reading and reasoning beyond the primary grades.* Boston, MA: Allyn & Bacon. [10] [13]

Vellutino, F. R. (1987). Dyslexia. *Scientific American, 256*, 34-41. [1]

Vickery, K. S., Reynolds, V. A., & Cochran, S. W. (1987). Multisensory teaching for reading, spelling, and handwriting, Orton-Gillingham based, in a public school setting. *Annals of Dyslexia, 37*, 189-202. [8]

Vinsonhaler, J. F., Weinshank, A. B., Wagner, C. C., & Polin, R. M. (1987). Computers, simulated cases, and the training of reading diagnosticians. In D. Reinking (Ed.), *Reading and computers: Issues for theory and practice* (pp. 127-40). New York: Teachers College Press. [3]

Volf, C. A. (as cited in Johansen, K. (1984, December)). *Man laerer at laise ved at laese—maske (you learn to read by reading—maybe). On diagnosis and treatment of reading difficulties emphasizing some non-acknowledged methods.* Unpublished doctoral dissertation, Pacific Western University, Los Angeles, CA. [12]

Vygotsky, L. S. (1962). *Thought and language*. Cambridge: MIT Press. [9] [7]

Vygotsky, L. S. (1978). *Mind in society: The development of higher psychological process*. (M. Cole, V. John-Steiner, S. Seribner, & E. Souberman, Eds.). Cambridge: Harvard University Press. [7] [10]

Wade, S. E., & Reynolds, R. E. (1989). Developing metacognitive awareness. *Journal of Reading, 33*, 6-14. [13]

Wade, S. E., & Trathen, W. (1989). Effects of self-selected study methods on learning. *Journal of Educational Psychology, 81*, 40-47. [13]

Wade, S. E., Trathen, W., & Schraw, G. (1988). *An analysis of spontaneous study strategies*. Paper presented at the meeting of the American Educational Research Association, New Orleans, LA. [13]

Wade, S. E., Trathen, W., & Schraw, G. (1990). An analysis of spontaneous study strategies. *Reading Research Quarterly, 25*(2), 147-66. [13]

Waern, Y. (1977a). Comprehension and belief structure. *Scandanavian Journal of Psychology, 18*, 266-74. [5]

Waern, Y. (1977b). On the relationship between knowledge of the world and comprehension of texts. *Scandanavian Journal of Psychology, 18*, 130-39. [5]

Wagoner, S. A. (1983). Comprehension monitoring: What it is and what we know about it. *Reading Research Quarterly, 18*, 328-46. [4]

Walker, D. F., & Schaffarzick, J. (1974). Comparing curricula. *Review of Educational Research, 44*, 83-112. [7]

Wallace, I., & Wallechinsky, D. (1980). *The Book of Lists #2*. New York: William Morrow & Co. [10]

Walter, R. B. (1974). *History and development of the informal reading inventory*. Unpublished study prepared at Kean College of New Jersey. (ERIC Document Reproduction Service No. ED 098 539) [4]

Wark, D. M. (1964). Survey Q3R: System or superstition? In D. M. Wark (Ed.), *College and adult reading*. Third and fourth annual yearbook of the North Central Reading Association (pp. 161-70). St. Paul: University of Minnesota, Student Counseling Bureau. [13]

Warrington, E. G. (1971). Neurological disorders of memory. *Br. Med. Bull., 27*(3), 000. [12]

Watson, G., & Glaser, E. M. (1964). *Critical Thinking Appraisal*. New York: Hartcourt Brace Jovanovich. [13]

Weaver, C. (1986, May). *Reading as a whole-brain process: Both reality and metaphor*. Paper presented at the Fourth International Conference on the Teaching of English, Ottawa. Educational Resources Information Center, no. ED 273926. [13]

Weaver, C. (1988). *Reading, process and practice: From socio-psycholinguistics to whole language*. Portsmouth, NH: Heinemann. [12]

Weaver, W. W., & Kingston, A. J. (1963). A factor analysis of cloze procedure and other measures of reading and language ability. *Journal of Communication, 13*, 252-61. [4] [10]

Wechsler, D. (1974). *Manual for the Wechsler Intelligence Scale for Children - Revised*. New York: Psychological Corporation. [4] [5]

Weiderholdt, J. L. (1990). A preface to the special series. *Journal of Learning Disabilities, 23*(10), 588. [12]

Weiner, E. (1980). The diagnostic evaluation of writing skills (DEWS): Application of DEWS criteria to writing samples. *Learning Disability Quarterly, 3*(2), 54-59. [4]

Weiner, M., & Cromer, W. (1967). Reading and reading difficulty: A conceptual analysis. *Harvard Educational Review, 37*, 620-43. [3]

Weiss, S. C. (1980). Culture Fair Intelligence Test and Draw-a-Person scores from a rural Peruvian sample. *Journal of Social Psychology, 111*, 147-48. [5]

Wepman, J. (1973). *Wepman Auditory Discrimination Test*. Chicago: Language Research Associates.

Werner, P. H., & Strother, J. (1987). Early readers: Important emotional considerations. *The Reading Teacher, 40*(6), 538-43. [11]

Wernicke, C. (1874). *Der aphasiche Symptomenkomplex*. Breslau, Germany: Cohn and Weigert. [12]

Wesson, C. L., Vierthaler, J. M., & Haubrich, P. A. (1989). An efficient technique for establishing reading groups. *The Reading Teacher, 42*(7), 466-69. [2]

Wheelock, W. (1990). Defense mechanisms of the ego. Class Handout, University of Missouri-Kansas City.

Whimbey, A., & Lochhead, J. (1980). *Problem-solving and comprehension: A short course in analytic reasoning* (2nd. ed.). Philadelphia: The Franklin Institute Press. [9]

Williams, J. P. (1975). Training children to copy and discriminate letter-like forms. *Journal of Educational Psychology, 67*, 790-95. [9]

Williamson, K. E., & Young, F. (1974). The IRI and RMI diagnostic concepts should be synthesized. *Journal of Reading Behavior, 6*(2), 183-94. [4]

Willmore, D. J. (1967). A comparison of four methods of studying a college textbook (Doctoral dissertation, University of Minnesota, 1966). *Dissertation Abstracts, 27,* 2413A. [12] [13]

Wilson, R. M., & Gambrell, L. B. (1988). *Reading comprehension in the elementary school*. Boston: Allyn & Bacon. [10]

Witte, P. L. (1982). Glossing content area texts: A vehicle for inservice training. In G. H. McNinch (Ed.), *Reading in the disciplines*. Second Yearbook of the American Reading Forum (pp. 23-25). Athens, GA: American Reading Forum. [10]

Witty, P. A. (1985). Rationale for fostering creative reading in the gifted and the creative. In M. Labuda (Ed.), *Creative reading for gifted learners: A design for excellence* (pp. 8-24). Newark, DE: International Reading Association. [13]

Wixson, K. L. (1979). Miscue analysis: A critical review. *Journal of Reading Behavior, 11*(2), 163-75. [4]

Wixson, K., & Lipson, M. (1991). Perspectives on reading disability research. In B. Barr, M. L. Kamil, P. Mosenthal, & P. D. Pearson (Eds.), *Handbook of reading research* (Vol. 2, pp. 539-70). New York: Longman. [2]

Wixson, K. K., & Lipson, M. Y. (in press). *Reading diagnosis and remediation*. Glenview, IL: Scott, Foresman. [3]

Wolf, D. P. (1980). Portfolio assessment: Sampling student work. *Educational Leadership, 46*(7), 4-10. [6]

Wolf, M. (1986). Rapid alternating stimulus naming in the developmental dyslexias. *Brain and Language, 27*, 360-79. [12]

Wolf, M. (1991). Naming speed and reading: The contribution of the cognitive neurosciences. *Reading Research Quarterly, 26*(2), 123-41. [12]

Wolff, D. E., Desberg, P., & Marsh, G. (1985). Analogy strategies for improving word recognition in competent learning disabled readers. *The Reading Teacher, 38*, 412-16. [8]

Wollman-Bonilla, J. E. (1989). Reading journals: Invitations to participate in literature. *The Reading Teacher, 43*(2), 112-20. [11]

Wolpe, J. (1958). *Psychotherapy by reciprocal inhibition*. Stanford: Stanford University Press. [11] [12]

Wolpe, J., & Lazarus, A. A. (1966). *Behavior therapy techniques*. New York: Pergamon Press. [11, 12]

Wood, E., & Middleton, D. (1975). A study of assisted problem-solving. *British Journal of Psychology, 66*, 181-91. [7]

Wood, K. D. (1984). Probable passage: A writing strategy. *The Reading Teacher, 37*, 496-99. [10]

Wood, K. D. (1988). Guiding students through informational text. *The Reading Teacher, 41*, 912-20. [6] [10]

Wood, K. D., & Mateja, J. A. (1983). Adapting secondary level strategies for use in elementary classrooms. *The Reading Teacher, 36*, 492-96. [10]

Woodcock, R. (1978). *Woodcock-Johnson Psychoeducational Battery*. Hingham, MA: Teaching Resources Corporation. [5]

Woods, M. L., & Moe, A. J. (1981). *Analytical Reading Inventory*. Columbus, OH: Charles C. Merrill. [4]

Wooster, G. F. (1958). Teaching the SQ3R method of study: An investigatio. of the instructional approach (Doctoral dissertation, The Ohio State University, 195.). *Dissertation Abstracts, 18*, 2067-68. [12] [13]

Yopp, H. K. (1988). The validity and reliability of phonemic awareness tests. *Reading Research Quarterly, 23*, 159-77. [7]

Zabroske, B., & Klever, K. (1991). Diagnostic teaching. *Illinois Reading Council Journal, 19*(2), 47. [2]

Zaslow, R. W. (1966). Reversals in children as a function of midline body orientation. *Journal of Educational Psychology, 57*(3), 133-39.

Zenker, E. R., & Frey, D. Z. (1985). Relaxation helps less capable students. *Journal of Reading, 28*, 342-44. [12] [13]

ACKNOWLEDGMENTS

Box 1–3   Adapted from Broder, L.A., and Wiesendanger, K.D. (1986), University based reading clinics: Practices and procedures. *The Reading Teacher, 39*(7), pp. 698–702. The International Reading Association.

Figure 4–2   LaPray, M. & Ross, R. (1969). The graded word list: quick gauge of reading ability. *Journal of Reading, 12*(4), 305–307. Reprinted with permission of LaPray and the International Reading Association.

Figure 4–3   Cunningham, P. (1990) The name test: A quick assessment of decoding ability. *The Reading Teacher, 44*(2), 124–129. Reprinted with permission of Pat Cunningham and the International Reading Association.

Figure 4–5   Used with permission of Robert E. Leibert.

pp. 90–91   Adapted from Kinney, M.A., and Harry, A.L. (1991). An informal inventory for adolescents that assesses the reader, the text, and the task. *Journal of Reading, 34*(8), pp. 643–647. The International Reading Association.

p. 97   Excerpt from *A Language-Thinking Approach to Reading* by Lenore H. Ringler and Carol K. Weber, copyright (c) 1984 by Harcourt Brace Jovanovich, Inc., reprinted by permission of publisher.

pp. 97–98   Clark, C.H. (1982). Assessing free recall. *The Reading Teacher, 35,* 764–768. (c) International Reading Association.

Box 4–3   Mitchell, J.N. & Irwin, P.A. (1989). The reading retelling profile: Using retellings to make instructional decisions. In S.W. Valencia, W. McGinley, P.D. Pearson (1990). Assessing reading and writing in G.G. Duffy (Ed.), *Reading in the Middle School* (2nd ed., p. 147) Newark, DE: International Reading Association. Reprinted by permission of Pi Irwin and the International Reading Association.

Figure 4–4   Irwin, P., & Mitchell, J.N. (1983). A procedure for assessing the richness of retellings. *Journal of Reading, 26*(5), 391–396. Reprinted with permission of Pi Irwin and the International Reading Association.

Figure 4–8   Gilmore, J.V., and Gilmore, E.C. (1968). *Gilmore oral reading test.* New York: The Pscyhological Corporation.

Figure 4–11   Rogers, D.B. (1984) Assessing study skills. *Journal of Reading, 27*(4), 346–354. Reprinted with permission of Douglas B. Rogers and the International Reading Association.

Figure 4–12, Figure 4–13   Schmitt, M.C. (1990) A questionnaire to measure children's awareness of strategic reading processes. *The Reading Teacher, 43*(7), 454–461. Reprinted with permission of Maribeth Cassidy Schmitt and the International Reading Association.

Figure 5–7   Used with permission of John E. George.

Box 6–1   Kirk, C. (1990). What Mitch taught me: A student at risk becomes a writer. *Wisconsin State Reading Association Journal, 34*(2), p. 11–14.

Figure 6–2, Figure 6–3   Flood, J. & Lapp, D. (1989) Reporting reading progress: A comparison portfolio for parents, *The Reading Teacher,* March 1989, pp. 508–514. Reprinted with permission of James Flood and the International Reading Association.

Figure 6–4, Figure 6–5   *Reading Psychology* 11(3) 1990 J.C. Carney and G. Cioffi "Extending Traditional Diagnosis: The Dynamic Assessment of Reading Abilities" pp. 177–192. Used with permission.

Figure 6–6   Used with permission of the National Reading Conference, Chicago, Illinois.

pp. 187–188   From "An ecological approach to learning," by Roselmina Indrisano, *Topics in Learning and Learning Disabilities, 1*(4), 11–15. Copyright 1982 by PRO-ED, Inc. Reprinted by permission.

Figure 7–1   "Hierarchy of Needs" from MOTIVATION AND PERSONALITY by Abraham H. Maslow. Copyright 1954 by Harper & Row, Publishers, Inc. Copyright (c) 1970 by Abraham H. Maslow. Reprinted by permission of HarperCollins Publishers.

pp. 233–234   From HANDBOOK OF READING RESEARCH VOL II edited by Rebecca Barr, Michael L. Kamil, Peter Mosenthal, P. David Pearson. Copyright (c) 1991 by Longman Publishing Group.

Figure 8–1   Used with permission of DLM, Inc. Allen, TX 75002

| Figure 8–2 | Fry, E.B. (1980) The new instant word list. *The Reading Teacher, 34,* 284–289. Reprinted with permission of Edward B. Fry and the International Reading Association. |

Figure 8–2 — Fry, E.B. (1980) The new instant word list. *The Reading Teacher, 34,* 284–289. Reprinted with permission of Edward B. Fry and the International Reading Association.

Figure 8–3 — Eeds, M. (1985) Bookwords: Using a beginning word list of high frequency words from children's literature K–8, *The Reading Teacher, 38,* 418–423. Reprinted with permission of Maryann Eeds and the International Reading Association.

Figure 8–4, Figure 8–5 — Fry, Edward, "A Frequency Approach to Phonics," *Elementary English,* November 1964. Copyright 1964 by the National Council of Teachers of English. Reprinted with permission.

pp. 251, 254 — *Letter Sound Labels.* The A.D.D. Program: Auditory Discrimination in Depth by Charles H. Lindamood and Patricia C. Lindamood. Copyright 1975, reproduced with permission from DLM, Allen, TX.

Figure 8–6 — Used with permission of Gerald G. Glass and Easier-to-Learn, Box 329, Garden City, NY 11530.

pp. 261–262 — McCormick, S. (1990, December). *Task dimensions and effects of a Multiple-Exposure/Multiple Context Strategy for teaching nonreaders.* Paper presented at the meeting of the National Reading Conference, Miami, FL.

Figure 8–10 — Koskinen, P.S. & Blum, I.H. (1986) Paired repeated reading: A classroom strategy for developing fluent reading, *The Reading Teacher, 40,* 70–75. Reprinted with permission of Patricia S. Koskinen and the International Reading Association.

Figure 8–11 — Reprinted by permission of Scholastic Inc.

Figure 9–6 — Adapted excerpt and figure from *Teaching Reading Vocabulary,* Second Edition by Dale D. Johnson and P. David Pearson, copyright (c) 1984 by Holt, Rinehart and Winston, Inc., reprinted by permission of the publisher.

p. 287 — Moore, D.W. and Moore S.A. (1986). Possible sentences. In E.K. Dishner, T.W. Bean, J.E. Readence, and D.W. Moore (Eds.), *Reading in the Content Areas* (pp. 174–178). Dubuque, IA: Kendall-Hunt. Copyright 1986 by Kendall-Hunt.

pp. 287–288 — Bowman, J.D. (1991). Vocabulary development by "twosies." *Arizona Reading Journal, 19*(2), 66.

Figure 9–9, Figure 9–10 — Gable, R.A., Hendrickson, J.M., Meeks, J.W. (1988) Assessing spelling errors of special needs students. *The Reading Teacher, 42*(2) 112–117. Reprinted with permission of Robert A. Gable and the International Reading Association.

pp. 326–327 — Adapted from DeWitz, P., Carr E.M., and Patsberg, J.P. (1987) Effects of interference training on comprehension and comprehension monitoring. *Reading Research Quarterly, 22,* 99–121. Reprinted with permission of the International Reading Association.

Figure 10–1 — From *The Book of Lists #2* by I. Wallace and D. Wallechinsky, 1980.

p. 333 — Maring, G.H., and Furman G. (1985) Seven "whole class" strategies to help mainstreamed young people read and listen better in content area classes. *Journal of Reading, 28,* 694–700. Reprinted with permission of Gerald H. Maring and the International Reading Association.

Figure 10–2 — Muth, K.D. (1987) Teacher's connection questions: prompting students to organize text ideas. *Journal of Reading, 28,* 254–259. Reprinted with permission of K. Denise Muth and the International Reading Association.

Figure 10–3 — Reprinted with permission of Deborah Fidler.

Figure 10–4 — Heimlich, J.E. & Pittelman, S.D. (1986) *Semantic mapping: Classroom applications,* Newark, DE. International Reading Association. Reprinted with permission of Joan E. Heimlich and the International Reading Association.

pp. 339–340 — Adapted from "K-W-L Plus: A strategy for comprehension and summarization," Eileen Carr and Donna Ogle, *Journal of Reading,* April 1987, pp. 628–629. International Reading Association.

p. 343 — Babbs, P. (1983). The effects of instruction in the use of a metacognitive monitoring strategy upon fourth graders' reading comprehension and recall performance (Doctoral dissertation, Purdue University, West Lafayette, IN). *Dissertation Abstract International, 5,* 44/06A. Reprinted with permission of Patricia J. Babbs.

pp. 347, 348 — Adapted from "InQuest: A listening and reading comprehension strategy," Mary E. Shoop. *The Reading Teacher,* March 1986, pp. 670–674. International Reading Association.

p. 350 — Henk, W.A. & King, G.T. (1984). Helping students follow written directions. In G.H. McNinch (ed.), *Reading Teacher Education.* Fourth yearbook of the American Reading Forum (pp. 62–64). Athens, GA: American Reading Forum. Reprinted with permission of the American Reading Forum Yearbook.

pp. 365–366	Adapted from "Correlates of effective reading instruction," Barbara J. Guzzetti and Robert J. Marzano, *The Reading Teacher*, April 1984, pp. 754–758. International Reading Association.
p. 366	Cecil, N.L. (1990). Diffusing the trauma: An exit interview for remediated readers. *Journal for Affective Reading Education, 10*, pp. 27–32.
Figure 11–1	Hoffman, J.V. (1977). Intra-Act: A language in the content areas teaching procedure (Doctoral dissertation, University of Missouri-Kansas City). *Dissertation Abstracts International, 38*, 3248A.
Figure 11–2, Figure 11–3	Schell, L.M. (1980). Value Clarification via Basal Readers. *Reading Horizons, 20*, 215–220.
Figure 11–4	Gentile, L.M. & McMillan, M.M. (1987) *Stress and reading difficulties: research assessment intervention.* Newark, DE. International Reading Association. Reprinted with permission of Lance M. Gentile and the International Reading Association.
Figure 11–5	Reprinted from Koeppen, A.S. (1974). Relaxation training for children. *Elementary School Guidance and Counseling, 9*, 14–21. Copyright AACD. Reprinted with permission of American Association for Counseling and Development.
p. 378	"Positive suggestion: It helps LD students learn" by O.A. Oldridge (1982), *Academic Therapy, 17*, 279–287. Copyright 1982 by PRO-ED, Inc. reprinted by permission.
Box 11.1	Reprinted with permission of Warren Wheelock.
pp. 385–386	Adapted from "A method for teaching sight words to disabled readers," George H. McNinch, *The Reading Teacher*, December 1981, pp. 269–272. International Reading Association.
pp. 395	Henk, W.A. (1991). Technology advances in the study of reading: An introduction. *Reading Research Instruction, 30*,(4), 1–19. Reprinted with permission of William A. Henk and *Reading Research Instruction*.
Figure 12–1, Figure 12–2	Adapted from "Dyslexia: Neuroanatomical/neurolinguistperspectives," George W. Hynd and Cynthia R. Hynd, *Reading Research Quarterly*, Vol. 19, No. 4, pp. 482–489. International Reading Association.
Figure 12–4	THE TEACHING OF READING IN THE ELEMENTARY SCHOOL by Paul McKee. Copyright (c) 1948 by Houghton Mifflin Company. Reprinted by permission of Houghton Mifflin Company.
Figure 13–1	Figure 2 from "Developing a strategic reading program," Joy N. Monahan, *Reading in the Middle School*, Gerald G. Duffy, ed., 1990. reprinted with permission of Joy N. Monahan and the International Reading Association.
pp. 438–439	Adapted from "A Notetaking System for Learning," Robert A. Palatier, *Journal of Reading*, October 1973, pp. 36–39. International Reading Association.
pp 433–434	Adapted from "Strategy families for disabled readers," Carol Dana, *Journal of Reading*, October 1989, pp. 30–35. International Reading Association.
pp. 440–441	Adapted from "The directed notetaking activity: A self-questioning approach," Hiller A. Spires and P. Diane Stone, *Journal of Reading*, October 1989, pp. 36–39. International Reading Association.
pp. 443–444	Cecil, N.L. (1990b). Where have all the good questions gone? Encouraging creative expression in children. *Contemporary Issues in Reading, 5*(2), 49–53. Reprinted with permission of *Contemporary Issues in Reading*.
pp. 443, 445	Adapted from "Reading instruction that increases thinking abilities," Cathy Collins, *Journal of Reading*, April 1991, pp. 510–516. International Reading Association.
Figure 13–3	Figure 2 from "Developing metacognitive awareness," Suzanne E. Wade and Ralph E. Reynolds, *Journal of Reading*, October 1989, pp. 6–14. International Reading Association.
pp. 460–461	Adapted from "Help students GRASP the knack of writing summaries," David A. Hayes, *Journal of Reading*, November 1989, pp. 96–101. International Reading Association.
Figure 13–10	Short, K. (1986). *Literacy as a collaborative experience.* Doctoral dissertation, Indiana University.
p. 479	Chase, F. (1961). Demands on the reader in the next decade. *Controversial Issues in Reading and Promising Solutions. Supplementary Educational Monographs, 91*, 7–18. Chicago:University of Chicago Press.
pp. 494–501	Excerpted and adapted from *The Living Word Vocabulary* by Edgar Dale and Joseph O'Rourke, (c) 1981 World Book-Childcraft International, Inc. By permission of World Book, Inc., 525 W. Monroe, Chicago, IL 60661.

Index